DATE DUE

APR 0 7			
MAY 0 6			
DEC 4			

Demco, Inc. 38-293

Saudi Arabia
The Ceaseless Quest for Security

SAUDI ARABIA

The Ceaseless Quest for Security

NADAV SAFRAN

The Belknap Press of Harvard University Press
Cambridge, Massachusetts, and London, England
1985

This book is printed on acid-free paper, and its binding materials
have been chosen for strength and durability.

Library of Congress Cataloging in Publication Data

Safran, Nadav.
Saudi Arabia: the ceaseless quest for security.

Bibliography: p.
Includes index.
1. Saudi Arabia—National security.   2. Saudi Arabia
—Defenses.   3. Saudi Arabia—Armed Forces.
4. Saudi Arabia—Military policy.   I. Title.
UA853.S33S24   1985   355'.0330538   85-5484
ISBN 0-674-78985-7 (alk. paper)

To Liz, Abby, Nina,
and Anita

Preface

I set out to write this book about Saudi Arabia because I have been a lifelong student of the Middle East and international politics, and Saudi Arabia came to occupy an important place in both. My reasons for choosing to focus on the issue of security and to adopt the approach I did are explained in the Introduction.

I write this preface to state one or two points, but mainly to fulfill the pleasant duty of thanking the institutions and persons who helped make this work possible.

This book was written entirely on the basis of open sources and declassified documents available to the public. No privileged information of any sort, from any source, has been used.

While doing the research and writing the first drafts of this book, I could not think of a better place to do the work than my home institution, whose resources and facilities continue to amaze me after thirty years of using them. No field research was necessary for my subject, except perhaps in certain spheres that are usually barred to academic investigators even in countries that have "right to know" laws.

After living with my subject for more than five years and completing a satisfactory draft, I did feel the urge to visit the Kingdom to get something of its flavor. However, when I was ready to go I could not, and when I received an invitation to attend an academic conference, time and circumstances were not convenient. I still hope to visit the Kingdom in the future.

I say all this because there is a notion abroad that "having been" to Saudi Arabia is a warrant of validity for one's work, regardless of what one did when one was there. I like to think that other qualifications, such as the methods used by certain types of historians and social scientists, can be far more important than a visit or a sojourn in yielding an understanding of the country's contemporary history. I leave it to the critics and readers to assess this proposition, make comparisons, and reach a judgment.

In 1979–80 I was awarded a Rockefeller Foundation Fellowship, which afforded me the leisure to advance my project to the point of no return. The Rand Corporation provided substantial support for research leading to a preliminary paper on defense and security allocations and Saudi defense concepts. Harvard's Center for Middle Eastern Studies gave me unstinting logistical help for several years. I am most heavily indebted, however, to generations of students, graduates and undergraduates, Saudi and others, who participated in my seminars and contributed, through their perspectives and insights, much more than they realized. Of these students, four who became my assistants at different times deserve my most profound gratitude. Gary Samore has since earned a doctorate for his work on the Saudi royal family; Laurie Mylroie is completing her thesis on Saudi Arabia and the Gulf emirates, and Gregory Gause is writing his on Saudi Arabia and the Yemens. Arie Ofri has been a wizard at ferreting out and making available to me material that I did not suspect existed. The dedication and enthusiasm of these young collaborators sustained me in the inevitable moments of near despair.

The long labor on this book deprived my family of much of my time and attention to which they were rightfully entitled. In gratitude, I dedicate the book to them.

Cambridge, Massachusetts

Contents

Tables

Figures

Conversion of Hijra years and fiscal years
to Gregorian dates, 1380–1400 H.Y.

Hijra year (Muharram through Dhu al-Hijjah)	Starting Gregorian date	Hijra fiscal year (1 Rajab through 30 Jumada II)	Starting Gregorian date
1380	June 25, 1960[a]	1380–81	December 19, 1960
1381	June 14, 1961	1381–82	December 9, 1961
1382	June 4, 1962	1382–83	November 28, 1962
1383	May 25, 1963	1383–84	November 17, 1963
1384	May 13, 1964[a]	1384–85	November 5, 1964
1385	May 1, 1965	1385–86	October 25, 1965
1386	April 21, 1966	1386–87	October 16, 1966
1387	April 11, 1967	1387–88	October 4, 1967
1388	March 30, 1968[a]	1388–89	September 23, 1968
1389	March 19, 1969	1389–90	September 12, 1969
1390	March 9, 1970	1390–91	September 2, 1970
1391	February 26, 1971	1391–92	August 22, 1971
1392	February 15, 1972[a]	1392–93	August 10, 1972
1393	February 4, 1973	1393–94	July 30, 1973
1394	January 23, 1974	1394–95	July 19, 1974
1395	January 13, 1975	1395–96	July 9, 1975
1396	January 2, 1976[a]	1396–97	June 28, 1976
1397	December 22, 1977	1397–98	June 16, 1977
1398	December 11, 1978	1398–99	June 6, 1978
1399	November 30, 1979	1399–1400	May 26, 1979
1400	November 19, 1980[a]	1400–1401	May 15, 1980

Source: Richard Nyrop et al., *Area Handbook for Saudi Arabia,* 3d ed. (Washington, D.C.: Government Printing Office, 1977).

a. Leap year.

How long halt ye between two opinions?

1 Kings 18:21

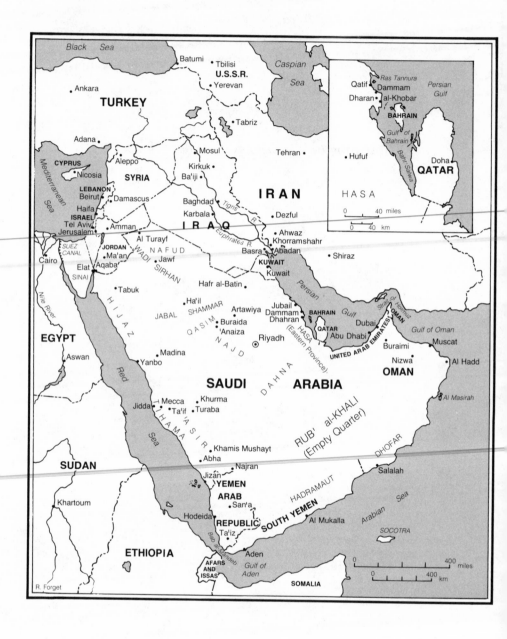

Black Sea

Batumi
Tbilisi
U.S.S.R.
Ankara
Yerevan
TURKEY

Caspian Sea

Tabriz

Aleppo
Mosul
Tehran

CYPRUS
Nicosia
SYRIA
Kirkuk
Ba'iji

LEBANON
Beirut
Damascus
Baghdad
IRAN

Mediterranean Sea

Haifa
ISRAEL
Tel Aviv
Jerusalem
Amman
IRAQ
Karbala
Dezful

SUEZ CANAL
Cairo
JORDAN
Al Turayf
Ma'an
Jawf
NAFUD
Ahwaz
Khorramshahr
Basra
Abadan
Shiraz

SINAI
Elat
Aqaba
WADI SIRHAN
KUWAIT
Kuwait

Tabuk
Hafr al-Batin

HIJAZ
Ha'il
SHAMMAR
Artawiya
Jubail
Dammam
Dhahran
BAHRAIN
QATAR
Abu Dhabi
Dubai
OMAN

EGYPT
JABAL
QASIM
Buraida
'Anaiza
HASA
(Eastern Province)
UNITED ARAB EMIRATES
Buraimi
Muscat
Gulf of Oman

Aswan
Madina
Yanbo
NAJD
Riyadh
Nizwa
OMAN
Al Hadd

Nile River
SAUDI
DAHNA
ARABIA
Al Masirah

Red Sea
Jidda
Mecca
Ta'if
Khurma
Turaba

'ASIR
RUB' al-KHALI
(Empty Quarter)
DHOFAR

TIHAMA
Khamis Mushayt
Abha
Najran
Salalah

SUDAN
HADRAMAUT
Arabian Sea

Khartoum
Jizan
YEMEN
ARAB
San'a
SOCOTRA

Hodeida
REPUBLIC
Ta'iz
SOUTH YEMEN
Al Mukalla

ETHIOPIA
AFARS AND ISSAS
Aden
Gulf of Aden
SOMALIA

Bab al-Mandeb

R. Forget

0   400 miles
0   400 km

Inset (upper right):

Qatif
Ras Tannura
Dammam
Persian Gulf

Dharan
al-Khobar
BAHRAIN

Gulf of Bahrain
Hufuf
HASA
Bahr-Salwa
Doha
QATAR

0   40 miles
0   40 km

Introduction

This study analyzes the national security policy of the Kingdom of Saudi Arabia from the perspective of its rulers since the creation of the Kingdom through 1982 in order to provide insight into the rulers' modus operandi and the country's behavior in the international arena. The importance of that behavior was demonstrated beyond doubt by the 1973 oil embargo, which shook the foundations of the Western alliance as no Soviet campaign has since the onset of the Cold War; and by the Saudi action and inaction on oil prices in 1974 and 1979, which affected the world economy and distribution of wealth more than any single acts by any other power. The centrality of regime and national security as a determinant of Saudi behavior is suggested by a few facts of geography and history and is indicated by clear evidence of the Saudi rulers' perceptions and actions.

Saudi Arabia is a vast, desolate country with a relatively sparse population. It forms a rough rectangle more than 1,000 miles long and 800 miles wide, comprising about 860,000 square miles — approximately the size of the United States east of the Mississippi River. There are no rivers or significant perennial streams, and rainfall is scarce except in the southwest; less than 1 percent of the country is suitable for settled agriculture. Most of the country consists of great sand deserts — the Rub' al-Khali, stretching across the entire south; the Dahna in the east, between Najd and the Persian Gulf coast; and the Nafud, across most of the north. The rest is wilderness covered by gravel or jumbled lava beds.

The size of the Saudi population is something of a mystery; the best estimates put it at some 5–6 million indigenous Saudis in 1980, plus more than 2 million foreign workers and their dependents (for a discussion of this subject, see Chapter 8). The population is distributed along three belts that correspond to geographic and historical divisions. About half the population lives and moves in the Hijaz and 'Asir regions, which form a mountainous belt along the Red Sea. This area, conquered in the 1920s, includes the holy cities of Mecca and Madina and the ports of Jidda and Yanbo. The second belt of population consists of an archipelago of oases extending from Ha'il in the north to beyond Kharj in the south. This is the Najd power base of the House of Saud and includes Riyadh, the Saudi capital. The third belt begins on the coast of the Persian Gulf near Qatif, a Shi'ite population center, and extends south and west to the oasis of Haradh. This region, known as the Eastern Province, was conquered in 1913 and is the site of Saudi Arabia's main oil fields and facilities, the Dhahran airport and military base, and the new port of Jubail. The three belts are separated from each other, and each in turn is surrounded and split by vast thinly inhabited spaces, resulting in a multitude of subregions that historically supported the division of the population into some twoscore major tribal groupings and many more subgroupings.

The vastness of the country, its topography, its ecology, and its poverty have made it extremely difficult for any central power to hold it together for any substantial length of time. Indeed, the area occupied by the present Kingdom was politically united only twice before in historical times, in the seventh century and at the turn of the nineteenth, and for only brief periods, before the centrifugal tendencies inherent in the environment reasserted themselves. Since the 1940s, oil revenue has provided the wherewithal for attempts by the rulers to mitigate those tendencies; but these efforts have so far not been decisive and have generated their own problematic consequences.

In addition to vastness, fragmentation, and sparse population, critical features of Saudi geography in terms of defense include the specific location of the Kingdom's oil wealth and the vulnerability of its lines of communication with the outside world. Most of Saudi Arabia's oil-producing capacity derives from five fields and 475-odd wells clustered in a core area 250 miles long and 50 miles wide on the Persian Gulf coast and offshore. In 1979 these fields produced about 6.5 million barrels a day (mbd) out of a total daily production of 9 mbd.[1] Terminal facilities serving all Saudi oil fields occupy a 50-mile arc along Tarut Bay between Ras Tannura and al-Khobar. All Saudi oil was loaded at Ras Tannura until recently, when the additional terminal of Ju'ayma became operative. The entire area is studded with power plants, pumping stations, gathering places, and tank farms that provide targets for prodigiously damaging sabotage or air attacks, and hostage objects for small hostile forces.

Although Saudi Arabia has a coastline of 1,300 miles on two seas, it has access to the open sea only through two choke points on the Red Sea and one on the Persian Gulf. The 20-mile-wide Strait of Bab al-Mandeb, adjacent to South Yemen, controls passage between the Red Sea and the Gulf of Aden, while the Suez Canal links the Red Sea to the Mediterranean. The Strait of Hormuz, 30 miles wide at its narrowest point and bordered by Oman on one side and Iran on the other, links the Persian Gulf to the Arabian Sea. Until recently, nearly all Saudi oil exports had to go through the Strait of Hormuz. The completion of the 750-mile cross-Arabian pipeline from the Ghawar oil field across the Kingdom to Yanbo on the Red Sea has provided an alternative outlet for about 2 mbd but has also increased the Kingdom's dependence on the Suez Canal and Bab al-Mandeb. Nearly all Saudi imports are vulnerable to blockage of the choke points. Ironically, these facts did not matter much when imperial Britain controlled all three passages; access became a problem for the Saudis only when indigenous neighboring governments took over, in 1955, 1967, and 1971.

History and geography have also combined to produce yet another major security problem. Saudi Arabia was created by recent conquest, and conquest almost always leaves unresolved boundary problems. In the case of Saudi Arabia, the nature of the terrain of the Arabian Peninsula makes precise demarcation of boundaries virtually impossible. A much more serious problem is that the Kingdom is surrounded by a dozen states that are either too strong or too weak: the former threaten aggression, and the latter invite it, especially since several of both are also extremely rich; and vital Saudi interests can suffer in the process. Again, until the end of World War II, Britain's control or strong influence over nearly all these neighbors permitted an understanding between it and the Kingdom wherein Britain restrained the stronger powers in exchange for Saudi self-restraint vis-à-vis the weaker powers. That understanding began to lapse as British control and influence waned in the 1940s and 1950s, and came to an end when Britain pulled out of Aden in 1967 and the Persian Gulf in 1971, leaving the Saudis to confront problems around their entire perimeter.

These basic vulnerabilities have helped make defense and security a primary concern for the rulers of the present Saudi realm. For instance, in 1952, when one of the first rudimentary state budgets was issued, the founder of the Kingdom devoted 30 percent of the $210 million total revenue to defense and security. Twenty-nine years and profound changes later, in 1981, the Kingdom's revenues had increased 383 times, to about $79 billion; but allocations to defense and security had multiplied 415 times, to $25 billion, or 32.4 percent of the state's revenue.

The amounts allocated by the Saudis to defense and security in 1981 were exceeded only by the defense allocations of the United States, the Soviet Union, and China. On a per capita basis they were by far the highest in the world, twice as high as Israel's, the next highest, and more than three times as high as those of the United States, the third in rank. In absolute amounts, the Saudi allocations were equivalent to four times the combined defense spending of India and Pakistan, with their 760 million population and their thirty-five years of strife, or about twice the combined defense budgets for that year of Egypt, Syria, Jordan, Iraq, and Israel — the principal antagonists in the Arab-Israeli conflict.[2]

Just as striking as the extremely high level of Saudi allocations to defense throughout the years is the relatively small military establishment that these have generated so far. With between one-half and the same amount of defense spending as Saudi Arabia in recent years, the five Middle Eastern countries last mentioned could field in 1981 about 60 divisions, 10,000 tanks, and 2,000 combat aircraft. In the same year Saudi Arabia could field at most the equivalent of 5 divisions, 500 tanks, and 200 combat aircraft. Except for the air force, this was about the same size military force that Jordan could muster in 1981, with less than one-sixtieth of Saudi Arabia's defense allocation for that year. The reasons for this seemingly fantastic low cost effectiveness include the multiplication of defense and security instruments; the lack of an initial infrastructure; the lavish scale on which that infrastructure was developed; scarce, underdeveloped, and underutilized manpower; the extreme slowness of the process of training personnel for a modern force; and false starts, waste, and spoilage. The ratio of the amounts spent on hardware to amounts spent on construction, training, and personnel over the last decade has been 1:3 or 1:4.

The disparity between the real and perceived vulnerability of the Kingdom, on the one hand, and its rather limited military capability, on the other, made the thrust of this inquiry clear from the outset: foreign policy — the endeavor to neutralize or deter threats through alliances and alignments, diplomatic maneuverings, foreign aid, and so on — was bound in the case of Saudi Arabia to be at least as important as the military component of national security. Moreover, foreign policy was likely to be more reactive than active; thus an understanding of Saudi reactions would require attention to actions by others and would involve discontinuities in the Saudis' own policies. Finally, as in the case of other countries, analysis of Saudi national security would have to refer to the domestic dimension, including shifts in the structure of power and in the resources at the command of the rulers, relevant changes in the political and social systems, and modifications in demographic and even geographic factors.

Although the broad parameters of this study were thus clear, its execution presented difficulties. Until 1973 the literature on the Kingdom in general and on Saudi defense and foreign policy in particular was thin.

To all but the personnel of interested oil companies and a few foreign service specialists, adventurers, explorers, and scholars, Saudi Arabia was much like the Yemen Arab Republic today — a remote, exotic part of the Middle East hinterland that occasionally made news in connection with the antics of some of its princes or with the impact on it of developments originating in other parts of the region. The indifference of outsiders accorded well with the Kingdom's strong religious-cultural isolationism, the secretiveness of its rulers, and a traditional political system that lacked even the kind of forums for the articulation of policy and opinion that have existed in other restrictive Middle Eastern countries. The result was that Saudi Arabia remained essentially terra incognita, and the behavior of its rulers remained much as Winston Churchill described that of the Kremlin: "A riddle wrapped in a mystery inside an enigma."

Since 1973 there has been an explosion of literature on the Kingdom, but most of it deals with oil issues and other more or less technical subjects. In the area of defense and foreign policy, more information became available as outsiders poured into the Kingdom in connection with its massive development projects, as Congress pressed successive administrations to justify and account for the greater American involvement with the Kingdom, and as the world media began to report more extensively on the expanded regional and international role of the Kingdom itself. However, no comprehensive study of the subject has been produced, except for one imaginative and useful work in Arabic by the Lebanese political scientist Ghassane Salameh. A few articles and monographs have shed some light on various facets of the subject, but vast areas remain obscure. The long list of works cited in the Bibliography is somewhat deceptive. Many are either too general or too formal, too impressionistic or too spotty; most are tediously repetitive, reflecting more the greatly increased demand for knowledge about the Kingdom than any increased supply of it, either through the tapping of new sources or the application of new methods.

To execute this study, it was therefore necessary to assemble and present the accessible data as well as to analyze and synthesize them, and to pursue a strategy that combines several approaches and techniques. One is historical and traces the security problems from the simpler times of the Kingdom's inception to the complex present. Because of the traditional nature of the Saudi political system, the analysis proceeds in terms of reigns, to underscore the centrality of the royal family and of power relations within it. Within this framework each reign is also examined in terms of stages, defined by domestic and external strategic problems or opportunities and the rulers' responses to them. If a particular stage spans two reigns, the analysis does likewise.

This study also uses a structural approach that is calculated to make the most of scarce data about the rulers' policy decisions. The method places strategic problems facing the rulers in the context of carefully constructed analytical frameworks that depict the alternative courses theoretically available to deal with these problems and assesses the implications of the various options on the basis of logic and the historical record. Once that matrix has been constructed, an act or a statement by the rulers often suffices to give a clue not only about the course they probably chose but also about the attendant considerations that affected their choice. This approach may yield equivocal results in individual instances; but when it is applied to scores of cases in historical sequence, as is done in the following chapters, it becomes possible to test inferences by sequels, "predictions" by subsequent events, and thus to validate the analysis.

At the point when the scope of the Kingdom's security policy expands as a result of new problems or opportunities, a spatial or functional differentiation is introduced in the analysis. Thereafter Saudi security policy is examined in the context of several "theaters," such as the Arab-Israeli arena, the Gulf, south Arabia, and in terms of the Kingdom's American connection. Detailed analysis of developments in each arena includes general discussion of related developments in the other arenas, as necessary. This examination of some of the same problems from different perspectives in varying degrees of detail, though involving some repetition, provides a useful check on the overall analysis and approximates the situations that the Saudi policymakers confronted.

Finally, at all stages a study of Saudi defense policy parallels the analysis of foreign policy. The defense analysis proceeds along two lines. One focuses on the evolution of the defense and security establishment, including concepts, strategies, development programs, orders of battle, and capabilities; the other involves a systematic, detailed analysis of defense and security allocations over time to the various defense and security instruments. Because the defense studies use different data from those used in the foreign policy analysis, the two sets serve as counterchecks to each other and reinforce confidence in the validity of insights and conclusions on which they both converge.

The book is divided into four principal parts and eighteen chapters, all of which open with more or less extensive overviews. The conclusions to each part assess the Kingdom's security standing at that point and seek to identify enduring structural developments and recurrent patterns of behavior of the Saudi rulers. The final set of conclusions attempts to use some of the findings of the entire study to cast some light on the future and to cite some general implications for American policy, as Saudi Arabia continues its ceaseless quest for security.

PART ONE

The Origins of
Saudi Arabia

Saudi Arabia as presently constituted is barely fifty years old. The present king and other senior officials are the sons of the remarkable man who created the Saudi Arab Kingdom[1]—Abd al-Aziz ibn Abd al-Rahman Al Faisal Al Saud,[2] generally referred to as Ibn Saud. Ibn Saud started his empire-building endeavor with a handful of followers from an exile base in Kuwait in 1902 and completed it with a victory over the Yemen in 1934 that unified nearly 900,000 square miles. His success, however, depended in large measure on the fact that he had set out to *recover* a realm that his ancestors had created, ruled, and lost, and that his grandfather had recreated before his uncles and father lost again.

The first two Saudi realms gave legitimacy to Ibn Saud's restoration effort and endowed it with a source of potential power that increased and became actualized *pari passu* with his successes. Moreover, the record of the first two realms is highly relevant to an understanding of the formation and evolution of the third, not only because Ibn Saud was guided in his endeavor by some acutely sensed lessons derived from that record, but also because many of the factors that affected the history of those realms continue to affect the present Kingdom of Saudi Arabia.

For these reasons this study of the Kingdom begins with a concise history of the first two Saudi realms, including some reflections relevant to understanding aspects of present-day Saudi Arabia. Chapters 2 and 3 furnish a more elaborate narrative of Ibn Saud's creation of the third realm. Part One concludes with reflections on features of his accomplishments that have relevance to the present and future of Saudi Arabia.

1

The Rise and Fall
of the
First Two Realms

The First Realm, 1744–1818

The origin of the first Saudi realm was an encounter in 1744 between two men and two ambitions in a desert townlet called Dar'iyya. One of the men was Muhammad ibn Abd al-Wahhab, a religious preacher possessed of a sense of mission such as arose from time to time in the lands of Islam and left their mark on the course of history. Substantively, ibn Abd al-Wahhab's message was neither novel nor radical in Islamic terms. It was indeed a reiteration of the teachings of the great fourteenth-century revivalist Ahmad ibn Taimiya, who in turn was inspired by the great ninth-century founder of one of the four orthodox schools of Islamic jurisprudence, Ahmad ibn Hanbal. Ibn Abd al-Wahhab called for a return to the simple and pure beliefs, austere living, and strict application of the law of early Islam and condemned prevalent saint worship and animistic rituals, indulgence in "luxuries" such as smoking, music, and the wearing of silk, and laxity in the application of the Qoranic prescriptions and penalties. What was new was the length to which he carried his message. Ibn Abd al-Wahhab regarded the practices he denounced not as mere sins and shortcomings of imperfect believers, but as departures from the central belief in the absolute unity of Allah and the mission of His Prophet, which were tantamount to apostasy and merited the maximum penalty. Like other prophets, ibn Abd al-Wahhab found few disciples in his own town. He encountered some success elsewhere before being driven out, and in 1744 he landed in Dar'iyya in search of a new base of support.

The other man in that encounter was Muhammad ibn Saud, the shaikh[1] of a small clan of one of the large tribes that had settled for several generations in two agricultural villages that had grown into the town of Dar'iyya. At the time of ibn Abd al-Wahhab's visit, the Sauds and their domain were one of the less important of several Najd shaikhdoms, none of which matched the realm and power of the sharifs (a title borne by descendants of the Prophet Muhammad) of the Hijaz, the Banu Khalid of Hasa and the coastal district, the Sa'dun of lower Iraq, the Sadat of Najran, the imams of Yemen, or the sultans of Oman. Yet, after meeting ibn Abd al-Wahhab, Muhammad ibn Saud concluded a compact with him in which he undertook to defy and fight one and all powers for the sake of God and empire. Ibn Saud had sought explicit assurance that ibn Abd al-Wahhab would not ask him to forgo taxes on his subjects, and the latter had agreed and promised that if ibn Saud exerted himself and held fast to the doctrine of God's oneness, "the Almighty will hopefully conquer your conquests and recompense you with spoils of war far more ample than your present revenues."[2]

The first expedition out of Dar'iyya consisted of seven camel riders who fell on an unsuspecting company of bedouins and brought home booty. During the next fifteen years or so, the combination of additional successes, the desire of some tribes to avoid exposure to Saudi-Wahhabi raiding and to share in the loot from raiding others, and the appeal of the Wahhabi religious message enabled ibn Saud to bring much of Najd, excluding Riyadh, under his control. These successes, however, brought the Wahhabis into conflict with the powers beyond the Najd region — the lords of Hasa, Najran, and the Hijaz. A critical moment occurred in 1764, when, after many skirmishes and battles, the Hasa and Najran leaders mounted large combined expeditions from the east and the south to put an end to the movement. Muhammad ibn Saud's son set out to meet the forces advancing from Najran but his forces were crushed not far from Dar'iyya. Fortunately for ibn Saud, the leader of the Najran forces agreed to come to terms with him and returned home. When the Banu Khalid arrived on the scene, they withdrew after learning that their Najrani allies had made peace.

One year later Muhammad ibn Saud died and was succeeded by his son Abd al-Aziz (r. 1765–1803). Under Abd al-Aziz, the Wahhabi jihad gained new momentum, and the Wahhabi forces, ably led by Abd al-Aziz's eldest son, Saud, were victorious in all directions, reaping vast booty and often sowing terror along their way. To the east, the Wahhabis captured Qatif, an oasis inhabited by sectarian Shi'ites, and destroyed their places of worship. They also conquered Hasa, subjected Bahrain to their suzerainty, submitted what are now called the United Arab Emirates to Wahhabism, and reached the Arabian Sea. The sultan of Muscat (part of the present Oman) was intermittently forced to pay tribute but was able to escape subjugation by seeking and receiving timely support from British, Persian, and other Arab allies.

To the south, the Wahhabis reached the great Empty Quarter and made descents into the Hadramaut beyond it although they were unable to annex that region. The leaders of the 'Asir tribes joined the cause and from there the Wahhabi movement spilled down into the lowland of the Tihama along the Red Sea, reaching as far south as the ports of Yemen, although in the highlands of Yemen the Zaidis (a Shi'ite sect) preserved their independence. To the north, the Wahhabis advanced into the Iraqi and Syrian deserts, subduing tribes and harassing settled areas and cities. In 1801 a force of 10,000 men on 6,000 camels broke into Karbala, site of the tomb of the Prophet Muhammad's martyred grandson, Hussein, and one of the holiest places of Shi'ism. In an eight-hour orgy of violence they indiscriminately massacred some 5,000 people, wrecked Hussein's mosque-tomb, looted the city, and then pulled out with 200 camels loaded with treasure.[3] On the Syrian side, the Wahhabis raided in the vicinity of Damascus and further north.

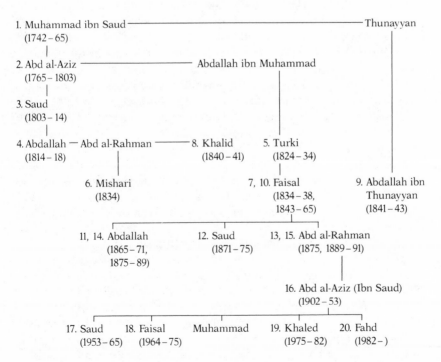

Figure 1. Abridged genealogy of Saudi Arabia's rulers (with years of reign)

To the west, the Wahhabis culminated a fifteen-year struggle with Sharif Ghalib by capturing Ta'if and massacring its inhabitants in 1802, and then marching into Mecca in 1803. Before the victorious Abd al-Aziz, the 'ulama of the holy city declared their acceptance of Wahhabism, and Ghalib accepted Saudi sovereignty; but after Abd al-Aziz returned to Dar'iyya, Ghalib reoccupied the city. Shortly thereafter Abd al-Aziz was assassinated in his capital while performing the Friday prayers in the mosque. The assassin was a Persian whose three sons had been massacred in Karbala. He had pretended to convert to Wahhabism and had worked in the Wahhabi capital for a year awaiting an opportunity to avenge his children.[4]

Abd al-Aziz was followed by his eldest son, Saud (r. 1803–1814), whose succession had been secured as early as 1787 by Shaikh ibn Abd al-Wahhab. The Shaikh himself had died in 1792 but had left four sons who continued his work and further tightened the alliance with the Saudi dynasty. Saud was an enthusiastic Wahhabi and a most capable military leader; he was responsible for most of the conquests during his father's lifetime, and during his own reign he brought the movement to the height of its power. He recaptured Madina the following year and extended the frontiers of Wahhabism in all directions. In 1808, 1810, and 1812 Wahhabi forces threatened Baghdad. In 1810 a large force sacked dozens of villages immediately south of Damascus and later that year exacted taxes from tribes forty miles south of Aleppo. Internally, Saud institutionalized Wahhabism and dealt severely with tribal lawlessness. Over a century later, King Ibn Saud liked to tell of how when Imam Saud had imprisoned some shaikhs from the Mutair tribe, a party of the tribe's leaders came to remonstrate with him and became threatening.[5] Saud ordered the heads of the prisoners to be cut off and dished up on the table before their kinsmen, whom he then ordered to proceed with their meal.[6] Saud left Sharif Ghalib in charge of the Hijaz so as not to provoke the Ottoman sultan, Ghalib's suzerain and the self-proclaimed Guardian of the Two Holy Places (that is, Mecca and Madina). But he antagonized the sultan and Muslims everywhere by ordering Ghalib to remove the domed tombs of saints and by interfering drastically with pilgrim traffic to enforce Wahhabi standards against long-established customs.

The effective loss of the holy cities was more than the Ottoman sultan could countenance. After failing to engineer counterattacks from Iraq, Sultan Selim appointed Muhammad Ali of Egypt viceroy of the Hijaz with orders to combat the Wahhabis. Muhammad Ali first took time to consolidate his rule in Egypt, but in October 1811 he sent a force of 1,000 Albanian infantry, which landed in Yanbo and was joined two weeks later by 800 cavalry who had marched overland through Sinai and Aqaba. In January 1812 the expeditionary force, under the command of Muhammad

Ali's son Tusun, advanced on Madina but was ambushed by Saud's forces and nearly destroyed at the Judaida pass. In October 1812 the reinforced Egyptian army, supported by tribes that had deserted the Wahhabis, reached Madina and, after a fourteen-day siege, stormed and captured the city. One thousand Wahhabis were killed and 1,500 captured. In January 1813 Mecca was occupied without opposition and Ta'if fell soon after. In August of that year Muhammad Ali himself landed at Jidda with 2,000 cavalry and 2,000 infantry and performed a triumphant pilgrimage. Negotiations between agents of Muhammad Ali and Saud based on Saudi recognition of Ottoman/Egyptian dominion in the Hijaz failed over side issues. Despite Muhammad Ali's obvious strength, Saud, who had kept most of his forces intact, trusted in his ability to use them effectively against regular forces, taking advantage of distances and terrain as he had done at Judaida and was to do again at Turaba in 1814. But in April 1814 Saud died suddenly of fever at Dar'iyya; his death was a grievous setback to the Wahhabi cause.[7]

Saud was succeeded by his son Abdallah (r. 1814–1818), a man known for wisdom and intelligence but lacking his father's firmness and military abilities. At the very beginning of his reign he was challenged by his great-uncle, Abdallah ibn Muhammad, who considered that he had a prior claim because he was the son of Muhammad ibn Saud, the founder of the Saudi-Wahhabi realm. Abdallah ibn Saud defeated his great-uncle, but dissension had set in and opponents of Abdallah and of the Sauds generally, as well as the fickle bedouin tribes, turned to Muhammad Ali for support.

In March 1815 Tusun marched on the Qasim, a region halfway between Madina and Dar'iyya, with a force of 1,000 regulars, plus contingents from the Mutair and Harb tribes, hitherto themselves Wahhabis. In June of that year Abdallah and Tusun reached an agreement wherein the former renounced any claim to Mecca and Madina and recognized Tusun as overlord while the latter agreed to withdraw to Madina; but Muhammad Ali refused to ratify the agreement. Instead he recalled Tusun to Cairo, where the latter died soon after, and sent another of his sons, Ibrahim Pasha, with a fresh force and with instructions to destroy Wahhabi power and lay waste all the territories under their control. He sought to ensure that no aspirant to supremacy over the holy cities should arise for a long time to come.

Ibrahim Pasha landed in the Hijaz with 2,000 infantry and 1,500 cavalry in September 1816 and advanced systematically, rallying defecting tribes as he went. In April 1818 he finally appeared before the walls of Dar'iyya with a force of 2,000 cavalry, 5,600 infantry, 12 guns, and a multitude of tribesmen. A rapid assault on the town failed and gave way to a five-month siege, after which Abdallah sued for terms including pardon for the troops that had remained faithful to him, pardon for his brothers and family, the preservation of the town, and safety for his own person. Ibrahim agreed to the first two requests but would make no promise with respect to the town. As to the fourth request, he would guarantee Abdallah's safety only until he arrived in Cairo, where further decisions would be made. Abdallah complied. He was sent to Cairo and thence to Constantinople, where he was paraded for three days before being beheaded and impaled. Ibrahim Pasha razed Dar'iyya and then swept into all adjacent territories — into Jabal Shammar, Hariq, Hasa, and the borders of Oman. He razed all forts, dismantled every fence, and collected some 400 members of the House of Saud and the Shaikh family whom he deported to Cairo. In 1819 the Egyptian forces pulled back to the Hijaz, leaving only a garrison in the Qasim. They restored Hasa to the Banu Khalid to rule but left central Arabia to be torn asunder as before by its own tribal enmities. Thus ended the first Saudi-Wahhabi realm, seventy years after its modest beginnings and less than twenty years after reaching its zenith.[8]

The Second Realm, 1824–1891

Muhammad Ali withdrew his forces from Najd because he had accomplished his main object of recapturing and securing Mecca and Madina, because Najd itself was too poor and too restless to tempt him, and because he believed he had completely destroyed Wahhabi power. Within five years, however, a grandson of the founder of the first Saudi realm and son of the pretender defeated by Abdallah ibn Saud, Turki ibn Abdallah ibn Muhammad ibn Saud (r. 1824–1834), established a new Saudi-Wahhabi power base in Riyadh, south of Dar'iyya. Like his forebears, Turki began by consolidating his rule in Najd through constant campaigning and then proceeded to expand, conquering Hasa in 1830 and exacting recognition of Wahhabi rule along the entire coast of the Persian Gulf by 1833. Unlike his predecessors, however, Turki, though a faithful Wahhabi, was careful not to fan the embers of Wahhabi fanaticism and endeavored to avoid clashing with Ottoman/Egyptian power in the Hijaz and with the increasingly assertive British power in the Persian Gulf and along its shores. The challenge that Turki faced stemmed rather from a combination of tribal lawlessness, rivalry within the Saudi family, and discontent within the religious leadership, which split over the question of responsibility for the 1818 disaster.

In 1831, while on a punitive expedition against some tribes, Turki received word that a distant cousin of his, Mishari ibn Abd al-Rahman ibn Saud, whom he had appointed governor of Manfuha, had revolted with the support of some tribal elements. By the time Turki got back to

Riyadh, Mishari had fled. The latter tried in vain to mobilize additional tribal backing and to enlist the support of the sharif of Mecca, then submitted to Turki, who put him and his family under some kind of house arrest. In 1834, however, Mishari successfully plotted the assassination of Turki while the Saudi forces under Turki's son Faisal were occupied in a war with Bahrain. Turki was killed while coming out of the mosque on Friday. Members of the Shaikh family remained in the mosque and asked for *aman* — assurance of safety. When this was given, they acknowledged Mishari as imam.

Mishari's rule did not last long. Within forty days Faisal ibn Turki (r. 1834–1838, 1843–1865) rallied tribal support, marched on Riyadh, defeated Mishari, and had him executed. But the dissensions within the Saudi family encouraged the Banu Khalid of Hasa to revolt and the rulers of Qatar and Bahrain to repudiate Saudi suzerainty. Moreover, in the year that Faisal seized power, Muhammad Ali of Egypt, having broken with the Ottoman sultan, defeated his forces, and brought what is now Palestine, Syria, and Lebanon under his rule, looked to incorporating the entire Arabian Peninsula in his growing empire. The Egyptians began by putting pressure on Faisal to recognize their overlordship over Najd and to assist them in their long-unsuccessful effort to subdue the 'Asir highlands. Faisal sent his brother Jilwi to Mecca with presents, submissive words, and offers of some camels for transport while he secretly helped his 'Asiri allies. In 1836, however, the Egyptians landed an expeditionary force in Yanbo that marched on Najd. With them came a Saudi pretender in the person of a cousin of Faisal, Khalid, son of Saud and brother of the Abdallah they had defeated in 1818. Faisal assembled a force and went out to meet the invaders, but his troops melted away as word spread about the superior Egyptian forces. The people of Riyadh, too, were intimidated by the approaching enemy and refused to fight. Faisal then slipped out with a small number of followers, and Khalid entered Riyadh with the Egyptian forces in 1837. For a while the Egyptians accepted a submission by Faisal and left the two Saudi chiefs ruling a partitioned Najd under them. But in 1838 they marched against Faisal, defeated and captured him, and sent him for detention in Cairo.

The Egyptians went on to conquer all of Arabia except 'Asir, this time with intent to stay. The fact that they now worked with Khalid and were allies of the Wahhabis, coupled with their superior forces and energetic military leadership, enabled them to exercise firm control. But events elsewhere soon led to the termination of Egyptian rule. In the wake of a second war and a decisive victory by Muhammad Ali against the Ottoman sultan in 1839, the European powers intervened and forced on Muhammad Ali a settlement that confined him to the hereditary rulership of Egypt. In 1841 the bulk of the Egyptian forces were withdrawn from Najd, leaving Khalid ibn Saud in charge of Riyadh with the support of a small Egyptian garrison.

Soon after the Egyptian withdrawal, Abdallah ibn Thunayyan, a descendant of Muhammad ibn Saud, captured Riyadh and was proclaimed imam in 1841. Khalid made several unsuccessful attempts to recover his fortunes before giving up and finding refuge in the Hijaz. Ibn Thunayyan met his doom through another challenger. In 1843 Faisal ibn Turki escaped from his jail in Egypt, made his way to Najd, and raised a force with which he challenged him in Riyadh. Ibn Thunayyan surrendered, and Faisal had him thrown in jail, where he was poisoned shortly thereafter.

Faisal's second reign (1843–1865) was the golden age of the second Saudi realm. Territorially, the realm was much smaller than the first and had little of its dynamism; but it had far greater acceptance externally and internally, representing as it did a transition from "revolutionary Wahhabism" to "Wahhabism in one country." Faisal's ideal notion of the "one country" comprised all the domains once conquered by his ancestors, but in practice he was careful not to press beyond the limits of his power. He not only refrained from challenging Ottoman rule in the Hijaz but also acknowledged the sultan's suzerainty and paid an annual tribute in exchange for Ottoman recognition of himself as "ruler of all the Arabs."[9] In the opposite direction, Faisal endeavored to assert his authority in Bahrain, Qatar, the Gulf shaikhdoms (known then as the Trucial Shaikhdoms and now as the United Arab Emirates), and northern Oman but was careful not to clash with the British, who in 1835 sponsored a treaty that established a "maritime truce" among the rulers of these lands and recognized Britain as arbitrator of disputes between them.

Toward the end of his life Faisal tried to tempt the British into an alliance with him against Ottoman power, although he had long used his Ottoman connections and the title granted him by the sultan to resist British pressure to recognize the independence of the Gulf statelets. When the British declined his offer, he tried to take advantage of dissension in Oman in order to advance his claim there. The British responded by bombarding Dammam and Hufuf, on the coast under his control, in January 1866, after which they reached an understanding with Faisal's son Abdallah to prevent further clashes.

Just as Wahhabism ceased under Faisal to be a driving force for an unlimited holy war externally, so it ceased to be a major issue internally. On the one hand, all the territories under Faisal's authority willingly accepted Wahhabism, and on the other hand acceptance came to signify merely willingness to accept judges and religious teachers appointed by the imam. The bedouin tribes were exempted even from that requirement, as were the Gulf states and Oman in the intermittent periods when they paid tribute to Riyadh. Although the practice of Wahhabism was strictly enforced in places such as Riyadh and central Najd and more or less loosely followed elsewhere, the differences provided little or no ground for conflict.

Politically and administratively, Faisal adopted an even more flexible policy to keep his realm together. In remote and insecure areas such as Buraimi and Qatif, he appointed governors supported by garrisons; in the central districts, he appointed governors chosen mostly from the local citizenry; in distant, strong, but nominally loyal districts such as Jabal Shammar, he accepted the Rashidi leadership that emerged locally. Among the bedouin tribes he dealt directly with the shaikhs and made them responsible for enforcing order and paying taxes, which varied with the extent of grazing rights and support against raiding by other tribes granted by the imam. The Gulf states and Oman paid tribute intermittently but had no other connection with Riyadh. Everywhere, he sought to reinforce the "administrative" connection with family bonds — his son Abdallah, for instance, had a Rashidi wife, and another son, Saud, married into the 'Ajman tribe.

Since the "government" disposed of a very small revenue, had no bureaucracy and no standing army beyond a royal bodyguard of a few hundred, and depended entirely on tribal militias, it is clear that the entire realm was essentially a precarious confederation of tribes held together by the energy, will, and wisdom of the chief.[10] Faisal had these qualities, but even so he had to campaign constantly to keep the bedouins in line and to subdue recalcitrant tribes. His sons-successors not only lacked these traits but also engaged in a long fratricidal strife that resulted in the destruction of the second Saudi-Wahhabi realm. The main episodes of the debacle were as follows.

Faisal had four sons: Abdallah, Saud, Muhammad, and Abd al-Rahman. In his own lifetime he had given administrative responsibilities to the first three in various parts of the realm and had nominated Abdallah to succeed him. (Abd al-Rahman, born in 1850, had been too young to play a significant role.) After his accession as imam, Abdallah tried to "centralize" his power by forcing his appointees and enlarging their jurisdiction, thus antagonizing important families, sections, and tribes. Saud, who coveted the succession for himself and had sources of support of his own, particularly within the powerful 'Ajman tribe, to which both his mother and his wife belonged, took advantage of his brother's mistakes to challenge and eventually defeat him and captured Riyadh in February 1871. Before that happened, however, Abdallah, feeling the ground slip from under him, had appealed to the Ottoman authorities, the nominal suzerains of Najd, to help him against his rebellious brother. The Ottoman governor of Iraq, the energetic and able Midhat Pasha, took advantage of the situation to send a strong expedition that conquered the eastern province of Hasa in July 1871. Abdallah, who went to greet his ostensible saviors and to obtain further help from them, found himself their virtual prisoner. Soon afterward, however, a brother of the late Imam Faisal, Abdallah ibn Turki, ousted Saud from Riyadh, and Abdallah ibn Faisal escaped and joined him. Abdallah ibn Faisal wrote to Midhat Pasha that he was willing to acknowledge Turkish suzerainty in return for recognition as imam of the Wahhabi territories, but Midhat reacted by dismissing all Saudis and appointing a Turkish governor for Najd. The dismissals and the appointment meant little as far as Najd was concerned, but the eastern province remained in the hands of the Turks until Ibn Saud recovered it in 1913.

As the strife between the brothers continued, the Ottomans took advantage of the opening of the Suez Canal to send a powerful expeditionary force that finally overcame Wahhabi resistance in 'Asir and brought the province under their control. The leader of a fundamentalist Ibadi upheaval in Oman captured the Buraimi oasis from Abdallah's forces and retained it in alliance with Saud, who continued to contest his brother. The Qasim towns and Jabal Shammar ceased to make any contribution to Riyadh, so that the Saudi state shrank to the central Najdi districts, and even there, whoever ruled in the Saudi capital was unable to control the bedouins.

In 1873 Saud captured Riyadh for the second time. His brother Abdallah eluded him but his uncle, Abdallah ibn Turki, was seized and thrown into jail, where he died shortly thereafter. Two years later, Saud himself succumbed to smallpox. Abd al-Rahman, the youngest brother, who was with Saud in Riyadh, took over, but Abdallah and Muhammad fought him. Abd al-Rahman emerged victorious but was soon challenged by Saud's sons and was forced to flee Riyadh. He joined his brothers Abdallah and Muhammad and together the three were able to drive the nephews out of Riyahd though not to defeat them decisively. This was the eighth change in supreme authority in Riyadh in the eleven years since Faisal's death.

After being reinstalled in Riyadh for the second time, Abdallah tried to take advantage of a conflict between 'Anaiza and Buraida, the principal towns of Qasim, to reassert his authority throughout the province. He backed 'Anaiza; but Muhammad ibn Rashid, the very able ruler of Jabal Shammar, supported Buraida in order to check the resurgence of Saudi power. In the ensuing confrontation Abdallah backed down without giving battle, with the result that not only did Jabal Shammar break away but also whatever authority remaining to Abdallah in Najd was undermined.[11]

In 1879 Abdallah and his brothers temporarily patched up their quarrel with their nephews (the sons of Saud), and they all sought intermittently to regain Hasa and to reassert Saudi control. In the process, Abdallah clashed once more with Muhammad ibn Rashid in 1884 and this time was decisively defeated. Ibn Rashid, however, not only refrained from marching into Riyadh but also, in an attempt to pacify Abdallah, agreed to relinquish his conquest of the districts of Washm and Sudair. The following year, the quarrel between brothers and nephews flared up again, and two years later the nephews marched from their base in Kharj, captured Riyadh, and took Abdallah prisoner. Abdallah managed to send an appeal for help to ibn Rashid, who advanced on the Saudi capital with an overwhelming force. The nephews negotiated an *aman* and returned to Kharj. Ibn Rashid entered Riyadh; liberated Abdallah; took him to Ha'il, Shammar's capital, as a "permanent guest"; and appointed a Rashidi governor of the Saudi capital.[12] The second Saudi realm thus came to an end, the victim of dissension in the ruling family, the inherent centrifugal forces in the region, and the chance presence of a rival of stature in the person of Muhammad ibn Rashid.

Two or three more episodes round out the story of the fall of the second Saudi realm and shed an interesting light on subsequent events. From their base in Kharj, Saud's sons (the nephews of Abdallah) plotted a restoration of Saudi rule. To quash this threat the Rashidi governor of Riyadh, Salim ibn Subhan, in an operation that anticipated a better-known one by Ibn Saud in 1902, launched a surprise dawn raid on Kharj in 1888 with thirty-five men who had scaled the town's walls under cover of darkness. Salim killed one of the nephews and foiled the attempted escape of a second. When the third, who was on a mission with the 'Ajman tribe, heard of what had befallen his brothers and their town, he went to Ha'il and threw himself on ibn Rashid's mercy. (The sons of this nephew, grandsons of Saud, were to challenge Ibn Saud in 1911 and 1916.)

Muhammad ibn Rashid behaved generously toward the Sauds. He disclaimed any knowledge of the attack on Kharj and later dismissed Salim. He allowed Abdallah to return to Riyadh and retain the title of imam, and after Abdallah's death in 1889 he appointed his brother Abd al-Rahman governor. In 1890 Abd al-Rahman revolted and successfully surprised and defeated the Rashidi garrison. Ibn Rashid besieged Riyadh but came to an agreement with Abd al-Rahman that confirmed him as governor of Riyadh and of neighboring districts under Rashidi suzerainty. Later that year the Qasimis, including 'Anaiza and Buraida, apparently encouraged by the "weakness" shown by ibn Rashid toward Abd al-Rahman, revolted against the former. In addition to backing from Abd al-Rahman, they enlisted the support of powerful tribes hostile to Shammar. Ibn Rashid met the rebels in 1891 in the battle of Mulaida, said to have been the biggest military encounter in central Arabia since the rise of Islam. Ibn Rashid prevailed before Abd al-Rahman and his forces were able to join the battle; Abd al-Rahman headed for the desert and eventual exile in Kuwait, where family members joined him. Mulaida was the last twitch of the dying second Saudi-Wahhabi realm.[13]

Lessons from the First Two Realms

The history of the rise and fall of the first two Saudi realms provides many insights helpful to an understanding of the emergence of the third Saudi state, its character, and its mode of functioning. Although present-day Saudi Arabia is in many ways vastly different from the first and second realms, and even from the third realm as bequeathed by its founder to his successors, more features of the earlier states remain relevant today than might be suspected from a superficial impression of the changes that have taken place since. Moreover, an appreciation of certain features of the earlier realms also helps to highlight the scope and significance of the changes that have occurred. The remainder of this chapter presents the most important of these insights.

1. The Arabian Peninsula is by nature inhospitable to any comprehensive political entity.

This conclusion is based not only on the fact of the turbulent existence and relatively brief duration of the first two Saudi realms, but also on the fact that for thousands of years before them no political entity embracing most of Arabia had arisen, except for a short period under the Prophet Muhammad and his immediate successors. The reasons for this circumstance are related to the geography and ecology of Arabia.

With the exception of Yemen and Oman, the Arabian Peninsula is essentially a vast arid territory of more than 1 million square miles that until recently was too poor to provide any resources beyond the needs of subsistence sufficient to support a central power. Its sparse population comprised two groups. The majority consisted of nomadic herdsmen — bedouins — roving over large expanses to graze their flocks on scarce brush and ephemeral grass that sprouted after the scanty winter rains. The remainder consisted of small agricultural communities in the few areas where the availability of water made cultivation possible. In this environment, where individuals and limited families could not survive, both the settled and nomad populations were organized into tightly knit tribes, clans, and extended families for mutual support and security. Before the rise of Islam, some settled tribes were able for various periods to organize and secure a transit trade through Arabia to and from the rich, fertile lands at its periphery. After Islam was established, some towns and tribes secured an additional source of income by providing services, transport, and protection to caravans of pilgrims passing through their territories. However, the benefits of trade and pilgrimage reached only small portions of the population, were subject to frequent and prolonged disruptions as a result of disorder, and thus failed to provide a basis for an enduring large-scale political entity.

The difficulties of earning a livelihood, the dearth of surplus resources, the vast distances of the peninsula, and nomadism and tribalism combined to place Arabia in a kind of Hobbesian state of nature in which each tribe was permanently at war with all the others, except for short and temporary alliances. Hostility between the settled and bedouin tribes was particularly profound, assuming an added "cultural" dimension of contempt for each other's occupation and way of life. Yet, contrary to Hobbesian theory, this state of affairs was not deemed to be an unbearable evil to be escaped at all costs. On the contrary, the bedouin tribes especially regarded war, mutual raiding, and looting not as deplorable necessities from which they would escape if they could, but rather considered them to be exciting features of a desirable way of life, providing occasions for the display of various kinds of virtuosity to be immortalized in heroic verse and song.

That state of affairs was sustained by an inherent tendency to produce an equilibrium of power among the tribes, bedouin or settled. Weak units tended to merge or ally themselves with others for protection against stronger units; overly large entities tended to split up from lack of sufficient living space or because they became unwieldy. For this reason, wars were not as destructive or as one-sided in their outcomes as they might otherwise have been. More important, no unit could achieve a sufficiently superior power to develop into a political leviathan that could impose itself on all. The exceptions to this rule, under the Prophet Muhammad and the Saudis, occurred precisely when a new factor, in the form of a religious impetus, upset the equilibrium.

2. Religious fervor coupled with the tribal ethos was the essential driving force in the creation of the first Saudi realm, and also its ultimate nemesis.

The dynamics of the creation of the first Saudi realm were similar to those that had brought about the unification of the Arabian Peninsula under the Prophet Muhammad. Muhammad had delivered a message that sublimated but did not eliminate the tribal ethos and provided a bond that transcended but did not abolish tribal divisions. The adoption of Islam by several tribes and sections of tribes and their submission to a single firm leadership created a mass of power that was too strong for any other tribe to resist. Consequently other tribes, whether or not they were convinced by the Prophet's message, were impelled one after the other to join his cause in order to avoid reprisals and to share in the booty to be taken from the remaining recalcitrant tribes.

When all the tribes of Arabia were thus united, their formidable combined energies, previously dissipated in mutual hostility, were directed outward against the infidels of neighboring lands. Each success achieved there confirmed the merit of the new dispensation, brought additional material rewards, and gave the movement further impetus, until a vast empire was created in an astoundingly short time. The conquest of rich lands and cities provided more than ample revenues to support a central power; but the seat of that power shifted to more natural centers of gravity in the new empire, and arid Arabia became a neglected backwater province, except for the holy cities of Mecca and Madina. Before long, under the impact of its environment, it reverted to pre-Islamic beliefs and practices under an Islamic veneer.

The creators of the first Saudi-Wahhabi realm consciously emulated the model of the Prophet's career, tapped the same motives, and by a similar process achieved similar results up to a certain point. Using Wahhabism as the supratribal and intertribal bond, and coupling militancy on behalf of "true Islam" with the tribal ethos of loot and conquest, they established a firm base in Najd from which they overran the rest of Arabia and spilled over into the neighboring lands. At that point, however, they confronted the power of the Ottoman Empire, which not only disposed of different, superior, and modern material power but also was acknowledged by most Muslims as the bulwark of Islamic orthodoxy. That confrontation stopped the increasing momentum of the Wahhabi thrust; and once the drive was checked, a reversal of the process began: tribes that had accepted Wahhabism abandoned its promoters in increasing numbers as their cause appeared to be losing, and joined the successful Egyptian-Ottoman forces that finally destroyed the Saudi-Wahhabi realm.

3. The dynastic principle coupled with routinized Wahhabism was the driving force in the creation of the second Saudi realm and also contained the seeds of its ultimate destruction.

The fate of the first realm having demonstrated the perils of militant Wahhabism, the founders of the second realm based their drive on their right to rule the domains once conquered by their ancestors in the name of Wahhabism. That dynastic principle provided the creators of the second realm with a more conventional and therefore safer foundation than their ancestors had had, but it was also less inspiring and therefore less strong. Since Wahhabism without militancy had become generally accepted or acceptable, other rulers could and did contest the House of Saud's claim to exclusive association with that creed. Moreover, since the Saudi claim was based on inheritance, various members of the House of Saud itself could and did lay competing claims to it. To be sure, Wahhabism as a subsidiary to the dynastic principle kept alive the ideal of a large unified realm in Arabia, and this fact altered Arabian politics by giving them a new focus; but it no longer ensured unified leadership, as it had in the first realm.

The advantages and disadvantages of the dynastic principle in the Arabian environment are clear from the historical record. Whereas Muhammad and Abd al-Aziz, the founders of the first realm, starting from Dar'iyya and using militant Wahhabism, took nearly half a century to subdue most of Arabia, Turki and Faisal, starting from a claim to the inheritance of their ancestors, were able to assert their rule over most of the same territory within a few years. On the other hand, whereas the creators and rulers of the first realm, having founded their right on achievement in the service of the cause they had espoused, met with no challenge to their leadership, the creators and rulers of the second realm, having based their right on inheritance, were constantly challenged from both within and outside the House of Saud. Turki was challenged by Egyptian-supported Khalid, who was challenged by ibn Thunayyan, who was challenged by Faisal again. After Faisal's death, his brother, his own four sons, and his grandsons fought one another in alliance with outsiders, giving the Ottomans the chance to encroach upon the Saudi realm and Muhammad ibn Rashid to liquidate it altogether.

4. During internal power struggles, the religious establishment contributed little to an orderly resolution of the conflict, tending to take neutral positions when the issue was in doubt and to sanction the authority of whoever prevailed.

Muhammad ibn Saud and his son Abd al-Aziz had a personal compact with Shaikh Muhammad ibn al-Wahhab, who created and headed the Wahhabi religious establishment. The third ruler, Saud, had a personal compact with the descendants and successors of the Shaikh. But when Saud's son Abdallah was challenged by his uncle, the religious establishment wavered. After the destruction of Dar'iyya by Ibraham Pasha, the religious establishment itself was rent by bitter arguments about the wisdom of identifying the cause of religion with the person and policies of a particular ruler, and by charges of blame for the disaster leveled by some members of the establishment against the leaders.[14]

During the second realm, the religious establishment adopted from the outset an attitude of cautious neutrality toward the power struggles among the Saudis and between them and outsiders, a stance that amounted in fact to sanctioning whatever outcome the struggles produced. The blood of Imam Turki had not been wiped off the floor of the mosque where he was assassinated when the attending members of the Shaikh family recognized his assassin, Mishari, as imam. Nor did the fact that Khalid was installed in 1837 by the bayonets of the returning Egyptian forces prevent the religious establishment from acknowledging his legitimacy. It maintained the same position throughout the fratricidal struggles that led to the destruction of the second realm and throughout the major crises of the third realm, when Ibn Saud confronted the Ikhwan and when King Saud and Emir Faisal quarreled. To all appearances, once the era of militant Wahhabism was past, the religious establishment reverted to the traditional Sunni political doctrine advanced by al-Ghazzali (1058–1111), wherein all power was viewed as legitimate regardless of how it was achieved, as long as its holder was prepared to support the application of the Shari'a (the Islamic religious law). Perhaps this attitude protected the continuity and integrity of the role of religion against political fluctuations, but only at the cost of forfeiting whatever contribution the religious establishment might have made toward diminishing those fluctuations by regularizing the transfer of power.

5. The Saudi realms have been particularly vulnerable to the problem of succession.

All hereditary regimes have been periodically troubled by the issue of succession, but the Saudi and other Arabian regimes (the Rashids, for instance) have been particularly vulnerable to the problem. The first two successions in the first Saudi realm took place smoothly, but the third, Abdallah's, already encountered some difficulty. In the three-quarters of a century of the second Saudi realm there was not one peaceful transfer of power.

One reason for the difficulty is the environmental conditions that made the Arabian Peninsula inherently inhospitable to large-scale political entities. An exceptionally able leader, or one who is identified with a religious cause transcending existing loyalties, could temporarily overcome the environmental limitations and establish a substantial realm; however, because of the dearth of surplus resources, even such a ruler could not create institutions of power—such as standing armed forces, a bureaucracy, and police—that, if transmitted to his successor, could give him a critical edge over potential challengers. Consequently, if a successor was a weaker personality than the original ruler or was not exclusively identified with the religious cause, as was the case with Abdallah after Saud and Abd al-Aziz, or if the transcendent religious bond itself weakened, as was the case in the second realm, the inherent centrifugal tendencies reasserted themselves and encouraged challengers to contest the transfer of power.

Another reason has to do with the rules for succession followed by the House of Saud. Like other Arabian (and Muslim) ruling families, the Saudis have shunned the Western principle of primogeniture in favor of the tribally rooted rule that invests the succession in the oldest and most capable member of the ruling family. Perhaps in the circumstances of tribal life, where the criteria of ability are simple, obvious, and related to survival, the rule is logical and natural, but in the more complex circumstances of a large state, even one that consists of a confederation of tribes, the criteria become more difficult to ascertain and capability becomes accordingly subject to division and revision of opinion. The problem might have been overcome if there were a recognized body empowered to make authoritative decisions, and a neutral state power to enforce them, but such was not the case in the disputes that developed in the first and second Saudi realms, nor has such a body matured in the third realm.

The criterion of seniority is fairly straightforward, but even that has not been without problems. In the extensive House of Saud, some have sought to confine the rule to one branch, while others have sought to extend it to the entire family tree. The problem arose in the second Saudi realm and troubled even the great Ibn Saud early in the third. The greater the ramification of the family, the greater the potential for problems, and the more difficult it becomes for a particular incumbent to establish lineal succession within his own family against the opposition of all the others.

The House of Saud, like other Arabian and Muslim dynasties past and present, has tried to resolve the problem by a procedure wherein the incumbent ruler nominates his successor and secures for him confirmation from "the people with the power to loosen and bind," subject to reconfirmation upon the nominee's accession. This device has worked often but not always. It did not work in the case of the fatal conflict between Abdallah, who had been nominated by his father Faisal (the first) and his brother Saud in the 1860s and 1870s, or in the case of the conflict between King Saud and his brother Faisal (the second) some hundred years later. These cases also illustrate the point that attempts to appease potential rivals of the nominee by giving them shares of power could just as well place them in a better position to challenge him.

6. Except perhaps at the height of the Wahhabi movement, the politics of the Saudi realms, like all other Arabian politics, have been dominated to an unusual extent by an ethos of opportunism.

Even if one accepts the adage that in politics there are no permanent friends and enemies, only permanent interests, Arabian politics seem to demonstrate the point to an unusual degree. The following examples are by no means exhaustive: the tribes rallied to the Wahhabi cause when it appeared to be winning and joined its enemies when the latter appeared to be stronger; Khalid ibn Saud joined the Egyptians, who had destroyed the first realm and his brother Abdallah, in their campaign against Faisal; the Rashidis began their career as lieutenants of Faisal and went on to dispossess his successors; Faisal overtly helped the Egyptians against the 'Asiri rebels and covertly helped the rebels against the Egyptians; he vowed loyalty to his Ottoman suzerain and broached a revolt against him with the help of the infidel British; his son Abdallah invited Turkish power against his brother Saud, while Saud allied himself with the sectarian Ibadi chiefs of Oman against his brother Abdallah; Abd al-Rahman sided with Saud against Abdallah and Muhammad, then with the latter against the sons of Saud, and so on.

This tendency is rooted in the Arabian environment and its previously described effects. Because Arabia was composed of almost entirely self-sufficient tribes, there were very few bonds even of self-interest to tie them into *enduring* associations. Among the bedouin tribes, who were predominant in numbers, the only interest in association related to power balances; and since the power constellations always changed because they lacked a firm "substructural" base, the associations and alliances also constantly shifted. Among the settled tribes there was a larger measure of shared interest in common defense against the bedouin tribes, but the wide dispersal of their settlements and the rivalries among themselves also limited the possibility of enduring associations and tempted the chiefs of the individual towns and oasis-clusters to make their own arrangements with the bedouin tribes and thus be drawn into the orbit of their politics. Neither settled nor bedouin tribes had a lasting interest in an overarching state unless their particular tribe controlled it, since the state merely exacted taxes and tribute and was in no position to offer desirable services. A chief who would attempt such an enterprise was therefore to be intitially resisted, joined if he appeared to be succeeding, shaken off if he appeared to be faltering, and deserted in favor of his enemy if the latter seemed stronger. From the point of view of the would-be founder or ruler of a realm, it was necessary to treat some defeated opponents harshly to impress or deter others, but to treat most of them generously because enemies could easily become allies.

This ethos was modified but not fundamentally altered by Wahhabism. Once the first Saudi chiefs were able to build momentum for their drive, religious fervor and identification injected a certain measure of constancy into the previously fluid politics of Arabia. However, since the momentum itself had been built largely through the play of the Arabian political ethos, once that momentum was stopped, the ethos reasserted itself and contributed to its reversal. Abdallah, the unfortunate last ruler of the first realm, exceptionally fought almost to the end at Dar'iyya; but he did so only after Muhammad Ali had rejected the accommodation Abdallah had worked out with Tusun.

7. The quality of the ruler has been of vital importance for the Saudi realms.

If the quality of leadership is important for democratic states and crucial for absolutist ones, it has been a matter of life and death for the Saudi (and other Arabian) realms. Because the dearth of surplus resources has prevented the development of standing instruments of power, and because the natural and human environment has fostered centrifugal tendencies, the creation and maintenance of the Saudi realms has depended entirely on the strength and wisdom of their leaders. The first realm was forged by powerful chiefs who maintained it by directing tribal energies and greed outward against "unbelievers." The failure of these leaders to recognize the limits of their power led to Egyptian intervention and destruction under a weaker leadership. Turki and Faisal, who forged the second Saudi realm, were strong but knew the limits of their power and maintained their territory by constant campaigns against recalcitrant tribes and careful accommodation of amenable others. Their successors, however, dissipated their energies in fratricidal strife in which none had the strength to prevail against the others or the wisdom to compose their quarrel, with the result that they all forfeited their inheritance to third parties.

The story of the House of Saud might have ended with the second realm and the history of Arabia might have been quite different, but that a scion of that house emerged who combined enough strength and wisdom to create a third realm as vast as the first and to steer it safely until fate introduced a new, critical factor into Arabia's destiny: oil.

2

The Third Realm:
Creating an Empire,
1902 – 1932

Eleven years after the destruction of the second realm, a twenty-year-old son of Abd al-Rahman named Abd al-Aziz and later known to the world as Ibn Saud seized Riyadh in a surprise raid and began an effort to restore the realm of his ancestors. The enterprise seemed hopeless because, although the Sauds had once before recreated their realm after total destruction and regained their independence after losing it, the authors of the previous restorations, Turki and Faisal, had essentially taken advantage of the chaos and power vacuum left behind by the withdrawing Egyptian forces to establish themselves. Ibn Saud, on the other hand, had to contend with the strong established power of the ibn Rashid dynasty. Unlike the alien Egyptians, the Rashids were Arabians, had a strong power base in the powerful Shammar tribe, were themselves adherents of Wahhabism, occupied a strategic territory linking the Turkish possessions of Hasa, Syria, and Iraq to the east and north and the Hijaz, 'Asir, and Yemen to the south and west, and were loyal allies of the sultan. But Ibn Saud was a truly extraordinary man. H. St. John Philby may have let his enthusiasm get the better of his judgment when he likened Ibn Saud to the Prophet Muhammad and described him as probably the greatest of Arab leaders who have acted in a desert setting;[1] but even the judicious, unromantic Sir Percy Cox, who had much to do with Ibn Saud and followed his career closely, made the extraordinary assertion that Ibn Saud made no serious mistake in thirty turbulent years following the start of his enterprise.

Early Reconquests, 1902–1914

After his final defeat at the hands of Muhammad ibn Rashid, Abd al-Rahman Al Saud spent his time in Kuwait brooding over his family's fate and entertaining impractical schemes of recovery. In 1897 the death of the formidable Muhammad ibn Rashid suddenly gave Abd al-Rahman grounds for renewed hope. The year before, his Kuwaiti host, Muhammad ibn Sabah, and the latter's brother had been assassinated by a third brother, Mubarak, who assumed the chieftainship of the shaikhdom and its tribes. Mubarak was as ambitious and clever as he was ruthless, and upon the death of Muhammad ibn Rashid set out to supersede him as the dominant power in Arabia and to use the Sauds to advance his goal. He first tried to neutralize the power of the Turk, his own nominal suzerain and the ally of the Rashids, and to accomplish that he sought to involve British power on his side. The British, long the masters of the Persian Gulf, had been concerned about a Turkish-German project for a Berlin-to-Baghdad railway that envisaged using Kuwait as a Persian Gulf terminal, and they therefore responded to Mubarak's overture by concluding with him in 1899 a treaty similar to the ones they had with chiefs of other Gulf principalities. Mubarak committed himself not to alienate any Kuwaiti territory or to grant any concessions to subjects of powers other than Britain, in exchange for British protection and a guarantee of his independence. The British tried to keep the treaty secret because it ran counter to their long-established general policy of upholding the integrity of the Ottoman Empire in order to preserve the European balance of power; but the Turkish government somehow got wind of it and, keeping its own knowledge of the pact secret, secretly incited the new Rashidi ruler, Abd al-Aziz ibn Mut'ib ibn Rashid, to attack Mubarak.

Mubarak welcomed ibn Rashid's provocations and responded early in 1901 by mounting a major expedition against him that included a small contingent of Saudi supporters under Abd al-Rahman. Mubarak and his allies were thoroughly defeated, but when ibn Rashid sought to follow up his victory by attacking positions in the vicinity of the town of Kuwait, a British gunboat opened fire on him and forced him to withdraw. Later in 1901 the Turks massed troops in Basra and tried to land some of them in Kuwait from one of their warships, but British naval units prevented them; the result was a diplomatic uproar. In the negotiations that followed, Britain, Turkey, and Germany agreed to maintain the status quo in Kuwait, which meant nominal Turkish suzerainty but de facto Kuwaiti independence. Mubarak's hegemonic scheme and Saudi hopes had failed for the moment, but Mubarak had succeeded in playing off Britain against Turkey to secure his own rule and independence, and Ibn Saud had learned a lesson he was later to perfect.

During the fighting that preceded the defeat of Mubarak and Abd al-Rahman, Ibn Saud had ventured with a small force to the vicinity of Riyadh, far from the main battlefield. He had actually entered the town and was pondering an attack on the Rashidi garrison, which had entrenched itself in the fort, when he received word of the defeat and hurriedly returned to Kuwait. After spending some time with his dejected father, Ibn Saud set out with sixty men in January 1902 for a new desperate attempt on Riyadh, counting this time more on surprise and luck than on strength. Upon reaching the vicinity of the town, he left thirty men behind with instructions to return to base unless they heard otherwise from him within twenty-four hours. Still closer to the town he left twenty more men just outside the walls, which ibn Rashid had partly demolished, and with the remaining most trusted companions stole under cover of darkness into one of the houses in the main square near the citadel's gate and lay in wait for the governor. Ibn Saud and his band knew that the governor and his retinue customarily came out of the castle every morning and marched across the square to a place where a levee was held. At the proper time the castle's gates were thrown open and the usual march began, whereupon Ibn Saud and his men fell upon the governor and his party and within moments killed him and others, broke into the castle, and rushed the unwary garrison with the help of the acolytes who had waited outside the walls. The thirty reserves were called in to help secure the town, whose population welcomed the return of the native Saudis.

Twenty years before, in Kharj, the Rashidi governor of Riyadh, Salim ibn Subhan, had executed against the Saudis a coup de main very similar to Ibn Saud's coup against his successor in Riyadh. But on that occasion ibn Subhan had had the triumphant Rashidi power to back him up after his exploit, whereas Ibn Saud had little force with which to face the expected reaction of Abd al-Aziz ibn Rashid. To deal with that problem, he began by putting the Riyadhis to work frantically to rebuild and reinforce the town walls. He also brought his family from Kuwait and arranged with his father that the latter should retain the title of imam and take charge of administrative affairs while he took on the tasks of military and political chief. Ibn Saud then left Riyadh and went out to elicit the support of the towns of the southern districts and to impress his authority on the region's bedouin tribes.

Ibn Rashid was still busy with projects connected with his war against Kuwait and did not attribute too much importance to Ibn Saud's seizure of Riyadh. Not until the autumn of 1902 did he send a strong force south to try to undo Ibn Saud's work, picking as a target the town of Dailam, capital of the Kharj district. Ibn Saud, however, had been following ibn Rashid's moves closely, and the night before the attack he had arrived on the scene unnoticed and deployed his small force in the palm groves outside the town. When the Rashids attacked at daylight they were surprised by the ambush and, despite their superior forces, could not regain their balance and prevail. At the end of a day of fighting they accepted a draw and pulled away during the night. Ibn Rashid next tried the stratagem of a feint, and when Ibn Saud's forces rushed to the point of threat, another Rashidi force launched a surprise attack on Riyadh. The plan failed because the citizens had been alerted and had manned their restored walls in strength. Ibn Rashid thereupon withdrew northward, leaving southern Najd under Ibn Saud's uncontested control.

By the time Ibn Saud returned to Riyadh he learned that his father had already dispatched expeditions into the Washm and Sudair districts and that these had encountered important successes. Ibn Saud reinforced and developed those efforts and by June 1904 had captured 'Anaiza and Buraida, the principal towns of the Qasim, and all the western part of that vital province, from which the links between the eastern and western possessions of ibn Rashid's Turkish ally could be disrupted. While that was happening, however, ibn Rashid called on the Turkish government for help, and the latter responded with unwonted alacrity and determination.

Ibn Rashid had justified his request for help by charging that the British were helping Ibn Saud against him. The charge happened to be untrue, but the circumstances of the time made it highly credible. For one thing, there was the recent case of Kuwait, in which the British had concluded a secret agreement with Shaikh Mubarak and then obstructed the Turks when they sought to act against him. For another thing, European rivalry in the Persian Gulf had been mounting to a climax in connection with the Berlin-Baghdad railway, as was illustrated by the grandiose tour of the Persian Gulf made by the viceroy of India, Lord Curzon, at the head of a powerful flotilla in November 1903. The significance of the visit was underscored by a statement made by the foreign secretary, Lord Lansdowne, in the House of Lords six months before, on May 5, 1903: "I say it without hesitation — we should regard the establishment of a naval base, or a fortified port in the Persian Gulf by any other Power as a very grave menace to British interests, and we should certainly resist it with all the means at our disposal."[2] Third, an emissary of Ibn Saud had in fact met secretly with the British political agent in Bahrain, Captain Prideaux, in 1903 and broached with him the idea of driving the Turks out of Hasa with British help. The British government, informed by Prideaux, had turned down the suggestion;[3] but word of the encounter may have reached ibn Rashid, and in any case the logic that had led Ibn Saud to make his proposal to the British may have occurred to ibn Rashid and the Turks as well. Finally, early in 1904 Turkey had begun to construct a railway from Damascus to Madina under the supervision of German engineers. This project formed a central part of an overall design by Sultan Abdul Hamid to tighten his grip on his Arab empire, advance pan-Islamism, and promote his role as caliph. The undertaking was promoted as a service for Muslim pilgrims and was partly financed by popular subscriptions. It did not take much for the ever-suspicious Turks to find possible connections between Ibn Saud's successful campaign against their Rashidi ally and their railway project, and in any case they could not but fear that control of Najd by an enemy of their ally would jeopardize completion of the project.

The Turks therefore sent ibn Rashid large amounts of arms and money with which he raised substantial new forces from Shammar and other tribes, and followed up by dispatching a contingent of eight battalions of regular troops and six guns from Iraq and Madina to help. Ibn Saud had no choice but to rally all the forces he could muster from the territories under his control and go out to meet the enemy. A series of battles began in the summer of 1904 near a locality called Bukairiya and lasted for the better part of two months. Initially things went badly for Ibn Saud — at one point his camp was overrun and he was wounded and had to flee; but then success shifted back and forth, and the fighting tapered off after each side had suffered about one thousand killed — a very high level of casualties by Arabian standards. The battle ended in an agreement wherein Ibn Saud acknowledged Turkish suzerainty and was "appointed" qaimaqam (deputy governor) of Najd; the Qasim was to be a buffer between Ibn Saud and ibn Rashid under native rule, also subject to Turkey; and the Turks were to keep a small garrison there for some time.

On the face of it, the agreement appears to have been a severe setback for Ibn Saud, involving as it did "submission" to Turkey and renunciation of his Qasim conquests.[4] In fact, however, the outcome of Bukairiya was a tribute to Ibn Saud's superior statecraft just as the battle itself was a tribute to his courage. The Turks had come into the battle with their vital interest in securing the Damascus-Madina railway wedded to the cause of ibn Rashid, who sought the destruction of Saudi power. By denying to the enemy coalition victory in the battlefield through his effective resistance, and then satisfying the particular interest of the Turks through nominal and temporary concessions, Ibn Saud broke up the coalition, placed himself with the Turks on an equal footing with ibn Rashid, and secured from both recognition of his power in the domains other than the Qasim that he had acquired so far. Ibn Rashid realized that he had got the worse end of the deal and subsequently tried to encroach on the agreement by intriguing with the native Qasim rulers and by taking military action while the Turkish forces were still in Buraida and 'Anaiza. Ibn Saud responded with counterintrigues and limited operations until he was able one day to launch a successful surprise attack on Abd al-Aziz ibn Rashid's camp in April 1906, in the course of which Abd al-Aziz himself was killed and his troops broke up and fled. The defeat of Abd al-Aziz confirmed the Turks in the conclusion they had reached after Bukairiya, that it was best to protect their interests by balancing Rashids and Sauds rather than by supporting an unattainable Rashidi hegemony. They reaffirmed the post-Bukairiya understanding with Abd al-Aziz's successor and Ibn Saud, granted them a monthly subsidy of 200 and 90 sterlings respectively as a kind of protection money for the railway project, and withdrew their forces from the Qasim. Once the Turks were out, Ibn Saud took advantage of strife in Ha'il over the Rashidi succession to depose the native Qasimi ruler and annex the province outright.

Early in 1909 the turmoil in the Rashidi capital finally subsided and the succession settled for a while on a young son of Abd al-Aziz who was assisted by two able regents. The new rulers formed an alliance with Sa'dun Pasha, the head of the powerful Muntafiq federation of tribes of Iraq, which was countered by an alliance of Ibn Saud, Mubarak of Kuwait, and various chiefs in revolt against Rashidi rule. In a battle fought at Hadiya, near the Iraqi border, early in 1910, Sa'dun inflicted a heavy defeat on the combined forces of Ibn Saud and Mubarak. The battle of Hadiya was significant not only because it resulted in one of Ibn Saud's rare defeats but also because it triggered a conflict within the House of Saud and hostilities on a new front.

Back in 1904, when Ibn Saud had made his first sallies into the Qasim, he had found in one of the captured Rashidi positions six grandsons of his uncle Saud ibn Faisal, whom ibn Rashid obviously hoped to use against him. Ibn Saud had taken his relatives — subsequently dubbed 'araif (lost and recovered camels) — to Riyadh, where they were treated with the honor due to members of the senior branch of the Saudi family but were carefully excluded from any position from which they might assert their right to the throne. In 1910, while Ibn Saud was away on the Hadiya expedition, they slipped out of Riyadh, joined the rebellious 'Ajman tribe, and sought to rally additional support for their pretension to the Saudi succession. Ibn Saud, occupied by the war with the Muntafiq tribes and the Rashids, could not react promptly to the threat, and the pretenders were thus able to establish a base for themselves in Hariq and Hauta, south of Riyadh. Eventually, in 1912, he defeated them, but out of excess generosity or for political considerations, he offered them a choice between returning to the fold or going into exile. The senior among them, Saud ibn Abd al-Aziz ibn Saud, chose to return, eventually married Ibn Saud's sister Nura, and became a loyal supporter of Ibn Saud for the remaining forty years of his life. Saud's brother Muhammad also returned. But one had fled to Hasa and the others preferred refuge with

Sharif Hussein of the Hijaz, who was emerging as a formidable new enemy and had started a lifelong hostility to Ibn Saud by inflicting on him a humiliation he was never to forget or forgive.[5]

Sharif Hussein had been appointed to his post in the Hijaz in 1908, the year the railway reached Madina, and had already proved his usefulness to the Turkish government by occupying the highlands of 'Asir and Abha while the Turks were engaged in suppressing a rebellion by Imam Yahya in Yemen. Hussein's success in the south encouraged him to assert himself in the east, and at the end of 1911 he was leading a strong force through the 'Utaiba country, straddling the Hijaz and Najd, when he encountered a group led by Ibn Saud's favorite brother, Sa'd, who was seeking to enlist recruits for the campaign against the 'araif. Hussein took Sa'd hostage, pending Ibn Saud's agreement to acknowledge anew Turkish suzerainty through himself and to pay tribute for the Qasim, which Ibn Saud had occupied some years before. Beset by his recent reverses in the east, worried about the pretenders' revolt, and anxious to rescue his brother, Ibn Saud signed the humiliating document presented to him by Hussein.[6] Even as he did so, however, he was nurturing plans that were soon to come to fruition to despoil the Turks of much more tangible assets than Hussein had secured for them.

In 1903, shortly after Ibn Saud had seized Riyadh, one of his emissaries had vainly broached with Captain Prideaux the idea of driving the Turks out of Hasa with British assistance. In 1904, during the battle of Bukairiya, Ibn Saud once more sought British material support in vain, although this time the British made representations to the Turkish government not to upset the balance of power in central Arabia by supporting Rashidi hegemony, a goal that the Turks had renounced on their own after Bukairiya. In 1906 Ibn Saud made several additional overtures to the British, offering to subscribe to the Trucial System — including suppression of slave trade, nonalienation of territory to other powers, British control of foreign relations — in exchange for a guarantee of his independence against the Turks. The political resident in the Persian Gulf, Major (later Sir) Percy Cox, wrote to the government of India urging a favorable response, but the secretary of state for India rejected the recommendation on the general ground of supporting the integrity of the Ottoman Empire and on the specific ground of avoiding entanglement in the Arabian interior, where Britain had no interest. The secretary did, however, recommend that Cox maintain a friendly dialogue with Ibn Saud to avert the latter's encroachment on British interests in the Gulf, and this as well as the specific reason given to Ibn Saud for the rejection of his request (that his was not a Gulf state) kept alive his hopes of changing the British position by making himself a riparian power.[7]

In 1910 Ibn Saud met personally for the first time with a British Gulf official, Captain Shakespear, the political agent under Cox. Although no specific business was discussed, the meeting was significant because it prepared the ground for other, substantive meetings and because it took place at a time when the Young Turk government suspected the British of fostering Arab agitation for autonomy within the Ottoman Empire. In 1911 Ibn Saud met Shakespear again, expressed a desire to drive the Turks out of Hasa, and asked for British support against a Turkish invasion of the province from the sea, in exchange for his acceptance of a British political agent there. Shakespear and Cox wrote to their superiors in favor of the proposal, but the latter decided on a polite rejection. The British government was about to engage in negotiations to settle all outstanding issues with the Turkish government, including the German-backed Baghdad railway, at a delicate juncture in European politics, and it did not want complications over a change in the status quo in an irrelevant part of the Persian Gulf coast.[8]

Ibn Saud repeated his proposal the next year and this time told Shakespear that he intended to seize Hasa because it was his ancestors' patrimony, and the time was opportune in view of Turkey's troubles with the Italian and Balkan wars. Shakespear and Cox again recommended giving Ibn Saud the reassurance he sought against invasion from the sea, while the latter, as if to give point to his advocates' argument, made threatening noises against the shaikhs of Qatar, Abu Dhabi, and Dubai. In London, however, Ibn Saud's fear of naval attack was used as an argument to discount the likelihood of any threat from him to British interests even if he should seize Hasa independently. This line of reasoning, together with the prospect of a comprehensive settlement with Turkey, led the British to ignore Ibn Saud's overture.

Finally, on May 9, 1913, Ibn Saud acted on his own. At dawn that day his fighters surprised the Turkish defenders of the fort of Hufuf, the inland capital of Hasa, after scaling the walls under cover of darkness. The Turkish garrison, some twelve hundred strong, scrambled to the big mosque and entrenched itself there. Ibn Saud surrounded the place and offered the Turkish commander safe evacuation of his troops to Bahrain if he surrendered. The commander accepted. The Turks made an attempt to recover by landing again at 'Uqair, a coastal village further northeast, but the effort was foiled and the prisoners were allowed to reembark for Bahrain. The tiny Turkish garrison at Qatif gave no trouble and was also evacuated, and the entire province from Kuwait to Qatar was thus secured with little effort and with minimum provocation to the Turks.[9] Even as he was completing his conquest, Ibn Saud wrote to the Turkish vali (governor) of Basra affirming his continued subservience to the Porte and explaining that his action was due to the mismanagement of the affairs of Hasa and his desire to restore the traditional state of affairs in the province.[10]

Ibn Saud had hoped that by making himself a Gulf power he would force the British to change their position and enter into some form of protective agreement with him; but in fact just the opposite happened. In July 1913, after two years of desultory negotiations, the British and Turkish governments finally signed the Anglo-Turkish Convention, which ostensibly settled all issues between the two countries. In the case of the Arabian Peninsula, a line was drawn from the base of the Qatar Peninsula to the border between Aden and Yemen, and everything north of that line, including Najd and Hasa, was recognized as falling under Turkish sovereignty. In the wake of the agreement the foreign secretary, Sir Edward Grey, issued a directive enjoining Cox and his subordinates from any communication, other than of a purely formal nature when inevitable, with Ibn Saud or any other Arabian chief with whom his majesty's government had no treaty relations.

The Turks, taking Ibn Saud's protestations of loyalty at face value and feeling reinforced by the agreement with Britain, invited him to negotiate a regularization of his relations with them. In the meantime they supplied the Rashidi chief with money and 12,000 rifles and incited him to put pressure on Ibn Saud. Ibn Saud invoked a truce that had existed for some time between himself and the Rashidis, but the latter replied frankly that they were on the side of the Turks as the suzerain power and would act in their interests against Riyadh. Disillusioned by the British and fearing worse from the Turks, in May 1914 Ibn Saud finally signed a treaty that formalized his status as a Turkish vassal. An imperial firman appointed him governor general with power of vali for Najd and Hasa, in exchange for which Ibn Saud agreed to allow limited Turkish garrisons on the coast and to refrain from concluding any treaties or engagements with foreign powers. However, although the first part of the agreement was duly executed, the other two were soon rendered moot by the outbreak of World War I.

Overpowering Peninsular Opponents, 1914–1926

The war freed Britain from its traditional policy of preserving the integrity of the Ottoman Empire and impelled it instead to seek Arab allies against it. Ibn Saud now had the chance to obtain from Britain the treaty he had sought for twelve years. By the time the treaty was signed and ratified, however, the problem it was supposed to solve had become irrelevant as far as Ibn Saud was concerned, and new and more severe problems confronted him in regard to which the treaty was of limited use. Preventing Turkish action from the sea, Ibn Saud's original concern, had become a British military objective regardless of any treaty. On the other hand, the danger from the direction of Jabal Shammar had increased as the war gave the Turks a strong interest in reinforcing their Rashidi allies, and a new and much more serious threat had developed from the Hijaz as a result of a British decision to invest massively in an alliance with Sharif Hussein. Both problems were complicated by renewed tribal rebellions and family dissension, by unrest stemming from the disruptions caused by the British blockade, and by extremist pressures from the fanatic Ikhwan fighters, whom Ibn Saud had fostered as a power instrument. Nevertheless, Ibn Saud not only steered his way through these difficulties to the end of the war but also was able a few years thereafter to defeat definitively his external enemies and capture their domains, to master the internal situation, and to force Britain to recognize him as the sole ruler of Arabia more or less within its present boundaries.

On November 3, 1914, the government of India sent Ibn Saud a note asking him to cooperate in keeping the peace in the Gulf and to assist the British in taking Basra in exchange for a treaty that would recognize him as independent ruler of Najd and Hasa, guarantee him protection against attack from the sea, and help secure him against Turkish reprisals. Soon after a preliminary favorable response from Ibn Saud, Captain Shakespear reported that Ibn Saud would remain neutral and seek to keep all his options open until he got a signed and sealed treaty with the British government that included a solid guarantee of his position, a judgment that was brilliantly confirmed by events in the next four years. Nevertheless, while the British government pondered the terms of the treaty, Ibn Saud went out to do battle with the Rashids, and Shakespear accompanied him. Whether Ibn Saud was trying to demonstrate his value to the British or whether it was ibn Rashid who took the initiative to attack is not clear. At any rate, the battle fought at Jarrab on January 15, 1915, went badly for Ibn Saud, and Captain Shakespear was killed during it. Having compromised himself by fighting against the Turks' ally, and having been defeated as well, Ibn Saud now pressed hard to obtain the protective treaty promptly, threatening that otherwise he might have to make some move to appease the Turks. The British hastened to submit a draft treaty the following month, but once Ibn Saud had it he prolonged the negotiations until December 1915, when the treaty was finally signed.[11]

In the treaty the British acknowledged Najd, Hasa, Qatif, Jubail, and their dependencies, territories, and ports to be "the countries of Ibn Saud and of his fathers before him" and recognized Ibn Saud as the independent ruler thereof and absolute chief of their tribes, "and after him his sons and descendants by inheritance provided the successor shall not be a person antagonistic to the British government in any respect." The British also undertook to help Ibn Saud protect his interests and countries against aggression committed by any foreign power without reference to the British government and without giving Whitehall a chance to compose the matter by other means. In exchange Ibn Saud undertook, "as did his father before him," to "refrain from all aggression or interference in the territories of Kuwait and Bahrain, and of the shaikhs of Qatar and the Oman coast who had treaty relations with the British government." He also obligated himself not to enter into "any correspondence or agreement or treaty with any foreign power, and absolutely not to cede, sell, mortgage, lease or otherwise dispose" of his territories or grant concessions within them to any foreign power or the subjects of a foreign power without the consent of Great Britain. In a final article the two parties agreed to conclude a further detailed treaty regarding matters concerning them.

The treaty thus formally foreclosed Ibn Saud's option of siding with the Turks but did not obligate him, as the government of India would have liked, to side actively with Britain in the war; nor did Britain obligate itself to assist Ibn Saud, apart from a sweetener of 20,000 pounds and 1,000 rifles to help him out of some internal difficulties. The final article anticipated the possibility of a more extensive offensive and defensive agreement, but Ibn Saud continued for another two years to resist British pressure to assume an offensive commitment, and when he finally did, he acquitted himself perfunctorily and in a pro forma manner.

One reason Ibn Saud did not want to play a more active role in the war, even of the kind exemplified by the battle of Jarrab, was that for a long time after that battle he was fully occupied in suppressing tribal revolts. His defeat at Jarrab had encouraged the 'Ajman of Hasa to rise against him in alliance with the *'araif,* and when he lost one battle to them in which his brother Sa'd was killed and he himself was wounded, other tribes rebelled and still others failed to help in what they felt to be a losing cause. When Ibn Saud, through extraordinary exertions, finally defeated the 'Ajman in battle (the pretenders — Faisal, brother of Saud, and Faisal, Fahd, and Saud, sons of Sa'd ibn Saud — were all killed in the 'Ajman battles), they were given refuge by the new, hostile, rulers of Kuwait, whose territories he could not touch because of their treaty relationship with Britain.

Another reason for Ibn Saud's passiveness was that by the time the treaty was signed, the British themselves were not doing well in the area to which he was most sensitive. After advancing toward Baghdad, the bulk of the Mesopotamian Expeditionary Force was thrown back on Kut al-Amara, where it was besieged and destroyed in the first months of 1916, leaving the impression that the Central Powers might well win in the region, or at least badly hurt small powers such as Ibn Saud's. Finally, in June 1916, six months after Ibn Saud had signed his treaty with Britain and before the government of India had formally ratified it, Sharif Hussein of Mecca proclaimed a general Arab revolt against Turkey in return for far-reaching British commitments to help him establish independent rule in all the "Arab-inhabited" territories of the Ottoman Empire. Ibn Saud viewed the British pledges to Hussein as a case of double dealing, and British material support to his enemy as a mortal threat to his own position. And although he could not afford to break with the British and switch camps, neither was he prepared to commit what forces he had in a manner that exhausted them or helped his enemy.

Following Sharif Hussein's revolt, the British called on Ibn Saud to help the movement by taking action against the Rashidis. Ibn Saud wrote directly to Hussein offering cooperation in exchange for a guarantee of his independence, but Hussein rejected the offer in insolent terms. Ibn Saud then sought to discuss the whole situation with his old friend Sir Percy Cox, and the two met at 'Uqair at the end of 1916. Cox assured Ibn Saud that his independence was in no way prejudiced by Britain's commitments to Hussein and offered him a subsidy of 5,000 pounds a month, plus 3,000 rifles, 4 machine guns, and ample ammunition on the understanding that he would maintain a force of 4,000 men continuously in the field against ibn Rashid and attack his capital. Ibn Saud took what was offered, went to Kuwait to a durbar of Arab chiefs allied with Britain and made a vague public declaration in support of the Arab revolt, visited the British forces in Iraq, and then returned to his capital and did nothing. On the contrary, he maintained a secret contact with Jemal Pasha, the Turkish governor of Syria, explained to him that he was humoring the British because of their naval stranglehold, and assured him of his good intentions by allowing supplies to move through his territories to Shammar and beyond to the Turkish forces.[12]

In the autumn of 1917 the British authorities in Cairo tried to impart new momentum to the flagging Arab revolt and in that connection urged their Baghdad counterparts to press Ibn Saud to take action against the Rashids. Baghdad suggested that a joint mission from Cairo and Baghdad first attempt to work out an understanding between Hussein and Ibn Saud, but the mission sent to Jidda in December 1917 failed to achieve its objective. The immediate cause of the failure was a conflict that had broken out earlier between Hussein and Ibn Saud concerning control of the oasis of Khurma, whose chief had espoused Wahhabism and defected to Ibn Saud but whose territory and tribe were claimed by Hussein. The basic reason, however, was that both Hussein and Ibn Saud had for some time been playing games of their own that did not quite correspond with the British interests and desires.

Hussein, whose ambition embraced all the Arab lands of the Ottoman Empire, did not want to enter into any commitments with Arab chiefs until the power of the Turks was broken and he could deal with those chiefs from a position of strength. Ibn Saud, fearing just that, wanted to assure his position in advance as much as possible and, failing that, to let the sharif and ibn Rashid exhaust themselves against each other while he preserved and built up forces for the day of reckoning. One key difference in approach between Ibn Saud and Hussein was that the former appreciated the power and crucial role of Britain, the more so the more the tide of war in the Middle East turned in its favor, whereas Hussein became more cantankerous, megalomaniacal, and stubborn in his relations with the British the closer he thought he came to the moment when his dream should be fulfilled. That difference was to prove critical in the eventual dismal failure of Hussein's strategy and the brilliant success of Ibn Saud's.

After the failure of the British mediating mission, the British authorities in Baghdad worked through H. St. John Philby, their newly appointed permanent representative with Ibn Saud and a fervent admirer of his, to keep Ibn Saud from fighting Hussein over the Khurma dispute and to address himself instead to the Rashidi enemy. Ibn Saud obliged the British in their first desire with great difficulty in the face of internal pressure; and he responded to the second by belatedly launching a series of probes against ibn Rashid's forces and making an appearance before Ha'il in August 1918 and then pulling back. Shortly thereafter Turkey withdrew from the war and Ibn Saud, having come through it unscathed and with a treaty with Britain, was ready to face both the challenges he had anticipated and others he had not. In the meantime, however, another force was beginning to play a crucial role: the famous or infamous Wahhabi Ikhwan (Brethren).

From the time of his 1902 raid against Riyadh until 1912, Ibn Saud had fought to create the third Saudi realm more or less in the way his ancestors Turki and Faisal had fought to create the second. He had carried the war (mainly against the Rashid family) on a dynastic rather than a religious basis, and probably for the same reasons Turki and Faisal did: that vibrant Wahhabism led to disastrous excesses, and mild Wahhabism was also espoused by the enemy. Sometime before 1912, however, he decided to fan the embers of Wahhabism and to use it in a new way. He sent missionaries to revive the message among the bedouin tribes, and whenever a sufficient number of tribesmen were sufficiently aroused, he helped them establish *hijar*, colonies (plural of *hijrah*, "migration," supposedly modeled after the first Muslim community established by the Prophet Muhammad in Madina after he migrated to it from Mecca). The first settlement, begun in 1912 at the wells of Artawiya by fifty men from the Mutair and Harb tribes, had grown within a decade to a town of several thousand. More than threescore additional settlements were created capable of yielding more than sixty thousand arms-bearing men.[13]

The settlers were supposed to form communities of brethren in the faith — Ikhwan — transcending tribal loyalties, but in fact most settlements were formed by members of single tribes, and the others had elements of two or three tribes. The Ikhwan were supposed to abandon the tribal way of life and to lead a religiously inspired, settled existence, but they did so only in varying degrees. Most abandoned nomadism and raiding, many sold their camels and tents and built mud huts, but far fewer were able to take up agriculture and trade and to support themselves productively. All practiced the rituals faithfully and the majority attended religious instruction regularly, but most of the instruction was given by unqualified preachers and amounted to little more than revivalist sessions that stirred up militant fanaticism. The Ikhwan were supposed to be ready to respond immediately to the imam's call to carry on *jihad* against the *mushrikun* (literally, "polytheists," but in the Ikhwan view practically all non-Wahhabis). This was one duty they were all eager, indeed overeager, to fulfill. The zeal of the Ikhwan for jihad and the exploitation of that zeal by some of their ambitious leaders eventually presented Ibn Saud with what was probably the most serious threat in his fifty-year career.

Several considerations led Ibn Saud to stimulate and use militant Wahhabism when and as he did. His defeat at Hadiya in 1910; his trouble suppressing the revolt of the *araif* pretenders, the 'Ajman, and other tribes in 1911; and the setback inflicted on him by Sharif Hussein in that same year drove home to him a sense of both the vulnerability of his claim to legitimacy and the weakness of his power base. The pretenders challenged his claim to the succession within the House of Saud with a better one, while Sharif Hussein presented a potential challenge to the entire House of Saud based on his Hashemite lineage going back to the Prophet. Moreover, Hussein could draw on the superior resources of the Hijaz to raise forces, and he and the Rashidis had the backing of the power of the Ottoman state, made more available since the completion of the Damascus-Madina railway in 1908; whereas Ibn Saud depended entirely on the meager resources of Najd, with its loyal but small settled tribes and its completely fickle bedouin tribes, ever ready to join the enemy just when their support was most needed. In these circumstances, the revival of Wahhabism appeared to Ibn Saud to offer a needed buttress to his legitimacy, both internally and externally, while the coupling of the revival with the establishment of Ikhwan settlements promised to provide him with a new power base and at the same time give him sufficient control over it to prevent the kind of excess zeal that had led to the destruction of the first Saudi realm. Experience was to vindicate Ibn Saud on all but the control question: in the end he had to destroy rampant Ikhwan power to protect his own. In the meantime, however, he controlled it sufficiently to accomplish all he had set out to do.

In the summer of 1918 Ibn Saud undertook action against the Rashidis only after he had overcome strong resistance by the Ikhwan, who had already become a significant force. The latter had wanted to go first to the assistance of the fellow Wahhabis of Khurma, who had been attacked again by Hussein's forces. Ibn Saud, who did not want to antagonize the British by fighting their ally, had been able to divert the Ikhwan only because the defenders of Khurma were eventually able to repel Hussein's forces by themselves. At the beginning of 1919, however, with Turkey out of the war and with the sharifian forces that had been occupied in the siege of Madina finally freed and available, Hussein thought the time ripe to deal with Ibn Saud and began by reviving the issue of Khurma. In May 1919 he sent an army of 4,000 regulars supported by artillery and 10,000 bedouins under the command of his son Emir Abdallah to enforce his demands. Ibn Saud wearily advanced his forces to meet the well-equipped enemy, but before he had a chance to act, an Ikhwan force advanced stealthily from Khurma and surprised the slumbering enemy camped at Turaba. Abdallah's army was annihilated in a few hours, his bedouin contingents evaporated, and Abdallah himself barely escaped with his life. The road to Ta'if and Mecca lay open and the Ikhwan were eager to take it, but Ibn Saud ordered them to halt, partly because of British pressure.

For more than two years before the events at Turaba, the British government had grappled periodically with two mutually hostile powers in Arabia, each with its own advocates in British councils. After all attempts to conciliate the Arabian antagonists had failed, various proposals were discussed but no conclusion was reached until the end of the war. When the tension over Khurma began to build again at that time, a ministerial committee chaired by Lord Curzon decided in March 1919 to take the easy way out by backing the stronger party in the expectation that it would force the other to come to terms. Hussein, with his British-trained regular troops and modern equipment, seemed an easy favorite against the ragtag troops of Ibn Saud, and he was given the green light to try his hand at Khurma. The disaster at Turaba not only upset the calculations of the British government but also raised immediate fears about the consequences in Arabia, the Middle East, and India of a Wahhabi-Ikhwan invasion of the holy cities. Whitehall therefore reacted promptly by issuing an ultimatum to Ibn Saud to withdraw his forces from the Hijaz and the disputed area or be considered to have adopted an attitude of definite hostility toward Britain. In that event the subsidy would at once be discontinued and Ibn Saud would forfeit irrevocably all the advantages secured under the treaty of December 1915.[14]

Ibn Saud, anxious to avoid a clash with Britain, sent a conciliatory reply expressing willingness to withdraw his forces to Najd if he received a satisfactory guarantee against aggression and to submit to British arbitration. Hussein, who had panicked after Turaba, recovered in the wake of the British ultimatum and refused arbitration, to the irritation of the British. The latter then tried to arrange a meeting between Hussein and Ibn Saud to settle things, but the discussion went on for a year, with Hussein making most of the difficulties. Finally, representatives of the two chiefs met and agreed on an armistice pending British arbitration, but Hussein insisted that he would agree to the results of arbitration only if they gave him the disputed areas. At that point, in October 1920, Lord Curzon commented: "I don't think we shall have peace until he [Hussein] has gone. But I do not want to administer the final kick."[15] The British continued reluctantly to follow a "Hussein policy," but more on account of the position of his sons Faisal and Abdallah, whom in February 1921 they decided to make respectively king of Iraq and emir of Transjordan, than of Hussein himself.

Even before the armistice with Hussein had been concluded, Ibn Saud had turned his attention to an opportunity in the 'Asir uplands and began operations that led to the annexation of that region in 1920. During the world war, the Idrisi ruler of that relatively rich and ill-defined area had risen against the Turks, who were, however, able to maintain their position in the capital, Abha, with the help of the local 'Aid chieftains. In 1919 the Turks evacuated Abha, and the local chieftains appealed to Ibn Saud for help against the Idrisis. Ibn Saud responded, but after defeating the Idrisis his forces remained in place and he reasserted his claim to the province on the ground that it once belonged to his ancestors. By the time the armistice with Hussein was concluded, Ibn Saud had absorbed the 'Asir highlands and was ready to turn his energies in another direction where danger and opportunity beckoned: the Rashidi capital and dominions.

Among the ideas considered by the British government during the war in connection with the hostility between Hussein and Ibn Saud was one that had been presented to it jointly by its representatives in Cairo and Baghdad in March 1918, which called for retaining the power of the Rashidis intact to serve as a balancer between the two antagonistic allies. Whitehall had rejected the proposal on the old grounds of not wanting to become involved in central Arabian affairs; but after the war two events — the reconquest of the northernmost province of Arabia with its capital, Jawf, by the Rashids, bringing them between the British-controlled territories of Iraq and Transjordan; and the failure of Hussein's attempt to assert himself against Ibn Saud — led the British to reconsider. The government agreed to the idea in principle, and Ha'il was approached informally; but while discussion went on in London as to which British agency was to foot the bill, the situation in Ha'il suddenly deteriorated and gave Ibn Saud a chance to destroy the Rashidi state and foil the British design.[16]

Late in 1920 the Rashidi Emir Saud was assassinated by a cousin who aspired to his throne. The assassin was immediately cut down by one of Saud's slaves, and the succession reverted to Abdallah ibn Mut'ib, who immediately imprisoned a brother of the assassin, Muhammad ibn Talal, also a potential pretender. Ibn Saud reacted by sending Wahhabi emissaries to work on tribes disaffected by the unrest while his forces undertook a series of operations against Rashidi territories at the same time that the chief of the Ruwala tribe was reasserting his independence in the Jawf district, in the north. Pressed from all directions, Abdallah ibn Rashid let his cousin Muhammad out of jail and sent him at the head of an expedition against the Ruwala; but upon returning to Ha'il, Muhammad staged a revolt against Abdallah, who fled and joined Ibn Saud. In the meantime Ibn Saud had had himself declared sultan of Najd and its dependencies to give himself a status matching that of his ultimate sharifian rivals. Encouraged by better prospects of success, he now pressed his campaign and by October 1921 was investing Ha'il. He rejected an offer by Muhammad ibn Talal to surrender on condition of remaining emir of Shammar under Saudi overlordship, which he might have welcomed under different circumstances. Finally, after Ibn Saud threatened to bombard the city with cannon, its gates were opened to him, and not long thereafter, on November 4, 1921, Muhammad himself surrendered the citadel after receiving a guarantee of personal safety.

The Rashidi realm, which had begun in 1834, was thus brought to an end and the surviving members of the Rashid family were taken to Riyadh, where they were kept in comfortable captivity and eventually married into the Saud family. Like the second Saudi realm it had once liquidated, the Rashidi state met its end as a result of fratricidal strife within the ruling family at a time when external enemies pressed it.

After taking Ha'il, Ibn Saud immediately sent his forces to assert his control over all the territories that had come under Rashidi rule at any time, including Jawf and Wadi Sirhan, in the far north. This northern campaign brought him into contact on a wide front with the territories of Iraq and Transjordan placed under Sharif Hussein's sons, and before long the entire region was live with raids and counterraids by Ikhwan and tribes from those territories only partly controlled by their respective sovereigns.

The British, who held mandates over Iraq and Palestine (including Transjordan) and were seriously considering building a strategic railway from the Persian Gulf to the Mediterranean through the agitated territory, acted quickly to try to stabilize the situation. They called a conference of representatives of Iraq, Najd, and Kuwait to settle their border problems, and the result was the Treaty of Muhammara, signed on May 5, 1922. The treaty drew the boundaries on the basis of a prior assignment of the various tribes in the region to the respective three sovereigns, and in addition confirmed the security of other Persian Gulf principalities under British protection. Ibn Saud, however, refused to ratify the treaty, claiming that his negotiators had exceeded their authority by agreeing to assign some of "his" tribes to the sovereignty of King Faisal. He proposed a reconsideration of the whole matter in a personal discussion with Sir Percy Cox, now British high commissioner for Iraq.

Cox agreed, and their meeting in November 1922 resulted in what came to be known as the 'Uqair Protocols, which in turn became part of the Treaty of Muhammara. Cox persuaded Ibn Saud to agree to boundary lines that favored Iraq's claims by compensating him with lines that greatly favored his claims against Kuwait. Provisions were also made to assure access by tribes of both sides to wells and pastures in the area, including the barring of military posts there. Neither the treaty nor the protocols prevented the outbreak of serious border warfare in the following years. However, their ratification did allow Ibn Saud to keep on good terms with the British, who held positions around all his domains, and helped neutralize Iraq's Faisal in the decisive rounds that Ibn Saud next fought against his father, Hussein, in the Hijaz.

Even before the signing of the 'Uqair Protocols, which ostensibly settled matters with Iraq and the Gulf principalities, trouble had flared up between Najd and Transjordan, and the dispute between Sharif Hussein and Ibn Saud had been resumed. In the case of Transjordan, an Ikhwan group of about two thousand advanced on one occasion as far as the Hijaz railway in the vicinity of Amman and raided a village near Ziza, killing its entire population. It was a typical Ikhwan operation and was carried out without authorization from Ibn Saud, who was more anxious than ever to avoid provoking the British after having recently rejected the Treaty of Muhammara. The sequel to that incident demonstrated the good sense of Ibn Saud's policy of caution in dealing with Britain: the Ikhwan raiders were pursued by British armored car detachments and by Royal Air Force squadrons stationed in Amman and virtually annihilated. The eight raiders who survived to tell about the uneven match between rifle-armed cameleers and air power in the open desert were themselves punished by Ibn Saud for the provocation they offered.

The resurgence of the dispute with Hussein also involved Ikhwan pressure, but on grounds that Ibn Saud himself felt were justified. Since the first fighting over Khurma, Najdi pilgrims had abstained from going to the Hijaz; but the year after the 1920 armistice the Najdis felt that they should be able to perform the very important obligation of the hajj. The problem was that the Ikhwan and Ibn Saud did not trust Hussein's protection and wanted the pilgrims to provide their own, whereas Hussein saw in the Najdi demand both a derogation of his sovereignty and a threat to his security. In the 1921 pilgrimage season Ibn Saud, preoccupied with his anti-Rashidi campaign, allowed the issue to pass by not sending a Najdi contingent; but as the 1922 season approached, he could not or would not restrain Ikhwan demands and threatened to let his pilgrims go armed. The British intervened once more to prevent fighting between their allies, only this time, ominously for Hussein, they did not take his side, but rather called for a conference of representatives of Najd, the Hijaz, Transjordan, and Iraq to settle all problems among them.

Ibn Saud agreed and in the meantime contented himself with sending a small number of pilgrims. Hussein, as usual, made difficulties before agreeing and strained British patience to the limit. The previous year he had turned a deaf ear to an attempt by T. E. Lawrence to win his endorsement of the British policy in Palestine as enunciated by Colonial Secretary Winston Churchill in February 1921. Now he compounded his misdeeds in British eyes by communicating to Ibn Saud that he, Hussein, would be willing to abdicate in his favor if the latter joined him in expelling all European powers from Arabia — a communication that Ibn Saud made certain reached the British.[17]

The British-sponsored conference convened in Kuwait in December 1923. Its complicated agenda and the fact that representatives of the three sharifian or Hashemite states were brought together to face the representatives of Najd did not bode well for its success, nor did the announcement by the British government at the outset that it was terminating all subsidies to the parties as of March 31, 1924. Nevertheless, the British representatives kept the conference limping along until the first week of March, when Hussein dealt it a fatal blow. On March 3, 1924, the Grand National Assembly of Turkey set the Muslim world astir by proclaiming the abolition of the caliphate held by the Ottoman dynasty for four centuries, and two days later King Hussein added to the agitation by having himself proclaimed caliph in the Friday mosque of Amman, where he had been visiting with his son Abdallah. Ibn Saud could hardly be expected to be the first Muslim or Arab ruler to lend credence to Hussein's unilateral act by concluding an agreement with him and his sons, and so the conference trailed into inconclusion.

Shortly thereafter the pilgrimage issue arose once more, and the doubly outraged Ikhwan petitioned for a campaign against the Hijaz. This time their demand was backed by Ibn Saud's more sober advisers, who saw in Hussein's provocative unilateral action an opportunity to strike at him with the approval of Muslim opinion and especially of leaders and rulers who considered themselves more worthy of the caliphal dignity than Hussein. Ibn Saud decided to act, but only after the end of the pilgrimage season in order not to offend Muslim opinion; even then he authorized a limited strike directed against Ta'if only, in order to test the capacity of the bedouin Ikhwan to fight in the Hijaz mountains and to watch the reaction of the British. As events unfolded, the latter concerns proved to be unwarranted, and his precaution to avoid giving offense to Muslims proved to be of no avail, owing to the excessive zeal of the Ikhwan.

The Hijaz campaign began in late August 1924 with a series of diversionary moves and raids in Iraq and Transjordan while the main forces jumped off from Khurma and Turaba. One of the raids in Transjordan resulted in another massacre of villagers and another devastating reprisal by the Royal Air Force; but before the flurry over that event subsided, the Saudi forces lunged at Ta'if and occupied it on September 3. An attempt by 'Ali, son of Hussein, to counterattack at Hadda, some twenty miles to the northwest, failed for lack of local tribal support, and 'Ali's force retreated all the way to Jidda amid a stream of refugees, bypassing doomed Mecca. The victorious Ikhwan indulged their passion for loot and indiscriminate killing of *mushrikun,* including a few British subjects.

Hussein, Abdallah, and Faisal appealed to the British government for help, the first recalling his services during the great war and the latter two invoking the menace of the Wahhabis to their realms and thrones; but this time the British adopted a neutral position in what they decided to consider a conflict among Muslims over the holy places, as long as the rights of Muslim British subjects were respected. Most important, at the end of September 1924 Britain declared that "it would give no countenance to interference in the Hedjaz by Transjordan and Iraq."[18] Three days later, on October 3, 1924, the hapless King Hussein was forced to yield to the demand of notables of Mecca and Jidda to abdicate in favor of his son 'Ali and go into exile. 'Ali lost no time in offering to negotiate with Ibn Saud, but the latter promptly turned him down and his forces entered Mecca without a fight on October 12, 1924. Strict orders prevented any massacre by the Ikhwan this time but did not stop them from committing other forms of violence. In the words of Ibn Saud's newly appointed civil governor of the holy city, "their violence . . . was beyond description . . . the Ikhwan set themselves to annihilating personally, with bare hands, sticks or rifles, anything they considered evil."[19]

The fall of Mecca was followed by the capture of several coastal towns north and south of Jidda, leaving 'Ali in command of an area comprising only Jidda, Madina, and Yanbo. At this point Ibn Saud's predominant concern ceased to be 'Ali's capacity to continue military resistance on his own and focused on two other problems: the possibility of foreign intervention in response to Ikhwan excesses, which might rob him of the complete victory now within his grasp; and the reaction of the Muslim world to his invasion of the Hijaz and capture of the holy city. To meet the first problem he indicated to Whitehall his willingness to come to an understanding regarding the death of British subjects at Ta'if and assured it that he had made strict provisions to protect all foreigners. At the same time he ordered his troops to refrain from assaulting the cities still under 'Ali's control and to put them under siege instead, in order to avoid incidents that might involve foreign residents and especially members of the diplomatic and consular corps established in Jidda . As the war dragged on, Ibn Saud went further to appease the British and keep them neutral. In the summer of 1925 the British, having concluded that the Hijaz was bound to fall to Ibn Saud, engineered a dubious cession of the Aqaba-Ma'an district by 'Ali to his brother Abdallah of Transjordan and then sent their forces to occupy it. Ibn Saud protested the act and never recognized its legitimacy; nevertheless, in November 1925 he concluded with Sir Gilbert Clayton two agreements that ostensibly settled most of the issues with Iraq and Transjordan left unsettled by the abortive 1923 Kuwait Conference.

To meet the problem of Muslim opinion, Ibn Saud endeavored to isolate his enemy diplomatically and to gain support for himself by disclaiming for some time any ambitions of his own in the Hijaz and indicating that, once the "Sharifian evildoers" were expelled, the Muslim world would be free to decide the future of the Holy Land. This line also served to justify Ibn Saud's rejection of 'Ali's repeated pleas for peace and the many offers of mediation made by various parties, including one by the Soviet consul at Jidda together with the Dutch and Persian vice-consuls.[20]

At that stage Ibn Saud concentrated his attention on the Muslims of India because of the possible effect of their attitude on the position of Britain, and on King Fuad of Egypt, as ruler of the strongest neighboring Arab country. He accepted a proposal made in October 1924 by Indian Muslim leaders that a constitution for the Holy Land "must be drawn up by the whole Islamic community" and that the area "must be placed under a democratic government" after the expulsion of Hussein and his sons;[21] and he intimated to King Fuad that he supported his aspiration to the caliphate and would like him to convene the Islamic congress that would decide the future of the Holy Land. However, as the initial impact of the fall of Mecca wore off and as it became apparent that 'Ali had been successfully isolated, Ibn Saud's pronouncements about the future of the Hijaz became more and more ambiguous, and those about the role of the envisaged Islamic congress more and more qualified. By the time 'Ali finally surrendered Jidda peacefully after a yearlong siege and sailed away in December 1925, the only promise of Ibn Saud's that was still operative was one to convene an Islamic congress with an unspecified agenda to be determined later. Whatever function the congress was meant to have, it did not impede Ibn Saud from "accepting" on January 8, 1926, his proclamation as king by an assembly of Hijazi notables and his assumption of the formal title King of the Hijaz and Sultan of Najd and Its Dependencies.[22]

The conquest of the Hijaz was followed by the establishment in 1926 of a Saudi protectorate over the remainder of the 'Asir, this time as a result of an invitation by the incumbent Idrisi ruler, who sought to save his domain from the encroachment of Imam Yahya of Yemen in collusion with a rival pretender. The Hijaz and the 'Asir lowlands added to Ibn Saud's domains an immense strip of territory 1,000 miles long and 250 miles wide. Their annexation marked the end of his expansion and defined, with one minor exception, the limits of the third Saudi realm as it exists today. All around that enormous realm there was either sea or political entities dominated or protected by British power; and that power Ibn Saud had no intention of challenging even when respect for it threatened to undermine his rule over the domains he had conquered.

Mastering the Ikhwan and Rounding Off the Empire, 1926–1932

The real political considerations that in Ibn Saud's view set the limits for the expansionist drive of the Saudi-Wahhabi state did not accord well with the theopolitical conception of jihad held by the Ikhwan, which called for unrelenting war against *mushrikun* and infidels. This opposition of views blended with other ostensibly religious issues that arose in connection with the conquest of the Hijaz and became the basis for a conflict between Ibn Saud and the Ikhwan that threatened to undo all of Ibn Saud's labors of a quarter of a century. When he finally mastered that most serious of challenges, Ibn Saud set not only the boundaries of the Saudi state but also the limits of Wahhabism.

The conflict germinated during the Hijaz war. On the one hand, the massacre of the "unbelievers" at Ta'if had created a host of unnecessary complications for Ibn Saud, which he was able to overcome only with great difficulty and at the cost of prolonging the war by a year. On the other hand, as he took control of Mecca and then of the rest of the Hijaz, he found it necessary to leave in place much of the sharifian administrative apparatus, including personnel, taxation, regulations, and physical instruments such as telegraph, telephones, and cars. All of these were anathema to the Ikhwan, who were prompt to express their feelings. In 1924, on the first holy day of Id al-Fitr celebrated in Mecca under Saudi rule, one of their leaders, Faisal al-Dawish, made a speech at an Ikhwan gathering in which he said ominously that the Ikhwan were pledged to enforce the word of God and to correct departures from the ways of Islam regardless of who committed them, be it the sharif or anyone who followed in his footsteps.[23] Ibn Saud tolerated that kind of arrogant zeal for the duration of the war, but immediately afterward he sent the Ikhwan off to their respective *hijar* while he turned his attention to the multitude of problems he faced in the conquered lands.

A year later, at an Ikhwan conference at Artawiya, the participants freely criticized Ibn Saud for many practices that they deemed contrary to the true faith and for allowing tribes from Iraq and Transjordan to pasture their herds in "true Muslim" territory. They also upbraided him for prohibiting commerce with Kuwait, saying that if that country was infidel it should be invaded, and if not it should not be boycotted. When news of this reached Ibn Saud in the Hijaz, he hurried back to Najd and invited all the secular and religious leaders to a conference in Riyadh in January 1927 to discuss the affairs of the realm. Ibn Saud arrived at the conference with chests full of treasure acquired in the Hijaz, which he distributed differentially among the assembled chiefs to mollify and divide them. He then proposed that the conference proclaim him king of Najd and its dependencies as well as of the Hijaz, as if that were its principal business, and the conference did so by acclamation. Regarding the problem that was foremost in his mind, he addressed to the 'ulama a number of questions concerning issues on which he had been criticized and asked them to provide authoritative *fatwas* (rulings according to religious law) to deal with them. When the conference dispersed, it looked as though Ibn Saud had defused the crisis, but events were to show otherwise.

The 'ulama reported in February 1927, and their rulings were an interesting mixture of decision, ambiguity, and evasion, typical of their position in situations of internal power conflict. On the question of use of the telegraph, for instance, the 'ulama stated that the legal sources provided no guidance on the matter and that they could not provide a ruling until the exact nature of the device was understood. On the question of administration in the Hijaz, they ruled that any un-Islamic laws, "if any such exist," should be abolished in favor of pure Islamic law. Regarding treatment of the Shi'ites in Hasa and Qatif—a question that Ibn Saud had apparently raised voluntarily—the answer was decisive enough: they should not be allowed to perform their misguided religious practices, and if they violated the prohibition they should be exiled from Muslim lands. On the explosive question of grazing across the borders, the 'ulama ruled somewhat irrelevantly that the Shi'ites of Iraq should be forbidden entry to Muslim pastures or, for that matter, to other Muslim territory. On the question of jihad, they replied clearly enough that "we leave this to the Imam, whose duty it is according to our religious teaching to see what is best for Islam and the Muslims."[24] As for the levying of taxes other than the traditional *zakat* they reported, unhelpfully under the circumstances: "Taxes, we have ruled, are completely illegal and it is the King's duty to remit them; but if he refuses to do so, we do not feel it is permissible to break up Muslim unity and revolt against him *solely on this account.*"[25]

The rulings of the 'ulama took some specific questions out of the discussion but failed to settle the principal issue between Ibn Saud and the Ikhwan chiefs, which centered on jihad against Iraq. In April 1927 Ibn Saud convened another conference, which was attended by all the Najdi chiefs and three thousand Ikhwan but was boycotted by Sultan ibn Bijad, chief of the 'Utaiba and the Ghatghat *hijrah* and conqueror of Ta'if. Ibn Saud tried to appease his critics by explaining that his attitude toward Iraq was not different from theirs, but that because of the attitude of a certain foreign power he must exercise discretion in handling the problem until circumstances were right, at which time the Ikhwan would have the honor of submitting that country to the law of God. His words, however, must have sounded hollow the next month, when on May 20 he signed the Treaty of Jidda with Britain. This instrument annulled the 1915 treaty and included British recognition of "the absolute independence of the dominions" of Ibn Saud in return for the latter's undertaking to respect British treaties with the trucial shaikhs, suppress slavery, and facilitate the pilgrimage of British subjects.

In any case, some of the Ikhwan leaders were unpersuaded at the April conference, probably because they had decided to try to overthrow Ibn Saud and take power themselves.[26] Thus, in October 1927 Faisal al-Dawish, chief of the Mutair and Artawiya, led a small Ikhwan force against a party engaged in building a controversial Iraqi garrison post at Bosaya and wiped it out together with its police guard. The British authorities in Iraq demanded the immediate withdrawal of the Najdi frontier tribes and launched air attacks on them that continued for three months. Ibn Saud had no choice but to protest against the British and the Iraqis and to advance his own grievances in justification of his subjects' actions, until an agreement was reached to hold negotiations in April 1928. In the meantime, however, the Ikhwan plotters had succeeded in provoking a conflict with Iraq and the British, in arousing the anger of the Najdis, and in depicting Ibn Saud as a frightened and weak leader in the face of the infidels.

The British sent Sir Gilbert Clayton to Jidda to negotiate on behalf of themselves and the Iraqis. The talks went on for several months but ended in failure. The heart of the problem was that the British did not trust Ibn Saud's ability to prevent raiding from his side and Ibn Saud failed to convince them of the contrary. They therefore insisted on continuing to build frontier posts and using other defensive measures, while Ibn Saud insisted that the frontier posts were contrary to previous agreements to keep the borders demilitarized. The Ikhwan thus succeeded in causing the failure of the negotiations just as they had succeeded in stirring up the problem in the first place. Ibn Saud tried to underplay the consequences of the fiasco by taking time to go on pilgrimage, but the resumption of the raids and counterraids, the Iraqis' continued construction of new posts, and the agitation by the Ikhwan brought the situation in Najd close to anarchy.[27]

In September 1928 Ibn Saud ordered another conference of Najdi and Ikhwan chiefs to convene the following month to discuss the situation. This time Faisal al-Dawish (of Mutair) joined Sultan ibn Bijad (of 'Utaiba) in refusing the summons, as did Dhaydan ibn Hithlain, chief of the 'Ajman, ever ready to revolt against constituted authority, and Farhan ibn Mashhur, leader of a group of Ruwala Ikhwan. In the absence of the rebels an understanding could not even be attempted, so Ibn Saud used the occasion to try to rally support for himself. In the presence of eight hundred shaikhs and chiefs, both town dwellers and bedouins, he reviewed his efforts to unite and pacify the Arabian Peninsula and referred to signs of disaffection in some quarters. He spoke about his negotiations with the British and their insistence on the frontier posts but blamed their decision on Faisal al-Dawish's raid on the Bosaya post. He then called upon those present, if dissatisfied, to choose another member of the Saud family to take his place as leader and pledged himself to support whomever they chose.[28]

Of course those present did not choose a successor but pledged themselves anew to support and obey him. The fact that Ibn Saud offered to abdicate, however, was an interesting reflection of his state of mind and of the gravity of the situation he confronted. He could not bring himself to declare war on the Iraqi unbelievers and their infidel British supporters, especially since the Ikhwan had deliberately provoked them; but neither could he ask his people to rally behind him to fight the Ikhwan, because they were fighting unbelievers and infidels. All he could do for the moment was to elicit a demonstration of trust in his leadership, continue his efforts to split the ranks of the rebels by gifts of money and the encouragement of rivals to their tribal leaderships, and wait for them to make a mistake that would allow him to change the issue and fight them on more promising grounds.

Before long his opponents played into his hands. For several months after the conference dispersed, the rebels and their Ikhwan bands buzzed threateningly along the frontiers of Kuwait and Iraq, launching an occasional raid but failing to deliver a serious blow, because of the alertness of the enemy and the vigilance of the Royal Air Force. Then on February 22, 1929, Sultan ibn Bijad for some unknown reason suddenly attacked simultaneously the Najd Shammar and a group of Najdi camel merchants — both under the jurisdiction of Ibn Saud — and the Ya'jib, under Iraqi jurisdiction. The latter fled and lost only property, but the Shammar suffered heavily and the camel merchants, mostly natives of the Qasim, were massacred almost to a man. At the same time, other minor Ikhwan groups massacred a group of unarmed Sulaba tribesmen, subjects of Ibn Saud, while Faisal al-Dawish maneuvered to surprise some Iraqi prey. Whether the rebels had been driven by frustration and greed or whether they meant to undermine Ibn Saud's position by sowing terror among his subjects, their actions backfired completely. The massacre of the merchants raised a storm of indignation among the townspeople of Najd, and the great bedouin tribes were outraged. The rebel leaders' claim to be "true Muslims" while they labeled Ibn Saud a renegade was shown to be completely hypocritical by their attacks on fellow Muslims.

Ibn Saud responded with speed and determination. As soon as he got word of the massacre he proceeded to Buraida and called out a double levy of the townspeople of Najd, who responded with alacrity. He appealed to the tribes to join him and received a massive response, including sections of the rebel tribes. The rebel forces under al-Dawish and ibn Bijad, smaller but highly confident, advanced to meet Ibn Saud's gathering forces, while the 'Ajman under ibn Hithlain covered the flank in Hasa. Negotiations went on while the armies converged: Ibn Saud tried to split the rebels or to get them to surrender without battle, and the rebels tried to lure Ibn Saud into a trap and kill or capture him. Nothing came of these efforts, and the battle was joined at Sibla, between Buraida and Artawiya, on March 30, 1929.[29] The battle was sharp, lasted only a few hours, and ended in a total rout of the rebel forces. Ibn Bijad fled to Ghatghat; al-Dawish was wounded and carried from the battlefield by his men to Artawiya. Ibn Saud pursued the latter thither, seized him, and then let him go to die peacefully — or so he believed.

After Sibla, Dhaydan ibn Hithlain visited the camp of Fahd ibn Jilwi, the son of Ibn Saud's governor of Hasa, who had been watching the 'Ajman movements with a small force, to assure him of his peaceful intentions. A failure of communication and mutual suspicion of treachery caused the 'Ajman to approach Fahd's camp in force, Fahd to kill Dhaydan, and the 'Ajman to kill Fahd, defeat his forces, and raise the banner of rebellion again under Dhaydan's son and successor, Naif ibn Hithlain. Not long thereafter Faisal al-Dawish recovered from his wounds, left Artawiya, rallied a force of Mutair Ikhwan, and resumed operations against Kuwait and Iraq north of the 'Ajman region. Ibn Mashhur of the Ruwala Ikhwan raided further north, and most of the 'Utaiba ravaged the land between Najd and the Hijaz. The rebellion thus raged again more fiercely than ever, cut off Najd from the Persian Gulf, and disrupted communications between Riyadh and Mecca for months. However, since the rebels' claim to be the bearers of the banner of jihad and upholders of "true Islam" had been exploded, Ibn Saud had no trouble rallying the loyalist forces of Najd and other tribes for a final campaign against them. The rebellious 'Utaiba were defeated and mercilessly dispossessed; a raiding group of seven hundred Ikhwan under the command of a son of Faisal al-Dawish was defeated, pursued, and defeated again.

The denouement was rather ironic. The ringleaders of the rebellion, Faisal al-Dawish, Naif ibn Hithlain, and Farhan ibn Mashhur, made their way to Iraq with a small number of followers, surrendered their arms to the authorities, and sought asylum in the land of the unbelievers (Sultan ibn Bijad had surrendered earlier to Ibn Saud and was in jail in Riyadh). Adding to the irony, King Faisal of Iraq refused for a while to surrender the refugees to Ibn Saud, giving rise to a crisis that threatened to erupt into hostilities. In the end the British mediated an "unconditional" extradition on the understanding that Ibn Saud would not execute the rebels. The trouble was over by January 1930, and the British fittingly capped it by arranging a meeting between King Faisal and King Ibn Saud aboard HMS *Lupin* on February 22, 1930, which resulted in an agreement of friendship and *bon voisinage* between the heads of the two hostile dynasties.[30]

After Sibla, Ibn Saud declared that religious issues would be decided only by the 'ulama and banned all meetings for any purpose without prior approval by the ruler. Artawiya and Ghatghat, the most notorious of the Ikhwan colonies, were razed and other *hijar* brought under strict control. The Ikhwan were not banned and were used to good effect in the 1934 war with Yemen; but as the events of that war showed, their sting had already been drawn and Ibn Saud felt free to pursue with Yemen a realistic and even generous policy without fear of internal repercussions.

The immediate cause of the Yemen war was a dispute over the oasis of Najran, on the border between the two countries, which the forces of Imam Yahya seized and from which the Ikhwan ousted them in the spring of 1932. Ultimately, however, the war occurred as a result of the convergence of the forces of two expansionist leaders on the territory of the dissolving 'Asiri state. Hemmed in by British power elsewhere, Ibn Saud and Yahya were tempted to test their strength against each other, and this is why two years of negotiations led nowhere. In April 1934 Ibn Saud gave Yahya an ultimatum to comply with his demands, and when the latter failed to answer, two Saudi columns led by Ibn Saud's sons Saud and Faisal marched in. Saud's army, starting from Najran and heading for San'a, made some progress before becoming bogged down in the mountains. Faisal's forces, however, moving along the coast, advanced rapidly after defeating Yahya's forces and reached the port of Hodeida, halfway down Yemen's coast, within three weeks.

By that time Yahya had sent appeals for help in every direction, some of which elicited prompt responses. The Italians, entrenched in Eritrea and Somalia since 1885 and fearing eventual Saudi control of Bab al-Mandeb, sent two destroyers to Hodeida and landed a company of marines. Two days later the British sent in their own naval units to balance the Italians and to try to keep Ibn Saud from becoming their neighbor at the Aden Protectorate. Both powers demanded that Ibn Saud halt his forces and enter into negotiations, and Arab leaders chimed in with a call to end the fighting among Muslims and an offer to mediate the dispute. Ibn Saud yielded and negotiations took place under the supervision of a concilia- tion commission composed of Egyptians, Syrians, and Palestinians. The resulting agreement recognized Ibn Saud's sovereignty over all of 'Asir, including Najran, and stipulated withdrawal of his forces from Yemen and payment to him of reparations of 100,000 sterling in gold.[31] With these rather modest gains, Ibn Saud concluded the remarkable career of con- quest begun thirty-two years before and turned his attention to consoli- dating the empire he had rebuilt and the dynasty he had restored. Symbo- lizing the shift, at about the same time he changed the name of his realm from the Kingdoms of Hijaz and Najd and Its Dependencies to the King- dom of Saudi Arabia (more accurately, the Arab Saudi Kingdom) and nominated a crown prince in the person of his son Emir Saud.

Observations on the Creation of the Third Realm

A few general observations concerning the creation of the third realm are worth underscoring for their possible bearing on key features of the Kingdom and on subsequent developments there.

1. In his endeavor to create the third realm, Ibn Saud based his drive on the dynastic principle, like the founders of the second realm, as long as he confronted tribal adversaries. When facing established powers with strong traditional Islamic credentials, such as the Hashemites and the Turks, he based his drive on militant Wahhabism, like the founders of the first realm.

2. Despite the fact that Ibn Saud personally rebuilt the fortunes of the House of Saud from zero, he was not spared serious challenges from pretenders belonging to another branch of the family, who were able to draw considerable support from disaffected tribal chiefs. Conscious that family strife had brought about the destruction of the second realm, Ibn Saud endeavored to forgo retribution and to conciliate the pretenders after defeating them.

3. Whether he pursued the dynastic principle or militant Wahhabism, Ibn Saud was acutely aware from the history of the first realm of the imperative to avoid an all-out confrontation with a superior imperial power all by himself. He strove to obtain British support against the Turkish power behind ibn Rashid and to neutralize the British power behind Sharif Hussein before launching his final assaults on the realms of those enemies. In pursuing these strategic goals, he went to great

lengths to appease the big powers, accepting for tactical reasons humiliating terms from the Turks and their allies and seeking and agreeing to a
British alliance on highly constricting terms.

4. The high point of Ibn Saud's strategy of caution toward big powers
came when the Ikhwan sought to embroil him in an all-out confrontation
with the British-backed Hashemites in Iraq and Transjordan. He resisted
their pressure at great risk to himself and eventually turned on them and
destroyed them rather than fight the powerful "infidels" (the British) and
their protégés, the Iraqi "unbelievers."

5. The confrontation with the Ikhwan carried an additional lesson.
Although Ibn Saud was aware from the outset of the need to control
militant Wahhabism and devised ways that he thought would do so, the
Ikhwan eventually eluded his control, divided or paralyzed his own con-
stituencies and sources of support, and threatened to take over supreme
power.[32] Only because of the lack of coordination among the leaders of
the challengers and their excesses against fellow Muslims was Ibn Saud
eventually able to prevail against them.[33]

6. After subduing the Ikhwan, Ibn Saud did not revert simply to the
dynastic principle, notwithstanding the name he adopted for his realm.
The justification of his conquest and control of the Hijaz and the holy
cities; the continuing need to counter the danger of irredentism from the
Hashemites installed in Iraq and Transjordan, with their superior lineage
and prescriptive religious legitimacy; and the general requirement of
providing a cement for his heterogeneous empire made it as necessary as
ever for him to rest the legitimacy of his house on superior religious
ideology and performance.[34] The suppression of the Ikhwan may thus be
seen as ending a stage of "revolutionary Wahhabism" in favor of "Wahhabism in one country."

7. Although Ibn Saud alternately appeased and defied the Turks and
their local allies until he prevailed over them, he was careful not to
attempt the same approach with the British and their local allies. He did
agree to a constricting treaty with Britain in 1915, which he subsequently
nullified in 1927, but he achieved this end by negotiations rather than by
defiance. His absolute respect for British power was seen in the fact that
he pressed his attack against Sharif Hussein only after the British had
abandoned him, that he did not encroach on the British-protected Gulf
emirates, and that he turned on his own Ikhwan when they threatened to
embroil him with the British in Iraq and Transjordan. In Yemen, too, he
demonstrated considerable moderation and renounced most of his conquests in the face of a possible clash with British and Italian power. The
result was that historically it was British power that effectively set the
limits of Ibn Saud's process of expansion on practically all sides.

3

Preserving the Empire,
1932–1953

Having created an empire out of disparate sections and anarchic tribes in a vast inhospitable environment, Ibn Saud in the last two decades of his life faced the problem of how to preserve that unusual creation. Two dangers threatened its existence: the internal centrifugal pulls that had historically barred the emergence of any enduring political entity the size of the one he had forged; and the hostility of the Hashemite rulers of Iraq and Transjordan, whose family he had dispossessed of the Hijaz.

In the 1930s and early 1940s, Ibn Saud neutralized the Hashemite threat by reaching an understanding with their British patrons. His main preoccupation was the danger of disintegration from within. Although he had, and was believed to have, the necessary personal leadership qualities and a suitable strategy to appease or deter the restless tribes and sections of his realm, he lacked sufficient financial resources to uphold that strategy.

Eventually Ibn Saud was tided over by British and American assistance until the flow of oil revenues after World War II provided the necessary means. No sooner did this happen, however, than he was confronted with a resurgence of the Hashemite threat owing to the weakening of Britain's control over Iraq and Britain's suspected collusion with Iraq and Transjordan (later Jordan) in projects that could give the Hashemite rulers the capability to defeat him and to destabilize and break up his empire.

Ibn Saud responded with a three-pronged strategy: he strove to conclude a military alliance with the United States, endeavored to contain the Hashemites and frustrate their designs through political friendships and alliances in the Arab arena, and attempted to build up a regular armed force for purposes of internal and external deterrence. By the time of his death in November 1953, he had achieved none of his goals fully. He had scored a measure of success with the first and perhaps a larger measure with the second, but the third remained more of an objective than a reality. Altogether, although he transmitted his empire intact to his successors, its continued existence was far from assured.

Defense and Foreign Policy during the Lean Years

In 1932, the year in which Ibn Saud formally signified the unification of the territories he had conquered over the previous three decades by renaming his realm the Kingdom of Saudi Arabia, the American vice-consul in Aden, who followed developments in Arabia, wrote to the secretary of state that the kingdom was not destined to survive its founder: " . . . a unified Arab state, even if established today by Ibn Saud, would evidently collapse after his death under the influence of the schismatic tendencies of his heirs."[1] He added: "Undoubtedly the Wahhabi family [sic], as it has done twice before, will abandon the Hijaz and retire to Najd soon after Ibn Saud's death, or possibly even earlier."[2] Seven months later the same vice-consul predicted the fall of Ibn Saud and of his realm much sooner indeed as a result of penury. In August 1933 he wrote that "neither he [Ibn Saud] nor his government can be expected to last much longer without money."[3] After describing Ibn Saud's desperate efforts to raise money by "pandering to foreigners" to the detriment of his religious standing, the vice-consul concluded: "The Consulate, which has for some time predicted the beginning of ibn Saud's fall as a world personage and his retirement to Nejd, if the 1933 pilgrimage were a failure, feels that its views were greatly strengthened by the recent events in Saudi Arabia of which an outline has been furnished above."[4]

The American vice-consul proved to be wrong, of course, but he was in excellent company. Only a few years before, T. E. Lawrence and David Hogarth, two of the foremost British experts on Arabian affairs, had made similar predictions based on similar grounds. Lawrence had argued that the vastness and poverty of Arabia and the ethos of the tribes inhabiting it precluded the establishment of enduring large political entities. A leader of exceptional abilities such as Ibn Saud might be able to create such an entity by dint of extraordinary exertions and good fortune, but in the absence of the necessary resources and instruments of established states, it was bound to fall apart after his disappearance from the scene, as had happened to the realm of the Rashids (the archrivals of the House of Saud) and many others before. H. St. John Philby, another British Arabist, who was particularly close to Ibn Saud, had argued against Lawrence that Ibn Saud's espousal and promotion of Wahhabism gave his endeavor an element of cohesiveness which other tribal empire builders had lacked and which assured its durability. Hogarth shared Philby's view of the critical importance of Wahhabism, but precisely for that reason he had categorically predicted the collapse of Ibn Saud's empire within a few years after the conquest of the Hijaz, on the grounds that the Wahhabi spirit would give way to the lure of the fleshpots of Jidda and leave Ibn Saud's enterprise exposed to the inexorable anarchic pressures of Arabian politics.[5]

Although the vice-consul and the experts were wrong in their predictions, they accurately diagnosed Ibn Saud's basic security concern and associated practical problem in the period up to World War II. That concern was internal rather than external threats, and the practical problem was money. The Kingdom was surrounded on all sides except its southwestern corner by waters and territories under British control. The territories bordering on the Arabian Sea and the Persian Gulf consisted of small emirates vulnerable to Saudi encroachments — Ibn Saud had conquered and absorbed stronger ones inland. To the north and east, the territories had recently been organized into the state of Iraq and the emirate of Transjordan, both under the rule of princes of the Hashemite family whom Ibn Saud had dispossessed in the Hijaz, and presented a real potential danger. Ibn Saud had dealt effectively with that threat by entering into an agreement with Britain, anticipated in the 1927 Treaty of Jidda, wherein he in effect committed himself to refrain from encroaching upon the weak emirates in exchange for Britain's restraining the potentially strong Hashemites from hostile action against his realm. This kind of deal had been expected at the time the experts spoke and was an established reality when the vice-consul reported.

Ibn Saud's basic security problem was how to keep together the empire he had created out of many diverse scattered regions and a multitude of armed tribes, with the very limited means at his disposal. In dealing with that issue Ibn Saud had adopted an approach that was more akin to interstate relations than to the relations of a ruler to his subjects. He could not disarm the tribes and establish a monopoly over the means of coercion — probably the thought did not even occur to him. His only way to maintain intertribal peace and acquiescence in his rule was a strategy based on deterrence, diplomacy, and blandishment. He had inherited from the sharifian administration of the Hijaz a regular, uniformed army of several thousand, trained by Turkish officers and possessing some "modern" equipment, including motor transports and some guns, but he neither valued its capability nor trusted its loyalty. He kept some two or three thousand of these troops and distributed them in small detachments among the Hijaz cities to perform supplementary police duties, and in border posts to fight smugglers. His real deterrent force consisted of a core of up to one thousand royal guards backed by tribal levies provided by loyal tribes from the vicinity of Riyadh and other towns of Najd. That force attracted as well as deterred another set of tribal forces in the more remote areas, and this wider combination at least deterred and secured the acquiescence of still others.

The entire system was finely interwoven and needed constant tending to prevent a tear that would unravel it all. As one kind of tending activity, Ibn Saud entered into a multitude of marital alliances with families of tribal chiefs, including former foes as well as allies, and held members of formerly hostile chiefs as security in gilded captivity in his court. Another device that Ibn Saud deemed essential was to maintain a flow of largesse to the tribes to sustain his own prestige, to compensate the tribes for the flow of tribute in the opposite direction, and to reduce the temptation of tribal raiding as a supplementary means of livelihood in times of scarcity.

The problem that confronted Ibn Saud in 1933, and the one that the American vice-consul expected to lead to his prompt downfall, was shortage of money to support the system. Hafiz Wahba, who spent half a century in Saudi service, reported for instance that during the financial crisis of 1932 there was a tribal revolt in northern Hijaz led by ibn Rifada, instigated by Emir Abdallah of Transjordan, and financed by the former Egyptian khedive Abbas Hilmi II. Not long afterward there was a revolt of the Idrisis in 'Asir; and not long thereafter there was the border conflict with the imam of Yemen that led to war.[6]

The financial crisis resulted from a drastic decline in the number of pilgrims, the country's main source of revenue, in connection with the world economic depression. Figures for that period are difficult to obtain. According to Philby, the number of pilgrims fell from an average of 130,000 a year in 1926–1929 to 80,000 in 1930, 40,000 in 1931, and less thereafter. At the highest level of pilgrim traffic, the revenue of the state amounted to 4 to 5 million sterling — 20 to 25 million dollars[7] — so that in 1933 the revenue must have been between one-third and one-fourth that amount. Nearly 80 percent of the revenue was used to support the internal political system in one way or another. A rare sheet of government appropriations for 1930, published in the official gazette, *Umm al-Qura,* listed appropriations amounting to 106 million piasters. The value of a piaster in more familiar currencies is not known. However, about 17 million piasters were assigned for debt repayment, 18 million for administration and public service functions, and the remaining 89 million were assigned to the court, defense and security, grants to tribes, and so on.[8] The drastic drop in revenue was therefore a critical problem, and from 1930 until the end of World War II Ibn Saud's financial anxieties and his basic security concern were one and the same thing.

In 1933 Ibn Saud's desperate need for money drove him to grant to

Standard Oil of California (SOCAL) the historic concession to explore and develop his country's oil resources in exchange for relatively small payments even in his own terms. The agreement provided for the payment of an annual rent of $35,000, plus a loan of $210,000 in the first year and another of $140,000 in the second year recoverable from future royalties if any should be forthcoming. Two additional loans of $350,000 each would be given if oil in commercial quantities were discovered. Royalties on such oil would be at the rate of $7 per ton. The agreement was bitterly opposed by the religious leaders on the grounds that it would let into the country infidels who would corrupt the people and introduce liquor, phonographs, and other instruments of the devil,[9] but Ibn Saud overrode the opposition on what might be called *raison d'état.* The following year he obtained additional relief in the form of $700,000 in reparations exacted from Yemen at the conclusion of the 1934 war, but the financial bind persisted. In 1938 SOCAL struck oil in commercial quantities, and the following year Ibn Saud collected $3.2 million in revenues; but the outbreak of World War II suspended further development, oil revenues dropped to $1.2 million, the traffic of foreign pilgrims came to a nearly complete halt, and a succession of droughts brought hunger to the tribes.

The British, fearing the development of trouble in an area on the flank and in the rear of their restless Middle Eastern territories, provided emergency shipments of food, and SOCAL, renamed CASOC (California Arabian Standard Oil Company), provided some funds on account of future royalties. Neither, however, felt able to comply with Ibn Saud's request for a loan of $6 million a year to help meet his minimal annual need of $10 million. Eventually CASOC was able to persuade the U.S. government to help Ibn Saud under the terms of the Lend-Lease Act, first through the British in 1942 and 1943, and thereafter directly. In a memorandum to President Roosevelt CASOC stated, with some exaggeration, that "unless this is done, and soon, this independent kingdom, and perhaps with it the entire Arab world, will be thrown into chaos."[10] In the next few years direct American aid was at twice the level of Ibn Saud's indicated budgetary need.

The end of the war allowed the resumption of oil development and exports, which finally resolved Ibn Saud's political-financial problem. Revenue from oil amounted to $10 million in 1946, $53 million in 1948, $57 million in 1950, and $212 million in 1952, the last full year of Ibn Saud's reign.[11] Because of the profligacy of the ruler and primitive financial management, neither these amounts nor multiples of them sufficed to prevent endemic budgetary deficits and indebtedness for the next fifteen years; but the Kingdom was never again to be politically endangered by lack of the minimal financial means necessary to lubricate the nexus between the ruler and the tribal chiefs.

Even as the money problem was on its way to solution, however, Ibn

Saud confronted a serious security problem in the shape of a resurgence of the Hashemite threat. Britain had emerged from the war as the sole dominant power in the Middle East after having ejected the Italians from Libya and eased the French out of Syria and Lebanon. However, Britain was also exhausted and, facing what Lord Keynes called a "financial Dunkirk," sought to reduce drastically its global commitments. Within two years of the end of the war, it had been compelled by penury at home and nationalist pressure abroad to concede independence to India, Burma, and Ceylon and to divest itself of responsibility for the defense of Iran, Turkey, and Greece. In the Middle East heartland, its endeavor to reduce its commitments while protecting its interests in the region (defined in terms of access to oil and imperial communications and defense) led it to pursue a complex policy, including two features that particularly affected Saudi Arabia. One was to replace existing treaties with Iraq, Egypt, and Transjordan, which were anathema to local nationalists, with new treaties that would concede full independence to those countries in exchange for their granting to Britain certain minimal base rights. To create a favorable climate for achievement of this goal, Britain unilaterally minimized the extent of its interference in the affairs of those countries even before the negotiations yielded the desired results, and took a pro-Arab stance in the surging Jewish-Arab conflict over Palestine.

The other feature of British policy particularly relevant to Saudi Arabia was an attempt to encourage various schemes of association among Arab states, partly the better to keep out rival powers, partly in the hope that association would either facilitate conclusion of the desired treaties with individual states or make possible a collective substitute for them. Even before the end of the war King (then Emir) Abdallah of Transjordan had advanced one such associative scheme, known as Greater Syria, which sought to unite Syria, Lebanon, and most of Palestine with Transjordan under his rule. Iraq's perennial prime minister, Nuri al-Sa'id, had advanced another scheme in the name of his Hashemite masters known as the Fertile Crescent, which sought to unite all the previously cited countries with Iraq. The British were known to be sympathetic to both schemes at the time they were enunciated; but when these triggered a process that led to the formation, with active British encouragement, of the League of Arab States in 1945, Britain ostensibly ceased to back the Iraqi and Transjordanian plans even though their authors continued to pursue them.

From the point of view of Ibn Saud, the prospect of his Hashemite opponents' realizing either of their schemes with British help was alarming. Britain's profession of neutrality toward those projects after the formation of the Arab League was hardly credible to the old king, who had seen British officials create the Hashemite states, determine their boundaries, choose and depose their rulers, and prescribe their policy at will. Least of all was he disposed to believe Britain's claim after it had emerged victorious from a world war and was without rival in the Middle East. But even if he were to take the British at their word, the Hashemites would have acquired or been granted freedom of action to a degree that would allow them to contemplate all sorts of hostile initiatives toward him. Either way, his historic understanding with the British, wherein they had undertaken to restrain the Hashemites in exchange for his exercising restraint toward the British-protected Persian Gulf emirates, appeared to him to have become inoperative.

Ibn Saud expressed his concerns in diplomatic exchanges with the British, who reassured him of their desire to preserve and develop their traditional friendship with the Kingdom. He pretended to take the British protestations at face value for the time being; he even took them as a basis for seeking their assistance in creating for him a modern army formation similar to Transjordan's Arab Legion. However, to protect himself against the dangers he perceived, he strove to bring in the United States as a counterweight to Britain and as a substitute buttress for the Kingdom's security. He specifically sought to have the United States put pressure on Britain to restrain the Hashemites and asked it to supply him with arms and even to conclude a full-fledged treaty of alliance with him. In a dogged pursuit of that aim, he tried to play upon the element of rivalry that existed between Britain and the United States and to use the leverage of oil, military bases, and even the Soviet danger. After four or five years, however, he achieved only partial success. The following paragraphs recount some of the landmarks of these efforts.

In mid-January 1947 Crown Prince Saud made a monthlong visit to the United States, culminating in a meeting with President Truman on February 18. According to a memorandum submitted to the president by the State Department in preparation for the meeting, the crown prince had expressed in his talks with government officials a fear that the British were behind King Abdallah's plan for Greater Syria. Later in the crown prince's visit, the memorandum informed the president, King Ibn Saud himself had sent an urgent message to Washington claiming that he had "obtained definite information" that the British were indeed "planning to have King Abdallah made ruler of Greater Syria" and requesting that the U.S. government "intervene in this matter immediately." The State Department memorandum went on to say that the crown prince had been assured that the United States would support the integrity and independence of the countries of the Near East in the United Nations should these countries be threatened with aggression, and recommended a reassertion of that position. It also informed the president that the American chargé d'affaires in London had been requested to tell the British that the

United States was "disturbed" by reports that had reached it from Near Eastern capitals in regard to King Abdallah's plans for a Greater Syria, and to ask for a statement of the British position in this matter.[12]

On December 12 the Arab League Council was due to meet to react to the UN resolution to partition Palestine, adopted on November 29, 1947. Well before the meeting there was talk that the league might consider a resolution calling for cancellation of American and British oil concessions in member countries (at that time, Saudi Arabia and Iraq) because of their role in connection with the UN resolution. On December 3 Ibn Saud received the American minister in Jidda to express his view of the situation and to make a general request for American political and military aid. He told the minister that the talk about canceling the concessions was an example of the increased pressure being put on him by the "Shereefian states" in order to harm his relations with the United States. He indicated agreement with the Arab states regarding the dispute with Zionism but said that he wanted to make "a distinction between such an attitude and the attempts being made by my antagonists in the Arab world to draw me into direct conflict politically or economically with the United States." He was prepared to oppose the pressure being put on him, but for him the "crucial question" was to know "whether and to what extent I can count upon United States aid in enabling me to resist any incursion from Iraq or Transjordan which may be the result of my failure to yield to the pressure."[13] After the audience Ibn Saud indicated that he had requested aid consisting of arms and political support.

The United States responded promptly that it was barred from providing him with arms by the embargo it had just declared on all arms shipments to the Near East. However, it sent Ibn Saud a note expressing support for the "territorial and political integrity of Saudi Arabia."[14] Ibn Saud was not content with the American reply and four months later returned to the chargé with another request for arms and a proposal for an American-Saudi treaty of alliance.

In early April 1948, when they were evacuating Palestine and when Transjordan's Arab Legion was expected to move in, the British tried to assuage Ibn Saud's suspicion of their support for Hashemite schemes by offering to conclude a military alliance with Saudi Arabia. Ibn Saud tried to use the British offer to induce the United States to conclude such a treaty with him in addition to, or instead of, the British.[15] Later that month he took advantage of a visit by the commander of the U.S. Air Transport Command in connection with programs to develop the Dhahran air base, to make, in the words of a State Department memorandum, "the strongest plea which he has yet registered for provision of military equipment by the United States." The memorandum reported the king to have said that if his country were armed to share in its self-defense, the United States would be granted whatever strategic facilities it might require in Saudi Arabia.[16] Washington replied that it could not undertake "to discuss assistance of any sort" to any of the Near Eastern states before a settlement of the "Palestine situation" — that is, the Arab-Israeli war, which had started a few days before.[17]

In April 1949 Transjordan followed Egypt and Lebanon in signing an armistice agreement with Israel that left Transjordan in control of the Arab part of Palestine (later known as the West Bank) and eastern Jerusalem with its Islamic holy places. By then the tensions between West and East were assuming the character of a cold war. In May 1949 Ibn Saud received the American representative in Jidda in an audience from which even interpreters were excluded, to express his concern and to reiterate his demands for American assistance. He mentioned the danger of Communism, stating that he did not fear it at home but was concerned about its taking hold in some neighboring Arab countries. He said that Britain's attitude toward him had cooled and its interest had been deflected to Iraq and Transjordan as American interests in Saudi Arabia had increased. He then dwelt at length on the problem of the "innate Shereefian hostility." He said that Yemen was flirting with Transjordan and Iraq and that Saudi Arabia might find itself encircled by enemies. He emphasized that King Abdallah would never give up the idea of Greater Syria, and asserted that he had reliable information that Abdallah had told the Jews that he would make concessions to them in Palestine if they would support him in efforts to regain the Hijaz. He argued that there was a time when Saudi Arabia could rely on the splendid fighting qualities of its soldiers to defend itself, but that now it was defenseless against tanks and military aircraft "in possession of/or available to" his enemies. He concluded by addressing an urgent request "for the last time" for help, adequate armaments, and advice. He was prepared to send one of his sons to Washington to make his views known, but he did not want to advertise unduly his concern and feared disastrous consequences should their mission fail.[18]

The American representative remarked in his cable that "we cannot continue to give King brush off indefinitely" and recommended that the United States agree to train 10,000 mobile airborne Saudi troops in exchange for a long-term agreement on the Dhahran Air Facility to replace the one due to expire in 1951.[19] This proposal became the subject of extensive discussion in Washington. In the meantime relations between Ibn Saud and the British deteriorated further. At the end of 1949 Ibn Saud reopened with Oman and Abu Dhabi the long-dormant dispute over the Buraimi oasis. The prospects of oil there had something to do with the move, but it was also a signal from Ibn Saud to Britain that his strategic understanding with them was a two-way street, and that if they did not restrain the Hashemites he was exempt from the obligation to restrain himself. Early in 1950 the British reacted by announcing plans to create a "Persian Gulf Frontier Force," later known as the Trucial Oman Levies.[20]

By April 1950 Washington had crystallized a set of specific proposals in response to Ibn Saud's requests. These were conveyed to the king by Assistant Secretary of State George McGhee during a meeting in Riyadh on April 10 and were summarized in a memorandum submitted to the president the following month. The memorandum recapitulates nicely both Ibn Saud's views and the American position at that point.

According to McGhee, the king dwelt at length on his concern about "possible aggression from the Hashemite Kingdoms of Jordan and Iraq, with whom the United Kingdom has treaty relations." He expressed his need for military forces to protect his realm against Hashemite attack, to assure internal security, and to secure a defense against Russia. McGhee attempted to allay the first of these fears by pointing out that the British were capable of restraining Hashemite aggression and had assured the United States that they would do so, if necessary; but the king said "he did not trust the British," had refused a treaty of alliance they had offered him, and wished to look to the United States, "to whose companies he had given his oil concessions," for support. He wanted "to assure Saudi Arabian security by concluding a military alliance with the United States" and by obtaining military assistance on a grant basis. He called attention to the Dhahran air base as well as to America's interest in Saudi oil to show that Saudi Arabia's security should be vital to both countries.

McGhee replied that the United States was fully aware of the importance of maintaining the security of Saudi Arabia and wanted to do what it could to assist. It could not consider concluding a treaty of alliance with Saudi Arabia "since it was contrary to our traditions," but McGhee suggested "certain other means which should achieve virtually the same end." These included (1) a treaty of friendship, commerce, and navigation; (2) providing technicians as Saudi Arabia might desire under the Point IV Program; (3) loans by the Export-Import Bank, subject to approval by the bank; (4) a long-term Dhahran airfield agreement, which would include or follow (5) a program of military aid providing arms on a cash-reimbursable basis and a military mission to help train Saudi Arabian forces.[21]

Ambassador Childs, who accompanied McGhee, submitted a report on the conversation that differed from the memorandum to the president in two particulars. According to Childs, McGhee followed his expression of American concern for Saudi security with a statement that the United States "will take most immediate action at any time that the integrity and independence of Saudi Arabia is threatened." That was a much stronger and more specific statement than any previous assurances. Childs also reported that McGhee explained America's reluctance to conclude a military alliance by saying that the United States had already assumed numerous commitments and that "although our friendship is unbounded, our resources are not."[22]

After the April 1950 talks Ibn Saud finally reconciled himself to the fact that he could not obtain an American alliance. He accepted the package he was offered but held back on the long-term agreement on the Dhahran air base. On June 18, 1951, he signed an agreement extending for five years the lease on the base, along with a mutual defense assistance agreement. As part of the latter, the United States began to supply Saudi Arabia with military equipment, and an American military mission arrived to start a training program for the Saudi armed forces.

In addition to his efforts with Britain and the United States, Ibn Saud sought to check the Hashemites by cultivating friends and influence among Arab leaders. The formation of the Arab League in 1945, partly as a result of British exertions, had created an arena for inter-Arab politics, and Ibn Saud maneuvered within and outside it to check Hashemite designs. In January 1946 he paid a state visit to Egypt to nourish a budding diplomatic alliance with its leaders, and one report has it that he watered it with a handsome secret retainer to King Faruq.[23] He developed an equally flourishing relationship with Syria's President Shukri al-Kuwatly until the latter was overthrown in 1949, and with other leaders and personalities in Syria, Lebanon, and even Jordan and Iraq. These exertions proved to be of considerable value. They helped shield Ibn Saud against Hashemite efforts to embarrass him by publicly advocating the cancellation of oil concessions to countries that supported the creation of a Jewish state; and they helped him foil the movement for a union between Syria and Iraq that developed after the overthrow of Kuwatly. However, the exertions did not prevent King Abdallah from annexing the Arab part of Palestine, which his army had occupied and defended in the 1948 war, and from thus becoming the protector of Jerusalem's Al Aqsa mosque and the Dome of the Rock, after Mecca and Madina the holiest places of Islam.

The Palestine war also showed the weakness of Ibn Saud's security position vis-à-vis the Hashemites in another way. King Abdallah's Arab Legion was the only Arab force that was able to hold on to its initial conquests after the Israelis passed to the counteroffensive, in contrast to the Egyptian, Syrian, and Lebanese forces and the Palestine Liberation Army. The Iraqis, although they did not exactly cover themselves with glory, at least were able to field and maintain an army of up to ten thousand men in Palestine by the end of the war. In contrast, Saudi Arabia was able to contribute to the war only a small battalion of two companies that fought under Egyptian command.[24] Members of that unit had been recruited solely from Najdi tribes; the Hijazis and others had been excluded because their loyalty was suspect.[25] After the war, particularly after the conclusion of the 1951 mutual defense assistance agreement with the United States, Ibn Saud began to acquire some modern arms and devoted large amounts of revenue to building his armed forces. These efforts, however, were very slow to mature, and in any case the Hashemites improved their forces even more under their long-standing treaty arrangements with Britain, on top of the headstart they already had on Ibn Saud.

Defense Establishment and Strategy

The arrival of the American military advisory group and training mission marked Ibn Saud's second major attempt to develop his armed forces after World War II. The first effort, begun six years before with the help of a British military mission, had failed almost completely before it was formally terminated. The reasons for the fiasco included insufficient allocations of funds for equipment needed, the "disappearance" of most of the allocations that were made, restrictions on the movement of the training mission personnel and on their contact with Saudi troops, lack of adequate officer material, and the arbitrary granting of commissions to the king's relatives and friends.[26] Typically, construction of a large army base designed to include a small-arms and ammunitions factory, warehouses, training facilities, and living quarters was begun at Kharj, southeast of Riyadh, in 1950 but was suspended halfway to completion because of official bungling.[27] The effect of the entire British effort was so small that officers with the American mission did not know the number of existing Saudi troops even though they had the findings of a nine-month-long survey of the Saudi defense establishment and needs, undertaken before their arrival.

American officers estimated the number of regular Saudi troops in 1953 at between 7,500 and 10,000. With the royal bodyguard, paramilitary police, and bedouin levies included, the number would be more than doubled.[28] The American mission's program, based on the survey, envisaged the creation of an army of three to five regimental combat teams with appropriate artillery, engineer, signal, and other technical units over a period of three years.[29] As in the earlier British program, these troops were to be specially equipped for desert warfare; but according to the American plan they were also to be endowed with a substantial element of air mobility to permit rapid deployment to any part of the vast country.

In addition to air transport, the Saudi armed forces were to acquire an air combat component. This had been an obsession with Ibn Saud ever since the RAF had annihilated a party of two thousand Ikhwan after they had raided in Transjordan in 1922. In 1923 he had acquired a few surplus DH-9 light bombers from the British and had hired foreigners to fly and maintain them. In 1931 he had bought four ex-RAF Wapitis and secured a few seconded RAF personnel to operate them under a two-year contract. When the British left, other foreign personnel were hired and a start was made on the construction of a new airfield at Jidda. Work was interrupted repeatedly by lack of funds until 1937, when the Italian government took over and completed it as a gesture of goodwill. For the next thirteen years military aviation stagnated until the British military mission was asked to revive it. A handful of de Havilland Tiger Moth primary trainers was provided from RAF surplus stock, but the mission was soon withdrawn and gave way to the American mission.[30] By the time of Ibn Saud's death in November 1953, six troop transports and twenty armable trainers had been provided under the American program — six Douglas C-47 transports and ten Temco TE-1A Buckaroo trainers in 1952, and ten NA T-6 Texan trainers in 1952–53. In addition, two Convair C-131Ds were provided for royal use in 1952.[31] Because of the importance Ibn Saud attached to aviation and because the U.S. Air Force was already present at the Dhahran airfield, the military advisory group and the training mission were headed by a U.S. Air Force brigadier general.

Defense and Security Allocations

A close and systematic study of budgetary data provides a parallel approach to the study of Saudi defense and security that can highlight, check, or supplement key points presented in the historical analysis of defense and foreign policy and in the review of the information on the military establishment.

Budgetary data for the period 1932–1953 are scarce and rudimentary, reflecting the primitive condition of the Saudi realm at the time. Only three budgets of any sort are available for the latter part of that period, covering fiscal 1948, 1952, and 1953. (The Saudi fiscal year is based on the Hijra, or lunar, year and runs from 1 Rajab through 30 Jumada II. The table at the beginning of the book provides conversions to the Gregorian calendar for the years 1960–1980.) Moreover, in principle as well as in practice, Ibn Saud regarded the entire revenue of his country as his own personal wealth and disposed of it accordingly, without having to account to anyone and without even self-imposed constraints. Still, although the data for the period may be irrelevant as an indication of actual performance, they can shed considerable light on Ibn Saud's perceptions and intentions at the time, as well as on the realm's general status in terms of defense and security. Table 1 presents the relevant information culled from the three available budgets. The following points emerge from or are reflected in the table.

Table 1. Revenues and defense and security allocations, fiscal 1948, 1952, and 1953 (million SR)[a]

	1947–48	1951–52	1952–53
Revenues and allocations			
Total revenue	215	490	758
Oil revenue	141	341	372
Total defense and security allocations	91	157	400
% of total revenue[b]	42	32	53
Specific defense and security allocations[c]			
1. Ministry of Defense	64	88	61
2. Aviation	4	12	10[d]
3. Royal Guard	—	—	7
4. Grants to tribes	11	34	—
5. Riyadh and its dependencies	—	—	152
6. Cash and kind annuities	—	—	11
7. Regions and principalities	4	10	—
8. Public Security Department	6	12	—
9. Ministry of Interior	—	—	63
10. Coast Guard	1	2	2
11. Emergency expenditures	—	—	2
12. Unanticipated expenditures	—	—	5
13. Kharj factory and materials	—	—	87

Source: Kingdom of Saudi Arabia, *Statistical Yearbook, 1965.*

a. Rounded to nearest million.

b. Rounded to nearest percentage.

c. Items 1–13 are official Saudi budget categories.

d. Recategorized as "Kingdom's airports."

1. In general, allocations to defense and security represent a very high percentage of revenues, reflecting the preeminence of the ruler's concern with the problem. With the very large increase in revenues between 1947–48 and 1951–52, the percentage allotted to defense shrank, although the absolute amounts increased substantially; but in the following fiscal year the percentage caught up despite a continuing increase in revenues.

2. The table reflects generally the structure of the defense and security concept previously described: its heavy concentration on internal security, its central concern with deterring and appeasing tribes and sections, and the incipient effort at institutionalization.

3. Although a Ministry of Defense had been created in 1944, its function in 1947 was not confined to handling a regular defense establishment. The 1952–53 budget suggests that the allocation for the tribal levies around Riyadh and in the Najd localities (item 5) had previously been

included in the allocations to Ministry of Defense and was separated that year; it was alternately reincluded and separated again in subsequent budgets. The allocation for the Royal Guard had apparently also been previously included under Ministry of Defense but was permanently separated that year. Item 6 in the 1952–53 budget seems to represent the portion of grants to non-Najd tribes that had previously been included under the item "grants to tribes" (item 4).

4. The specific allocation to "aviation" (later included in the larger category "Ministry of Defense and Aviation") reflects Ibn Saud's special interest in the subject because of past experience and the importance of aviation in the absence of other rapid means of communication.

5. A Ministry of Interior (headed by Emir Abdallah al-Faisal) came into being with the 1952–53 budget, taking over the previous Public Security Department, and evidently also the allocations to "regions and principalities," reflecting an incipient effort to institutionalize the handling of certain aspects of internal security.

6. The allocations for "emergency expenditures" and "unanticipated expenditures" (items 11 and 12) reflect a continuing tendency toward the proliferation of discretionary budget items.

7. Item 13 represents an attempt to resume the Kharj project (military base and factories) begun and dropped before; it was dropped again before long.

Conclusions

After the creation of the Kingdom of Saudi Arabia, the central security concern of its founder and first ruler was the preservation of the Kingdom's very existence.

The threats to the existence of the Kingdom sprang from a combination of internal fragility and the hostility of the Hashemite rulers of Iraq and Transjordan (Jordan), who had been dispossessed by Ibn Saud of their Hijaz patrimony.

By a shrewd strategy and policy, Ibn Saud was able to enlist the British to contain the Hashemite threat during the lean years before oil revenues began to flow, when the internal situation was precarious. When the British became less able or willing to continue in that role, at least in Ibn Saud's eyes, he tried to use his newly acquired oil wealth to obtain a security guarantee from the United States, gain diplomatic allies and friends among Arab leaders opposed to the Hashemites, and build up armed forces and instruments of security for purposes of internal and external deterrence.

By the end of his reign Ibn Saud had succeeded in gaining a security assurance from the United States but not the military alliance he sought.

He had managed to obstruct the Hashemites' moves in the Arab arena but not to stop them from scoring some real gains, notably in Palestine. He had perhaps enhanced his hold on the country by the use of traditional means, but he had made little headway in building up a suitable military deterrent of his own. On balance, therefore, the original threatening combination to the Kingdom's existence remained real: the Hashemites probably did not have the military capability to invade and occupy Saudi Arabia or large parts of it; but they did have the means to encroach upon its borders and, with their modern weapons, to defeat Ibn Saud's forces in a major encounter. This could suffice to unleash internal forces hostile to the House of Saud—Hijazis, Shammaris, and others—which would in turn undo the delicate balance on which it rested and bring about its destruction.

PART TWO

The Reign of Saud

1953 – 1964

The formal reign of King Saud witnessed some critical threats to the survival of the Kingdom. These threats were the result of an interplay between external developments and internal structural changes stemming mainly from the demise of Ibn Saud as the undisputed master of the realm he had created. The way in which these threats were dealt with had a formative influence on subsequent Saudi positions and behavior in the sphere of defense and security.

The problem began with two interrelated external developments that undermined key elements of Ibn Saud's basic strategy. One was the adoption by the United States and Britain of major new initiatives regarding the Middle East; the other was the polarization of the Arab countries in reaction to these initiatives along a neutralist versus pro-Western axis, which stimulated a conflict between rival versions of pan-Arabism. Ibn Saud had been able to cultivate the American connection and seek to preserve his understanding with Britain and at the same time cooperate with Egypt in seeking to check the Hashemites. However, the emergence of Egypt under Nasser as the champion of neutralism and anti-imperialism made the pursuit of that strategy problematic by injecting an element of contradiction between cooperation with both Egypt and the West. The problem was further complicated by two additional factors: (1) Nasser's position became ever more radical, with the result that the Saudis found it increasingly difficult to withstand the contradiction on domestic as well as external grounds; and (2) within Saudi Arabia itself, unrest among newly mobilized social sectors and rivalries among members of the ruling family impinged on whatever courses were pursued.

The actual courses pursued during Saud's formal reign fell into two broad stages: from 1953 to early 1958 the Saudis tried to muddle through the contradiction; from early 1958 to 1964 and beyond, they confronted the contradiction and made clear policy decisions.

Each of these stages, in turn, had two phases. Until about the end of 1956 the Saudis stressed their anti-Hashemite alliance with Egypt much more than their connections with the West; from then until 1958 they sharply reversed their priorities. Early in the second stage the Saudis almost completely suppressed their Western connections in an attempt to appease Egypt; but in 1962 they unequivocally strove to revive and cultivate their Western connections in a context of total confrontation with Egypt. All these shifts were accompanied by substantial, sometimes drastic, changes in the allocation of resources to the various instruments of defense and security.

The developments of the period may be outlined as follows. With the accession of King Saud, there was a resurgence of the Hashemite threat in more intense form as Iraq responded to Western initiatives by making its way during 1955 into what came to be known as the Baghdad Pact, and by seeking to draw Syria and Jordan along with it.

In response, King Saud developed the Egyptian connection begun by his father into a full-fledged military and political alliance. The alliance was effective in containing Iraq and putting it on the defensive, although it did not prevent that country from joining the pact. But for Saudi Arabia, the association with an ever more radical Egyptian leadership entailed a complete sacrifice of the British connection, a straining of the American connection, and the adoption of positions and actions that had detrimental effects on internal security and stability.

The latter effects became more manifest as Nasser emerged in 1956–1959 as the dominant influence in the Arab world, and as the United States took the lead in trying to halt him because of his association with the Soviets. King Saud responded in 1957–1958 by attempting simultaneously to cooperate with the United States, to effect a rapprochement with the Hashemites to counterbalance Nasser, to continue overtly to cooperate with him, and covertly to seek to destroy him. His endeavor backfired and exposed Saudi Arabia to an unequal confrontation with Nasser at the peak of his power. In March 1958 the crisis brought to a head a long-simmering conflict within the royal family over distribution of power, which resulted in a transfer of all effective power from King Saud to Crown Prince Faisal and the latter's adoption of a new defense concept and strategy.

Faisal, like Saud, recognized that Nasser's Arab nationalist drive represented a critical threat to the Saudi realm and regime. However, believing that open resistance to it was hopeless, he adopted a strategy based on appeasing Nasser while reinforcing the country internally. He proclaimed formally a policy of neutrality and sympathy with Arab nationalism and accordingly suppressed the American (and Hashemite) connections almost entirely. He even put in abeyance the buildup of Saudi Arabia's armed forces, which depended on the continued supply of American arms, and instead emphasized the development of internal security forces. At the same time he endeavored to strengthen the country internally through institutional reforms and better management of its finances.

Faisal's strategy saw Saudi Arabia through a critical period, but at the end of 1960 Saud removed him and took over with the help of a group of "liberal princes." For a while he attempted to take Faisal's strategy even further internally and externally; but then he relented and rid himself of the liberal princes on September 11, 1961. Saud's backtracking, which was followed less than three weeks later (on September 28) by Syria's secession from the United Arab Republic, contributed to the excuses or reasons that led Nasser to proclaim openly a strategy aimed at the overthrow of all "feudal-reactionary" regimes, including, in the first place, Saudi Arabia's.

The September 1962 military coup in Yemen and the arrival of an Egyptian expeditionary force to support it converted Nasser's previous media war against the Saudi regime into an immediate, real, mortal threat. It also resulted in Faisal's return to power and ushered in a long period of confrontation between the two countries. The strategy openly adopted by the Saudis against Egypt was reminiscent of the strategy that Ibn Saud had discreetly followed in dealing with the Hashemites. It consisted in trying to revive and develop the American and British connections; in seeking an alliance with Egypt's opponents in the Arab and Muslim worlds, starting with the surviving Hashemite state of Jordan; and in building up the armed forces of the country while endeavoring to strengthen the regime internally. Partly because of persisting power struggles at the top and internal unrest, the strategy did not fall entirely into place until the deposition of Saud and the accession of Faisal.

Throughout the reign of King Saud money was far more plentiful than in the best years of Ibn Saud; revenues from oil exports ranged between $236 and $366 million. However, the government experienced moments of financial difficulty as a result of misuse of funds and improvision in the face of fluctuations in the rate of increase of oil revenue.

4

Tribulations under the First Successor

Muddling Through, 1953–1958

Alliance with Nasser

Saud started his reign on a note of continuity. He intended to follow his father's strategy of trying to check the Hashemites diplomatically through informal understandings (for example, with Egypt and Syria) while building up a deterrent force for internal and external purposes. But almost immediately he met with complications. One of the most serious of these came as a consequence of an American initiative. In the spring of 1953 Secretary of State John Foster Dulles toured the Middle East capitals, including Riyadh, to explore the possibility of creating a regional alliance as part of his global defense scheme vis-à-vis the Soviet Union. The Truman administration had broached such projects before but had encountered objections from Egypt, which wanted to end the British occupation of the Suez Canal bases before considering any new alliance, and more general Arab objections to including Israel in any regional scheme. The Saudis had looked rather favorably on an all-Arab alliance with the United States and Britain jointly, which promised a decisive containment of the Hashemites, but they had given way in the face of Egypt's decisive opposition to this idea. Dulles discovered that the situation had not changed essentially since the previous attempt to forge a pro-Western alliance in the region, in 1951. Unlike his predecessors, however, he sought to circumvent Egyptian and other Arab objections by proposing that an alliance begin with the mostly non-Arab countries of the "northern tier" of the Middle East, which had shown greater sensitiv-

ity to the Soviet danger, and be augmented later by other countries whenever they felt ready to join.

The proposal was welcomed by the Iraqi regime and eagerly espoused
by the British. The former saw it as an opportunity for aggrandizement
with Western support; the British saw it as a means to replace their
expiring treaty with Iraq with a more acceptable, multilateral alliance.
The Iraqi government sought to secure the assent of the members of the
Arab League to its intent to join, but when it failed, it nevertheless signed
an alliance with Turkey in February 1955. This treaty paved the way for
the conclusion in November of the Baghdad Pact, which included Iran,
Pakistan, and Britain in addition to Turkey and Iraq. The United States,
although it had originated the idea and helped promote it, among other
things by granting Iraq economic and military assistance, preferred to
hold back for various reasons, including regard for Egyptian and Israeli
opposition.

As far as the Saudis were concerned, the fact that the United States
stayed out probably made the pact more rather than less obnoxious, for
that meant they could not count on Washington to restrain the Hashemites from within as Britain had done in the past. At any rate, King Saud
and his advisers saw in Iraq's participation a resurgence in a most viru-
lent form of the old Hashemite threat. They had visions of Iraq with
Western help wooing Syria, Jordan, and Lebanon into the alliance, realizing its scheme of the Fertile Crescent, and then turning on them. At the
very least, they saw Iraq using its access to the best equipment in the
Western arsenals to build up its military power and then using it independently in direct or indirect ways to recover the Hijaz and avenge the
defeat inflicted on its ruling family by Ibn Saud. The reaction of Saud and
his advisers was accordingly far-reaching.

While the pact was still being discussed, Saud made common cause
with Egypt in trying to dissuade Iraq from going ahead with it. In the
process he espoused the themes of neutralism and Arab nationalism that
Egypt was using in the joint struggle, even though these were highly
charged concepts that could undermine Saudi rule domestically and
endanger Saudi-American ties. After Iraq signed the alliance with Turkey, Saud concluded a mutual defense treaty with Egypt in October 1955
and cooperated with Nasser in efforts to isolate Iraq and to prevent Syria
and Jordan from joining the pact. In that endeavor he did not hesitate to
emulate the tactics used by revolutionary Egypt of appealing to the publics of Iraq, Syria, and Jordan over the heads of their governments and
inciting them to disobedience and rebellion. At the same time he pursued
the more congenial methods of discreetly trying to buy off politicians and
supporting opposition groups in those countries.

Once Saud committed himself to following Egypt's line, he felt compelled to support actions by its leader that went far beyond the immediate

issue of Iraq. Thus, when Nasser announced in September 1955 the conclusion of an arms deal with the Soviet Union, which brought the latter into the Arab region for the first time, Saud supported the move and went on to sign the military alliance with Egypt the next month. In December 1955 two Saudi princes visited Prague, allegedly to discuss an arms deal, and Polish and Chinese trade delegations subsequently traveled to Saudi Arabia.[1] In July 1956 Saud also supported Nasser's nationalization of the Suez Canal, which was avowedly done in retaliation against the United States for withdrawing a promise to help Egypt build a high dam at Aswan. Three months later, when Britain and France responded to the nationalization of the canal by invading Egypt in the wake of an Israeli invasion of Sinai, Saudi Arabia broke off diplomatic relations with the two European powers and declared an embargo on oil shipments to them.

The break with Britain marked the culmination of a deterioration in Saudi-British relations that had been going on for some time. Ibn Saud himself had raised the issue of Buraimi before his death but had not pressed it forcefully. His intent was more to recall the British to a faithful pursuit of the joint understanding concerning the Hashemites and the Gulf principalities than to contest the issue itself. Saud, on the other hand, resenting Britain's role in promoting what became the Baghdad Pact and acting on the themes he had espoused as part of his cooperation with Nasser, turned the issue into a contest between Saudi "national rights" and British "imperialism" and extended the hostility to other fronts as well. He supported the imam of Yemen's claim to the British colony of Aden and incited and assisted a tribal revolt in Oman, headed by its imam, against the British-backed sultan, in the name of Arab nationalism. In December 1955 and January 1956 Saud joined forces with Egypt in inciting, with Arab nationalist propaganda and Saudi gold, massive riots and rebellion in Jordan to compel its government to reverse its intention to join the Baghdad Pact and force it to break away from Britain.

The practical results of Saud's anti-British campaign were mixed. In the case of Buraimi, the British-officered troops of Oman and Abu Dhabi eventually occupied the oasis in October 1955 and expelled the Saudi police units that had held it. In Oman the sultan's forces, also British led, captured the rebel stronghold of Nizwa in December 1955 and won at least that round of a contest that was to flare up again. In the case of Jordan, however, the Saudis and Egyptians had their way, keeping it out of the Baghdad Pact after causing the downfall of several governments within a few weeks and shaking King Hussein's throne. The net effect of all this, even before the final break in relations, was to terminate, indeed to reverse, the historic Saudi-British understanding, and to that extent to remove one of the pillars of Saudi security, leaving the Kingdom more dependent on the supports that remained.

The line pursued by Saud in fighting the Baghdad Pact also threatened to damage the American connection, which his father had carefully nurtured and which was paying handsome dividends in security and military assistance as well as in oil development. As part of the nationalist posture that he assumed, Saud concluded in February 1954 an agreement with Aristotle Onassis, the Greek shipping magnate, to create a tanker fleet to transport Saudi oil and clashed on this score with Aramco, which claimed infringement of its concessionary rights.[2] In August of the same year Saud rejected the American Point IV allotment in a demonstrative way and ordered the Point IV aid mission, which had been active for three years, to leave the country. The reason given was that the allotment was insultingly small compared with that awarded to Israel; but American assistance to Iraq was probably as much of a factor.

After concluding the mutual defense treaty with Egypt in October 1955, Saud invited an Egyptian military mission to help organize and train the Saudi forces alongside the American mission. The arrangement entailed practical inconveniences and reflected a certain amount of mistrust of the American personnel. It also provided the Egyptians with opportunities to indoctrinate the trainees with nationalist notions that were ultimately inimical to the Saudi political system. Saudi Arabia's participation with Egypt in the campaign against the Baghdad Pact and in the successful efforts to destabilize the pro-pact government of Jordan and to pressure fence-sitting Syria to stay out added further to the strain. Finally, in June 1956, the agreement on the lease of the Dhahran air base expired and the Saudis decided to renew it for one more year only, pending renewed negotiations. The fact that they did not terminate the lease indicated their ultimate appreciation of the contribution of the American military presence at the base to their security; but the fact that they dared not at this point renew the lease for more than one year (and referred to it as involving the lease of an airport) was symptomatic of the contradiction in which they had become embroiled by opportunistically espousing Nasser's nationalist, neutralist, anti-imperialist line.

The contradiction manifested itself also in disturbing developments inside Saudi Arabia. Even as he espoused the nationalist themes in his fight against Iraq, Saud tried to promote traditionalism at home as an antidote, with such measures as barring Saudi pupils from going to foreign schools and extending the reach and power of the religious police. Trouble ensued on both scores. For instance, the Iraqi ambassador to Saudi Arabia, who was a keen and cautious observer, reported toward the end of September 1955 that some time earlier the al-Rith tribe in northwest Jizan had rebelled and entrenched itself in Jabal Qaha because the Saudi authorities had suddenly interfered with its customs (presumably trying to enforce religious rules). The government sent planes and tribal forces but failed to subdue the rebels and finally had to come to terms with their chief, Shaikh Mudawi ibn Shahira.[3]

The same observer wrote that in the early summer of that year the authorities stamped out with great cruelty what appeared to be a "free officers' movement" modeled on the Egyptian prototype that overthrew King Faruq's regime in 1952. The movement was led by a certain Abd al-Rahman al-Shamrawi and included at least twelve officers.[4] An intelligence report by the State Department's NEA research and intelligence division on January 18, 1956, stated as a "well established" fact that a group of senior army officers had plotted in April and May 1955 to assassinate Prime Minister Faisal and other ministers and to force the abdication of the king if not to assassinate him as well. The conspirators had intended to establish a "revolutionary command council," as in Egypt. These officers were executed and a purge of army officers was carried out.[5] Other reports from the same period spoke of the marshaling and deployment of tribal forces at strategic points in the country and of sudden shifts and disappearances of Saudi personnel.[6]

Other troubles were beyond the government's capacity to conceal. In May 1956, on the occasion of a visit by King Saud to the Aramco facilities in eastern Saudi Arabia, at a time when the lease on Dhahran air base was about to expire and rumors were circulating about its renewal, thousands of workers held a demonstration in which they carried banners condemning "imperialism" and demanded elected trade unions. The demonstration was suppressed with violence, but on June 17 a strike broke out that lasted for several weeks despite a government decree on June 16 that banned all strikes and political demonstrations on pain of jail or deportation. On September 23, 1956, Nasser landed in Dhahran to confer with King Saud and Syria's President Kuwatly. Although the visit had not been announced in advance, Nasser was met by tumultuous popular demonstrations hailing him as the savior of the Arab world; this welcome was repeated on an unprecedented scale when he arrived in Riyadh. A keen observer inside King Saud's court reported that in the wake of that visit, the king's advisers reversed themselves and, instead of supporting the project of a Syrian-Egyptian-Saudi federation that Nasser had come to discuss, determined to destroy him.[7]

In November 1956, following the British-French-Israeli attack on Egypt, violent demonstrations broke out in Bahrain and Kuwait, and Kuwaiti oil fields were sabotaged. Saud avoided similar disturbances by decreeing "general mobilization," breaking off diplomatic relations with the British and French, and imposing an embargo on oil shipments to them.

Ambivalence toward Nasserism

By the time the Suez War was over, Saud and his advisers were seriously reconsidering the alliance with Egypt. On the one hand, the Hashemite threat, which had been the *raison d'être* of the alliance, seemed to have abated; Iraq was contained and Jordan was altogether destabilized. On the other hand, Nasser had emerged as an increasingly popular Arab hero, and the association of the Saudi government with him appeared to give license and legitimacy to expressions of identification with him among the peoples of Saudi Arabia. Moreover, Nasser seemed to have embarked on an ever more extreme revolutionary course and to have developed the habit of taking drastic decisions without consulting his ostensible allies and without regard to the effect of his decisions on them.

The nationalization of the Suez Canal was a case in point. It exposed Egypt's allies to military attack by strong powers; it stirred up popular nationalist hostility against the oil companies, the Western countries to which they belonged, and the Arab governments that had granted them the concessions, thus forcing the latter to take decisions about their only resource without regard to cost and benefit. It specifically resulted in the blockage of the Suez Canal oil transit route and led to a considerable loss of revenue for Saudi Arabia.[8]

After he had wrested political victory from the jaws of military defeat in the Suez War, Nasser's appeal to the Arab masses became greater than ever, and all restraints on whatever new initiatives he chose to take seemed to have collapsed. What course he would choose next was not quite clear; but his increased cooperation with the Soviets, who had spoken of sending "volunteers" to Egypt and had offered to replenish its arsenal, destroyed during the war, did not bode well.

Reconsideration of the situation led Saud in 1957 to try to revitalize the American connection as a security asset against Nasser, to reverse his relationship with the Hashemite monarchs from one of hostility to one of cooperation for the same reason, and at the same time to handle his relations with Nasser so as not to incur his open hostility. For a while circumstances helped Saud manage this seemingly impossible feat; but as the year wore on, the pretense behind this diplomatic and strategic reversal wore off, and Saud and Nasser came to a mortal confrontation.

On January 30, 1957, Saud began a state visit to the United States during which the American government sought to enlist his support for its new Middle East policy, known as the Eisenhower Doctrine. The doctrine was prompted by fear of a Soviet move to fill the "vacuum" created by the collapse of British and French influence in the Middle East in the wake of the Suez fiasco. Formally, it proclaimed the determination of the United States to use force to support any Middle East country seeking assistance against open aggression by any country under the control of "international communism." In fact the doctrine was meant to cover a policy of trying to check and roll back Nasser's Soviet-supported nationalist, anti-imperialist drive, and the Americans invited Saud to Washington with the aim of building him up as a counterpoise to Nasser in the Arab world.[9]

Saud gave his support to the doctrine and promised to help promote it in the Arab world. He also agreed to a five-year renewal of the lease on the U.S. Air Force base at Dhahran. In exchange he obtained a commitment of economic and military assistance, which was formalized in specific agreements in April 1957, for additional supplies of arms and a program to create a small Saudi navy.[10] Saud felt able to conclude that deal without risking Nasser's open hostility; at that time Arab nationalist opinion was still favorable to the United States because the latter's strong opposition had contributed decisively to the failure of the British-French-Israeli compaign against Egypt. On his way home Saud stopped in Egypt to brief Nasser about his American visit and to explain his support of Washington's anti-Communist objective.

While in the United States, King Saud took another action, which he must have had more difficulty explaining to Nasser. Iraq's Crown Prince Abdul Ilah, the son of the last Hashemite king of the Hijaz (whom the Saudis had dispossessed) and the man they believed to be the most determined proponent of Hashemite irredentism in Syria as well as in Saudi Arabia, happened to be in Washington at the same time. Saud met with the crown prince, and the two agreed to bury the hatchet and cooperate in meeting the real danger to their realms and thrones, which lay in the revolutionary ideology promoted by Nasser.[11] Although both the Iraqi and Saudi governments had previously engaged in double-talk and double-dealing with each other,[12] the meeting between these two men at that particular place and under the particular circumstances prevailing at the time established at least a presumption of earnestness to be tested by their respective future behavior. The record of that behavior was to show that the meeting was of substantial consequence.

In January 1957, ten days before leaving on his visit to the United States, Saud had given active support to the pro-Nasser nationalist government of Jordan. He had specifically supported its initiative to terminate Jordan's treaty with Britain by agreeing to share with Egypt and Syria in replacing the subsidy of about $25 million a year that Britain had given Jordan under the treaty.[13] In April King Hussein dismissed the pro-Nasser government and precipitated a crisis that lasted several weeks, during which he received discreet American backing as well as open support under the terms of the Eisenhower Doctrine. King Saud backed King Hussein squarely and even placed at his disposal the Saudi troops that had been in Jordan since the Suez War, on the grounds that he had been the victim of an attempted military coup. Nasser did not react publicly against Saud, perhaps because he knew that Saud's excuse was not without foundation. According to John Bagot Glubb, all fourteen officers arrested during the crisis had been in the pay of the Egyptian secret services.[14] But on April 21, 1957, the Riyadh police uncovered a plot to assassinate Saud by blowing up his Nasiriya palace; the principal culprits were five Palestinians who had made their way from Egypt.[15]

The Saudi media did not dwell on the possible Egyptian connection, presumably because Saud was not prepared to draw the consequences publicly. Nasser probably acted on similar reasoning when, after a state visit by Saud to Baghdad in May, he declared on July 1, 1957, that his personal relations with King Saud were good and that the latter's policy was definitely "Arab."[16]

The next test of Saud's post-Suez policy came not long thereafter. In August 1957 an American-sponsored plot to overthrow the Syrian regime was uncovered and the Syrian government ordered the expulsion of the American military attaché in Damascus along with two other diplomats. The incident triggered a "crisis" that lasted several months before petering out, in the course of which the United States invoked the Eisenhower Doctrine on behalf of Syria's neighbors, deployed the Sixth Fleet in the eastern Mediterranean, and called upon the Syrian people to rise against their government. Turkey and Iraq massed troops along Syria's borders; the Soviet Union threatened Turkey when it persisted after Iraq had backed away; while the United States countered the Soviet threats, and the Egyptians sent a battalion of troops to help defend Syria against Turkey.

Saud's position throughout the crisis was one of concern but nonpartisanship, unlike his behavior in the Jordanian crisis in April. Worried though he was about Syria's close alliance with Egypt and its increasing drift to the left, he did not want to see it fall under Iraqi domination either, notwithstanding his rapprochement with the latter. Early in the crisis he had told the United States privately that he believed the trouble in Syria was due to overambitious army officers rather than to Communists,[17] with the implication that Washington's swift aid to Iraq and Turkey was unwarranted. Later he publicly offered to mediate between Syria and Turkey and called on all sides to avoid interference in Syria's affairs. Nasser was pleased by his position and showed his appreciation by sending to Saudi Arabia another batch of his obsolete fighter planes, thus giving renewed expression to the military alliance between the two countries.

After the phony crisis over Syria's Communist-inspired threat to its neighbors subsided, Saud resumed and intensified his rapprochement with Iraq. A reflection of this trend was a state visit by Iraq's King Faisal to Riyadh at the beginning of December 1957, returning Saud's visit to Baghdad the previous May. Saud had very good grounds for closing ranks with Iraq; even as he feted the Iraqi monarch and signed a series of economic and cultural agreements within him, Syrian delegations were following one another to Cairo in an endeavor to persuade Nasser to respond to a resolution adopted by the Syrian parliament in November 1957 calling for an Egyptian-Syrian union. A few weeks later, after the Syrians had met all the terms he had set, Nasser agreed, and on February 1, 1958, he and President Kuwatly of Syria jointly proclaimed the union of the two countries, which became known as the United Arab Republic. Other Arab countries were invited to join.

The proclamation of the union had an electrifying effect on all the Arab peoples, who saw in it the beginning of the realization of the Arab nationalist dream and looked to other Arab states to respond to the call to enlarge it. Iraq and Jordan responded by forming their own federal union, the United Arab Kingdom, on February 14, 1958. Yemen joined the United Arab Republic in a federative arrangement called the United Arab States. Lebanon began a slide toward civil war as its population became polarized between Muslims who favored union, and Christians and others who opposed it.

In Saudi Arabia itself, pro-Nasser and Arab nationalist sentiments swelled among the urban public and the educated elite, many of whom foresaw an imminent end of the monarchy.[18] In that charged climate, both the United Arab Kingdom and the United Arab Republic invited Saudi Arabia to join, but Saud asked for time to consider. It was clear to Saud that his country would lose its independence if it joined the UAR, would be threatened by the UAR if it joined its rival, and would be vulnerable and isolated if it did neither. Caught in that dilemma, he turned to conspiracy in search of a solution and displayed the feverishness and simplemindedness of a desperate man.

The Egyptian-Syrian agreement had called for a plebiscite to be held in both countries on February 21, 1958, to ratify the union, to be followed by the proclamation of a provisional constitution that would establish the instruments of government of the new state. One of the conditions on which Nasser had successfully insisted was that all Syrian parties and political organizations be dissolved in order to make way for a single political organization called the National Union, as in Egypt. Saud sought to capitalize on the resentment of politicians and groups who would have to terminate their political careers, in order to foment a coup d'état before the union became a reality. His quest for a leader for the coup led him to the head of the Syrian Deuxième Bureau (security service), Colonel Abdel Hamid Sarraj. The conditions set by Sarraj might have aroused the suspicions of a professional in the dirty-tricks business, but Saud apparently handled the matter personally through an emissary and let himself be trapped into providing damning evidence against himself.[19]

On March 5, 1958, Sarraj revealed to a press conference that Saud had commissioned him to carry out a coup aimed at foiling the union and to arrange for the assassination of President Nasser. He substantiated his story by producing photostatic copies of a memorandum issued on royal stationery and discussing particulars of the plot, three incriminating cables, and checks issued him by Saud to the amount of 1.9 million pounds sterling, representing an advance on a total of more than 20 million pounds to be paid after completion of the job. Saudi Arabia formally denied the story; but even if the affair had been entirely fabricated, its publication with the certain approval of Nasser could only mean that Nasser had decided to go after Saud, if not after the entire Saudi regime. And, in a way, he did get Saud.

While these external developments were taking place, a critical evolution was under way at the center of the Saudi political system. The key to that evolution was the demise of the founder of the Saudi realm and the hub of its political system. Saud's succession appeared to have occurred smoothly, temporarily belying the experts and delighting the emerging band of interested partisans of the country. However, the facts that Saud had acceded to the throne not by virtue of demonstrated achievement, as in the case of his father, but on the basis of seniority and *presumed* ability; that he had to demonstrate ability of a different kind from that underlying the principle of succession; and that, unlike his father, he was surrounded by a multitude of brothers, uncles, sons, and nephews who deemed themselves entitled to a share of power, altered fundamentally the political situation of the Kingdom. From the outset of Saud's reign, there developed a political struggle that, significantly, centered for the most part on institutions and issues about which tradition provided little guidance. The struggle centered on the powers of the Council of Ministers, decreed by Ibn Saud just before his death and beginning operation after Saud's accession; on the distribution of top positions in the modern-type administration initiated by Ibn Saud; on control of the emerging regular armed forces and the refurbished tribal forces; and on the disposal of the revenues of the state as they fluctuated even while increasing. An outline of the complex political alignments and maneuvers during that period is essential for an understanding of later developments regarding Saudi defense and security.

Even while Ibn Saud was alive, rivalries had begun to develop among his many sons as they came of age to take on whatever positions he chose to assign to them. By the late 1940s the rivalries had crystallized into two cliques or factions, one headed by Prince Saud, who was governor of Najd as well as crown prince, and one by Prince Faisal, who was viceroy of the Hijaz and titular foreign minister. A third, smaller, and at the time less well-defined clique headed by Prince Talal was beginning to jell independently of the other two but was for some reason more hostile to Faisal than to Saud. Upon Saud's accession to the throne, an informal understanding was reached wherein Faisal was to be in charge of the Council of

Ministers—first as deputy prime minister and after August 1954 as prime minister—while the king would ostensibly retain all the absolute power that his father had held.

This diffuse arrangement, intended to promote harmony through the sharing of power, became instead a prescription for a constant tug-of-war between the two and their respective supporters and clients. Faisal tried to establish regular "legislative," administrative, and financial procedures for their own merit as well as to check the king's power, but he was constantly frustrated by the king's use of his royal prerogative to ignore or circumvent these procedures. Of particular importance in this respect was Faisal's failure to get the king to adopt and abide by a regular budget. Saud's persistence in treating the revenues of the state as his own and the extravagant use he made of them naturally antagonized those in the power circle who felt they got less than their share of the bonanza and also stirred resentment of the system among segments of the public that were exposed to the nationalist winds blowing from the outside.

Saud's behavior exhausted the treasury and ran the country into serious financial troubles the moment revenues, which had been rising by leaps and bounds, diminished and leveled off in 1956 and 1957. In 1954 oil revenue was $236 million, up 39 percent over 1953. In 1955 it rose another 44 percent, to $340 million. In 1956 it fell 15 percent, to $290 million, and remained static for the next two years.[20] The results were a soaring public debt, inflation, the fall of the riyal to half its official value, denial of credit by Aramco and international banks, and suspension of public projects, all while numerous palaces were being built and the orgy of royal spending remained otherwise unabated. It was against this background of immediate financial strains and underlying political struggle that Saud attempted his ill-fated plot against Nasser.

Within two days of revelation of the plot, Prince Faisal resigned his prime ministership and other positions and precipitated a crisis within the ruling establishment. In the meantime, Egypt's Voice of the Arabs Radio, heard throughout the Middle East, had begun a campaign calling for the overthrow of the Saudi monarchy, and a Saudi National Liberation Front was formed in Cairo under Nasir al-Said, the leader of the 1956 oil workers' strikes. Saud and his supporters tried to enlist other princes and the 'ulama in an effort to persuade Faisal to relent at a time of great internal and external peril, but Faisal and his supporters saw greater dangers in letting matters drift along. They insisted on certain drastic conditions, and Saud, in despair, conceded. The king was to transfer to Faisal by decree all his statutory powers; formal governing procedures were to be instituted and consistently pursued; the king and his court were to refrain from any interference in the management of the internal and external affairs of the state. Saud retained the title of king and issued the March 24 decree authorizing the change, but otherwise the transfer of power was as complete as could be.

Facing the Contradictions, 1958–1964

Appeasing Nasserism

Faisal was well placed to weather the storm raised by Saud's plot and to deal with the underlying issue of Nasser and Arab nationalism, because he had been absent from the country for nine critical months starting in April 1957, when Saud's policy turned against Nasser. For most of that period Faisal was undergoing medical treatment in the United States (Saudi Arabia watchers know that extended medical trips abroad by key princes tend somehow to occur in the wake of flare-ups of royal family disputes in which those princes have been bested), but he had spent the entire month of January 1958 in Egypt, part of it as Nasser's state guest, just weeks after his brother had entertained the king of Iraq in Riyadh. Faisal had observed from close quarters the last stages of the negotiations leading to the proclamation of the Egyptian-Syrian union, had discussed their progress with Nasser, and had perhaps even hinted that, in his view, Saudi Arabia should associate itself in some way with the emerging union.[21] He certainly conveyed to Nasser the impression that he believed Saudi Arabia could live with the union, and his first actions upon assuming power confirmed that impression.

One of Faisal's first acts was to order the withdrawal of Saudi troops from Jordan (which had been placed at Hussein's disposal in the April 1957 crisis) and to change the policy of rapprochement with the Hashemites to one of neutrality. He also did nothing to correct the interpretation advanced by the media at the time that his accession to power represented a setback for the American anti-Nasser policy, and rather tended to confirm it by adopting a distant attitude toward the United States. This position provided a respite from external pressure that allowed him to devote most of his energies to reorganizing the structure of power and government through a new statute for the Council of Ministers and to reforming and rationalizing the country's finances. But the respite was soon disrupted by another storm, which confronted Faisal with the necessity of making drastic decisions regarding the country's basic security concept. On July 14, 1958, the Iraqi monarchy was overthrown by a revolution led by Arab nationalist officers believed to be partisans of Nasser, and within days American marines landed in Lebanon and British paratroopers in Jordan to shore up the regimes of those countries against the Nasserist tide and to be in a position to intervene in Iraq if the opportunity arose.

Faisal's immediate problem was what stand to take in the face of an apparent showdown between the United States and Nasserism whose outcome was totally unpredictable. He dealt with that problem by playing for time till the dust settled, refraining from condemning the American and British interventions but at the same time scrupulously avoiding any hint of action that might be interpreted as condoning them.[22] Beyond that, however, he confronted the basic problem of developing a new defense concept that would take into account three critical factors underscored by the events surrounding the Iraqi revolution: the seemingly irresistible tide of Nasserism, the failure of the United States and Britain to stave off the collapse of an allied regime, and the added evidence of the unreliability of the regular armed forces as an instrument of security for the regime — indeed, the confirmation of their role as the spearhead of revolution.

The task was complicated by the reassertion of the divisions within the royal family itself, which began as soon as the storm over Saud's plot to assassinate Nasser had subsided, and was further fueled by resentment of Faisal's reform measures. The divisions manifested themselves among other ways in the unseemly rush of members of rival factions of the royal family to cultivate Nasser's support. During a six-week period, for example, members of the royal family engaged in the following activities: Emir Talal, who headed a faction of liberal princes, was in Cairo on July 2, 1958; Emir Fahd ibn Saud, son of King Saud, former defense minister and at the time chief of the royal cabinet, returned from Cairo to Riyadh on July 17; Emir Fahd ibn Abd al-Aziz, minister of education and a fervent Faisal supporter, arrived in Cairo on July 19; on August 6, King Saud conferred with Field Marshal Abd al-Hakim Amer, Nasser's second in command and commander-in-chief of the UAR armed forces; finally, on August 15, Faisal went to Cairo for three days of discussions with President Nasser.[23]

By the end of the discussions Faisal had agreed to denounce the American and British military interventions in Lebanon and Jordan as "aggression"[24] and practically to put in abeyance the mutual security agreement with the United States. He had tried to secure Nasser's understanding for Saudi Arabia's necessary connection with the American oil companies while explaining away the significance of the Dhahran lease and promising not to renew it after its expiration. He had proclaimed his support for Arab nationalism and apparently indicated his willingness to try to get Saudi Arabia to join the United Arab Republic.[25] He had also distanced himself from the regimes of Jordan and Lebanon, the only independent governments in the eastern Arab world that still resisted Arab nationalism. In short, Faisal appeared to have settled on a defensive strategy that was in essence the opposite of Ibn Saud's: it consisted in appeasing, rather than opposing or seeking to counterbalance, the main source of threat — in this instance Nasser; renouncing all other Arab links; suppressing the American — as well as the British — connection; putting in abeyance the development of an internal/external deterrent power based on the regular armed forces; and relying for internal deterrence on other instruments of public security.

Faisal himself was too shrewd not to recognize the long-term dangers involved in a strategy that depended so completely on appeasing the principal potential opponent. He had subscribed to it at a time of stress when no viable alternative appeared to exist, but he was bound to modify it as soon as an opportunity presented itself. Such an opportunity arose by the autumn of 1959, when a bitter struggle following the initial friendship between Nasser and the revolutionary leadership of Iraq finally settled into a hostile stalemate. The seemingly irresistible tide of Nasser's personal and ideological sway over the Arab world had been checked by Baghdad's new regime, supported by Moscow, and Nasser was looking everywhere for forces to counter his opponent. Faisal took advantage of the situation to steer what he called in a declaration in October 1958 an "independent" Saudi policy based on "neutrality and Arab nationalism."[26] The policy continued to keep the United States at arm's length and paid obeisance to the prevailing dogma of Arab nationalism but regained some room for maneuver by capitalizing on the hostility between Nasser's UAR and Kassem's Iraq.

The next development in Saudi policy came as a result of internal political change. Faisal's success in riding out the Nasserist storms and putting the country's internal affairs into some order stimulated efforts by King Saud to recover his powers. The king first approached the United States for help, then went on to seek it from none other than Nasser — the man whose assassination he had plotted personally.[27] Ahmad Shuqairy, an adviser of King Saud whom Faisal barred along with other advisers from attending meetings of the Council of Ministers in 1958, reports in one of his many books that both Saud and Faisal indiscriminately sought help against each other from American and Arab quarters. In that volume he reproduces a photocopy of a note from King Saud to him while Shuqairy was in Cairo, informing him of developments in the May – June 1959 crisis between himself and Faisal and asking him to convey to Nasser and company that he, Saud, was "on their side."[28] Nasser, for his part, feeling deceived by Faisal, was anxious to play on the rivalries among the Saudi princes and preferred to deal with the erratic but emotional and amenable king rather than with his coldly calculating brother. All the more so since Saud sought political allies at home among the liberal princes headed by Talal, who professed to be convinced adherents of Nasserist ideological tenets.

In May 1960 Faisal needed to go abroad for medical treatment and

sought authorization from the king to appoint two princes of his choice
—Fahd ibn Abd al-Aziz, a supporter of his, and Musa'id ibn Abd al-Rahman, a presumed neutral—to replace him in his absence. Saud refused
on the grounds that the powers conferred on Faisal were not transferable
and should revert to himself if Faisal ceased to be able to exercise them. A
crisis ensued that lasted for several months, split the royal family
sharply, and spilled over into the Lebanese and Egyptian press before
Faisal finally decided to forgo his planned trip despite his failing health.[29]
In December 1960 King Saud brought the persisting strain between himself and his brother and their respective camps to a climax by refusing,
for some technical reason, to sign into law a budget submitted to him by
Faisal. When Faisal wrote the king a note complaining that he could not
carry out his duties under the circumstances, the latter construed it as a
formal resignation, which he promptly accepted. He then formed a government with himself as prime minister, thus circumventing the division
of powers between king and prime minister that Faisal had labored to
establish. Moreover, Saud loaded the Council of Ministers and other key
positions in the government and armed forces with his own sons, liberal
princes, and commoners and technocrats who owed their promotion to
him. Faisal turned down a pro forma invitation to join the government,
and no known supporter of his was included in it.

Prodded by his advisers and the liberal princes, Saud adopted a program that sought to outdo Faisal both in internal reforms and in swinging
Saudi Arabia closer to the UAR and Arab nationalism. In a speech delivered on his behalf at the first meeting of the new Council of Ministers he
proclaimed "Arabism" as a foundation of Saudi existence on a par with
Islam. He promised to work for the elimination of poverty, ignorance, and
disease; to march on the "correct scientific paths"; to create a special
apparatus to undertake comprehensive economic planning and good
management of the economy; and to guide educational policy to achieve
those objectives "while benefiting from the experience of others who
preceded Saudi Arabia in this domain." Saud also promised to establish a
"basic order of government" that would define the functions of groups
and individuals and their rights and obligations in accordance with the
prescriptions of the Qoran and the Prophet's Tradition. Apart from the
obligatory references to Islam, all this was vintage Nasserism. In matters
of foreign policy specifically, Saud pledged to cooperate with "sister Arab
countries"; to support efforts to recover Arab rights in Palestine, Algeria,
Oman, and the "Arab South" (the Arab nationalist term for the British
colony of Aden and the protectorate of South Arabia); and to resort to all
means to recover Buraimi. Reference to the United States was conspicuous by its absence.[30]

The fate of King Saud's program was illustrative of the extent to which

Saudi policy during that period had come to be determined by internal power struggles and the accident of external events. Saud's government began by giving indications of the earnestness of its intent at home and abroad. It adopted some measures of liberalization and welfare projects and started to consider constitutional reform. In May 1961 it announced its intention to terminate the American presence in Dhahran when the lease expired the following June. The head of the newly created Ministry of Petroleum and Minerals, Abdallah Tariqi, adopted a contentious nationalist line toward Aramco and played an active role in the efforts that resulted in the creation of OPEC. In June and July Saudi Arabia joined Egypt in opposing Iraq's moves to annex the newly independent state of Kuwait and later sent a brigade of troops along with Egyptian, Jordanian, and Sudanese contingents assigned by the Arab League to replace British forces that had come to assist Kuwait. The king, however, was being constantly buffeted by opposite pressures: from the liberal princes, who were demanding more action in line with the government's program; from his own sons, who were growing jealous of the power of the liberal princes; from advisers who cautioned him against antagonizing conservative religious and tribal leaders and playing into the hands of Faisal's faction; and from conciliators who feared the consequences for the dynasty and the realm of permanently alienating Faisal and his supporters. By September 11 the strains resulted in the dismissal of Talal, the resignation of two liberal princes, and a turn toward conservatism. The vacancies were filled by a son of Saud and by other princes whom the king was trying to win to his side.

Later in the same month, quite by coincidence, a military coup took Syria out of the United Arab Republic and installed a conservative civilian government in Damascus. Nasser took stock of the reasons for Syria's secession, concluded that it was due to the machinations of "exploitative capitalists, feudalists and colonialists," and accordingly proclaimed that the pursuit of Arab unity must henceforth proceed by an effort first to destroy those forces everywhere in the Arab world through an alliance of toilers, soldiers, intellectuals, and "national capitalists." The Saudi regime, which had rid itself of such "progressive" elements just before the secession, was designated as a prime target in this social revolutionary metamorphosis of Arab nationalism.

Resisting Nasserism

Forced to abandon appeasement, Saud was at a loss to devise a coherent alternative strategy to face the Nasserite threat. He was too committed to an anti-British line to be able to reverse course without giving ammunition to his enemies. The United States had some time before given up its campaign against Nasser and, since the advent of the Kennedy administration, was on the contrary engaged in an experiment of supporting Nasser's Arab Socialism as an antidote to Communism. In the Arab arena, Iraq was too antagonized by the Saudi position on Kuwait to be of any assistance, and Syria's secessionist regime was too weak. Jordan was a potential exception, but relations with it required a great deal of tending to repair the damage they had suffered in the previous phase, when both Faisal and Saud had abandoned King Hussein. Nor was the internal situation reassuring. The weak armed forces presented no deterrent externally and were more of a threat than a buttress internally after years of exposure to Arab nationalist ideology with the license of the government. Other internal security instruments were not immune to the nationalist virus and had been weakened by the conflicts among members of the royal family. The king's political base was narrower than ever, now that he faced the hostility of the liberal princes as well as the opposition of Faisal and his supporters.

Saud's response under these circumstances consisted of improvisations. Initially, these betrayed more nervousness than sense. In November 1961, for example, he repudiated the "erroneous" previous policy that had succumbed to the "lure of alien doctrines," proclaimed Islam and the Shari'a (religious law) to be the Kingdom's only policy, and issued decrees prohibiting support of any contrary ideology such as socialism or Communism.[31] Subsequently he made some moves that ameliorated but did not fundamentally alter the situation. In December he called on Faisal to act as regent while he left the country for medical treatment abroad. This move paved the way for Faisal to rejoin the government together with some of his supporters in March 1962, although Saud was careful this time to retain for himself the post of prime minister. In August Saud signed with King Hussein at Ta'if a comprehensive treaty of alliance that included among other things a provision for the forces of each country automatically to enter the other country to assist in case of internal upheaval. However, before the Treaty of Ta'if was ratified, another Nasserist storm shook the Saudi regime to its foundations, contributed to the final toppling of King Saud, and forced his successor to adopt a fundamentally new course for the realm.

On September 26, 1962, Imam Muhammad al-Badr of Yemen was overthrown by a military coup led by Colonel Abdallah al-Sallal, who immediately proclaimed the Yemen Arab Republic. The imam survived the attack on his palace and surfaced in the north of the country a short time later to lead the resistance already rallied by his uncle, Emir Hassan. Within days of the coup, Egyptian paratroopers landed in Yemen to spearhead a combined expeditionary force of many thousands, including air force and naval units. The speed and scope of the Egyptian intervention clearly indicated Nasser's prior knowledge of and preparation for the coup.

The coup and the Egyptian intervention presented a threefold threat to the Saudi regime. At a minimum, the consolidation of a Nasser-backed radical regime on the peninsula would present the Saudis with a persistent security threat. Next, were the Egyptian military presence to endure, it might encourage dissidents in Saudi Arabia to follow the Yemeni example, attempt a coup and call for Egyptian military assistance. Several ominous developments made that threat particularly serious. Emir Talal, who had attacked the regime in the pages of the Beirut press after his dismissal by King Saud, went to Cairo before the Yemen coup and was apparently held in reserve by Nasser to head a revolutionary regime in Saudi Arabia. Shortly after the coup Talal was joined in Cairo by three liberal princes who formed with him a Committee of Free Princes, harking back to the Committee of Free Officers that had overthrown King Faruq. At the same time the armed forces justified the regime's mistrust of them: several Saudi pilots sent to ferry supplies to the Yemeni loyalists in the first days after the coup defected with their planes and their cargo to the Egyptian side. A third threat was that of an Egyptian-initiated invasion of the country, ostensibly in response to Saudi provocation, in the expectation that the first major defeat of the regime's forces would trigger uprisings of dissident and separatist elements.

These threats, severe in themselves, were made worse by panic, divided counsel, and conflict within the ruling establishment and by the physical and mental breakdown of King Saud. According to one report, the commoners in the Council of Ministers submitted a petition to the king urging recognition and appeasement of the Yemen Arab Republic, while princes within and outside the government urged various courses of resistance and proceeded on their own to organize help to the royalists.[32] King Hussein, according to all accounts, pressed for joint Saudi-Jordanian military intervention and sent a brigade to the Yemeni border. King Saud was inclined toward military action but feared that a defeat of the Saudi forces might trigger a revolution, and the strains he suffered were exacerbated by combinations of princes who plotted to depose him or to force him to transfer all his powers to Faisal once more. The U.S. Central Intelligence Agency summarized the situation as follows in its October 15, 1962, daily intelligence "checklist" to the president: "(a) King Saud, in extremely poor health and in a psychopathic state of suspicion and worry over the Yemenis, may not last much longer. (b) Among other plots, a group of Saudi princes, anxious to pre-empt the field before pro-Nasirites make a try at taking over, are laying plans to force Saud to abdicate in favor of Faysal."[33] Three days later, the CIA checklist reported that King Saud, "to avert a revolt against the Saudi monarchy," had named Crown

Prince Faisal prime minister and given him authority to form his own cabinet — "which amounts to forced abdication."[34]

Egyptian intelligence, which at the time was good on Saudi Arabia, essentially confirmed the CIA report and added significant details. In a column published in the daily *al-Ahram* on November 20, 1962, Nasser's confidant, Muhammad H. Heikal, reported that the defection of the Saudi pilots had caused King Saud to suffer a nervous breakdown for fear of a plot. Heikal added that a group of princes had gone to see Saud and asked him to transfer power to Faisal to avert revolution. In the argument that ensued, Saud reportedly said that the real source of trouble was the cities — Jidda, Mecca, Madina, Riyadh — because of their educated people; and he told his interlocutors to warn those people that if they made a revolutionary move against him, he would let the tribes march on them and despoil them. In the end, the princes convinced him to transfer power on the grounds that Faisal could manage things, especially the United States, to save what could be saved.[35]

While these events were taking place, Faisal was in the United States attending the United Nations General Assembly session and therefore did not take part in the wrangles that compelled the king to call on him. Once he returned home, however, he became involved in a dispute over the terms of his appointment, as is evident from the fact that he did not announce the formation of his government until November 6, nearly three critical weeks after he was assigned the task. Moreover, the cabinet that he formed did not include any of King Saud's sons for the first time since 1953; indeed it included none of the members of Saud's 1960 cabinet and only two carry-overs from the reshuffled cabinet of March 1962. Faisal held the portfolio of foreign affairs in addition to the prime ministership and assigned the key posts of defense and interior to ardent partisans of his, Sultan ibn Abd al-Aziz and Fahd ibn Abd al-Aziz, respectively. Other important positions held by sons of Saud — notably the governorship of Riyadh and command of the National Guard — were later taken away from them and given to Faisal loyalists.

With the question of supreme leadership settled for the moment — it was to flare up again and again before being finally resolved with the deposition of Saud — Faisal evolved a three-point strategy to deal with the Egyptian-Yemeni threats. First, he decided to avoid direct Saudi military intervention at all costs. Instead, he chose to fight the Egyptians and republicans by proxy, through providing all possible support to the royalists and to any tribes that could be bought. Faisal realized that the loyalists could not defeat the Egyptian forces decisively and that his strategy could at best result in a long war of attrition, stalemate, and negotiations; but he also realized that he had no other choice. The Saudi armed forces, even with a Jordanian contribution, were no match for the Egyptians, and their loyalty was questionable. Were they to suffer a serious defeat, the consequences could be fatal. Moreover, intervention would give the Egyptians an excuse to extend the war to Saudi Arabia itself and thus encourage internal uprisings, while placing the regime in an unfavorable position to obtain assistance from friendly outside powers.

Second, now that the Nasserite threat was so close to home, Faisal decided to drop all pretense of nonalignment and incur the liability of seeking the help of the United States and Britain. Ironically, he had more success with the latter, with which Saudi Arabia had broken diplomatic relations in 1956, than with the United States, whose friendship had been taken for granted.

Even before he had assumed full powers, Faisal had personally sought to enlist American support during a meeting with President Kennedy in Washington on October 4, 1962. Behind the diplomatic phraseology, Faisal was given to understand that the United States would help Saudi Arabia only in case of an Egyptian invasion of its territory. Otherwise, even though it spoke of self-determination for the people of Yemen, the United States did not in principle oppose the advent of a "progressive" Arab nationalist regime in Yemen. Moreover, although it favored a "hands off" policy in Yemen, it did not view the Egyptian military intervention with any particular alarm, as long as the Egyptians did not actively encroach upon Saudi sovereignty and integrity.

With regard to the indirect effects of the Yemeni revolution on Saudi Arabia, Faisal was advised by the United States that these were best combatted through political, economic, and social reforms that would strengthen the loyalty of the people to the regime and thus immunize it against subversion. Faisal barely managed to convince Kennedy to postpone American recognition of the republican regime at least until it became apparent that it actually controlled the country.

Even the "guarantee" against direct Egyptian attack, Faisal was to learn before long, was construed in a rather limited way. On November 2, 1962, for instance, the Egyptian air force and navy began a series of almost daily attacks on Saudi border and coastal towns and positions that ostensibly served as supply bases and staging points for loyalist forces. On November 10, American combat planes based in Dhahran made demonstrative sorties over some of the principal Saudi cities to support the morale of the population and ostensibly also to warn the Egyptians. However, as the Egyptians continued to bomb and shell the Saudi border areas without being molested by the U.S. Air Force, it became apparent that the American "protection" extended only to the oil facilities and to an "unprovoked" extension of the war into the interior of Saudi Arabia. The border areas, insofar as they served as bases for the forces opposing the Egyptians, were apparently fair game as far as the United States was concerned.

President Kennedy's reticence in assisting the Saudis was based upon a broad policy of trying to work with Nasser's Arab Socialism to stem the appeal of Communism. The British did not labor under any such constraint; on the contrary, they had every reason to seek to frustrate Nasser's intervention in Yemen and to overthrow the republican regime in order to protect their position in Aden and South Yemen. Consequently, once Faisal turned to them and restored diplomatic relations in January 1963, they cooperated with him in every possible way in supporting the loyalists and his own defense plans. Among other things, in June 1963 they sent a military mission to help modernize and upgrade the training of the Saudi National Guard. Later that year, as Faisal looked for some rapid ways to counter the increasing Egyptian air attacks, they put together an emergency assistance package providing for a dozen Lightning and Hunter combat jets, some taken directly out of RAF stock; a battery of Thunderbird surface-to-air missiles; and pilots and personnel to operate the equipment while Saudi personnel were taken to Britain for training. Later in the war, when the United States had become disappointed with Nasser, the British and Americans together contracted for a much more ambitious $300 million nationwide air defense system. The British were to provide forty Lightnings and twenty-five Strikemasters, an up-to-date radar network, plus 1,000 maintenance and training personnel; the Americans were to supply Hawk surface-to-air missiles and a communications network. That program was realized only after the Egyptians withdrew from Yemen in the wake of the 1967 Six Day War with Israel.[36]

The third element of Faisal's strategy was a plan to reinforce the home front that was interesting for what it excluded as much as for what it included. Faisal inaugurated his government on November 6, 1962, with an impressive ten-point reform and development program, headed by the promise of a constitution or basic law and concluding with the announced intention of outlawing slavery and emancipating all existing slaves. Many believed at the time that the program was mainly an exercise in public relations designed to counter Egyptian propaganda and to please American and world opinion. However, despite the failure of Faisal (and his successors to date) to deliver on the basic law promise, it is apparent in retrospect that the program led logically and practically to the first five-year plan (1969), which in turn marked a watershed in Saudi history. Hitherto the Saudi rulers had approached the question of modernization gingerly, taking one step forward and then halting or retreating for fear of the unknown. Faisal's program eventually led the country to take the plunge, on the basis of his own declared conviction that modernization and traditional Islam, on which the Saudi political order and regime rested, were mutually compatible. Whether or not Faisal actually believed what he said, he definitely decided that political necessity required him to act as if he did.

Another aspect of Faisal's internal effort was to arouse and appeal to the Saudis' sense of patriotism against the menace of the alien Egyptians. In January 1963 he declared a national emergency and proclaimed a general mobilization of the "working forces of the country." As the conflict went on, Faisal assumed the (for a Saudi chief) novel role of a political leader, addressing mass rallies and using populist and even democratic-nationalist rhetoric. For example, at a mass rally in Ta'if on September 5, 1963, Faisal said: "We find ourselves in the position of one who is defending himself, his country, his homeland. The Egyptian leaders, on the other hand, have said that they went to Yemen and fight in Yemen in order to threaten the very existence [*kayan*] of this country, to conquer it and destroy it." He concluded by telling his audience: "You are the owners of this country; you are the party to any agreement; you are responsible for everything in the country. The government is nothing but a representation expressing your will, your feelings and your wishes."[37] However, notwithstanding his call for national mobilization, Faisal enlarged and reinforced the National Guard and strengthened the instruments of internal security but was careful to avoid building up the regular army until much later, when the internal front appeared to be secure and the danger of Egyptian subversion seemed to have passed its peak.

Faisal's strategy stemmed the panic at home and before long brought about a stalemate in the Yemen battlefront. These successes, however, underscored the limitations inherent in that strategy: it could deny Nasser's broad objectives but could not achieve Faisal's own of getting rid of the Egyptians and the republican regime. Moreover, the passing of the critical moment encouraged a dangerous resurgence of the struggle for power between Faisal and Saud, which threatened to undo whatever gains were achieved. The struggle blended with diplomatic-military developments in the conflict.

Already in the latter part of November 1962, Nasser realized that the prospects of quickly achieving control over Yemen and toppling the Saudi regime with a limited military investment had eluded him. (Heikal's November revelations, mentioned above, were an indication that Nasser had decided to escalate the political-propaganda war against the Saudi regime, as the military operation in Yemen failed to achieve quick results.) His choice became either to negotiate for some compromise or to escalate his military commitment and make another attempt to achieve his goals. Since the United States was attempting to mediate a solution to the conflict and had given indications of a not unfriendly disposition, Nasser decided to try negotiations first. By December 19, 1962, he had arrived at a deal with the United States: in exchange for his accepting an American proposal for a simultaneous withdrawal of Egyptian forces and an end to all intervention, the United States agreed to recognize the Yemen Arab Republic.

Faisal himself had agreed earlier to the principle of simultaneous withdrawal and an end to intervention, but Washington's recognition of the republican regime seemed to him to reflect a disturbing tilt toward Nasser and an acceptance of the outcome that Faisal had desperately sought to avoid; he therefore balked. The United States corrected the impression of a tilt by making public on January 8, 1963, a letter from Kennedy to Faisal written the previous October in which the president expressed America's support for the Kingdom's territorial integrity. Faisal, however, continued to oppose any recognition of the republican regime and demanded a supervised consultation of the Yemeni people once all foreign intervention had ceased.

Encouraged by the American recognition, Nasser redoubled his efforts to subdue the loyalist forces and bring Faisal to heel. By February 1963 the Egyptian forces engaged in the fighting in Yemen had reached 40,000. The raids on Saudi border areas continued, and Egyptian planes dropped arms in various spots in the Hijaz to encourage putative dissident tribes to rebel. However, Yemen's geography and topography, together with an incessant flow of Saudi funds and arms to the Yemeni loyalists, frustrated Nasser's campaign, and this lack of progress in turn discouraged any substantial expression of dissidence in Saudi Arabia. By March 1963 Nasser was ready to negotiate again, and by April 15 he and Faisal had agreed to a United Nations proposal for simultaneous withdrawal and cessation of intervention, to be preceded by a disengagement of forces and the creation of a UN-supervised demilitarized zone of twenty kilometers on each side of the Yemeni-Saudi border. However, since neither party had given up on its political objective, both violated the agreement, the Egyptians in an effort to buttress the republican regime and the Saudis to reinforce further the opposition to it. By June 1963 the fighting had resumed and Egypt was again bombing Saudi territory.

Once more the fighting produced no decisive results, and once more, at the end of 1963 and the beginning of 1964, there was an attempt to negotiate. This time, however, the negotiations were to be direct and to be held at the highest level, under the auspices of an Arab summit called by Nasser to deal with Israel's diversion of the Jordan River waters. The fact that it was Nasser who engineered the summit suggested that he was tiring first in what had become a war of attrition. Earlier, in August 1963, the Free Princes had asked for permission to return home, indicating that they, at least, had given up on Nasser's chances of toppling the regime in Saudi Arabia. Had other things remained equal, Faisal would have been in a superior bargaining position and might have been able to extract some advantages from it if not to secure his principal objectives. As things were, however, King Saud decided to take advantage of the situation to attempt to recover his powers and thus got the negotiations tangled up with the struggles within the royal family. The result was that the negotiations were damaged and the intrafamily struggle deteriorated into a showdown that ended with the deposition of Saud. Precise details are, of course, unavailable, but on the basis of scattered bits of information, the following picture can be reconstructed.

In September 1963 King Saud returned to Riyadh after an eleven-month absence abroad, interrupted by a brief home visit. During his absence Faisal had consolidated his power by removing sons of Saud from key positions, notably from the posts of commander of the National Guard and governor of Riyadh, and replacing them with his own men. At the time of Saud's return, the situation in Yemen was stable, and Saud began to maneuver to recover his powers, urged on by his sons, who had lost theirs, too. Nasser's call for a summit precipitated matters. Saud insisted that he, as the head of state, should represent the country, like the other Arab heads of state, whereas Faisal maintained that, as the person effectively in charge of policy, he should be the one to speak for the country. The dispute degenerated into a series of confrontations and threats of violence. Fahd ibn Abd al-Aziz was said to have demanded Saud's abdication and to have threatened to kill him if he did not.[38] Saud was reported to have mobilized the Royal Guard, the most effective force in the country, deployed it around his palace, and used it to threaten Faisal. Faisal was reported to have countermanded plans made by Saud for a ceremonial entry into Jidda — Faisal's power base — and deployed the National Guard to face the Royal Guard.[39] That episode of the crisis was temporarily resolved by arbitration of the 'ulama, who decided that, because of Saud's poor state of health, Faisal should continue to exercise effective power, but that because Saud remained the sovereign, he should represent the country at the summit while referring all decisions to Faisal.

Saud abided by the letter of the 'ulama's decision, but in his talks with Nasser he paved the way for restoration of diplomatic relations between the two countries, broken off since November 1962, and for peace negotiations to be undertaken with Faisal. An Algerian-Iraqi conciliation commission was to go to Riyadh in mid-February 1964, to be followed at the end of that month by an Egyptian peace delegation headed by Vice President Abd al-Hakim Amer. Saud naturally took credit for this achievement, while Faisal tried to limit its significance. Before the arrival of the

Egyptians, Faisal voiced unusually tough positions, stating on February 6, for instance, that his government would never recognize a Yemeni government controlled by a foreign state and that he might seek compensation for the Egyptian attacks on Saudi territory.[40] On February 18 a "Saudi source in Beirut" told the Arab News Agency that Saudi Arabia did not intend to discuss the Yemen in the forthcoming talks with the Egyptians since that was a problem for the Yemenis themselves to settle. When Faisal finally met with the Egyptians, the two sides agreed on March 3, 1964, to the restoration of diplomatic relations, and the Egyptians conceded the principle that it was for the Yemenis to determine the future of their country, but Faisal nevertheless put off further negotiations to a meeting between himself and Nasser scheduled for two months later, in late April or early May. Saud, however, felt sufficiently reinforced by his achievement, and perhaps also by the return of the Free Princes in January, to reopen the question of recovering his powers.

On March 13, 1964, Saud wrote Faisal a letter asking him to resign his position as prime minister in his favor on the grounds (harking back to the 'ulama's argument the previous January) that his health was now perfectly restored and there was no longer any reason for him not to exercise the powers that were his. The next day Faisal showed the letter to some of his brothers, who unanimously rejected the king's request and insisted that Faisal carry on as prime minister. Some of Saud's sons distributed leaflets in Riyadh and Jidda criticizing Faisal's government, and slogans appeared on the walls of Riyadh saying "No king and no ruler but Saud."[41] Faisal's partisans, on the other hand, endeavored to secure the support of the army and of tribal leaders, while Faisal himself mobilized support in his Jidda power base. Among other things, he approached the mufti of the city on March 17, and the latter convened a conclave of 'ulama the next day to consider the situation. The Jidda 'ulama then adjourned to Riyadh to join a council of the senior religious leaders of the realm, where they probably constituted a solid pro-Faisal caucus. By March 22 the council had decided that Faisal should be vested with full powers while Saud retained the title of king, although it did not issue a formal *fatwa* to that effect until March 29.

On March 22 Faisal went to Riyadh at the behest of his partisans who had succeeded in the meantime in securing the city and rallying most of the senior princes behind the 'ulama's judgment. The judgment was then conveyed to King Saud, who rejected it and deployed his personal guard and the Royal Guard around his palace. Faisal ordered the National Guard to surround the palace and the Royal Guard to withdraw,[42] but the latter stood its ground, presumably on Saud's counterorders. On March 26 a group of officers loyal to Faisal, moving in taxis for disguise, raided the home of Sultan ibn Saud, the commander of the Royal Guard, and arrested him.[43] Two days later Saud gave in, and during the next two days the permanent transfer of power from Saud to Faisal was formalized. On March 29 a *fatwa* was made public in which the 'ulama harked back to the ruling they had issued in the dispute in January, pointed to the exacerbation of the dispute between the two brothers since, stated that the conflict threatened to produce "civil strife and chaos" the consequences of which God only knew, alluded to Saud's health, and concluded that he should remain king of the realm while Faisal should carry out the internal and external affairs of the Kingdom without referring back to the king.[44] On March 30 a petition signed by sixty-eight princes from different branches of the royal family was made public, which alluded to the *fatwa* and called upon Faisal as prime minister to expedite its execution. He and the Council of Ministers did so the same day. The council also ordered the transfers of the Royal Guard to the authority of the Ministry of Defense and of the king's personal bodyguard to the Ministry of Interior, abolished the royal Diwan (cabinet), and cut the king's allowance of $40 million a year by half.

Partly because of these events, Faisal's anticipated trip to Egypt to pursue the Yemen peace talks was put off until September 1964, when the second Arab summit met in Alexandria. Another reason for the delay was the development of strain between Faisal and the Yemeni royalists over ways to give effect to the principle of letting the people of Yemen determine their own future, agreed to between Faisal and Amer. The dispute was serious enough to cause Faisal to stop the flow of assistance to the imam in the summer of that year. The grounds for that friction became apparent in the agreement reached between Faisal and Nasser when they met in September. The two leaders decided to cooperate "to help the people of Yemen towards stability, security and freedom," specifically agreed on a seven-month cease-fire during which Egyptian troops would withdraw gradually and Saudi Arabia would halt its aid, and pledged themselves to support a Yemeni coalition government that would include royalists as well as republicans but exclude both President Sallal and Imam al-Badr.[45] A start was made in implementing the agreement when republican and royalist representatives met for the first time at Erkwit, Sudan, in October 1964 and agreed to convening a national reconciliation congress in Haradh, Yemen, in November to realize the agreement fully.

The reconciliation congress did not meet as scheduled. Instead the cease-fire broke down and fighting resumed, with the Egyptians bombing royalist positions in late November and the royalists resuming ground operations shortly thereafter. Given the opposition of Sallal and the imam to the Alexandria agreement, it is not difficult to see why the cease-fire did not hold. What is not clear, however, is the connection, if any, between these events and the final denouement of the Saud-Faisal struggle on November 2, 1964. All the sources that provided some details about the events of March are silent about those of November, except for a few general allusions. These suggest that in October 1964 Saud and his entourage reopened the question of the king's powers in the context of the wider issue of a basic law, that rumors circulated that some neighboring governments (Egypt and the imam, for different reasons) were behind the move, and that the princes, 'ulama, and leaders met continually and decided that Saud must go.[46] The king was given a choice to abdicate voluntarily, to comply with a demand to abdicate, or to be deposed and exiled by a resolution of "the people." Saud refused to make a choice and entrenched himself in his palace, whereupon the princes decided to depose him and proclaim Faisal king. The 'ulama issued a *fatwa*, which, in accordance with traditional Sunni doctrine, reported the facts of the deposition and succession and then legitimized the latter.[47]

Defense Establishment and Policy

In 1952 the American military advisory and training missions had set up a program aimed at creating a regular army of three to five regimental combat teams with a substantial element of air mobility and air combat support over a three-year period. Ten years later that goal had not been met despite redoubled American assistance in 1957 in connection with the endeavor to promote the Eisenhower Doctrine. The failure stemmed from a combination of internal developments, technical inefficiencies and limitations, and the sudden shift in the Saudi defense concept in 1958 in connection with Saudi foreign relations.

The effects of the shift in defense concept are reflected dramatically in the procurement of military equipment. Through 1958 there was a steady flow of heavy equipment to the air and ground forces from American and, to a lesser extent, British sources; after 1958 the acquisition of such equipment from any source ceased for six or seven years in the case of military aircraft and for nearly a decade in the case of heavy equipment for the ground forces. Specifically, from 1954 through 1958 Saudi Arabia received the following aircraft from the United States:

9 Douglas B-26 Invader tactical bombers (piston)
10 Lockheed T-33A trainers plus a number of Beech A-45s
6 C-123 Provider transports
12 F-86 Sabre jet fighters

In addition, in 1956 the Saudis acquired from Britain twelve DH Chipmunk T-10 trainers, and in 1957 Egypt presented them with two batches of Vampire fighters, one batch containing four and the other of unknown but probably similar size, as part of the Saudi-Egyptian military alliance. In contrast, from 1959 through 1965 no military aircraft were acquired from any source except for two Sud Alouette III helicopters received from France in 1965.[48] A $300 million air defense system including sixty-five aircraft, a radar network, and Hawk surface-to-air missiles was broached in 1963–1964 but was not realized until after 1965.

As for heavy equipment for the ground forces, the following armored fighting vehicles were acquired in the period through 1958:

30   M-6 Staghound and M-8 Greyhound armored cars from Britain
58   M-41 Walker Bulldog light tanks from the U.S.
15   M-24 Chaffee light tanks from the U.S.
55   M-47 Patton medium tanks from the U.S.

Some of the Chaffee tanks were delivered in 1959. The Pattons were ordered in 1956–1958 and delivered in 1959 and 1960.[49] In contrast, no armored fighting vehicles were ordered after 1958 until about 1969. In that year and in 1970 the Saudis received 220 Panhard AML armored cars from France, purchased for $95 million.[50]

The total halt in the acquisition of heavy military equipment was not due to any reluctance on the part of the suppliers. The American advisory and training missions continued to operate, and the United States had agreed in April 1957 to provide Saudi Arabia with more equipment than the latter subsequently ordered. Nor was the halt due to financial stringencies, as will be explained in the next section. It was basically the consequence of the change in defense concept that occurred after Faisal took over effective power in 1958 in the wake of the Egyptian-Syrian union. That concept, it will be recalled, viewed Arab nationalism under Nasser's leadership as the main threat and sought to meet it through a policy of neutralism, appeasement, and suppression of the American connection to the point of freezing the buildup of the regular armed forces. When the concept was changed in connection with the Yemen war, American coolness and Saudi internal considerations delayed the effective resumption of the flow of arms.

Even before the interruption in the procurement of equipment, the development of the regular armed forces was hampered by the intrusion of politics into the process. From the outset of his reign, King Saud sought to build up the White Army of tribal levies and the Royal Guard to buttress his personal power position against rival princes,[51] and thus diverted financial and manpower resources away from the regular armed forces. The discovery in May 1955 of a plot against the regime by senior army officers and the subsequent purge of the officer corps further increased Saud's fears and caused additional diversion or dissipation of resources. In 1956 Saud dismissed Minister of Defense Mishal ibn

Abd al-Aziz on grounds of corruption and alleged pro-Nasserism and replaced him with his own son, Fahd ibn Saud.[52] This move may have somewhat allayed Saud's fear of the regular armed forces but it stirred suspicion among his princely brothers because it extended his direct control over the country's armed forces (his sons already controlled the White Army and the Royal Guard) and caused those among them in a position to check that development, like Faisal, to try to do so.

At any rate, the double handicap under which the regular armed forces labored, as a suspected source of disloyalty to the regime as a whole and as a source of specific support for Saud against his rivals, made it easier for Faisal to contemplate freezing them in 1958, when the requirements of high policy also pointed in the same direction. When these requirements changed in 1962, new manifestations of disloyalty in the armed forces, such as the defection of pilots with their planes to Nasser and the culmination of the struggle between Saud and Faisal, helped prolong the stagnation.[53]

Finally, corruption, inefficiency, bureaucratic bungling, and lack of suitable personnel wrought havoc in the underlying assumptions and schedules of the original American-devised program. The need for additional time and effort to meet the program's targets of size and quality for the armed forces and to absorb the equipment already received made the halt of the flow of arms appear a plausible course under the circumstances.

At the time of the halt, the regular army comprised some 12,000 men organized in small infantry battalions of 400–600 troops loosely fitted into five regiments. After six years of assistance by an American training mission and three by an Egyptian mission of 200 men, a committee of the American Joint Chiefs of Staff reported in 1959 that the army still lacked an adequate trained officer corps and trained enlisted personnel, had inadequate logistical support in the field, and suffered from endemic disease among the troops and a low level of education. It had no field combat capability against a modern army except for harassment in desert warfare.[54]

The air force had a personnel strength of about 160, and one American intelligence report characterized most of its officers as being secretly in sympathy with Nasser.[55] Its organization was still embryonic and the training of its personnel rudimentary. Its combat capability was nil.

The civil air fleet under the Ministry of Defense comprised twelve DC-3s and 4s, five Bristol Wayfarers, and ten Convair 340s. TWA provided the flying and maintenance personnel under contract, but the commander of the Royal Saudi Air Force personally controlled all flight scheduling.

The navy was nonexistent. As part of the April 1957 agreements on military assistance, an American survey mission worked out a program for building up a modest navy, a naval base, and training facilities, but the program was delayed at the Saudi end and was eventually shelved after the 1958 defense concept switch.

The tribal levies (White Army) were estimated at 10,000 to 16,000 plus twice that number of inactive reserves by different American intelligence sources.[56] They were equipped with light arms, were poorly trained, and lacked motor transportation of their own. They were used as a kind of regime guard, were presumed to be loyal to the king, and were assigned to sensitive army duties — such as patrolling the Tapline and guarding the strategic points — in moments of trouble.

The Royal Guard was estimated at one battalion or one regiment of 2,700 crack troops by different American intelligence sources.[57] The disparity may be due to an unclear line of demarcation between the Royal Guard and some tribal units. In any case, all the sources agree that the Royal Guard was the most effective unit of the Saudi armed forces. One source estimated that the Royal Guard was more than a match against the White Army, and that together the two could defeat the entire regular army.[58]

The royal bodyguard, composed of a few hundred armed men, was responsible for close protection of the person of the king. Their military significance was negligible, but their existence was a reminder of the ruler's great exposure to assassination in a system of personal authoritarian government.

During the years that followed the halt in procurement, the American training mission continued to work (the Egyptian mission was withdrawn in 1958) so that some progress in organization and training may be assumed to have taken place. However, a participant in the American effort assessed the capacity of the Saudi air force by the end of 1962 to be still "purely nominal";[59] and the capability of the various armed forces probably did not improve much more than that of the air force in the intervening years.

Altogether, then, the regular armed forces remained incapable throughout the formal reign of King Saud of playing a deterrent role against the military power of actual or potentially hostile neighbors such as Jordan, Iraq, or Egypt, or of playing a significant offensive role against an enemy such as Israel. Provided they remained loyal, they could afford a measure of deterrence against internal tribal uprisings. Moreover, they could be used in politically profitable noncombat military missions, as they were in Jordan in 1956–1957 and in Kuwait in 1961–1963. In the former instance a contingent of two or three battalions was deployed in southern Jordan in a demonstration of support for Egypt during the 1956 war, and for King Hussein during the internal crisis he faced in early

1957. They were also meant to retain control of the territory they guarded, over which the House of Saud had claims, in case King Hussein's regime collapsed. In the case of Kuwait, a Saudi brigade served as part of an Arab League peacekeeping force that relieved the British troops who had effectively blocked Iraq's move to annex the newly independent emirate.

The Saudi forces, regular and tribal, had a theoretical offensive capability only against the neighboring shaikhdoms, over some of which the ruling family had irredentist claims; but, as the conflict over Buraimi showed, the British patrons of these shaikhdoms provided an effective deterrent.

Supplementing the various armed forces in their internal security roles and contributing to the system of checks and balances among them were various civil security apparatuses at the national and regional levels. The most important of these was the Department of Public Security of the Ministry of Interior, which controlled most of a 10,000-man police force. As with the various military forces, control of the ministry and the department became an issue in the power struggles within the royal family. For instance, Abdallah ibn Faisal ibn Abd al-Aziz was appointed minister of interior by King Ibn Saud and formally retained that post throughout the 1950s. But King Saud insisted on having the director of the Public Security Department report to him directly, and he often bypassed Faisal's son altogether even on such important matters as having Jidda's police chief arrested on grounds of disloyalty.[60]

Defense and Security Allocations

Table 2 presents the budgetary data on defense and security for the reign of King Saud. Examination of the data confirms key points in the previous analysis and sheds additional light on them.

1. The most general point reflected in the financial data is that the character of those data changed significantly after 1958. Although the Council of Ministers began to operate in 1954 under a statute that required it to follow a regular budget, King Saud continued to treat the country's revenue as his private wealth to the point that he did not even bother to formulate a budget for particular years (for example, 1955–56, 1956–57). Moreover, the budgets that were published did not follow a consistent format. Only after Faisal took over effective power in 1958 were budgets in a more or less consistent format published regularly.

2. The upper part of the table shows a drastic drop in the percentage of total revenue allocated to defense and security in the period starting with fiscal 1958–59. This decline reflects dramatically the change in defense

Table 2. Revenues and defense and security allocations, fiscal 1955–1965 (million SR)[a]

	1954–55	1957–58	1958–59	1959–60	1960–61	1961–62	1962–63	1963–64	1964–65
Revenues and allocations									
Total revenue	1355	1498	1410	1405	1786	2166	2452	2686	3112
Oil revenue	967	1241	1145	1149	1410	1682	1951	2284	2607
Total defense and security allocations	600	763	369	384	379	486	676	844	914
% of total revenue	44.3	50.9	26.2	27.3	21.2	22.4	27.6	31.4	29.4
Specific defense and security allocations[b]									
1. Ministry of Defense	472	310	196	197	187	265	314	345	405
a. Civil aviation	—	—	6	6	7	30	36	37	47
b. Army[c]	—	—	190	191	180	235	278	276	330
c. Air force	26	—	—	—	—	—	—	31	28
2. Grants to tribes/White Army	—	192	—	—	—	—	—	—	—
3. National Guard	—	60	55	54	55	57	61	134	145
4. Royal Guard	—	16	11	14	16	18	18	22	—
5. Ministry of Interior	82	87	107	119	121	146	183	244	265
a. Department of Public Security	47	—	48	55	66	67	82	105	112
b. Investigations	—	—	—	—	—	—	—	5	8
c. Coast and Frontier Guards	—	—	11	12	13	13	23	40	40
d. Emirates	—	18	20	24	20	22	22	20	22
6. National defense purposes	—	—	—	—	—	—	40	39	39
7. Emergency expenditures	102	75	—	—	—	—	60	60	60
8. Secret expenditures	10	5	—	—	—	—	—	—	—
9. Total non–Ministry of Defense	128	453	173	187	192	221	362	499	509
Ratio of item 9 to item 1	—	—	.88	.95	1.03	.83	1.15	1.45	1.26

Source: Kingdom of Saudi Arabia, *Statistical Yearbook, 1965.*
a. Rounded to nearest million.
b. Items 1–8 are official Saudi budget categories.
c. The actual category is "General Bureau and Army." The General Bureau accounts for a few million SR.

concept described in the preceding historical analysis and shown in the halt of procurement of heavy equipment.

3. The same point is reflected more specifically in two sets of facts: (a) the stagnation of the allocations to the army (item 1b) in absolute amounts for a cluster of years after 1958–59, and the declining share of these allocations as a percentage of total revenue; and (b) the shift of emphasis in defense and security to internal security apparatuses, as is shown (item 10) in the increasing ratio of allocations to the latter compared to Ministry of Defense. There is a clear indication of Faisal's putting in abeyance the buildup of the regular army as an external deterrent and his increased reliance on internal security instruments as part of his strategy toward the Nasser threat.

4. The grants to tribes and to the White Army (item 2) reflect Saud's effort to build up the tribal levies after his disappointment with the loyalty of the regular army. Whereas in 1954–55 he apparently included the allocations to the tribes in the allocation to the Ministry of Defense (item 1), by 1957–58 he had separated the former and assigned to them a vast amount. When Faisal took over the next year, the allocations to tribes were apparently reduced and distributed to an institutionalized National Guard (item 3), and probably also to the emirates (item 5d).

5. The allocations to national defense purposes and emergency expenditures (items 6 and 7) reflect at least in part the assistance given to the royalists in the Yemen conflict and the strategy of fighting the Egyptians and republicans by proxy.

6. The stagnant allocations to the army in the years of the Yemen conflict even as revenue was increasing reflect the mistrust of the regular army in that contest with Nasser. Fragmentary internal evidence suggests that the increase in the absolute amount allocated to the army in 1961–62, modest though it was when account is taken of the increase in revenue, went entirely to an increase in salaries aimed at acquiring the good will of its personnel when Nasser proclaimed a policy of confrontation with the Saudi regime in 1961.

7. The large increase in allocations to the National Guard (item 3) during the Yemen conflict reflects the regime's preference to rely on the institutionalized tribal forces to back up its support for the Yemeni royalists.

8. The allocations to the Royal Guard (item 4) reflect something of the vicissitudes undergone by that body in connection with the Saud-Faisal struggle before it was finally transferred to the army in the climax of that struggle. The Royal Guard allocation disappears altogether in 1964–65 and that to the army is increased.

9. Item 1c shows the beginning of the differentiation of the air force from the army in 1963–64 in preparation for the projects to build it up in response to the Egyptian air attacks on Saudi territory.

10. Item 5b shows the beginning of a new instrument of internal security — investigations — stimulated by the Yemen conflict.

Conclusions

The reign of King Saud was a period of severe trial for the survival of the empire built by Ibn Saud and of the dynasty he founded. As the threat of a combination of Hashemite irredentism/revanchism and sectional and tribal secessionism surged and then receded, a new and more severe threat crystallized in the shape of radical pan-Arabism led by Nasser's Egypt.

The threat was more severe because Nasser's movement commanded Soviet and occasionally American support, because it appealed to vast publics in the Arab countries, and because it had a substantial impact inside Saudi society itself, within the armed forces, and even among the Saudi royal family.

Although the divisions within the royal family were a consequence of the traditional rules of succession and of the large number of princely claimants to a share of power, the contests they generated often expressed themselves in rival policies and programs. The resulting alternation of approaches may sometimes have served the overall interests of the dynasty and the realm; but the arbitrariness with which competing factions and approaches prevailed constituted a basic danger to the system, especially in times of externally generated stress.

In dealing with the Hashemite and the Nasserite threats, the Saudis had to depend almost entirely on diplomatic maneuvering. The attempt to develop regular forces to support the defense of the realm collapsed because of suspicion concerning the army's loyalty, the intrusion of royal family rivalries, poor endowment in human resources, inefficiency, and the contradiction that developed between a higher policy based on appeasement of Nasserism and the active cooperation with the United States needed to build up the armed forces.

In the maneuvering to advance the defense interests of the realm, Saudi diplomacy during Saud's reign was basically reactive. The one attempt to shape a favorable situation, which was made in association with the United States under the Eisenhower Doctrine, never took off. Talk of initiatives based on Islam remained, in that period, at the level of talk.

The confrontation between the Saudi regime and Nasserism precipitated by the Yemen military coup and civil war put the Saudi regime and its defense policy to its most severe test. Diplomatic maneuvering elicited an effective American deterrent against outright Egyptian invasion of Saudi Arabia or raids on oil facilities, but it did not constrain Egyptian border attacks and active efforts at subversion, nor did it prevent the United States from recognizing the republican regime in Yemen. The strategy of avoiding a direct military encounter with Egyptian and republican forces and fighting them through the proxy of loyalist Yemeni tribes worked well enough by the end of 1964 to frustrate Nasser's war aims and compel him to resort to negotiations; but it did not suffice to bring about a resolution of the conflict that would safeguard the essential Saudi defense interests in Yemen. When Faisal acceded to the throne after the deposition of King Saud, the stalemate in Yemen could tempt Nasser equally to escalate the conflict or to seek to wind it down.

From a very broad historical view of the determinants of Saudi viability and behavior, the reign of King Saud demonstrated the ingrained vulnerability of the Saudi realm to complications arising from the problem of succession. The phenomena of the Free Princes seeking to ride to power in the wagons of the Egyptian forces and of Faisal and Saud seeking to promote their respective positions by competing for the favor and support of outside powers are reminiscent of the behavior of princes of the House of Saud that undermined the first realm in its difficult hours and contributed decisively to the destruction of the second realm. The deposition of King Saud resolved that particular episode, but the potential for additional episodes of perhaps different type, particularly in moments of external difficulties, remained inherent in the system because of the ambiguities of the rules of succession, the presence of numerous potential pretenders, and a vast and growing number of actual claimants to a share of power.

The reign of King Saud also demonstrated that the requirements of preserving the realm and the dynasty inexorably drove the regime willy-nilly to a course of action that altered the foundations of Saudi society. Ibn Saud took the first step when he granted oil concessions to obtain the revenues he desperately needed to keep his realm together, and the second step when he tried to use the increasing oil revenues to create an army and reinforce his regime in the face of resurgent Hashemite threats. Saud and Faisal were compelled to carry the process a long way forward, and Faisal to take it to the point of no return in his 1962 ten-point program, in the endeavor to meet the challenge of Nasser's radical Arab nationalist drive. Some consequences of the social change manifested themselves in unrest among the embryonic modern regular armed forces and contributed to holding back their development. Other consequences were averted by reforms and concessions that were bound to accelerate the dynamics for further reforms and concessions.

Finally, the behavior of the Saudi government, regardless of who was in charge, reflected a distinct diplomatic style, probably rooted in the tribal ethos, characterized by vagueness, discretion, and ambiguity in overt dealings and a penchant for covert action and intrigue, use of proxies, attempts to buy friendships, and avoidance of confrontation with and appeasement of powerful opponents. Above all, it reflected a capacity of the government — as if acting on the principle that there are no permanent friends and enemies, only permanent interests — to make sharp diplomatic turns and to reverse courses to protect the perceived security interests of the dynasty and the realm. When Saud was in charge he swung from a pro-Egyptian, anti-Hashemite policy to the reverse; then from a policy of appeasing Nasser to one of resisting him; and then again from resistance to seeking to collaborate with him. Faisal, too, made similar swings in relation to Nasser and Britain. In their dealings with the United States, both Saud and Faisal abruptly lowered and raised the temperature by many degrees, but both were also careful to avoid extremes that could bring about total rupture.

PART THREE

The Reign of Faisal

1964–1975

From the perspective of defense and security, the reign of Faisal was infinitely more complex and witnessed far greater changes than the reign of Saud, which was of almost equal duration. The Kingdom's strategic environment was repeatedly altered by major events such as the 1967 Arab-Israeli war; the British withdrawal from south Arabia in the same year and the announcement of their intent to withdraw from the Persian Gulf the following year; the 1969–70 war of attrition; the death of Nasser in 1970; the Jordanian civil war the same year; violent changes of regime in Iraq, the Sudan, Libya, and Syria in 1968–1970; Iran's assertion of territorial claims in the Persian Gulf; Iraq's conclusion of a friendship and cooperation treaty with the Soviet Union in 1972 and its violent encroachment on Kuwait's border in 1973; and, finally, the October 1973 war and the critical developments associated with it. All these events, singly and in clusters, posed serious problems and called for reactions and initiatives at both the political-strategic and strategic-military levels.

The options available to the Saudis to meet these problems varied, of course, with changes in the environment and circumstances at any given moment. Underlying all the choices, however, were the means and leverage provided by Saudi Arabia's main asset. The conditions affecting the increasing importance of Saudi oil under Faisal's reign are complex, but a crucial feature of that evolution is reflected in the changes in the level of Saudi revenues in that period. At the beginning of Faisal's reign, in 1964, these amounted to roughly 3 billion Saudi riyals (SR), in 1968 to SR 5.5

billion, in 1972 to SR 13 billion; and in the last year of Faisal's reign, 1975, they reached the astronomical figure of SR 96 billion.[1]

The Saudis' ability to use their revenue resources to develop their strategic-military capabilities to deal with changing contingencies continued to be heavily constrained under Faisal, as it had been under Saud. The population base remained small; and, although the Saudis resorted increasingly to importing foreign labor for civilian purposes, they could use only a limited number of foreign personnel in the defense and security forces without creating risks that would outweigh the benefits. Indeed, the Saudis under Faisal continued to discriminate against non-Najdis in recruitment to the armed forces and in promotion to officer ranks because of persisting doubt regarding their loyalty to the regime. This policy deprived the armed forces of the full benefits to be had from an expanding system of public education by reducing the already small pool of manpower suited for training in modern military skills. Finally, accessibility continued to be a major limitation, despite considerable construction of transport and communication facilities.

The administrative structure was another major constraint. Although new ministries were created, existing ones differentiated, a civil service code adopted, foreign personnel recruited, training programs established, and so on, the actual ability of the system to perform remained, with few exceptions, weak and uneven. Above all, the system continued to be severely handicapped by the built-in contradiction of combining bureaucratic norms with the ascriptive norms designed to secure the power and privileged position of the thousands of members of the royal family, their allies, and their clients and to regulate their distribution. Nowhere was this more evident than in the various defense and security apparatuses. The Ministry of Defense, controlling the regular armed forces, remained totally separate from the National Guard, comprising the tribal forces, and both were separate from the Ministry of Interior, controlling among other things the Department of Public Security and Frontier and Coast Guards, and from the Royal Intelligence. Different, and in some cases rival, senior princes were in charge of these institutions, and many younger princes and allies and clients occupied important posts in them.

Because of all of these constraints, Saudi Arabia through most of Faisal's reign as under all of Saud's had to rely primarily, in dealing with ever-changing security problems, on means other than conventional military power. To deter or avert hostile action it relied on alliances and alignments supported by its oil leverage, dispensation of funds, and appeals to Islamic values and interests. In the conflicts in which it actually became involved, it relied on the traditional methods of buying proxy forces and promoting sedition and subversion in the enemy's ranks. To be sure, at intervals efforts were made to develop, within the limits of what seemed possible, certain regular military capabilities. These, however, played only a secondary, noncombat role or none at all in dealing with the defense and security problems that were actually confronted. A much more ambitious project was begun toward the end of Faisal's rule to build up the Saudi armed forces to a level where they could be the mainstay of the Kingdom's defense strategy; but that attempt was still in its infancy when Faisal died.

About the only change toward less complexity under Faisal was the fact that he had no challenger or rival as supreme leader. Inevitably he had to delegate power to his princely brothers and distribute it carefully among them to avoid conflicts, but he managed to do this while retaining for himself full ultimate control in both theory and practice. This was a factor of inestimable importance for the Kingdom's defense and security in a period fraught with so many major events; for, although Saudi Arabia could for the most part only react to these events rather than shape them, the fact that the same steady hand was at the helm throughout helped to see the Kingdom through many perilous situations and to steer it to unprecedented security and seemingly dazzling prospects.

In terms of nearly all the relevant variables for defense and security, Faisal's rich and complex reign can be divided into three stages: 1964–1967, 1967–1973, and 1973–1975. The first was essentially a continuation of a stage that had begun two years before. It witnessed the consolidation of Faisal's power base after the deposition of King Saud and was dominated by the twists and turns of the conflict in Yemen. It ended with the withdrawal of the Egyptian forces from Yemen in the wake of Egypt's defeat in the 1967 war.

The second stage was characterized by the eruption of an array of problems around the entire perimeter of the Kingdom and also within it. By 1971 or 1972 Faisal had managed, with the help of some lucky breaks, to cope with these problems, but the durability of this success hinged on the United States' making some move to break the stalemate that enveloped the Arab-Israeli conflict. When the United States failed to do so and when Egypt and Syria found a way to neutralize Israel's military deterrent, the 1973 war erupted and led to fundamental changes in the Middle East strategic environment in general and in Saudi Arabia's position in particular.

The third stage was dominated by Saudi Arabia's leadership in using the "oil weapon" in the last days of the 1973 war and the unanticipated consequences of that act, especially the enormous leap in the price of oil. These developments not only transformed the previous strategic environment but also gave Saudi Arabia its first opportunities to try to shape events instead of merely reacting to them. By the time Faisal was assassinated in March 1975, the Kingdom had already made one critical, definitive choice: it had renounced its earlier intention of reducing the price of oil from the level it had reached in the midst of the war and embargo and had decided instead to let it stand. The implications of that decision were fateful for Saudi Arabia and the world. Other important decisions initiated projects whose practical consequences were not yet apparent when Faisal's reign ended.

5

Strivings and Probings, 1964 – 1973

Consolidating Power, 1964 – 1967

One of Faisal's first acts upon acceding to the throne was to amend the statute of the Council of Ministers so as to reunite the powers of the king and the prime minister that he had labored so hard to separate when he was prime minister and Saud was king. The same decree affirmed the responsibility of the Council of Ministers to himself as king, thus undoing the collective responsibility of the council that he had tried to establish earlier. Faisal took these precautions even though the ministers had all been chosen by him in the course of his struggle with Saud, and even though fervent, proved partisans of his controlled the key positions: Fahd ibn Abd al-Aziz in Interior, Sultan ibn Abd al-Aziz in Defense, Abdallah ibn Abd al-Aziz in command of the National Guard, and others in the most important governorship posts. To leave no doubt about the concentration of all powers in his hands, Faisal did not nominate a crown prince and presumed successor to the throne until March 29, 1965, four months after his own accession, and then saw to the appointment to that post of Emir Khaled ibn Abd al-Aziz, an amiable, low-key prince with useful connections with the Najdi tribes, bypassing Khaled's senior, but tougher and irascible, full brother, Muhammed ibn Abd al-Aziz.[1]

Once he centralized supreme power in his own hands, Faisal was able to retain control of it throughout his reign while making important and timely adjustments. As long as the conflict with Egypt in Yemen continued, Faisal kept his initial power structure and tight team intact in order to confront possible renewed challenges from the deposed King Saud and his vast offspring. Indeed, in late 1966 and early 1967, when the fighting in Yemen reached a new level of intensity and was accompanied by an Egyptian-instigated campaign of sabotage inside Saudi Arabia, five of Saud's sons and then Saud himself established themselves in Cairo and lent their support to the Egyptian war effort. Saud broadcast appeals to his people over Cairo Radio reasserting his right to the throne and calling for the overthrow of the "usurpers." In April 1967 he went to San'a, accompanied by two of his sons, to explore the possibilities of doing from a base in Yemen what the imam of Yemen was doing in reverse from his base in Saudi Arabia. Saud's entire endeavor collapsed before getting very far as a result of the termination of the Egyptians' Yemen campaign following Egypt's defeat in the 1967 Arab-Israeli war.

After the failure of Saud's last feeble challenge, Faisal addressed himself by stages to consolidating and stabilizing his power. In October 1967 he appointed Fahd second deputy prime minister and second in the line of succession, after Khaled. The move was meant to give Faisal a working deputy besides the ailing Khaled to help with the tasks of governing, and to avert possible conflict within the royal family over the succession question in case Faisal's own precarious health suddenly failed. Five months later Faisal consummated the process of bringing the former Free Princes back to the fold by appointing all the members of the group except their former leader, Talal, to important albeit supervised positions.[2] Through the remainder of his reign Faisal further broadened his governmental power base by allotting political and security positions to younger princes — half-brothers, cousins, nephews, and so on — as they reached maturity and by co-opting into the highest administrative posts commoners with newly acquired technical education.

Impressive as was Faisal's political achievement, it was not without problems. Although, precisely because of Faisal's unquestioned predominance, less is known about Saudi politics under him than under either his predecessor or his successor, indications of various difficulties do exist. For instance, the fact that Faisal promised but did not deliver a basic law — the one item in his 1962 ten-point program that was entirely ignored — suggests that there was a continuing conservative-reformist division on the issue within the royal family. In an incident that is possibly related to that division, in September 1965 a nephew of the king, Khaled ibn Musa'id, led a group of demonstrators in seizing the broadcasting house in a religiously inspired protest against the introduction of television. Khaled was killed in a shoot-out with the police; ten years later his full brother killed Faisal in an ostensible act of personal revenge.

Another sign of strain, probably having to do with power rivalries among the princes working with Faisal, was Prince Fahd's departure in October 1969 on a leave that lasted until May 1970. The absence of Faisal's working deputy, who was also minister of interior, for nearly eight months, at a time when the authorities were dealing with the aftermath of two coup attempts foiled the previous September and June, clearly points to major confrontations within the government if not to an actual crisis of power. Finally, former Secretary of State Henry Kissinger has pointed out in his memoirs that he was constantly confronted with conflicting signals from different Saudi sources in connection with the postembargo crisis, probably reflecting rival currents within the government. However, as Kissinger avers, only what Faisal said proved to be authoritative and this fact testifies that he remained ultimately in full control.

Managing the Yemen Conflict, 1964–1967

As soon as he had established a firm hold on power, Faisal proceeded to apply and adapt the three-pronged general strategy he had adumbrated earlier to deal with the Egyptian-Yemeni threat.[3] Internally, after setting aside the item in his ten-point program promising a basic law, he went on to apply slowly but systematically all the other points, with a view to strengthening the country's fabric and reinforcing its moral posture in relation to external friends and foes. He was favored in this effort by a rapid increase in revenues during the first two years of his reign, which rose at about double the 11 percent annual rate of the previous two years. It is not clear whether the increase, which derived mainly from greater oil production, was the result of a deliberate move by Aramco and its parent companies to help Faisal, but it is clear that the American government adopted a more cooperative attitude toward other components of Faisal's strategy. Disappointed by Kennedy's attempt to woo Nasser, the United States under President Johnson was more willing to support Faisal's plan to build up the Saudi armed forces to enhance the realm's long-term internal and external deterrent capability. In addition to participating with the British in a $400 million air defense program, the United States also authorized in 1965 an agreement for the U.S. Corps of Engineers to supervise the construction of a vast network of military facilities, and in 1966 sponsored a $100 million program to provide combat vehicles, mostly trucks, to increase the mobility of the Saudi armed forces.

Faisal also attempted to take the initiative in developing an Islamic alignment, which he called the Islamic Conference, to counter Nasser's Arab Socialism and his hold on the Arab camp. Typically, however, Faisal pursued this project and the other components of his strategy in a discreet rather than confrontational fashion, preserving as long as he could the dialogue with Nasser begun at the September 1964 Arab summit, and using an innocuous resolution that he had put through the Arab summit of November 1965 (about the desirability of mobilizing the support of

Muslim and other powers to the Arab cause) as a sanction for his endeavors on behalf of the Islamic Conference.

While pursuing that higher defense policy, Faisal continued his effort to use Yemeni tribal proxy forces to lever the Egyptians out of that country and at least tame its republican regime. The September 1964 agreement with Nasser, providing for Egyptian withdrawal and a Yemeni coalition of royalists and republicans but excluding the current chiefs of both, had given Faisal a good start, but the agreement broke down because the excluded chiefs balked and were able to cause a resumption of the fighting and to compromise their Saudi and Egyptian supporters.

In the first half of 1965 the royalists took advantage of a crisis among the republicans that had developed in the wake of the September 1964 agreement, and launched an offensive against their forces. The latter, after some setbacks, repelled the attack with Egyptian help, and a stalemate set in once more. Nasser, however, was becoming impatient with the strains of his Yemen commitment and made a determined effort to ease it. On August 22–24, 1965, he came to Jidda to confer with Faisal, and the two reached an agreement similar to the September 1964 accord. This time the royalists and republicans were actually brought together at a national conference in Haradh the following November to work out a constitution and government. Halfway through the conference, however, it became apparent that the Egyptians had had a change of heart and were encouraging the republicans to take a recalcitrant position, which produced a deadlock. Possibly the Egyptian military, headed by Marshal Abd al-Hakim Amer, sabotaged the peace effort out of a desire to have another try at a military solution; in any case Nasser developed his own reasons to go along.

In late August 1965 Nasser, who had hitherto kept the Soviets out of his Yemen venture, decided to involve them in order to ease his own burden and to secure continuing support for the republicans. He convinced them to cancel a $500 million debt that he had incurred up to this point in the conflict and to provide military aid to the republicans. One result was that while the Haradh conference was in session, 6,000 new Egyptian troops landed in Yemen and two large shiploads of arms arrived from the Soviet Union. At about the same time, Nasser felt extremely provoked by Faisal's campaign on behalf of an Islamic Conference, which the latter began with successful visits to Iran (December 1965) and Jordan (January 1966) to enlist their rulers' support. Nasser saw in Faisal's project another attempt inspired by the United States, similar to the Eisenhower Doctrine, to organize an alliance against him led by the Saudis under the banner of Islamic solidarity; and he found support for this conviction in the increasing coldness that had crept into the United States' relations with him, in contrast to the Americans' increasing military cooperation

with the Saudis. Finally, in February 1966 the British government announced its intention to withdraw from Aden and South Yemen by 1968.
The prospect of using the Yemen base to extend his influence into south
Arabia gave Nasser an added, decisive incentive to maintain and expand
his position there and rededicate himself to his original purpose. The
result was that the Yemen conflict, which had been edging slowly toward
a political resolution, took a sudden reverse and accelerated toward
greater violence than ever before.

In February 1966 Nasser made one of those dramatic speeches that
punctuated his career, in which he virtually tore up the Jidda Agreement,
derided Faisal's Islamic Conference proposal as a tool of imperialism,
and charged him with supporting a plot by the Egyptian Muslim
Brethren to overthrow the Egyptian regime. Nasser declared his determination to stay in Yemen "even five more years" if necessary to protect
the republican regime. In March 1966 the Egyptian forces, whose numbers had been reinforced to nearly 60,000, launched the biggest offensive
yet in an attempt to crush the royalist resistance. The royalists, with
increased Saudi support, lost some ground but were able to recover and
in the summer to launch a counterattack, which also eventually faltered
and resulted in yet another stalemate in the field. This time, however,
Nasser did not go back to negotiations but adopted instead a so-called
Long Breath Strategy: he withdrew his forces from outlying areas; concentrated them in a triangle based on the cities of Ta'iz, San'a, and Hodeida; and used air power, sabotage, and subversion to try to break the
enemy's will. In November 1966 and for the next six months the Egyptian
air force resumed periodic bombings of Saudi border towns and staging
areas while constantly attacking villages and positions under royalist
control. In their fury and frustration, the Egyptians even used poison gas
against hostile Yemenis on at least two occasions, in January and February 1967.[4] Egyptian-supported groups, mostly Yemeni expatriates, executed a series of sabotage bombings against targets throughout Saudi
Arabia, including the Ministry of Defense, the headquarters of the American military mission in Riyadh, the public security building in Dammam,
two royal palaces, the Saudi air base near the Yemen border, and the
Tapline. Various "liberation movements" declared themselves to be active, while former King Saud, in exile in Egypt, was enlisted to broadcast
to Saudi Arabia that he considered himself to be the rightful ruler and
that he would return to save the people and the country from their
present predicament.[5]

Faisal's response was to redouble his efforts along the already established lines. He continued to pursue his Islamic Conference project by
traveling to Pakistan, Turkey, Morocco, Guinea, Mali, and Tunisia between April and September 1966 in search of supporters. He visited the

United States in June 1966 to confer with President Johnson and obtained renewed assurances of American support for Saudi independence, security, and territorial integrity. In September he concluded an agreement for American equipment and assistance to improve the mobility of Saudi forces. He obtained from Britain on an emergency basis elements of an air defense system operated by seconded British personnel pending the realization of the larger air defense package contracted for earlier. He tightened internal security and clamped down on convicted or suspected saboteurs and oppositionists. And he patched up the disagreements that had developed between him and the Yemeni royalist leadership and increased his support in funds and arms. However, while all these measures enabled Faisal to hold his own in the contest with Nasser, they did not offer him a promising chance to prevail. Indeed, they did not suffice any longer to cause Nasser to make another attempt at a political settlement, as he had done after earlier episodes of fighting. The Long Breath Strategy and Soviet material support appeared to have put Nasser in a position to sustain the pressure on Saudi Arabia indefinitely, and perhaps even to extend his position into south Arabia. That was the situation when, suddenly, the outbreak of the crisis and war of May–June 1967 changed things radically.

Dealing with Proliferating Problems, 1967–1973

The Six Day War marked a turning point in Saudi Arabia's security position. Already, during the weeks of crisis that preceded the war, Nasser had begun to pull some of his troops out of Yemen to reinforce the army he deployed against Israel in Sinai. After the total destruction of that army, Nasser agreed at the Khartoum summit of August 1967 to withdraw unconditionally the remainder of his Yemen expeditionary force and actually did so by the end of November. Israel's victory not only accomplished what five years of Saudi and royalist resistance had failed to achieve, but it definitively stymied Nasser's ten-year-long drive for integral Arab unity, which had posed challenge after challenge to Saudi Arabia and convulsed the Arab world. Henceforth Nasser was forced to concentrate on "eliminating the consequences of the Six Day War" and was reduced to a position of financial dependence on Saudi Arabia, Libya, and Kuwait. The leaders of the three conservative monarchies agreed at Khartoum to provide Egypt with an annual subsidy of $266 million, of which Saudi Arabia's share was $154 million, to be paid in quarterly installments.

Even as the Egyptian threat was abating, however, a new array of menaces emerged in the following years as a result of developments in south Arabia, the Persian Gulf, and the wider Arab arena, and the interaction of some of these with developments inside Saudi Arabia. None of these dangers was as clear and grave as the Egyptian threat at its height, but their multiplicity, diversity, and complex intertwining made their management much more difficult and the chances of failure greater than was the case when the Saudis confronted a single overriding threat.

1. Despite the Egyptians' withdrawal from Yemen, a troublesome republican regime remained in place in the center and south of the country. Although the forces of that regime were divided by personal and ideological rivalries and by differences regarding the various Egyptian attempts to reach a political settlement, they were united after the Egyptians' departure by a common fear of royalist restoration and anxiously sought help from any source to prevent it. The Soviets were already providing assistance, and the Syrians and the Algerians contributed money, arms, and advisers after the Egyptians' departure.

2. In addition to the continuing threat presented by the republican regime, a new and even more serious threat crystallized in South Yemen. While the Egyptians were completing their withdrawal from North Yemen, the British withdrew from Aden and the South Arabian Federation, which promptly fell under the control of the Marxist National Liberation Front — subsequently renamed the National Front — after the latter had defeated its Egyptian-supported rival in a bloody struggle. The NLF established the People's Republic of South Yemen and proclaimed its dedication to the overthrow of all the traditional regimes in the Arabian Peninsula. Although some of the North Yemeni republican leaders and factions feared and resented the NLF, others favored it and most viewed it as a useful source of support against royalist restoration. Moreover, union between the two Yemens was seen as an overriding national ideal by leaders of both countries regardless of political coloring, including North Yemeni royalists. This aspiration further complicated the already bewildering Yemeni politics and presented the Saudis with the constant latent threat of a large, populous, irredentist or revolutionary neighbor to the south.

3. Under the influence of the National Front, the long-smoldering rebellion against the sultan of Oman in South Yemen's neighboring province of Dhofar, originally supported by the Saudis, took a decidedly radical turn. In 1968 the rebels adopted a Marxist-Leninist ideology, purged the traditional elements from their ranks, proclaimed themselves the Popular Front for the Liberation of the Occupied Arab Gulf (PFLOAG), and began to receive Soviet and Chinese help through South Yemen. Were the rebels to succeed in Oman as the NLF had in the South Arabian Federation, they would be in a position to endanger traffic through the Strait of Hormuz and to spread the rebellion to the neighboring weak shaikhdoms. That threat became all the more real after the British announced

in 1968 their intention to withdraw from the Persian Gulf by 1971, terminating their historic obligation to defend those shaikhdoms.

4. Even more important than its effect on the shaikhdoms, the British announcement forecast the end of Britain's more than century-old role as protector of free navigation and of peace in the Persian Gulf. That development could awaken dormant regional conflicts that had been kept in check by the British presence, produce a scramble among Saudi Arabia's more powerful neighbors (such as Iran and Iraq) to fill the vacuum left by the British, impel them to draw in their superpower supporters, and destabilize altogether both the Gulf waters through which the bulk of Saudi (and other) oil traveled and the countries bordering those waters.

5. Although Egypt's defeat in the Six Day War finally forced Nasser out of Yemen, it also led him to develop an ever tighter cooperation with the Soviets in a desperate endeavor to "eliminate the consequences of the 1967 war" and recover the territories and position he had lost. This in itself placed the Soviets in a favorable position to deepen and extend their influence throughout the region, including countries that were already threatening to Saudi Arabia, such as the two Yemens, Iraq, and Syria. Moreover, Nasser's partnership with the Soviets and his identification of them as the champions of the Arab cause automatically put Saudi Arabia and other Arab countries in a bad light for maintaining close and friendly relations with the United States, Israel's friend and protector. Although Nasser himself did not dare openly attack the Saudis, Libyans, and Kuwaitis on that score for fear of losing their badly needed financial support, other radical Arabs did so and prepared the ground for his later demand that oil-rich Arab countries use their resource as a weapon in the service of the cause he led.

6. The patent failure of the Arab states to help the Palestinian cause they had espoused since 1948, as manifested in their defeat in the 1967 war, stimulated the growth of various resistance movements among the Palestinians that aimed to carry on the struggle for their cause themselves, in their own ways. These movements enlisted the support of the large concentrations of Palestinians in Jordan and soon managed to establish themselves as a force that threatened to swallow the Jordanian state, install a radical nationalist regime next door to Saudi Arabia, and bring the Arab-Israeli conflict to its borders. The Palestinian movements were also disposed to resort to threat, sabotage, and terror to extract political and financial support from some Arab governments and to punish those deemed to be insufficiently cooperative. Because of their relationship with the United States and the virtual impossibility of protecting the thousands of members of the royal family against terrorist action, the Saudis had particular reasons to fear that disposition.

7. Finally, intensifying most of the previously mentioned threats was

the danger of their combining with the consequences of the modernization programs launched by King Faisal, to generate internal upheavals. Saudi Arabia's past experience and that of neighboring countries indicated that the armed forces were particularly prone to lead such an upheaval because of the more concentrated degree of modernization they must go through and because of the greater temptations that control of instruments of force presented to the discontented among them. Indeed, in 1969 two plots against the regime were uncovered in Saudi Arabia, while two military coups succeeded in overthrowing the monarchy in Libya and the civilian regime in the Sudan, underscoring the persistence and pervasiveness of that danger, switching those two states to the hostile camp, and sharpening the polarization of the Arab world between radicals and conservatives.

In dealing with these threats, Faisal adapted his three-pronged strategy (avoidance of direct Saudi military intervention; pursuit of close relations with the United States; adoption of political, economic, and social reforms) to pursue several different approaches depending on his assessment of the possibilities and limitations in each case. In the case of the Yemens, Faisal first tried to use the North Yemeni client tribes to overthrow the country's republican regime, and then to use North Yemen as a proxy to overthrow the radical regime to the south. When the first part of that strategy failed, Faisal reconciled himself to a republican regime in San'a but sought to control its policy through representatives of his client tribes and to embroil it in the conflict with South Yemen. That effort encountered both successes and setbacks, and some of the successes boomeranged and generated agreement on unity between the two Yemens.

Regarding South Yemen itself, Faisal's relentless efforts to subvert and overthrow its regime through the use of proxies only contributed to further radicalization of its government and to its responding in kind through support of subversion and sabotage inside Saudi Arabia. At one point in late 1969 the confrontation between the two countries erupted into an encounter between their regular forces, contrary to a long-standing strategic Saudi imperative. Altogether, Faisal's strategy toward the two Yemens failed to resolve the problem and at best only managed to contain it.

With respect to Oman, Faisal felt able only to put aside his past conflict with its sultan, especially after Qabus ibn Sa'id overthrew his father in 1970, and to help through the pressure that he put directly on South Yemen. Otherwise he was content to let the sultan's British-officered forces deal with the Dhofar rebels and other opponents, and subsequently resigned himself to the intervention of an Iranian expeditionary force on the sultan's side.

In the Gulf, Faisal adopted a low profile for nearly two years after the

British announced their intention to withdraw, first in the hope that Britain might relent or that the United States might take its place, and then to avoid involvement in a dispute between the British and the shah of Iran over the future of Bahrain. When the latter issue was settled and the shah emerged as the candidate to fill the power vacuum left by the British, Faisal reached an unequal understanding with him based on a tacit division of spheres of influence that left the Gulf emirates in the Saudi sphere but allowed Iran to seize the Abu Musa and Tunb islands belonging to two of those emirates. The United States was at least presumptively a guarantor of that understanding by dint of its close relations with the two parties. The agreement withstood one serious test in March 1973, when Iraq encroached upon part of Kuwait's territory: the implicit threat of Iranian intervention and the deployment of Saudi troops in Kuwait, coupled with intensive diplomatic action within the Arab League (in which the Saudis and the Kuwaitis had strong friends), forced the Iraqis to pull back.

In the wider Arab arena, Faisal strove for some time with rather inadequate means to protect Saudi Arabia against the fallout from the war of attrition. He paid his subsidy to Nasser in quarterly installments, kept his American connection as inconspicuous as possible under the circumstances while pleading with the United States to limit its identification with Israel, and revived his endeavor to create an Islamic alignment to counter the Arab radical movement. These defensive measures barely diminished the threats. By the latter part of 1970, however, events beyond Faisal's control, including the end of the war of attrition, King Hussein's victory over the PLO in the Jordanian civil war, the death of Nasser and Sadat's accession to power, and a military coup that brought Hafez al-Assad to the presidency of Syria, combined to ease some of the dangers and to create room for policy maneuvers, of which Faisal promptly availed himself.

Faisal endeavored in this new phase to cultivate a close relationship with the new leaders of Egypt and Syria and persisted despite both seeming and real difficulties. The connection with Cairo and Damascus seemed crucial to the entire range of Saudi Arabia's security problems. It could end direct hostile action from these capitals of radicalism; terminate their political and material support for regimes such as South Yemen and for the radicals and rebels of North Yemen, Oman, and the Gulf; isolate and counterbalance Iraq; and, finally, make it easier for Saudi Arabia to cooperate with the United States in defense and development projects. Faisal succeeded in his endeavor to a large extent; but for his success to endure, it was necessary to bridge the gap between the United States and the two Arab leaders, or at least Sadat, on the Arab-Israeli problem. Faisal tried hard to accomplish that to no avail, with the result that a confrontation developed by the latter part of 1973 that forced him to make a choice between alienating either Washington or Cairo and Damascus. His decision and action on that question were to have momentous consequences.

Finally, the multiplicity of external threats and problems caused Faisal to persist in the effort to build up the armed forces despite the attendant risks. As a measure of insurance, he also continued the development of the National Guard and other internal security apparatuses. In a broader sense, he endeavored to protect the regime by combining severe internal repressive measures with wider economic and social-welfare development programs, expressed in the adoption of the first five-year plan.

The Yemens

Even as the Egyptian forces were completing their withdrawal from Yemen in the latter part of 1967, the royalists launched an offensive to regain full control of the country. Although Faisal had been distancing himself from the imam and his family, he gave them a last major infusion of funds and arms to help them mount and lead the offensive. Faisal's hope was to bring about the destruction of the republican regime and then enlist the restored royalist regime in a campaign to overthrow the regime of South Yemen. The offensive went well at first, and by December 1967 the royalist forces had cut off and laid siege to San'a, the capital. However, in the subsequent fighting the royalists were assailed by divisions and defections and were unable to mount a decisive final assault. The republicans, on the other hand, faced with the danger of annihilation in the event of defeat, closed their own ranks temporarily, fought well, and, with the help of sorties of MIG-19s and Ilushin bombers flown by Syrian personnel, beat back the uncoordinated enemy attacks. In March 1968 the royalists withdrew in failure and the republicans subsequently regained some lost ground in partly successful counterattacks.

With his scheme gone awry, Faisal sought to advance his objectives through a two-tiered strategy. For the long run, he reverted to a policy of trying to bring about an agreement among moderate royalist and republican forces and to enlist the support of the new government against South Yemen. In the meantime he endeavored to disengage himself from the connection with the imam's family and to establish independent proxy control over the northern parts of North Yemen by providing direct support to tribal chiefs and moderate notables. In this way he hoped to facilitate the envisaged agreement with the moderate republicans and to safeguard the Saudi interests after such an agreement had been reached. The approach was also meant to secure for the Saudis a base of operations and tribal allies to help in mounting an immediate campaign against South Yemen.

The victory of the National Front in South Yemen had been accompanied by the flight or expulsion of shaikhs, tribesmen, and politicians who had opposed it. The Saudis used these elements and client North Yemeni tribes to try to destabilize the NF regime or at least to duplicate their achievement against the Egyptians in Yemen, of wearing down the regime's forces and containing them in a few urban enclaves. However, although the Saudis were able to stimulate several uprisings, in July, August, September, and December 1968, the NF was able to put them all down, and the troubles stirred by the Saudis only played into the hands of extremists, who gained the ascendancy in the country. Thus, in June 1969 a Marxist-Leninist faction headed by Abd al-Fattah Ismaʻil ousted the relatively moderate rival group led by Qahtan al-Shaabi and proceeded to tighten its grip on the country with ruthless purges and repression coupled with the application of revolutionary "socialist" economic and social programs. It sought and obtained additional help from the Communist countries: the Soviets provided arms and technical assistance; the East Germans, help in organizing the security system; the Cubans, assistance in training the air force and in agricultural projects; and the Chinese, medical aid and a road from Aden to the Hadramaut.[6] The new government of South Yemen also rededicated itself to the theory of permanent revolution and endeavored to extend it throughout south Arabia.

Already before the further swing to the left in Aden, radicals in the Dhofar rebellion had taken over control of the movement with the help of the NF in September 1968 and given it a Marxist-Leninist orientation. They had changed the name of the movement from the Dhofar Liberation Front to the Popular Front for the Liberation of the Occupied Arab Gulf (PFLOAG) to signify their commitment to a wider revolution and sought and obtained from the People's Republic of China arms and training assistance, which were channeled to them through South Yemen. In mid-1969 PFLOAG guerrillas, with South Yemeni help, launched a sustained drive into the western and central regions of Dhofar. By August 1969 they had captured key towns and the port of Rakhyut; by November they had isolated Salalah, the capital; and by the summer of 1970 they controlled nearly two-thirds of the province. The success of the PFLOAG encouraged the spread of revolutionary activity to central Oman, and in June 1970 an organization calling itself the National Democratic Front for the Liberation of Oman and the Arabian Gulf (NDFLOAG) launched night attacks on the sultan's garrisons at Izki and Nizwa. The attacks so alarmed the British, who were helping the sultan against the rebels but were frustrated by his tightfistedness and extreme conservativism, that they instigated his overthrow by his son, Qabus ibn Saʻid, in July 1970, in the hope of obtaining greater cooperation to do what they believed had to be done.

Despite the peril that the rebellion in Oman presented to vital Saudi interests, including the transit of oil through the Strait of Hormuz, Faisal was in no position to play any direct role to help the Omani ruler cope with it, not only because of the ingrained hostility between the two countries but especially because of the Saudi complicity in instigating the original rebellion against Sultan Sa'id. The accession of Qabus and his amenability to British advice held out the promise of an improvement in Saudi-Omani relations based on newly shared interest in Omani stability, but that promise took some time to materialize. It was not until December 1971, for instance, that the Saudis extended diplomatic recognition to Oman and began to offer it some modest assistance. Early in 1973 Qabus invited Iranian forces to help him put down the rebellion in Dhofar. Although Faisal, whose forces were then deployed in Jordan and Kuwait and along the Yemeni borders, was in no position to offer help, he nevertheless resented Qabus's action and feared that as a consequence Iran might become entrenched on both sides of the Strait of Hormuz.

Faisal's proxy war against South Yemen backfired not only in Yemen and Dhofar but also in Saudi Arabia itself. On May 30, 1969, the Popular Front for the Liberation of Palestine, an offshoot of the Arab Nationalist Movement that had also spawned South Yemen's National Front, blew up in the Golan a section of the Tapline, which carried 23 million tons of Saudi oil yearly to Mediterranean ports. In June the Saudis arrested scores of oil workers, many of them Palestinians, suspected as supporters of the PFLP. Later in the month the authorities uncovered an attempt at a coup d'état involving members of the Arab Nationalist Movement, which led to waves of arrests and dismissals among officers and senior civil servants over the next few months.[7] The plotters reportedly included sixty air force officers and the director of the air force academy in Dhahran. Their plan is said to have called for eliminating the king and senior princes by bombing the royal palace from the air and then proclaiming a Republic of the Arabian Peninsula. Also involved in the plot were the director of military operations, the director of the office of the chief of staff, the commander of the military garrison at Hasa, the former chief of staff of the army, the former commander of the Mecca garrison, the director general of the maintenance corps, the director of officers' affairs of the Internal Security Academy, officials of Petromin — the agency in charge of development of petroleum and minerals — the director of the Public Administration Institute, and other officials and a junior officer from the Sudairi family.[8]

Before the purges were completed, regular forces of South Yemen — said to amount to 1,000 troops — penetrated into Saudi Arabia and attacked and occupied the outpost of Wadi'ah on November 26, 1969. Wadi'ah occupies elevated ground controlling an area where the borders of Saudi Arabia, North Yemen, and South Yemen meet and was held only by a platoon of Saudi Frontier Guards. Its capture, especially at a time of unrest in the Saudi armed forces, was probably meant to demonstrate the impotence of the regime and thus encourage potential rebels and plotters against it.

The Saudi government, at any rate, reacted on that assumption both in what it did and in what it refrained from doing. It flew in large reinforcements and launched them in a counterattack. The action was preceded, accompanied, and followed by air strikes by a flight of Lightning F-53s led by a British pilot and by a flight of Sabres manned by Pakistanis.[9] The Saudi forces recaptured Wadi'ah on December 3, but the government refrained from sending them in pursuit of the enemy, even though the latter remained twelve miles inside Saudi territory after retreating from the outpost. This caution was due in part to the fact that the Saudi high command was unable to muster the larger forces needed for pursuit: one brigade was tied down in Jordan, and other forces had to stand watch on the Iraqi and Persian Gulf fronts. But it was also due to the government's fear of the reaction within the armed forces to a possible setback. This was the first time the Saudi troops had been used in combat since the 1934 Yemen War (with the minor exception of 1948, when two Saudi companies fought one engagement in Huleiqat, in southern Israel, as part of the Egyptian forces); and although the government was careful to send in National Guard units along with the regular army, it evidently did not want to risk any of them beyond the point of absolute necessity.

While the Saudis were waging their unsuccessful campaign against South Yemen, developments in the republican-controlled part of North Yemen took a somewhat more favorable turn for them. After the republican forces had repulsed the royalists around San'a, their forces splintered again over issues of power and policy. In March 1968, for instance, a dispute broke out concerning the custody of a shipment of Soviet arms that had arrived at Hodeida — the Soviets had intended the arms for the left-oriented militia, but government officers insisted on taking them. A shooting scuffle ensued, and the government called on tribal irregulars to support the army. But the army itself split over the issue and its ideological implications, and in August 1968 the contesting parties clashed in a pitched battle in and near San'a that left some two thousand dead. The leftist-led army units and tribes were soundly defeated; and although the army chief had the leaders of both sides arrested and expelled to avert further trouble, the setback to the leftists created a favorable ground for the Saudi endeavors to bring about a unified government of moderate royalists and republicans and involve it in the struggle against South Yemen.[10]

By that time the Saudis had rid themselves of the extreme royalists from the imam's family, and the combination of internal unrest, the Wadi'ah battle, and disturbing developments in the wider Arab arena (discussed below) caused them to redouble their efforts to achieve their goal in North Yemen. In March 1970 these efforts resulted in a meeting between King Faisal and North Yemeni Prime Minister Muhsin al-'Aini, who reached preliminary agreement on a formula to end the civil war and establish a unified government. In July of that year the agreement was confirmed by King Faisal and President Iryani, and Saudi Arabia announced its willingness to provide North Yemen with economic assistance.

For a while the Saudi scheme of implicating the Yemen Arab Republic in the conflict with South Yemen seemed to work. Over the next two years the two Yemens were involved in constant border conflicts and attempts to subvert each other's regime while the Saudis intensified their own efforts against South Yemen from the expanded base they had gained. The outcome of the scheme, however, ran counter to Saudi expectations. The South Yemeni regime not only withstood the increased pressure but responded to it by further tightening its hold on the country and further increasing its cooperation with Communist countries and radical Arab regimes. This movement toward the extreme left was symbolized by the change in the country's name from the People's Republic of South Yemen to the Popular Democratic Republic of Yemen (PDRY) in 1971, which made its Marxist-Leninist identification more explicit and proclaimed its rejection of the separateness of North Yemen.

The real surprise for the Saudis, however, came from the action of the ostensibly allied YAR government. In September 1972 the border clashes between the two Yemens culminated in open warfare, as YAR troops and armor attacked in force and PDRY forces counterattacked and seized the town of Qatab and its environs. The fighting continued through most of October while the Arab League sought to mediate an end to the conflict at the behest of both sides. The league's efforts bore fruit on October 28, 1972, when an agreement was signed in Cairo between YAR Premier 'Aini and PDRY Prime Minister Ali Nasser Muhammad not only to end the fighting but also to unify the two countries. The two leaders specifically agreed to ban all subversive activity and to close all camps being used in each country to train opponents of the other's regime. Special committees formed of representatives from both governments were scheduled to plan for combining the institutions of the two countries and for completing a draft of a constitution within one year. The agreement would be monitored by Libya, which in 1969 had come under a revolutionary regime headed by Colonel Mu'ammar al-Qaddafi; the latter promised financial assistance conditional upon progress in the pursuit of the agreement. A substantial bit of progress followed swiftly when Presidents Iryani of the YAR and Salim Rubaya Ali of PDRY signed the final agreement on unity in Tripoli, Libya, on November 1972.

The dream of Yemeni unity was widely shared by Yemenis everywhere. Imam Yahya had pursued it since bringing North Yemen under his rule at the end of World War I; his successors had struggled for it; the Saudis themselves had supported the Yemeni cause against the British in the 1950s; nationalists of South Yemen had fought for it; and the Yemen Arab Republic and the People's Republic of South Yemen had espoused it as their goal since their respective foundings in 1962 and 1967. However, developments in the two countries since they had achieved independence had seemed to drive them further apart rather than closer together, and it was therefore striking that their governments suddenly agreed on a unity plan so soon after having fought a war. Of course, each regime hoped to be able to dominate the envisaged united state, but what mattered was that both were willing to wager on that expectation and act upon it.

In the Saudis' view, Yemeni unity of any sort presented a serious threat to the Kingdom's security. Of course, the threat would be most drastic if a unified Yemen were to come under the control of the National Front, backed by radical, oil-rich Libya, other radical Arab regimes, and Communist countries. Nor did such a prospect appear to the Saudis to be so remote, in light of the NF's success in imposing its "atheist" Marxist-Leninist regime on the primitive society (except in Aden) of South Yemen and maintaining it for five years against all the opposition the Saudis could muster against it. But even a union in which the YAR somehow achieved preponderance was seen as a serious threat. It would create a vast but poor country, with a population considerably larger than Saudi Arabia's, adjoining a weak neighbor and entertaining irredentist aspirations in Oman as well as in Saudi Arabia's own richest agricultural province of 'Asir and coastal province of Tihama, while controlling the Red Sea oil route at Bab al-Mandeb. Apart from any actual prospects of unity, the agreement of the two Yemens to unite was in itself a serious setback to the Saudi design to embroil the YAR as a whole in a proxy war against PDRY. There was also the possibility that some strongly shared interest might bring the two Yemens together again sometime in the future to the detriment of Saudi security interests.

The Saudis' immediate reaction was to use their leverage with the tribes and their representatives in the YAR government to obstruct the union and eventually to force the resignation of Prime Minister 'Aini in December 1972. His successor, Abdallah al-Hajri, chose to work with the Saudis and they rewarded him with increased financial support and above all with military assistance designed to win over the YAR armed forces. President Iryani, however, continued to feel committed to the union project and pressed for its realization. As a result, for a while the YAR government pursued at the same time two diametrically opposite courses, which threatened to plunge the country back into civil war. On the one hand, training camps for anti-PDRY elements were reopened and multiplied and incursions into South Yemen were resumed and intensified, leading to PDRY counteraction with border raids, acts of terrorism against pro-Saudi personalities, and support for pro-union groups. On the other hand, the unity talks continued and political organizations were set up to advance it in accordance with the agreed-on union plans.

In September 1973 President Iryani tried to put an end to the chaotic situation. He tendered his resignation to the Council of Ministers, and when it was rejected he used his reinforced mandate to dismiss Hajri, ask for the recall of the intrusive Saudi ambassador, and agree with PDRY's President Rubaya Ali on an extension of the unification deadline and an end to border incursions. Iryani accommodated the Saudis to the extent of not reappointing 'Aini prime minister as he had first intended; but the compromise candidate he appointed in March 1974, Hassan Makki, turned out to be too leftist-oriented and pro-union for the Saudis' taste, and they once again encouraged their client tribal leaders to oppose him. In June 1974 Iryani tendered his resignation once more, but this time a group of army officers led by Colonel Ibrahim al-Hamdi stepped in and assumed complete power.

Hamdi, as will be discussed in a later chapter, was able to balance the YAR's various forces and pursue a fairly coherent policy before being felled by an assassin's bullet; but the pattern of subsequent developments in the two Yemens and the elements of the dilemma that the Saudis confronted in dealing with them had already been established by the time of his accession to power. That dilemma may be summed up as follows. The PDRY regime faced the Saudis with a many-faceted threat that they could neither abide, nor remove by using their own armed forces. Use of South Yemeni opponents and client tribes of the YAR as proxies to combat PDRY proved insufficient and threatened to perpetuate the division of North Yemen and the loss of the republican-controlled part of the country to PDRY. On the other hand, the effort to support a central YAR regime and embroil it in the war against PDRY backfired when the YAR's government joined in an agreement on union, which entailed even greater dangers to the Saudis than the ones they were attempting to meet. How to escape that dilemma has been the Saudis' problem ever since.

The Gulf

One reason the Saudis under Faisal refrained from committing their regular forces against PDRY was their fear of internal repercussions if those forces suffered a severe setback. Fear of such a setback was based partly on the poor quality of the regular Saudi forces at that stage, particularly on their lack of combat experience; and partly on the limited number of forces that could be marshaled against PDRY because of the need to deploy substantial forces to face threats on other fronts. One of those fronts was the Persian Gulf, where a situation fraught with both threats and opportunities was developing as a result of Britain's decision, announced in January 1968, to withdraw from the region and to terminate its peacekeeping responsibilities there by the end of 1971.

Britain's peacekeeping responsibilities at the time of the announcement had two facets. One involved its relations with nine emirates on the Arabian coast of the lower Gulf: Qatar, the island of Bahrain, and the seven shaikhdoms that make up the present United Arab Emirates (Abu Dhabi, Dubai, Sharjah, 'Ajman, Umm al-Qaiwain, Ras al-Khaimah, Fujairah). Britain's relationship originated in a series of treaties going back at least a century that bound these tribal entities to observe peace among themselves in exchange for British protection of each and all, and evolved into a role of adviser and mentor to their rulers as several of them came into vast oil fortunes. Beyond this function but related to it, Britain had assumed the responsibility of ensuring free navigation throughout the Persian Gulf, which in turn had entailed a responsibility to preserve a balance and keep the peace among all the countries bordering on it. In the interim between the 1968 announcement of their intent to withdraw and the 1971 deadline set for that withdrawal, the British hoped to work out an orderly transfer of both responsibilities; but the announcement itself unleashed dynastic animosities, tribal feuds, and territorial disputes among the shaikhdoms and rivalries, ambitions, and fears among the other Gulf powers that made the prospects of an orderly transition highly problematic.

Specifically, on February 27, 1968, the British induced Bahrain, Qatar, and the seven shaikhdoms to sign an agreement to establish a Federation of Arab Emirates to take effect the following month. The idea was that the federation would take over the limited functions the British had hitherto fulfilled among the emirates and enter, with their advice, into engagements that would help fulfill the larger function of establishing a new balance and order in the Gulf basin as a whole. The nature of those engagements was not quite clear, but there was speculation at the time that these might involve the United States, in an operation similar to its taking over from Britain responsibility for the defense of Greece and Turkey in 1947, or that they might produce a security arrangement combining American power and British political experience in the region.

The signing of the federation agreement immediately aroused strong Iranian opposition on two accounts. One was Iran's claim to sovereignty over Bahrain, harking back to the eighteenth century; the other was the shah's aspiration to succeed Britain as the arbiter of the Gulf's destiny and guarantor of its peace, to the exclusion of any outside power. The Iranian claim, in turn, caused the signatories of the federation agreement to fall out among themselves. Qatar and the seven shaikhdoms had been fearful anyway that the federation might be dominated by Bahrain, whose population of 200,000 outnumbered them all and was more energetic and developed than theirs. Iran's assertion of its claim compounded that apprehension with the fear of involvement in a conflict with Iran on account of Bahrain and caused them to think of excluding the latter from the federation. Two years later, in May 1970, Iran renounced its claim to Bahrain in order to facilitate Britain's withdrawal, after having found out that the field would then be clear for itself (as the United States declined to take on the responsibilities relinquished by Britain). By then, however, the divisions among the prospective members of the federation had taken hold and were exacerbated by Saudi territorial claims on Abu Dhabi, the largest and richest of them.

Faisal had initially favored a comprehensive federation of the nine Gulf entities supported by the United States as a means of filling the vacuum that would be created by the British withdrawal. However, when Iran asserted its claim over Bahrain and objected to any American or British security role in the Gulf, Faisal decided to keep a low profile until the situation became clearer. He was, of course, vitally interested that Iran should not gain control over Bahrain, just a few miles off the Saudi coast and oil region, but he left the burden of resisting Iran's claim to the British and to the pressure of general Arab opinion. He did not want to risk antagonizing the shah; on the contrary, he endeavored to sustain the friendly discourse established earlier in connection with the project of an Islamic Conference, at least until the larger picture of the security of the Gulf, and particularly of the American role, became clear. Faisal's cautious approach proved justified in two respects: (1) by the end of 1969 the British succeeded in inducing the shah to renounce his claim to Bahrain, and (2) by the same time it had become apparent that the United States, paralyzed by its Vietnam burden, was not going to take the relay from Britain and was prepared to rely on the shah to be the guardian of the Gulf and of Western interests there. Faisal, however, was still left with the problem of finding an accommodation with the shah and with the emirates and shaikhdoms that would serve Saudi Arabia's security interests.

Starting in 1970, Faisal emerged from the passive phase to pursue a two-pronged policy to meet those problems. First, he reached an understanding with the shah on a tacit division of spheres of influence in the Gulf, wherein Iran recognized the emirates and shaikhdoms as falling within the Saudi purview while Saudi Arabia acknowledged Iran's primary role as guardian of the Gulf waters. This understanding was underscored by a declaration issued by Saudi Arabia, Iran, and Kuwait in July

1970, some two months after a Conservative government committed to reconsider its Labour predecessor's position on the Gulf came to power in Britain. The declaration asserted the wish of the three countries that Britain leave at the date already announced and thus gave the Conservative government an excuse to back off from its commitment.

The Saudi-Iranian understanding on spheres of influence included one exception, involving the islands of Abu Musa and the two Tunbs, near the entrance to the Strait of Hormuz. The islands belonged to the shaikhdoms of Sharjah and Ras al-Khaimah respectively, but the shah insisted that he absolutely needed them to secure Gulf navigation, and the Saudis tacitly assented to his demand. The shah then reached an understanding with the British wherein he would occupy the islands after the termination of their treaty commitment to the shaikhdoms, but he actually did so one day before, on November 30, 1971. Whether the shah advanced the date in order to demonstrate that he wrested the islands from Britain rather than from the weak shaikhdoms or in order to spare the Saudis the embarrassment of failing to protect their new clients is not known. At any rate, the uproar that ensued among the Arab countries centered mainly on Iran and Britain, and some of them adopted sanctions aimed exclusively at the latter. Iraq broke off relations with London and completed the takeover of Iraq Petroleum Company, and Libya nationalized the possessions of British Petroleum Company in its territory.

Saudi Arabia received minimum blame for the time being, though almost two years afterward it still felt it necessary to explain its role. In July 1973, for instance, Defense Minister Sultan ibn Abd al-Aziz revealed that Saudi Arabia had tried to arrange for Iran to lease the islands from their owners, but that the outcry of the radical Arab countries against Iran's demand to control the islands caused the Iranians to annex them instead.[11]

Once he obtained a relatively free hand with respect to the emirates and shaikhdoms in the wake of his understanding with Iran, Faisal used this leverage to seek a modification of the original federation plan advanced by Britain, both for the sake of better security and for territorial gains as well. Instead of a union of the nine entities, Faisal now supported the independence of Bahrain and Qatar and qualified his backing for a union of the seven shaikhdoms. Because the House of Saud had got along quite well historically with the ruling Al Khalifa of Bahrain and Al Thani of Qatar (the latter also being Wahhabis), Faisal felt he could count on fuller cooperation from them in security and other matters as independent rulers than as members of a wider federation. This approach was also useful in advancing a long-standing Saudi claim to part of the territory of Abu Dhabi lying between Qatar and the shaikhdoms, which Faisal chose to assert vehemently in May 1970. If Qatar were included in the union, the Saudi claim would appear as driving a wedge through the union's territory of the seven shaikhdoms at Abu Dhabi.

As the deadline for Britain's withdrawal approached, Bahrain and Qatar did proclaim their independence in August and September 1971 and that part of Faisal's policy was satisfied. But his claim on Abu Dhabi's territory remained unsettled when the United Arab Emirates was inaugurated on December 2, 1971. Faisal chose not to obstruct the union of the shaikhdoms on that account, but he indicated his reservation by withholding recognition of the UAE until 1975, when the Saudi demand was met.

The understanding with Iran, the independence of Bahrain and Qatar under friendly rule, and the formation of the United Arab Emirates resolved the immediate problem posed for the Saudis by the British decision to withdraw from the Gulf and created a framework within which they could deal with the region's security problems. These developments, however, did not in themselves assure Saudi security in the region. For one thing, the understanding with Iran was a partnership between two militarily unequal parties with different overall aspirations; and although for the moment Iran appeared to be reasonably accommodating, there was no assurance that it might not someday choose to use its superior power in ways detrimental to Saudi security and interests.

Second, the United Arab Emirates was a fragile creation, riven by rivalries, feuds, and unsettled conflicts, which had been put together rather hurriedly by the British under the pressure of their self-imposed deadline. Ras al-Khaimah, for example, stayed out of the union for a while to protest the indifference of its would-be partners to Iran's seizure of the Tunbs. Sharjah's ruler, on the other hand, was slain within two months of the formation of the UAE, during an attempted coup by his deposed predecessor supported by Iraq, for acquiescing in the Iranian seizure of Abu Musa. Sharjah and Fujairah, both members of the UAE, fought a small war in the summer of 1972 over local territorial issues. The chiefs of Abu Dhabi and Dubai vied for predominance within the union, and the latter demonstratively maintained a close connection with Iran and an implicit threat of secession to check the ambition of Abu Dhabi's ruler. The latter, in turn, yielded to Faisal's pressure to the extent of stopping oil drilling operations in the area claimed by Saudi Arabia, but he resisted Faisal's demand for settlement even after the latter withheld recognition of the UAE. Finally, even the limited resolution of the immediate problem raised by the British withdrawal stirred up other problems involving Iraq.

Iraq's relations with Iran and Saudi Arabia had been hostile for quite some time, but the Iranian-Saudi understanding appeared to the Iraqi leadership as a qualitative escalation of hostility. They viewed it as a combination of two strong local powers backed by the United States that threatened Iraq's vital access to the world through the Persian Gulf, and they reacted accordingly by intensifying their support for PDRY and for subversive movements in Oman and the Gulf states and by seeking closer Soviet support. In April 1972 they signed a fifteen-year treaty of friendship and cooperation with the Soviet Union and followed up with increased military cooperation and with permission to the Soviet navy to use Iraqi facilities at Umm al-Qasr, near Basra. Partly in reaction to the Iraqi-Soviet treaty, President Nixon and National Security Adviser Henry Kissinger stopped in Tehran on the way back from a May 1972 Moscow summit and promised the shah almost unlimited access to American conventional weapons. From the Saudi point of view, the closer American special relationship with the shah was useful in countering Iraq's hostility and its Soviet connection; but in the longer run it involved the danger of American-supported Iranian hegemony in the Gulf.

On March 20, 1973, Iraqi troops seized a Kuwaiti border post near the naval base of Umm al-Qasr and laid claim to two Kuwaiti islands — Bubiyan and Warba — that controlled the entrance to it. If successful, the Iraqi moves would not only enhance greatly the strategic position of the port used by the Iraqi and Soviet naval units but could also trigger a collapse of the Kuwaiti regime and perhaps even bring Iraqi troops within striking distance of Saudi Arabia's oil region. The Saudis responded by giving Kuwait immediate political support, sending in some 15,000 troops nine days later to stiffen its government's resistance, and mustering diplomatic pressure on Iraq within the Arab League. Iran remained in the background to give the Arab countries a chance to settle the issue; but its power was foremost in the mind of the Iraqis. The latter withdrew their forces but did not give up their claims, which they revived three years later.

The Arab-Israeli Arena and the Big Powers

Even as Faisal was grappling with problems around the rim of the Arabian Peninsula, from the Yemen Arab Republic to Kuwait and in the Persian Gulf, the respite he had had from the Egyptian problem after the Six Day War was coming to an end. After a period of rapid rearmament and preparation with Soviet help, Nasser declared in March 1969 a "war of attrition" against Israel designed to force it to renounce its 1967 conquests on his terms. The war went on until August 1970, and during that time each side's fortunes fluctuated sharply. Each time the fighting took a bad turn for Egypt, Nasser called upon the Soviets for further assistance to recover and keep going, and the latter responded positively and appeared to entrench themselves deeper and deeper in the country. By the first months of 1970, Soviet missile crews and combat pilots were defending Egypt's interior against an Israeli campaign of bombing in depth, some 17,000 Soviet "advisers" were distributed among Egyptian installations and forces down to battalion level, Soviet aircraft had exclusive use of some Egyptian air bases, and the Soviet navy had privileged access to Egyptian ports and naval facilities. In July 1972, when President Sadat expelled the Soviets by the stroke of a pen, their presence and role in 1969 and 1970 appeared in retrospect to have been tenuous. At the time, however, it looked to most observers, and certainly to the Saudis, as though the Soviets were well on their way toward turning Egypt into a dependent proxy if not a satellite. This apparent entrenchment, added to the strong Soviet presence in Syria, Iraq, and PDRY and the Soviet-supported subversive activities of those regimes, suggested to the Saudis a systematic Soviet design to encircle and subdue the Kingdom.

Second, Egypt's grueling struggle against Israel, regardless of the balance of its successes and failures, went a long way toward restoring Nasser's prestige and the credibility of the Arab nationalist cause that he led after the setbacks they suffered in the 1967 defeat. This became apparent when, in May 1969, a military group headed by Colonel Jaafar al-Numeiry overthrew the conservative parliamentary regime in the Sudan, proclaimed its adherence to Arab socialism, and moved the country toward cooperation with Egypt and the Soviet Union. Four months later, in September 1969, another military coup, headed by Colonel Mu'ammar al-Qaddafi, overthrew Libya's King Idris al-Sanussi, proclaimed the new regime's adherence to Arab nationalism, and offered to merge Libya with Egypt and other Arab countries. The Saudis' anxiety in the face of this resurgence of revolutionary pan-Arabism was particularly acute because in the months between the Sudanese and Libyan coups they uncovered and suppressed similar coup attempts in the Kingdom, involving a large number of senior military officers and civilians, some with Egyptian intelligence connections.

Third, although Nasser, because of his absorption in the struggle against Israel, deflected Qaddafi's offer to merge his country with Egypt with an "agreement to agree to unite" that included the Sudan, he nevertheless tried to use the renewed Arab nationalist momentum to impose on the Saudis policies detrimental to their interest or to embarrass and undermine them. Thus, at the December 1969 Arab summit in Rabat, Nasser surprised Faisal, with whom he had ostensibly coordinated positions a few days before, by making an impassioned speech calling upon the Arabs to close ranks in their struggle against Israel, and concluded with a tacit demand that Saudi Arabia and other Arab oil-producing countries confront the United States and the West by using their oil as a political weapon.[12] Faisal, who needed American support more than ever before in view of the many troubles he faced, ably parried Nasser's thrust on this occasion. He expressed willingness to use all his resources provided the Arabs made the struggle exclusively their own — that is to say, provided Nasser got rid of the Soviet connection as he was asking Faisal to get rid of his with America; whereupon Nasser left the conference in a huff and went on to Moscow to seek and obtain Soviet arms and participation of Soviet personnel in the combat. However, the encounter at Rabat showed that Nasser had recovered much of his old punch and wiliness and was prepared to strike surprise blows at Saudi Arabia where they could hurt most.

Fourth, Nasser's resort to war of attrition was emulated intermittently by Syria and Jordan and continually by the reformed Palestine Liberation Organization, operating mainly from Jordan. As the war dragged on, the PLO was able to establish a virtual state within a state in Jordan, the majority of whose population was Palestinian, and threatened to take over the country. Were it to do so, Jordan would cease to be a buffer state shielding Saudi Arabia from radical Syria and Iraq and from the Arab-Israeli war, and become a springboard for hostile activity by a radical bloc and a battlefield for Arabs and Israelis right next door.

Finally, the war of attrition involved a constant escalation in violence, force levels, scope, and damage inflicted and threatened to get out of hand and lead to total war. Were that to happen, the Saudis could get caught in it one way or another and their oil production could be disrupted, or they themselves might be forced to interrupt it, as had happened in previous wars.

Against that formidable combination of dangers there was not much that Faisal could do on his own initiative. One of the things he tried was to revive his pet project from the early 1960s of an Islamic organization as a means to counter the resurgent Arab radical trend. Taking advantage of an incident in which a deranged Australian set fire to the Al Aqsa mosque in Jerusalem, Faisal took the lead in arranging an Islamic summit at Rabat in September 1969 to consider a Muslim response. The conference condemned Israel roundly but rejected Egyptian proposals for concrete sanctions against the Jewish state; and Faisal got his chance to lay the foundation for a permanent organization under the control of Saudi Arabia and other friendly powers. But whatever Faisal's expectations may have been, the organization produced no recognizable effect of any kind until well into the 1970s, when the issue of radical Arab nationalism had become largely moot. For the moment, Faisal's success in assembling the conference probably contributed to provoking Nasser to spring his surprise call at the Arab summit in Rabat three months later to use the oil weapon.

Another course pursued by Faisal was to plead with the United States

—he was not yet in a position to threaten it—to exert pressure on Israel on behalf of a settlement based on UN Security Council Resolution 242 as interpreted by the Arab side.[13] The United States under the Nixon administration had abandoned President Johnson's policy of leaving the promotion of a settlement of the conflict to the UN representative, Gunnar Jarring, and had instead engaged in talks with the Soviets intended to produce a framework for a settlement that the big powers would then press on the parties. By June 1969 the American and Soviet negotiators had come close to an agreement, and Soviet Foreign Minister Andrei Gromyko had gone to Cairo to seek Nasser's assent to it. When Nasser rejected the proposed terms, however, the Soviets backed away from their tentative agreement and the Soviet-American talks reached a deadlock.[14]

In the meantime, the war of attrition escalated as the Israeli air force reacted to Egyptian attacks at the Suez Canal front line with raids deep into Egypt. The May 1969 military coup in the Sudan was followed by an attempted coup in Saudi Arabia and the successful coup in Libya in September. In the same months the Saudis were encountering frustration in their attempts to deal with PDRY, the rebellion was making headway in Dhofar, the Tapline had been blown up by the Popular Front for the Liberation of Palestine, and the efforts to cope with the planned British withdrawal from the Gulf were stymied by Iran's claim to Bahrain. In that context, Faisal desperately pleaded with the United States to do something to end the situation wherein, in his view, the continuing Israeli occupation of Arab lands fueled the spread of Soviet influence and Arab radicalism, or at least to do something to ease Saudi Arabia's exposure because of its association with the United States while the latter was viewed as supporting Israel unconditionally.

Partly in response to Faisal's pleas, the United States made public in December 1969, just before the Rabat Arab summit, its own unilateral plan for settling the Arab-Israeli conflict. What came to be known as the Rogers Plan, after the American secretary of state who enunciated it, called essentially for Israeli withdrawal from all the occupied territories in exchange for a contractual peace agreement coupled with international security guarantees. In substance the plan was similar to the proposal rejected by Nasser when conveyed to him by Gromyko, and had also been turned down by Israel before it was made public. Consequently, its enunciation was meant not so much to start a diplomatic process as to define the American position and to underscore its distance from Israel's for the benefit of Saudi Arabia and other friendly Arab countries. In this respect, Israel's public rejection of the proposal and the dispute that developed openly between its government and the American secretary of state fitted exactly into the latter's intended scenario. The only flaw was that it did not help the Saudis much.

As was pointed out before, Nasser used the Rabat summit to excoriate the Saudis implicitly but clearly for their association with the United States, and then went on to Moscow to conclude agreements that escalated qualitatively the Soviet involvement in the conflict and their presence in Egypt. Moreover, the subsequent participation of Soviet missile personnel and pilots in the defense of Egypt introduced a new element in the war of attrition and caused the United States to undertake moves in support of Israel that largely nullified the distancing effect achieved by the announcement of the Rogers Plan. Relief for the Saudis from the implications and ramifications of the war of attrition was not to come until several months later, in the summer of 1970; and when it came, it was at least partly associated with America's narrowing rather than widening its distance from Israel.

The injection of the superpower rivalry into the war of attrition created a real danger of an eventual clash between the superpowers themselves. This, coupled with continued indecisiveness in the fighting even after the limited Soviet intervention, finally created a favorable climate for a cease-fire. A timely initiative by Secretary of State Rogers calling on the parties to stop fighting and start talking found receptive ears. After Nasser failed during yet another trip to Moscow to induce the Soviets to increase their involvement further, and after President Nixon gave Israel certain diplomatic and military assurances, an agreement was reached to cease hostilities on August 7, 1970, and to resume negotiations through UN Ambassador Jarring. The cease-fire was supposed to be limited to three months, renewable only if negotiations were making progress; however, although the negotiations were late in starting and early in failing, the cease-fire continued for more than three years until it was shattered by the October 1973 war.

The cease-fire halted the previous drift toward general war and the increasing Egyptian dependence on the Soviets so feared by the Saudis. Although general war did erupt three years later, several crucial changes in the interim made its advent the occasion for major gains, rather than setbacks, to the Saudi security position. In the meantime, the fact that the cease-fire and related agreement to negotiate had been initiated by the United States and that Nasser had assented to these proposals made it much easier for the Saudis to cooperate openly with the United States in major defense and security projects as well as in civilian projects connected with the first five-year plan. Thus in 1970 the Saudis asked the U.S. Department of Defense to assess their defense needs and to formulate a program for modernizing parts of their armed forces. In 1971 they asked it to assess the role of the National Guard and work out a program to upgrade its capabilities. In the same year they concluded an agreement with the United States on a twelve-year program to develop a Saudi naval capability in view of the withdrawal of Britain's naval forces, including construction of ports, supply of materiel, and training of personnel. In 1972 they signed an agreement on a program for developing a logistical system for the armed forces, and the following year concluded an agreement to arm and train the National Guard.

The cease-fire also triggered a chain of events involving Jordan and Syria that resulted in a decisive resolution of one of Saudi Arabia's major security anxieties. The cease-fire agreement had been subscribed to by Egypt and Jordan as well as by Israel but was vehemently opposed by the PLO. As part of an attempt to sabotage it, the Popular Front for the Liberation of Palestine hijacked four airliners in the first days of September 1970, landed one at the Cairo airport, and blew it up after evacuating its passengers. It brought the other three planes to a desert airstrip in Jordan and threatened to blow them up and kill their 425-odd passengers, most of them American, unless all the Palestinians held prisoner in West Germany, Switzerland, and Israel as a result of previous guerrilla actions were released. Deadlines were set and extended, but Israel, backed by the United States, refused to yield. On September 12 the guerrillas released most of the hostages, transferred the remaining 50 to refugee camps under their control, and blew up the planes. Three days later King Hussein, whose authority had been eroded by the PLO long before this final act of defiance, launched an all-out campaign to crush the guerrillas. The latter fought back fiercely, but as the tide began to turn against them Syrian armored units crossed the frontier on September 19 to help them in their avowed aim to overthrow Hussein's regime. Hussein called on the United States for help, and the latter responded swiftly with a plan of action worked out in coordination with Israel. Israeli forces, already mobilized, were to deploy menacingly against the Syrian forces in the Golan Heights and in northern Jordan while the United States warned the Soviets to call upon their Syrian protégés to pull back. If the warning was not promptly heeded, Israel's forces would act against the Syrian forces while the American Sixth Fleet and other forces in the region would hold the line against Soviet intervention.[15]

Hussein, apprised of the essential elements of the plan, took courage and launched his air force against the Syrian armor, while the Syrians, cautioned by the Soviets, lost heart and held back their own air force. The result was a victory for Hussein, and by the end of the day of September 22 the Syrian tanks began to withdraw to their own border. In the next few days Hussein completed the defeat of the PLO forces, and this success enabled him subsequently to liquidate the PLO presence in Jordan altogether.[16]

King Hussein's victory rendered enormous services to Saudi security interests. It not only removed the specter of a PLO-dominated state engaged in war with Israel and allied with radical Iraq and Syria right next door; it also resulted indirectly in highly favorable changes in Syria itself. Two months after the intervention of the Syrian forces in Jordan and because of its failure, General Hafez al-Assad overthrew the radical leadership that had ordered and managed the intervention. One of Assad's first acts was to reverse his predecessors' position and allow the repair of the Tapline, blown up in 1969, in a gesture of rapprochement with the Saudis. He also ended Syria's open support of revolutionary and subversive groups in the Yemens, Oman, and the Gulf principalities; signed an economic and trade agreement with Saudi Arabia in April 1972; and, because of continuing hostility to Iraq, provided a welcome counterpoise to it from the west in addition to that provided by Iran from the east.

All these gains were secured at minimal risk and cost to the Saudis. While Hussein's fate was still uncertain, the Saudis had kept a low profile in order to avoid reprisals from the Palestinian guerrilla movements. A Saudi brigade had been stationed in southern Jordan, in the Aqaba-Ma'an area, since 1967; but, contrary to what King Saud had done in similar circumstances in 1957 when he placed Saudi forces at the disposal of King Hussein, Faisal ordered his forces to remain neutral and merely hold on to their positions.[17] Presumably he wanted to secure the area for Saudi Arabia in case Hussein's regime collapsed. Faisal did refrain from cutting off the subsidy to Jordan under the Khartoum agreement, unlike Kuwait and Libya, the other contributors; but his position on this score was covered by the mediating role he played together with Nasser. While the fighting was still going on, the latter had called a rump Arab summit in Cairo to deal with the crisis, and Faisal discovered that for once his interest coincided with that of the Egyptian leader. Both wanted the PLO disciplined and cut down to size without appearing to sanction all of Hussein's actions; and both therefore pushed for a cease-fire and mediation without pressing Hussein too hard to comply and without punishing him as other Arab parties were demanding.

Before the Jordanian crisis was completely settled, President Nasser died of a heart attack on September 28, 1970, and was succeeded by Anwar al-Sadat. This event removed from the scene a formidable adversary and the foremost leader of pan-Arabism and brought in his place a man who was much more disposed to accommodate the Saudis than to seek to dominate them. Moreover, President Sadat was soon to reverse dramatically Egypt's relations with the Soviet Union and to alter the region's political-strategic configuration in a way that was much more favorable for the Saudis. Before that happened, however, the Saudis endured another period of uncertainty and danger, arising mainly from Sadat's initial insecure hold on power and his tendency to resort to improvised and mutually contradictory policies.

In January 1971 negotiations finally began between Egypt and Israel through Ambassador Jarring, and in the following months Sadat indicated in reply to a formal inquiry by Jarring that he was prepared to conclude a formal "peace agreement" with Israel if Egypt's territorial conditions were met. Israel promptly rebuffed this crucial departure from Nasser's policy, but the exchange led the United States to enter the picture in the role of mediator in an attempt to reach a partial "interim agreement." This development was favorably viewed by the Saudis, who were very uncomfortable in their position as the principal Arab friend of America; but another move by Sadat ran counter to it and worried them. Partly to cover his Arab flank and partly to gain credit at home, in April 1971 Sadat concluded an agreement with Libya and Syria to form a federation of the three countries to be called the United Arab Republics. Although the agreement had limited credibility, it was disturbing to the Saudis because it kept alive the prospect of radical Arab nationalism and because it revealed inconsistency and uncertainty on the part of Sadat. More indications of the latter were to follow.

Sadat's signing of the agreement with Libya and Syria was used as an issue against him by a coalition of opponents headed by ex-premier Ali Sabri, Defense Minister General Muhammad Fawzi, Presidential Intelligence Chief Sami Sharaf, Interior Minister Sha'rawi Gom'a, and others. The opponents plotted to remove Sadat, but he preempted them and had them arrested on March 15, 1971. The Soviets, alarmed by the arrest of their friends and by Sadat's cooperation with the Americans on an interim agreement that might make their military presence in Egypt unnecessary, rushed to Cairo a high-level delegation headed by President Podgorny to try to shore up their position. Podgorny presented Sadat with a draft of a fifteen-year treaty of friendship and cooperation and made his acceptance of it a test of his proclaimed dedication to continuing good relations between the two countries. Caught in a weak moment after the recent shake-up and fearful that the Soviets might incite the armed forces against him by withholding military supplies if he refused, Sadat signed the treaty on May 27, 1971. Thus within three months Sadat had made five moves in the internal, inter-Arab, Arab-Israeli, and big power arenas that ran counter to one another and necessarily entailed additional subsequent contradictions.

Despite Sadat's patently inconsistent actions, Faisal had reason to believe he might be able to woo the Egyptian president and steer him in a desirable direction. In November 1970, shortly after Nasser's death, Faisal had sent his brother-in-law, chief of Saudi intelligence, and confidant, Kamal Adham, on a confidential mission to explore the possibility of an understanding with Sadat. Among other things, Adham had stressed to Sadat the Saudis' concern over the extent of the Soviet presence and influence in Egypt and had pointed out how that factor also caused the

Americans to associate themselves with Israel much more strongly than they would have liked. Sadat had replied that he needed the Soviets as long as he faced the probability of war with Israel, but that if he were able to achieve even only an interim agreement, he would be prepared to send the Russians home. That particular exchange had a rather embarrassing sequel: the Saudis, with Sadat's specific approval, conveyed the message to the United States, but its content was leaked by Senator Jackson to the embarrassment of Sadat and the dismay of the Soviets.[18] But Sadat's startling statement of his basic disposition and his willingness to have the Saudis convey it to the United States encouraged Faisal to persist in the endeavor to lure him despite all the difficulties.

On May 27, 1971, the same day that Sadat signed the Soviet-Egyptian treaty, Faisal arrived in Washington and met with President Nixon to "explain in detail the Arab views on the Middle East," as the Saudi media put it. Under different circumstances, it could be assumed that Faisal sought reassurances from the United States on account of the treaty; but given the context of the Adham-Sadat dialogue, the reverse was most probably the case. Faisal presumably reiterated to Nixon the view that Sadat had expressed to Adham, and urged the United States to persist in the effort to achieve an interim agreement, which is what Secretary of State Rogers did through the remainder of the year.

Three weeks after the signing of the Soviet-Egyptian treaty, on June 19, Faisal began a weeklong visit to Egypt in which he accomplished at least two things: he secured Egypt's endorsement of the Saudi-Iranian understanding on the Persian Gulf, which was being attacked by Iraq and PDRY;[19] and he helped form a joint Saudi-Egyptian mission to mediate the remaining conflict among King Hussein, the PLO, and Syria. Over the next four months the mission traveled to Jordan, Lebanon, and Syria, and leaders of these countries and of the PLO visited Saudi Arabia in search of a formula for reconciliation. Although the mission did not achieve its goal, its efforts kept the lid on the conflict and, most important from the Saudi point of view, prevented a dangerous fragmentation or polarization among the Arab countries over the PLO issue, and sustained the Saudi-Egyptian cooperation.

In July Sadat sought to increase pressure on the United States to accelerate its mediation efforts by proclaiming 1971 to be the "year of decision," meaning that he would go to war if no progress was made toward a political settlement by the end of the year. On October 11 Sadat went to Moscow in order, as he said, to coordinate action with the Soviets in connection with the year of decision and obtained from the Soviet leaders promises of additional types of arms that, it turned out later, they did not fulfill. However, the joint communiqué concluding the visit spoke of the agreement of the parties to seek a peaceful settlement based on

Israeli withdrawal from all the occupied territories and of the Soviet Union's decision to bolster Egypt's military capacity, thus seemingly supporting Sadat's call for war or peace in 1971. Sadat's attempt to put added pressure on the United States boomeranged. One week before Sadat left for Moscow, Secretary of State Rogers had made one more attempt to promote an interim agreement by advancing, in a United Nations speech, a "Six Point Program" linking the interim agreement with a comprehensive settlement, as the Egyptians had been demanding against strong Israeli opposition. The Soviet-Egyptian communiqué, with its implication of Soviet support for an Egyptian war initiative, caused the United States to close ranks with Israel publicly and to promise it additional military support, and took the wind out of Rogers's Six Point Program. As the year drew to a close and the diplomatic process remained completely stymied but Sadat did not go to war, his year of decision appeared to all to be a bluff and he suffered a grievous loss of face and credibility.

Sadat tried to recover by verbally attacking the United States, speaking of war as inevitable, and planning another trip to Moscow for February 1, 1972, ostensibly as part of the war preparations. Faisal, worried that the developing confrontation between Sadat and the United States would rebound with damage to Saudi-Egyptian relations, made an extraordinary gesture to retain Sadat's good will. On the eve of Sadat's departure to Moscow, he offered to make him a present of twenty Lightning fighter-bombers that the Kingdom had recently acquired from Britain.[20] Sadat responded with a noble gesture of his own: he let the Saudi defense minister know through his Egyptian counterpart that the Egyptian army command had been instructed to take orders from King Faisal should an emergency arise while Sadat was in Moscow.[21] Faisal's offer was accepted but never consummated, and Sadat's instruction was purely symbolic to begin with, but the exchange of gestures helped reassure Faisal and sustain the Saudi-Egyptian relationship.

Faisal's cultivation of the connection with Sadat was finally vindicated when, on July 8, 1972, Sadat suddenly ordered the Soviet advisers and military personnel — by then numbering 21,000[22] — to leave the country within ten days. Despite the Soviet-Egyptian treaty and all the exchanges of visits and joint communiqués, Sadat's relationship with the Soviets had been caught from the outset in a web of contradictions and mutual suspicion. Basically, the Soviets had had several indications, including the leaked message conveyed by Adham to the United States, that Sadat would want to get rid of them if he could obtain even the beginnings of a political settlement. They also knew that, failing a settlement, he would want to embroil them in war to advance his interests even if this should bring them into a dangerous confrontation with the United States. The first problem required them to obstruct the possibility of an American-sponsored settlement, among other things by underscoring their own close involvement with Egypt; whereas the latter problem required them to withhold from Sadat such arms as would encourage him to venture war. From Sadat's point of view this meant that, short of a peace arranged by them — which they were in no position to deliver — the Soviets were interested in perpetuating the state of neither-war-nor-peace that he could not abide. Consequently, after failing to persuade the Soviets to provide him with the arms he thought he needed — or, more accurately, after extracting several times promises of such arms that they subsequently failed to fulfill — he decided to break with them, and thus at least to remove the handicap they placed on his dealings with the Americans. The breaking point came in the wake of the Soviet-American Moscow summit of May 1972, when, in Sadat's view, the Soviets formally agreed with the United States to freeze the military situation in the Middle East, even though the two superpowers had failed to agree on ways to settle the problem by peaceful means.

The expulsion of the Soviets brought immense relief to the Saudis and opened the way for a solid strategic alliance between Saudi Arabia and Egypt. There were still problems to be overcome before that alliance could become a reality, but with Faisal exercising characteristic patience and flexibility in his dealings with the Egyptian leader, they were. One of these problems related to a sequel of Sadat's anti-Soviet action. In what seemed to be a paradox, the Soviets, after a period of sulking, showed greater willingness to provide Egypt with arms, which might have averted their expulsion had they demonstrated it before. In October 1972 they promised to renew arms shipments, and in March 1973 they concluded the biggest arms transaction they had ever signed with that country and delivered "promptly and in record time."[23] Faisal, far from being disturbed that this development might portend the return of the Soviets, actually provided money to help finance the big arms transaction.[24] He did so on the strength of Sadat's assurances that he intended to keep the Soviets out, and perhaps because he realized himself that the Soviets' greater willingness to provide arms stemmed precisely from their recognition that they were out and therefore were unlikely to be implicated against their will in case of war.

The other problem had to do with Libyan-Egyptian relations. Right after Sadat's announcement of the expulsion of the Soviets, in July 1972, Colonel Qaddafi proposed to Sadat an immediate merger of Libya and Egypt with a view to reviving the movement for Arab unity and building a strong Arab entity capable of confronting Israel independently of any superpower. Sadat could not reject Qaddafi's offer or object to his logic, especially since the Libyan leader readily provided vast financial assistance that Egypt desperately needed.[25] Consequently, on August 1, 1972,

Sadat signed an agreement providing for an integral union between Libya and Egypt, to take place after one year of preparation. Faisal, who had argued in Rabat in December 1969 that the Arabs should pool all their resources for the struggle against Israel after detaching themselves from any superpower,[26] could not very well object to the Libyan-Egyptian project; but neither could he agree to Qaddafi's sponsorship of a revived drive for Arab unity, especially because Qaddafi carried his drive to Faisal's own backyard by promoting, in October–November 1972, the union agreement between the Yemen Arab Republic and the Popular Democratic Republic of Yemen.[27] Faisal therefore competed with Qaddafi's financial lure by providing financial assistance to Egypt, argued to Sadat the importance of enlisting American support for an agreeable settlement and the reasonable chances of gaining such support after Sadat got rid of the Soviets, and waited for Qaddafi to overplay his hand. The policy worked, and in due course Sadat backed out of the projected union before the date set for its consummation.

Thus by the latter part of 1973 Saudi Arabia had managed to survive the formidable array of problems that had converged on it in the years 1968–1971, thanks partly to the steady and subtle leadership of Faisal, partly to good fortune. It is perhaps an indication of the extent of the role played by fortune that, probably contrary to his preferred priorities, Faisal fared considerably better in the wider Arab arena than in the Arabian Peninsula itself. In the south, his campaign against PDRY continued to meet with failure and frustration, and his effort to enlist a united YAR against it had backfired and ignited the agreement on Yemeni unity. However, he was able to use his continued control over the tribes of the northern YAR to check the union project and to keep open the possibility of promoting an amenable regime in San'a that would provide a solid buffer against PDRY.

In the southeast, a more effective and friendly ruler had taken charge in Oman, and the Dhofar rebels had passed the peak of their power and were thrown on the defensive. Sultan Qabus, however, continued to tend to disregard Saudi wishes and go his own way, and the presence of Iranian forces in his territory was a potential threat to vital Saudi interests even as it underscored the Saudis' inability to provide alternative military assistance.

In the Gulf, the crisis of the British withdrawal had been weathered without too much trouble, but the newly independent entities that emerged, particularly the United Arab Emirates, were fragile, and their weakness could spell difficulties for Saudi Arabia in the future. The understanding with Iran protected the vital Saudi interest in Gulf navigation for the time being and was at least tacitly endorsed by Arab countries important for Saudi Arabia. However, it also intensified the hostility of

Iraq and provoked it to deepen its connection with the Soviet Union and to put military pressure on Kuwait, which forced the Saudis to deploy their forces against Iraq to protect their buffer and ally.

In the wider Arab arena, the gains for Saudi security were much more clear-cut and dramatic. The war of attrition and its nefarious implications had ended. The threat of a PLO takeover of Jordan had been decisively quashed, and that country had reverted to King Hussein's firm control and to its crucial role as a buffer and a shield for Saudi Arabia. Syria's hostile regime had been replaced by the more cooperative one of Hafez al-Assad. An entire troublesome era for the Saudis had come to an end with the death of Nasser, and a new, more hopeful one had begun with the accession of Sadat. A friendly dialogue, initiated at the outset of Sadat's rule, had helped prevent serious misunderstandings and sustained the promise of better relations until Sadat's expulsion of the Soviets created the foundations for a broad-based strategic alliance. The end of the war of attrition and the subsidence of threats from several outside sources had in turn eased the atmosphere at home and provided a chance for the first five-year plan to begin to take effect. Most important, these developments allowed the Saudi regime to cultivate its American connection openly to strengthen the Kingdom's security without fear of condemnation from Cairo and Damascus, now that these had come to see the usefulness of that connection. That gain, however, also entailed an obligation for the Saudis to exert themselves to alter American policy in favor of the Arab cause in the Arab-Israeli conflict, which became particularly relevant after Sadat expelled the Soviets from Egypt. The obligation was to have momentous consequences when the Saudis acted on it in the context of the Yom Kippur War.

6

The October War
and Its Aftermath,
1973–1975

Faisal's success by 1971 or 1972 in managing the problems that had arisen
over the previous four years or so depended ultimately on his ability to
cultivate reasonably good relations with Cairo and Damascus as well as
with Washington. The relationship with Egypt and Syria not only ob-
viated direct threats from them but also made it easier for Faisal, absent
their interference, to cope with the problems of south Arabia. The American connection was essential for his economic and military development
programs and for ultimate insurance against more powerful neighbors
in the Gulf such as Iran and Iraq. However, Faisal's ability to sustain both
sets of relations was jeopardized by the persisting stalemate in the Arab-
Israeli conflict, which the United States tolerated or upheld and which
Egypt and Syria could not abide. The United States hoped that the pressure of the stalemate would eventually facilitate a settlement, whereas
Faisal feared that it might sooner stimulate radicalism or explode in war.

When the explosion of the 1973 war did occur, Faisal found himself
trapped. The initial Arab military successes gave him a reprieve from
decision, but as the tide of battle turned he felt compelled to line up with
Egypt and Syria and, along with other Arab countries, to impose an oil
embargo on the United States coupled with general cuts in production.
The oil sanctions had no effect on America's position with respect to the
war itself, but they had an important influence on its postwar diplomacy.
Far more important, the sanctions triggered a chain of unanticipated
events that led to the quadrupling of oil prices, and this in turn caused an
upheaval in the world economy, and a revolutionary transformation of

Saudi Arabia's domestic, regional, and international political-strategic position.

Because of the epochal consequences of the embargo, the background and specific reasons that led Saudi Arabia to resort to it and the circumstances that accounted for its effectiveness warrant detailed examination. This chapter describes political developments before and during the embargo period and analyzes the unintended consequences of the embargo on Saudi Arabia's position — indeed, on its destiny.

The Embargo

Background to the Decision

Immediately after Sadat ordered the Soviets out of Egypt, the Saudis urged the United States to undertake a new initiative to advance a settlement acceptable to the Arabs, now that the Americans' previous excuse or reason for high-level support for Israel — putting pressure on the Soviets — had become almost invalid. The United States took some time before responding. First it awaited the outcome of Israeli deliberations on a proposal by Defense Minister Moshe Dayan for a limited agreement on Sinai. After the deliberations on this and other proposals ended inconclusively in September 1972, the imminence of the presidential elections precluded any new serious American move. Finally, in February 1973 secret talks began between President Nixon's national security adviser, Henry Kissinger, and his Egyptian counterpart, Hafez Ismail, but they quickly revealed that the United States, far from proving more accommodating to the Arab position after the expulsion of the Soviets from Egypt, had in fact reneged on its previous proposals as expressed in the Rogers Plan. Washington now argued that a return to the 1967 borders was not possible, and that Egypt with American assistance should enter into a secret dialogue with Israel to find some formula for reconciling the Arabs' concern for sovereignty with Israel's concern for security. One such formula might be a settlement by stages over a number of years to allow the parties to overcome gradually their mutual hostility and mistrust.

The change in the American position reflected the triumph of Kissinger's views over those of Secretary of State Rogers in an intra-administration debate going back at least to the latter part of 1969. Rogers had advocated the need for the United States to maintain a certain distance from Israel in order to protect friendly Arab regimes, such as Saudi Arabia's and Jordan's, against their radical Arab critics and to avoid driving Egypt and Syria into greater dependence on the Soviet Union. Kissinger, on the other hand, had argued that any attempt by the United

States to distance itself from Israel was likely to encourage the Soviets to increase their commitment to the Arab side and cause the latter to persist in their intransigence. American policy should, on the contrary, provide Israel with all the military and political support necessary to enable it to foil Soviet pressure, cause the Arabs to despair of the effectiveness of Soviet support, and compel them to turn to the United States and moderate their position to a point that would make a settlement feasible.

Until the August 1970 cease-fire that concluded the war of attrition, President Nixon was inclined to let his secretary of state have his way, albeit with increasing reluctance. After the Jordanian crisis that year, which Kissinger successfully managed in accordance with his own conception, the president tended increasingly to espouse the views of his national security adviser. In that context, Sadat's expulsion of the Soviets, far from suggesting any need for the United States to change course, appeared only to confirm the effectiveness of the one it was following. Unequivocal support for Israel, having driven a wedge between the Soviet Union and Egypt, was now expected to lead Egypt, deprived of any war option, to moderate its position so as to facilitate a settlement. In the meantime the Israeli deterrent would also help protect friendly Arab regimes by preserving the status quo.[1]

Faisal's perspective on the situation was quite different. In the first place, he had stood warrant to Sadat for the earlier American position to the effect that if Egypt loosened its connection with the Soviets the United States would be more willing to press Israel for a favorable settlement. Now, as it became apparent that the United States was not about to deliver on its presumed promise after Sadat had altogether expelled the Soviets, Faisal felt personally deceived and embarrassed before Sadat.

Second, however much Saudi Arabia may have benefited from the consequences of Israel's military superiority—the defeat of Nasser in 1967, helping to save Hussein's regime in September 1970, and now contributing to the strains that led to the expulsion of the Soviets from Egypt—Faisal was naturally loath to admit that, much less to accept the idea of a virtual *pax Israeliana*.

Third, to compensate for their loss in Egypt and prevent a repetition elsewhere, the Soviets became much more solicitous toward Syria, Iraq, and PDRY, entrenching themselves more deeply in those countries and making their regimes potentially even more radical. This may not have made much difference in the broad American strategic view, but in the case of Saudi Arabia the change could both defeat its effort to appease Syria and impel the others to cause a great deal more trouble.

Finally, Faisal had intuitively a keener appreciation than the Americans of the psychological, domestic, and inter-Arab constraints on Sadat's ability to make concessions. Faisal feared that Sadat, sooner than yield as the

United States expected him to, might revert to the Soviet connection in circumstances that would give the Soviets greater leverage on Egypt than ever before. The fact that Sadat did not repudiate the Soviet-Egyptian treaty, concluded an arms deal with the Soviets in October 1972, invited Leonid Brezhnev to visit Egypt and sent Hafez Ismail to Moscow before sending him on his February 1973 mission to Washington was ominous in that connection. Alternatively, if Sadat failed to restore the Soviet connection and at the same time could not offer his hard-pressed countrymen the prospects of either an honorable peace or a promising war, he might himself be overthrown and replaced by a leadership of unpredictable orientation or even by chaos.

As Faisal became gradually aware of the American perception, he tried to bring about its modification by placing increasing Saudi weight behind Sadat and Syria's Assad. After offering Sadat the symbolic present of the twenty Lightnings and helping to finance an arms transaction with the Soviets, Faisal began to drop hints about tying Saudi oil policy to American Middle East policy. In April 1973 he sent oil minister Zaki Yamani to Washington with a message that Saudi Arabia would not significantly expand its oil production as it was being asked to do unless the United States changed its pro-Israeli stance.[2] Earlier in the same month he announced a substantial grant to Syria "to help it in the battle against Israel."[3] In May Faisal and Sadat made a set of diplomatic and military moves designed to impel the United States to change course that foreshadowed subsequent action. While Egypt initiated a UN Security Council debate to give Resolution 242 a more specific content in line with its own position, Egyptian forces deployed threateningly on the Suez Canal front line. At the same time Faisal summoned Aramco's parent companies, warned them that American interests in the Middle East "will be lost" unless the United States gave more support to the Arab cause, and urged them to impress that view on the American government and public.[4] As if to underscore Faisal's warning, the previous month armed men had attacked the Tapline terminal at Sidon, destroyed one storage tank, and damaged two others.[5] On July 6 Faisal told the *Christian Science Monitor* that Saudi Arabia would like to continue friendly ties with the United States but that this would be difficult unless the latter adopted a "more even-handed policy in the region."[6]

The United States remained unimpressed; indeed, in July 1973 it was the only country to veto a Security Council resolution that merely deplored Israel's continuing occupation of territories seized in 1967.

Washington's unresponsiveness was partly due to the fact that even as the Saudis were venting their unhappiness with mild threats, they were negotiating and concluding deals with the United States for arming and training their National Guard and for supplying their air force and navy with modern weapons. In March 1973, for instance, the United States signed a seven-year agreement for the modernization of the National Guard. On May 26 Pentagon officials reported that negotiations were under way to sell the Saudis $500 million worth of arms.[7] On the same day the *Washington Post* reported that Saudi Arabia was negotiating the purchase of nineteen warships from the United States.[8] On May 31 the State Department announced that the United States was willing to sell Saudi Arabia a limited number of F-4 Phantom jets. All this made the Saudi complaints and threats look like a cover for the deals, and at any rate discounted their significance considerably.

More important, perhaps, Kissinger and Nixon had reason to believe in the summer of 1973 that their strategy for the Middle East was working well and that it was only a matter of time before it would yield its full fruits. In June the second Soviet-American summit took place in Washington, in which discussion of the Middle East occupied an important place. Although the conferees failed to agree on ways and means to advance a settlement, they concurred on the need to avoid a superpower conflict in the area. In Kissinger's and Nixon's view, this agreement removed the principal danger of the policy of maintaining the status quo until the Arab side moderated its position and, by the same token, intensified the Arab motivation to do so.

In fact the solidification of the status quo produced quite opposite effects. Back in October 1972 Sadat had ordered his newly appointed minister of war to prepare plans for a limited war designed to seize and hold a bridgehead on the east bank of the Suez Canal and thus break the diplomatic stalemate and force negotiations under more favorable conditions.[9] Sadat realized that this strategy involved enormous risks — its military component depended entirely on achieving strategic surprise, and failure could involve the destruction of the Egyptian armed forces; but from his point of view there was no less danger either in indefinite prolongation of the state of neither-war-nor-peace or in making concessions to Israel without a fight. So, after failing to induce or press the United States to use its leverage on Israel to advance an acceptable settlement, he decided to take his chances on the war option and found a willing ally in Syria. As part of his preparations, he visited King Faisal in Riyadh in August 1973 to inform him of his intent and to enlist his support and cooperation. Faisal went along with Sadat's decision, agreed to contribute $500 million to Egypt's war chest, and promised to weigh in by using the oil weapon. According to Heikal, who reported that promise, Faisal added: "But give us time. We don't want to use oil as a weapon in a battle which goes on for two or three days and then stops. We want to see a battle which goes on for [a] long enough time for world opinion to be mobilized."[10]

Timing of Application

On October 6, 1973, Egypt and Syria launched simultaneous surprise attacks, beginning what came to be known as the Yom Kippur War. Two weeks later, on October 20, the Saudis declared an embargo on all oil shipments to the United States and the Netherlands and, with other Arab oil producers, announced drastic cuts in oil production and in the amounts to be made available to other consumer countries. Unlike previous occasions when the Saudis had used the oil weapon, in 1956 and 1967, this time their action had a devastating immediate effect and momentous long-term consequences for the world, the Middle East, and Saudi Arabia itself. Of the multitude of commentaries that have since been written on the subject, most have viewed the Saudis' decision as being simply a fulfillment of their promise to Sadat or of their warnings to the United States before and after that promise. Virtually all accounts have related the timing of the Saudi decision to President Nixon's request to Congress on October 19, 1973, for a $2.2 billion appropriation for military assistance to Israel. A careful review of the relevant facts, however, suggests a different interpretation, which is much more revealing of Saudi diplomatic-strategic thinking and behavior.

The key to understanding the Saudis' fateful October 20 decision is the question: What triggered it just then? Nixon's request to Congress by itself cannot suffice as an explanation when viewed against the background of previous pertinent events. On October 11, for instance, King Faisal had written to the president asking the United States to stop assisting Israel in the war, in the wake of press reports that it was doing so. Nixon's reply is not known, but three days later the United States launched a massive airlift of military supplies to Israel. Two days afterward, on the sixteenth, Faisal had written to Secretary of State Kissinger saying that he was "pained" by the American action and urging the United States to stop sending arms to Israel and instead to call upon it to withdraw. The only hint of a threat was a statement that, otherwise, Saudi-American relations could become "lukewarm."[11] What, then, was the reason for the Saudis' acting when they did?

On October 9, four days into the war, Kuwait had called for a conference of the Arab oil-producing countries in order to determine how oil could best be employed in the service of the "Arabs' war of liberation." At the time Faisal held his own private consultations on the subject with an Egyptian delegation, which then left him to consult with leaders of other oil-producing countries;[12] thus the conference did not begin until October 17, three days after the start of the American airlift. The conferees included representatives of Saudi Arabia, Kuwait, Bahrain, Qatar, Abu Dhabi, Iraq, Syria, Egypt, Libya, and Algeria. All except Iraq agreed to reduce their oil production by at least 5 percent from their average September output and to make further cuts of 5 percent every month thereafter until a total evacuation of Israeli forces from Arab territories should be completed and the legitimate rights of the Palestinians restored, or until further reduction would hurt the individual producing country. States that supported the Arabs actively or took significant steps to pressure Israel to withdraw would be exempted from the cuts and would receive their full supply based on September imports. A proposal to impose a total embargo on the United States was set aside because of Saudi opposition. The purpose of the decision was clearly to recruit support for the Arab cause over the long run rather than to target the United States immediately.

On the same day as the Kuwait conference, a delegation of Arab foreign ministers, led by Saudi Arabia's Omar Saqqaf and including the foreign ministers of Algeria, Morocco, and Kuwait, met with President Nixon and Secretary of State Kissinger to discuss the situation. The Arab ministers complained that as soon as Egypt and Syria had shown signs of winning, the Americans had started an airlift to Israel. Nixon replied that the United States had taken this step only after the Russians had started an airlift of their own. The Saudi minister expressed the Arabs' concern to achieve a prompt settlement of the conflict based on complete Israeli withdrawal and restoration of Palestinian rights in accordance with Resolution 242. Kissinger explained that American policy was first to end the current fighting and prevent its spread, and then to engage in a diplomatic effort for a just and lasting peace. Saqqaf argued to Nixon the United States' responsibility to force Israel to withdraw to the 1967 lines; Nixon answered by pledging to work for "the implementation of Resolution 242" but emphasized that he could not promise that Israel would withdraw to the 1967 lines. The president and the secretary of state told their interlocutors that the Arabs had made their point and that the United States was not seeking to defeat them, but otherwise yielded nothing either on continuing military assistance to Israel or on the terms for a settlement. Indeed, the tenor of the entire discussion was one of apparent pleading by the Arab representatives for consideration from the party that held all the cards in its hands, without a hint of a threat except in the composition of the delegation. According to the Tunisian foreign minister, its members had been deliberately chosen so that "the smell of oil should be present without being overpowering."[13] At the end of the meeting Omar Saqqaf told the press, gathered in the Rose Garden, that the talks had been "friendly and constructive."[14]

This sequence of events does not suggest the image invoked by most accounts, of a strained camel whose back is broken by the added straw of the October 19 request for aid. Why, then, did the Saudis react strongly the next day? The answer lies in the perceived change in the military situation, its interpretation by the Saudis, and its implications for them.

Unlike the case of the 1967 war, the Saudis this time were given a chance to keep close track of the course of the hostilities. On October 8, 1973, when the Egyptian delegation went to Riyadh to discuss the oil question, Sadat had sent along a senior officer to brief Faisal personally about the fighting. Subsequently a special line of communication was set up between the presidential palace in Cairo and the royal palace in Riyadh and was used freely by Saudi liaison officers in Cairo.[15] Saudi princes were permitted access to the military operations room of the Egyptian high command.[16] As long as the war appeared to be going well for the Arabs, both Faisal and Sadat sought to press the United States to recognize the need to advance an acceptable settlement, while being careful to avoid provoking Washington to commit itself to seeking an Israeli military victory. In that context, the American airlift to Israel underscored the danger that Faisal and Sadat feared, but because the military situation continued to appear favorable from the Egyptian vantage point, they reacted to it cautiously in the manner described and were satisfied with the assurances offered by Nixon and Kissinger on October 17. By October 20, however, the military situation had changed drastically, and that put a totally different complexion on the aid request to Israel as well as on all previous and anticipated American actions.

The tide of the war had actually turned against the Arabs and in favor of Israel well before October 20, but the Egyptian high command had failed to recognize the fact. On October 16 Israeli Prime Minister Golda Meir had said in a speech in the Knesset that Israeli forces were fighting on the west side of the Suez Canal, but President Sadat, after checking with his military chiefs, had dismissed the statement as mere propaganda. On the same day Soviet Prime Minister Kosygin had arrived in Cairo and for the next two days had tried in vain to convince Sadat that the war was turning against the Arabs and that it was time for them to seek a cease-fire on the best obtainable terms. It was not until he produced satellite photographs of a major Israeli armored force operating west of the Suez Canal, in the rear of the Egyptian forces, that Kosygin began to convince Sadat.[17]

Kosygin left Cairo on the morning of October 19 with a mandate from Sadat to seek a cease-fire, but by that evening the Israelis, according to Egyptian estimates cited by Heikal, had a formidable force west of the canal, including four tank brigades, one mechanized brigade, and one parachute brigade.[18] Later that night or in the first hours of the twentieth, according to Heikal's account, Sadat was called by the Egyptian high command to arbitrate between the commander-in-chief, General Shazly, who feared the imminent destruction of the Egyptian forces east of the canal and urged their retreat, and the minister of war, General Ismail, who thought the Egyptian forces would be better off remaining in place while a cease-fire was sought. Sadat decided in favor of Ismail, dismissed Shazly, and thereafter wrote to Syria's President Assad to inform him of his decision to accept a cease-fire in place. In his message to Assad, Sadat said, significantly, that for the last ten days he had been fighting the United States, through the arms it was sending, as well as Israel, and that "to put it bluntly" he could not go on doing this "or accept the responsibility before history for the destruction of our armed forces for a second time."[19]

The sudden drastic change in the perception of the military situation put an entirely different light on the whole of Washington's policy. Even apart from the president's October 19 request for aid, previous measures of assistance to Israel came to be viewed as intolerable when assessed in terms of the situation they had helped produce. Moreover, in the same retrospective reassessment of cause from effect, Nixon and Kissinger appeared strongly suspect of having deceived the Arabs all along when they said that they were striving to end the fighting and to prevent its spread in preparation for negotiations. At the very least the United States seemed to be deceiving itself about its control over the situation, or else it was being deceived by Israel; in any case its policy was wreaking disaster upon the Arabs. From that perspective, the aid request only added insult to injury. It provided a convenient reason for the Saudi sanctions — the communiqué announcing the embargo against the United States referred to "the increase in American military aid to Israel"[20] — and perhaps a cover for the failure to act sooner; but the sanctions would probably have been imposed even without the aid request because of the changed perception of the military situation.

This assessment is supported by reference to the record of 1967. The disaster suffered by the Arab armies at that time had led Faisal to declare an embargo against the United States and Britain even though he had been fighting Nasser by proxy in Yemen for years and the United States had played no visible role in the war itself. He had done so simply to appease aroused Arab opinion and to ward off trouble at home. In 1973, in contrast, Faisal had been an associate in Sadat's strategy and plans and had promised him to use the oil weapon under certain circumstances; and the United States had played a conspicuous role in support of Israel almost from the outset of the war, at least in the eyes of the Arab public. In these circumstances, there was no way that Faisal could have refrained from applying sanctions against the United States regardless of the aid request, once the impending military disaster occurred, or once word of the perilous state of the Arab armies spread, which could be a matter of only a few days at most. By resorting to sanctions against the United States when he did, Faisal made a last-minute attempt to affect American policy even while doing what he was convinced could not be avoided in any case.[21]

In one of the many ironies of the 1973 drama, word of the Saudi declaration of embargo reached Secretary Kissinger on the plane that was carrying him to Moscow at Brezhnev's urgent invitation to arrange for a cease-fire. Kissinger had gone on that trip, and the next day agreed with Brezhnev on a cease-fire resolution, because of strategic considerations that had nothing to do with the Saudi embargo. From the outset of the war he had wanted to bring about its termination at a time when Israel enjoyed a military advantage and therefore retained bargaining cards that the United States could use in advancing a settlement, but before Israel could achieve a total victory, which might cause it to stiffen its terms and cause upheavals in Arab countries. That moment appeared to Kissinger to have struck two days after the Soviets, who had been taking their time in discussing the terms for a cease-fire, suddenly called urgently for an end to the fighting. Kissinger was thus essentially sincere when he told Arab interlocutors on the seventeenth that he sought to end the fighting without having the Arabs suffer defeat; it was his timing that did not correspond with that of the Arabs and led the Saudis to feel he had deceived them. Conceivably the Saudis might never have imposed an embargo had Kissinger informed them of his plan to go to Moscow to seek a cease-fire, or had the Saudis held back for another two days. In that case, the most devastating consequences of the embargo decision might have been avoided.

Immediate Effects

Materially, the direct effect of the Arab embargo, production cutbacks, and supply sanctions was not all that serious. World crude oil production declined during the six months of the embargo by only 4.5 percent — from a high of 59.2 mbd in September to an average of 56.9 mbd in October 1973 through March 1974. At the lowest point, in November 1973, world crude production fell to 54.8 mbd, less than 7.5 percent from the September high.[22] The cutback in Arab production had been mitigated by an increase in non-Arab production. In the period January–April 1974, when the cuts in production took full effect after all oil in transit at the beginning of the embargo had been cleared, consumption of petroleum products in the major consuming nations declined by 6.3 percent from the same four months of the previous year. During the embargo Canada and Japan actually experienced a rise in consumption of 6.5 and 1 percent respectively, while the United States and Western Europe experienced a 6.9 and 11 percent decline respectively.[23] These figures do not take into account the increase in consumption that would have occurred if supplies had been as available as before; but neither do they take into account the drop in consumption that would have taken place naturally, quite apart from availability of supply, as a result of the jump in price from $2.74 or less per barrel in the period before April 1, 1973, to $11.65 in the period after January 1, 1974.[24]

The real effects of the embargo were the vast and lasting political and economic changes that occurred as a result of panic first among the European nations and then in the United States. Underlying that panic was a set of crucial developments. For some years before the embargo, an unprecedented simultaneous economic boom in the United States, Western Europe, and Japan had accelerated the rise in demand for oil and created a taut market. This trend had facilitated a shift in power away from the international oil companies in favor of OPEC and led to a considerable increase in prices. Whereas the price of oil throughout the 1960s had remained stable at $1.80 or less per barrel, between December 1970 and August 1973 it had risen by 70 percent, to $3.07 per barrel.[25]

During approximately the same period there had been a major shift in the sources of world crude production in favor of Middle East producers generally and Saudi Arabia in particular. In 1969 total world crude production had amounted to 43.6 mbd. The Western Hemisphere accounted for 39.7 percent of this, with 17.3 mbd; the Middle East for 28.4 percent, with 12.4 mbd; and Saudi Arabia for 7.3 percent, with 3.2 mbd. In 1973 total world production had increased by 32.6 percent, to 57.8 mbd. The Western Hemisphere's share had dropped to 31.8 percent, with 18.4 mbd; the Middle East's had risen to 36.5 percent, with 21.1 mbd; and Saudi Arabia's to 13.1 percent, with 7.6 mbd.[26]

The increased demand for oil and the shift in the sources of supply led to greater European dependence on Middle East oil. In 1966, the year before the Six Day War, oil accounted for 57 percent of the energy needs of the OECD nations, of which 71 percent was imported from the Middle East and North Africa and 12.9 percent from Saudi Arabia specifically. By 1972, the year before the 1973 war, oil had come to account for 68.8 percent of Europe's energy needs, 76 percent of which came from the Middle East and North Africa, 21.6 percent from Saudi Arabia specifically.

The increased European dependence on Middle East oil was made more troublesome by the disappearance of the American production "cushion." In 1966 the United States already imported 22 percent of its oil (oil accounted for 43.8 of its total energy requirements), but only 15.6 percent of its imports — 3 percent of its oil needs — came from the Middle East and North Africa and a very small part from Saudi Arabia — 5.3 percent of imports, 1 percent of needs. More important, the United States had a "spare" production capacity, which it had used in the 1967 emergency to fill the shortfall in Europe's needs caused by the Six Day War —

an average of 260,000 barrels per day between June and December of that year. In 1972 that spare capacity no longer existed, and the United States itself was on the eve of a major increase in its dependence on imported oil, particularly from the Middle East and Saudi Arabia. In 1972 the United States imported 27.8 percent of its oil needs and 34.9 percent the following year, compared with 22 percent in 1966. Imports from the Middle East and North Africa were 13.9 percent in 1972, less than the 15.6 percent of 1966, but in 1973 they shot up to 22.1 percent. Saudi Arabia's share of America's imports declined from 5.3 percent in 1966 to 3.8 percent in 1972, but shot up in 1973 to 8.1 percent.

In these circumstances the European governments were naturally sensitive to the dangers that an Arab-Israeli explosion presented to their oil supply. For this reason, several of them had tried after the 1967 war to explore ways in which, either individually or collectively as the European Community, they might help advance a settlement of the conflict that would protect them against those dangers. However, as these efforts bore no fruit and as the conflict seemed to subside into an indefinite stalemate, the European governments gradually fell back on an approach that tried to secure their interest by insulating themselves from the conflict: they gave symbolic or nominal support to the Arab side but left the management of the conflict entirely to the superpowers. Implicit in that approach were two assumptions. One was that the superpowers themselves would be able to stay out of a war, in accordance with the spirit of detente and the specific understandings to that effect reached in the Moscow and Washington summits in 1972 and 1973. The other was that, in a crunch, the American special relationship with Saudi Arabia, the pivotal producer, and the latter's own dominant influence with the UAE, Qatar, and Kuwait would somehow prevent unbearable damage to Europe's interests.

The first assumption was shattered when, a few days after the outbreak of the Yom Kippur War, the Soviet Union and then the United States became involved on opposite sides with massive resupply operations. The worried European governments reacted by trying in varying degrees and at different paces to distance themselves from the United States, some going so far as to deny it the use of their air space and facilities in connection with the airlift and others even to oppose it publicly. Most of them, however, continued to hold on to the second assumption, concerning the American-Saudi connection, as the Arab oil producers talked about sanctions but collectively held their hand and, when they did act on October 17, adopted measures that were relatively mild, slow in their anticipated effect, and containing ample escape provisions. Indeed, press reports at the time described European governments as being more worried about the 17 percent price increase adopted by the Gulf producers the previous day than by the decisions on cuts in production. In that context the Saudi decision of October 20 came as a tremendous shock. With Saudi Arabia openly confronting the United States, indeed singling it out as the target of a total embargo, the dams appeared to have been broken and there was no telling how far and wide the disaster might reach. That was when panic set in.

Two sets of developments, one political and one economic, unfolded over the next two months. In the political sphere the Europeans openly split from the United States and desperately tried to appease the Arab producers by subscribing to political formulas desired by them. The split became manifest after Secretary Kissinger had President Nixon, who was preoccupied with the last stages of the Watergate affair, proclaim a strategic alert on October 25 in order to deter a possible Soviet military intervention on the Egyptian-Israeli front. The Europeans took strong exception to Washington's taking such grave action affecting world peace and their own destiny without consultation with them, while President Nixon defended his decision as a well-calculated move to secure Europe's oil supply, without which the Europeans "would have frozen to death" in the coming winter.[27]

Subsequently the United States and the Europeans went their own ways demonstratively. Secretary Kissinger sought to persuade the Arabs to relent by continuing the strategy of inducement and pressure he had pursued so far, but with a change in the mix. He began his famous shuttle diplomacy to achieve a separation-of-forces agreement that saved the beleaguered Egyptian Third Army and promoted a peace conference at Geneva, making stopovers in Riyadh to report to Faisal on progress. At the same time he continued the flow of arms to Israel and dropped occasional reminders, as on November 21, that the United States might consider countermeasures if the embargo continued "unreasonably and indefinitely." The Europeans, for their part, felt they had no choice but to comply with Arab political demands. On November 6 the ministerial council of the EEC issued a statement formulated after an all-night session, reaffirming Resolution 242 with a modification in favor of Palestinian national rights as the Arabs were demanding, and urging the belligerents to withdraw to the October 22 cease-fire lines, a disputed issue that Kissinger was trying to resolve in a different way. The Arab producers showed their appreciation of the statement by deciding on November 18 not to implement the slated 5 percent cut for the month of December for any of the EEC countries except the Netherlands. But on December 14 a delegation of Arab ministers virtually broke into an EEC meeting in Copenhagen to tell the assembled heads of government and foreign ministers that they must do more to influence a political settlement favorable to the Arabs before the embargo, which by then included the Netherlands and Portugal as well as the United States, would be lifted.[28] Two days later the EEC issued another statement favorable to the Arabs, "balanced" by a decision reached after long and bitter argument to face the oil crisis together.[29]

In the economic sphere, the Europeans' initial reaction was simply *sauve qui peut*, particularly after the embargo was extended to the Netherlands on October 30 because of its alleged pro-Israeli stance. Europe had fuel reserves of thirty days, and the OECD had contingency plans for sharing supplies in an emergency, but calls to apply those plans were resolutely turned down for fear of antagonizing the Arab producers, who had warned against any consumers' combination. Countries that thought themselves to be in a "privileged" position according to the Arabs' classification, such as Britain and France, insisted on getting their full September supply quota and clashed with the international oil companies, and indirectly with the United States and their fellow Europeans, because the companies diverted non-Arab oil to countries in the penalized class. Several governments pleaded with the Arab producers to continue shipping oil to them through the Rotterdam distribution point by pledging to cooperate in denying the Netherlands any supplies, while the latter threatened to cut off its substantial gas supply to other European countries unless they helped in relieving its crisis. Importers and refiners in Europe and the United States scrambled for every barrel of non-Arab oil and drove prices in the spot market to astronomical heights. Uncertainty and uncoordinated conservation efforts produced gas lines and industrial cutdowns in Europe, the United States, and Japan and contributed everywhere to a spreading sense of chaos and doom. By the time the EEC countries mustered courage to decide to face the oil crisis together, in the Copenhagen meeting on December 16, the most severe damage had already been done.

On December 22–24, 1973, the Persian Gulf producers, including Iran, met in Tehran to discuss oil prices. On October 19 Libya had unilaterally raised the price of its oil from $4.90 to $8.92 per barrel,[30] but other producers had continued to meet contracts on the basis of OPEC's price. Just before the Tehran meeting, however, Iran held an oil auction that brought in $17.34 per barrel, and the shah proposed that that price be adopted as a standard. The Saudi representative argued for a considerably lower price. Eventually the participants decided on a price of $11.65 per barrel effective January 1, 1974, which was promptly adopted by OPEC as a whole. Immediately after the Tehran meeting, the Arab oil producers announced a 10 percent increase in production for January, starting a process of deescalation that led to the termination of the embargo against the United States in March 1974. But the unintended consequence of the use of the oil weapon — the fourfold increase in the price of oil since October 1, 1973 — was to persist and give a permanent new dimension to the problem of access to oil.

Termination

Although the Saudis resorted to the oil weapon only reluctantly and late, once they took the decision and observed what they deemed to be its benefits to themselves, their attitude toward its continued use changed markedly. The oil weapon was successful against the United States mainly because the latter's policymakers were already inclined to move in the direction that Saudi Arabia wanted them to for their own broad strategic considerations. Kissinger had sought to bring about a "negotiating situation" and a role for the United States as a peace broker from the outset of the fighting. However, this policy objective did not appear to be such, especially after the start of the airlift to Israel, and did not become evident until after the Saudi embargo decision. Furthermore, despite Kissinger's repeated protests to the contrary, the manner in which he carried out his post-cease-fire diplomacy showed that the Saudi decision and its consequences in Europe did affect the pace of his peace mediation if not its substance. At any rate, as the United States appeared to be moved and Europe seemed to be thoroughly shaken by their action, the Saudis were freed of their initial apprehensions about possible damaging reactions and persisted in the sanctions even while gradually scaling down the objectives they sought from them. The landmarks in that process were as follows.

November 8, 1973: Secretary Kissinger stopped in Riyadh to see King Faisal after arranging an agreement between Egypt and Israel that settled the question of supply to the beleaguered Egyptian Third Army. That accord subsumed the problem of the demarcation of the cease-fire lines under the broader question of a disengagement of forces, which the two parties agreed to negotiate. Kissinger called on Faisal to remove the embargo in order to facilitate America's effort to bring about Israeli withdrawal from Arab lands. Faisal refused, but Kissinger was left with the impression that the embargo might be lifted once the Israelis actually began to withdraw.[31]

November 21, 1973: Kissinger, using the tactic of alternating pressure and inducement, stated that the United States might consider "countermeasures" if the embargo continued "unreasonably and indefinitely." The next day, Petroleum Minister Yamani countered with a statement on Danish television to the effect that if the United States, Europe, or Japan took countermeasures, Saudi Arabia would cut its oil production by 80 percent.[32]

November 26–28, 1973: An Arab summit met in Algiers. Saudi Arabia supported a resolution in favor of continuing use of the oil weapon until Israel withdrew from the occupied Arab territories and the national rights of the Palestinians were restored.[33]

December 9, 1973: Yamani, after a week of talks in the United States, announced that the Arab states had decided to lift the oil embargo "when Israel accepts withdrawal from occupied Arab territory and that acceptance is guaranteed" by the United States. At the outset of his talks in Washington, Senator Fulbright, chairman of the Foreign Relations Committee, had warned that consumers might move militarily against producers to obtain supplies.[34]

December 14, 1973: Kissinger stopped in Riyadh again to inform Faisal about his progress in promoting an Egyptian-Israeli disengagement agreement and in assembling a peace conference at Geneva, and to press for the lifting of the embargo. Faisal reportedly told Kissinger that he first wanted to see the beginning of actual Israeli withdrawal.[35]

December 25, 1973: The Arab oil producers canceled the scheduled 5 percent cutback for January and promised instead a 10 percent increase in production. The previous day, however, the Gulf producers, including Saudi Arabia and Iran, had agreed to set the price of oil at $11.65 per barrel starting January 1.[36]

January 3, 1974: Secretary Kissinger said that President Nixon would make a personal effort to persuade major oil consumers and producers to band together to ameliorate the oil shortage. (The producers had earlier warned against any consumers' combination.)[37]

January 17, 1974: Egypt and Israel signed a disengagement agreement mediated by Kissinger. The agreement envisaged the first Israeli withdrawal from territories occupied in 1967 and established a step-by-step approach to peace.

January 22, 1974: Kissinger declared that he expected an early end of the Arab oil embargo as a result of his role in bringing about the agreement between Egypt and Israel. He let stand a statement by Secretary of Defense James Schlesinger that public opinion might demand a show of force against the Arabs if the embargo went too far.[38]

January 30, 1974: President Nixon declared in his State of the Union message that the Arab oil-producing nations would hold an urgent meeting to discuss lifting the embargo against the United States following "Secretary Kissinger's role in bringing about the troop separation agreement between Egypt and Israel."[39]

February 11, 1974: Kissinger opened a conference of oil consumers in Washington. He proposed "Project Independence" to attack problems posed by the energy crisis and suggested the creation of an international program to protect consumers against supply interruption and manipulation. The conference overrode French objections, and on February 13 eleven nations joined the United States in a comprehensive-action program.

February 13, 1974: The Arab oil-producing states abruptly called off a meeting in Tripoli, Libya, that was supposed to consider lifting the oil embargo against the United States and the Netherlands. A preparatory meeting of Egyptian, Saudi, Algerian, and Syrian leaders earlier in Algiers had failed to come to an agreement. Egypt had argued for ending the embargo but Syria had insisted on its continuation until a separation-of-forces agreement was reached for the Golan.

February 27, 1974: Kissinger mediated a settlement of preliminary issues between Syria and Israel, opening the way to negotiations on separation of forces.

March 10, 1974: A meeting of Arab oil ministers called by Egypt to consider lifting the oil embargo floundered because representatives of Libya, Algeria, and Syria failed to show up.

March 13, 1974: The Arab oil ministers finally met in Tripoli and agreed to lift the embargo against the United States but to postpone the announcement of the decision.

March 18, 1974: Most Arab oil producers officially announced the lifting of the embargo against the United States but its continuation against the Netherlands and Denmark. Libya and Syria planned to continue the embargo. The majority decided to review their decision the following June and to reinstate the embargo if no separation-of-forces agreement had been reached by then between Syria and Israel.

Saudi Arabia after the Embargo

The use of the oil weapon and its consequences fundamentally altered Saudi Arabia's international, regional, and internal strategic position. It underscored the Kingdom's pivotal position within OPEC, brought it into open confrontation with the United States for the first time, and thrust upon it an unprecedented leadership role in the Arab world. Even more important than these developments and their implications, however, were the internal consequences for the Kingdom of the decision to uphold the leap in oil prices resulting from its use of the oil weapon.

The Price Decision and Its Implications

Analysts have agreed that the massive increase in the price of oil was an unintended result of the Saudi-led embargo, but they have disagreed as to who was responsible for actually bringing it about. Most blame the shah of Iran; a few blame the Saudis; but all take it for granted that the critical moment was the Tehran decision setting the price at $11.65 per barrel on December 24 of that year. Regardless of who did what in Tehran, however, Saudi Arabia had it in its power to bring about a substantial price cut, and for many months after the Tehran decision actively considered doing so for reasons of profound self-interest. Its final renunciation of that option in the last months of 1974 was therefore the real critical decision; and it was fraught with fateful consequences not only for the Kingdom itself but also for much of the rest of the world.

On January 27, 1974, less than one month after the Tehran price came into effect, Zaki Yamani declared in Tokyo that King Faisal would move to reduce oil prices to ease adverse effects on the world economy.[40] The motives for considering such a move were in fact much more complex. In the first place, the mere use of the massive revenues based on the Tehran price presented a basic problem for Saudi Arabia. Already before the October war, oil revenues had trebled in three years as a result of increases in production and in prices — from $949 million in 1969 to $2,745 million in 1972.[41] This increase had transformed a budget deficit of $89 million in fiscal 1969–70 into a surplus of $967 million in fiscal 1972–73, after provision had been made for financing the five-year plan, the program to build up the armed forces, and increased use of "riyal diplomacy." The massive revenue increase to $22,574 million in 1974, therefore, confronted Faisal's government with the question of what to do with these huge sums.

In theory the Saudi government had three choices: to expand and accelerate the development plan and other expenditures to match the new level of revenue; to expand and accelerate these at a measured pace and put the surplus in reserve; or to reduce production from the level of 7.5 mbd in 1973 to a level that would bring in sufficient revenue for a measured pace of development and conserve oil. Theoretically the Saudis had tremendous latitude regarding this issue: on the assumption that the government's "take" at the time was $7.00 out of the $11.65 price per barrel,[42] the 1973 revenue level of $4,340 million could be raised with a production of about 1.7 mbd, twice that level by a production of 3.4 mbd, and so on.

The third option — reducing production to the level of needed revenue — was really out of the question, although the Saudis subsequently claimed a great deal of credit for not espousing it. It would have entailed such a drastic cut in production as to be tantamount to perpetuating and even intensifying the embargo and sanctions adopted during the conflict. The damage to the Western economies would be so great that the Western powers collectively or the United States separately would be irresistibly provoked to drastic counteraction. Kissinger's and Schlesinger's threats to resort to force during the embargo were ominous in that respect. Alternatively, the United States could bring many sorts of indirect pressures to bear on Saudi Arabia, including manipulation of the Arab-Israeli conflict and denial of the military and technical assistance needed by the Kingdom to carry out even a measured development program.

The first two options were more realistic but not devoid of problems. One problem involved in the first choice was the paucity of Saudi manpower, especially the shortage of the technical and administrative personnel needed to realize it. Even at the pre-1974 level of activity, Saudi Arabia had had to import hundreds of thousands of foreign workers; a massive expansion and acceleration would require them to import millions, and this, as the Saudis already knew, would present severe practical problems and security risks. Moreover, the presence of foreign personnel and labor would aggravate further the severe social strains that were bound to result from rapid, massive development. Even at the modest level of development of the previous decade or two, such strains had been manifested in the form of seditious or rebellious acts by "leftist" nationalists or "rightist" traditionalists.

Similar difficulties attended the second choice. For one thing, there were practical problems involved in the placement, security, and preservation of the value of the massive reserves that would rapidly accumulate. More important, the accumulation of vast reserves when most of the population still lived in difficult conditions would create an explosive political situation. Attempts to explain it in terms of prudent social policy or inadequate administrative apparatus either would not be understood or would underscore the defects of the political system. Most likely, in view of the local tribal tradition and the example of some of the Gulf shaikhs, the conclusion would be drawn that the rulers were hoarding the reserves for themselves, as their own private wealth. Radical propaganda from hostile neighbors was certain to drive the point home to the Saudi people if they did not initially entertain it themselves. Thus, unstated by Yamani was the point that a reduction in prices would resolve or at least mitigate a major problem, allowing the Saudis to undertake a measured acceleration of development and a modest accumulation of reserves.

Another consideration not mentioned by Yamani was the long-term economic interest of Saudi Arabia. Yamani implied in general terms that the welfare of the Kingdom was somehow connected with the welfare of the world economy, but the Saudi interest in lower prices was more specific. Yamani and most economists were convinced at the time that the quadrupling of the price of oil within a period of a few months was bound to stimulate the development of alternative energy sources and drastically reduce demand, fundamentally reversing the condition of the oil market within a relatively short time. For oil-producing countries that had limited reserves and a vast existing capacity to absorb funds usefully, these considerations did not matter. But for Saudi Arabia, which had enormous petroleum reserves and relatively limited capacity to absorb funds then, preserving the oil market by keeping the prices competitive with alternative energy sources was a matter of crucial importance.

A third reason favoring a substantial price cut, omitted by Yamani although he was certainly aware of it, was the resentment throughout the world generally and in Washington in particular against the Tehran price. The punishingly high price appeared to be simply a perpetuation of the sanctions in different form after the reasons for the embargo had ostensibly been removed. They thus prolonged the strain between Saudi Arabia and the United States as the latter pressed the former to bring about a price cut and threatened to withhold needed political, military, and technological assistance if Saudi Arabia did not deliver.

A fourth and final reason favoring a major price cut, also not mentioned by Yamani, pertained to the long-term balance of power between Saudi Arabia and its Gulf neighbors. As a result of the Tehran price, Iran's oil revenues jumped from $4.1 billion in 1973 to $17.4 billion in 1974, and Iraq's from $1.5 billion to $6.8 billion. Since both of these countries, each in its own way, presented threats to Saudi Arabia's security, and since both were much better able in terms of population and infrastructure to convert their increased wealth into greater military power, a reduction of their revenue through a sharp price cut was of major strategic interest to Saudi Arabia.

For all these weighty reasons, through most of 1974 the Saudi leaders continued to voice their intention of achieving a cut in prices and of holding a large auction sale to accomplish that aim. Not until September of that year did Faisal finally renounce the idea of an auction and decide instead to cut Saudi production, if necessary, to sustain the current prices until OPEC addressed the issue collectively.[43] When OPEC did so, in December 1974, the Saudis were content with a symbolic reduction to $10.12 for the following nine months. The final decision not to challenge the Tehran status quo had crucial implications for Saudi Arabia, as the analysis of the case for reducing the price intimated. Why, then, did the Saudis eventually take that course?

The highly instructive answer is that the Saudis based their decision on short-term tactical views of some problems and on an instrumental and traditionalist conception of others. The immediate reason for not pressing with the auction was the fear of antagonizing Iran, whose ruler had declared he would consider any action to bring down the price of oil as a hostile act. Another motive was to avoid provoking Iraq and other Arab producers, especially since an important Arab summit was scheduled to meet in Rabat in October 1974.

Encouraging the Saudis in their decision was the sense, by September

1974, that the world had managed to absorb the initial shock of the Tehran price and that the hostility of world opinion had abated. This perception in turn helped allay their concern about their own long-term economic interest, at least to the point where they were now willing to take time to watch the world's economic reaction further. If it appeared that their concerns were justified, they could then take the appropriate counter-action.

Also contributing to the Saudis' decision was the ambiguity they perceived in the American attitude toward the Tehran price. On the one hand, Washington pressed throughout 1974 for a price reduction and made occasional threatening noises to support its demand. On the other hand, some of its actions seemed to belie its concern or at least to undercut its credibility. During the second quarter of 1974 an American Defense Department mission was in Saudi Arabia surveying the country's defense position and needs and preparing programs for massive Saudi purchases of American arms, equipment, and services. In Washington that June, Crown Prince Fahd signed a series of agreements on economic and military cooperation that were said to define formally a "special relationship" between the United States and Saudi Arabia. In November 1974 Kissinger visited Tehran for talks with the shah on American-Iranian strategic and technological cooperation and oil prices. The shah was adamant on the last issue, yet Kissinger declared himself to be highly satisfied with the overall results of the talks. The shah made sure the Saudis were informed about what transpired. Finally, and perhaps most important, the American Defense Department mission that surveyed the Saudi's defense position and needs formulated a defense strategy for Saudi Arabia that depended in crucial respects on major Iranian supporting roles. For the Saudis, this conception made the idea of confronting Iran over the issue of a major price cut absurd, and Washington's demand that they should do so both incomprehensible and incredible.

With the weight of tactical considerations favoring the Tehran status quo, the Saudis convinced themselves that they could find ways to manage the problems involved in the massive expansion and rapid acceleration of their development plans. At the purely practical level, it was already apparent by mid-1974 that they would have no trouble obtaining from the United States, Europe, and Japan all the technical assistance they would need for development. Unskilled and semiskilled labor was readily available from Yemen and other Arab countries. The security problem posed by the massive influx of foreign labor would be handled by administrative regulations and police measures designed to insulate the foreigners as much as possible and to monitor their behavior. Money and technical assistance to establish the instruments of control were no problem.

As for the social impact of rapid, massive development, two sets of considerations, one conceptual and the other instrumental, encouraged the Saudis to take the plunge that was the concomitant of keeping up the Tehran price. Conceptually, the Saudi rulers — in contrast to some of the Western-educated Saudi technocrats — viewed development as a single, one-time act to overcome backwardness, perhaps comparable to a surgical operation to remove an ailment; they therefore believed that the faster it was done, the better. This view was related, in turn, to two complementary notions: one was that development was a package of value-free instruments and techniques that could be implanted in any ideological-ethical environment; and the other was that the beliefs and values of Islam, which underpinned and legitimized the Saudi regime, were eternal, perfect for all times and circumstances and therefore suitable to any level of development. This view ignored through sheer definition the problem of a potential crisis between beliefs and reality, which is ultimately the most serious threat to the Saudi sociopolitical order. The Saudi rulers were, of course, aware from their own experience that past development had produced strains and unrest between and among modernizing and strongly traditionalist groups, but these were viewed as incidental aberrations rather than as necessary consequences of the process of modernization. As such, they could be dealt with by the traditional method of blandishment and deterrence; and the Kingdom's vastly increased wealth provided ample means to do both on a grand scale.

On the basis of these kinds of considerations, the Saudis took what was probably the most fateful decision since the creation of the Kingdom: to refrain from bringing down the Tehran price and to use the resultant huge revenues for massive economic, social, and military development. By the end of 1974 they adopted a second five-year plan due to start in 1975 and involving an outlay of $142 billion, in contrast to the allocation of a "mere" $9.2 billion for the first five-year plan.

Relations with the United States

The aftermath of the embargo also involved a profound transformation in the character and scope of the Saudi-American relationship. The previous simple client-patron connection gave way to a much more complex relationship of interdependence, involving shared as well as divergent interests between the two parties and therefore the potential for adversarial bargaining as well as agreement, antagonism as well as cooperation.

The United States now needed Saudi cooperation in connection with the supply and prices of oil and the recycling of petrodollars, while Saudi Arabia needed continued American support for its ultimate security, and immensely increased assistance in devising and realizing gigantic development plans for its economy and defense and security. The translation of this interdependence into specific tradeoffs, however, naturally involved maneuvering and bargaining by each side to obtain the most advantageous terms. Moreover, because the two countries' shared interests in the dual relationship were connected with divergent interests in third-party relationships, the maneuvering between the two sometimes took on an antagonistic character. Saudi Arabia, for instance, while using its pivotal position in OPEC to restrain price increases, ultimately lent its power to keep the price at the generally high level it had attained at the peak of the embargo period. It sought to use its leverage not only to secure American technical and military assistance but also to press the United States regarding its policy toward Israel and third Arab parties. The United States, for its part, provided Saudi Arabia with the assistance it sought and at the same time directed thinly veiled threats at it to affect its production and price decisions. It responded in part to the Saudi wishes regarding the Arab-Israeli problem but also used its position with Israel as leverage on the Saudis. Saudi Arabia tried to play off Europe against the United States and the United States to play off Iran against Saudi Arabia as each sought to enhance its bargaining position or to achieve particular ends.

In the year between the end of the embargo, in March 1974, and the assassination of King Faisal, in March 1975, the new Saudi-American relationship manifested itself as follows.

April 5, 1974: A few days after the lifting of the embargo against the United States, the two governments held talks to expand economic and military cooperation. The signing of specific agreements was put off until after the conclusion of a Syrian-Israeli disengagement agreement through American mediation. Nevertheless, on April 14 Prince Abdallah ibn Abd al-Aziz and U.S. Ambassador James Akins signed a preliminary $335 million agreement on a project to modernize the National Guard. From April through June 1974 an American Defense Department mission was in Saudi Arabia at the latter's request to study Saudi defense needs and make recommendations.

June 6–8, 1974: A few days after the conclusion of a Syrian-Israeli disengagement agreement, Saudi Deputy Prime Minister and Minister of Interior Fahd ibn Abd al-Aziz visited Washington and signed a wide-ranging agreement for American-Saudi military and economic cooperation. The agreement, described by Secretary of State Kissinger as "a milestone in U.S. relations with Saudi Arabia and Arab countries in general,"[44] involved massive American assistance to Saudi Arabia in pursuing its economic and security development plans, in exchange for Saudi cooperation in meeting the energy problems of the United States and its Western allies. In the latter connection Fahd reiterated the Saudi intent, previously expressed by oil minister Yamani, to strive for a substantial reduction in the price of oil.

June 14 and 15, 1974: President Nixon visited Saudi Arabia as part of a triumphant tour of several Middle Eastern countries.

September 9, 1974: King Faisal decided to cancel plans for a large-scale Saudi oil auction aimed at reducing prices and, on the contrary, to cut Saudi oil production in order to sustain current prices. The reason stated for the decision was opposition by Iran and other Arab oil producers.[45] Unstated were the Kingdom's reluctance to antagonize several Arab countries on the eve of a preparatory conference for an Arab summit meeting, and its resentment of American efforts to set up an organization of Western oil consumers. (Plans for the creation of the International Energy Agency — IEA — were announced on September 30, 1974. The organization was actually established on November 17, 1982.)

September 23, 1974: President Ford and Secretary of State Kissinger reacted to the Saudi decisions with tough speeches. The president declared that continued high oil prices involved the risk of a world depression and the breakdown of world order and safety. The secretary of state stressed that the current oil prices were based not on economic factors but on a deliberate decision to restrict production and maintain an artificially high price level. He added that if the producers failed to cooperate with consuming countries in lowering prices, the United States might be forced to change its policies of helping the producers diversify their economies and channel their resources.[46]

November 2, 1974: Secretary Kissinger visited Tehran for talks with the shah. Although the shah refused to support a reduction in oil prices, he agreed not to seek an increase at the coming OPEC meeting. The two parties favored cooperation between consumers and producers and agreed to set up joint commissions to develop cooperation between the United States and Iran in various fields — including technical and security — as the United States had done with Saudi Arabia the previous June.[47]

December 13, 1974: Following an initiative by Saudi Arabia, Qatar, and the UAE the previous month, OPEC established a unified oil price of $10.12 per barrel for the next nine months, far less than the reduction sought by the United States.

January 1975: In an interview given to *Business Week* at the beginning of the year but published on January 13, Secretary Kissinger seemed to have given up on his effort to bring about a reduction in prices but said he could not rule out completely the use of military force against oil-producing countries if faced with "some actual strangulation of the industrialized world."

The remarks set off widespread discussion in the American and world media in the next weeks about the use of force to secure access to oil. On January 7 Algerian President Boumedienne said that American aggression against any Arab state would bring about the destruction of all Arab oil fields. Egypt's President Sadat made a similar statement on January 9. Yet President Ford, in an interview published in *Time* magazine January 13, supported Kissinger's remarks, observing that the secretary of state had said that force would be used only in the event of "some actual strangulation."

January 9, 1975: In the midst of the furor about the use of force, the United States signed a $750 million contract with Saudi Arabia for the sale of 60 F-5E/F fighters.[48] On February 9 it was reported that the Vinnell Corporation of Los Angeles, under a $77 million Defense Department contract, would use 1,000 Vietnam War veterans to train Saudi National Guard troops. That program was part of the $335 million contract signed by the U.S. government with Saudi Arabia in 1974 for the modernization of the National Guard.[49] Altogether, in its fiscal year 1975, the United States concluded with Saudi Arabia military agreements valued at $1,993 million, more than with any other country except Iran.[50]

February 15, 1975: Kissinger paid a last visit to Faisal in Riyadh to discuss a second Egyptian-Israeli disengagement agreement and to accelerate Saudi-American cooperation.[51]

March 25, 1975: King Faisal was assassinated in his Riyadh palace by a nephew, Prince Faisal ibn Musa'id ibn Abd al-Aziz.

Position in the Arab World

The use of the oil weapon also thrust Saudi Arabia into an unwonted position of leadership in the Arab world. During the October fighting and shortly thereafter, Egypt and Syria naturally occupied the center of the Arab stage while Saudi Arabia played an assisting part. However, as the war gave way to diplomacy and as the oil weapon had its tremendous impact on Europe and its perceived effect on the United States, the roles were gradually reversed. By the end of December 1973, when the surge in the price of oil had brought immense new wealth and more political power to Saudi Arabia, it had emerged as the foremost country in Arab councils.

Saudi Arabia's new preeminence in the Arab world was a mixed blessing and confronted it with dilemmas with which it has struggled ever since. On the one hand, its wealth and political influence opened up the alluring possibility of forging a broad Arab alignment that would assure its security and transcend the previous polarization between radicals and conservatives that had underlain so many of its troubles. On the other hand, the pursuit of such an alignment meant that Saudi Arabia had to adjust its own policies to denominators that were low enough to accommodate the more extreme members of the alignment, even when its particular interests indicated more moderate positions. In the case of the Arab-Israeli problem and in matters relating to oil policy, for instance, this requirement could (and did) conflict with the Saudis' need to maintain an overall cooperative relationship with the United States for the sake of obtaining necessary technical and military assistance and retaining the ultimate American insurance of Saudi security.

Even apart from any attempt to forge an Arab alignment, Saudi Arabia's effective use of the oil weapon and its preeminence and wealth meant that it could no longer maintain a low profile in matters of importance to the Arabs even if it wanted to. Thus in the Arab-Israeli dispute Saudi Arabia was forced into the position of a "confrontation country," first diplomatically and financially and then increasingly also militarily, with severe implications for its security, especially if the dispute were to erupt again into large-scale war. In more strictly inter-Arab issues, Saudi Arabia could no longer easily avoid taking a position, and thus ran the risk of suffering from the fallout of inter-Arab quarrels regardless of what stance it adopted.

Despite these dilemmas, Faisal was able on the whole to maneuver so as to reap the benefits of Saudi Arabia's new position of Arab leadership while averting its pitfalls. He maintained the oil sanctions against the United States long enough to cement the cooperative relationship he had begun with Egypt and Syria before the war into the core of an Arab alignment that comprised all the Arab countries except Iraq, Libya, and South Yemen. When that was accomplished, he encouraged Egypt to take the lead in urging the easing and then the removal of the sanctions; afterward he concluded, without any serious Arab demurral, the Kingdom's most comprehensive agreement on economic and military cooperation with the United States.

In matters of oil policy, he managed to gain credit for moderation by speaking against the drastic price increase and for a substantial price reduction, and yet ended up with the jacked-up price virtually intact and Saudi Arabia in possession of undreamt-of wealth. In the process he managed both to appease the more extreme Arab producers and Iran and to assert Saudi Arabia's predominance within OPEC and the Organization of Arab Petroleum Exporting Countries (OAPEC).

In strictly inter-Arab affairs, at the 1974 Rabat summit he came down decisively on the side of the PLO in its quarrel with King Hussein and thus checked potential hostility from that quarter; yet he managed to retain Hussein's alliance and his proven value to Saudi security. At the same summit Faisal played a leading role in institutionalizing the depolarization of the Arab world by establishing an annual contribution of $2.5 billion from the oil-rich countries to the "confrontation countries" and the PLO. He also tried to bring South Yemen into the Arab mainstream and incidentally to protect one of Saudi Arabia's oil routes by promoting an Arab League ninety-nine-year lease on Perim Island, strategically located at the mouth of the Red Sea. Faisal achieved all this at an immediate cost of a certain amount of strain in the Kingdom's relationship with the United States, which was balanced by an extension of the scope of cooperation with it.

Position in the Gulf and the Peninsula

In the Persian Gulf arena, too, the aftermath of the use of the oil weapon had a profound effect on Saudi Arabia's position. As mentioned earlier, the Tehran price caused Iran's oil revenues to jump from $4.1 billion in 1973 to $17.4 billion in 1974 and Iraq's to increase from $1.5 billion to $6.8 billion in the same period. In basic strategic terms, this development represented a deterioration in Saudi Arabia's relative position because those two powers were much better able than Saudi Arabia to convert their increased financial wealth into military power. But in the immediate term, the accession of Iran and Iraq to vast new wealth had additional and rather ironic consequences for the Kingdom. Iran, hitherto a party to an understanding with Saudi Arabia on Gulf security, began to act more assertively and became more menacing as the shah acquired more means to pursue his hegemonic aspirations. On the other hand, Iraq, which had hitherto engaged in relentless hostility against the Saudis and the Gulf emirates, eased or ceased its subversive activities and groped toward rapprochement with its neighbors as it gained the means to reduce its dependence on the Soviets and to pursue policies premised on a comprehensive domestic development program.

The moderation of Iraq's policy and behavior, whatever its implications in the long run, came as a welcome relief to the Saudis. Iran's greater assertiveness, on the other hand, was doubly problematic because it enjoyed the tacit encouragement of the United States. During the height of the embargo, Iran's importance had increased greatly in the view of the United States as it made available to the Western countries all the oil it could produce. The shah temporarily lost some of that credit when he engineered the massive price increase in December 1973 and subsequently resisted Washington's efforts to bring the price down with Saudi help. However, when Saudi Arabia relented and the Tehran price stuck, the United States went on to develop with Iran a closer relationship than ever before. For, although the shah remained hawkish on the question of price, he was otherwise deemed much more dependable than the Saudis on the question of continuity of supply, because he had no political quarrel with the United States that might cause him to tamper with the flow of oil, as the Saudis had in connection with the Arab-Israeli problem. Moreover, Iran appeared to have the potential of becoming a strong power that could, in accordance with the recently enunciated Nixon Doctrine, contribute significantly to the defense of the Gulf region against any direct or proxy Soviet threat. Finally, the shah's regime was thought to be more stable and less likely than the Saudi to suffer an internal upheaval. Indeed, Iran was thought to constitute an American proxy intervention force to put down any disruptive upheavals in the Kingdom and the weak Gulf emirates. Symbolizing the importance of this "special relationship," the United States opened up an almost unlimited military supply line to Iran, whereas with Saudi Arabia it haggled over the quality and quantity of the equipment it was prepared to provide.

Iran's greater assertiveness manifested itself in the final year of Faisal's reign in the scope of its military intervention in Oman. Early in 1973 it had sent some helicopters complete with crews to help the sultan against the PFLOAG. By early 1974 the Iranians had a full combat brigade, a substantial air force complement, and supporting services in Oman, and these were rotated periodically to give combat experience to as many troops as possible. By the beginning of 1975 the Iranian forces had helped the sultan decisively turn the tide against the rebels. Although this development relieved the Saudis and the Gulf principalities of a major source of trouble, it set a precedent of Iranian intervention on the Arab side of the Gulf that was all the more ominous for the lack of an alternative to it.

Elsewhere in the Arabian Peninsula, the aftermath of the embargo had little or no effect on the Saudi position. Possibly Saudi Arabia's new prominence in the general Arab arena influenced Shaikh Zaid of Abu Dhabi finally to settle his territorial dispute with the Kingdom on terms favorable to the latter. Zaid yielded to Saudi Arabia a considerable tract of land that gave it a corridor to the Gulf between Qatar and the UAE, in exchange for Saudi recognition of Buraimi as Abu Dhabi's territory, minus the Zarrara oil field.[52] Regarding the much more serious problem of the Yemens, however, neither the Kingdom's vastly increased wealth nor its newly acquired political prominence availed to improve its position. For a while, Colonel Hamdi's military regime in the YAR appeared to be a reasonable candidate to serve the Saudi objective of effectively uniting the country and checking PDRY. The Saudis accordingly agreed to provide him with substantial financial assistance and considered giving him funds to reequip the YAR's armed forces with Western weapons and thus terminate its Soviet arms connection. That strategy, however, eventually stumbled on the Saudis' reluctance to help Hamdi enforce San'a's will on their own client tribes, and on opposition within the

Yemeni armed forces to severing the Soviet connection entirely and increasing the YAR's dependence on Saudi Arabia. The Saudis therefore had to content themselves with a reversion to partial control over the YAR through client tribes and support for subversive efforts against PDRY.

The Saudis' failure to make any significant headway with the problem of the two Yemens and the relatively passive role they were forced to play in Oman underscored the Kingdom's persisting basic weakness despite its massive increase in wealth and influence. That weakness consisted in its inability to translate its financial and political power into military clout because of manpower, technical, and psychological-political constraints. Saudi Arabia could not aspire to develop a military establishment commensurate even with the means at its disposal. The limited establishment that these allowed was hampered by division into several bodies, and the use of some of these was inhibited by fear of defeat, stemming from suspicion of the loyalty of its members. Consequently, in situations in which military power was the only possible solution, Saudi Arabia for all its wealth and global political influence remained almost impotent. Ironically, the only such situations faced by Saudi Arabia at the end of Faisal's reign were the ones nearest to home, in the Arabian Peninsula.

7

The Defense and Security Perspective, 1963–1975

Defense Allocations: Fluctuations, Trends, Significance

Analysis of the budgetary allocations to defense and security bodies under King Faisal confirms some of the main trends detected in the analysis of the political-strategic sphere and sheds light on some additional features of the Kingdom's defense and security concerns.

Table 3 provides the global data on defense and security allocations in relation to total revenue during Faisal's reign and for the last two years of King Saud's formal reign, during which he was the effective ruler. The table also lists the allocations for the main components of defense and security in absolute amounts and as a percentage of revenue. Several general trends are immediately apparent.

1. In absolute amounts, allocations to defense and security increased more than twentyfold in the fourteen years of Faisal's rule—from SR 676 million in 1962–63 to SR 14,115 million in 1974–75. In relative terms, defense and security allocations accounted for a high percentage of rising total revenue, reflecting a continuing anxiety about the Kingdom's internal and external security.

Although in some years the percentage of revenue allocated to defense and security declined as a result of an exceptionally high increase in revenue, shortly thereafter it caught up to the new, higher level of revenue, even when the jump in revenue was of dramatic proportions. Thus, because of the large increase in revenue in 1971–72, the percentage of defense and security allocations dropped sharply from 42.9 in the previous year to 32.9, but the following year it rose to 38.2 percent of the higher revenue levels. Similarly, a sharp rise in revenue in 1973–74 and a massive increase the following year caused the percentages of defense and security allocations to drop to 33.4 and 14.4 respectively despite substantial increases in the absolute amounts. But in 1975–76 a huge increase in defense and security allocations brought the percentage back up to 37.5 percent of the new level of revenue.

This pattern suggests a tendency to seek to allay anxiety about security by devoting large resources to defense and security purposes independently of specific, considered plans for their use. Further indication of that tendency will be seen in the accumulation of large amounts of sophisticated hardware regardless of the ability to use it effectively.

2. Table 3 shows a continuation of a pattern already discernible in the reign of King Saud: a constant proliferation of instruments of defense and security. The Royal Guard (item 4) is eliminated in connection with the last stage of the Saud-Faisal struggle, but several other categories emerge: "national defense purposes" appears in 1962–63 and remains in the budget for a decade before disappearing. "Emergency expenditures" appears at the same time and becomes a permanent feature. The amounts allocated to these two components remain comparatively modest until the last year or two of Faisal's reign, but the creation of new components further reflects security anxiety and a desire to multiply the checks and balances among various security instruments and the personnel in charge of them.

In addition to the proliferation of defense and security categories, the budgetary data reveal a progressive differentiation within the major categories, giving rise to new services, arms, or agencies. At the beginning of Faisal's rule, Ministry of Defense allocations were differentiated into only two line items: the army and "civil aviation." In 1963–64 the air force was assigned its own budget line; a Meteorological Department line followed in fiscal 1966–67; the navy and "military industry" in 1972–73; followed next by "military academies" and "medical services."

A similar process occurred in the Ministry of Interior. At the beginning of Faisal's rule, it had five line departments: "General Bureau," "public security," "Frontier and Coast Guards," "passports and nationality," and "emirates." By the end of his reign, the ministry had further differentiated an Investigations Department (1963–64), a Mujahideen (Holy Warriors) Department (1963–64), "civil defense" (1965–66), Public Security College (1966–67), "prisons" (1968–69), "special security" (1974–75), and a National Security Council (1975–76). (For a typical budget in the period of Khaled's rule, see the Appendix.) Altogether, defense and security became differentiated into seventeen budget lines at the end of Faisal's rule, in contrast to seven lines at the beginning.

The process of differentiation reflects the continuous institutionalization and bureaucratization of the defense and security apparatuses; the

Table 3. Revenues and defense and security allocations, fiscal 1963–1976 (million SR and percent of revenue)

	1962–63	1963–64	1964–65	1965–66	1966–67	1967–68
Revenues and allocations						
Total revenue	2452	2686	3110	3961	5025	4937
Defense and security allocations	676	844	910	1233	1872	1984
% of total revenue	(27.6)	(31.4)	(29.2)	(31.1)	(37.3)	(40.2)
Specific defense and security allocations[a]						
1. Ministry of Defense	313 (12.8)	345 (12.8)	402 (12.9)	622 (15.7)	1235 (24.6)	1365 (27.6)
2. National Guard	61 (2.5)	134 (5.0)	146 (4.7)	188 (4.7)	197 (3.9)	202 (4.1)
3. Ministry of Interior	183 (7.5)	244 (9.1)	263 (8.5)	333 (8.4)	342 (6.8)	350 (7.1)
4. Royal Guard	18 (0.7)	22 (0.8)	—	—	—	—
5. National defense purposes	40 (1.6)	39 (1.5)	39 (1.3)	31 (0.8)	31 (0.6)	20 (0.4)
6. Emergency expenditures	60 (2.4)	60 (2.2)	60 (1.9)	44 (1.1)	46 (0.9)	31 (0.6)
7. Intelligence Bureau	—	—	—	15 (0.4)	21 (0.4)	16 (0.3)
8. Total non–Ministry of Defense	356 (14.5)	499 (18.6)	508 (16.3)	611 (15.4)	637 (12.7)	619 (12.5)
Ratio of item 8 to item 1	1.1	1.4	1.3	1.0	0.52	0.45

Source: Kingdom of Saudi Arabia, *Statistical Yearbooks,* 1965–1976.
a. Items 1–7 are official Saudi budget categories.

proliferation of these instruments is another indication of the Kingdom's security anxiety.

3. On the assumption that the Ministry of Defense comprises the regular military establishment and that the other components (except perhaps "emergency expenditures") constitute instruments of internal security, the bottom line of Table 3 shows a decisive shift of emphasis between the two starting in fiscal 1966–67. In the previous year, allocations to internal security equaled those to the Ministry of Defense, and in the preceding years, from the beginning of Faisal's rule, allocations to the former sub-

1968–69	1969–70	1970–71	1971–72	1972–73	1973–74	1974–75	1975–76
5535	5966	6380	10782	13200	22810	98247	95847
2110	2515	2738	3544	5041	7619	14115	35988
(38.1)	(42.2)	(42.9)	(32.9)	(38.2)	(33.4)	(14.4)	(37.5)
1375	1743	1866	2347	3547	5409	8814	23725
(24.8)	(29.2)	(29.2)	(21.8)	(26.9)	(23.7)	(9.0)	(24.8)
234	234	282	348	404	649	1296	2613
(4.2)	(3.9)	(4.4)	(3.2)	(3.1)	(2.8)	(1.3)	(2.7)
415	459	507	743	980	1297	2307	4880
(7.5)	(7.7)	(7.9)	(6.9)	(7.4)	(5.7)	(2.3)	(5.1)
—	—	—	—	—	—	—	—
30	20	20	—	—	—	—	—
(0.5)	(0.3)	(0.3)					
40	41	41	60	61	200	1602	4500
(0.7)	(0.7)	(0.6)	(0.6)	(0.4)	(0.9)	(1.6)	(4.7)
16	18	22	35	49	64	96	221
(0.3)	(0.3)	(0.3)	(0.3)	(0.4)	(0.3)	(0.1)	(0.2)
735	772	872	1197	1494	2210	5301	12262
(13.3)	(12.9)	(13.7)	(11.1)	(11.3)	(9.7)	(5.4)	(12.8)
0.53	0.44	0.47	0.51	0.42	0.41	0.60	0.52

stantially exceeded those to the latter. In 1966–67 allocations to internal security dropped to slightly over half the amount allocated to the Ministry of Defense and remained at that level or lower until the last year of Faisal's reign, when an extraordinary allocation to emergency expenditures lifted that year's ratio to 0.6:1.

The high level of allocations to internal security until 1965–66 reflects the point previously made that three years into the Yemen war, Faisal still viewed the Egyptian military intervention in Yemen and the rise of the Yemen Arab Republic more as threats to the Kingdom's internal front

Table 4. Comparative allocations to Ministry of Defense, army, internal security, and National Guard, fiscal 1963–1976 (million SR and percent of defense and security)

Allocations	1962–63	1963–64	1964–65	1965–66	1966–67	1967–68
Total defense and security	676	844	910	1233	1872	1984
Ministry of Defense[a]	313 (46.8)	345 (40.9)	402 (44.2)	622 (50.4)	1235 (66.0)	1365 (68.8)
Army and General Bureau[a]	278 (41.6)	276 (32.7)	329 (36.2)	428 (34.7)	969 (51.8)	736 (37.1)
Internal security[b]	278 (41.6)	417 (49.4)	448 (49.2)	567 (45.9)	591 (31.6)	588 (29.6)
National Guard[a]	61 (9.1)	134 (15.9)	146 (16.0)	188 (15.2)	197 (10.5)	202 (10.2)

Source: Kingdom of Saudi Arabia, Statistical Yearbooks, 1965–1976.
a. Official Saudi budget category.
b. Includes National Guard, Ministry of Interior, "national defense purposes," and Intelligence Bureau.

than as a danger of external invasion. The subsequent shift in favor of the Ministry of Defense reflects the decision, taken only in 1965, to build up the Kingdom's regular forces, starting with the acquisition of an Anglo-American air defense package, in response to renewed Egyptian bombings of Saudi border areas.

4. A comparison of items 1 and 2 (Table 3) seems to negate the widespread notion that the National Guard is meant to be a check on the regular armed forces represented by the Ministry of Defense. The gap in both absolute amounts and percentages of revenue allocated to the two components is simply too large to begin with (and gets larger over time) to sustain such simple interpretation. A more plausible notion of balance emerges from a comparison of all the internal security instruments (bottom line) with the Ministry of Defense, and a still better notion if the comparison is made with the army only, as is done in Table 4.

Table 4 shows that whatever relationship may be discerned between any components holds true for the first and last three or four years but not for the middle years—between fiscal 1966–67 and 1970–71. This pattern reflects once more the fact that in these middle years the regular armed forces—the Ministry of Defense and its components—were being developed on a piecemeal basis. Before that they were relatively stagnant; afterward, all the defense and security instruments were developed on the basis of longer-term programs.

5. Even when viewed in terms of three stages as above, no plausible

1968–69	1969–70	1970–71	1971–72	1972–73	1973–74	1974–75	1975–76
2110	2515	2738	3544	5041	7619	14115	35988
1375	1743	1866	2347	3547	5409	8814	23725
(65.2)	(69.3)	(68.2)	(66.2)	(70.4)	(71.0)	(62.4)	(65.9)
825	990	1137	1431	1601	1941	4122	8888
(39.1)	(39.4)	(41.5)	(40.4)	(31.8)	(25.5)	(29.3)	(24.7)
695	731	831	1126	1433	2010	3672	7714
(33.0)	(29.1)	(30.3)	(31.8)	(28.4)	(26.3)	(26.2)	(21.5)
234	234	282	348	404	649	1269	2613
(11.1)	(9.3)	(10.3)	(9.8)	(8.0)	(8.5)	(9.2)	(7.3)

relationship of balance seems to emerge from a comparison of the National Guard and the Ministry of Defense.

A somewhat more plausible three-stage relationship emerges from a comparison of the National Guard and the army. A far better relationship appears to exist between internal security and the Ministry of Defense, and the most plausible balance relationship of all emerges between internal security and the army.

These relationships suggest that, at least as far as the allocation of financial resources is concerned, the Saudi leadership thought in terms of balancing the various instruments of internal security against the regular forces generally and the army specifically. The leadership acted in this respect in three stages. Through fiscal 1965–66 they tilted slightly in favor of internal security; in the period 1966–1971 they tilted considerably in favor of the army; and in the years 1972–1975 they reverted to a near balance between the two. The relative position of internal security instruments in the second and third stages would appear more advantageous if it is kept in mind that a considerable part of the allocations to the army went in fact for surface-to-air missile (SAM) and radar components of an air defense system, which are not very relevant to the actual relation of forces. To the extent that there remains an element of truth in the National Guard as a counterpoise to the army, this must be sought in the specific deployments of elements of the two forces. This point is discussed further on.

Table 5. Annual revenues and allocations to defense and security instruments, with percent change from previous years, fiscal 1963–1976 (million SR)

	1962–63	1963–64	1964–65	1965–66	1966–67	1967–68
Total revenue	2452 (13.2)	2686 (9.5)	3110 (15.9)	3961 (27.3)	5025 (26.9)	4937 (−1.8)
Total defense and security	676 (39.1)	844 (24.9)	910 (7.8)	1233 (35.5)	1872 (51.8)	1984 (6.0)
1. Ministry of Defense[a]	313 (18.1)	345 (10.2)	402 (16.5)	622 (54.7)	1235 (98.6)	1365 (10.5)
a. Army	278 (18.3)	276 (−0.7)	329 (19.2)	428 (30.1)	969 (126.4)	736 (−24.0)
b. Air force	— —	31 —	28 (−9.7)	115 (310.7)	121 (5.2)	503 (315.7)
c. Navy	—	—	—	—	—	—
2. National Guard	61 (7.0)	134 (119.7)	146 (9.0)	188 (28.8)	197 (4.8)	202 (2.5)
3. Ministry of Interior	183 (25.3)	244 (33.3)	263 (7.8)	333 (26.6)	342 (2.7)	350 (2.3)
4. Intelligence	—	—	—	15 —	21 (40.0)	16 (−23.8)
5. Emergency expenditures	60 (0.0)	60 (0.0)	60 (0.0)	44 (−26.7)	46 (4.5)	31 (−32.5)

Source: Kingdom of Saudi Arabia, *Statistical Yearbooks,* 1963–1976.
a. Items 1–5 are official Saudi budget categories.

So far the discussion of Saudi defense and security perceptions has focused on budgetary allocations at the political-strategic level: the very high level of allocations to defense and security, the proliferation and differentiation of defense and security instruments, and the allocations among broad defense and security categories. Insight into Saudi security perceptions at the operational level requires an examination of the fluctuations in allocations to security instruments from stage to stage and year to year. Because the level of revenue has varied greatly over the years, it is necessary to consider the fluctuations in terms of annual percentage changes in revenue as well as in the defense and security components. In order to pursue the clues as far as the data would allow, some composite categories such as Ministry of Defense will be broken up into their principal subcomponents, and the allocations to the parts themselves will occasionally be examined in terms of titles that distinguish between salaries and projects.

1968–69	1969–70	1970–71	1971–72	1972–73	1973–74	1974–75	1975–76
5535	5966	6380	10782	13200	22810	98247	95847
(12.1)	(7.8)	(6.9)	(69.0)	(22.4)	(72.8)	(330.7)	(−2.4)
2110	2515	2738	3544	5041	7619	14115	35988
(6.4)	(19.2)	(8.9)	(29.4)	(42.2)	(51.1)	(85.3)	(155.0)
1375	1743	1866	2347	3547	5409	8814	23725
(0.7)	(26.8)	(7.1)	(25.8)	(51.1)	(52.5)	(63.0)	(169.2)
825	990	1137	1431	1601	1941	4122	8888
(12.1)	(20.0)	(14.8)	(25.9)	(11.9)	(21.2)	(112.7)	(115.3)
383	594	590	750	1461	2339	2363	5408
(−23.9)	(55.1)	(−0.7)	(27.1)	(94.8)	(60.1)	(1.0)	(128.9)
—	—	—	—	55	227	240	2322
				—	(312.7)	(5.7)	(867.5)
234	234	282	348	404	649	1296	2613
(15.8)	(0.0)	(20.5)	(23.4)	(16.1)	(60.6)	(99.7)	(101.6)
415	459	507	743	980	1297	2307	4880
(18.6)	(10.6)	(10.5)	(46.5)	(31.9)	(32.3)	(77.9)	(111.5)
16	18	22	35	49	64	96	221
(0.0)	(12.5)	(22.2)	(59.1)	(40.0)	(30.6)	(50.0)	(130.2)
40	41	41	60	61	200	1600	4500
(29.0)	(2.5)	(0.0)	(46.3)	(1.7)	(227.9)	(701.0)	(180.9)

Table 5 presents the percentage changes from year to year in revenue, the aggregate allocations to defense and security, and the allocations to the main components of the latter. Figure 2 presents the aggregate data in graphic form.

6. Table 5 and Figure 2 indicate two stages in the relationship between fluctuations in revenue and fluctuations in allocations to defense and security. In the first stage, extending from fiscal 1962–63 through 1970–71, allocations to defense and security tend to increase at a faster rate than revenue. For those nine years, the average annual increase in revenue amounts to 13.1 percent, whereas the average annual increase in defense and security allocations comes to 22.2 percent. For the period 1971–72 through 1974–75 (the last year of Faisal's reign), the reverse is generally true. The average annual increase in revenue in those four years is 123.7 percent, whereas the average annual increase in defense and security is 52 percent. If the first fiscal year after Faisal's death is computed in this average (which it should be, for reasons that will presently become clear), then the average annual increase in revenue comes

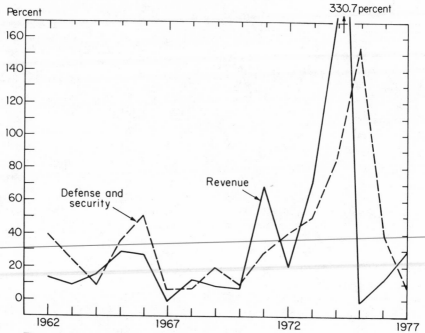

Figure 2. Percent change from previous year in revenues and defense and
security allocations, fiscal 1962–1977 (Source: Table 5)

to 98.5 percent, while the average annual increase in defense and security
allocations comes to 72.6 percent, still leaving a substantial differential.

These data confirm the point made in the historical analysis that in the
first stage (1962–1970) the Saudis were pushing against a revenue constraint and therefore the specific allocations to the various components
involved choices among alternatives. In the second stage, with no revenue
constraints, allocations to components reflected, on the whole, the Saudi
view of the optimal.

7. Table 5 and Figure 2 also show that although defense and security
allocations increased from year to year throughout the two stages, the
increases were erratic in the first stage but followed a steady upward
pattern in the second. The same is true of the three major defense and
security components listed in the table: the Ministry of Defense, the
National Guard, and the Ministry of Interior. This contrast confirms the
point previously made that through 1970, defense and security projects
were undertaken on a piecemeal basis through ad hoc transactions,
whereas after 1970 they were based on a more comprehensive approach
and on longer-term plans. The change was a function of the greater
availability of funds, the new security problems stemming from the Brit-

ish withdrawal from Aden and the Persian Gulf, and the Kingdom's adoption of a five-year overall development plan.

8. Table 5 and Figure 2 contain many striking year-to-year fluctuations, including the exceptions to the trends of the two stages mentioned in point 5 above. The following sections treat the most important of these fluctuations as individual issues and discuss their significance in some detail.

8a. Fiscal 1963–64 (November–November)

The issue: A negative increase for the army that is not accounted for by change in revenue, which increases by 9.5 percent. The Faisal-Saud struggle is not a likely explanation, for by November 1963 Faisal was in full control and the minister of defense was his trusted man, Sultan ibn Abd al-Aziz. The issue is particularly puzzling because allocations to aggregate defense and security increase at a much higher rate than revenue, reflecting the emergency of the Yemen war, which had been going on for nearly one year.

Probable explanations: The explanation of the puzzle confirms the point made in the historical analysis, that Faisal viewed the danger of the Yemen conflict not in terms of a possible invasion by regular Egyptian and Yemeni republican forces (except for air action), but in terms of the creation of a base next door to support subversive activities inside Saudi Arabia. With revenue still comparatively scarce, Faisal decided at first to give priority to the instruments best suited to meet that danger, and to do so at the expense of the regular army, which was in any case suspect because it was the regular army that overthrew the imam in Yemen. Hence allocations to the National Guard were increased in the same year by nearly 120 percent, and to the Ministry of Interior by exactly one-third. (Here, too, is a specific illustration of the point previously made, that when the balance operated, it was between the army on one hand and the National Guard and Ministry of Interior on the other.)

The Saudi air force also began to receive attention. Its differentiation in the budget for the first time, with an initial modest allocation of SR 31 million, signifies the beginning of its development.

8b. Fiscal 1964–65 (November–November)

The issue: One of only two instances before 1971 in which aggregate allocations to defense and security increase at a substantially lower rate than revenue. The phenomenon is concentrated in components other than Ministry of Defense and is particularly puzzling because it took place during the climax of the Saud-Faisal struggle. Those circumstances indicated an increase rather than a decrease in allocations to internal security.

Probable explanations: The Saud-Faisal struggle did involve larger internal security allocations, but these probably took the form of payments to tribes that were not recorded in the allocations to formal instruments of internal security even though they were made at their "expense." Partial confirmation of this hypothesis may be found in the fact that a Mujahideen (Holy Warriors) Department was differentiated in the Ministry of Interior the previous year. It is also known that the allocation to the Royal Guard, amounting to SR 22 million in previous years and included in the aggregate defense and security category, was eliminated in fiscal 1964–65; the Royal Guard was partly dissolved and partly merged with the National Guard in connection with the climax of the struggle.

8c. Fiscal 1965–66 (October–October) and 1966–67 (October–October)

The issue: Two successive massive increases in allocations to the Ministry of Defense far exceeding the rate of increase in revenue, in contrast with increases to the main internal security instruments, which match or fall far below the rate of increase in revenue. Table 6 compares the average for these two years with the allocations for 1964–65.

Probable explanation: The allocations were made close to the end of the third and fourth years of the Yemen conflict and reflect a basic political-strategic decision to build up the regular Saudi armed forces. The decision was made so late in the Yemen conflict for two reasons: (1) the need to develop a modern air defense system and air force, revealed by the Saudi vulnerability to Egyptian air attacks that recurred at the time, in contrast to the Saudi successes in frustrating the Egyptian ground forces in Yemen through proxy Yemeni tribal fighters; and (2) the announce-

Table 6. Comparative allocations to defense and security instruments, fiscal 1965 and average fiscal 1966–1967 (million SR and percent change)

	1965	Average 1966–1967	Percent Change
Total revenue	3110	4493	44.5
Total defense and security	910	1553	70.6
Ministry of Defense	402	926	131.1
Army	329	699	112.3
Air force	28	118	97.3
National Guard	146	193	32.2
Ministry of Interior	263	338	32.2

Source: Table 5.

ment by the British in February 1966 of their intent to leave Aden and South Yemen, which impelled the Egyptians to renew their intent to remain in North Yemen and seek to extend their influence into South Yemen.

The seemingly disproportionate share allocated to the army as compared to the air force is somewhat misleading, since much of the allocation to the army was for the ground air defense system, which was placed under its authority rather than under the air force's.

8d. Fiscal 1967–68 (October–September)

The issue: The very large negative rate of increase for the army, −24 percent, far exceeding the small negative increase in revenue due to blockage of the Suez Canal oil route, in contrast to the massive 316 percent increase in the allocation to the air force and the overall 10.5 percent increase to the Ministry of Defense.

Probable explanations: Two related explanations are likely. One is that the schedule of payments for the aircraft and other elements of the air defense system previously contracted for called for that kind of distribution; the other is that the Saudis felt safer for a while after the Egyptian forces proceeded to evacuate Yemen in the wake of the 1967 defeat. Confirmation of the first explanation is to be found in the overall fluctuating pattern of allocations to the air force, and of the second in the fact that the rate of increase in the aggregate defense and security category was lower that year than in any other year recorded.

8e. Fiscal 1968–69 (September–September)

The issue: For the second and last time during the first nine years of Faisal's rule, the rate of increase in allocations to defense and security is lower than the rate of increase in revenue. Unlike the first occasion (fiscal 1963–64), the phenomenon is concentrated in the Ministry of Defense; the National Guard and Ministry of Interior enjoy increases at a higher rate than revenue.

Probable explanation: This was the first budget in which the Saudi subsidy to the confrontation countries, to the tune of SR 409 million, appeared. Evidently much of that amount was taken from allocations that would otherwise have gone to the Ministry of Defense. Here is specific probable evidence that the Saudis view defense and security as a package of substantially interchangeable components, including not only regular armed forces and other security instruments but also aid to other countries to buy their good will or to neutralize their ill will.

If the SR 409 million were added to the aggregate category of defense and security, the increase in that category would come to 27 percent, bringing this year into conformity with the pattern of the first nine years of Faisal's rule. In subsequent years, defense and security allocations increased faster than revenue even with no account taken of the subsidies.

8f. Fiscal 1970–71 (September–August)

The issue: A slight negative increase for the air force when allocations to virtually all other categories and components increase at substantially higher rates than revenue.

Probable explanations: On the face of it, the phenomenon may be readily explainable in terms of the flow of hardware and contracts, especially in view of the fact that the previous year the air force enjoyed a very high rate of increase. It is also possible, however, that the negative rate of increase reflects the consequences of the two coup attempts in 1969 in which air force personnel were heavily involved (see Chapter 5). This hypothesis cannot be confirmed from internal air force data because the budget for that year does not provide the usual breakdown by titles. On the other hand, the internal air force data for 1969, which should reflect the first coup attempt, do provide some supporting evidence: whereas allocations to projects increased by 91.5 percent over the previous year, the allocation to salaries remained virtually static, contrary to the trend in previous years. This fact indicates that the negative increase for the air force may have been due at least in part to a purge of personnel in the wake of the coup attempt.

8g. Fiscal 1971–72 (August–August) through 1973–74 (July–July)

Starting in 1971, revenue increases by extraordinarily large leaps, which are overtaken by allocations to defense and security only in following years. This lag makes it necessary to consider several years at a time. Table 7 compares the combined average for fiscal 1971–72 through 1973–74 with the allocations for fiscal 1970–71.

The issues: Three issues are immediately apparent: (1) the extraordinary rate of increase for the navy; (2) the very high average rate of increase for the air force, exceeding the high rate of increase in revenue; and (3) the higher rates of increase for the National Guard and Ministry of Interior than for the army.

Probable explanations: In the case of the navy, the explanation is obviously related to the 1971 British withdrawal from the Persian Gulf. What is rather surprising is that although the British announced their intention in 1968, it was not until 1972 that the Saudis differentiated the navy from the Ministry of Defense, and not until 1973 that they made a substantial

Table 7. Comparative allocations to defense and security instruments, fiscal 1971 and average fiscal 1972–1974 (million SR and percent change)

	1971	Average 1972–74	Percent change
Total revenue	6380	15597	144.5
Total defense and security	2738	5401	97.3
Ministry of Defense	1866	3768	101.9
Army	1137	1658	45.8
Air force	590	1517	157.1
Navy	55[a]	227	312.7
National Guard	282	467	65.6
Ministry of Interior	507	1007	98.6

Source: Table 5.
a. Data for fiscal 1971–72.

allocation to it. This underscores the point made in the historical analysis about the Saudi dependence on Iran to police the Gulf and keep its sea lanes open. It also probably illustrates a Saudi distaste for naval service, apparent from their repeated failure from 1957 on to fulfill plans to develop a naval capability.

In the case of the air force, the probable explanation is the reverse of that for the navy. Ever since the late 1920s, when the RAF pursued and annihilated Ikhwan raiding columns in the open desert, the Saudi leaders have been immensely impressed by the capabilities of air power and have viewed it as the key to their defense problems. As soon as Ibn Saud acquired some revenue beyond the bare subsistence necessities, he bought a few planes and hired a motley of foreign personnel to operate them. Since then, every defense program proposed by British and American advisers and accepted by the Saudis has involved a strong air power and air mobility component.[1] The failure of previous programs never deterred the Saudis from attempting a new one each time they felt a heightened sense of insecurity.

In 1971–1973 the heightened insecurity was related to the following events: the British withdrawal from the Gulf; Iraq's signing of a Treaty of Friendship and Cooperation with the Soviet Union; the continuing conflict with South Yemen, culminating in the December 1969 battles over the Saudi Wadi'ah outpost; the conflict between the two Yemens, culminating in war in September–October 1972, followed by the agreement between the two to unite; and the ongoing Dhofar rebellion and Iran's intervention in the fighting.

Strategic perception of the nature of the perils facing the Kingdom also

Table 8. Comparative allocations to defense and security instruments, fiscal
1974 and average fiscal 1975–1976 (million SR and percent change)

	1974	Average 1975–1976	Percent change
Total revenue	22810	97047	325.5
Total defense and security	7619	25052	229.0
Ministry of Defense	5409	16270	207.2
Army	1941	6505	235.1
Air force	2339	3886	66.1
Navy	227	1281	464.3
National Guard	649	1955	201.2
Ministry of Interior	1297	3594	177.1
Emergency expenditures	200	2050	1425.0

Source: Table 5.

probably accounts for the fact that allocations to the Ministry of Interior
and National Guard were increased on the average at a much higher rate
than allocations to the army during that period. The experience of the
1969 coup attempts was a reminder to the Saudi leaders, if such was
needed, that one of the main dangers of external pressures was their
effect on internal affairs. It may be relevant in this connection that
Minister of Interior and Second Deputy Prime Minister Prince Fahd ibn
Abd al-Aziz was out of the country from October 1970 to May 1971, to all
appearances sulking as a result of a dispute over the handling of the coup
attempts; and that following his return and the appointment of Prince
Nayef ibn Abd al-Aziz as deputy minister of interior, the ministry was
allotted the largest percentage increase in 1971 next to intelligence.

8h. Fiscal 1974–75 (July–July) through 1975–76 (July–July)

The budget for fiscal 1975 was the last prepared under Faisal's reign.
However, because the full effect of the huge increase in revenue for that
year took some time to manifest itself, it is useful for some purposes to
consider that year together with fiscal 1976. Table 8 compares the combined average for fiscal 1975 and 1976 with the data for fiscal 1974.

Before consideration of the issues raised by the data in Table 8, two
crucial observations should be made on the basis of Table 5. One is the
dramatic increase in the aggregate allocation to defense and security in
fiscal 1975 and 1976 — 51.1 percent and 85.3 percent respectively — to
catch up with the astounding 330.7 percent leap in revenue in fiscal 1974.
The defense figures dramatically reiterate the points made earlier about

the extent of Saudi security anxiety and about the perception that a high level of defense spending serves in itself to mitigate that anxiety.

The other point that emerges from Table 5 is that although the Saudis increased allocations to aggregate defense and security and each of its components by large percentages in fiscal 1975, they still kept them far below the rate of increase in revenue. Not until fiscal 1976 did the Saudis increase the rate of allocations in additional massive increments, far in excess of the rate of increase in revenue (which was actually negative), to the point where the average allocations for each of the two years approached the average rate of increase in revenue. This fact suggests that when the Saudis set the budget for 1974–75, sometime before July 1974, they did indeed expect to bring down the price of oil very substantially after the massive increase of the previous year, and therefore restrained their allocations. Only later did they decide to let the high price stand and acted accordingly.

Another probable explanation for the second and higher round of increases in defense and security allocations in 1975–76 has to do with the increased anxiety following the assassination of King Faisal in March 1975. This explanation is supported by data on allocations to salaries, shown in Table 9. In fiscal 1975–76 there was an across-the-board salary increase for all the major components and key subcomponents of defense and security, ranging from 87 percent for the army to 137 percent for the Ministry of Interior, in contrast to much more modest increases in previous years. The fluctuations in the following years rule out an increase in manpower as the explanation and strongly support the proposition that the Saudi authorities sought to curry the favor of the defense and security personnel in a difficult period of transition by nearly doubling their salaries.

The issues suggested by the data in Table 8 for fiscal 1975 and 1976 and fiscal 1974 are obviously: the massive rate of increase for the navy, the much larger rate of increase for the army than for the air force, and the phenomenal increase in "emergency expenditures."

Probable explanations: Again, the case of the navy is easy to explain in terms of the flow of hardware and contracts, once the decision was made to build a naval force in the wake of the British departure from the Gulf. The different rates of increase for the air force and army are probably explainable in similar terms, and also by the fact that the doubling of salaries in fiscal 1976 cost the army much more than it did the air force. The enormous average increases in emergency expenditures reflect the uncertainties and anxieties of the Saudi leadership as it assumed a pre-eminent role in Arab and world affairs after the 1973 war and in the face of unforeseeable events such as Faisal's assassination.

Table 9. Salary allocations for defense and security instruments, with percent change from previous year, fiscal 1963–1978 (million SR)[a]

	1962–63	1963–64	1964–65	1965–66	1966–67	1967–68	1968–69
Ministry of Defense[b]	—	204	232 (13.7)	234 (0.9)	266 (13.7)	295 (10.9)	333 (12.9)
Army	—	185	216 (16.8)	224 (3.7)	238 (6.3)	248 (4.2)	276 (11.3)
Air force	—	19	16 (−15.8)	19 (18.8)	28 (47.4)	47 (67.9)	57 (21.3)
Navy	—	—	—	—	—	—	—
National Guard	49 (2.1)	86 (75.5)	94 (9.3)	104 (10.6)	124 (19.2)	124 (0.0)	150 (21.0)
Ministry of Interior	73 (2.8)	111 (52.1)	131 (18.0)	148 (13.0)	150 (1.4)	161 (7.3)	174 (8.1)

Source: Kingdom of Saudi Arabia, *Statistical Yearbooks,* 1963–1978.

a. SR rounded to nearest million.

b. This and the following items are official Saudi budget categories.

Strategic-Military Concepts and Programs: Scope, Aims, Results

Faisal acceded to power at a time of severe confrontation with the Egyptian and republican forces in Yemen. During his reign, both the strategic environment of Saudi Arabia and the means at the disposal of its government changed drastically. Yet, until practically the last year of Faisal's reign, the basic Saudi strategic-military concept remained the same as the one that had been evolved with the help of the American military advisory missions in 1952 and 1957. The changes that did occur centered on specific programs, which were adopted piecemeal to meet particular new problems or to remedy failures of earlier programs. Not until 1974 did what looked like a new, comprehensive strategic-military concept that took account of the changed conditions begin to emerge and to be coupled with a coherent set of defense programs. Faisal died before the results of these revisions began to be apparent.

The general scope and character of the military programs adopted during Faisal's reign are shown in Table 10, which presents major defense acquisitions by the three branches of the regular armed forces.

An initial survey of dates of orders and quality and quantity of weapon systems reveals many correspondences with major points made in the previous discussions of foreign policy and defense allocations. The pattern of procurements clearly reflects, for example, the three main stages

1969–70	1970–71	1971–72	1972–73	1973–74	1974–75	1975–76	1976–77	1977–1978
359	—	—	604	695	921	1751	1585	3175
(7.8)			—	(15.1)	(32.5)	(90.1)	(−9.5)	(100.3)
300	—	—	475	529	704	1319	1194	2326
(8.7)			—	(11.4)	(33.1)	(87.4)	(−9.5)	(94.8)
59	—	—	119	152	194	381	343	745
(3.5)			—	(27.7)	(27.6)	(96.4)	(−10.0)	(117.2)
—	—	—	10	14	23	51	48	104
			—	(40.0)	(64.3)	(121.7)	(−5.9)	(116.7)
169	—	—	258	280	398	796	769	1526
(12.7)			—	(8.5)	(42.1)	(100.0)	(−3.4)	(98.4)
193	192	—	311	346	559	1323	1313	2695
(10.9)	(−0.5)		—	(11.3)	(61.6)	(136.7)	(−0.8)	(105.3)

discerned in the discussion of foreign policy (1964–1967, 1967–1973, and 1973–1975) and the similar division discerned in the pattern of allocations between the periods before and after 1970. Also readily apparent is the emphasis on air defense and air power to the relative detriment·of the army's combat capability until about 1973.

There are also, however, some phenomena that are not immediately understandable from the previous discussions — for instance, the comparatively limited acquisition efforts in the period 1966–1970, which witnessed the high point of the Yemen conflict and the total transformation of the Saudi strategic environment. The following analysis of strategic-military concepts and programs during Faisal's reign will help clarify these apparent divergences as well as the correspondences.

The 1952 and 1957 defense surveys had started from the premise that an outright invasion of Saudi Arabia by potentially hostile neighbors would be deterred by geography, an American security guarantee, and Saudi diplomatic alignments. The main danger was seen as a combination of encroachments upon the Saudi borders aimed at undermining the credibility of the regime's control of the realm, coupled with attempts to subvert restless tribal and sectional elements. Countering the latter threat was the mission of the National Guard and other internal security apparatuses. The task of the armed forces was to deal with the former threat and assist with the latter. To that end, a program was adopted to

Table 10. Major defense acqusition programs, 1964–1975

Year[a]	Army	Air force	Navy
1964	300 BAC Vigilant antitank guided weapons (U.K.)		
1965	Construction of military facilities (U.S. Corps/Eng.)[b] 150 Hawk surface-to-air missiles (SAMs) (U.S.) 37 Thunderbird I SAMs (U.K.)	14 C-130 Hercules transports (U.S. company) 40 Lightning interceptors (U.K.) 9 Lightning F-52 interceptors and T-54 trainers (U.K.)	
1966	Army mobility, parts, and maintenance program (U.S. Corps/Eng.)[c]		
1968	220 AML-90 Panhard armored fighting vehicles (France)	25 BAC-167 Strikemaster counterinsurgency/ trainers (U.K.)	
1971		55 F-5B/E fighters (U.S.)	
1972	Program for logistical support system (U.S. Corps/Eng.)		8 hovercraft for Coast Guard (U.K.) 22 patrol boats for Coast Guard (U.K.) Agreement on naval modernization program (U.S.)
1973	200 AMX-30 medium tanks (France) 250 armored personnel carriers (APCs) (France)		
1974	250 M-60 medium tanks (U.S.) 250 APCs (U.S.) 350 105 mm howitzers (U.S.) 1200 Hawk SAMs (U.S.) 250 Scorpion light tanks (?) 550 armored cars (U.K. and France)	11 C-130 Hercules transports (U.S. company) 38 Mirage III fighters (France)[d] 34 Alouette II helicopters (France)	

Table 10 (continued)

Year[a]	Army	Air force	Navy
1975	300 AMX-30 medium tanks (France) 250 AMX-10 APCs (France)	60 F-5E and F fighters (U.S.) 10 KC-130 Hercules transports 8 C-130 Hercules transports	4 MSC-322 coastal minesweepers 1 large missile patrol boat 14 patrol boats 100 Harpoon surface-to-surface missiles

Sources: Stockholm International Peace Research Institute, *World Armaments and Disarmament: SIPRI Yearbook, 1976* (London and Philadelphia: Taylor and Francis, 1976); International Institute for Strategic Studies, *The Military Balance, 1974–75* (London, 1974); U.S. General Accounting Office, *Perspectives on Military Sales to Saudi Arabia*, Report to Congress, October 2, 1977.

a. Years refer to initiation of orders or agreements.

b. Program repeatedly renewed. Starts with base facilities at Khamis Mushayt. In the 1970s expands into projects for military cities and other construction worth several billion dollars.

c. Extended the following year, for a total worth of $147 million. Agreement renewed periodically. By 1978 10,000 vehicles had been ordered through the program.

d. Intended for Egypt.

create an army of five regimental combat teams endowed with a substantial element of air mobility and supported by a strong air combat element.

The situation that Faisal confronted in Yemen was similar in principle to the ones anticipated by the 1952 and 1957 defense surveys. Although these may have looked to the north and east rather than to the south as the direction from which threats were apt to materialize, the danger he faced was one of a combination of encroachment upon the Kingdom's border and domestic subversion rather than of an outright invasion. Moreover, the latter was indeed deterred by geography and by the American security guarantee, which Faisal took care to burnish constantly. The problem, however, was that the actual threat that materialized was much more intense than had been expected, and that he did not command even as many forces as had been planned to deal with the less severe contingencies.

The danger was more intense because the Egyptian forces in Yemen were far stronger and better equipped than the anticipated hostile neighbors, and because the subversion effort was made in the name of Arab nationalism, which had already seduced some members of the Saudi royal family itself as well as elements of the armed forces. As for the armed forces program conceived in 1952 and reaffirmed in 1957, it had failed entirely, the victim of overriding tactical foreign policy considerations, struggles within the royal family, suspicion of non-Najdi elements of the population, poor manpower resources, inadequate institutional support, lack of adequate infrastructure, corruption, and so on. By 1962 the army may have had a paper strength of five infantry brigades and several armored battalions; but these lacked the training, equipment, and logistical support to operate as field combat formations. The inventory of M-47 and M-15 tanks, for instance, had been decimated by poor maintenance and misuse, and the few that remained could not be operated effectively. The air force had a paper strength of several transport, training, and combat squadrons; but in fact there were only about half a dozen trained Saudi pilots altogether, the F-86 jet fighters were confined to Dhahran air base and were barely operational, and the entire air force was grounded at the outset of the Yemen conflict after several pilots ferrying supplies to the Yemeni loyalist forces had defected to the Egyptians with their cargo and planes.

Up to a point, the failure of the 1957 program proved to be a blessing in disguise in that it compelled Faisal to devise an alternative response to the threat from Yemen that eschewed any use of Saudi armed forces. The alternative strategy was to fight the Egyptians and the republicans by the proxy of the Yemeni royal family and the tribes that it could rally, while protecting Saudi Arabia's home front by strengthening the internal security instruments, advancing a domestic reform program, and appealing to religious and patriotic loyalties. The strategy worked to the extent of seeing the Kingdom through the initial period of shock and panic, leading to a stalemate in the battlefield, and forcing Nasser to attempt to negotiate. However, as neither negotiations nor additional fighting proved to be decisive and the conflict turned into a war of attrition, a serious problem took shape.

On the whole, the Saudis and their proxies were better placed to withstand a long war of attrition than the regular Egyptian expeditionary force. But the Egyptians used their critical advantage of command of the air to bomb Saudi border towns and areas. As a result Faisal confronted two distinct problems. One was the possibility that Nasser might carry the air war to the Saudi interior and inflict all kinds of severe damage. Although the United States had warned Nasser against such action, there was no assurance that he would heed the warning or that the United States would react effectively if he did not. After all, the United States was tolerating the bombing of the border areas on the grounds advanced by the Egyptians that these were staging points and bases for the royalists. The other problem was that even if the Egyptian bombings remained confined, they threatened to undermine the Saudi regime by demonstrating its helplessness and inability to protect the country. To meet these problems, the Saudis contracted in 1965 with Britain and the United States for an air defense package worth $400 million.

The program began with an American study of Saudi air defense needs undertaken at Saudi request, which recommended a package based on American F-104 aircraft and Hawk SAM missiles. But then, to offset British purchases of American F-111 aircraft, the United States and Britain agreed to offer the Saudis a package including 40 BAC Lightning interceptors adapted for ground capability, British radars and communication equipment, 150 American Hawk SAMs, and British training and support services based on the use of staff of private contractors.[2] Along with this package the Saudis bought a smaller, stopgap one to meet immediate needs until the components of the larger program could be delivered and absorbed: 37 British Thunderbird I SAMs, and 9 Lightning F-52s and T-54s and 6 Hawker-Hunter fighters to be taken out of RAF stock and operated and serviced by seconded British military personnel.

The Anglo-American program was, theoretically, the centerpiece of the Saudi defense strategy until the acquisition of the F-5 aircraft six years later and continued, also theoretically, to play an important role even afterward. In December 1964, shortly after Faisal's accession, Minister of Defense Sultan ibn Abd al-Aziz made a brave declaration that a modern Saudi army would soon be developed, that three major military bases would be built, near Hafr al-Batin, at Tabuk, and at Khamis Mushayt, and that allocations had already been made for the creation of a modern air defense system.[3] In fact, however, partly because of revenue constraints, partly because of Faisal's persistent mistrust of a modern army, and partly because Saudi Arabia was doing well on the ground in Yemen with the means at its disposal, only the last of these objectives was promptly and urgently addressed. The army was not necessarily deprived of a proper share of allocations; but a large proportion of the funds allotted to it was used for the ground component of the air defense system, for construction of facilities, transportation, and logistical support systems, and relatively little was used to acquire combat hardware. Thus, in 1965 a private contract was signed for the first five of fourteen C-130 Hercules transport planes intended to facilitate the supply of proxy Yemeni forces and, as envisaged in the 1957 strategic plan, to build up a capability to transport troops and equipment to any point of crisis. In the same year the Kingdom signed a contract with the U.S. Corps of Engineers for the construction of base facilities at Khamis Mushayt, including airfields to receive some of the aircraft ordered. In 1966 and 1967 two contracts worth $147 million were signed with the corps for the supply of trucks and the development of a spare parts and maintenance system to improve the army's mobility.

The Anglo-American air defense program proved to be a complete failure. In 1966 and 1967 the Egyptian air force repeatedly bombed Saudi border towns and staging areas without any interference from the British-manned "emergency" missiles and other parts of the air defense package, presumably because of inadequate warning and control. That element of the package came into play in a limited way in December 1969, when a few Lightnings manned by British and Pakistani personnel supported the Saudi counterattack that dislodged the South Yemeni forces from the Wadi'ah border outpost. The main part of the program became mired in difficulties that prevented its absorption for many years after the hardware had been delivered. In the first place, the Lightnings turned out to have been built for too specific an interceptor role, and their conversion to multirole weapons, including ground attack, was largely unsuccessful. Altogether, the aircraft proved to be extremely difficult to keep serviceable, and the British contract support effort was poorly organized and inadequately capitalized and staffed.[4] The Saudi trainees were deficient in preliminary qualifications and thus forced a slow and low standard of instruction, and the Saudi bureaucracy added more problems than it helped resolve. Finally, compounding the difficulties were the extensive arrests and purges of air force personnel in connection with the 1969 coup attempts, and the intensification of the already cumbersome security procedures to guard against disloyal acts.

The result is illustrated by the following episode, reported by General Saad al-Din Shazli, the Egyptian chief of staff before and during the 1973 war. In November 1971, or six years after the inception of the Anglo-American program, Saudi Arabia agreed to contribute two squadrons of Lightnings to a collective Arab military effort in anticipation of war, but said that it could not provide the pilots and asked Egypt to supply them instead. As mentioned earlier, Faisal offered the twenty Lightnings to Sadat on the eve of one of Sadat's trips to Moscow. The fact that at this time the Saudis received the first twenty of 55 F-5s ordered in 1971 suggests that the Saudis switched to the F-5s pilots who had been assigned to the Lightnings and did not have enough pilots to man both groups of aircraft. At any rate, Shazli's report says that in May 1972, at Sadat's insistence and contrary to his own judgment, he sent a first contingent of seven Egyptian pilots and thirty-three mechanics to Saudi Arabia to receive instruction in operating and servicing the Lightnings before bringing them over. "It was a waste of time," he concluded: "There were so many problems with the serviceability of the aircraft and the standards of instruction and administration, that after wasting a year, our pilots finally returned to Egypt. The Lightnings never came."[5]

Fortunately for Saudi Arabia, the immediate problem that had prompted the adoption of the 1965 air defense program was resolved independently by the withdrawal of the Egyptian forces from Yemen in the wake of Egypt's defeat in the 1967 war. However, the longer-term defense problem remained and was rendered infinitely more complex by developments around the entire perimeter of the Kingdom: the persistence of the Yemen problem and its aggravation by the conflict that developed with South Yemen; the ramifications of the war of attrition; the instability of the Jordanian regime, caught between Israel and the PLO; the advent of an actively hostile radical regime in Iraq; the consequences of the scheduled termination of Britain's peacekeeping role in the Persian Gulf; and the rebellion in Oman's Dhofar province supported by South Yemen. The way in which the Saudis addressed this profound change in the Kingdom's strategic environment constitutes one of the most instructive episodes about their defense behavior.

After the Six Day War, in the crucial period 1967–1970, the Saudis did less to build up their military combat capability than at any other time in Faisal's reign. As Table 10 shows, the only initiatives to buttress the armed forces' combat capabilities were two arms transactions concluded in 1968: one for 220 AML-90 Panhard armored fighting vehicles from France, and the other for 25 BAC-167 Strikemaster counterinsurgency and training aircraft. The planes, much simpler to operate and maintain than the Lightnings, were meant to give the Saudis a measure of capability against South Yemen or potential internal trouble within a relatively short time. Nevertheless, they were not used in the Wadi'ah incident at the end of 1969 and the beginning of 1970. The armored cars were a potentially useful addition to Saudi capability against the Yemens and the Gulf emirates; but they were not very relevant to the kind of threats that might emanate from Iraq, Iran, Syria, Egypt, or Jordan under hostile rule.

The reasons for the absence of a more substantive response comprise the entire mix of factors affecting Saudi defense behavior. First, financial resources were constrained from 1967 through 1970 by an unusually slow rate of increase in revenue: the average annual increase was only 6 percent compared with an average annual increase of 20 percent in the previous four years. Second, the pool of personnel trainable in modern technology was already largely committed to the effort to absorb the Anglo-American air defense package. Third, the 1969 coup attempts and the subsequent purges of military personnel further drained the pool of appropriate manpower and made the Saudi leaders less enthusiastic about projects to strengthen the combat capability of the armed forces. Fourth, many of the new defense problems did not seem readily amenable to solution by military projects within the Kingdom's existing capability—for instance, a major threat from Iraq, Syria, Iran, a hostile Jordan, Egypt, or indeed a number of lesser threats from several directions at once. Finally, the Saudis were inhibited in those years from seeking American military and financial assistance in devising suitable and affordable defense programs by the hostility and criticisms of the radical Arab camp comprising Egypt, Syria, Iraq, South Yemen, and others. It is significant in this respect that the only two arms transactions signed in that period were concluded with France and Britain, not with the United States. In these circumstances, the Saudis felt compelled to rely in their defense endeavor on cautious diplomacy and keeping a low profile rather than on military programs.

Starting in the second half of 1970, two of the most critical constraints were nearly removed and others were greatly eased, allowing the Saudis to undertake military projects more appropriate to the Kingdom's changed strategic environment. In fiscal 1971, revenue leapt 69 percent, and in the period 1971–1973 it increased at an annual average of 53 percent. Cooperation with the United States became much more feasible again after it successfully mediated the ending of the war of attrition in August 1970. The death of Nasser and King Hussein's suppression of the PLO the following month, and the accession to power of Hafez al-Assad in Syria in November further contributed to that effect while removing or easing several sources of threat. All this encouraged the Saudis to think of military projects to improve their capability to deal wholly or partly with the remaining defense problems.

Their first step was to ask in 1970 for a special American military mission to study their contemplated projects and make recommendations. The United States obliged by sending a high-powered Defense Department mission under Major General O. A. Leahy. From what is publicly known about the mission, it seems that the Saudis asked it to address itself to defense problems arising from the impending withdrawal of the British from the Gulf and to various organizational matters but excluded from its purview the army and internal security forces, notably the National Guard. The latter exclusion is perhaps readily explainable in terms of the Saudi insistence, on internal political and security grounds, on keeping the National Guard and internal security apparatuses separate from the regular armed forces in every respect. The exclusion of the army is more problematic. Possibly there was still a lingering suspicion of the army. Perhaps King Faisal and Defense Minister Sultan were content with the existing definition of the army's mission and were satisfied that, within the limits of the available resources, adequate measures were being taken to enhance its capability to defend the Kingdom's borders and assist in internal security. It is also possible that Faisal and Sultan were already contemplating what they did two years later, namely, contracting with France to create an armored brigade — including equipment, support, and training — in order to avoid possible American constraints about its deployment on the Arab-Israeli front.

The Leahy mission recommended the development of a comprehensive five-year defense program and reorganization of the Ministry of Defense and Aviation. It also recommended that the navy and air force be placed on the same level as the army, that a program be drafted for the expansion and modernization of the navy, and that the air force be reinforced and the obsolete F-86 and T-33 aircraft be retired.[6]

In the following years the Saudis undertook some reorganization of the Ministry of Defense but this apparently did not meet the intended purpose, since another American mission was to make the same recommendation four years later. Nor was a comprehensive five-year defense program developed in the interim. Instead, several separate programs for the various branches of the armed forces were commissioned and adopted at different times in the next three or four years, until another drastic change in the strategic environment led to another American mission, another defense study, and a new program. Thus, in 1971 the Saudis ordered from the United States 55 F-5B/Es at a cost of $171 million, and the following year they signed a $277 million contract for the construction, equipment, and training part of the program. In the same year they extended the contract with the U.S. Corps of Engineers for a logistical support system for the army. Also in 1972 the Ministry of Interior ordered from Britain 22 coastal patrol boats and 8 Hovercraft for the Coast Guard under its jurisdiction, while the Ministry of Defense commissioned from the United States a phased naval expansion plan which was eventually approved in 1974. Finally, in 1973 the Saudis signed an agreement with France for 200 AMX-30 medium tanks and 250 armored personnel carriers as part of a program to create an armored brigade.

Starting in the last months of 1973, Saudi Arabia's strategic position underwent an upheaval as a result of the 1973 war, Faisal's use of the oil weapon, and the consequences of that action. First, the explosion of oil prices caused Saudi revenues for fiscal 1974– 75 to increase by 330 percent over the previous fiscal year, jumping from SR 22.8 billion ($6.4 billion) to SR 98.2 billion ($27.7 billion). This effectively eliminated any financial constraint on Saudi defense and security aspirations.

Second, the constraints previously imposed by suppliers of arms, equipment, and services were drastically reduced. On the one hand, the United States and Europe were eager to provide almost any arms and services requested by the Saudis to meet the balance-of-payments problem created by the leap in the price of oil as well as to improve their prospects of access to oil. On the other hand, the Saudis could readily avail themselves of that disposition as Europe distanced itself from Israel, as the United States took the lead in advancing an Arab-Israeli settlement, and as Saudi Arabia emerged as a leader of a largely united Arab world instead of being a target for radical forces.

Third, the same processes that had gained for the Saudis the new means and possibilities also generated new threats or increased existing ones. In general, the emergence of Saudi Arabia as a global oil and financial power underscored for the Saudi leaders the contrast of the Kingdom's virtual military nakedness. The bonanza of increased oil revenues had also benefited and opened up new opportunities for Iran and Iraq, thus intensifying the threats from that direction. Moreover, the embargo and the Kingdom's newly acquired political preeminence thrust it into the center of the Arab-Israeli conflict and exposed it to more severe challenges and threats. The Arab parties expected it to bankroll their military effort, to use its oil and financial leverage for the benefit of the Arab cause, and even to contribute forces in a future confrontation with Israel. These responsibilities in turn made Saudi Arabia a logical target for possible Israeli military counteraction.

Finally, the massive increase in revenue led to a massive expansion and acceleration of civilian development plans. This in turn required a parallel expansion and acceleration of defense projects to ensure political balance at the top and to mitigate the sense of increased internal vulnerability arising from the social strains of development.

Despite these far-reaching transformations in the strategic environment, the Saudis' first impulse was to deal with the change through piecemeal defense programs, and they proceeded differently only at the behest of the United States. As mentioned earlier, in December 1973, at the height of the embargo controversy, the Saudi Ministry of Defense approached its American counterpart for assistance in developing a five-to-ten-year program for the modernization of the Saudi air force. The U.S. Defense Department agreed, but strongly urged that the air force study be done as part of a comprehensive survey of Saudi defense problems and needs over a ten-year period. The Saudis assented but excluded the National Guard, which was, however, covered by a separate American survey undertaken at about the same time.

The forty-five-man Defense Department mission made a field survey in April–June 1974 and completed its report by October.[7] From the information available about the report from open sources, it seems that this mission, like its predecessors, estimated that there was little danger of an outright invasion of the Kingdom by or through any of its neighbors. Unlike its predecessors, however, the 1974 mission sought, apparently at Saudi insistence, to provide even against that remote contingency. The principal danger was seen as coming from the direction of Iraq, where the terrain favors a thrust by fast-moving armored columns toward the vital oil fields and facilities 400 miles away, in contrast to the conditions from the direction of Jordan and Israel in the northwest and the two Yemens in the southwest, where the terrain favors the defense, and vital targets are more distant.

The 1974 survey, like its predecessors, also viewed the defense of the Kingdom's borders as a principal objective, although, unlike them, it saw such threats as potentially emanating from all directions. Most important, however, the 1974 survey added as another principal objective the defense of the Kingdom's oil resources, facilities, and transit routes against external attacks, previously left to the care of Britain.

To address the various defense tasks, the survey adopted a force design that sought to compensate for the constraints of limited manpower and vast distances with a high level of technology. It envisaged the creation of relatively small but highly mechanized forces endowed with great firepower, ground and air mobility, strong air support, and the best infrastructure that money could buy. Withal, the survey recognized that even the best-designed forces that the Kingdom could aspire to develop could not, by themselves, meet all the anticipated contingencies, and therefore built into its defense concept the basic premise that the Kingdom would have to depend in some situations on friendly foreign powers to deter or overcome threats. Specifically, the survey relied on Iran to deter an outright Iraqi invasion; and if such an invasion nevertheless took place, it envisaged a Saudi capability to fight a delaying action until Iranian, and ultimately American, forces came to the rescue. Similarly, the survey envisaged the creation of a first-line Saudi air defense of the oil facilities based mainly on Dhahran; and if that line were breached, it counted on the intervention of Iran's air force, and ultimately on the American air force if necessary. A similar approach underlay the concept for the development of the Saudi navy.

The force design program recommended by the survey envisaged a relatively modest increase in personnel. Over a ten-year period the army was to be expanded from 45,000 to 72,000; the air force from 14,000 to 22,000; and the navy from a few hundred to 3,900. The National Guard was to remain at the 1974 level of 35,000.[8] The capabilities of the various forces, however, were to be vastly increased. The army was to develop two armored brigades, each with three armored and one mechanized infantry battalions; four mechanized brigades, each with three mechanized infantry and one armored battalions; one airborne brigade with three infantry battalions and support groups; and a helicopter force with two assault helicopter battalions and one attack helicopter battalion.[9] Equipment recommended for purchase included 440 helicopters, M-60A1 tanks, armored personnel, cargo and command carriers, M-109A1B howitzers, TOW missile system launchers, Dragon systems, and Redeyes.[10] All this was in addition to the equipment of one armored brigade based on AMX-30 tanks and other French equipment, and to Hawk SAMs directly contracted for with the Raytheon Corporation.

Within five years the air force was to complete the absorption of the 55 F-5B/E aircraft acquired in 1971, which were to be retrofitted to enhance their ground attack role. In the same period it was also to acquire and

absorb 60 F-5E/F aircraft reconfigured for offense as well as interception, at a cost of $769 million.[11] This purchase was to be accompanied by a
construction, training, and support program executed by Northrop Corporation, the manufacturer of the aircraft, at a cost of $1,574 million.[12] At
the same time, the program for the C-130 Hercules transport aircraft and
logistics support, contracted with Lockheed, was to continue.

The modernization program developed separately by another American mission aimed at creating a trained Saudi naval force largely independent of contractor support. Equipment recommended for purchase
included nine 300-ton guided-missile patrol boats, four MSC-332 coastal
minesweepers, eight other smaller craft, plus utility landing craft, mechanized landing craft, and large harbor tugs. In addition to the equipment,
estimated at $944 million, deepwater port facilities were to be built at
Jubail and Jidda, as well as facilities for docking, repair maintenance,
administration, and naval headquarters, at an estimated cost of $1.7 bil-
lion.[13]

The National Guard was not directly covered by the 1974 or the 1970
surveys because of Saudi insistence on keeping the affairs of that body
completely separate from those of the regular forces. However, in March
1973, after a separate survey, an agreement was concluded with the U.S.
Defense Department for the modernization of the guard by three private
contractors working under the supervision of the Defense Department.
The goal was to structure, over a seven-year period, four of the National
Guard's twenty battalions into mechanized infantry battalions with artillery support and air defense capability to enable it to fulfil its regime
guard duty and other internal security functions and to serve as a reserve
for the army. The basic equipment of the modernized guard was to be the
V-150 armored vehicle, TOW missiles, and Vulcan antiaircraft guns. In
1974 the estimated cost of the program was $335 million: $123 million for
equipment, $63 million for construction, and the rest for training and
management. By 1976, however, the total cost had escalated to $1.9 billion,
largely as a result of a twentyfold increase in construction costs — to
$1,366 million — to provide the guard with elaborate base and housing
facilities comparable to those of the regular forces.[14]

The basic military strategy endorsed by the survey expressed an uneasy compromise between dispersing the limited forces available to meet
any of several possible border threats, and concentrating them to meet a
major invasion. It envisaged the permanent deployment of substantial
parts of the Saudi forces in elaborate "military cities" consisting of bases,
airfields, hangars, depots, maintenance and repair shops, and living
facilities for the military, their families, and the civilian population providing services. The cities were located in the vicinity of threatened
frontiers: in Khamis Mushayt, near North and South Yemen; in Tabuk, in

the vicinity of Jordan and Israel; and at Hafr al-Batin, next to Kuwait and Iraq. Another substantial force was to be concentrated in the Riyadh-Kharj-Dhahran area to provide for the defense of the oil region and to constitute a strategic reserve; and a fifth force was to be deployed in the Jidda-Ta'if-Mecca region. In the event of a local border attack, the forces from the nearby military city, assisted if necessary by contingents flown in from the central reserves, would deal with the situation. In case of serious invasion, the local forces would try to block it with assistance from the central reserves. Failing that, they would fall back and join in the defense of a central corridor extending from Dhahran through Riyadh to Jidda and comprising the Kingdom's political center, its oil resources, and most of its population, pending the arrival of help from friendly powers.

The National Guard study endorsed its deployment to guard the oil facilities from its base in Hufuf and to provide protection to the regime from bases in Jidda, Riyadh, Ha'il, and Hufuf. In addition, the National Guard was to assist the army and the Frontier Guard in the area bordering the Yemens. Initially, the survey envisaged the construction of only improved cantonments for the guard, but shortly thereafter the character of the cantonments was modified to approximate the concept of military cities adopted for the regular forces.

The following points about the 1974 defense plans deserve emphasis:

1. The plans represented the most comprehensive and ambitious effort of the kind undertaken by the Saudis, and a new, significantly expanded defense concept.
2. The effort was undertaken not when the change in the strategic environment seemed to call for it, but when funds and political opportunity made it possible.
3. Conceptually, the defense plans sought to compensate for the constraints of vast space and limited manpower with a defense design and force structure requiring the kind of technological, administrative, and leadership aptitudes that past endeavors had shown to be conspicuously scarce.
4. Even on the best assumptions, the defense plans did not aim to prepare the Kingdom to meet the whole range of plausible regional threats by itself, but depended with regard to some important contingencies on a major Iranian, and ultimately American, role.
5. Although the forces envisaged by the plans were inadequate to meet all the defense threats, they were, if realized, sufficient to endow the Kingdom with a capability for offensive missions against weaker neighbors and could contribute substantially to an Arab military coalition against Israel.

Table 11. Order of battle and inventory of weapons, 1969 and 1975

	1969	1975
Personnel		
Army	28,000	40,000
Navy	1,000	1,500
Air force	5,000	5,500
National Guard	16,000	28,000
Coast Guard and Frontier Guard	—	6,500
Organization		
Army		
Infantry brigades	4–5	4
Armored brigades	—	1
Royal Guard battalions	1	1
Parachute battalions	1	1
Artillery battalions	—	3
SAM batteries	6	10
National Guard		
Infantry Battalions	20	20
Air force		
Fighter/bomber squadrons	1 (F-86)	2 (F-5E)
Counterinsurgency (COIN)/training squadrons	2 (see inventory)	2 (BAC-167)
Interceptor squadrons	2 (Lightnings)	2 (Lightnings)
Transport squadrons	2 (see inventory)	2 (C-130)
Helicopter squadrons	1 (AB-206, AB-205)	2 (AB-206, AB-205)

6. The entire defense design was supposed to be implemented over a ten-year period starting in 1974, during which, if the past were any guide, both the strategic environment and the Kingdom's internal political environment could change drastically.

In the meantime, despite the very substantial amounts spent on defense in the course of King Faisal's reign, the size of the armed forces, the number of organized formations, and their equipment remained comparatively modest because most of the defense allocations went for construction, training, and support and because cost efficiency was low. Table 11 summarizes the relevant data for 1975, the year of Faisal's death, and for 1969, the halfway point of Faisal's reign and the time when the radical change in the Kingdom's strategic environment began.

Judging by the Saudi estimates as reflected in actual use made of the armed forces, their actual capabilities were even less than the figures for inventory and formations might suggest. Throughout the period 1968–1975, for instance, the Saudis were engaged in conflict with South Yemen and had vital interests at stake there as well as in the Dhofar rebellion in Oman. Yet, except for the clash over Wadi'ah at the end of 1969, which was

Table 11 (continued)

	1969	1975
Inventory of weapons		
Army	85 M-47 medium and M-41 AMX-13 light tanks	85 M-47 medium and M-41 AMX-13 light tanks 150 AMX-30 main battle tanks
	60 AML-90 armored cars	200 AML-60/90 armored cars (plus some Staghounds, Greyhounds, and Ferret Scouts)
		150 mm guns; 75 mm recoilless rifles; SS-11 Harpoon antitank guided weapons; antiaircraft guns
	Hawk surface-to-air missiles (SAMs)	Hawk SAMs
Navy	1 patrol boat coastal patrol craft	1 patrol boat 3 fast patrol boats (Jaguar class) 50 small patrol boats 8 SRN-6 hovercraft under Coast Guard
Air force	11 F-86 Sabres	35 F-5Es 20 F-5Bs
	40 Hunter, Lightning jet Provost, and T-41A jet trainers 28 Lightning F-52/F-53s 4 Hunter interceptors	30 BAC-167 COIN/trainers 3 Lightning T-55 trainers 35 Lightning F-52/F-53s
	9 C-130 transports 10 C-47 transports 2 C-118 medium transports	21 C-130 transports 4 KC-130 transports
	20 AB-206 and AB-205 helicopters 2 Alouette III helicopters	45 AB-206 and AB-205 helicopters 6 Alouette III helicopters

Sources: International Institute for Strategic Studies, *The Military Balance, 1968–69, 1969–70,* and *1975–76* (London, 1968, 1969, 1975), and miscellaneous other sources.

forced on them by South Yemeni action, they refrained from committing their forces to battle for fear they might suffer a defeat that could have severe internal repercussions. Instead, they contented themselves with using their forces to supply and hold the ring for proxy tribal forces that did the actual, ultimately ineffective, fighting.

On the other hand, the Saudis made frequent and extensive use of their armed forces in noncombat deterrent or political-support roles. Thus in 1967 they deployed a brigade group in Jordan in connection with the Arab-Israeli crisis and war and left it there through the end of Faisal's reign, but carefully refrained from committing it to action in 1967, in the war of attrition, or in the 1970 civil war. In addition, they deployed another brigade in Syria in connection with the 1973 war in a support role, which accidentally saw some action. The forces sent to Syria had been sent earlier into Kuwait as part of a larger force that was committed in March 1973 to stiffen Kuwait's resistance to Iraqi encroachment on its border. These deployments may have made it impossible for the Saudis to marshal enough forces in the south to give them an acceptable option for combat action. If that was the case, it underscores a serious limitation on Saudi capabilities that even the 1974 plans do not seem to have addressed — namely, the inability of the Saudis to confront simultaneously a number of threats on several widely separated fronts.

Conclusions

Faisal took over from Saud the Kingdom founded by their father at a moment of grave danger to its very existence and left it at the zenith of its wealth, security, and influence. He saw it safely through historic events that impinged on its security and transformed its strategic environment, including a proxy armed confrontation with Egypt in Yemen, the end of Britain's secular peacekeeping role in southern Arabia and the Persian Gulf, three Arab-Israeli wars, the oil embargo, and the first open confrontation with the United States.

However, although Faisal's achievements gave the Kingdom a new lease on life, they did not ensure its security against future shocks, nor did they even equip it to deal better with all the problems identifiable at the time of his death. This was partly because the achievements were due in large measure to the strength of Faisal's individual personality and the unchallenged power position he held rather than to any decision-making institutions and procedures that he instituted. But this mixed result also stemmed from decisions made and not made and from inherent limitations in the Kingdom's basic conditions.

One of the most remarkable features of Faisal's success in seeing the Kingdom safely through a sea of potential defense and security problems was that he did so by relying on a variety of means other than conventional military power. From the 1973 crisis on, he of course relied heavily on the leverage of oil power and enormous wealth, but even before that he used mainly a mixture of conventional diplomacy and Arabian tribal relations methods in conducting relations with his neighbors. To be sure, Faisal, like his two predecessors, made several attempts to build up a military capability that could serve as a major component of the Kingdom's defense strategy and policy endeavors. These attempts, however, were halfhearted and partial and fell far short of their goal because of fluctuating financial and diplomatic constraints, vast space and a slowly evolving infrastructure, and severe manpower limitations, aggravated by fear of sectionalism, suspicion of the regular armed forces, and the entrenchment of vested interests in multiple security instruments. As a result, throughout Faisal's reign the Kingdom's defense policy centered on the conceptualization and management of its foreign relations and its internal policy. The last, most ambitious and comprehensive, attempt to build military power as a serious instrument of national security was still embryonic and held an uncertain promise at the time of Faisal's death.

The lack of a significant military capability contributed to Faisal's pursuit of a defense–foreign policy style that had substantial roots in Arabian tribal culture. The principal features of that style included the following:

1. A disposition to appease rather than resist a powerful opponent if at all possible, and to avoid irreparable confrontation if a clash is inevitable. This approach was illustrated in Faisal's relations and dealings with Nasser throughout.
2. A tendency to wait for events to unfold before reacting, rather than seek to anticipate them. A clear example was Faisal's response to the British announcement of their intent to terminate their peacekeeping responsibilities in the Persian Gulf.
3. A propensity to give priority to immediate, clear demands rather than to long-term strategic considerations when the two come into conflict. A demonstration of this tendency was apparent in what was probably the most fateful decision for Saudi Arabia since King Ibn Saud granted to SOCAL the original oil concession, namely, Faisal's renunciation of his initial intent to bring about a reduction in the December 1973 Tehran oil price, a move that was prompted mainly by a desire to avoid an immediate clash with Iran.

Apparent exceptions to this mode of operation only confirm it. For instance, Faisal's relentless open hostility toward South Yemen was largely founded on an assessment that it was within his power to destroy its regime. When events proved otherwise, he tried to shift to a policy of accommodation. His confrontational resort to an oil embargo against the United States was delayed until the prospects of an imminent Arab military disaster made it seem inevitable. His retention of the embargo for several months afterward was carefully calibrated to allow him to stay within the limits of American tolerance while bringing the interested Arab parties around to easing the conditions for its removal.

Regarding the substance of the defense-oriented foreign policy, Faisal's handling of the momentous events of his reign was guided by certain consistent conceptions and positions. Once the British announced their intention of withdrawing from south Arabia and the Persian Gulf, the Saudis under Faisal gradually developed at least a tacit political-strategic conception that viewed their defense–foreign policy problems in terms of a matrix comprising their relationship with the United States and three distinct but interrelated arenas: south Arabia, the Gulf region, and the Arab-Israeli arena.

In south Arabia the main problem involved the hostility of the PDRY regime, the instability of the YAR, and the syndrome of Yemen unity. The Saudis felt capable of dealing with this problem by themselves. South Yemen's position abutting Bab al-Mandeb presented a potential threat to the security of that oil route, and the Soviet positions in the Horn of Africa across the strait presented a wider potential problem; but if these threats became actual, the Saudis expected the United States to react effectively for its own reasons.

Oman linked the problems of the Yemens and the Persian Gulf. The rebellion supported by PDRY increased the danger of that country's hostility to Saudi Arabia and presented a potential threat to oil transit through the Strait of Hormuz and to the vulnerable United Arab Emirates. The Saudis felt they could contribute to dealing with that problem by pinning down most of PDRY's resources, thus limiting the extent of its assistance to forces hostile to the Omani regime. The remainder of the solution they were reluctantly willing to leave to Iran and, ultimately, the United States.

In the Persian Gulf the problem was two-tiered: at one level there was the threat of radical, hostile Iraq to the regimes of Saudia Arabia and the Gulf emirates, and the related threat to oil facilities and transit; at another level there loomed the threat of Iranian hegemony and its potential implications. The Saudis could not do much by themselves to counter either danger. They essentially counted on Iran to check Iraq, and on the United States to check Iran. They saw no basic difficulty in cultivating a close relationship with the United States to that end, since the interests of the two countries almost completely coincided.

In the Arab-Israeli arena the problem had two aspects. First, the persistence of the Arab-Israeli conflict stimulated Arab radicalism and Soviet penetration in the region, which in turn threatened the Saudis in many ways. The Saudis needed the United States' support to deal with some of those threats and depended on it entirely for a basic solution of the problem. In this case, however, American support was not assured, and the American view of a solution to the problem differed, sometimes greatly, from the Saudis' and, in their eyes, tended to perpetuate the problem. The second aspect of the problem was that the persistence of the conflict exposed the Saudis to attack for cooperating with the United States in other arenas, where American support was both forthcoming and essential or important. This is why Faisal and the Saudis asserted again and again that the Arab-Israeli conflict and the American position toward it was their chief defense–foreign policy issue, even though the record shows that they faced a multitude of other problems.

PART FOUR

The Reign of Khaled

1975–1982

The motto and actual supreme wish of Faisal's successors was continuity; yet the reign of Khaled was marked by discontinuities and qualitative changes in all spheres of Saudi existence. Indeed the Khaled era as a whole may be viewed as a vivid demonstration of the proposition that, regardless of appearances to the contrary and the wishes of the rulers, discontinuity and profound change have become almost the defining characteristics of the Kingdom.

That proposition was demonstrated at the center of power and decision making, where a basic structural change with far-reaching implications took place as a result of the mere fact that a collective leadership replaced Faisal's unitary rule and became entrenched during Khaled's reign instead of reverting to the single-leader pattern. It was demonstrated at the level of society at large, where the implementation of the massive second five-year plan devised under Faisal and the continuation of that policy through another, even more massive, plan resulted in vast economic and social changes that altered the Kingdom's grand strategic posture and generated a potential for radical political change or upheaval. The proposition was above all demonstrated in the sphere of defense and security, where challenges to the Kingdom were essentially defined by developments beyond its control, and where its ability to meet those challenges effectively was impaired by the absence of a single captain at the helm and constrained by the problems attending the process of development.

The central concern of this book is, of course, developments in the third sphere. However, because changes in the other two had a crucial bearing on Saudi responses to external defense and security challenges, it is useful to outline the principal features of the changes at the power center and in the domestic environment that are most relevant to the Kingdom's defense and security policies. Because developments in the latter sphere were highly complex, a chapter providing an overview precedes the chapters of detailed analysis.

8

A Time of Change: Overview

Changes at the Power Center

Khaled's predecessor, upon acceding to the throne, had sought to avoid a repetition of his own experience with King Saud, wherein an informal diarchy became the basis for a relentless power struggle that nearly wrought disaster upon the dynasty and the realm. Faisal reunited the prime ministership and the crown and kept both to himself, diminished the collective power of the Council of Ministers, and saw to it that the man designated crown prince was incapable of either challenging him or serving as a rallying point for a hostile coalition. He managed to get the eldest half-brother after him, the strong but irascible Muhammad ibn Abd al-Aziz, to renounce his claim to the succession in favor of the next eldest, Muhammad's full brother Khaled, who was known to be ailing, devoid of political ambition, and lacking in any demonstrated talent beyond an ability to get along with the tribes.[1]

Later in his reign, when he needed the help of a working lieutenant and the ailing Khaled sought to retire, Faisal created in 1967 the post of second deputy prime minister, which he conferred upon the energetic and able minister of interior, Fahd ibn Abd al-Aziz, and convinced Khaled to stay on in the relatively inactive positions of crown prince and first deputy prime minister. At the same time Faisal proceeded to balance Fahd's increased power by delegating more power to other key princes, and to check anyone's ability to build a threatening coalition by expanding and diversifying the royal family power circle, bringing back to the fold the alienated Free Princes, and initiating the career of younger princes as they came of age. When necessary, Faisal did not hesitate to come down against his second deputy prime minister and minister of interior, as he did in connection with a policy dispute that developed in the wake of the 1969 plots against the regime and caused Fahd to leave the country in a huff for a self-exile that lasted from October 1969 to May 1970.[2]

Faisal's management of royal family politics averted the strife that had characterized the previous reign and enabled him to exercise undisputed authority throughout his reign; but this achievement contained the seeds of trouble for his successors. Observers unanimously noted the smooth formal succession, as Khaled was proclaimed king immediately after Faisal's assassination, Fahd was made crown prince and first deputy prime minister, Abdallah became second deputy prime minister, and all members of the family spoke of continuing Faisal's well-established policies. However, no one noticed either then or since that, because Faisal had created a power structure tailored to his abilities, concerns, and aims, his death necessarily entailed a major change in the power structure. Whereas Faisal's rule was a single leadership mitigated by the need to preserve the consent of important supporters, that of his successors was essentially a collective leadership headed by a recognized final arbiter in the person of King Khaled, mitigated by the presence of a more prominent wielder of delegated responsibility in the person of Crown Prince Fahd.

The basic change in the power structure was obscured by the fact that Fahd did indeed play the most prominent and active role during the first few years of Khaled's reign. Actually, however, Fahd's prominence was due to the fact that the foreign and domestic conditions of the Kingdom during those years allowed him to pursue the policies laid down by Faisal (see below), which commanded the consensus of the collective leadership. When those conditions changed and new situations required crucial decisions and initiatives, differences of view among the leaders asserted themselves, shifting coalitions were formed around personalities and positions, and Fahd's standing was reduced to that of a caucus leader who managed to have his way in some instances but failed in others. In those other instances, the rallying point of the opposition was often Abdallah ibn Abd al-Aziz, the second deputy prime minister and commander of the National Guard, who shared with King Khaled the disposition of a beleaguered conservative.

The turning point in royal family politics occurred in the first months of 1979, when the nearly simultaneous collapse of the shah's regime in Iran, the signing of the Egyptian-Israeli peace treaty, and the outbreak of war between the two Yemens triggered a critical policy debate among the Saudi leaders that resulted in a defeat for Fahd and in his leaving the Kingdom for a self-imposed exile. That episode came close to causing the kind of split that had afflicted the royal family during King Saud's reign, and incidentally demonstrated once more the opposite of the conventional wisdom that the royal family tended to close ranks in the face of adversity. Circumstances helped the Saudi leaders heal that split through compromise, but thereafter the characteristics typical of collective leadership manifested themselves clearly in the Kingdom's policies and behavior. Those characteristics were aptly described by Max Weber: "Collegiality unavoidably obstructs the promptness of decision, the consistency of policy, the clear responsibility of the individual, and the ruthlessness to outsiders combined with maintenance of the discipline within the group."[3]

Another relevant development within the royal family was the coming of age of the younger sons and older grandsons of Ibn Saud and the proliferation of the royal family as a whole. By the end of Khaled's reign various estimates put the number of male members of the Al Saud family at between 3,000 and 5,000. The senior princes have dominated the central and provincial governments, while the junior members have pervaded the upper ranks of the civil service and the armed forces, the quasi-governmental agencies and corporations, and large private businesses.

It is often argued that the size and ubiquity of the royal family provide a formidable defense for the regime and endow it with other assets not available to other modernizing regimes, monarchical or republican. This argument, though valid, is counterbalanced by various factors that make the size and role of the royal family serious potential liabilities.

First, the increasing size and diversification of the royal family tend to dilute its sense of unity and weaken its cohesion. Second, the size and diversity of the royal family also tend to dilute the aura of royalty in the eyes of others and thus debase the status of the royal family to that of a privileged class or caste perpetuating itself by restrictions on marriage to commoners, especially for female members. Third, the royal family's involvement in the affairs of the country tends to exacerbate the tension between the ascriptive norms that underlie its privileges and the achievement-oriented values of the large and growing middle classes. Although commoners have been co-opted into high offices and have prospered in entrepreneurial fields, many positions and advantages have remained the exclusive preserve of the members of the royal family.

Fourth, the size and involvement of the royal family have also increased the incidence both of abuses by its less responsible members and of public exposure of those abuses. The effect is to mar the reputation of the royal family as a whole and to undermine its legitimacy. Finally, and perhaps most important, the coming of age of younger sons, older grandsons, and even great-grandsons of Ibn Saud has multiplied the number of claimants to a share of power and thus added to the complexity of the already complicated succession problem that rocked the dynasty after the death of its founder.[4]

Strategically Relevant Domestic Developments

In the domestic sphere, Faisal took in 1974 what was probably the most fateful single decision in Saudi history since his father granted the oil concession to SOCAL: he let the December 1973 Tehran price hike stand and opted to spend the resultant huge increase in revenue on development (see Chapter 6). Faisal presided over the elaboration of the second five-year plan, involving a planned outlay of $142 billion (compared with $9.2 billion for the expanded first five-year plan), but it was left to his successors to launch and execute it. They did, spending $40 billion more than initially planned, and followed up with an even more ambitious third plan for the period 1980–1985, which involved projected outlays of $237 billion on civilian expenditures and unprojected expenditures of at least $100 billion for defense and security and foreign aid.[5] In both cases the level of planned expenditure was approximately based on a projection of the level of oil revenue in the year in which the plans were formulated or launched. This fact confirms the conclusion reached in Chapter 6 that the Saudis felt they had to spend the bulk of the anticipated revenues regardless of how huge they were. Table 12 shows the revenues from oil during the last years of Faisal's reign and throughout Khaled's.

The following observations are directly or indirectly pertinent to a consideration of Saudi defense and security.

1. The first five-year plan was officially reported to have achieved an annual compounded growth rate (in 1969–70 prices) of 13.4 percent, with the oil sector growing at 14.8 percent and the nonoil sector at 11.7 percent. The second five-year plan was reported to have achieved an estimated annual growth rate of 8 percent, with the oil sector growing at 4.8 percent and the nonoil sector at 15 percent. National income was projected to grow in 1980–1985 at an annual average rate of 19 percent, per capita income at 15.5 percent.[6]

2. The second plan aimed at strengthening defense, building the country's physical infrastructure, developing its social services, and beginning to reduce long-term dependence on oil by developing other productive sectors. In their annual budgeted outlays, the Saudis exceeded the planned expenditures in the first two sectors and fell far short of the targets in the last. Construction, which cut across most sectors, accounted for nearly 50 percent of budgeted outlays. Planned outlays for defense were 15.7 percent of the total, whereas budgeted outlays came to

Table 12. Saudi oil revenues, 1972–1982

Year	Billion $[a]
1972	2.7
1973	4.3
1974	22.6
1975	25.7
1976	30.8
1977	36.5
1978	32.2
1979	48.4
1980	84.5
1981	102.1
1982	70.5

Source: Ministry of Petroleum and
Natural Resources, *Petroleum Statistical
Bulletin,* 13 (1982), 14.
a. Rounded to nearest hundred million.

27.3 percent. For health, education, and labor and social affairs, the planned outlays were 17.2 percent, the budgeted outlays 17.9 percent. Likewise, for transport and communications and public works and housing, planned outlays were 13.9 percent and budgeted outlays 13.2 percent. On the other hand, for industry, commerce, electricity, and agriculture, planned outlays were 15.9 percent but the budgeted outlays were only 3.7 percent. The government simply could not find ways to spend nearly the amounts it had planned to spend in these sectors.[7]

3. The third five-year plan sought to shift the emphasis from the building of infrastructure, where the second plan generally succeeded, to diversification of the economy, where the second plan did not do so well. The returns on the third plan on this score are not yet in, but the prospects do not look much more promising than in the past. In industry, the main barriers to growth will probably continue to be the paucity of entrepreneurial Saudis and the attractiveness of the "throughput" sectors — construction and distribution — where huge profits are relatively easy to attain. In agriculture, the problems are more deeply rooted — small landholdings, the dispersion of farms over vast areas, inadequate water supplies, and harsh climate. To the extent that these problems can be overcome, much time will be required. In the meantime, the combined contribution of non-oil-related industry and agriculture to GDP was 2.6 percent in 1980–81, less than 4 percent of the contribution of the oil sector.

4. One of the cornerstones of the Saudi development drive—construction of the huge petrochemical plants in Jubail and Yanbo—is unlikely to increase the potential for diversification. Whatever the potential economic viability of these plants—and opinion has varied to extremes on this question—there is no doubt that the dependence of the petrochemical industry on associated gas will not decrease the Kingdom's dependence on oil and indeed may reduce its flexibility regarding oil policy. In early 1983, for instance, oil minister Yamani stated in an interview that Saudi oil production at the time had fallen to a level "beyond which it can fall no further unless we close down some of our plants which operate on associated gas. This would mean reducing the quantity of sweet water we produce from sea water and cutting down on electricity consumption . . . "[8] Yamani may have exaggerated the point for tactical reasons related to OPEC production quotas; but it is noteworthy that he made this statement even before the huge Jubail and Yanbo plants, with their vast requirement of associated gas, came on line.

5. While the Saudis' efforts to alter their grand strategic position by reducing their dependence on oil have met with limited success, their vastly increased imports as a result of greatly heightened economic activity have altered their position in the opposite direction. The Kingdom's imports soared more than ninefold in six years, from SR 14.8 billion in 1975 to SR 135.3 billion in 1981.[9] Thus the Saudis became vulnerable to retaliation by suppliers of essential goods if they should attempt to use the oil weapon again. More important, they became far more vulnerable to disruption of the flow of essential as well as nonessential goods, since nearly all imports have to pass through at least one of the three choke points, the Suez Canal, Bab al-Mandeb, and the Strait of Hormuz.

6. At the strategic level, one of the clearest and most tangible effects of the development effort was to alter the constraint of a vast, disconnected territory by means of a massive transport and communications network. A 750-mile, 48-inch-diameter pipeline from the eastern oil fields to Yanbo on the Red Sea was begun in the summer of 1978 and was scheduled for completion in 1981.[10] The pipeline, with a throughput capacity of 2–2.3 mbd, was designed for the multiple purposes of providing an alternative outlet to the Strait of Hormuz, filling a strategic petroleum reserve on the western side of the Kingdom, and supplying the petrochemical complex at Yanbo. Existing ports were enlarged and new ones built, increasing the number of berths from 25 in 1975 to 123 in 1981.[11] Air transport was substantially developed. By the late 1970s a regularly scheduled service touched twenty airports throughout the Kingdom. Some, such as Jidda, Riyadh, and Dhahran, were international; others, such as Dhahran, Tabuk, and Turaif, were primarily designed as military bases; all, how-

ever, served a double function in varying degrees. The paved road network was expanded from 9,660 miles in 1973–74 to 21,154 miles in 1980–81.[12] The Kingdom's patchwork telecommunications system, which in 1970 provided 50,000 telephones in ten cities and towns, was replaced by 1982 with one of the world's most sophisticated systems, maintaining more than 800,000 telephones throughout 90 percent of the country.[13]

Although these achievements greatly improved the conditions that prevailed during Faisal's reign, in some respects they were still inadequate to the requirements of so large a country. For instance, in March 1983 Prince Abdallah pointed out in a press interview that "our road network is absurd; Saudi Arabia is a huge continent and is not only Riyadh and Jidda."[14] For the sake of comparison, in 1978 the Commonwealth of Massachusetts, which is about one hundredth the size of Saudi Arabia, had some 33,000 miles of paved roads, or 50 percent more than the Kingdom at that time.[15] More appropriate perhaps, Israel, which is also one hundredth the size of Saudi Arabia, had proportionally about forty times as many miles of paved roads as the Kingdom.[16]

7. To meet the manpower requirements for their development plans, the Saudis have imported foreign labor on a massive scale, thus altering the size and profile of the Kingdom's population — its other strategic constraint besides geography. In 1975, the final year of the first plan, foreign workers amounted to 314,000.[17] In 1980 their number had reached 2.1 million, plus about 400,000 dependents.[18] About 1 million were from North Yemen. Egyptians and Jordanians-Palestinians accounted for about 200,000 each. Sudanese, South Yemenis, Lebanese-Palestinians, Pakistanis, Indians, South Koreans, and Filipinos contributed 50,000–100,000 each. In the late 1970s the Saudis made a conscious switch in favor of Pakistanis and Filipinos at the expense of others. Westerners numbered about 100,000, including 40,000 Americans, 25,000 Britons, 15,000 French, 13,000 Italians, and 10,000 West Germans.[19]

The foreign workers and their dependents amounted to half the total national Saudi population, estimated at about 5 million in 1980.[20] Their economic and social weight, however, was much greater, for they constituted twice the nominal Saudi work force and an even higher percentage of the "effective" national labor force. More than half the Saudi population was under the age of fifteen,[21] and half the remainder were women, most of whom are excluded from the labor force on religious grounds. Thus the national labor force amounted to about 1 million, or a scant 22 percent of the population, compared with 42 percent for Egypt and 50 percent for Israel. Furthermore, the Saudi labor force was itself divided in half between a persisting subsistence sector scattered throughout the country and a "modern" sector concentrated in urban centers, where

nearly all the foreign workers are also to be found. The effectiveness of
even the urban Saudi workers was restricted by lack of education among
the older age groups and by the persistence of traditional and tribal
values, such as resistance to external discipline, contempt for manual
labor, and placing a high value on idle leisure.

8. The use of foreign labor on a vast scale had a mixed effect on the
Kingdom's security position. On the one hand, it made possible the pursuit of the ambitious development plans and thus greatly enhanced its
overall strategic potential. Also, foreign labor made it possible for the
Kingdom to maintain a larger and more sophisticated defense establishment than would otherwise have been possible. Although foreign personnel have been sparingly used in the "teeth" component of the defense
and security forces, they have been used on a large scale in training and
maintenance and in various "tail" functions. Finally, the massive use of
foreigners in civilian activities has released Saudi manpower for use in
defense and security.

On the other hand, the masses of foreign workers have raised serious
security problems, creating the need for a much larger security apparatus to control them than would otherwise have been necessary. Although the well-paid foreign workers are unlikely to be the source of
major upheavals themselves, they could easily serve as havens and provide recruits for outside saboteurs, as they did in the 1960s at the height of
the clash between Nasser and the Kingdom, or for domestic rebels, as
they did in part for the Islamic fundamentalists who seized Mecca's
Grand Mosque in 1979. Perhaps more serious because more difficult to
control, the presence of so many "modernized" foreign workers could
convey to the Saudi populace, however indirectly, political notions and
values that run counter to those on which the Saudi political order rests.
Above all, the very notion of using Muslims and Arabs as "foreign"
workers, who are denied the rights enjoyed by Saudi citizens, introduces a
discrimination based on nationality that runs counter to the basic Islamic and Arab principles proclaimed by the regime as the foundations of
its legitimacy. This contradiction leaves the regime vulnerable to devastating criticism by potential domestic opposition and hostile outside
powers, and the workers themselves receptive to agitation on those
grounds.

9. While enlarging the total manpower pool at their disposal by importing foreign workers, with all the advantages and disadvantages that
this practice entailed, the Saudis also made great efforts to raise the
educational level of their own population and potential labor force. The
total number of students at all educational levels rose from 746,000 in
1972–73 to 978,000 in 1974–75 and to 1,581,000 in 1980–81. The number of
students enrolled in postsecondary institutes and universities increased

even more dramatically, from 11,300 in 1972–73 to 19,100 in 1974–75 and to 32,100 in 1980–81.[22] In addition, some 9,500 Saudi students were enrolled in undergraduate and graduate studies in universities abroad in 1979–80 — nearly double the number of three years before — 70 percent in colleges and universities in the United States.[23]

Impressive as these figures are, their significance in terms of developing a modern labor force must be discounted by at least two factors. One is that the quality of Saudi education has been mixed for various reasons, not the least of which is the haste with which the quantitative expansion has taken place. The other factor is that 39 percent of the school population in 1980–81 consisted of females, whose education has had little bearing on the labor force so far. The Saudis have realized that they must educate their women in order to make them fit wives and mothers for their educated husbands and children; but they have persisted in excluding them on ostensibly religious grounds from all but a few occupations outside the home. The record of comparable societies and the pressures of Saudi Arabia's own needs for qualified labor suggest that sooner or later the Kingdom's rulers will have to give way on the employment of women. However, the sooner the adaptation is made the more politically risky it will be, and the later it is done, the longer the waste of educated women as members of the labor force will persist.

10. Altogether, the enormous acceleration of the pace of development in the Khaled era put the entire Saudi society in motion and released powerful forces for further change that the regime has been unable to comprehend, let alone control. The dizzyingly rapid growth of a few urban conglomerations gave rise to a pronounced split between urban and rural-tribal ways of life, social organization, values, and standards of living. Within the urban sector itself, a widening fissure divided several emerging new classes from surviving traditional urban groupings and recent rural migrants, and both of those from the masses of foreign workers. The tensions and strains accompanying these changes exploded in the November 1979 seizure of the Grand Mosque in Mecca by Islamic fundamentalist insurgents, who included students of religion, foreign workers, 'Utaiba tribesmen, and even disaffected members of the National Guard reserves. After putting down the insurrection by force, the regime responded, typically, with some measures designed to appease the underlying concerns of the rebels and to enhance its image as an enforcer of tradition, and others designed to reassure the new classes, whose interests were bound with continuing development and change.

The new classes include an industrial proletariat, a mercantile bourgeoisie, and a so-called new middle class. The first of these, though comparatively small, is concentrated in the critical oil industry and has a tradition of activism going back to the 1950s. The second consists of traditional Hijazi trading families and newcomers who have flourished as a result of the massive development projects. Because that class has fed directly or indirectly on government expenditures rather than being itself a major source of government revenue through taxation, it has so far lacked the incentive that has prompted Western bourgeoisies to seek participation in and control of political power. However, as that class gets used to its vast new wealth, it, too, is likely to press for a voice in government. In the meantime, its "collusion" with members of the vast royal family in amassing wealth by fair and foul means and its conspicuous consumption have constituted an increasing provocation to traditional and other new elements of society.

The emergence of the so-called new middle class is probably the most politically relevant result of the Kingdom's ultrarapid modernization effort. That class is composed of teachers of modern subjects (as distinguished from the traditional religious teachers), middle- and upper-grade civil servants, military officers, and self-employed professionals. The common characteristic of these groups is that they owe their status and income to their modern education, which is not only their means of earning a living but also a key determinant of their consciousness and a driving force in their behavior. It has been shown that throughout the Third World a new middle class is initially brought forth by traditional regimes seeking "defensive modernization," but that eventually it tends to become alienated from its progenitors, as its pressure for ever further modernization begins to encroach upon the rulers' sphere of prerogative or upon the ideological underpinnings of their power. Although the class as a whole lacks the cohesiveness to act as a revolutionary class, its alienation undermines the regime and creates a favorable atmosphere for insurrectionary action by other groups, most often the military. A symbolic military defeat or a major economic failure usually provides the spark that ignites the insurrection.[24]

The number of people belonging to the new middle class in the Kingdom increased nearly fourfold in a decade—from 22,200 in 1970 to 86,200 in 1980, representing an increase from 2.5 percent of the Saudi labor force to 7.2 percent.[25] Elsewhere in the Middle East and in the Third World, that class has frequently acted as an agent of coup d'états and revolutionary change, according to the dynamics described, once it has attained a comparable mass level.[26] Although Saudi Arabia's abundant wealth, its huge and socially involved royal family, and its vast and disconnected territory endow it with special conditions, a recent study has shown that these have aggravating as well as mitigating effects and thus do not exempt the Kingdom from the essential dynamics of regime–new middle class relations.[27] The regime itself has shown a partial awareness of that reality by scrupulously avoiding military encounters that might result in a defeat, which could in turn trigger an upheaval. But the regime's relationship to the new middle class is best illustrated by its approach to the issue of a basic law, historically a typical aim of that class's drive for rationalization.

Ever since the mid-1950s, each time the regime has experienced difficulties at home or abroad, it has promised to issue a basic law that would define the rights and obligations of citizens while providing for their participation in the political process; and each time the immediate crisis has passed, the promise has been shelved, to be reiterated with some variation during the next crisis. This sequence occurred in 1958, in connection with the first crisis in the Saud-Faisal struggle; in 1960, in another expression of that struggle; in 1962, in connection with the Yemen war; in 1970, in the aftermath of the 1969 coup attempts and subsequent purges; in 1975, after Faisal's assassination; in 1979, in the wake of the takeover of the Grand Mosque by fundamentalist insurgents; and in 1982, after King Khaled's death. The fact that various Saudi leaders have felt it necessary to make those promises shows the extent of their awareness of an unsatisfied demand that needed to be appeased. The fact that those who made the promises have been unwilling or unable to deliver on them betrays an ingrained opposition within the regime's power center that paralyzes its capacity for political adaptation and bodes ill for its future.

Political-Strategic and Strategic-Military Developments: Two Stages

In the sphere of defense and foreign policy, Khaled's reign was marked by two distinct stages. During the first three years or so, the regime endeavored to pursue Faisal's overall strategy and, with the help of favorable external circumstances, not only accomplished that but even improved on Faisal's performance. Starting in 1978, however, difficulties began to develop independently in the Arab-Israeli, Gulf, and south Arabian arenas, and in 1979 they all erupted simultaneously in a set of crises that became interlinked and compelled the regime to make critical new strategic choices. Any of the options entailed a break with the specific courses set by Faisal. The choice actually made also proved impossible to sustain and soon gave way to an increasing tendency to improvisation to meet immediate problems or take advantage of fleeting opportunities, with a resultant loss of consistency or continuity in overall high policy.

The transition from the first to the second stage was closely related to the latent change in the center of the Saudi power structure as a result of Faisal's death. As long as Faisal's policies seemed to be working, key members of the royal family were content to let Crown Prince Fahd make the operational decisions and assume the position of first among equals.

But once events changed the relevant configurations and imposed the need for new, critical choices, some of those family members challenged the choice favored by Fahd, had their way in the family councils, and drove Fahd, in protest, to leave the country in a self-imposed exile. The split in the royal family was healed and Fahd returned to office within a few months; but the reconciliation was effected on the basis of an ad hoc policy compromise that signaled the entrenchment of collective leadership with its attendant typical traits.

One by-product of the combined foreign and domestic crises of 1979 was another devastating oil shock. The roots of the problem lay in the disruption of Iran's production by the revolution, but it was the ill-timed reduction of Saudi production in January and March 1979 that precipitated a panic in the world market and sent oil prices soaring. It was typical of Saudi behavior in the second stage that, unlike the 1973 embargo, the Saudi action in early 1979 had no ultimate political strategic objective but was taken for entirely local tactical reasons related to appeasing the Iranian revolutionaries. Also typically, the action brought some short-term benefit to the Kingdom in the form of redoubled revenues in the next two or three years but ran counter to its own well-established conception of its long-term interest. It accelerated processes that produced an oil glut already in 1982, which in turn led to strains in OPEC, a drastic cut in the Kingdom's production, and a sharp and sustained drop in revenue.

The political-strategic crisis naturally affected the strategic-military sphere by altering the premises underlying the defense concept and related plans inherited from the Faisal era. The new view of potential friends and foes, of the nature of the most likely threats, and of the resources at the Kingdom's disposal that emerged by early 1979 led to a revision of the defense concept worked out in 1974–75. The Saudis now sought to achieve as independent a defense capability as possible to take account of their changed relations with the United States, placed greater reliance than ever on high technology to compensate for the constraints of vast space and scarce manpower, emphasized air and naval defense in the face of threats from revolutionary Iran, sought defense coordination with the small Gulf countries to protect their flanks, and endeavored to enlist military contributions from Pakistan and Jordan to buttress their thinly stretched armed forces.

Whatever plausibility the revised plans had in the abstract, they were riddled at the practical level with serious contradictions, or else they ran up against domestic political considerations. In general, the very idea of a military establishment that is short on elementary maintenance awareness and skills going for supersophisticated technology seems highly dubious. More specifically, the emphasis on highly advanced air and

naval defense programs necessitated greater and more prolonged dependence on American assistance than before. This aspiration ran counter
to the goal of independence and obstructed the aim of promoting defense
cooperation among the Gulf countries, some of which precisely feared
greater American involvement in their affairs. As for the regime's effort
to establish a Pakistani military connection, this became entangled in
disagreements over jurisdiction and substance among key members of
the royal family and was ultimately reduced to modest proportions. The
net overall result was that in the second stage of Khaled's reign the
Saudis' defense strategy lost the coherence it had had in the first and was
reduced to a series of disparate, often contradictory objectives in almost
the same way that political strategy was.

These general political-strategic and strategic-military trends unfolded
through many shifting currents and crosscurrents of major events, actions, and reactions. The following sections summarize these trends in
four distinct but interrelated arenas during the two major stages of
Khaled's reign. Subsequent chapters will discuss these arenas and stages
in detail.

Stage One: Success and Crisis, March 1975 – March 1979

THE ARAB-ISRAELI ARENA Faisal's successors inherited a position of
Saudi leadership, anchored in a Riyadh-Cairo-Damascus strategic alignment that protected them from attack by Arab radicals, strengthened
their security position in the Gulf, facilitated their handling of the south
Arabian problems, and allowed them to cultivate their American connection.

In the next four years, however, the strategic triangle was exposed to a
series of developments that pitted Cairo and Damascus against each
other and threatened to repolarize the Arab countries, force the Saudis to
take sides, and forfeit their advantageous position. These developments
included: (1) Egypt's signing of the American-mediated Sinai II agreement
with Israel in September 1975; (2) Syria's intervention in the Lebanese
civil war in 1975–1976; (3) Sadat's dramatic visit to Jerusalem in quest of
peace in November 1977; (4) the American-mediated Camp David agreements of September 1978; and (5) the signing of the American-sponsored
Egyptian-Israeli peace treaty in March 1979.

The Saudis managed to balance support for Cairo in connection with
Sinai II with partial support for Damascus in connection with its involvement in Lebanon and thus to keep their lines to both capitals open. They
even succeeded in mediating a reconciliation between Egypt and Syria
and thus briefly restored the triangular alliance in late 1976, in anticipation of working with the new American administration on a comprehen-

sive peace conference. When Cairo and Damascus flew apart again in the wake of Sadat's visit to Jerusalem, the Saudis managed to preserve their lines to both powers, albeit with greater difficulty, even after the Camp David agreements. The signing of the Egyptian-Israeli peace treaty, however, finally exhausted the Saudis' ability to keep their two allies in harness and forced them to make a choice.

By the time the treaty was signed, a strong Arab opposition front had formed around an unheard-of Damascus-Baghdad axis, which threatened any party that would not actively ostracize and penalize Egypt. This threat came at a time when the collapse of the shah's regime in Iran and the outbreak of war between the Yemens confronted the Kingdom with additional critical dangers. The Saudis were thus forced to choose between two strategies: (1) to espouse unequivocally an American-oriented strategy, of which the Egyptian-Israeli treaty was a central part, and in that context confront the Damascus-Baghdad coalition as well as revolutionary Iran; or (2) to join the Damascus-Baghdad coalition, use appeasement and the Arab alliance to deal with the dangers of Iran and the Yemens, and in that context risk the American connection. The Saudi ruling establishment agonized and split over the issue but came down in favor of the latter choice. In that connection it decided to cut oil production to satisfy Iran and triggered a panic in the world oil market.

THE GULF ARENA   In the Gulf, the signing of the Algiers agreement on March 6, 1975, settling the long-standing disputes between Iran and Iraq, promised an auspicious beginning for Khaled's reign. The agreement, which was made possible by Iraqi concessions to Iran, also marked a turn by Iraq toward moderation in its relations with its Arab neighbors and transformed the strategic configuration in the Gulf in favor of the Kingdom. Previously the Kingdom had been forced by Iraq's active hostility to depend on Iran for protection at the risk of enhancing the latter's hegemonic aspirations; now the Saudis could play off Iraq against Iran to neutralize dangers from both directions and to advance their own aspirations for predominant influence among the smaller Gulf countries. Moreover, with the abatement of the Iraqi danger, the Saudis could afford to use their oil policy to challenge Iran's position as the regional favorite of the Nixon and Ford administrations and to encourage the Carter administration's cooler disposition toward Iran.

The maneuvering among the parties of the newly formed Riyadh-Tehran-Baghdad triangle focused heavily on the issue of Gulf security. The Saudis managed for some three years to use Iraq's opposition to neutralize the shah's scheme of a regional collective security pact, which was bound to be dominated by Iran, and the shah's opposition to neutralize Iraq's aspiration for a series of bilateral pacts between itself and individual Arab countries of the Gulf, in which Iraq would have been the senior partner. In the first half of 1978, developments in the Horn of Africa and Afghanistan boosted the shah's continuing exertions and created a more favorable climate for his security schemes; before he could avail himself of the chance, however, his energies were diverted to growing troubles at home, which resulted in his overthrow by the turn of the year.

The fall of the shah's regime nullified all the previous Saudi gains, turned the strategic configuration in the Gulf topsy-turvy, and confronted the Kingdom with grave potential dangers. The problem was made much worse by the fact that the American ultimate strategic backstop was proving to be problematic just when it was most needed. The United States had not only failed to save the shah and flirted with alternatives to his rule, but after the final collapse of the monarchy Washington proposed to link protection of the Kingdom against the Iranian revolution to Saudi support for the Egyptian-Israeli peace treaty, in defiance of the Arab front that had formed to oppose the latter. The belated American help in connection with the simultaneous eruption of war between the Yemens somewhat redeemed the American image in the eyes of some Saudi leaders, but not enough to prevent a decision by the ruling establishment to turn away from the United States and seek protection elsewhere.

THE YEMENS AND SOUTH ARABIA   The initial success of Faisal's successors in managing the Kingdom's relationship with both Damascus and Cairo, and with both Tehran and Baghdad, encouraged them to attempt to bring about a similar result with regard to Aden and San'a. They started by renouncing Faisal's stubborn but futile policy of seeking to use the YAR to undermine PDRY and at the same time prevent the consolidation of a strong YAR. Instead, they attempted to tame PDRY and loosen its Soviet connection through recognition and cooperation, to give YAR's government more leeway, and to balance the two against each other.

The Saudis' strategy was favored by the fact that the Aden government was headed by Salim Rubaya Ali, who was responsive to their new approach for his own domestic political and international policy reasons, and that the San'a government was headed by Colonel Hamdi, who was able, strong, and popular yet disposed to cooperate with the Kingdom. These circumstances helped advance matters to the point where the Saudis exchanged ambassadors with PDRY in April 1977, extended economic assistance to it, and maintained a high level of aid to Hamdi even as he tightened his hold on power and engaged PDRY in ritualistic unity talks.

The Saudis' progress toward their goal was real but slow. Their strategy was hampered on the one hand by strong factional opposition to Rubaya and by residual hostility toward the Kingdom within PDRY, and on the other hand by tribal resistance to Hamdi's excessive centralizing efforts and the Saudis' own apprehensions about his excessive independence, particularly as it might lead to a serious advance toward Yemeni unity. These difficulties erupted in the last quarter of 1977, when Hamdi was assassinated by unknown assailants and was succeeded by the completely pro-Saudi Ahmad al-Ghashmi, and when Rubaya facilitated Soviet intervention on Ethiopia's side in its clash with Somalia and provoked the Saudis to withdraw their ambassador from Aden. The chain reaction continued in 1978, as Ghashmi was blown up in June by a bomb carried in the case of a PDRY emissary, and Rubaya was overthrown and executed two days later. The Saudis backed the YAR in its confrontation with PDRY, while border clashes and attempts at mutual subversion intensified until the situation exploded in war in February–March 1979.

THE AMERICAN CONNECTION　　Through most of the first three years of Khaled's reign, as the Saudis successfully managed their triangular relations with Cairo and Damascus, Baghdad and Tehran, and San'a and Aden, their post-1973 relationship of interdependence with the United States also prospered. The two sides cooperated quietly on a day-to-day basis in economic and military affairs, and the few demands they made on each other at the political-strategic level did not raise undue difficulties for either. The Saudis' "special relationship" with the United States worked as an asset rather than as a liability in their efforts to manage the various sets of triangular relations.

Starting in late 1977 and throughout 1978, as problems gradually built up in one arena after another, the Saudis and the United States made more and more demands on each other that neither was able to meet fully or consistently, and residues of disappointment and doubt were created. In early 1979 the relationship reached a critical point when the United States urged the Saudis to make a fateful commitment to its political strategy for the region, centering on the Egyptian-Israeli peace treaty. At that time such a commitment entailed for the Saudis outright confrontation with the Arab coalition opposed to the treaty, association with the United States in opposing the revolutionary regime in Iran, and support for the YAR in the showdown with PDRY. The alternative to the American proposal involved active association with the Arab bloc opposing the Egyptian-Israeli peace, termination of the link with Cairo, a strain on the American strategic connection, and reliance on the Baghdad-Damascus axis to balance Iran and settle the Yemen conflict by political means. When the Saudis rejected the American proposal, the relationship between the two countries plunged to the lowest point since the 1973 embargo.

Stage Two: Elusive Quest for Recovery, March 1979 – June 1982

THE ARAB ARENA   After joining with the Arab bloc in rejecting the Egyptian-Israeli peace and the American strategy centered on it, the Saudi rulers sought to mend some of the consequences of their choice within their own ranks and abroad, once the crisis had passed. They agreed among themselves to try to mend their American connection and at the same time to cooperate with the Arab bloc opposing Egypt. The United States, concerned about the short-term strain in its relations with the Kingdom, complied by agreeing to separate the issue of the Egyptian-Israeli peace from other aspects of the two countries' relations, "agreeing to disagree" on the former while continuing to cooperate on the latter.

The Saudis' attempt to preserve the American strategic connection while working with the Baghdad-Damascus axis was flawed from the outset. It reflected more the need to achieve a compromise among the Saudi leaders than any tenable political-strategic scheme. Even after the short-lived Baghdad-Damascus axis broke down and Iraq and Syria reverted to their traditional mutual hostility, both remained independently opposed to the Saudis' American connection; Iraq because it obstructed its ambitions for predominance in the Gulf and beyond, and Syria because it negated use of the Saudi leverage against the United States in the Arab-Israeli conflict and might even lure the Saudis to support the American peace process. As events exposed the contradictions in the Saudi orientation, the leadership collectively compromised and improvised or various factions pulled it now this way now that way. Two features, however, remained constant throughout: (1) the Saudis never seriously contemplated a strategic reorientation toward Egypt as long as Sadat lived; (2) although they intermittently defied Damascus or tried to isolate it, they almost always yielded ultimately before the Syrians' counteractions. By the end of Khaled's reign Saudi policy was virtually enthralled to Syria.

The lack of consistency and continuity in Saudi policy was reflected in the following developments. (1) In the summer of 1979 the Saudis attempted to promote an American-PLO dialogue and lure the PLO away from Syrian control. They were defeated by Syrian opposition and American mishandling of the issue. (2) In November of that year the Syrians mobilized pressure on the Saudis at the Tunis summit to use the oil weapon against the United States. The Saudis foiled that pressure with help from Iraq, but joined with the others in condemning the United States. (3) Following the Soviet invasion of Afghanistan, the Saudis moved closer to the United States and used the Islamic Conference Organization to condemn the Soviet Union and to undermine Syria's position as a friend of the Soviets. Shortly thereafter, however, they pulled away from the United States under Iraqi and Syrian pressure, and themselves began a cautious understanding with the Soviets regarding the Yemens. (4) The outbreak of the Gulf war led the Saudis to invite direct American military assistance; but Syrian reaction and the subsidence of the crisis caused them to restore some distance between the Kingdom and the United States. (5) Their quest for American arms and a successful mediation of a crisis in Lebanon prompted Fadh to advance in 1981 a peace plan that could legitimize the Kingdom's American connection; but Fahd dropped his plan in the face of Syrian opposition and, to deal with a recrudescence of dangers in the Gulf, the Kingdom moved toward greater strategic understanding with Syria. (6) Israel's invasion of Lebanon and Syria's defeat and abandonment of the PLO gave the Saudis a rare opportunity to work more closely with the United States to promote a favorable change in the strategic configuration in the Arab arena. However, although the Saudis went so far as to espouse the American goal of seeking the withdrawal of all foreign forces from Lebanon, they were inhibited by fear of Syria and the delicate transition following King Khaled's death from lending any active support to the American peace plans that they favored.

THE GULF ARENA   The triumph of the revolution in Iran confronted the Saudis with a critical threefold problem: it turned Iran from a strategic shield to a major threat; it placed the Kingdom in the middle between two mutually hostile regimes in Baghdad and Tehran; and it presented an immediate danger to vital navigation in the Gulf. The problem was compounded by the simultaneous strain in American-Saudi relations as a result of the signing of the Egyptian-Israeli treaty.

In trying to deal with the problem, the Saudis pursued several mutually incompatible approaches. They sought to appease Iran without antagonizing Iraq, to rely on the Damascus-Baghdad axis and then on Iraq alone to balance Iran without antagonizing the latter, to rally the small Gulf countries around itself exclusively without antagonizing Iraq, and to maintain American support without provoking the hostility of the anti–Camp David coalition. In addition, they tried to develop a long-term independent defense capability by espousing programs that increased their short-term dependence on the United States and others.

External events and reactions forced the Saudis to make choices they would rather have avoided, confronted them with new problems, or provided them with opportunities to correct course and even score some temporary advantage. Altogether, they managed to make their way through the currents and crosscurrents, but not to get on a clear course toward safety or to check the drift of their strategic orientation into incoherence and inconsistency.

Among the events that affected the Saudis' initial approach were the seizure of American hostages by the Iranians, the seizure of Mecca's Grand Mosque by fundamentalist insurgents, and the Soviet invasion of Afghanistan, all occurring in the last two months of 1979. The first event helped bring the Americans and the Saudis closer in their attitude toward Iran and encouraged Iraqi belligerency toward the Tehran regime. The Mecca incident undermined the Saudi regime's image of stability and its Islamic credentials and prompted it to compensate by leading Islamic opposition to the Soviet invasion. The latter Saudi move was also seen as helpful in isolating Syria and momentarily brought the Kingdom closer to the United States, which enunciated the Carter Doctrine, adopted plans for the development of a Rapid Deployment Force, and sought bases and facilities in the Gulf region and its vicinity. But the Saudis pulled back when the Carter Doctrine was countered by Saddam Hussein's pan-Arab charter and other Arab opposition, and they traded their withdrawal for a Soviet promise of forbearance in regard to the Yemens, which facilitated a modus vivendi there.

The 1980 Iraqi invasion of Iran implicated the Saudis. The failure of the Iraqi gamble on dealing a knockout blow to Iran exposed Saudi vital interests to mortal danger and forced them to call publicly for American military help. As the war bogged down into stalemate, however, the Saudis edged back toward neutrality and the position of a mediator and took advantage of Iraq's preoccupation with the war to promote a Gulf security organization under their own leadership. They tried to reinforce that approach by exploring a strategic connection with Pakistan and by seeking advanced American arms. They rejected a U.S. proposal for open strategic alignment ("strategic consensus"), which was consistent with the actual help provided by and sought from the Americans, because it conflicted with their own Gulf security project, their understanding with the Soviets on the Yemens, and their Syrian and Iraqi connections. Nevertheless they pressed forward the Fahd Plan as a possible bridge to the United States in the face of (eventually successful) Syrian and Iraqi opposition.

The advantageous stalemate in the Gulf war unexpectedly broke down in late 1981 when Iran launched a series of successful counteroffensives. At the same time an Iranian-instigated plot to overthrow the Bahraini regime and to destabilize the Saudi regime was uncovered. The Saudis, horrified by the prospect of an Iranian victory, turned to Syria for help. The latter agreed to suspend hostility toward Iraq and Jordan in exchange for Saudi endorsement of Syria's Soviet connection and a promise to adopt a more neutralist position between the superpowers. The agreement did not hold, and the Syrians shortly thereafter shut off Iraq's oil pipeline and deployed forces against it, just when the latter suffered its greatest defeat at the hands of the Iranians.

The Saudis next used the newly established Gulf Cooperation Council (GCC) and Oman to explore with Egypt's new President Mubarak the possibility of Egyptian military intervention on Iraq's side, in exchange for GCC support for its reinstatement in the Arab fold. When Mubarak refused, the Saudis turned to Syria once more and tried to persuade it to use its influence to dissuade Iran from invading Iraq proper. The Syrians agreed verbally to the Saudis' request in order to keep them from moving closer to the United States, but they continued to back Iran when the latter actually invaded Iraq. The Saudis were spared the consequences of a total Iranian victory, at least temporarily, by the failure of the invasion.

THE YEMENS   The termination of the 1979 war with an agreement between the two Yemens to unite confronted the Saudis with a new, more severe version of the problem they faced after the 1972 war between those two countries. Because the new unity agreement was the result of mediation by key Arab countries and was embedded in the dynamics that produced the anti–Camp David coalition led by Baghdad and Damascus, the Saudis were less able to try to subvert it by manipulating the YAR's political forces, as they had done with the 1972 agreement. The Saudis eventually found a new way to deal with the problem, but this involved a minor revolution in the south Arabian diplomatic constellation, which had a significant bearing on the Saudi position in other arenas.

The fact that Saudi Arabia and PDRY were part of the anti–Camp David bloc led PDRY and the Soviet Union to adopt an accommodating stance toward the Kingdom in order to keep it within that bloc. That stance was helped by the fact that the Oman issue, which had previously complicated Saudi-PDRY relations, was simplified by the withdrawal of all Iranian forces in the wake of the revolution. The Saudis used the Soviets' and PDRY's cooperative disposition to foil the effort of YAR's President Saleh to capitalize on the Arab-sanctioned unity agreement in order to carve for his country an independent policy course.

The Saudi policy of using the Soviet Union to moderate PDRY's policy was temporarily endangered by increased Saudi cooperation with the United States in the wake of the Soviet invasion of Afghanistan. However, Saudi second thoughts about such cooperation and Soviet fears that the Americans and Saudis might combine to put pressure on their position in PDRY led to a firmer tacit Saudi-Soviet understanding concerning the Yemens, which also influenced the Saudi position in the Gulf and Arab arenas. The understanding was enhanced by the Soviets' support of a March 1980 coup in PDRY, which replaced the intransigent Abd al-Fattah Ismaïl with the more accommodating Ali Nasser.

The modus vivendi was endangered again by the Saudis' call for American help after the outbreak of the Gulf war, and their subsequent endeavor to create the GCC while excluding from it either Yemen. The YAR's relations with the Kingdom became strained, and PDRY countered with a treaty of alliance with Ethiopia and Libya. Ultimately, however, all three parties either adjusted their positions or managed to tolerate the strains in their mutual relations for the sake of preserving the modus vivendi, which survived through the end of Khaled's reign. A key to that measure of success was that Saudi Arabia for the first time accepted PDRY for what it was and renounced all efforts to subvert it or to lure it away from its Soviet connection.

THE AMERICAN CONNECTION   The split decision of the Saudi rulers in March 1979 to reject an American-oriented strategy anchored in the Egyptian-Israeli peace and to opt instead for an Arab-oriented strategy was followed by a decision at the end of that month to cut oil production by 1 mbd in order to appease Iran. Together, these two moves triggered a panic in the world oil market and a rapid escalation of oil prices and marked the most severe crisis in Saudi-American relations since 1973. Although the worst of the crisis at the domestic and political-strategic levels was mended a few months later, residual effects have persisted just as they have in the sphere of oil, albeit less conspicuously.

The crisis within the royal family was mended in May 1979 by a compromise aimed at preserving the American strategic connection even while working with key Arab parties opposed to the Egyptian-Israeli peace. The compromise was based on the leaders' unanimous recognition that despite recent disappointments the American connection remained essential for three reasons: to protect certain Saudi interests that coincided with America's, such as resisting Soviet encroachments and keeping navigation open; to ensure the supply of advanced American arms and military assistance; and to preserve a source of help in emergencies. However, whereas Abdallah and others believed that Saudi cooperation with the United States in oil matters was a sufficient quid pro quo for American cooperation, Fahd and others believed that more effort was necessary at appropriate occasions to secure the American connection. These differences manifested themselves in subsequent swings in Saudi policy, as now one approach now the other prevailed.

The understanding within the royal family was translated in the political-strategic sphere into a reconciliation with the United States in mid-1979, based on an agreement between the two sides to put aside their disagreement on the Arab-Israeli peace process. The Saudis followed up with a decision to increase oil production by 1 mbd starting July 1, 1979, which, however, had only a marginal effect on the escalating oil prices.

The attempt to preserve both the American connection and the align ment with the anti-American Arab parties placed the Saudis in a difficult position from the outset, and the difficulty was exacerbated by the reactions of all parties to constantly shifting relevant situations. Specifically, when the Saudis, under the impetus of Fahd, sought to influence the American position toward the PLO by nonconfrontational means in the middle of 1979, the Syrians suspected their designs and frustrated them. When the Saudis subsequently pulled back and merely tried to remain aloof from the United States on the Arab-Israeli question, the Syrians and their allies pressed them, during and after the 1979 Tunis summit, to use their presumed leverage on the United States to compel it to modify its policy. When the Saudis cooperated with the United States in areas other than the Arab-Israeli question, as they did briefly in the wake of the Soviet invasion of Afghanistan, the Iraqis and Syrians and their respective allies opposed their move, the former because it might obstruct their own pan-Arab designs, and both because it might presage the Kingdom's acceptance of the American-sponsored peace process. The same pattern was repeated, *mutatis mutandis,* in connection with the Gulf war, the Saudi quest for arms from the United States, and so on.

The United States, for its part, resented the Saudis' partial yielding to the pressures to express their disagreement with it on the peace question more sharply, as they did in the 1979 Tunis summit, in the 1980 Islamic Conference at Islamabad, and in the 1981 Islamic Conference in Riyadh; and at least some elements of the U.S. government sought to penalize the Kingdom by restricting American cooperation with it. When the Saudis needed American support regarding critical issues outside the Arab-Israeli sphere, as they did after the Soviet invasion of Afghanistan and particularly after the outbreak of the Gulf war, the United States, without distinction of elements, personalities, or administration, sought to use the opportunity to press the Kingdom into a comprehensive strategic association.

These pressures and counterpressures put added strain on the collective Saudi leadership. Although the leadership did not visibly split again, the policies pursued showed all the marks of an intermittent tug of war, punctuated by improvisations, compromises, and zigzags. The overall result was that in the brief period of three years or so between the crisis of 1979 and Khaled's death, the Saudi connection with the United States underwent at least five distinct changes after the crisis itself.

(1) In the summer of 1979 the Saudis made an effort to consolidate their reconciliation with the United States, which was foiled by Syria; by November they felt compelled at Tunis to take a public stance critical of the United States. (2) The Soviet invasion of Afghanistan drew the Saudis closer to the United States; soon thereafter, however, Syrian and Iraqi opposition and an opportunity to achieve an understanding with the

Soviets caused them to revert to ambivalence. (3) The Gulf war impelled the Saudis to seek American military help; but Syrian reaction, the apparent passing of the emergency, and the opportunity to mediate between Iran and Iraq led them to move away from the United States. (4) The Saudis' quest for American arms, coupled with their success in mediating the summer 1981 crisis in Lebanon, encouraged Fahd to advance his peace plan in a bid to promote better conditions for Saudi relations with the United States; but Syrian opposition and American moves favorable to Israel caused him to drop the plan. (5) When the Gulf war turned in Iran's favor and when Iran intensified subversive efforts against the Gulf countries, the Saudis relied on the United States for military protection but turned to Syria for diplomatic support.

9

The Arab-Israeli Arena, 1975–1979: The Cairo and Damascus Connections

One of the most important results of the 1973 war and the events related to it was to thrust the Kingdom into a leadership role in Arab affairs, anchored in a triangular Riyadh-Cairo-Damascus strategic alliance. Because the interests of various Arab parties diverged on some critical issues even while they converged on others, that role involved potential trouble for the Saudis as well as major advantages. On the one hand, the Kingdom's new position enabled it to transcend the previous polarization of the Arab world that had exposed it to assaults by the radicals, allowed it to cultivate its American connection once Washington committed itself to pursuing an Arab-Israeli settlement, improved its security in relation to Iraq and Iran, and generally facilitated its handling of remaining problems in the Gulf, in southern Arabia, and at home. On the other hand, its new position of prominence also made it much more difficult for the Kingdom to avoid being drawn into every inter-Arab dispute and could saddle it with new heavy burdens. Saudi foreign and defense policy in the Arab-Israeli arena during the first few years after Faisal's death was largely dominated by the manifestation of this problem and the efforts of Faisal's successors to deal with it.

A preview of the problem had presented itself in the last two months of Faisal's reign. In February and March 1975, Secretary of State Kissinger had undertaken two expeditions of shuttle diplomacy aimed at bringing about a second, limited agreement on Sinai between Egypt and Israel. The Syrians had vehemently objected to the attempt and tried to enlist the Saudis and other Arab parties against it on the formal grounds that it violated the unanimous resolutions of the Rabat Arab summit in October 1974, which had enjoined the confrontation parties against any separate political agreement and had called upon them to seek only a comprehensive settlement based on return of all the occupied Arab territories and satisfaction of the Palestinians' national rights. Egypt's President Sadat had rationalized his participation in the Kissinger attempt and called for Saudi support by invoking two rather contradictory arguments: that it envisaged a purely military, not a political, agreement; and that he would insist on linking any Egyptian-Israeli accord with a similar one between Syria and Israel. Faisal had come down discreetly on Egypt's side and tried to get the leaders of Egypt, Syria, Jordan, and the PLO to meet to coordinate policies. Having failed in that, he had sought to reassure the Syrians and the others that he would continue to use the Kingdom's resources to advance a settlement that met their needs after the step at issue, and in the meantime would try to influence Sadat to keep the scope of any agreement with Israel as limited as possible.

That particular manifestation of the problem had subsided of its own accord before it could inflict any severe damage on the Kingdom's prized triangular alliance. On March 22, 1975, three days before Faisal's death, Israel had rejected the final terms of a proposed agreement worked out by Kissinger, causing the United States to declare angrily that it was going to reassess its entire Middle East policy, including relations with Israel. Although these developments gave Faisal's successors a welcome respite during the delicate period of succession, they did not affect the essence of the problem, which continued to recur in different and more disturbing forms. Indeed, within a period of four years after Faisal's death, King Khaled's government confronted with varying degrees of success half a dozen manifestations of the problem of trying to preserve the triangular alliance or of avoiding getting caught in a new polarization centered on Cairo and Damascus, before being finally overcome by it.

Sinai II

Immediately after the collapse of Kissinger's effort in March 1975, Khaled's government tried to mend the damage done by that endeavor to the Cairo-Damascus-Riyadh axis. It took advantage of the presence of Presidents Sadat and Assad at Faisal's funeral to arrange a meeting between them that ostensibly eased previous "misunderstandings," elicited renewed vows of unity, and prepared the ground for a full-fledged policy conference of the two leaders with King Khaled in Riyadh on April 21 and 22, 1975. In the interim, the Egyptians and Syrians consulted with Moscow and with various Arab parties and reassessed their positions and options in light of the experience of the aborted Egyptian-Israeli negotiations.

In the April meeting in Riyadh the conferees easily agreed on common "principles," but the Egyptians and Syrians alluded to profound differences with regard to the strategy to be followed in pursuing them. The Syrians, realizing that their own leverage with Israel and the United States was limited, believed that their best hope to achieve what they deemed a satisfactory settlement lay in a united Arab front. They suspected that the American step-by-step diplomacy was designed to lure Egypt out of the war and then to confront them, when and if their own turn came, with the choice of either accepting whatever terms Israel could be made to offer or else confronting it by themselves. They therefore urged at the conference that all the Arab parties go to Geneva together or not at all. If the Geneva Conference did not materialize or if it met and failed to make progress, then all the Arabs together would engage in confrontation with Israel and, if necessary, with the United States.

Sadat was in a different position, had different needs, and operated under a different time constraint from the Syrians. He thought little of the Arab chances in another military confrontation with Israel, wanted to cultivate the American connection that he had nurtured, and trusted that the United States could ultimately be induced to deliver what he wanted from Israel. In the immediate run, Sadat was anxious to continue rebuilding the devastated cities bordering on the Suez Canal, resettle the million refugees who had fled the area, complete the clearance of the canal itself, and reopen it, and he felt inhibited in all those endeavors by the presence of the Israeli army in force a few miles from the canal. He feared that the approach proposed by the Syrians would allow Israel to procrastinate over the question of Palestinian representation at Geneva, give the Soviets at the conference an opportunity for mischiefmaking, and, after the ensuing deadlock, recreate a solid front between the United States and Israel that the Arabs could not confront. He therefore argued at Riyadh that the conferees should agree on the principles of no surrender of Arab territory, no separate settlement, and no final settlement without securing the Palestinians' rights, while leaving ample flexibility in method and tactics. In short, he wanted to keep open the option of another attempt at a limited Egyptian-Israeli agreement.

The Saudis were strongly inclined toward Sadat's position for very similar reasons. They shared his eagerness to keep the Soviets out of the peacemaking process, and they had their own concerns about the consequences of a stalemate and renewed military confrontation with Israel and political confrontation with the United States. At the same time, they wanted to avert a clash between Egypt and Syria and alienation of either.

They therefore promoted agreement on the creation of a joint strategy committee to coordinate the moves of the parties.

Coordination, if there was any, proved to be short-lived. In late May 1975, Sadat arranged to meet with President Ford and Secretary of State Kissinger in Salzburg, Austria, on June 1 and 2 to discuss the results of the American policy reassessment. Kissinger expounded three options to Sadat: trying to reconvene the Geneva Conference, attempting a complete Egyptian-Israeli peace treaty, and making a new effort to achieve a limited Egyptian-Israeli agreement if the parties showed willingness to compromise over the differences that had caused the failure of the first attempt. Sadat agreed with Kissinger about the difficulties involved in the first option — the problem of Palestinian representation, the Arab parties' outbidding one another in extremism, Soviet catering to the more extreme Arab positions in a bid to embarrass the United States, and so on. He rejected the second option as premature and too divisive of Arab ranks. But he indicated his willingness to support the third option and, to give the new attempt a better chance to succeed, proposed a compromise on the question of an early warning system in the Sinai passes on which the Israelis had insisted, by suggesting that American personnel might man it. This set in motion a process of preparatory negotiations among the United States, Israel, and Egypt that culminated in a new round of shuttle diplomacy starting on August 21, 1975.

In the meantime the Saudis hedged their bets by periodically expressing positions designed to appease all parties. Thus, on May 25, 1975, the *Washington Post* quoted Khaled as being willing to recognize Israel within the 1967 boundaries — a position in line with the scenario of seeking to go to Geneva. On July 15, 1975, a meeting of the Islamic Conference under Saudi sponsorship at Jidda called for the expulsion of Israel from the United Nations, asserted the right of the Palestinians under the PLO to statehood, and affirmed the Islamic character of Jerusalem — a position calculated to please hardline Muslim and Arab audiences. The resolution carefully refrained from criticizing the United States but was hardly helpful to the Geneva project. In the next five days — July 16–20, 1975 — King Khaled was in Egypt on a state visit, during which he reportedly expressed sympathy for Sadat's case for a second limited agreement in Sinai,[1] which had already been set in motion. Two weeks later, on August 2, Crown Prince Fahd told a Kuwaiti newspaper that Saudi Arabia would use the oil weapon if another Middle East war broke out[2] — a statement designed to reassure the Syrians and seemingly to put pressure on the United States, without being incompatible with support for Sadat's limited-agreement project.

On September 1 the Saudi problem with their Egyptian and Syrian allies took a new turn as Kissinger concluded a ten-day shuttle with the

signing of an Egyptian-Israeli agreement that came to be known as Sinai
II. The agreement returned to Egypt some 400 square miles of Sinai
territory, including the Abu Rodeis oil fields and the passes; provided for
a careful separation and limitation of forces; and included an array of
provisions that practically ended the state of war between the two countries. No link was established between that agreement and a Syrian-
Israeli agreement. On the contrary, a renewed personal promise by Secretary Kissinger to President Sadat to make a serious effort to bring
about further Israeli-Syrian negotiations was more than counterbalanced by an explicit written commitment from Kissinger to Israel that
the Egyptian-Israeli agreement stood on its own and did not depend on
any act or development between Israel and other Arab states. Moreover,
the United States assumed the obligation to coordinate with Israel all
policy regarding the Geneva Conference and committed itself not to
recognize or negotiate with the PLO as long as the latter did not recognize
Israel's right to exist and refused to accept Resolutions 242 and 338. It also
promised to put military assistance to Israel on a long-term basis and
gave it some assurances against possible Soviet threats. Altogether, Sinai
II ended the period of estrangement between the United States and Israel
and replaced it with a virtual alliance between the two countries.

The Saudis, who had been consulted throughout the negotiations, endorsed the agreement promptly but in a manner designed to downplay its
importance. A statement delivered by Minister of State for Foreign Affairs
Saud al-Faisal in Riyadh on September 2, while Secretary Kissinger was
in town, simply said that the Kingdom viewed it as "a step toward a final
settlement." The Saudis knew from the experience of the aborted negotiations of February–March 1975 that the agreement would be anathema
to Damascus and would cause a breach between it and Cairo. They
nevertheless supported it for three reasons. They not only sympathized
with Sadat's need for the agreement but also believed that the alternative
strategy proposed by the Syrians was problematic from their own point of
view. Second, although they expected a disruption of the Cairo-Damascus side of the strategic triangle, they believed they had enough leverage
with Damascus to keep open their line to it as well as to Cairo. Finally, the
Saudis believed that once the storm over the agreement subsided, the
equal need of the Syrians and the Egyptians for the Saudi leverage with
the United States would enable them to mend the Cairo-Damascus line
and restore the triangle. Events were to prove the Saudi calculations to be
alternately right and wrong, with qualifications.

The Syrians predictably denounced Sadat in violent terms and sought
to mobilize Arab opinion against him, but they refrained from attacking
the Saudis for supporting the agreement. President Assad's sectarian
minority regime needed the legitimation that good relations with Saudi

Arabia bestowed upon it as much as it needed the Kingdom's financial support. Moreover, in the exposed position in which it felt itself to be after Egypt ostensibly pulled out of the war, Syria needed the Saudi leverage with the United States to restrain a feared American-Israeli collusion to deal with it by force. Finally, Syria needed Saudi support for the immediate measures it took to enhance its defensive capability in case of a military encounter with Israel. Suspecting that in such an encounter Israel would seek to score a quick victory by enveloping their strong defense line in the Golan, the Syrians sought to strengthen their flanks in Jordan and Lebanon through political and military measures that needed Saudi blessing. Since Jordan believed the danger of an Israeli strike against Syria through its territory to be highly plausible, they had no difficulty convincing King Hussein to establish a joint supreme command to coordinate the defense of the two countries. With respect to Lebanon, however, the task proved to be much more complicated for the Syrians themselves and problematic for the Saudis, who initially supported them.

The Lebanese Civil War

Since April 1975 a civil war had been raging in Lebanon between a coalition of rightist-Christian armed factions and a coalition of leftist-Muslim forces allied with the PLO. Among the issues involved was the determination of the rightist-Christian side to bring the PLO in Lebanon under control and to disengage the country from the hostilities with Israel caused by PLO incursions across the border; and the opposite determination of the leftist-Muslim coalition to replace the confessional state, which gave the Christians dominant influence, with a secular state and to commit the country unequivocally to the Arab struggle against Israel. On the face of it, the Syrians should have favored the leftist-Muslim-PLO grouping, and to some extent they did. However, they were not sure that they could effectively control such a coalition if it prevailed and prevent it from embroiling Syria in war with Israel at a time not of its choosing. Moreover, the Syrians feared that the act of crushing the rightist-Christian forces and converting Lebanon into a radical confrontation state might itself trigger Israeli military intervention supported by the United States and alienate Arab countries such as Saudi Arabia and Jordan, which would feel threatened by such a development. Consequently, in their endeavor to reinforce their Lebanese flank the Syrians strove to end the civil war in a way that would make them the arbiters of Lebanon's destiny and policy. They wanted a moderate revision of the pre–civil war distribution of power in favor of the leftist-Muslim coalition while keeping the rightist-Christian side strong enough to restrain its opponents and, if necessary, check them with Syrian help.

From the point of view of the Saudis, the Syrian strategy regarding Jordan and Lebanon was quite acceptable. It not only conformed with their interest in maintaining stability and preventing war in the region, but support for it also gave them a chance to compensate the Syrians for the Kingdom's support of Egypt's Sinai II agreement and thus retain their good will. The trouble was that events in Lebanon caused the Syrians, while pursuing their strategy, to make some sharp tactical turns that antagonized other Arab parties besides Egypt and put the Saudis themselves on the spot. Among the bewildering details of the Lebanese conflict, the following were the main developments that bore on the Saudi position and policies.

September 1975 – January 1976

In the wake of the Egyptian-Israeli agreement, the Syrians redoubled their effort to end the fighting and bring about a settlement of the civil war but to no effect. They mediated cease-fires that repeatedly broke down, and promoted the formation of a Committee of National Reconciliation and then a Committee of Coordination, but neither was able to advance matters. The fortunes of war alternated, but by the turn of the year they favored the rightist-Christian forces, who were successfully bringing the core area of Mount Lebanon under their control and expanding it. There was talk of secession or partition of the country. The leftist-Muslim-PLO forces appealed to Syria first to increase the help it was giving to them and then to intervene on their behalf.

At this stage the Saudis demonstrated their support of Syria through an official visit by King Khaled to Damascus on December 25–27. Khaled's simultaneous effort to heal the rift between Syria and Egypt did not succeed, but this visit helped keep the Kingdom on good terms with both sides.

January – March 1976

In response to the leftist-Muslim-PLO appeal, Syria sent into Lebanon on January 18 a brigade of the Palestine Liberation Army (PLA), which Damascus controlled. The Syrian-led formations quickly checked the rightist-Christian forces but did not attempt to defeat them decisively, and made it possible for the Syrians to bring about a cease-fire and a new attempt at a political solution. On February 14 the Syrians convinced Christian President Suleiman Franjieh and Muslim Prime Minister Rashid Karami to endorse a seventeen-point program to settle the conflict, which envisaged a mild redistribution of power in favor of the Muslims, counterbalanced by the imposition of effective restrictions on the PLO. The rightist-Christians were inclined to accept it, but the leftist-Muslim-PLO coalition rejected it.

While the Syrians endeavored to persuade the latter, the Lebanese army began to break up into its confessional components. On March 11 a group of Muslim senior officers of the Lebanese army staged a "television coup" and demanded the resignation of President Franjieh, and in the next two days they got a majority of the members of parliament to sign a petition supporting that demand. When Franjieh refused, units of the Lebanese army that had defected to the leftists and their allies marched on the presidential palace. The Syrians viewed these developments as an attempt to sabotage their efforts to achieve a settlement and a defiance of their authority, and consequently ordered the PLA to block the way before the attackers. This move marked the beginning of a reversal of the Syrian position vis-à-vis the parties in conflict.

The initial intervention of the PLA and the Syrian program for settling the conflict were compatible with Saudi interests as far as Syria and Lebanon were concerned. The Saudis were somewhat concerned at first that the Syrian proxy intervention through the PLA might provoke an Israeli military intervention and a larger war, but these concerns were eased by the attitude of forbearance taken by the Americans, who were in touch with the Israelis and who had been notified in advance by the Syrians of their intent and aims.[3] The Saudis' problem at this stage stemmed from the hostile reactions of Iraq and Egypt, the former because of ingrained enmity to the rival Syrian Ba'thist regime and the latter because of Sadat's clash with Assad over Sinai II. Regarding Iraq, the Saudis could do nothing beyond continuing to cultivate the improved relations that had begun the previous year. Egypt they tried to compensate for their tacit support of Syria with new gestures of friendship. On February 21–26 they received President Sadat on a state visit, committed to him additional sums of financial aid, and promised to help mobilize larger development funds from the neighboring oil-rich emirates.

March–May 1976

After blocking the leftists' attempt to overthrow President Franjieh by force, the Syrians initiated a move to have Franjieh replaced through constitutional processes in order to put that issue out of the way and get back to their program for settling the conflict. The leftists, however, remained unsatisfied. The Syrians stopped all military assistance to them, blocked their line of supply through the port of Sidon, and leaders of the two sides openly attacked each other. On April 9, the day Lebanon's parliament met to amend the constitution so as to permit the removal of Franjieh, the Syrians advanced their own forces several miles inside Lebanon to deter attempts by the leftists to sabotage the move. A week later the Syrians made an abortive attempt to split the leftists and their PLO allies by reaching a short-lived agreement with the latter. By May 8, when a new, Syrian-supported president, Elias Sarkis, was elected, the cease-fire had broken down, fighting had engulfed the country, and the PLA had clashed with both PLO and leftist forces. In the following weeks the tide of battle favored the leftist-Muslim-PLO coalition, which seemed to be in a position to overrun its enemies. The Syrians charged that the leftists and their allies were courting foreign intervention and partition of the country, and threatened to intervene militarily themselves to stop them.

The Saudis continued to favor the overall objectives of Damascus but were anxious about Syria's actions at this stage. The advancement of Syrian troops into Lebanon increased the danger of a wider war. Israel's Prime Minister Yitzhak Rabin warned the Syrians against crossing "a definite red line," and Secretary of State Kissinger gave tacit endorsement to the warning.[4] More disturbing for the Saudis, the Syrians' tactical reversal and their use of the PLA against the PLO and its leftist-Muslim allies placed them in opposition to the Arab formal consensus, stirred up demand for a collective Arab initiative, intensified the attacks on Damascus from Cairo and Baghdad, and risked putting the Saudis with the Syrians in the middle of the crossfire.

The Saudis' first impulse was to press their attempts at mediation, but their effort backfired. On May 5 they were able to bring together representatives of Egypt and the PLO, but the agreement reached by the two parties to cooperate on the Lebanon question and the PLO's promise to tone down its criticism of Egypt on account of Sinai II appeared to the Syrians as a Saudi-promoted collusion to undercut their policy in Lebanon. Consequently, the Syrians turned down at the last moment a further Saudi attempt to bring together representatives of Egypt and Syria in Riyadh for conciliation talks on May 19. The Saudis continued in their endeavor to mediate but quietly suspended payment of their assistance installments to Syria to the tune of $700 million a year.[5]

June 1976

On June 1 the Syrians carried out a previously voiced threat and threw powerful armored formations against the leftist-Muslim-PLO forces. The Syrian troops advanced rapidly, bypassing or driving away enemy forces, but were soon halted in Bhamdoun, east of Beirut on the highway from Damascus, and in Sidon, south of Beirut. While the Syrians pondered their next move a political storm broke out all around them. The Iraqis bitterly attacked the "fascist ruling clique in Damascus for this hideous crime against the people of Palestine,"[6] and on June 9 they dispatched troops to the Syrian border "to execute their historic duty."[7] Egypt and Syria recalled their diplomatic missions from each other's capital amid violent mutual recriminations. The Arab League sprang into action and on June 10 decided to send its own "peacekeeping force" to Lebanon. The Soviets condemned the intervention, and Leonid Brezhnev sent Assad a note calling for an immediate end of Syrian operations against the "Palestinian Resistance and the Lebanese National Movement" and the withdrawal of Syrian troops.[8] The Soviets gave point to their displeasure by reducing to a trickle the flow of their military supplies to Syria. In addition, there were signs of disquiet inside Syria itself. Statements by Israel to the effect that it saw no need to intervene and American statements to the effect that Syria was playing a constructive role in Lebanon were at least as damaging to the Syrian regime politically as they were reassuring militarily.

The Saudis could not fail to find some satisfaction in the strain that developed between Damascus and Moscow and in the tacit understanding between Syria and the United States, but these advantages were outweighed by the danger of either losing their Syrian connection or being caught in an exposed position on Syria's side. They therefore went along with the Arab League's project of establishing a peacekeeping force, which was anathema to the Syrians, and even agreed to contribute a small contingent to it, while they endeavored once more to mediate an understanding among the parties that concerned them most. Once again, they had no great difficulty in bringing about an accord between Sadat and Arafat at a meeting headed by King Khaled in Riyadh on June 21; and once again they failed to reconcile the Egyptians and Syrians. The prime ministers of the two countries did meet in Riyadh on June 23 and 24; but in the absence of Assad and Sadat, who were not yet ready to talk to each other, no agreement proved to be possible. All the Saudis were able to achieve was to salvage the possibility of a later meeting at the presidential level.

July – October 1976

After the initial advance of their forces came to a halt, the Syrians reinforced their troops to a total of nearly two divisions but did not commit them directly to battle. Instead they used them to draw and pin down leftist and PLO forces, thus allowing the rightist-Christian forces to go on the offensive and concentrate against selected and weakened targets. The Arab League's peacekeeping force was entirely stymied, and the rightist-

Christian forces made considerable headway. But the Syrians' attempt to subdue the leftist-Muslim-PLO forces through the Christian-rightist proxy was frustrated by the practical support given to the former from various Arab quarters. Egypt and Iraq, in particular, sent Palestinian formations that were part of their own armed forces to fight against the Syrians and their allies. The indecisive all-Arab proxy civil war dragged on until late September, punctuated by bloody and passion-stirring episodes such as the fall of the Tel Zaatar refugee camp to the Christian forces amid great slaughter in early August after a siege of more than sixty days.

On September 28 the Syrians finally decided to bring matters to a conclusion. After giving the leftists and the PLO an ultimatum, which was rejected, Syrian regular forces moved against them en masse and decisively defeated them within two days. Shortly after the start of the Syrian offensive, Arafat sent passionate appeals to Arab heads of state to save the Palestinians "from this new massacre," and several of them responded by calling for a small summit meeting in Riyadh on October 2. But the Syrians refused to attend and made their own attempt to conclude a peace with the PLO and thus separate it from the leftist forces. When that attempt failed, they launched a second and final offensive on October 11, which overcame the last resistance. Only then did they agree to attend the Riyadh minisummit, rescheduled for October 16.

During July the Saudis had endeavored to mediate between Syria and the PLO, and on the twenty-ninth they seemed to have succeeded in bringing about an understanding between the two. A week later, however, Tel Zaatar fell and the repercussions hit the Saudis close to home for the first time. The Kuwaiti parliament, responding to agitation by the 250,000 Palestinians in the country and a major press campaign, moved to cut off aid to Syria and condemn it. The government suspended the constitution, dispersed the assembly, and clamped down on the press, but the situation remained explosive. The Syrian offensive in September and Arafat's passionate appeals made matters worse. The Saudis, now joined by the Kuwaitis, urgently called upon the leaders of Egypt, the PLO, Lebanon, and Syria to meet in Riyadh on October 2, and when Assad refused, the Saudis sought to distance themselves from him publicly by ordering home the reinforced brigade they had stationed in the Golan since the 1973 war.[9]

These developments, coming on top of previous Saudi frustrations with Syria, the discreet suspension of financial aid, and the not-so-discreet criticism of Syria in the Saudi press, threatened to snap the Riyadh-Damascus connection. But the success of the final Syrian offensive not only averted that outcome but prepared the ground for the achievements of the minisummit of October 16–18. At that meeting the participants agreed on a cease-fire; on the creation of an Arab Deterrent Force of 30,000 under nominal Lebanese command, by the addition of small contingents from Saudi Arabia, the United Arab Emirates, and the Sudan to the 22,000 Syrian troops already in Lebanon, to enforce the cease-fire; and on the cessation of hostile propaganda between Egypt and Syria. A week later, a full Arab League summit meeting in Cairo endorsed the agreement and provided for financing the Arab Deterrent Force by the Gulf oil producers; Iraq and Libya were the only two countries to demur.

The Riyadh agreement in effect amounted to recognition by Cairo of Syria's primacy in Lebanon in exchange for Syria's *post facto* acknowledgment of Sinai II. It also marked a success of the Saudis in restoring the Riyadh-Cairo-Damascus triangle after its disruption by Sinai II and the events of Lebanon. The success was confirmed two months later when, at another conference in Riyadh involving only the leaders of the three countries, Sadat and Assad sealed their reconciliation by agreeing to establish a "unified political command" and to put their forces under joint military command as they had done in the heyday of their alliance.

The Saudi-mediated Egyptian-Syrian reconciliation of October 1976 proved, however, to be not much more viable than the reconciliation promoted by Riyadh in April 1975, after the quarrel over the first, abortive Sinai II negotiations. The reasons for the second failure were essentially the same as in the earlier instance, except that this time they operated in a different, much more crucial context. Earlier, Sadat had broken ranks with the Syrians and engaged in separate negotiations that produced Sinai II because he needed an agreement more than they did and because he believed that the Syrian-proposed alternative of collective negotiations for a comprehensive settlement was impractical. This time, Sadat broke the second Riyadh agreement and went to Jerusalem on his own in pursuit of total peace because he needed a settlement and because he had found out, after pursuing with the Americans the option favored by the Syrians, that the alternative was impractical.

The Geneva Project

As in the case of Sinai II, Sadat was tempted to venture the Jerusalem initiative alone because he had ascertained beforehand that the chances of securing his goals for Egypt were excellent. As before, he justified his move by asserting that he was merely paving the way for general peace and by vowing that he would conclude no separate agreement. As before, the vehemence of the Syrian and other Arab opposition, on the one hand, and the dynamics of the negotiations, on the other, impelled him to qualify his vow and conclude a quasi-separate agreement. And as before, the Saudis tried to keep their lines to both Cairo and Damascus open as long as possible while making periodic attempts to reconcile the two. Unlike the previous occasion, however, this time the Saudis eventually failed in their endeavor and were compelled by Syria and the majority of the other Arab parties to make a choice. In the circumstances in which they found themselves when that moment came, they opted to go against Cairo.

While the Lebanon conflict was raging the United States was absorbed in the last phases of a presidential election, and the combination of these two factors had put in abeyance the American peacemaking effort, which had been sustained for almost two years after the Yom Kippur War. America's diplomatic activity through much of 1976 was confined to managing the Lebanon crisis so as to prevent a clash between the Syrian intervention forces and Israel and to cultivating the new relationship with Egypt. However, by election time a consensus had developed in American foreign-policy circles, underscored by the events in Lebanon, that step-by-step diplomacy had run its course and that the next American peace initiative must aim at a comprehensive peace settlement. The advent of a Democratic administration under Jimmy Carter, eager to steer its own course, ensured the translation of the consensus into actual policy.

President Carter immediately made it clear that he favored an early convening of the Geneva Conference and in February 1977 sent Secretary of State Cyrus Vance to the Middle East to explore the positions of the parties and arrange for visits of their leaders to Washington for preparatory consultations. Israel's Prime Minister Rabin came in March, followed the next month by King Hussein and President Sadat. Syria's President Assad, significantly, refused to come to Washington but conferred with President Carter on the neutral ground of Geneva in May, after having gone first to Moscow for consultations. The last to come to Washington was Crown Prince Fahd, who arrived on May 24.

Fahd's visit was significant in several respects. First, the fact that he was one of the succession of leaders who took part in the consultation process underscored the point that Saudi Arabia had become a confrontation country in the Arab-Israeli conflict at least diplomatically if not militarily as well. Second, before coming to Washington Fahd and King Khaled had conferred in Riyadh with Sadat and Assad, unlike either of the latter before meeting with President Carter. This move underscored the Saudis' anxiety to allay suspicions about their American connection and to keep the strategic triangle in good repair. The anxiety to allay suspicions was also reflected in the fact that Fahd's was the first official visit to the United States by any ruling member of the royal family since Faisal's death, and came only after a multitude of exchanges of visits between Faisal's successors and leaders of Arab and European countries. Finally, the fact that Fahd's discussions with Carter dealt with questions of oil supply as well as with the Arab-Israeli conflict underscored the connection that had become established between the two issues as well as the particular Saudi leverage with the United States.

On that occasion, Fahd defined that leverage in positive terms. He specifically declared that "oil will not be used as a weapon" and agreed to assist the United States in building up a six-month "strategic petroleum reserve." Moreover, earlier that year Saudi Arabia had defied a majority decision of the OPEC conference at Doha to increase oil prices, and in May 1977 it was producing at near its maximum capacity to give effect to its defiance. Fahd made it quite clear, however, that Saudi forthcoming-ness was contingent on the expectation that the United States would exert itself to the utmost for a "just solution" of the conflict.[10]

The American preparatory activities for a peace conference were mo-mentarily thrown off track by an unexpected change of government in Israel. The May 1977 elections terminated three decades of Labor party rule and brought to power a more militant nationalist coalition headed by Menachem Begin that was dedicated to the idea of permanent Israeli control of the West Bank (Judea and Samaria). After a series of verbal skirmishes between the American and Israeli governments, a meeting between Carter and Begin took place in July 1977 and was concluded with an agreement to go to Geneva on the basis of the principle that "everything is negotiable." In August Secretary Vance went on another trip to the Middle East to try to work out a specific agreement among the parties on the modalities and procedure of the conference, especially on the question of Palestinian representation.

Vance quickly found that there were entrenched differences among the key Arab parties as well as between the Arabs and Israel. Begin invoked an Israeli consensus against any negotiations with the PLO and reminded the United States of the obligation it had assumed in the Sinai II agree-ment with the Labor government to do the same as long as the PLO did not recognize Israel's right to exist and failed to accept Resolutions 242 and 338. Sadat, more eager than ever to get down to the business of negotiations and to take advantage of the favorable disposition of the Carter administration toward the Arab positions on territorial issues, urged linking the Palestinian delegation to the Jordanian one in order to circumvent the Israeli objections, get the formal conference going, and carry on the real negotiations secretly in its shadow. The Syrians, as suspicious of Sadat as ever, insisted on a unified Arab delegation and a specific PLO representation within it to check Egyptian separatist tend-encies and to enhance their own bargaining position (since taking over in Lebanon the Syrians felt they could control the PLO). Jordan formally adhered to the position that the PLO should be specifically represented but hoped that the difficulties raised by this position would compel the

Arab parties to turn to it to represent the Palestinians and the West Bank. The Saudis, as might be expected, took a more complex stance, which incidentally revealed the strengths and limitations of their position.

The Saudis shared Sadat's keenness to get the conference going and at the same time could not ignore the Syrian and Jordanian insistence on specific PLO representation. They therefore endeavored to persuade Yasser Arafat to accept a modified version of Resolution 242, thus making the PLO eligible for participation at least in the eyes of the Americans, and thought they got Arafat's assent. They then put the proposal to Vance, and the secretary of state was so impressed by it that he cabled the president a recommendation to act on it even before he returned home.[11] The president promptly agreed, and on August 8, 1977, declared that acceptance by the PLO of "the applicability of 242" would satisfy the conditions that the United States had set for dealing with it and would permit the opening of an American-PLO dialogue, presumably as a prelude to PLO participation in the peace process. A meeting of the PLO Central Council was called in Damascus on August 28 to respond to the American call, and the Saudis were convinced that approval by the council was assured. The Syrians, however, more concerned about the Saudis' detaching the PLO from their control than about facilitating the representation of the PLO as such, used their leverage within that organization and their control over its base of operation in Lebanon to bring about a defeat of the Saudi project. Although the PLO council's rejection of even a modified version of 242 obstructed the convening of the peace conference in which the Syrians themselves were interested, the Syrians apparently felt that it was more important for them at that moment to make the point that they were the only ones who could deliver the PLO.

The Saudis resented this rebuff by the Syrians and even more the resultant loss of face with the United States. They refrained from putting themselves forward again for quite some time and were more inclined to favor at least passively the initiatives taken by Egypt.

Vance's visit having proved inconclusive, the United States invited the foreign ministers of the principal parties to Washington for further talks. Since the purpose of the talks as far as the United States was concerned was to find a way to Palestinian representation around the constraint on dealing with the PLO, the negotiations were most intense between the U.S. government and Israel's foreign minister, Moshe Dayan. On September 19, 1977, the two sides ostensibly agreed on a formula that solved the problem, but after the Arab parties rejected it, the United States disagreed with Israel as to what had been agreed to. While the search for a new American-Israeli formula continued, Secretary Vance and Soviet Foreign Minister Gromyko suddenly concluded discussions held on the margins of the UN General Assembly by issuing, on October 1, a paper on guidelines for settling the Arab-Israeli conflict. The paper reiterated the language of Resolution 242 but did not mention it by name and modified its content to include the necessity for "ensuring the legitimate rights of the Palestinian people." It stated that a settlement of the conflict should be achieved by reconvening the Geneva Conference not later than December 1977, with representation of all parties involved in the conflict, including the Palestinian people. Although the PLO was not mentioned by name, one of the main points of the exercise was to clear the way for its participation through its acceptance of the Soviet-American paper.

The omission of any reference to 242, hitherto the only agreed-upon basis for a settlement, and the two powers' unilateral amendment of its language on the Palestinians, coupled with the sudden reintroduction of the Soviet Union into the center of the peace diplomacy, after former Secretary of State Kissinger had done his utmost to relegate it to a marginal role, immediately triggered strong negative reactions. Israel and its American supporters were joined in their opposition by hard-liners, conservatives, and people within the administration itself who saw no point in the gratuitous concession made to the Soviets. In the Arab camp, the Syrians and the PLO did not think that the paper went far enough, while Sadat was indignant at the role given to the Soviets, after he had abrogated his friendship treaty with them in March 1976. The Saudis did not react officially but were inclined toward the Egyptian view.

Alarmed by the reaction, President Carter himself engaged Moshe Dayan in a marathon discussion that resulted in an American-Israeli working paper made public on October 5, 1977. In it the two sides agreed that the Arab parties should be represented at Geneva by a unified delegation that would include Palestinian Arabs not identified as PLO; that after the opening session, the conference would split into three working groups consisting of Israel and Egypt, Israel and Syria, and Israel and Jordan together with the Palestinian Arabs; and that the agreed basis for the negotiations would be Resolutions 242 and 338. Sadat was inclined to accept the paper, but the Syrians and the PLO vehemently opposed it. The Saudis took no stand, although in this instance too they leaned toward Egypt.

With the United States finally committed to a hard-fought-for position that the Arab side collectively rejected, the American drive to Geneva came to a final halt. In the retrospect of subsequent events, the Syrians and others were to argue that the path for further promising negotiations had not been blocked altogether, but Sadat and the Carter administration thought otherwise at the time. They feared that the only prospects henceforth were for a prolonged stalemate, strained relations among all the parties concerned, renewed confrontation, and probably new violent eruptions. It was to avert these prospects that Sadat launched the startling initiative that took him to Jerusalem on November 19, 1977, in quest of a new road to peace, and that the United States promptly veered direction and supported him.

Sadat's Initiative and the Egyptian-Israeli Peace

Sadat's trip to Jerusalem was viewed at the time as an impulsive leap into the dark, triggered by the American media's taking him up on a hyperbolic statement he had made ten days before in Egypt's National Assembly. Actually, Sadat's initiative was a bold act that was rooted in a sober recognition of the relevant political-strategic realities. It was based on a clear-sighted assessment of the preceding diplomatic process and on a cautious scouting of the grounds on which he proposed to advance.

Sadat's move rested on three political-strategic premises. The first was that the Arabs had no option of seeking to achieve by war their minimal objectives of recovering the territories lost in 1967 and securing Palestinian rights. That fact had been demonstrated in the 1973 war, which was fought under almost ideal circumstances for the Arabs. Since then the Arabs had perhaps gained much diplomatic leverage, but their military position relative to Israel had, if anything, deteriorated, as Israel rapidly rebuilt its military power with American help while Egypt's stagnated for several reasons, including difficulties with the Soviet Union.

The second premise was that a prolonged stalemate and continuing confrontation were highly problematic and dangerous. Egypt's economy was in ruins after two decades of confrontation. Arab assistance was insufficient to stave off popular discontent, as the outbreak of massive riots in January 1977, which nearly brought down the regime, demonstrated. Increased Arab help, even if it were forthcoming, entailed the mortgaging of Egypt's national decisions to the timid and fluctuating policies of Saudi Arabia and the other oil producers. Moreover, stalemate and confrontation would compel Egypt to revert to its unhappy experience of depending on the Soviets for arms, which would in turn strain its relations with the conservative oil-producing countries. Finally, in the unlikely event that the Arabs were able to maintain a united front and build up their military capabilities, Israel was likely to preempt before the balance began to tilt against it. Indeed, with the new, militant government of Prime Minister Begin, Israel might strike at Egypt and Syria much sooner to avenge the Yom Kippur War and try to nullify its political consequences.

The third political-strategic premise underlying Sadat's initiative was that the prospects of achieving the Arabs' objectives by peaceful means seemed to be highly promising as the United States came to view its national interest as being bound with the achievement of an Arab-Israeli settlement. This transformation had been demonstrated in the exertions of two previous administrations in step-by-step diplomacy, and even more in the endeavors of the Carter administration to bring about a comprehensive settlement. The problem, as Sadat saw it, was that some of his Arab partners — specifically the Syrians and the PLO — doubted that premise or suspected its applicability to themselves, and that the Carter administration, rather than circumvent that difficulty as Kissinger had done, sought to attack it directly and got inextricably tangled in the web of inter-Arab differences.

Even before the American endeavors to lead the parties to Geneva had reached a dead end, Sadat had begun to explore on his own the feasibility of an alternative approach. On September 16, 1977, he had sent Deputy Prime Minister Hassan Tuhami to Rabat to meet secretly with Israeli Foreign Minister Moshe Dayan, under the auspices of Morocco's King Hassan, to discuss peace possibilities. Dayan had told Tuhami that Israel was prepared to return all of Sinai to Egypt in exchange for a separate, full-fledged peace, and the two had discussed the desirability of additional meetings between themselves and also between their chiefs.[12] The idea of a secret Egyptian-Israeli summit did not appeal to Sadat, because he felt it necessary to involve the Americans and to avoid the impression that he was only seeking a separate peace. But the Rabat discussions had confirmed Sadat's sense that the alternative strategy he had been meditating was workable: that Egypt and Israel could easily reach a peace agreement, which would then be used to advance other peace agreements through the leverage of linkage and through American pressures and inducements applied to Israel. So, when the American initiative definitely faltered, Sadat was ready to launch his own.

Sadat's visit to Jerusalem immediately produced several effects that proved to be crucial for what developed next. The first and most tangible was Washington's abandonment of the Geneva approach and its commitment to Sadat's strategy. The second effect, no less crucial for being less tangible, was the tremendous impact that the initiative had on the minds of the Israelis. Sadat's visit broke through the psychological barrier of mistrust and alienation in the minds of Israelis of all stripes and planted the seeds of the possibility of genuine Arab-Israeli mutual acceptance. The third was the psychological effect produced on Sadat himself by the previous effect and the tremendous impact of his visit on the world's imagination. Sadat developed a profound vested psychic interest in proving the rightness of his approach, which became all the more entrenched in the face of criticisms by some Arab parties and passiveness by others. Those three factors combined again and again in moments of crisis to rescue the negotiations opened up by Sadat's initiative from final failure.

The actual negotiations went through three phases over a nine-month period culminating in the September 1978 Camp David accords. The first, the honeymoon phase, began with a pro forma preparatory peace conference in Cairo, which was attended by low-level representatives of Egypt, Israel, and the United States and boycotted by other Arab parties. It reached a climax in a Sadat-Begin summit conference at Ismailia on December 25 and 26, 1977. In that summit Begin "reciprocated" Sadat's initiative by offering a two-part peace plan that he had previously cleared with the United States. One part involved the return of all of Sinai to Egyptian sovereignty with some reservations, in exchange for a peace treaty and normal relations; the other consisted of a detailed scheme for self-rule for the Palestinians of the West Bank and Gaza, or, in Begin's words, the "inhabitants of Judea, Samaria, and Gaza." Sadat liked the first part and rejected the second, but he and Begin agreed to form two committees, one military and one political, to continue the negotiations. Although the committees were ostensibly functional, in fact the military committee dealt with the modalities of applying the first part of Begin's proposal while the political committee was meant to continue the negotiations on the Palestinian question.

The second phase, lasting for about eight months, was characterized by stumbling from crisis to crisis. It began with an abortive meeting of the political committee in Jerusalem in January 1978 with the participation of Secretary of State Cyrus Vance. It continued with unsuccessful bilateral negotiations in Washington between President Carter and President Sadat and Prime Minister Begin separately in February and March. The negotiations were next suspended for three months because of Israel's invasion of south Lebanon in reaction to a murderous attack by the PLO on the Haifa–Tel Aviv highway, designed to sabotage the peace negotiations. They were resumed in an abortive trilateral conference at Leeds Castle, England, on July 18 and 19, 1978, and reached a seemingly final crisis point with Sadat's suspension, a week later, of the military committee, which had been working regularly in Cairo since the beginning of the year.

The third phase began with the acceptance by Begin and Sadat of an invitation by Carter on August 8, 1978, to meet the next month at Camp David for a make-or-break effort to achieve agreement. It continued when the three leaders and their aides closeted themselves at Camp David for nearly two weeks of day-and-night negotiations on September 5–17, and ended when the parties reached and signed two agreements based essentially on the model presented by Begin at the Ismailia summit. One agreement spelled out nearly all the elements of an Egyptian-Israeli peace treaty based on the return of all of Sinai to Egyptian sovereignty, security arrangements, and provisions for normalization of relations. The other agreement outlined a "framework" for promoting a settlement of the "Palestinian question in all its aspects," involving negotiations for a self-rule regime for a transition period of five years, to be followed by negotiations for the determinations of the "final status" of the West Bank and Gaza. Jordan and the Palestinians were invited to participate in both stages of the negotiations, but it was understood that Egypt would start the first stage by itself if the others chose not to join.

The Saudis' attitude toward Sadat's initiative was essentially similar to the position they had taken toward his previous unilateral moves such as Sinai II: they wanted the potential benefit to their long-term interests that the initiative offered but wanted to avoid paying the price of supporting it in exposure to reactions of Arab opponents. However, the expressions of that attitude were affected by the momentous character of the new initiative and the circumstances attending its course.

The Saudis' initial concern in their first reaction was to make the point that, unlike the case of the negotiations for Sinai II, they had not been a party to Sadat's initiative, and to underscore that point by hinting at a reservation toward it. On November 18, 1977, one day before Sadat went to Jerusalem but two days after he had committed himself to go, the royal cabinet issued a statement expressing "surprise" at the move and stating that any Middle East peace initiative "must emanate from a unified Arab stand."[13] The Saudis felt it particularly necessary to make that point because a contrary impression might have been deduced from the fact that Sadat had visited Riyadh on November 2 for talks with Khaled and Fahd. The Saudis may have also been piqued that Sadat did not specifically consult them on his project, as he did Syria's Assad on November 16. Fahd vented such a feeling in retrospect after the signing of the Egyptian-Israeli peace treaty.[14] In any case, the Saudis tried to score on a technicality, since they must have conveyed to Sadat during his November 2 visit their common interest in finding a way around the Geneva logjam.

As the first results of Sadat's visit unfolded, the Saudis found themselves caught in a familiar dilemma. On the one hand, the tremendous impact of the initiative and the American support of it seemed to give it a real chance of leading to a breakthrough toward a settlement, which the Saudis devoutly desired. On the other hand, the move shattered the Arab near-consensus that they had painfully rebuilt after the events of Sinai II and Lebanon, and in particular destroyed once again the cherished Riyadh-Cairo-Damascus triangle. Therefore, their aim in this phase was to try to keep their lines open to both sides in the hope of bringing them together again if Egypt's initiative failed, or of getting Syria to join Egypt if its initiative succeeded. Their position thus became one of allowing the initiative to take its course, but without contributing visibly to it themselves and at the same time appeasing opponents of the initiative by expressing ambiguous reservations about it and asserting orthodox views about the desirable settlement.

Thus the Saudis refused to attend a summit at Tripoli called by Qaddafi for December 2, 1977, to mobilize opposition to Sadat, and encouraged others to do likewise. As a result, only a rump summit was held, involving Libya, Algeria, PDRY, Iraq, Syria, and the PLO, which violently attacked Sadat and led the latter to break off diplomatic relations with all five participating states. A few days later, however, on the ninth, the Saudis received Assad in Riyadh, and the next day Fahd told a Lebanese magazine that Saudi Arabia's view was actually "closer to the Syrians and the Palestinian organizations than to Sadat."[15] Six days later, on December 15, the Saudis swung the other way and indirectly endorsed Sadat's initiative. At the conclusion of a visit to Riyadh by Secretary of State Vance in which he sought to enlist support for Sadat, Foreign Minister Saud al-Faisal issued a statement expressing appreciation for the American efforts to advance a settlement and voicing the hope that these would result in achieving a "just and lasting solution in the area."[16] Finally, after a stopover of President Carter in Riyadh on January 3 and 4, 1978 (that is, after the Begin-Sadat Ismailia summit), Saud al-Faisal pointedly declared that any Middle East settlement must be based on return of all Arab lands and fulfilment of the legitimate rights of the Palestinian people.[17]

During most of the second phase of the negotiations (roughly January to August 1978) the Saudis kept a relatively low profile. For one thing, the negotiations were not getting anywhere of their own accord because of Sadat's insistence on consensual Arab positions. For another thing, Damascus and its Steadfastness Front supporters were embarrased by Syria's seeming helplessness in the face of the Israeli invasion of southern Lebanon, needed all the help they could get to cope with it, and were not in a position to put pressure on Saudi Arabia. Moreover, for three months starting on February 14, 1978, the U.S. Congress was hotly debating a proposal of the administration for a major arms package involving the sale of sixty F-15 aircraft and other equipment to Saudi Arabia together with arms and equipment for Egypt and Israel; the Saudis did not want to say or do anything that would jeopardize congressional approval. At the same time, disturbing developments in the Horn of Africa, Afghanistan, and the Yemens (see below) preoccupied the Saudis and made them anxious to keep their American connection in good order. One exception to the Saudis' inactivity was the support they gave to the convening of an Arab League meeting in Cairo on March 27–29 in the face of opposition of the Tripoli powers, which boycotted it. Typically, the Saudis promoted at that meeting the formation of a "committee for Arab solidarity" to mediate inter-Arab differences.

In late July 1978, after the American arms deal had been approved and when the failure of the Leeds conference and Sadat's dismissal of the military committee made it appear that the negotiations had definitely failed, the Saudis made a determined effort to bring about another reconciliation among key Arab parties on the basis of considering the Sadat initiative a closed chapter. Crown Prince Fahd visited Cairo on July 30 and 31 to urge the point on Sadat and proceeded from there to Damascus, Amman, and Baghdad. After Sadat's acceptance of the invitation to Camp David on August 8, Fahd declared that that was to be the last chance. "Either the matter will be decided in favor of peace or the gate will be finally closed."[18]

The success of the Camp David summit confronted the Saudis with a fateful problem. From a perspective of strict Saudi interest, the agreements represented a major historical gain. The Egyptian part of the package promised to bring to final consummation the attempt begun by Faisal seven years before to lure Egypt away from the Soviet Union and into the American sphere with the prospect of an American-promoted peace settlement, and thus remove one major source of trouble for Saudi Arabia and one major obstacle in the way of necessary Saudi-American cooperation. The Palestinian part of the agreements was disappointing in that it was most likely to be rejected by the parties chiefly concerned and thus leave the problem to fester. However, the Camp David framework still left ample room for addressing that question in subsequent negotiations, and even if these failed to produce an acceptable solution, the situation would certainly be no worse than before the Camp David agreements and would probably be a good deal better. With Egypt satisfied, the chances that the remaining conflict would lead to general war with its horrendous potential dangers for the Kingdom would be greatly reduced.

The trouble, however, was that some Arab parties — notably Syria, the PLO, and even Jordan — were bound to see things in a different light. From their perspective, the Camp David agreements bid fair to remove Egypt from the confrontation arena and thus to undermine fundamentally their bargaining position and even their security. Other Arab parties, such as Iraq, Libya, PDRY, and Algeria, were bound to rally to the former group if only for instrumental ends of their own. Were the Saudis to be seen to support the agreements in toto, hostile combinations of those countries could inflict grave harm on them. The Saudis' attempt to deal with the problem consisted, therefore, in trying to gain another chance for further negotiations on the basis of Camp David by maneuvering to prevent the formation of a hostile coalition against Egypt and, of course, in trying to ward off any combination against themselves in the process.

On September 19, 1978, two days after the signing of the Camp David agreements, the Saudi cabinet, after a meeting presided over by King Khaled, issued a statement that expressed rather nicely all the nuances of the Saudi position. The statement expressed appreciation of "the efforts made by U.S. President Jimmy Carter before and during the course of the conference." It characterized the agreement relating to the West Bank and Gaza as "an unacceptable formula for a *definitive* peace" and went on to list the reasons: there was no provision for Israeli withdrawal from all the occupied territory including Jerusalem, no stipulation of the right of the Palestinians to a state of their own, no recognition of the role of the PLO. As for the part relating to Sinai, the communiqué stated that Saudi Arabia did not consider itself entitled to "interfere in the *internal affairs* of any Arab country, nor to dispute its right to restore its occupied territories by armed struggle or through peaceful efforts, *provided that that does not clash with higher Arab interests.*"[19]

The September 19 statement anticipated pressures from different directions, and when these materialized, the Saudis tried to bend now this way now the other in the emphasis they gave to the various elements implicit in it. On September 22–24 Secretary of State Vance came to Riyadh to seek Saudi support for the agreements after having visited Amman for the same purpose the previous two days. The fact that Vance was to be received next by Syria's President Assad encouraged the Saudis to respond favorably and to state publicly that they viewed Camp David as "an initial step toward peace."[20] Three days after Vance left, Syria's Assad came to Riyadh, followed in rapid succession by Iraq's Saddam Hussein, Jordan's Hussein, and the PLO's Arafat, to press their different points of view but uniformly hostile response to the agreements and to urge the Saudis to support a summit conference at Baghdad the next month to react to them. The Saudis yielded to the latter demand but tried to head off the pressure they expected at the meeting by seeking to mobilize in advance support for resisting the imposition of sanctions on Egypt, and by pondering the possibility of luring Egypt back to the Arab fold with promises of massive economic assistance if that resistance failed. To this end Saud al-Faisal toured the Gulf oil-producing states from October 21 to 24, 1978, stating that the purpose of the envisaged summit was not to isolate Sadat but rather to restore trust within the family of Arab states.[21]

By the time the Baghdad summit convened (November 1–5), however, the Saudis had come to view the pressure of the anti–Camp David forces as irresistible and had concluded that the only thing they could do was to fight for an opportunity for Egypt to reconsider its course. One week before the summit, the rival Ba'thist regimes of Syria and Iraq had set aside years of bitter mutual hostility and agreed on October 26, 1978, to unite their countries, starting with an immediate military union. Syria had been driven to that act, as it had been to seeking greater military cooperation with the Soviet Union, by fear of American designs to isolate it and leave it at Israel's mercy militarily. Iraq had been prompted to make the overture to Syria by the ambition of its effective ruler, Saddam Hussein, to pick up the mantle of leadership of Arab nationalism that Egypt seemed to be casting away. Already before the rapprochement, Iraq had been assuming greater importance for Saudi security in the Gulf region because of the faltering of the shah's regime in the face of revolutionary forces. The combination of Iraq and Syria created a force that seemed to the Saudis to be at once potentially more useful vis-à-vis Iran and impossible to defy, especially since Saddam Hussein was inclined, by dint of his interest in not facilitating Sadat's return to the fold, to assume a relatively moderate posture in the summit he was hosting.

The result was that the Saudis joined the other summit participants in the unanimous decisions they took, after having exerted themselves, with the cooperation of Iraq and the Gulf countries, to limit the immediate damage. At their insistence, the summit rejected the calls for immediate sanctions against Egypt and condemnation of the United States; instead, it decided "not to endorse" the two Camp David agreements and "not to cooperate with the results arising from them" and to appeal to Sadat to renounce his signature. A mission was to go to Cairo to try to persuade Sadat to return to the fold and join an all-Arab strategy, and to inform him that the summit was prepared to place a vast fund of up to $9 billion at the disposal of the confrontation countries to continue the struggle, $5 billion of which would be earmarked for Egypt. On the other hand, the summit adopted a secret resolution, which was promptly leaked, providing for the expulsion of Egypt from the Arab League and for other sanctions if Egypt went ahead to sign a peace treaty.

Sadat refused even to receive the summit mission and denounced the attempt to "bribe [Egypt] with money," while the Egyptian media elaborated on this theme with specific attacks on Saudi Arabia for the first time in years. Nevertheless, the position taken by the Saudis contributed to making Sadat go slowly in the negotiations with Israel and the United States for a peace treaty by fighting for points of detail and resisting compromises, provoking Begin to do likewise. Sadat was convinced that the turn in the Saudi position was a temporary aberration or a tactical move made under the pressures of the summit and wanted to provide time for them to correct their course. In February and March 1979 the final collapse of the shah's regime, war between the two Yemens, and other domestic and foreign considerations caused President Carter to make extraordinary exertions, including shuttling between Cairo and Jerusalem, to bring the peace negotiations to a conclusion; and although the Saudis had not yet come around at that point, Sadat responded to Carter's endeavor, in the expectation that the Saudis would do so before long. Agreement on a treaty and a framework for the West Bank and Gaza along the Camp David lines was wrapped up on March 13, and the treaty was signed in a ceremony in Washington, D.C. on March 26, 1979.

One day after the signing of the treaty, a second conference convened in Baghdad, and after five days of sharp deliberations Saudi Arabia joined sixteen other countries and the PLO in resolving to apply the sanctions threatened in Baghdad I and more. In compliance with the resolutions, Saudi Arabia broke off diplomatic relations with Egypt, ceased economic assistance to it, and terminated almost all forms of cooperation with it. The breach marked the final collapse of the strategy bequeathed by Faisal, based optimally on a Riyadh-Cairo-Damascus triangle and minimally on simultaneous Riyadh-Cairo and Riyadh-Damascus connections, and signaled the adoption of an alternative course. That crucial change was connected to critical developments in other arenas, in Saudi-American relations, and at the center of power at home.

10

The Gulf Arena, 1975–1979: Balancing Baghdad and Tehran

In the Gulf arena, too, the reign of King Khaled began auspiciously thanks to a sudden change in the region's strategic configuration. Nineteen days before Faisal's assassination, on March 6, 1975, representatives of Iraq and Iran signed a surprise agreement in Algiers that ended the state of virtual war that had existed for some time between the two countries and opened the way for normalization of Iraq's relations with all the countries of the Gulf. The Saudis promptly took advantage of the new situation to reach toward Iraq and to maneuver between it and Iran to protect their security and other interests in the region against the threats they had previously faced from both quarters. Specifically, they endeavored to use Iraq to frustrate the shah's schemes to institutionalize his hegemonic aspirations through a Gulf collective defense pact, and to use Iran to check Iraq's aspiration to become the center of an alignment of the Arab countries of the Gulf. They also strove to play on the rival aspirations of the two powers in order to restrict the position of either one among the Gulf emirates and to assert their own predominance there. Within two years of Faisal's death they had succeeded remarkably in both endeavors, so that in 1977 they seemed to be in control of their destiny in the Gulf, even as they were at that same moment masters of the situation in the Arab-Israeli arena, in their relations with the United States, in their dealings with the Yemens, and elsewhere.

However, in the Gulf, too, the moment of success proved to be all too brief. By the middle of 1978, developments in the Horn of Africa, Afghanistan, the Yemens, and within Iran itself had cast a pall over all the countries of the area and shown the basic fragility of the Saudi position and the limitations of their previous achievements. Early in 1979 the fall of the shah, war between the two Yemens, and the signing of the Egyptian-Israeli peace treaty brought the entire Saudi diplomatic-strategic position crashing down and threw the Saudi ruling establishment itself into disarray. Still worse was to come before the end of 1979, so that within less than two years, the Kingdom's position and prospects turned from the brightest to perhaps the gloomiest in its existence.

On March 27, 1975, two days after Faisal's death, Crown Prince Fahd made a major speech outlining the policy of King Khaled's government in which he expressed the Kingdom's desire to cultivate brotherly relations with Iraq. The Iraqi regime, which three weeks earlier had concluded with Iran an agreement in which it had conceded national, treaty-based rights in the Shatt-al-Arab in exchange for Iran's ceasing to support the Iraqi Kurdish rebels, was more than willing to open up to the Saudis and the Arab Gulf countries in order to counter Iran's growing power by diplomatic means. The Iraqis were particularly anxious to do so at that time because the shah had recently proposed a Gulf collective security pact that would, if realized, give Iran a dominant role on the Arab side of the Gulf, which the Iraqis and the Saudis considered, in different ways, to be their particular turf.

On April 28, 1975, the shah visited Riyadh to take the measure of the new king and discuss his security proposal. The Saudis listened sympathetically but did not commit themselves, invoking the need for reflection and consultation with the other interested parties. On June 9–12 Fahd went on an official visit to Baghdad to consolidate the new relationship between the two countries that had been developing through earlier, lower-level contacts and to discuss issues of common interest, including the shah's proposal. One concrete result of the visit was the signing of an agreement to partition the neutral zone between the two countries created in the 1920s, which was formalized three weeks later.[1] However, when Fahd tried to mediate a settlement of the territorial dispute between Kuwait and Iraq he was rebuffed by his hosts, who were not disposed to accept a third-party intervention in what they saw as a bilateral issue between themselves and their neighbor.[2] Although the Iraqis' position on Kuwait was based on irredentist claims on that country, their rejection of the Saudis' offer to mediate was also a reflection of their more general attitude toward Gulf affairs. While the Iraqis were at one with the Saudis in opposing Iran's hegemonic aspirations and were prepared to abandon their own previous methods of indiscriminate subversion, they remained the Saudis' political rivals in the struggle for influence on the Arab side of the Gulf. In that rivalry, the Saudis had the advantage of propinquity with the Gulf principalities; but the Iraqis' stra-

tegic weight, which made them valuable in the eyes of the Saudis themselves as a counterbalance to Iran, also gave them an advantage over the
Saudis in the eyes of some of the weaker Gulf countries.

Three weeks after visiting Baghdad, Fahd visited Tehran on July 3,
1975, to keep Saudi relations with the two capitals even and to give the
shah his thoughts on Gulf security. The views he expressed were most
probably the same as those promoted by the Saudis in a different forum
two weeks later. On July 16 the Saudis assembled the foreign ministers of
the Gulf emirates attending an Islamic Conference meeting at Jidda and
elicited their agreement to a set of principles regarding Gulf security.
These recognized no external threats other than those that might arise
from an alignment of some Gulf countries with superpowers, viewed the
security issue mainly in terms of relations among the Gulf countries, and
called for a minimum of military cooperation and even that not necessarily on a fully collective basis. Specifically, the principles advanced by the
Saudis included: (1) exclusion of the superpowers from the region; (2)
denial of foreign military bases; (3) military cooperation among Gulf
countries to ensure freedom of navigation; (4) peaceful resolution of
regional disputes; and (5) a collective guarantee of the territorial integrity
of countries of the region.[3]

The shah agreed to the Saudi principles as far as they went but believed
they did not go far enough. He envisaged all sorts of threats to the region
emanating from the Soviet Union — direct and through proxies, near and
far, overt and covert. Weren't his troops engaged at that very moment in
fighting the Dhofar rebels, who were supported by PDRY, the Soviet
Union, and China? To meet those threats the shah thought it necessary to
have a tighter, more comprehensive defense arrangement involving a
substantial mobilization of the resources of the Gulf countries. The
Saudis suggested that they were prepared to be flexible, as was implied in
their proposal, but pointed out the necessity of securing agreement from
the other Gulf countries, especially Iraq.

The Iraqis, on the other hand, maintained that the Saudi proposals
went too far. From their point of view, there was no need for any collective
arrangement; only bilateral cooperation agreements were necessary (allowing them to bring their weight to bear on selected countries such as
Kuwait or the United Arab Emirates). Furthermore, they criticized the
ostensible exclusion of the superpowers as being directed at their Soviet
connection but as having no effect on the "organic" connection of Iran
and Saudi Arabia to the United States. They wanted the denial of foreign
bases to apply to American base rights in Bahrain but not to the Soviet
presence in their own Umm al-Qasr naval base. In the negotiations that
followed these initial statements of position, the Saudis availed themselves of the Iraqi objections to point out to the shah the difficulties with

his scheme; and at the same time they used the desire of the shah and of some of the emirates for some sort of security arrangement to justify to the Iraqis the need for a scheme like their own.

While discussions of Gulf security continued in a desultory fashion, the three big regional powers sought to deal with local situations and events in ways calculated to advance their respective interests and conceptions of a Gulf order. In that connection, the Saudis were able to make the most of their propinquity to strengthen their position on the Arab side of the Gulf. For instance, in August 1975 the Saudis put pressure on the ruler of Bahrain to suspend his experiment in representative government and to dismiss the National Assembly on the grounds that they were a source of danger to the area's stability. The shah, for his part, encouraged Oman, which he was helping militarily, to press his idea of a Gulf defense pact within the Arab camp. Partly to help counter the shah's leverage, Iraq established diplomatic relations with Oman in February 1976, after having terminated its assistance to the Dhofar rebels. In March 1976, partly with the same motive in mind, the Saudis established diplomatic relations with PDRY for the first time and in the same month mediated an agreement between it and Oman, formally ending the Dhofar rebellion on the basis of PDRY's withholding all aid to the rebels in exchange for Oman's asking all foreign forces (mainly Iran's) to leave the country.

The rivalry among the big three was also enacted at the personal and ceremonial levels, which were not without importance in a community of absolute and tribal rulers. Between March 21 and April 1, 1976, King Khaled made a grand goodwill tour of all the Gulf states — the first such campaign by a Saudi monarch — in which he emphasized the bonds between all the brethren neighbors. He was followed within less than two weeks by Iraq's vice president and strong man, Saddam Hussein, who included Riyadh in his itinerary and urged everywhere good bilateral relations. Careful to balance all the relevant parties and sensibilities, King Khaled next paid an official visit to Tehran on May 24–27, returning the shah's courtesy of a year before.

However, political courtesy and subtle diplomacy did not rule out resort to blunter means in pursuit of the same or related interests. Thus, even while King Khaled was the shah's guest in Tehran, the Saudi representative at the OPEC meeting in Bali was able, with help from the representative of the United Arab Emirates, to stymie a demand by Iran and Iraq for a 15 percent increase in the price of oil. The Saudis invoked economic reasons for their action, but the Gulf situation was relevant to it. The United States under President Ford and Secretary of State Kissinger viewed the shah as the main prop for Western interests in the region and favored his concept of a Gulf security pact. By their action at Bali, the Saudis sought to depict themselves as the better friend of the United States and to undercut American support for the shah's concept.

In addition, in July 1976 Saudi Arabia, together with Kuwait and the UAE, set up a $2 billion fund to help the economic development of Egypt, an emerging American strategic asset and counterweight to Iran. Iraq played on the superpower factor differently. In May 1976 it received Soviet Premier Kosygin in Baghdad and signed a substantial economic agreement with him.

Other external issues intruded into the Gulf game in a significant though not yet critical way. For instance, in August 1976 the Saudis bore down heavily on Kuwait after the latter concluded a $400 million arms deal with the Soviet Union with the intent of pleasing Iraq with its demonstration of "independence" and in the hope that the Soviet Union would advise Iraq to deal gently with it. The Kuwaitis were compelled by the Saudi pressure to bar Soviet advisers from coming to Kuwait and to insist that Kuwaitis be trained in the new weapons by Egyptians, with the result that the scope of the deal was eventually greatly reduced.[4] In the meantime, at the end of August the Iraqis came down hard on Kuwait, notwithstanding its deal with the Soviets, when its ruler suppressed the National Assembly and imposed restrictions on the press because of their pressure to denounce Syria's action in Lebanon. The Iraqi government denounced the action of the Kuwaiti ruler, deployed forces on Kuwait's border, and marched some of them one kilometer into it. The Saudis, who had not finished pressing the Kuwaitis over the Soviet arms deal, now comforted them and joined them in calling for a summit of the parties involved to try to settle the Lebanon situation.[5]

The Kuwaiti episodes — Soviet arms, internal agitation, and Iraqi military encroachment — gave a new sense of urgency to the idea of Gulf security in all its versions. In October 1976 Saudi Minister of Interior Prince Nayef ibn Abd al-Aziz toured the Gulf countries to promote a pact on internal security in the spirit of the Saudi scheme. The UAE, Bahrain, and Qatar were amenable but Kuwait, fearing Iraq, and Oman, with its special relationship with Iran, demurred and called for a conference of all the Gulf countries to consider proposals for the entire region. Such a conference assembled in Muscat, Oman, on November 25 and 26, with the participation of the foreign ministers of all the littoral countries. Five working papers were submitted by Iran, Iraq, Kuwait, Oman, and the UAE respectively — the Saudis typically avoided submitting one in their own name to avoid loss of face and to give themselves maximum room for maneuver. The proposals ranged from a comprehensive defense alliance suggested by Iran, through various proposals for loose cooperation in such matters as security information and nonaggression agreements, to a complete rejection of the need for any collective alliance. The deliberations took place in an atmosphere suffused with tension and mutual suspicions and ended with no agreement on any of the proposals.[6]

The failure of Muscat was above all a defeat for the shah's Gulf-wide defense scheme, since Iraq and Saudi Arabia, which had combined to bring about that result, could still pursue their respective limited plans, indeed pursue them better, after the conference. The shah, though disappointed, made it clear that he was going to pursue his goal piecemeal through various kinds of bilateral agreements, and began his new approach with discussions with Oman on relations between the two countries after the envisaged withdrawal of Iranian forces. However, before he could get very far with his new policy, the Saudis dealt him and Iraq a severe blow in the one area in which they commanded superior strength: oil prices.

On December 15–17, 1976, OPEC held its semiannual conference at Doha. As in the previous conference at Bali, the Saudis opposed demands by Iran and Iraq for substantial price increases (15 and 26 percent, respectively) and invoked economic reasons but also had political reasons. As before, they wanted to put Iran in a bad light in the eyes of the United States, which favored the shah's strategic aspirations, and put themselves in a good light. The Saudis were also particularly anxious to please the United States on this occasion because the impending new administration under President Carter had made clear its intent to seek a comprehensive settlement of the Arab-Israeli conflict.[7] At the same time, the Saudis were in a particularly confident mood because they had recently succeeded in restoring the Riyadh-Cairo-Damascus triangle after mediating the termination of the civil war in Lebanon and the Syrian-Egyptian clash over Sinai II. At Doha, the majority ultimately voted in favor of an immediate 10 percent increase and an additional 5 percent increase six months later, against a Saudi compromise proposal of 5 percent for the entire year. The Saudis, however, announced their intent to defy the majority and to increase their production up to full capacity to give effect to their defiance. Only the UAE and Qatar voted with Saudi Arabia. Kuwait, fearing Iraq's wrath, voted with Iraq, Iran, and the majority.

The Saudi position on oil prices gained the Kingdom the applause of leaders of the outgoing and incoming American administrations and severe condemnations from Iraq and Iran.[8] The latter two demonstratively drew together in an attempt to impress the Saudis; Iraqi Foreign Minister Sa'dun Hammadi was received ostentatiously in Tehran for a week-long visit from January 11 to 17, 1977, during which the two governments concluded a series of bilateral economic agreements. However, the shah ultimately had less of a shared interest with the Iraqis than with the Saudis and moreover could not afford to let the Saudis entrench themselves as America's favorites. Consequently, in April 1977 he made two moves to correct his position. Early in the month he signified his support for a proposal advanced by Prince Nayef for a conference to promote cooperation on internal security among Gulf countries, and on April 15 he sent a delegation to meet King Khaled in Riyadh and work out a compromise agreement on oil prices, wherein Iran (and presumably other OPEC members) would forgo the additional 5 percent increase in midyear while Saudi Arabia would raise its price by 5 percent to bring it into line with the others'. According to some reports, Saudi Arabia also agreed on that occasion to advance a $3 billion loan to Iran to help see it through the cash-flow difficulties it was experiencing.[9]

The reconciliation between Saudi Arabia and Iran enabled the shah to resume his policy of allaying fears and seeking bilateral agreements. Before the reconciliation, in January 1977, he had reached an agreement with Oman on the withdrawal of the bulk of Iranian forces and the retention of only air support elements in the country. After it, in May, he received UAE and Kuwaiti delegations in Tehran and concluded with them agreements on joint economic ventures. In July he received an Iraqi delegation and signed with it agreements on economic cooperation. At the beginning of November Saudi Minister of Interior Nayef visited Tehran to discuss internal security cooperation among Gulf countries and signed a bilateral agreement on the subject. On November 7 President Zayid of the UAE visited Tehran and concluded an agreement on internal security cooperation similar to that between Iran and Saudi Arabia. In the same month the shah capped his new approach with a visit to the United States, where he promised President Carter to seek no increase in oil prices in the next round and gave him assurances about human rights in exchange for securing greater American responsiveness to Iranian arms requests.

The Saudi-Iranian reconciliation and the shah's post-Muscat policy prompted the Iraqis in turn to launch a "goodwill offensive" of their own as a way of promoting their position in the Gulf. In May 1977 an Iraqi delegation headed by the minister of interior toured all the Arab Gulf countries to urge Arab solidarity and the conclusion of bilateral agreements. In July, as already mentioned, an Iraqi delegation signed a series of economic agreements in Tehran, and in December another delegation concluded another set of agreements in the Iranian capital. However, the most important Iraqi response to the situation that was shaping up in the Gulf was to relax pressure on Kuwait and achieve a detente with it. On June 27–July 3, 1977, the Iraqis hosted a Kuwaiti delegation in Baghdad and concluded with it an agreement calling for the mutual withdrawal of troops from the borders (in effect the evacuation of Iraqi troops from Kuwaiti territory they had seized); joint economic ventures, notably a railway between the two countries; and the establishment of a joint committee to solve the problem of the disputed control over the islands of Bubiyan and Warba.[10]

By the end of 1977, two and a half years after the Iranian-Iraqi Algiers

agreement, the Saudis had much reason to feel satisfied about their
position in the Gulf region. They had availed themselves of Iraq's help to
mediate an end of the Dhofar rebellion and to consolidate that achievement with an overture toward PDRY.[11] More important, they had successfully used Iraq to foil the shah's endeavor to establish his hegemony
through a comprehensive Gulf defense pact and ease him partly out of
Oman, and had then used the leverage developed with him to help get
Iraq to ease its hold on Kuwait and generally adopt a more benign approach toward all the Gulf countries. The Saudis still fell short of their
aim of achieving a network of cooperation on internal security, but they
had made a start in that direction through their bilateral agreement with
Iran and the latter's agreement with the UAE, and were pursuing the
subject further with the blessing of Iran. One subject that they had not
addressed sufficiently because of their absorption with the previous
issues was the promotion of an agreement on military cooperation to
ensure free navigation in the Gulf, through the Strait of Hormuz, and
along the oil transit routes beyond. In the absence of such an agreement,
Iran continued to monopolize that role and the enormous potential leverage it afforded. However, the Saudis could comfort themselves with the
thought that the general detente in the Gulf area had abated the dangers
to navigation from within the area, while no serious threat to it loomed
from without.

That favorable situation began to change in the first months of 1978,
and the deterioration gathered momentum as the year wore on, reaching
disastrous proportions by the beginning of 1979. The trouble began in the
Horn of Africa, where the Somali forces of Ziyad Barre's regime, which
had been receiving support from Saudi Arabia and all the other Gulf
countries, were thrown out of the Ogaden, and Somalia itself was threatened as a result of a counteroffensive launched in January 1978 by the
forces of Ethiopia's Marxist regime, supported by Soviet and Cuban arms
and personnel. PDRY had formally taken a neutral position in the conflict
but had put the port and airfield of Aden at the disposal of the Soviets as
staging and refueling posts for their airlift and sealift of weapons to
Ethiopia in December and January.[12] All the Gulf countries regarded
these developments as posing a danger to the oil route through Bab
al-Mandeb; and to some, including Saudi Arabia and Oman, they portended a renewed direct threat to the oil-producing countries themselves
through PDRY-supported rebellion and subversion. Saudi Arabia had
responded to the situation by putting direct pressure on PDRY, which led
to the mutual withdrawal of ambassadors in November 1977; by trying to
activate the Arab League against PDRY; and by seeking to promote American support for Somalia. The shah, however, took the initiative in trying
to activate the Gulf countries and used the issue to revive his idea of joint
defense arrangements.

On January 11, 1978, the shah visited Saudi Arabia to discuss that problem with his hosts. He found the Saudis more receptive to the idea of a Gulf security pact but still insistent on the need to accommodate Iraq, especially because Sadat's November 1977 visit to Jerusalem and the Saudis' tacit support of it had complicated their relations with the Iraqis. The shah sent his foreign minister to Baghdad the next month for consultations. The Iraqis apparently relented from their previous categorical opposition enough to encourage a visit by Saudi Defense Minister Sultan ibn Abd al-Aziz to Iraq and Iran in April 1978 to pursue the subject further, but not sufficiently to make an agreement possible. Probably the fact that the U.S. Congress was debating at that time a major package arms deal for Saudi Arabia, Egypt, and Israel made the Iraqis apprehensive about associating themselves just then in a pact with a country that was being depicted in the United States as part of the American Middle Eastern network of allies.

On April 27, 1978, however, a cabal of military and civilian plotters overthrew the Afghan government and installed a Marxist regime led by Nur Muhammad Taraki, which renamed the country the Democratic Republic of Afghanistan. At the same time, the Ethiopian forces, after completing their victorious campaign against Somalia in March, were mounting a successful campaign to suppress the Eritrean rebels, who had enjoyed the support of Iraq as well as that of all the Arab countries. Even the Iraqis became worried at this point by this apparent evidence of a Soviet design to squeeze the Arabian Peninsula and the Gulf between advancing pincers of satellite Marxist regimes. They were particularly alarmed by the fact that the Soviets were not content with the extensive cooperation they had been receiving from the previous Kabul government and promoted its overthrow by Marxists from within. Consequently, in the following months they clamped down on the Iraqi Communist party, starting with the arrest and summary execution of twenty Communist officers in the armed forces in May. Saddam Hussein also publicly upbraided the Soviet Union for its support of the Ethiopian suppression of the Eritreans and threatened to break off relations with it if it did not desist.[13] Such was Iraq's concern that it did not even protest Bahrain's decision to renew the lease of naval facilities to the United States. Finally, Iraq agreed to discuss a new proposal for joint Gulf security circulated by Oman in May 1978.

Negotiations among Iraq, Iran, and Saudi Arabia took place during May and June, and on June 18 the *New York Times* reported that the three powers were close to agreement on a security pact that could create "a major shift in the strategic balance of the oil producing area." Ultimately, however, Iraq's suspicion of the association of Iran and Saudi Arabia with the United States and Saudi Arabia's and Iraq's suspicion of Iranian ambitions prevailed, and a few days after agreement had been predicted, the Iranian prime minister announced the suspension of negotiations and charged Iraq and Saudi Arabia with responsibility for the failure.

Yet another few days later, on June 24, the president of North Yemen was blown up by a bomb carried in the case of an emissary of South Yemen, and two days after that the president of South Yemen was himself overthrown by more leftist and pro-Soviet opponents and was killed in the subsequent fighting. The Saudis put their armed forces on alert, marshaled their tribal support in North Yemen, got a rump session of the Arab League to suspend PDRY's membership, and called for American assistance to counter what seemed like an additional move in a Soviet systematic encirclement campaign. At the same time, the Saudis took the initiative to attempt a grand reconciliation of the Arab parties on the basis of closing the Sadat initiative chapter, following the failure of the July 1978 Leeds conference to break the deadlock in the Egyptian-Israeli-American peace talks. They also tried to combine that initiative with an attempt to revive the Gulf security talks.

On August 2, 1978, Crown Prince Fahd went to Baghdad to persuade its rulers to modify their views to facilitate an agreement in view of the added dangers and the prospects of putting aside the problems raised by Sadat's initiative. However, before the parties could follow up on that initiative, the political unrest that had been brewing in Iran for some time suddenly took on proportions that threatened the existence of the regime and absorbed all the attention of the shah. The next time that top Iraqi and Saudi leaders met — when Saddam Hussein came to Riyadh on October 2 — it was to discuss the dangers presented to them by the seeming political disintegration of the shah's regime and to consult on measures to protect themselves against them. They also discussed another development that had taken place in the interim and confronted them with critical choices, namely, the conclusion, through American mediation, of the Camp David agreements between Egypt and Israel on September 17.

Although the Iraqis and the Saudis feared the consequences of the shah's downfall, they could do little to help him. On October 4, 1978, the Iraqis expelled Ayatollah Khomeini from their country, where he had found refuge for the previous fifteen years, but the step proved to be counterproductive; the ayatollah found more freedom to lead the revolution from the Paris suburb to which he moved his headquarters than he had ever had in Iraq. Both the Iraqi and Saudi governments repeatedly voiced support for the shah, and Iraq received Empress Farah Pahlavi in Baghdad as late as November 11, 1979,[14] but this only compromised the Iraqis further in the eyes of the revolutionaries who were destroying the shah's regime. Both governments hoped or believed that the United States was bound in the end to do something to rescue its ally as it had done in similar circumstances back in 1953, especially since in the 1970s the shah's Iran had become the main pillar of Gulf security and the guarantor of Western access to its oil. However, whereas the Saudis could do nothing beyond wishing or expecting, the Iraqis also saw a major strategic opportunity in the crisis and proceeded to take advantage of it with hitherto unsuspected skill and deliberation.

Precisely because the demise of the shah's regime would destroy the strategic balance in the Gulf, Saddam Hussein and his colleagues saw in that eventuality an opportunity for Iraq to become the dominant power in the region and a major power well beyond. With the shah gone, Iraq could become the protector of the bewildered oil-rich Arab countries of the Gulf and parlay that position into preeminence in all Arab affairs and in the oil-dependent world at large. To achieve that potential, however, it was essential that Iraq act in such a way as not to drive the worried Gulf countries into the arms of the United States and/or Egypt for protection. The fact that Iraq had been loosening its ties to the Soviet Union for some time made it more acceptable to the Gulf countries' rulers. Furthermore, the fact that the United States had been perceived to be ineffective in countering Soviet advances in Afghanistan, south Arabia, and the Horn of Africa undermined America's credibility as a security asset. Nevertheless, to capitalize on the opportunity, Iraq needed to devise a nonprovocative stratagem to block entirely the Gulf countries' way to the United States and Egypt and leave them no choice but to rally to itself.

Egypt's coincidental signing of the Camp David accords under American aegis at that very time gave the Iraqis the perfect chance to attempt such a stratagem. If they could marshal the opposition of the Arab parties that vehemently rejected the accords (including Syria, PDRY, the PLO, Libya, and Algeria) to force the hand of the waverers who had reason to fear the rejectionists (Saudi Arabia and the Gulf countries), and if they could persuade the rejectionists to refrain from pressing extreme views for the sake of achieving consensus, then they could in one stroke achieve all three of their objectives. They could isolate Egypt, undercut the United States, and propel themselves forward as the leading power in both the Gulf and the Arab-Israeli arenas.

With a fine sense of timing, the Iraqis waited until the Saudis felt the agitation of key Arab parties against the Kingdom's initial accommodating position expressed to Secretary of State Vance. The Iraqis then issued a call on October 1, 1978, for an Arab summit at Baghdad, coupled with an offer of cooperation with Syria.[15] The next day, as already mentioned, Saddam Hussein visited Riyadh to persuade the Saudis to agree to Iraq's call and to discuss with them the deteriorating situation in Iran. By October 10 Saddam Hussein had obtained the agreement of Syria and Jordan as well as of Saudi Arabia, and by the twenty-fourth he had secured the most important condition for the success of the summit: he had effected a reconciliation with Syria and concluded with it an agreement on military cooperation. This step at once drew to Iraq the key member of the rejectionist camp and created a combination that the Saudis and their Gulf followers would find very difficult to oppose.

At the summit itself, which convened on November 2–5, 1978, the Iraqis set the tone by ruling out neutrality and equivocation, warning against division, and threatening that a split would not remain confined to Arab ranks but would lead to "dangerous international polarization."[16] After that warning to the Saudis and other waverers, the Iraqis were able to steer the conferees toward a consensus that refrained from attacking the United States specifically but rejected in toto the Camp David agreements it had sponsored. The agreements were denounced as an act of appeasement of the enemy, but the conference opted for an alternative, "just peace," based on Israeli withdrawal from all the territories occupied in 1967 and the establishment by the Palestinians of a state "on their national soil." The signing of the Camp David agreements was described as a betrayal of pan-Arab responsibilities, but, largely for the Saudis' sake, Sadat was offered a chance to rejoin the Arab fold and financial support to carry on the struggle. When, as expected, Sadat contemptuously turned down the invitation, the Iraqis steered the conference toward adopting a set of punitive measures against him but again accommodated the Saudis by confining application of the sanctions to the case and time when Egypt should actually sign a peace treaty.

The next few months saw the simultaneous culmination of all three critical issues that had been festering for some time, thrusting the Saudis into confusion and crisis and giving the Iraqis the chance to fulfill their objectives. On January 6, 1979, in a desperate attempt to save his throne, the shah appointed Shahpur Bakhtiar to head a government with total authority; on January 16 the shah left his country for the final exile; on February 1 Ayatollah Ruhollah Khomeini returned to Iran in triumph; and on February 12 the Bakhtiar government was overthrown and its leader went into hiding. On February 23 the long-simmering tension between the two Yemens erupted in open warfare, and by February 25 the Cuban-advised troops of South Yemen had advanced some twenty miles into North Yemen and captured the towns of Harib and Qa'taba.[17] Finally, on March 13 President Carter concluded a shuttle expedition to the Middle East by announcing that all the ingredients of an Egyptian-Israeli peace treaty were in place, and two weeks later the treaty was signed at a ceremony in Washington.

The approaching end of the shah's regime had caused the Saudis to turn to the United States in panic for some reassurance. The Carter administration, itself following a confused course in Iran and wishing to avoid the implication that that country's condition presented a danger to its neighbors, responded with the odd offer to send a squadron of *unarmed* F-15s and 300 support personnel on a demonstrative "visit" to the Kingdom. Such was the extent of the Saudis' fright that they agreed to receive the squadron, which arrived after some delays on January 15, 1979.

Less than three weeks later, the departure of the shah and the imminent collapse of Bakhtiar's government led the Carter administration to go to the opposite extreme in showing its concern for the security of Saudi Arabia. On February 10 and 11, 1979, Secretary of Defense Harold Brown visited the Kingdom on the first leg of a Middle East trip and presented his hosts with two proposals. He offered to speed up and increase the supply of American arms to North Yemen and the Sudan, in accordance with previously expressed Saudi wishes that the United States had been slow in meeting. He also startled his hosts with a proposal to establish an American military base in the Kingdom to enable the United States to take a direct part in its defense and the defense of the region as a whole.[18] With Crown Prince Fahd scheduled to visit the United States on March 1, at a critical moment in the Egyptian-Israeli peace talks, Brown's proposal seemed, in effect, to invite the Saudis to become openly the protégés of the United States, throw in their lot with it and Egypt, and defy the consensus of the Baghdad summit. Such a move was much more than they were willing to contemplate at that point, especially since Syria and Iraq had just consummated their rapprochement with an agreement to unite the two countries signed on January 31. The Saudis therefore instantaneously rejected the proposal for a base and instead requested American Lance missiles, which Brown declined immediately. Shortly thereafter they found it necessary to dissociate themselves actively from the American peacemaking effort by announcing on February 23 the cancellation of Crown Prince Fahd's planned visit to the United States and by making it a point to deny an American official explanation that the cancellation was for health reasons. In the meantime, on February 9 the Saudi minister of interior signed with his Iraqi counterpart an agreement on internal security cooperation to enhance the Kingdom's ability to deal with the possible fallout of the Iranian revolution.

While the Saudis were engaged in the altercation with the United States over the Fahd visit, the South Yemenis made their big thrust into North Yemeni territory. The Saudis responded with a series of reactions, not all consistent. They agreed to collective Arab mediation but then tried to undercut it with an attempt to settle the conflict on their own. When this attempt failed, they put their armed forces on alert, recalled their 1,500-man contingent with the Arab Deterrent Force in Lebanon, and proceeded to concentrate forces near the borders in support of North

Yemen. While the collective Arab mediation was going on, they dispatched American arms to North Yemen with U.S. approval even as the United States was rushing a naval squadron to the Arabian Sea. They next agreed to channel American emergency arms shipments to North Yemen, turned down an offer of an American squadron of F-15s to reinforce their own air capability, accepted an American offer to deploy two American-manned AWACS aircraft in the Kingdom, and supported the dispatch of American advisers to North Yemen.

The dispatch of American arms to North Yemen by the Saudis and the United States threatened to undermine the Arab mediation to end the conflict and gave rise to difficulties even between North Yemen and Saudi Arabia over questions of arms flow and control. Nevertheless, by March 16, 1979, the Arab efforts, led by Iraq, Syria, and Jordan, succeeded in promoting an agreement between the belligerents that brought about an end of the fighting and the mutual withdrawal of forces three days later. The contrast between the seeming effectiveness of the collective Arab approach and the dubious, provocative, and problematic character of the joint and separate Saudi and American military responses gave ground for satisfaction to Arab-oriented members of the Saudi ruling establishment. The satisfaction was marred by the fact that the successful Arab mediation was linked to the opening of a dialogue between the two Yemens aimed at implementing the 1972 accord on Yemeni unity, and that such a dialogue took place promptly in Kuwait under Arab aegis and led to a new specific unity agreement on March 30. On the other hand, what little could be said in favor of the American response was more than marred by Washington's endeavor to implicate the Saudis into associating themselves with the consummation of the negotiations for an Egyptian-Israeli peace treaty in return for American support.

On March 16, 1979, the day on which Iraq, Syria, and Jordan mediated the end of the war, President Carter's national security adviser, Zbigniew Brzezinski, came to Riyadh to enlist Saudi support for the Egyptian-Israeli peace treaty. He met with King Khaled and Foreign Minister Saud al-Faisal, argued that the treaty offered a basis for a comprehensive Arab-Israeli settlement, and, recognizing the Saudis' present anxieties and their fear of the reaction of Arab rejectionists, offered American protection of the Kingdom in exchange for compliance. The Saudis were not convinced that the treaty could satisfy the "just settlement which the Arab and Islamic nations and the Palestinian people desire."[19] Nor were they overly impressed by the American offer of protection, given their perception of America's record on that score in Afghanistan and the Horn of Africa, its recent failure to save the shah, and its dubious contribution in the Yemen crisis. Nevertheless, while turning down Brzezinski's offer they promised him that Saudi Arabia would not support a "precipitous" penalization of Egypt for signing the treaty. Even that proved to be more than they could deliver.

At the very same time Iraq, as the convener of the November 1978 Baghdad summit, issued an invitation for another meeting — this time of foreign ministers — in Baghdad for March 27, 1979, the day after the date scheduled for the signing of the treaty, to apply the contingent sanctions resolution decided upon earlier. Before the conference, the Saudis lobbied among the Gulf countries for the minimal sanctions compatible with the summit resolutions, while Oman, the Sudan, Somalia, and Djibouti —all countries with special actual or potential security interest in Egypt — decided not to attend the conference. However, these vacillations only prompted Iraq to adopt a much more aggressive stand than it had at Baghdad I. On March 23, for instance, Saddam Hussein declared through the Iraqi paper *al-Thawra:* "We regard every Arab ruler who does not implement the summit decisions as a traitor. It is therefore our duty to instigate his people against him and to provide them with all the necessary means to topple him." He repeated the warning in slightly more veiled terms at the opening of the conference while calling for the implementation of the summit sanctions as "the minimum" and inviting Arab states capable of adopting stronger and tougher stands to do so.[20]

The Syrians and the PLO picked up where the Iraqis left off. On the first working day of the conference, the PLO called for economic sanctions against the United States as well as against Egypt. The Saudis and their friends resisted the proposal on the grounds that it would only damage the interests of the Arab states themselves, but agreed to the suspension of economic assistance to Egypt. They also agreed to Egypt's suspension from membership in the Arab League as well as from membership in the various organizations sponsored by it, which was more than had been specifically resolved in Baghdad I. The critical point came the next day, the twenty-ninth, when the complete severance of diplomatic relations with Egypt was discussed. Saud al-Faisal opposed total rupture, hoping to prevent complete disruption of the strategic Riyadh-Cairo line. The PLO's Arafat led the countercharge, attacked Saud as a "disgrace to his father," and reportedly said: "Do not force us to become a band of assassins."[21] Later the conference was adjourned when Arafat stormed out of the meeting, followed by the Syrian and Libyan delegations. The conference reconvened on March 29 only to decide on a twenty-four-hour adjournment to allow for consultations among the delegations and between them and their governments. Saud al-Faisal returned to Riyadh to report and to receive new instructions.

The crisis at Baghdad II compelled the Saudis to make a choice they had devoutly tried to avoid. Even as the fall of the shah destroyed the strategic balance in the Gulf, the Saudis hoped to be able to build a new security structure based on greater cooperation with both Baghdad and Washington. The Camp David accords came in the way, but the Saudis temporized on that issue in the hope that the problem would go away by itself (through failure of the peace negotiations) or that further developments in the relevant areas would allow them to finesse their way out as they had done on similar occasions. The actual course of events disappointed them in both respects. On the one hand, agreement on a peace treaty was achieved as a result of dramatic American exertions; and on the other hand the Iraqis stiffened their stance against the treaty and greatly reinforced their strategic weight through the union agreement with Syria, an understanding with the PLO, and the formation of a powerful rejectionist coalition around themselves. These developments forced the Saudis to choose between the security strategy proposed by Brzezinski (that is, to become part of an American general Middle East defense scheme encompassing Egypt, Israel, and the Arabian Peninsula) and an Arab-oriented defense scheme with Iraq and Syria at its core. Either course involved a difficult balance of short- and long-term costs and benefits. The American orientation probably appeared sounder in the long run despite the recent weaknesses displayed by American policy; but it entailed the immediate danger of confrontation with Iraq, Syria, the PLO, and others. The Arab orientation, on the other hand, averted such confrontation and appeared to be effective in the short run, as seen in the Arab mediation of the conflict between the two Yemens; but it entailed a breach with Egypt and a dangerous straining of the relationship with the United States. Moreover, it left the Kingdom vulnerable to the pressures of a new movement for integral Arab unity that might develop out of the unity agreements between Iraq and Syria and between North and South Yemen.

The Saudi ruling establishment debated these choices during the maneuvering period preceding Baghdad II. As on previous critical occasions, the debate blended with rivalries and power struggles which had been going on among personalities and groups within the establishment and which had been exacerbated by the deterioration of King Khaled's health. (He underwent open heart surgery in September 1978.) Crown Prince Fahd and others, it seems, insisted on keeping open the line to Egypt and the United States even at the risk of a breach with the Baghdad coalition, whereas King Khaled, Abdallah, and others argued for the opposite.[22] The decision went against Fahd, although it was apparently mitigated by a vow by all to make an additional effort to avert the issue altogether, and to review the decision if that proved to be impossible. Fahd was nevertheless sufficiently upset to leave the country on March

22, 1979, when crises were brewing all around, and to go on a long holiday in Spain to brood on his defeat and recover his strained health.

Fahd's absence from the scene probably made it easier for the other members of the ruling establishment to accept Saud al-Faisal's report that the moment of decision had arrived and to reaffirm the choice they had made earlier. Saud went back to Baghdad on March 31, 1979, and accepted the conference's resolutions, which called for a complete severance of diplomatic relations with Egypt as well as a whole array of economic and other sanctions. Once more the Saudis opted to put at risk long-term strategic interests for the sake of meeting short-term tactical dangers.

11

The Yemens, Oman, and the Horn of Africa, 1975–1979: Accommodation and War

Faisal's death, coupled with an emerging favorable strategic configuration in the Persian Gulf region, a momentarily comfortable situation in the Arab-Israeli arena, and seemingly promising conditions within the YAR and PDRY, encouraged his successors to try a new approach in dealing with the hitherto frustrating problem of the Yemens. The old king had been adamant in his refusal to accept the National Front government in Aden and had geared all his efforts to vain attempts to destroy it through South Yemeni dissidents, a client government in San'a, or client North Yemeni tribes acting independently of San'a. Faisal's successors believed there was a chance of weaning PDRY away from fomenting revolution among its neighbors and from its dependence on Moscow; and to the extent that that chance proved to be real, it would considerably reduce the role that had been hitherto assigned to the YAR and would also facilitate the latter's stabilization. Instead of being thought of as a battering ram against PDRY, with the latter inevitably responding with subversive counteraction, the YAR could become merely a strategic counterweight and reinsurance against a tamed PDRY. Viewed in that role, the San'a government could be allowed much greater latitude by the Saudis in its attempts to bring the entire country under central control and end the state of semianarchy that had prevailed for so long.

Among the factors that encouraged Faisal's successors to try the new approach was the Kingdom's rapprochement with Iraq in the wake of the March 1975 Iranian-Iraqi agreement. The rapprochement not only held out the promise of ending Iraqi material support for PDRY militancy, but it also confirmed the Saudis' belief in the possibility of inducing PDRY itself to adopt a more benign course as Iraq was now doing, and as radical Syria and formerly radical Egypt had done before. The president of PDRY, Salim Rubaya Ali, was receptive to the Saudi approach for his own reasons. He wanted to play off the Saudis against the Soviets in order to obtain maximum economic aid from both, and he favored a detente with the Saudis as a means to end PDRY's isolation in the Arab world and to promote the shared interest of the two countries in terminating the Iranian military intervention in Dhofar as the PDRY-supported rebellion there faltered in mid-1975 and then collapsed at the end of the year.

In the YAR, too, conditions seemed to favor the new Saudi approach. Colonel Hamdi seemed to be a strong, able, and popular man, capable of playing the roles of unifier of the YAR and balancer of PDRY. After an initially disturbing start from the Saudi point of view, Hamdi corrected course in November 1974 by reconvening the Consultative Assembly, in which their client tribes had a dominant voice. In January 1975 Hamdi went further in appeasing Saudi sensibilities by dropping Prime Minister 'Aini, who, as signer of the 1972 unity agreement with PDRY, was strongly disliked by the Saudis. In 'Aini's place Hamdi appointed Abd al-Aziz Abd al-Ghani, a capable technocrat who surrounded himself with a like-minded cabinet. Hamdi himself took charge of the contacts on unity with PDRY and, at this stage, kept them going on a low key.

While these circumstances encouraged the Saudis to engage in their new policy and allowed them to make some headway, other elements in the situation of the two Yemens obstructed further progress and eventually defeated the policy altogether. In the first place, Rubaya's policy of seeking an understanding with the Saudis was opposed by powerful forces within PDRY, headed by Abd al-Fattah Isma'il, the leader of the country's sole political organization. Isma'il used every opportunity to slow down and sabotage Rubaya's efforts even before he managed to overthrow him altogether in mid-1978. In the second place, Rubaya himself, while seeking to play off the Saudis against the Soviets, was bound by conviction or political necessity to give primacy to the Moscow connection when and if a choice had to be made; and such a choice was forced on him in the latter part of 1977 by events in the Horn of Africa. Third, Rubaya was similarly committed to unity with North Yemen; and he could pursue a policy of detente with the Saudis only to the extent that he could demonstrate to his opponents that such a policy did not impede progress toward that unity. Fourth, from the Saudi point of view, the extent of the detente with PDRY depended a great deal on a conciliation between that country and Oman; but Rubaya's ability to effect such a conciliation was constrained by the continuing presence of Iranian forces in Oman and by his opponents' constant harping on that point. Finally, the ambivalence in PDRY's approach at its best stimulated a similar disposition among the Saudis, with the result that their endeavor to entice that country toward moderation never developed the kind of momentum that would have given it a better chance to succeed.

In the YAR, the difficulty for the Saudis was a variant of their classical problem in relation to that country. Granted that their new overall approach to the problem of the two Yemens allowed for giving Hamdi's regime greater latitude in pursuing a centralizing and nationalist policy, the question still remained as to how much latitude they could permit it without risking the loss of any control over matters that affected their own basic interests. The question was particularly acute with regard to the regime's attempts to assert central authority over the northern tribes because the latter were not disposed to tolerate the degree of central control acceptable to their Saudi patrons. This in itself placed the Saudis in a difficult position in the middle; but the issue had further, far-reaching ramifications. For instance, Hamdi wanted to develop a strong military relationship with the United States independently of the Saudis. To the extent that he could achieve such a relationship, he would be in a position to assert control over the tribes even beyond the point acceptable to the Saudis. And to the extent that the Saudis lost the leverage that the tribes gave them over the regime, the latter would also be freer to pursue unity with PDRY in more than a pro forma fashion.

The Saudis' efforts to steer their new policy through these complex problems went through two phases that coincided in large measure with the course of their endeavors in the Gulf and Arab-Israeli arenas. Until about the second half of 1977, they seemed to be making headway with their policy despite some setbacks. From the last quarter of 1977 on, their policy began to fall apart despite occasional successes until it disintegrated entirely in the February–March 1979 war between the two Yemens. The following paragraphs highlight the principal events and episodes of the four-year period that document the preceding analysis.

1. In January 1975 Hamdi dismissed Prime Minister 'Aini, who was objectionable to the Saudis, and replaced him with Abd al-Ghani, a technocrat. To compensate the radicals at home and in PDRY, Hamdi received a PDRY delegation at Ta'iz in February to continue unity talks and declared his willingness to accept Soviet arms as long as there were no strings attached.[1] Nevertheless, some elements in PDRY were unhappy, and in March and April YAR officials complained that PDRY was supporting acts of sabotage on the YAR border.[2]

In March 1975 PDRY Foreign Minister Muhammad Saleh Muti' visited the UAE, Qatar, and Bahrain seeking to normalize relations. This was one of the earliest indications of Rubaya's attempt to reach out to conservative Gulf countries and, through them, to Saudi Arabia in an endeavor to gain assistance and ease PDRY's isolation. Naturally, the Dhofar issue was central to the discussions,[3] and Muti' most probably hinted at PDRY's willingness to reduce its support for the rebels but linked such action to termination of the Iranian military intervention.

2. In May 1975 Hamdi visited Riyadh and received pledges of increased Saudi aid.[4] Earlier that month Hamdi had promised far-reaching reforms and begun a purge of officers with tribal affiliations from the Military Command Council, the real center of power. The purge continued in June.[5] In that month one of the dismissed officers, Lt. Colonel Mujahed Abu Shawarib, tried to raise a tribal rebellion in the northern areas but was put down.[6] The Saudis were thus allowing Hamdi to use his developing connection with them to curtail the power of the tribes.

In June 1975 a Beirut newspaper reported that a secret meeting had taken place in Cairo between Saudi Foreign Minister Saud al-Faisal and PDRY Foreign Minister Muti'.[7] In July there were unconfirmed reports from Saudi Arabia that a meeting would soon take place between Saudi and PDRY representatives as a result of mediation by Iraq's Saddam Hussein. The favorable conjunctures in the Arab-Israeli and the Gulf arenas were thus helping to bring about a Saudi-PDRY detente.

3. In August 1975 Saudi Arabia promised the YAR $100 million in budget support and $360 million in development aid. Hamdi announced that relations with the USSR were "frozen."[8] In October Hamdi disbanded the Consultative Assembly, dominated by representatives of the northern tribes, and concentrated all power in the Military Command Council.[9] In November a member of the command council, Ali Abd al-'Alem, headed a military delegation to Moscow, notwithstanding Hamdi's earlier declaration about "frozen" relations. In the same month, further unity talks between the YAR and PDRY were held in Aden.[10] Hamdi thus continued to use Saudi support to weaken the tribes and to satisfy the nationalists in the YAR, and at the same time tried to balance his developing relationship with Saudi Arabia with moves to appease PDRY and to keep an opening to Moscow.

In December 1975 Oman's Sultan Qabus declared his government's final victory in Dhofar after a three-month Iranian-Omani offensive. In the same month, it was reported that PDRY Foreign Minister Muti' had visited Jidda for talks, after the Saudis had begun moves to mediate a PDRY-Oman agreement.[11]

On March 10, 1976, Saudi Arabia and PDRY agreed to establish diplomatic relations for the first time since South Yemen's independence in 1967. The Saudis had failed to bring about a PDRY-Oman conciliation but had mediated a cease-fire agreement between the two countries based on the withholding of all aid to the Dhofar rebels and the withdrawal of all foreign forces from the country. The agreement underscored the common interest between Saudi Arabia and PDRY in getting Iran out of Oman, but was also a source of continuing friction between them, since the Saudis expected PDRY to cease aiding the rebels but could not themselves deliver the withdrawal of Iran's force.

4. On April 11, 1976, Saudi Defense Minister Sultan ibn Abd al-Aziz, the prince in charge of Yemeni affairs, visited San'a and agreed to increase aid to the YAR.[12] In June 1976 the United States agreed to supply the YAR with $140 million worth of arms, to be financed by the Saudis.[13] The move reflected the Saudis' willingness to give latitude to Hamdi's regime in order to build up the YAR as a counterweight to PDRY.

In April 1976 there were reports that PDRY expected to receive up to $400 million in Saudi aid over five years, almost double the total planned PDRY investment for that period.[14] The Saudis actually gave PDRY only $50 million before relations between the two countries soured again a year and a half later. In May, however, it was reported that the Soviet Union had offered expanded aid to PDRY.[15] Clearly, the Saudis were providing their aid slowly, and PDRY was trying to play them off against the Soviets.

5. For most of the remainder of 1976, Saudi relations with the YAR seemed to be on course even as Hamdi continued to tighten his hold on the country. In August the Saudi Development Fund gave the YAR $86 million in loans and aid, and in October Hamdi paid a five-day visit to Riyadh. Toward the end of the year, however, Hamdi began to display a measure of independence in foreign policy that later taxed the limits of Saudi tolerance. In December Hamdi visited Peking, where he signed an agreement on economic and technical cooperation between the two countries. China, which was keenly interested at the time in the Red Sea/Indian Ocean region, had earlier received Egyptian Vice President Mubarak, Pakistan's Prime Minister Bhutto, and Madagascar's President Rastiraka and in February 1977 would receive PDRY Foreign Minister Muti'.[16]

During the same period, Saudi relations with PDRY continued to be handicapped by the incomplete conciliation between PDRY and Oman because of the presence of Iranian forces in the latter country. Sultan Qabus wanted a Gulf security agreement before asking the Iranians to leave, and after failing to get that at the November 1976 Muscat conference (discussed in Chapter 10), he concluded an agreement with Iran in January 1977 calling for the reduction but not the complete removal of Iran's military presence. The mutual Saudi-PDRY recognition of the preceding March did not therefore lead to an exchange of ambassadors between the two countries, and Saudi assistance to PDRY remained at a modest level.

On February 15, 1977, Rubaya and Hamdi met in San'a and the two agreed to advance the unity process by setting up a joint council to cooperate in matters of economy, defense, and foreign affairs.[17] The following month the vow to cooperate in foreign affairs was given an impressive expression.

On March 22 and 23 Hamdi convened a summit conference on Red Sea security at Ta'iz, which was attended by the heads of state of PDRY, Somalia, and the Sudan in addition to himself. The conference produced no practical results, but Hamdi's initiative produced mixed feelings among the Saudi leaders. On the one hand, they were pleased to see the leaders of PDRY and Somalia take part in the project in association with two local friendly states just ten days after those same leaders had rejected a proposal, pressed by Cuba's Fidel Castro during a visit to PDRY, for a federation of Marxist East African states comprising PDRY, Somalia, and Ethiopia, including Eritrea. On the other hand, the Saudis saw and suspected China's influence behind the project, disliked the excessive independence shown by Hamdi, and resented his preemption of the initiative on a subject in which they had invested a great deal of attention. In an interview given to a Kuwaiti newspaper the following month, Crown Prince Fahd said that Saudi Arabia did not take part in the conference because "we were not informed on this subject in advance" and because "we believe" that the objectives sought "on such sensitive subjects" and the balance of political gains and complications that might result from them needed to be discussed "objectively and scientifically,"[18] implying that Saudi Arabia had done that but the participants in the conference had not.

6. In April 1977 the first Saudi ambassador to PDRY presented his credentials, over one year after the agreement to establish diplomatic relations between the two countries. In May Saudi Arabia agreed to supply the Aden refinery with one million tons of crude annually. In the same month, PDRY and Cuba signed a protocol on "ideological cooperation."[19] In June Abd al-Fattah Isma'il, Rubaya's rival, denied that PDRY would seek reconciliation with Oman.[20] At the beginning of July there were reports that PDRY Foreign Minister Muti' had met secretly with an Omani representative in Riyadh.[21] In mid-July PDRY Prime Minister Ali Nasser Muhammad attacked Oman and Iran and there were reports of border clashes on the PDRY-Oman border.[22] At the end of July Rubaya made an official visit to Saudi Arabia, the first ever by a South Yemeni head of state. Also in July there were reports that the Soviet Union was sending large quantities of oil to be refined in Aden.[23] These contradictory developments clearly reflected the ramified power and policy struggle within PDRY, which found a more conventional expression in September, when the Central Committee of the country's sole political organization stripped Rubaya of some of his functions.[24]

In the meantime, political developments inside the YAR took a more intense and violent course than they had for some time. On April 10, 1977, former Prime Minister Abdallah al-Hajri, known as pro-Saudi and favorable to the northern tribal chiefs, was assassinated in London, where he had gone to visit the ailing King Khaled. Suspicion centered heavily on the radicals of the NDF, whom Hamdi was using to counterbalance the tribes. In May and June leaders of the northern tribes, who had been restless for some time because of Hamdi's efforts to curb their power, intensified their previous acts of harassment against the government into what amounted to a guerrilla campaign. The Saudis sought to mediate. Hamdi went to Saudi Arabia in early May, his foreign minister in early June, and Hamdi again at the beginning of July. During the mediation process, tribal fighters — estimated to number 40,000 — attacked and occupied the towns of Khamir and Sa'da and the surrounding area. Hamdi used the air force to support a counterattack that recaptured the towns, but the rebels pulled back to their traditional strongholds in the northeast.[25]

7. At the beginning of September 1977 a reconciliation agreement was reached between Hamdi and the tribes in which Hamdi promised increased tribal representation in the Military Command Council and the government, the replacement of Prime Minister Abd al-Ghani with someone more acceptable to the tribal chiefs, the holding of elections to a Consultative Council, and various other significant concessions in exchange for the tribes' agreement to surrender their heavy weapons and pull back further from territory they had occupied in the recent fighting. On the face of it, the agreement conceded almost everything to the tribes in order to get at some of their weapons. Whether Hamdi thought the bargain worthwhile or felt compelled to accede to it, and whether he intended to fulfill it or thought of it as yet another political maneuver is not known. What is known is that by the end of September 1977 there was renewed strain with the tribal chiefs, that members of Hamdi's own government criticized the agreement, and that Hamdi planned to go on an important visit to Aden — the first visit to PDRY by a YAR head of state — on October 13. Also known, of course, is the fact that on October 11 Hamdi and his brother were assassinated in obscure circumstances by killers who were not apprehended, and that this act marked a turning point in the affairs of the YAR and its neighbors.[26]

Although Hamdi had a variety of enemies with an interest in his elimination, the belief in San'a has remained widespread ever since that the Saudis were behind the assassination because Hamdi had become too independent,[27] notwithstanding the Saudi government's strong condemnation of the "treacherous aggression." Certainly the fact that Hamdi's short-lived successor, Colonel Ahmad al-Ghashmi, followed a strong pro-Saudi orientation and that the Saudis reciprocated with all-out support for him helped to establish and perpetuate that notion.

8. On October 11, 1977, the day of Hamdi's assassination, the Military Command Council appointed Ghashmi, one of its members, to succeed Hamdi as chairman of the council and commander-in-chief of the armed forces. A statement by the Saudi government issued that day condemned the assassination and called upon the Yemeni people to rally around their new leadership.[28] On October 15 Saudi Deputy Minister of Defense Turki ibn Abd al-Aziz appeared unannounced in San'a to see Ghashmi. On October 16 a division commander loyal to Hamdi attempted to assassinate Ghashmi. In December the Saudis committed $570 million toward the YAR's $3.6 billion five-year development plan, which had started in 1976.

On November 25, 1977, mounting strain between Saudi Arabia and PDRY led to the mutual withdrawal of ambassadors. The Saudis accused PDRY of allowing itself to be turned into a staging post for Soviet and other Communist aid to Ethiopia. Earlier that month Somalia's Ziyad Barre had renounced the treaty of friendship with the Soviet Union, terminated Soviet use of naval facilities in Berbera, and ordered out 1,600 Soviet advisers. The Soviets then increased their pressure on PDRY for access to its facilities, and PDRY acceded to their demands. From PDRY's perspective, Rubaya's attempt at rapprochement with Saudi Arabia had never worked well because of the problem of Oman, nor had it justified itself in terms of the scope of Saudi aid. The assassination of Hamdi, which was viewed as the work of the Saudis aimed at defeating the prospects of YAR-PDRY unity, dealt Rubaya's policy a fatal blow and left him with no choice but to go along with his political opponents in acceding to the Soviet demands. The suspension of diplomatic relations marked the formal end of the Saudis' first experiment with a new approach to the problem of the Yemens and their reversion to the previous policy of confronting PDRY through a client YAR government, client YAR tribes, and South Yemeni dissidents.

9. In February 1978 Ghashmi appointed a Constituent People's Assembly in which the tribes had dominant influence. On April 22 the assembly voted to disband the Military Command Council and to elect Ghashmi president. Earlier that month a high-ranking Saudi delegation had spent four days in San'a — from the tenth to the thirteenth — amid speculation that a Saudi-YAR defense pact was to be concluded soon. A few days earlier, Colonel Mengitsu Haile Mariam, chairman of the Dergue (the Ethiopian provisional government), had visited PDRY for talks on the situation in the Horn of Africa after the successful Ethiopian counter-offensive in the Ogaden, supported by Soviet arms and Cuban troops. Also on April 10, a Kuwait-initiated visit by PDRY's minister of interior to Riyadh to address mutual complaints about border incidents and subversion produced no practical results.

10. In May – June 1978 a major rebellion against Ghashmi broke out near the PDRY border, led by Ali Abd al-'Alem, a leftist former member of

the command council disbanded by Ghashmi. After government troops put down the rebellion, 'Alem fled to Aden and joined forces with the NDF, which had been turning more radical since Ghashmi's accession to power.[29]

On June 24, 1978, Ghashmi was assassinated in a Byzantine plot that also framed PDRY's Rubaya, when a bomb rigged in the case of an emissary carrying a message from Rubaya to Ghashmi exploded, killing the hapless emissary as well. The next day Rubaya was "suspended" by the Central Committee of PDRY's political organization while a commission was established to investigate his role in Ghashmi's assassination. On June 26 fighting broke out in Aden between army units loyal to Rubaya and Popular Militia forces loyal to Abd al-Fattah Isma'il, ending in Rubaya's surrender and his execution on charges of rebellion, being in league with reactionary forces abroad, and undermining PDRY-USSR relations.[30] Rubaya was immediately succeeded by the hitherto pro-Isma'il prime minister, Ali Nasser Muhammad. After a one-month interim presidential council, Ghashmi was succeeded by Abdallah Ali Saleh, the commander of the forces that had put down 'Alem's rebellion.

11. The double killings polarized relations between the two Yemens and triggered several reactions in which the Saudis were involved. Saudi Arabia and the YAR called for an emergency meeting of the Arab League to deal with the events and with PDRY's threat to its neighbors and the Arab nation. The league met promptly on July 1 and 2, formally blamed PDRY for the murder of Ghashmi, and resolved to "freeze" diplomatic relations with it and to suspend economic, technical, and cultural aid to it "until its government shows respect for the Arab League's charter."[31] The resolution was less than the Saudi-YAR demand for PDRY's expulsion from the league, and its impact was weakened by the absence of the Tripoli bloc formed to oppose Sadat's peace initiative, whose members (Libya, Syria, Algeria, the PLO, and Iraq) boycotted the meeting because of Egypt's participation in it. However, Saudi comments tried to make the best of the situation by pretending that the absent members would have approved of the resolutions.[32]

Throughout 1977 and the first half of 1978 the United States had maintained sporadic contacts with Rubaya with a view of restoring diplomatic relations between the two countries, severed in 1969, and exploring the possibility of moderating PDRY's behavior. A congressional delegation had visited PDRY and met with Rubaya in January 1978, and a U.S. government mission was scheduled to come to Aden for negotiations at the end of June. After Rubaya's execution the mission was canceled and the idea of restoring relations was subsequently given up. Instead, the mounting tension between the two Yemens, coupled with the deteriorating situation in Iran, led the Carter administration to heed Saudi appeals and adopt a more forceful approach in the region. In September 1978 it decided to supply San'a with $400 million worth of arms to be funded by the Saudis, including 12 F-5s, 64 M-60 tanks, 100 armored personnel carriers, and 2 C-130s.[33] Notification of the decision to Congress was, however, delayed until February 1979, partly by the aftermath of Camp David.

The most serious consequences of the double killing occurred within and between the two Yemens. YAR President Saleh, besides pursuing Arab League sanctions against PDRY and seeking arms from the United States, severed relations with PDRY, conceded to the tribes a major role in his government, and supported operations against PDRY from YAR territory by the United National Front of South Yemen — a Saudi-supported organization comprising defectors from the South Yemeni armed forces, political dissidents, and tribal exiles, recently revived after having been kept in abeyance in the detente period.[34] PDRY's leaders, while blaming Ghashmi's assassination on Rubaya and carrying out a campaign against units of the armed forces loyal to the latter, supported operations against the YAR from PDRY territory by the National Democratic Front (an organization of North Yemeni leftists, urban, and Shafei elements) and tightened their hold on power by replacing the existing United Front–type political organization with the Leninist-type Yemeni Socialist party. Both sides massed troops and encroached on each other's borders, and both engaged in verbal warfare to back up their mutual subversion efforts.

12. Now and then attempts were made by third parties to mediate, but these achieved only brief respites at best, which soon broke down as a result of actions by the antagonists or of developments that eluded their respective control. Thus, a mission undertaken by the PLO's Yasser Arafat in September 1978 to establish a "dialogue" between the two sides collapsed in October, when PDRY created the Yemeni Socialist party and when leftist officers with ties to 'Alem attempted a coup d'état in the YAR shortly thereafter. During the November 1978 Baghdad summit (assembled to deal with Sadat's signing of the Camp David agreements), PDRY President Ali Nasser Muhammad was brought together with the YAR's vice president in a meeting attended by Saudi Crown Prince Fahd and UAE President Zayid; but the meeting failed to bring about any change, and hostilities by proxy were resumed and intensified. During the next three months the YAR reported clashes between PDRY and United National Front forces on PDRY soil, while PDRY cited clashes between YAR armed forces and the NDF in YAR territory. A new mediation effort in mid-February 1979 by Kuwait, Syria, Iraq, and the PLO did not produce even a respite. On the contrary, the border clashes escalated into open warfare by February 23 or 24.[35]

13. The war continued until mid-March despite a cease-fire agreed to on

March 1. The course of the fighting was more obscured than clarified by the reports issued by each side; however, it was apparent that PDRY's forces and their NDF allies had the upper hand. On February 25 these captured the North Yemeni towns of Harib and Qa'taba after an attack backed by tanks, artillery, and aircraft, and by March 15 NDF and PDRY troops had penetrated deep enough into YAR territory to threaten the Ta'iz-San'a road. Nevertheless the fighting in itself produced no major decision. Its principal impact was in the political effects it occasioned or generated.

14. On February 24, 1979, the YAR had called for an emergency meeting of the Arab League, and PDRY had agreed. In preparation for the meeting, a league fact-finding mission was sent to the border region. In the meantime, however, Saudi Arabia, feeling that the problem fell within its preserve and believing that its security interests were most affected by the war, decided to act independently. After inviting the foreign ministers of the two countries to come successively to Riyadh, it proposed a peace plan calling for an immediate cease-fire, withdrawal of all forces to their own borders, abstention of both sides from harboring or arming or backing dissidents, and the establishment of an Arab body to supervise the implementation of these measures. Both the YAR and PDRY turned down the Saudi proposal because it failed to address the question of unity between the two countries. The next day Saudi Arabia placed its forces on the alert, ordered the return of its contingent in the Arab Deterrent Force deployed in Lebanon, and proceeded to concentrate troops on the borders of the two Yemens.

On March 1 mediators from Syria, Iraq, Jordan, and Algeria persuaded the belligerents to agree to a cease-fire to take effect on March 3, in anticipation of the Arab League meeting due to begin in Kuwait the next day. The cease-fire was not observed, and fighting continued unabated. On March 5, while the league meeting was in session, it became known that Saudi Arabia had asked the United States for permission to transfer American-supplied arms to the YAR for use against PDRY. On the same day the United States demonstratively ordered a naval squadron to the Arabian Sea.

On March 6 the league adopted a set of resolutions submitted by Algeria, Iraq, Syria, and Jordan and agreed to by the belligerents, calling for a cease-fire, withdrawal of forces, end of intervention in domestic affairs, end of hostile propaganda, reopening of borders, and so on, but also calling for the formation of an Arab follow-up committee to supervise implementation of the resolutions and to initiate a summit-level dialogue between leaders of the two Yemens aimed at implementation of the 1972 unity accords. From the point of view of the Saudis, the resolutions were a mixed blessing. Although they promised to end the fighting at a time when the Kingdom was confronting major crises on other fronts, they represented a success for their promoters where they themselves had failed. More important, the resolutions revived and gave collective Arab sanction to the unity of the Yemens at a time when Iraq and Syria, two key promoters of the resolutions, had themselves just concluded, on January 31, 1979, an agreement to unite their countries. This raised the specter of Saudi Arabia's being squeezed between two new blocs in a revival of the integral pan-Arab drive of the 1950s and 1960s, which had threatened it mortally.

While the Arab League follow-up committee went to work, the fighting continued unabated as the YAR accused PDRY of launching air raids against its territory, and PDRY threatened to revoke the agreement because of the despatch of American arms to San'a. In the meantime, on March 7, 1979, President Carter decided to speed up the Saudi-financed supply of arms to the YAR by declaring the existence of an emergency situation to bypass normal congressional approval procedure. On the same day the United States offered Saudi Arabia the services of eighteen armed and manned F-15s, which the Saudis declined, but on March 9 it offered to station a squadron of AWACS aircraft at Saudi bases, and the Saudis agreed. Finally, on March 12 the United States announced that it was sending military advisers to the YAR to speed up instruction of its forces in the use of American equipment. Clearly, up to that point the Saudis had been pursuing simultaneously two rather incompatible courses; one relying on Arab mediation based on the principle of Yemeni unity, and the other relying on strong American military intervention based on the principle of repulsing and perhaps defeating the threatening South Yemeni regime. Similar ambivalences characterized their approaches to the other crises they faced at the same time, involving the fall of the shah and the accession of Khomeini's regime in Iran, and the impending signing of the Egyptian-Israeli peace treaty.

On March 16, 1979, the Arab League follow-up committee succeeded in bringing about an effective end of the fighting, and in the next three days it brought about the withdrawal of forces to prewar positions. On March 20 calm prevailed and commercial flights between San'a and Aden were resumed. The next day a new government was formed in San'a that excluded some of the public figures most objectionable to Aden. A week later the presidents of PDRY and the YAR met in Kuwait for the dialogue on unity called for by the league's resolutions. After talks on March 27–31, the two reached an agreement to implement the 1972 unity agreement in full. A constitutional committee was to draft within four months a constitution for a united Yemen, to be called the Yemen People's Republic and have its capital in San'a. The heads of state would then approve the "final formula" of the constitution and submit it to the People's Assemblies of the two parts of the Yemen for approval, after which there would be a popular referendum and election of a unified legislative authority.

While the two Yemeni presidents were deliberating in Kuwait, the foreign ministers of the Arab countries were meeting in Baghdad to consider sanctions against Egypt in the wake of its signing of the peace treaty with Israel. On the day the Yemeni presidents signed their unity agreements, the Saudis gave up their previous opposition and voted with the others in Baghdad to sever relations with Egypt and apply other sanctions against it. These developments, coupled with the Saudi rejection two weeks earlier of the American proposal on Persian Gulf and Middle East security brought to Riyadh by National Security Adviser Brzezinski, marked the final unraveling of the Kingdom's entire post-1973 defense and foreign policy strategy.

12

The American Connection, 1975–1979: Shifting Interdependence

The Saudi-American connection became much more complex in the wake of the 1973 embargo. The new relationship of interdependence, replacing the previous patron-client relationship, and the new roles and responsibilities assumed by the Kingdom as a result of the transformation of its financial and strategic position created a situation fraught with possibilities for both antagonism and cooperation (see Chapter 6). The challenge confronting Faisal's successors was how to manage that situation in a manner that best served the highest interests of the realm, and in the first instance its defense and security.

The American factor has been intermittently discussed in the previous chapters analyzing Saudi policy regarding developments in the Arab-Israeli arena, the Gulf, the Yemens, and related areas. To present a synthetic and continuous view of the Saudis' handling of the problem of the American connection during the first four years of Khaled's reign, this chapter fuses the disparate discussions and fills in the relevant background.

The Kingdom's relationship with the United States unfolded on two distinct levels. On one level, the relationship fluctuated in connection with major developments and policy decisions. On another level, there was a continuous relationship centered on trade, technical cooperation, and military and civilian contracts, which derived from the first and ultimately had a return effect on it but could be sustained independently of it for considerable periods. Thus, at the second level, Saudi trade with the United States grew from $2.6 billion in 1974 to $8.6 billion in 1976, to

$10.2 billion in 1978.[1] In 1976 the U.S. Corps of Engineers was engaged in contracts for planning and designing military construction projects valued at nearly $20 billion, all but $500 million worth to be completed in the following years.[2] The dollar value of arms and related military services purchased from the United States, though subject to major policy decisions, exceeded the 1974 $1.2 billion level in each of the next five years, averaging $4.8 billion a year for the period 1975– 1979.[3]

At the first, high policy level the Saudi relationship with the United States went through three phases, determined by the interplay between the fortunes of Saudi policy and American initiatives or dispositions in the various arenas. The first phase lasted from March 1975 until about the last quarter of 1977. During that period the Saudi and American governments managed to reconcile their interdependent interests with their respective independent policy objectives without undue difficulty. The second phase, from the last months of 1977 to January 1979, was characterized by mounting strains on the new relationship as events led Saudi Arabia and the United States to entertain mutual expectations and demands that were often disappointed. The third phase, from January to April 1979, saw the strains reach a crisis point as Saudi and American policies on critical issues clashed head on and seemed destined to collide again in the future.

Successful Management of the New Relationship, 1975– 1977

Starting from the strong international, regional, and domestic position of the Kingdom in the last year of Faisal's reign, his successors endeavored to pursue further and to improve upon the policies he had established. More specifically, they wanted to cultivate the American connection at the secondary level to the fullest extent possible while keeping the association at the primary policy level as low-key as feasible. They sought the latter aim partly in order to avert any inference being drawn from the former by potential critics at home and in the Arab world that they were clients of the United States. But they also wanted to keep their connection at the policy level discreet because they believed that this served their Arab policy better and that they possessed at the time sufficient resources to deal on their own with the other problems they faced. The American strategic connection was to be kept as a reserve resource in case of unexpected difficulties. Symbolic of that approach was the fact that the first visit to the United States by a senior member of the royal family did not occur until July 1976, sixteen months after Faisal's death, when Emir Abdallah was a guest of Secretary of Defense Donald Rumsfeld. In contrast, well before that, Crown Prince Fahd had visited Baghdad and Tehran, London and Paris; King Khaled had visited Cairo and Damascus and made a triumphal tour of the Gulf countries; and the shah, Sadat, Assad, and Saddam Hussein had been received in Riyadh.

The Saudi endeavor to play an active diplomatic role independently of the United States was favored by circumstances and seemed to work well during this phase. In the Arab-Israeli arena, the Saudis' objective was to sustain the peace process initiated by the United States largely through their own influence, and at the same time to preserve their Egyptian and Syrian connections if not the Riyadh-Cairo-Damascus triangle. This they were able to achieve despite some trouble. They managed to support Sadat's Sinai II agreement and steer their way through the complications of the Lebanese civil war, using mainly their financial and political leverage with Syria and Egypt. The American input in the Lebanese imbroglio was confined to discreet efforts to prevent an Israeli-Syrian clash, and as such was appreciated by the Syrians and their allies and cast no shadow on the Saudi-American connection.

During most of 1977, when the United States under President Carter assumed an active role in seeking to promote a comprehensive settlement through a Geneva peace conference, all the relevant Arab parties favored the American approach in principle, and the Saudis could therefore identify with it and indeed gain some credit for it. In May 1977 Crown Prince Fahd made his highly publicized visit to the United States, and in August of that year he submitted to Secretary of State Vance in Riyadh his proposal for enabling the PLO to take part in the envisaged general peace negotiations.

In the Gulf arena the Saudis' objective was to avail themselves of Iran's contribution to the security of the region while preventing it from asserting hegemony. Until the last days of Faisal's reign, the United States had been the only means to restraining Iran, and the Ford administration had seemed to be willing to give the shah much more latitude than the Saudis thought was safe, precisely to maintain a strong sense of Saudi dependence on it. However, the Iran-Iraq Algiers agreement of March 1975 opened an alternative way for Faisal's successors to pursue their objective by befriending and playing off the two Gulf powers against each other. This development did not altogether eliminate the Saudis' need for the United States as an ultimate safeguard, but it at least enabled them to foil, through their own independent maneuvers among the Gulf countries, the shah's scheme for a Gulf security pact throughout most of 1975 and 1976, until the U.S. approach to Iran tilted in their favor.

The election of Jimmy Carter in November 1976 brought to office an administration that was much less favorably inclined toward the shah because of his human rights record. The Saudis took advantage of the situation to widen further the gap between Iran and the United States by opposing firmly Iran's proposal to increase oil prices and casting it in an extremist role at the Doha OPEC conference in December 1976. Although this move also antagonized Iraq, the Saudis felt safe in making their challenge because the Riyadh-Cairo-Damascus triangle was in working order at that time and served to counterbalance Iraq. By the middle of 1977 the Saudis had achieved a reconciliation with Iran and Iraq on oil prices, but in the meantime they had for the most part achieved their policy objective of utilizing yet constraining the shah.

In the case of the Yemens, the Saudis felt no need for any American strategic input to advance their objective. In this arena the Saudis believed they had all the resources and connections they needed to pursue independently their new policy of trying to tame PDRY and to balance it with a strengthened but cooperative YAR regime. To the extent that American tactical assistance was needed, it was forthcoming without any difficulty. Thus under President Ford the United States agreed in April 1976 to the Saudi request to supply the YAR with $140 million worth of arms as part of an effort to wean its government away from Soviet arms, and under the Carter administration it seconded the Saudi efforts to lure PDRY by exploring at a deliberate pace throughout that period the possibility of restoring mutual relations.

In the related area of the Horn of Africa, the Saudis saw an opportunity in 1977 to capitalize on the conflict between Ethiopia and Somalia in order to detach the latter from the Soviet Union and use it against the former. They pursued that objective on their own, with the uncoordinated support of an assemblage of partners, including Egypt, the Sudan, Iraq, Syria, and Iran. The Carter administration cooperated passively by cutting off military assistance to Ethiopia in April 1977, and somewhat more actively by agreeing in July 1977, at the Saudis' urgings, to join with France and Britain in supplying Somalia with a small amount of "defensive arms." However, when Somalia invaded Ethiopia's Ogaden Province later that month, the United States, unwilling to be implicated in a wider conflict in the Horn of Africa because of Somalia's revisionist schemes, rescinded its decision.

Mutual Disappointments and Strains, Late 1977 – January 1979

Starting in the last months of 1977, events in all the key arenas caused Saudi Arabia and the United States to make increasingly major policy demands on each other. This trend negated the Saudis' desire to keep their strategic connection with the United States in reserve and to pursue an independent policy minimally linked to American policy except when supported by an Arab consensus. The interaction raised problems for both countries and confronted the Saudis with the necessity of defining their American relationship more precisely. For most of 1978 the Saudis muddled through the problems and avoided making fundamental choices; but by the end of that year and the beginning of the next, the pressures to make a choice became well-nigh irresistible.

In the Horn of Africa the Saudi effort to lure Somalia away from the Soviet Union and to use it against Marxist Ethiopia backfired when the Ethiopians launched a successful counterattack with massive Soviet and Cuban help at the turn of the year. PDRY's cooperation with the Soviets in preparing for the Ethiopian counterattack contributed to ending the Saudi attempt at accommodation with that country and led to a reversion to a policy of mutual confrontation. In April 1978, while the Dergue was seeking to carry its victorious campaign into Eritrea, there was a successful Marxist coup in Kabul. The Saudis and other Arab partners felt themselves caught in the middle of a systematic pincer campaign by Soviet proxies and looked to the United States to intervene effectively. The Carter administration responded by warning Ethiopia not to invade Somalia proper, which may have had some effect with regard to that contingency but, from the Saudi point of view, hardly addressed the larger problem.

After the assassination of Ghashmi and the execution of Rubaya, as relations between the Saudi-backed YAR and PDRY slid rapidly toward general armed confrontation, the United States showed greater responsiveness to the Saudis' call for help by agreeing, in September 1978, to supply the YAR with $400 million worth of arms. But the processing of that deal through Congress was delayed until war actually broke out in February 1979.

In the Arab-Israeli arena, the Saudis' American connection was forced to the foreground several times during that period. The first occasion was when the Americans requested the Saudis to support Sadat's November 1977 peace initiative. The Saudis, who deplored the breakdown of the highly prized Riyadh-Cairo-Damascus triangle as a result of Sadat's move, stopped short of active support in order to keep their line to Damascus open and to avert the wrath of Arab extremists. However, they helped deflect opposition to the initiative and thus gave it a chance to run its course. In the meantime the American connection was brought to the foreground again by the Saudi bid to purchase sixty advanced F-15 aircraft from the United States. The Carter administration, hitherto committed to reducing arms sales to nonallies, reversed itself and successfully pressed for congressional approval in May 1978 against fierce opposition, in order to gain political credit with the Saudis.

The signing of the Camp David agreements in September 1978 brought the American connection to the fore in a new, critical context for the

Saudis. In the first place, the agreements themselves were substantively crucial, envisaging as they did a fundamental transformation of the political and strategic configuration in the region, and the United States therefore placed an enormous premium on Saudi support. By the same token, however, Syria, the PLO, and other opponents of the agreements placed a similar if not greater premium on Saudi rejection of them. The Saudis could not realistically expect to be able to wriggle out of that situation and preserve their lines to both Cairo and Damascus, as they had when Sadat made his opening move by going to Jerusalem or in connection with Sinai II. Neither, however, could the Saudis make a simple clear-cut choice in the circumstances in which they found themselves. The mounting troubles of the shah's regime across the Gulf and the unsettled conditions in the Yemens and related areas made the American strategic connection, for all its recently revealed inadequacies, more essential than ever. At the same time, the crystallization of an Arab opposition front around the startling Damascus-Baghdad pact, for all the doubts about its durability, made it almost unthinkable for the Saudis to defy it. So, at the Baghdad summit of November 1978, the Saudis bargained their opposition to Camp David for the exclusion of anti-American decisions and the postponement of the application of sanctions against Egypt in the hope that time might give rise to an easier configuration.

In the Gulf arena, the Saudis' American strategic connection burst into prominence in the last months of 1978, at the same time that the connection was being most severely tested in the Arab-Israeli arena. A year or so before, the Saudis may have been slightly concerned by the warming of relations between the Carter administration and the shah, expressed in Iran's moderate stance on oil pricing at the December 1977 OPEC conference at Caracas and in President Carter's spending New Year's Eve of 1978 as a guest of the shah. The Saudis may have worried that this turn could spell a renewal of the favor shown by the previous American administration to the shah's power aspirations in the Gulf. Subsequent developments, however, must have allayed such concerns and perhaps even put a positive light on them. On the one hand, the F-15 arms deal that President Carter pushed through Congress in May 1978 clearly reaffirmed American interest in Saudi security in the Gulf in particular, in addition to providing the Kingdom with the means to strengthen its future capacity for self-defense. On the other hand, the U.S. failure to react meaningfully to the April 1978 Marxist coup in Afghanistan must have made the Saudis more appreciative of the role that a strong Iran could play as a shield against that new source of danger.

In the fall of 1978, as the shah's regime appeared to be losing control, the Saudis looked to the United States for help. In September and October they looked mainly to American measures to help shore up the shah. In

November, after the appointment of a military government in Tehran under General Gholam Azhari on the sixth and a State Department statement the next day that the United States supported it, the Saudis believed that the United States was doing what they had expected of it. On December 8, however, their hopes were dashed when President Carter publicly expressed the view that it might be too late for the shah's regime and disavowed any American intention to "intercede" in the country's political turmoil.[4] In the following days that turmoil reached a peak as the shah looked for candidates to head a coalition government and the candidates explicitly demanded his abdication as a condition for their taking on the task. By then the Saudis had begun to look to the United States not so much to save the shah as to protect them against the consequences of his downfall. Senator Robert Byrd, who visited Riyadh on December 4–7, 1978, as President Carter's special envoy, reported that the Saudis wanted the United States to defend the Persian Gulf.[5]

The United States took its time in responding, and then did so rather unconvincingly. On January 10, 1979, it announced that it was sending a flight of F-15s on a visit to Saudi Arabia. However, because the administration still hoped that the recently appointed Bakhtiar government might save the situation and wanted to avoid complicating his task by seeming to prepare a military intervention, the announcement specified that the planes would be sent unarmed. Nevertheless, so great was the Saudis' anxiety by then that they made the most of the American demonstration of support. When the planes arrived on January 15, Crown Prince Fahd and Defense Minister Sultan were on hand to watch the display they put on. However, that acquiescing disposition toward the United States did not last long.

While the Saudis were desperately looking to the United States for help, they reciprocated by being helpful in the matter of oil supply. As Iranian production tumbled from a high point of 5.9 mbd in August to 3.4 mbd in November and to 0.3 mbd in December, the Saudis increased theirs from 7.2 mbd in August to 10.3 mbd in November and to 10.4 mbd in December, their maximum capacity.[6] However, they were clearly uneasy about their action because stretching their capacity to the limit eliminated their leverage within OPEC. More important, they were anxious because their action identified them too closely with the United States at a time when the Arab producers along with all the other Arab parties of the Baghdad November summit were at odds with Washington over the Camp David agreements, when the shah's regime appeared increasingly to be doomed, and when the United States itself seemed to be giving only halfhearted support to the shah in the hope of opening up a line of contact with his opponents. The Saudi mood found expression in the message they conveyed to U.S. Treasury Secretary Blumenthal when he visited their country on November 17–19. In discussing the forthcoming OPEC meeting at Abu Dhabi on December 16, the Saudis told Blumenthal that they would seek a price freeze but would not go so far as to break ranks with their OPEC partners, as they had in 1976–77, if they did not have their way.

In the event, the Saudis were able to achieve a moderate decision at Abu Dhabi involving a series of quarterly incremental increases of 5, 10, and 15 percent during 1979. However, less than three weeks into the new year the Saudis took an action that nullified the Abu Dhabi resolution and contributed to pushing the world toward a second oil crisis. On January 16, 1979, the shah left Iran, ostensibly for an extended leave, and four days later the Saudis decided to cut their production for the first quarter of 1979 to 9.5 mbd. The Saudis actually announced that they had decided to *raise* the ceiling on production from the 8.5 mbd set for 1978 to 9.5 mbd for the first quarter of 1979; however, because effective production in November and December was well over 10 mbd (in the first nine months of 1978 it had averaged about 7.5 mbd), the decision amounted to a substantial reduction at a time when the market was already quite tight. Moreover, the Saudis announced that the new 9.5 mbd ceiling was to be averaged on a monthly basis starting January 1, which meant that for the remainder of January production had to be cut by more than 2 mbd to meet that month's average. That decision, coupled with the return of Khomeini to Iran at the beginning of the following month, greatly accelerated the ongoing rush for oil and drove up prices. In January 1979 the spot market price was $16.24 per barrel compared to the official contract price of $13.34; in February the contract price remained the same but the spot price jumped to $22.56.[7]

Analysts have reached far and wide in trying to interpret the Saudi January 1979 action; but when viewed in the context of the ambivalent Saudi-American relationship during this phase, the move indicates an intention to signal to the United States the Saudis' concern about and displeasure with its policy, while avoiding a confrontation with it at a time when its help was needed more than ever. More specifically, Washington's perceived resignation to the departure of the shah and its support of the Bakhtiar option reinforced latent suspicions among the Saudi rulers that the Americans were more interested in securing the flow of oil than in protecting a friendly regime. The Saudi action was a reminder to the United States that unless it paid more heed to the clear and present dangers confronting their Kingdom's security, its access to oil could be damaged immediately. A few months later, the Saudi rulers were to go further and take action based more rigorously on their own perceived self-interest in defiance of the American interest; in January 1979 they hoped that their move would make the United States more responsive to their needs and wanted to avoid giving it the appearance of a confrontational or punitive act. Hence on the one hand they formulated their decision in terms of raising the 1978 ceiling rather than in terms of lowering the previous months' actual production, and on the other hand they kept the United States on a short leash by setting the ceiling for one quarter rather than for a year and by doing the averaging on a monthly basis.

Crisis and Seeming Collision Course, January–April 1979

The Saudi decision of January 20 precipitated a dialogue with the United States concerning the strategic relationship between the two countries in the new circumstances. That dialogue in turn precipitated a basic policy debate within the Saudi ruling establishment itself even as the multiple crises in the Gulf, the Yemens, and the Arab-Israeli arena came simultaneously to a head in February and March, and even as the United States took some forceful initiatives in an attempt to influence its outcome. The turmoil of conflicting pressures produced a serious split in the Saudi ruling establishment and an ultimate decision in favor of an approach oriented to the Baghdad Arab consensus coupled with appeasement of revolutionary Iran. This decision entailed the danger of a disruption of the long-standing strategic relationship with the United States.

On January 26 President Carter announced that Crown Prince Fahd would be visiting the United States on March 1, presumably to discuss all outstanding issues between the two countries. On the same day, Secretary of Commerce Juanita Kreps arrived in Saudi Arabia for a three-day visit during which she elicited a promise from Crown Prince Fahd that Saudi Arabia would not cut oil production but would keep it at the level of 10–10.5 mbd.[8] The promise was not kept; either the crown prince had second thoughts or there was resistance within the ruling establishment to the "concession" he had made.

On February 1, 1979, Khomeini returned to Iran marking the beginning of the end of the Bakhtiar interlude. On February 10 and 11 Defense Secretary Harold Brown came to Saudi Arabia to present American proposals for security cooperation in view of the situation in the region and in anticipation of Fahd's planned visit to Washington. In meetings with the crown prince, Brown promised an increased supply of American arms to the YAR and the Sudan, pledged support for the Kingdom against external threats, and proposed to base U.S. forces in Saudi Arabia to assist in its defense. Fahd knew that such a proposal was out of the question for domestic as well as inter-Arab, regional, and international reasons and he promptly declined it. But the fact that it was made apparently eased some of Fahd's recent concern about the reliability of the American security connection, even though it remained necessary to find an appropriate expression for it. Brown could not obtain the reaction of other key Saudi leaders because Abdallah was in Syria and King Khaled was out in the desert. That no arrangements were made to solve this scheduling problem was perhaps another indication that the ruling establishment was, to say the least, not pulling together.

By February 23 it was evident that the establishment was in the midst of a sharp basic policy debate involving choices between reliance on the United States and other alternatives. On that day it was announced that Fahd's projected trip to the United States had been postponed to some indefinite date in order, as the Saudi embassy put it, "to give both sides time to make a comprehensive study of the issues of mutual concern."[9] Washington's attempt to save face and to minimize the significance of the postponement by attributing it to the crown prince's health backfired when the Saudis angrily denied that that was the reason.

At about the same time as the postponement announcement, and shortly after Khomeini took over power on February 12, the festering crisis of the Yemens erupted in open warfare. The Saudis followed an inconsistent two-track policy toward the conflict, reflecting probably the divergent tendencies within the ruling establishment. One track unilaterally supported the YAR militarily and diplomatically, while the other went along with collective Arab League mediation efforts. The American administration, aware by then of the debate going on within the Saudi establishment, sought to influence it by taking a series of energetic actions designed to impress the Saudis with its willingness and ability to protect their security interests. On March 5, 1979, President Carter ordered a carrier task force to the Arabian Sea. The next day, the United States offered to send a flight of F-15s, this time armed and equipped, to cover for the Saudi F-5s deployed against PDRY. The Saudis declined that offer but discreetly requested the United States to station two AWACS aircraft to help monitor and defend their airspace, and the United States did so on March 8.[10] On the ninth, President Carter announced an emergency supply of arms to the YAR, bypassing the need for congressional approval. While the United States used the Yemeni conflict to demonstrate its support and military muscle, Arab parties, including Syria and Iraq, were engaged in an effort to mediate a peaceful ending of it.

The American moves were intended not only to reassure the Saudis in connection with the problems of the Yemens and Iran, but also to gain credit with them for use in connection with the issue of Egyptian-Israeli peace. On March 13, 1979, President Carter successfully concluded a few days' shuttle between Egypt and Israel with an agreement on the terms of a peace treaty, and on March 17 and 18 National Security Adviser Zbigniew Brzezinski visited Riyadh to seek the Kingdom's support for the treaty, or at least its help in checking Arab reaction against Egypt. Brzezinski argued that the envisaged peace would advance the general Middle East peace process and was in the best strategic interest of the Kingdom. He granted that the position the Saudis were asked to take might expose them in the short term to the ire of the Arab rejectionists and perhaps of Khomeini, but he promised all possible American help to meet that danger. Secretary of State Vance indicated the extent of that help when he declared in Washington at the same time that the United States would use force to defend the vital Saudi oil fields.[11] While the Americans were making these points, the Arab mediators succeeded in bringing about an effective cease-fire between the two Yemens and arranged a meeting of their leaders to resolve the problem between the two countries on the basis of Yemeni unity.

Brzezinski received from the Saudis an ambiguous pledge that they would not support damaging sanctions against Egypt if it signed the peace treaty with Israel, which he interpreted as an approximation of acceptance of his minimal request and its attendant American quid pro quo.[12] In fact the answer merely masked the disagreement on basic policy that prevailed within the Saudi ruling establishment, which Brzezinski's mission brought to a head in the next few days. The disagreement was expressed in terms of two alternative approaches, one advanced by Crown Prince Fahd and probably some unidentified supporters, the other by King Khaled, Emir Abdallah, and probably others.[13] It is almost certain that power and personality considerations were embroiled in the debate, and that the give-and-take was not systematic; but the essence of the discussion was probably much as follows.

All involved agreed in principle that the Kingdom's security interests were best served by both preserving the American connection and humoring the Arab front that had formed around the new Baghdad-Damascus axis, but all were also agreed that the pursuit of both aims had been made impossible by the necessity to take a clear stand on the issue of sanctions against Egypt for signing the American-sponsored treaty with Israel.

The stand to be taken, all realized, had far-reaching implications for the basic Saudi security conception in the times ahead. Opposing the sanctions meant defying the Baghdad consensus and incurring the active hostility of nearby Arab powers such as Iraq, Syria, the PLO, and South Yemen at a time when revolutionary Iran was bound to constitute an additional source of danger. The inevitable corollary, if these dangers were to be confronted, was that the Kingdom had to depend more than ever for its security on the United States and accept its conception of defense for the region. That conception was based on an American alliance with Israel and Egypt and on the latter's providing a first strategic reserve for the defense of the Kingdom. Alternatively or additionally, there could be an American military presence on Saudi soil.

Going along with the sanctions, on the other hand, meant a breach with the most populous and powerful Arab country and a rejection of the United States at a time when its power was most needed to face the existing threats from Iran and PDRY, and probably future Soviet-inspired subversion from those and other quarters. The inevitable corollary was to rely for security on the Arab bloc around the Baghdad-Damascus axis and to try to turn the disjunction from the United States into an instrument to appease Iran and pacify the Soviets.

Fahd, who favored the American orientation, had also supported the shah's regime almost to the last moment and had expressed his conviction that the Communists would benefit from Khomeini's takeover.[14] He might have argued that appeasing Khomeini was a futile exercise, and that the Arab bloc was ineffective against a possible Communist takeover in Iran. He might have argued further that the entire Arab orientation was problematic. If the Iraqi-Syrian union that was at the core of the Arab bloc survived and prospered, it could revive the Arab nationalist danger to the regime and the Kingdom's independence. If it should prove ephemeral, it would be largely useless as a defense asset. In the meantime, he might have pointed out, the mediation of the Arab bloc in Yemen was already giving substance to the old specter of Yemeni unity.

Khaled and Abdallah, who favored the Arab orientation, might have pointed out that the United States had proved to be inept in helping against the kinds of danger the Kingdom would face if it defied the Arab bloc. It had proved unable to help the shah against internal subversion and had done more harm than good with its clumsy intervention in Yemen. As for the Soviet threat, the United States was bound to make every effort to counter it for its own self-interest. The same and other considerations of self-interest would also enable the Kingdom to repair its relations with Washington after the present crisis had passed, as happened after the 1973 oil embargo.

A few days after Brzezinski left on March 17, 1979, the Saudi ruling establishment decided reluctantly to go along with the imposition of sanctions on Egypt and, concomitantly, to espouse the security concept based on the Arab orientation, despite the vehement opposition of Fahd. In view of the grave implications of the decision, which Fahd underscored, it was agreed that an effort would be made to temporize and if possible to restrict the scope of the sanctions. Fahd, however, remained unreconciled to the decision and signified the strength of his dissent by leaving the country on March 22, 1979, for an indefinite holiday in Spain. He remained abroad for nearly three months.

On March 27, 1979, the foreign ministers of all the countries that had attended the November summit, minus the representatives of Oman, Somalia, the Sudan, and Djibouti, assembled again at Baghdad to discuss the application of the sanctions previously agreed to in principle. The Saudi foreign minister successfully resisted suggestions to penalize the United States, but his attempt to resist a proposal to break diplomatic relations with Egypt brought the conference to a crisis point on March 29. After an adjournment for consultations with other delegations and his government, he returned to Baghdad on March 31 and participated in the unanimous vote for the break as well as for economic and other sanctions.

The broad implications of the Saudi decision on sanctions began to manifest themselves immediately. On the day the second Baghdad conference assembled, OPEC concluded an emergency meeting in Geneva on March 26 and 27 to revise its December decisions in light of the market situation. The Saudis joined the others in an agreement to implement immediately the 10 percent increase previously scheduled to go into effect only in October. In an interview immediately after the conference the Saudi representative, Zaki Yamani, claimed that Saudi Arabia had defeated Iraqi and Iranian demands for increases of 25 and 32 percent, and defended the 10 percent increase as reasonable in view of the existing panic and tight market, which had brought spot prices $9 higher than the $13.34 contract price.[15] What Yamani did not say was that the Saudis satisfied the Iraqi and Iranian demands by agreeing to an OPEC-sanctioned surcharge system that in effect allowed members to charge what the market would bear, making major price increases inevitable.

Far more important than the price decisions was the position taken by the Saudis on production. The March 1979 OPEC meeting was the first to include a representative of revolutionary Iran, who demanded that Saudi Arabia cut its production to 8.5 mbd in order to enable Iran to increase its own to 3.5-4 mbd from its March level, estimated at 2-3 mbd.[16] Yamani agreed to do so *if* Iranian production actually reached 3.5-4 mbd.[17] However, on April 9, 1979, the Saudi deputy oil minister announced that Saudi Arabia had cut its oil production to 8.5 mbd as of April 1, without waiting to see if Iran attained the 3.5-4 mbd. Moreover, the Saudis maintained the lower rate during the following months even after it became apparent that Iran was unable to sustain its higher level. Given the existing tight and jittery market, the effect of the Saudi decision was devastating. The spot market price jumped to $28.94 in May and to $35.40 in June 1979, whereas the new contract price was only $14.55.

Yamani denied any connection between the Saudi decisions and the Egyptian-Israeli peace treaty, and in a certain sense he was right. Unlike the 1973 embargo, which sought to alter American behavior, the March-

April 1979 decisions were not intended to alter American policy with respect to the treaty or even to punish the United States for supporting it. They were merely part of the new Saudi security concept advanced by Khaled and Abdallah and adopted by the ruling establishment to deal with the Kingdom's situation, which simply disregarded, or at the very least greatly discounted, the interest of the United States. The Egyptian-Israeli treaty had contributed to creating the Kingdom's situation but was not relevant to the aims sought by the March–April decisions. Those aims were to maintain the association with Iraq and, above all, to appease revolutionary Iran, which had been charging Saudi Arabia before the OPEC meeting with overproducing in order to serve American interests in draining Iran's financial reserves and bankrupting the revolution. Khaled and Abdallah, unlike Fahd, believed in the efficacy of appeasement, as the following statement by Abdallah on April 23 shows:

> The new regime in Iran has removed all obstacles and reservations in the way of cooperation between Saudi Arabia and the Islamic Republic of Iran. Islam is the organizer of our relations. Muslim interests are the goals of our activities and the Holy Koran is the constitution of both countries . . . Our cooperation will have an Islamic dynamism against which no obstacles facing the Muslims can stand . . . The material potential—money and oil—possessed by the Islamic Republic of Iran and Saudi Arabia, and the Islamic and Arab worlds will be utilized and directed by an Islamic spirit . . . The fact is that we are very relieved by the Islamic Republic of Iran's policy of making Islam, not heavy armaments, the organizer of cooperation, a base for dialogue, and the introduction to a prosperous and dignified future.[18]

13

The Arab-Israeli Arena, 1979 – 1982: Opposite Pulls

The Khaled-Abdallah policy orientation as a whole proved to be short-lived and gave way within a few months to a revision that sought to combine some of its elements with elements of Fahd's orientation. The revised approach envisaged sacrificing the Egyptian connection definitively in order to avert the hostility of the rejectionists led by Iraq and Syria and using the Baghdad-Damascus axis as a counterweight to revolutionary Iran, as the Khaled-Abdallah faction had advocated. At the same time it sought to mend the strained American connection and to preserve it as an essential ultimate safeguard of Saudi security against all contingencies, including excessive pressure from Iraq and Syria, as Fahd had insisted. The immediate driving force behind the compromise was the anxiety of the ruling establishment over the split in their ranks; but a mixture of accidental and basic considerations made its adoption possible.

Agreement on sacrificing the Egyptian connection was facilitated by President Sadat's undifferentiated attacks on the Saudi royal family as a whole in the wake of Baghdad II, which caused even Fahd and his supporters to rally to a policy of earnestly ostracizing Egypt. However, the Saudi establishment could indulge this punitive approach only because it appeared to be cost free strategically and risk free tactically. To the extent that the Egyptian-Israeli peace treaty served a basic Saudi interest by reducing the chances of war in the region, that interest could be secured at no cost to the Saudis and regardless of their reaction toward the treaty and Egypt. Other Saudi strategic interests were protected by Egyptian self-interest and by the fact that Egypt had been completely weaned from its Soviet relationship and radical inclinations and was now safely ensconced in the American camp. This also meant that tactically the Saudis could afford to penalize Sadat without fear of retaliation beyond ineffective insults.

In view of Washington's sponsorship of the Egyptian-Israeli treaty, the Saudis' attitude toward Egypt might have been expected to obstruct their endeavor to mend and preserve the American connection; but this problem was resolved with surprising ease when the United States agreed to a Saudi suggestion to separate the differences between the two countries regarding the treaty from other aspects of their mutual relations. A more serious problem was the fact that this solution was profoundly repugnant to the parties that formed the core of the Baghdad consensus. Iraq, PDRY, and Libya, for instance, were keenly interested in perpetuating the Saudi break with the United States for their own strategic reasons, while Syria and the PLO wanted the Kingdom to confront the United States and to use its leverage with it actively in the service of the Arab cause in the conflict with Israel.

President Sadat had anticipated precisely that problem when he signed the treaty with Israel, and he counted on it afterward to force the Saudis to move away from the Baghdad powers and join the more compatible alignment of Egypt and the United States. However, neither that issue nor subsequent major developments that ostensibly pointed in the same direction, such as the Soviet invasion of Afghanistan and the outbreak of war between Iraq and Iran, would impel the Saudi rulers to alter their position toward Egypt. Sadat's assassination in October 1981 removed the element of personal vendetta from the situation, but by then the ostracism of Egypt had become too embedded in the Saudis' policies for them to be able to reverse it before King Khaled himself died in June 1982.

Instead of reconsidering their position toward Egypt, the Saudis tried to deal with the problem of the hostility of the key Baghdad powers to their American connection in two basic ways. One was to try to capitalize on potential or actual diverging interests among the dissatisfied parties in order to avert their combined pressure. This approach became easier to pursue the more Syria and Iraq reverted to their pre–Camp David pattern of hostility under the stimulus of major events originating outside the Arab-Israeli arena. The other way was periodically to advance their own ideas for a solution of the Palestinian question or to make tough declaratory statements on the subject with a view to serving a variety of purposes: to demonstrate continuing concern for a settlement; to try to wean the PLO away from Syria or to undermine its connection with it; to score some credit with the United States when that was needed, such as when major arms requests were under consideration; or to express anger against the enemy either as a substitute for action or as a cloak for greater cooperation with the United States. These maneuvers served their purpose more or less effectively, though not without difficulties, until the end of Khaled's reign. By then, however, whatever elements of a positive strategy—of a design aimed at shaping a secure environment—that may have been latent in the 1979 family policy compromise had been lost in the process.

Because Saudi policy in the Arab arena during this period lacked the thrust of a positive strategic objective and instead merely reacted to events and situations, the discussion of that policy necessarily focuses on a series of episodes rather than providing a continuous analysis.

Family Reconciliation and Policy Compromise

On April 23, 1979, the Saudis broke off diplomatic relations with Egypt in accordance with the Baghdad resolutions. The decision was taken by the Council of Ministers, which cited as reasons "the fact that Egypt has accepted and intends to exchange diplomatic representation with the Zionist enemy and has begun to establish normal relations without consideration of the minimum demands of the Arab nation." The council went on to express the Delphic hope that "the reasons which prompted the action will disappear so that relations will return to the unity of destiny which both countries used to enjoy."[1] A few days later, on April 27, Saudi Arabia went along with a decision by a consortium of Gulf countries to disband the Gulf Organization for the Development of Egypt, established in 1977 to assist Egypt economically.

On May 1, 1979, Sadat used the May Day celebration as an occasion to launch a broad public attack on the Saudi regime for the first time since the heyday of the Nasserist confrontation in the 1960s. He accused the Saudis of using pressure and bribery to impel certain Arab countries to break relations with Egypt, paid tribute to Faisal as a true and generous friend of Egypt but expressed contempt for his successors who were "not of his calibre."[2] The Egyptian media amplified the attacks, and the Saudi media responded in kind.[3] On May 7 the Saudi government announced that it would withhold credits previously approved for Egypt; on the eighth it voted with others to expel Egypt from the Islamic Conference meeting in Fez; on the thirteenth it banned the import of Egyptian newspapers into the Kingdom; and on May 14 Defense Minister Sultan announced the disbanding, as of July 1, of the Arab Organization for Industrialization, a corporation financed by Saudi Arabia and Gulf countries for the development of military industries in Egypt, on the grounds that Egypt's signing of the peace treaty with Israel contradicted the purpose for which the organization had been established. Finally, on May 20

Sultan announced that Saudi Arabia would not fund Egypt's purchase of fifty F-5 jet fighters from the United States as it had previously agreed.

The reneging on the agreement to finance the F-5s marked a turning point in Saudi Arabia's post–Baghdad II relations with Egypt. For one thing, the action involved the United States as a third party in a military transaction and thus symbolized a Saudi decision to repudiate the trilateral strategic connection that had been developing among the three countries for some time. For another thing, the act was particularly significant because it was the most important Saudi sanction against Egypt taken outside the frame of collective Arab action. Only a few days before Sadat's May Day speech, the Saudi defense minister had declared that the Kingdom had already paid for the planes, thus signaling the United States and Egypt, who knew that the fact was otherwise, that Saudi Arabia was intent on keeping its lines open to both and meant to evade or minimize the application of sanctions. The May 20 announcement indicated a deliberate reversal of position on both scores. It marked a decision of the Saudi government to ostracize Egypt of its own accord and to separate its attitude toward Egypt from its relationship with the United States.

The reversal was made possible by a personal and policy reconciliation among the Saudi ruling princes in the wake of Sadat's attack on the royal family. Ever since Fahd had left the country in the middle of multiple crises on March 22, Khaled and Abdallah had taken great pains to deny any rift between themselves and him and any disagreement among them all on policy toward Egypt. However, the very vehemence of the protestations—Abdallah said at one point that he had "no existence" except through Fahd—betrayed the denials and underscored the crucial importance of what was being denied in the view of those who were issuing them.[4] The anxiety over the rift naturally led to efforts to heal it, which culminated in a visit to Fahd in his "exile" in the second week of May by a delegation composed of Saud al-Faisal and Salman ibn Abd al-Aziz, two princes who had sided with Khaled and Abdallah against him. The reconciliation then achieved found expression in the participation of the three princes in a meeting with French President Valéry Giscard d'Estaing on May 12, and in a joint press conference in the wake of the visit in which they all denied the rumors of family dissensions.

Even before Sultan's announcement of the decision not to finance the F-5 aircraft for Egypt, Fahd had hinted at the other policy component of the family reconciliation. In an interview that appeared in *Le Monde* on May 15, 1979, the crown prince said, in his first public policy statement since March, that Saudi Arabia wanted to maintain good relations with the United States. He denied rumors that his country had lost interest in purchasing F-15 aircraft from the United States and urged the United

States to open talks with the PLO. The next day, the *New York Times* reported Carter administration officials to have said that the United States and Saudi Arabia had agreed to keep their sharp differences over the Egyptian-Israeli peace treaty from interfering with their close relations in other fields. On June 21 Fahd, back on active duty in Riyadh, used almost exactly the same words to define Saudi relations with the United States.[5] In early July the Saudis gave tangible expression to their new policy by announcing an increase in their oil production from 8.5 mbd to 9.5 mbd to ease the pressure that had been causing oil prices to rise by leaps and bounds.

Attempting American-PLO Dialogue

The Saudis' mending of their American connection on the basis of an agreement to disagree on the Arab-Israeli question represented a break with the policy initiated by Faisal in 1971, which had reached its sharpest expression in the 1973 oil embargo and the subsequent peace diplomacy. The new formula was also bound to displease both Sadat and the Baghdad powers, for opposite reasons. Sadat had counted on the Saudis' need for the United States as their ultimate security guarantor to give Washington leverage to force the Saudis to fall in line with the Camp David peace process, whereas the Syrians and the PLO had counted on America's need for Saudi oil to give the Saudis leverage to force the United States to espouse their views of a proper settlement. The Iraqis ostensibly supported the Syrian-PLO approach but were less interested in the aim of the Saudi pressure than in its likely result: alienation of the Saudis from the United States, leaving the Saudis more amenable to the Iraqis' own schemes for Arab security generally and for Gulf security in particular. Averting or mitigating the consequences of that displeasure remained a constant problem for the Saudis in the Arab arena over the next years.

Immediately after adopting the new formula, the Saudis tried to put forward ideas of their own for advancing a settlement, to demonstrate their continuing commitment to the Palestinian question generally and to the PLO in particular. In the same June 21, 1979, statement that affirmed the Saudis' willingness to separate disagreement on the Arab-Israeli issue from other aspects of Saudi-American relations, Fahd urged the United States to start an immediate dialogue with the PLO. He asserted, presumably on the basis of discussions with PLO leaders, that this dialogue could lead the PLO to accept Resolution 242, formally acknowledge Israel's right to exist, and thus open the way to peace negotiations on a better basis than that provided by the Camp David accords. Fahd added that if, as a result, Israel withdrew to the pre-1967 borders, Saudi Arabia itself would be ready to make peace with it.[6]

The Carter administration tried to pursue Fahd's idea over the next two months, but its attempt was defeated by a combination of its own bungling and opposition from diverse sources. In July 1979, after the Saudi decision to increase oil production, the Carter administration developed indirect contacts with the PLO with a view to reaching agreement on a formula to amend Resolution 242 and thus open the way to PLO participation in the peace process. In the course of these endeavors, the U.S. representative to the United Nations, Andrew Young, exceeded his authority by holding direct talks with a PLO representative and, when word of the meetings came out, Young compounded his trespass by giving a false version of what had gone on, before admitting to what had actually transpired. The uproar in connection with that episode led to Young's resignation on August 15 and contributed to Washington's renunciation of its effort a week later. However, the American initiative had by then been practically defeated by resistance from other sources.

One of the other sources was a coalition of some of the Baghdad powers that took a more demanding position. As a rotational member of the Security Council, Kuwait advanced a proposal to amend Resolution 242 by asserting the right of the Palestinians to self-determination, sovereignty, and independence. The proposal went much further than what the United States was prepared to accept and than what the Saudis had intended at that stage; but once it had been advanced, the PLO could not agree to any dilution in the face of Syrian and other Arab insistence on the proposal, and the Saudis could not oppose it. On August 12, 1979, the Palestinian Central Council, which had previously shown itself to be susceptible to Syrian pressure, formally rejected any UN resolution that did not recognize the Palestinians' right to an independent state. The council's spokesman added for good measure that reports that the United States might begin a dialogue with the PLO were maneuvers aimed at alienating so-called radicals from moderates.[7]

Another source that helped defeat the American initiative was the combined opposition of Israel's Prime Minister Begin and Egypt's President Sadat. Begin fiercely opposed any dealing with the PLO and any hint of a Palestinian state. Sadat justified his objection on the procedural grounds that the American move would sidetrack his own peace efforts based on the Camp David accords.[8] Implicit in Sadat's argument was also his resentment of the fact that the United States, rather than using its leverage with the Saudis to bring them over to the Camp David process, seemed prepared to accept their rejection of it and to espouse the alternative approach they proposed. When Begin and Sadat expressed their common opposition to President Carter's personal representative in the trilateral autonomy talks, Ambassador Strauss, the latter threw his weight against the administration's initiative. On August 22, 1979, the president formally dropped the plan to sponsor any resolution, and two days later the American representative in the Security Council succeeded, with the threat of a veto, in causing a postponement of the vote on the Kuwaiti resolution.

Although the Saudis' move thus ultimately came to naught, the results were not altogether negative from their point of view. Inasmuch as the Saudis' main point was to demonstrate their continuing concern with the Palestinian question despite their close American connection, that purpose was served regardless of the outcome. Furthermore, although the Syrians had their way with the PLO as a whole, to do so they had to ride roughshod over that organization once more. Finally whatever loss of face the Saudis suffered with the United States by proving unable to deliver the PLO was more than offset by the Americans' fumbling of the task they had taken upon themselves.

Averting Baghdad-Core Pressures: The 1979 Tunis Summit

While these developments were taking place, the Lebanese-Israeli front heated up as the PLO bombarded and raided Israeli northern settlements, and Israel responded with heavy punitive and preemptive bombings of PLO targets in camps and Lebanese towns and villages. Syrian attempts to intercept the Israeli aircraft resulted in air battles in which the Syrians were repeatedly worsted. The United States, fearing escalation of the fighting into general war, mediated a tenuous cease-fire through Saudi intermediaries in August 1979; and when that broke down, Washington sent former Under Secretary of State Philip Habib to the area in October to try to restore it and broaden it into a lasting truce. In the meantime Lebanon's President Elias Sarkis, invoking a resolution of the November 1978 Baghdad summit to convene again at least once every year, called for a prompt summit to regulate PLO military actions so as to protect Lebanon against Israeli reactions. Several Arab parties, including Jordan, Syria, and Iraq, supported Sarkis's call but sought to broaden the summit agenda to include issues of particular interest to themselves. The Saudis, wary of being exposed to pressure on account of their American connection and fearful of getting caught in the midst of conflicting positions on Lebanon, sought to keep the agenda as narrow as possible and to make the convening of the summit conditional upon prior agreement among the PLO, the Lebanese, and the Syrians on the broad lines of a solution. When that endeavor failed, they went along with a decision to convene the conference in Tunis on November 20, 1979, and made ready to capitalize on the divisions that had begun to manifest themselves among key participants and thus to ward off the formation of a strong combination against themselves.

Between the time the conference was broached and the time it actually convened, several events took place that had an important bearing on the situation the Saudis confronted. On October 16, 1979, the foreign ministers of Saudi Arabia and the five Gulf emirates met in Ta'if to consider an Iraqi proposal for a Gulf security pact. The participants disagreed among themselves but the Saudis steered the conference away from a negative vote, thus deflecting Iraq's bid to lead the region without rebuffing it bluntly, in order to keep its hopes alive and its behavior solicitous.

On November 1, 1979, members of the Steadfastness Front assembled in Algiers at Syria's initiative in anticipation of the summit. Originally created after Sadat's visit to Jerusalem, the front (comprising Syria, Libya, Algeria, PDRY, and the PLO) had ceased to function after the November 1978 Baghdad summit had created a wider opposition grouping centered on the Baghdad-Damascus axis and the January 1979 unity agreement between Iraq and Syria had promised to create a powerful state capable of facing Israel and dominating the Arab scene from the Mediterranean to the Gulf. However, subsequent negotiations to give effect to the unity agreement had stumbled upon resurgent mutual suspicions, so that by June 1979 the two countries could agree only on a meaningless joint political command. Syria's revival of the Steadfastness Front in November reflected an advanced degree of deterioration in Iraqi-Syrian relations and in the consensus politics of the Baghdad conferences. For the Saudis, this development meant a reversion of the Syrian-led front to extremist positions, particularly in relation to the United States; but it also promised to open greater room for them for maneuvering between Iraq and Syria to prevent irresistible pressure against themselves.

On November 4, 1979, Iranian militants seized the U.S. embassy in Tehran and held its personnel hostage, thus ending an American attempt to get along with Iran's revolutionary regime and initiating a period of outright confrontation between the two countries. The Saudis, though fearful of the complications that might ensue, appreciated the toughening of America's position because of its bearing on their own relations with Iran and because it created a potential Iraqi-American shared interest vis-à-vis Khomeini's regime that was apt to make the Iraqis less hostile to the Saudi-American connection. A hopeful sign in the latter respect was Iraq's condemnation of the detention of the American hostages as contrary to international law.

Finally, on November 20, the same day the summit conference opened in Tunis, Muslim fundamentalists seized the Grand Mosque in Mecca in an attempt to topple the entire Saudi system. During the three days of the conference, details of the incident were unknown, and official Saudi comments downplayed its significance and asserted that the misguided mutineers were about to be liquidated. Crown Prince Fahd, who represented his country at Tunis, did not even leave the conference. However, the rumors about the event were on everybody's mind, and apprehensions about the worst put the Saudis, their Gulf neighbors, and their other allies in no mood to court additional trouble by displaying too much resistance to other participants' demands that were not to their liking.

Three issues dominated the deliberations of the conference: the PLO's position in Lebanon, sanctions against Egypt, and ways and means to advance the Arab struggle against Israel. Syria, the PLO, and Libya took the lead in urging tough proposals on all three issues. On the first question, they opposed Lebanon's demand to freeze PLO operations from its territory against Israel and supported the PLO's insistence on its "right to exercise the struggle from all Arab fronts." On the second, they demanded additional sanctions against Egypt, including the enforced repatriation of Egyptian workers employed in Arab countries. On the third, they called for use of the oil weapon in the service of the Arab cause. Iraq competed with Syria on the third issue by proposing an Arab summit to work out a strategy for using the Arabs' resources to advance their "stand toward aggression" but also to promote cooperation among themselves. It tacitly opposed Syria on the second issue by expressing satisfaction with the effectiveness of the sanctions voted in Baghdad; and it again competed with Syria on the first issue by taking an independent position in support of the PLO.[9]

The Saudis of course were most concerned about the question of the use of the oil weapon, because it bore directly on their relationship with the United States. They maneuvered successfully to neutralize the Syrian proposal by a mixture of splitting tactics and appeasement. They espoused and modified part of the Iraqi position by advancing a proposal for a preparatory meeting of Arab *economic ministers* in Amman, to draft a comprehensive *economic* strategy to mobilize the Arab nations' resources and employ them to serve "Arab interests." They sought to secure PLO support for their proposal and to detach it from Syria's stance on using oil as a weapon by supporting the PLO position on the Lebanon question. As a consolation for Lebanon, they supported a grant to that country of $2 billion over a five-year period to finance reconstruction projects in the south. Finally, to appease the Syrians and their allies, the Saudis subscribed to a statement in the conference communiqué that condemned "the policy adopted by the United States and its role in concluding the Camp David agreements and the Egyptian-Israeli treaty" and emphasized that continuation of this policy would "reflect adversely on the relations and interests between the Arab countries and the United States."[10]

The issue of increased sanctions against Egypt also concerned the Saudis because of its indirect bearing on their relationship with the United States; however, widespread opposition at the conference to the Syrian proposal made it easy to dispose of it. The Syrians and their allies drew some consolation from the fact that the Sudan, Somalia, and Oman, which had absented themselves from the Baghdad II conference that had voted the original sanctions, subscribed to the reaffirmation of those sanctions at Tunis.

Thus the Saudis purchased at Tunis a reprieve from pressure by the core powers of the Baghdad summit at the cost of leaving the Lebanon-PLO problem unresolved, committing themselves to a vague collective Arab economic strategy, and subscribing to a tough verbal stance toward the United States. The reprieve proved to be quite valuable from the Saudis' point of view, not because they made any use of it on their own initiative, but because, as had happened so often in the past, unforeseen events came to the rescue.

The Soviet Invasion of Afghanistan and Arab Polarization

Syria and the Steadfastness Front on the one hand and Iraq on the other had accepted the Tunis compromises because they appeared to provide sufficient bases for a renewal of their respective charges at both the projected preparatory conference in Amman and the subsequent summit. Before the Amman conference convened, however, the Soviets invaded Afghanistan, and before the summit Iraq invaded Iran. These events triggered a chain reaction that the Saudis handled with mixed results.

The two invasions confronted the Saudis with severe security problems in the Gulf arena that made it necessary for them to tighten visibly their connection with the United States and thus expose themselves to more intense attacks on this score. The same events, however, precipitated a polarization between Damascus and Baghdad and undermined Syria's position, giving the Saudis the opportunity not only to prevent the coalescence of pressures against them but also to try to isolate Syria and loosen its hold on the PLO. The latter attempt backfired as Damascus took drastic action that severely threatened the Saudis' security interests and compelled them to relent and seek to appease it. (None of these developments altered significantly the Saudis' position toward Egypt.)

One of the first manifestations of the effect of the December 1979 Soviet invasion of Afghanistan on Arab alignments was a split vote on January 14, 1980, in an emergency session of the UN General Assembly on a resolution to condemn it. All the Arab countries except members of the Steadfastness Front, including Saudi Arabia and Iraq, voted in favor. The front itself was split several ways, with PDRY voting against, Syria and Algeria abstaining, Libya absenting itself, and the nonvoting PLO representative delivering a pro-Soviet speech. The division in Arab ranks found further, more serious, expression in connection with a Saudi-promoted endeavor to convene an emergency session of the Islamic Conference in Islamabad, Pakistan, to deal with the Soviet aggression against a Muslim country.

On January 16, 1980, two days after the UN vote, Syria assembled the foreign ministers of the Steadfastness Front in Damascus in an effort to close ranks and jointly oppose the proposed Islamic conference. The participants were unable to agree about the desirability or effectiveness of boycotting the conference altogether, but they achieved agreement on two issues. They subscribed to a statement asserting that the uproar about Afghanistan was fabricated by world imperialism, "led by the U.S. in collusion with Israel and the Egyptian regime," with the aim of diverting the Arab and Islamic peoples from their main object of liberating Palestinian and Arab territories, splintering the Arabs, and driving a wedge between the Arab nation and its Soviet friend. They also tried to weaken and diffuse the potential effect of the conference by demanding that its proposed opening on January 26 be postponed, that its venue be changed from Islamabad to Riyadh, and that its agenda be enlarged to include Egyptian-Israeli relations, Palestinian rights, Jerusalem, American threats of military aggression against Iran, and the establishment of U.S. military bases.[11] The Islamic Conference, in which the Saudis had the strongest influence, agreed to include the Palestinian question on the agenda and to postpone the opening by one day but rejected all the other demands. Algeria, Libya, and the PLO reluctantly agreed to participate, but PDRY and Syria definitely refused.

PDRY refused out of blind loyalty to the Soviet Union. The reasons for Syria's refusal were well expressed in the statement of the Damascus conference. One week later, on January 23, 1980, President Carter enunciated in his State of the Union message what came to be known as the Carter Doctrine, warning that the United States would use military force to resist an attempt by any "outside force" to "gain control of the Persian Gulf region." Syria's President Assad viewed Carter's statement as dramatic evidence that the United States sought to exploit the Afghanistan situation to further its own anti-Soviet and hegemonic designs, and clear confirmation of Syria's apprehensions that the Islamic conference would be playing into America's hands. He flew to Riyadh on January 26, the very eve of the conference, to impress his views on Crown Prince Fahd and persuade him to instruct the Saudi delegation to act so as to counter the American designs. Fahd stood firm on the necessity to condemn the Soviet invasion but tried to pacify Assad by reiterating the Kingdom's willingness to call on the Muslim countries to put pressure on Egypt on account of Camp David.

The Saudis genuinely feared that the Soviet invasion constituted an increased threat to the Gulf but had no illusion about the relevance of the Islamic conference to that threat. They promoted the conference partly in order to strengthen by activation an organization they had done much to create, partly to demonstrate their concern about the fate of a Muslim country to the public at home and to the world, and thus reinforce their Islamic credentials, which had recently been undermined by the Mecca incident. But the Saudis also wanted the Soviet Union to be condemned for some of the very reasons that worried the Syrians. They wanted precisely to destroy its image as a selfless friend of Arab and Muslim peoples and at least put those who would cooperate with it in no better position than those who cooperated with the United States. The implication was that if the higher interests of Syria justified its cooperation with the Soviet Union, similar interests justified Saudi cooperation with the United States.

Iraq supported the convening of the conference and voted with the rest to condemn the Soviet Union, but for somewhat different reasons from those of the Saudis. Its intent was to excoriate the Soviet Union as well as the United States in order to justify an *Arab* approach to regional and international affairs independent of either superpower, under its own leadership. Indeed, on February 8, 1980, President Saddam Hussein used the occasion of the anniversary of the coup that had brought the Ba'th to power to put forward a "Charter of Pan-Arab Action," and subsequently called for a special Arab summit meeting to discuss it. The charter called, among other things, for total neutrality and nonalignment of the Arab countries; rejection of the presence of any foreign armies, bases, or facilities in the Arab homeland; and the political and economic boycott of any regime that did so and opposition to its policies "by all available means." The charter called instead for Arab solidarity against any aggression and a joint endeavor to repulse it "by all methods and means, including military action" and "collective political and economic boycott."[12]

The Syrians, who were anxious to keep open the option of a closer defense link with the Soviet Union, especially after the projected union with Iraq had come to naught, opposed the Iraqi proposal for a special summit. Instead they held a summit of the Steadfastness Front in Tripoli, Libya, on April 13–15, 1980, to formulate their own "charter" of action and to counter the attempts to equate the Soviet Union with the United States. The conference created several institutions, including a political committee, and instructed the latter to draft a "program for joint Arab action" based on concentrating the main Arab effort against the Zionist enemy and on defining "clear-cut attitudes against the policy of the United States," which provided support and backing for that enemy. The committee was specifically enjoined to prepare a program to be submitted to the forthcoming meeting of Arab foreign and economic ministers to "use the Arab economy in negative and positive confrontation." In contrast to the attitude assumed toward the United States, the conferees adopted a resolution that called for promoting relations in various fields with "countries of the socialist community, first and foremost the Soviet Union." Nonalignment, the resolution polemicized, did not mean taking a neutral stand in the struggle against imperialism and Zionism; "friend and foe cannot be put in the same position."[13]

By the time the Amman economic conference convened on July 6 – 10, 1980, the rift between Iraq and Syria had reached dimensions that precluded any possibility of even the kind of converging pressures against the Saudis' American connection that had developed in Tunis the previous November. Syria, Libya, and the PLO did make extreme demands for using the oil weapon "positively and negatively": they called for an annual allocation of $5 billion to Syria to help restore the strategic balance between it and Israel and for the application of oil sanctions against the United States, Western Europe, Canada, and Japan, starting with a 25 percent reduction in supplies. The Saudis, however, left it to the Iraqis, embittered by Syria's obstruction of their pan-Arab scheme, to deride the demand for money for arms as shallow and shortsighted and, in a retreat from their position at Tunis, to reject the idea of using the oil weapon "unless all the Arabs agreed to use it as well." The Saudis themselves took on their favorite role of mediator. Although they endorsed most of the Iraqi positions, they also advocated some concessions to the Syrians to keep open the line to them. The final resolutions provided for setting up a fund to be financed by the oil-rich countries to help "narrow the development gap between the various parts of the Arab homeland" and specifically mentioned Iraq's proposal to start with an annual allocation of $1.5 billion. They also affirmed "the need to employ Arab international economic relations in the service of pan-Arab interests and issues" and referred the position papers submitted by Syria to the preparatory committee for the next summit conference, scheduled for November 1980. The United States came in for much milder criticism than it had in the Tunis resolutions. The Amman communiqué stated merely that "the Camp David policy and Israel's aggressive plans have ruled out the possibility of peace at present" because of the Egyptian regime's "going over to the hostile camp" and "the increasing U.S. support for the Zionist enemy in all fields."[14]

The Gulf War and Arab Polarization

Two months after the Amman conference Iraq made a move that fundamentally altered the political-strategic configuration in the Gulf and upset Arab alignments altogether for the remainder of King Khaled's reign and beyond. On September 17, 1980, Iraq's President Saddam Hussein brought to a climax the tension that had been mounting for some time between his country and Iran by repudiating the 1975 Algiers agreement and launching a full-scale invasion of Iran five days later. Iraq's reasons for going to war are better discussed in the Gulf context, but one must be mentioned here because of its bearing on developments in the Arab arena. That reason was Saddam Hussein's ambition to use the momentum generated by an expected easy victory over Iran in order to override Syria's obstruction of his pan-Arab scheme and realize for Iraq the position of predominance that he had believed was within his grasp ever since the 1978 and 1979 Baghdad conferences.

As often happens in wars, however, the actual course of events was nothing like what Saddam Hussein had anticipated. After some initial successes the Iraqi advances on the ground were decisively halted, and within a few weeks it became apparent that the hostilities would take on the character of a long and uncertain war of attrition. The prolongation of the war presented a serious danger to the transit of oil through the Strait of Hormuz; and because that danger could be averted only by the American naval forces deployed in the vicinity since the previous year, the United States was automatically placed in the position of protector of the oil interests of Saudi Arabia and the Gulf emirates. Moreover, Iraq's ground and air attacks on Iranian economic targets and oil facilities from the outset of the war had provoked Iranian air attacks on similar Iraqi targets. The two sides' lack of restraint in striking at each other's oil targets and the ease with which their aircraft penetrated each other's air defenses so alarmed the Saudis, whose relations with Iran had been hostile for some time, that they took the drastic step of openly asking for direct American military intervention to deter possible Iranian air attacks on their own oil facilities and territory. On September 30, 1980, the United States announced that "at Saudi request," it was sending four AWACS aircraft and several hundred American support personnel to Saudi Arabia as a "temporary deployment" for "defensive purposes."

Syria, Libya, and the PLO had vocally supported the Iranian revolution from the outset and had continued to support it on the grounds of its struggle against American imperialism even after the Tehran regime had clashed with Saudi Arabia and the Gulf countries. Now, as Iraq invaded Iran, the Syrians, concerned about Saddam Hussein's design and suspicious of the American role in the war, decided to tighten their connection with the Soviet Union for reinsurance. On October 7, 1980, they signed a treaty of friendship and cooperation with the Soviet Union (and began to negotiate a massive arms deal), after having resisted taking such a step for a long time to avoid giving ammunition to Islamic fundamentalist opposition at home and an excuse to the Saudis and others to conclude security agreements with the United States. At the same time the Syrians took active measures to help Iran and counter Arab support for Iraq, going as far as developing a military threat against Jordan.

Libya, for its part, directly attacked the Saudis for asking for the American AWACS and support personnel and demanded their immediate removal, even as it offered whatever aid it could to Iran. After angry exchanges between the Libyan and Saudi media, and after the Libyans circulated reports of an attempted military coup in Saudi Arabia in which many officers were allegedly executed, the Saudis broke off diplomatic relations with Tripoli on October 28. On the eleventh, Iraq had done the same with both Libya and Syria because of their support of Iran. The PLO was caught in the middle and spoke with many voices and different senses in public and private in an attempt to protect its interests.

In the midst of these conflicting currents, preparations began for the summit scheduled to meet in Amman in November 1980. Syria, backed by members of the Steadfastness Front, demanded postponement because it expected the Gulf war to dominate the deliberations and knew it was in a vulnerable minority position. It was particularly anxious to avoid being castigated by most of the participants as insufficiently "Arab" because of its support for Iran and as not Muslim enough because it had failed to condemn the Soviet invasion of Afghanistan at a time when it was having serious trouble at home with Muslim Brethren violence and subversion. The Saudis, however, in a departure from their previous concern to preserve the appearance of Arab consensus and avoid confrontation, pressed for holding the meeting on schedule even after the Syrians threatened to boycott it. They were angry with the Syrians for supporting Iran even though the latter deemed itself to be an enemy of Saudi Arabia and the emirates as well as of Iraq. They wanted to isolate the critics of their American connection by capitalizing on the revulsion in Arab ranks caused by the position of these critics on the Gulf war. Finally, the Saudis believed they had an opportunity to loosen Syria's hold on the PLO, which it had used on several occasions to frustrate their own initiatives to advance a settlement. This belief rested on the fact that the PLO had participated in the Islamabad conference, which the Syrians had boycotted, and on intimations given to them by some PLO leaders that they would break ranks with Syria and attend the summit.[15]

The Saudis' expectations were almost entirely disappointed. At the last moment, the PLO joined Syria and the other members of the Steadfastness Front in boycotting the conference. Indeed, the Syrians even managed to press Lebanon, too, to stay away. Worse still, as the rump summit assembled the Syrians suddenly deployed two armored divisions menacingly on Jordan's border. The Syrians justified their move on the grounds that Jordan supported the anti-regime activities of the Muslim Brethren and that it intended to break Arab ranks and join an expected new round of American-sponsored peace negotiations. In reality they had several other reasons. They wanted to intimidate the conferees, particularly the Saudis and their friends, by intimating to them what Syria could do if it were isolated. The Saudis did not need much imagination to figure out the consequences for their own security if Syria invaded Jordan or destabilized its regime. By developing a threat against Jordan the Syrians also sought to deter it from sending any of its armed forces to help Iraq against Iran. King Hussein had thrown in his lot with Iraq as early as the previous May, when during a visit to Baghdad he had compared Iraq's stand against Iran to Jordan's against Israel and had declared that his country "stood at Iraq's side with all its strength and resources."[16] With the outbreak of war, Hussein had put Jordan's port and transportation facilities at the service of Iraq and was the most unequivocal among all Arab leaders in expressing support for it.

King Hussein met the Syrian threat by deploying two divisions of his own and declaring bravely that Jordan would cut the arm that attempted to hurt it. But the summit conferees took due heed of Syria's warning. Their resolutions reasserted the familiar anti–Camp David line and refrained from condemning Syria. They called for a cease-fire and negotiations in the Gulf war and expressed only general, verbal support for "Iraq's legitimate rights." Instead of isolating Syria, the Saudis felt compelled after the summit to court its goodwill visibly. As soon as Crown Prince Fahd returned home from Amman, Emir Abdallah went on a mission to Damascus to mediate the dispute between Syria and Jordan. He shuttled between the two capitals from November 30 to December 3, and on the fourth announced that the crisis was resolved. Altogether, the only result the Saudis achieved by insisting on holding the summit was to deflect attention from their closer American connection, and even that modest gain was achieved at the price of a dramatic display of the divisions and splits in the Arab ranks and a barely disguised surrender to Syrian blackmail.

Keeping Egypt at Arm's Length

The events from the summer of 1979 until about the end of 1980 naturally changed Egypt's "objective" position within the shifting political and strategic configurations of the region. Sadat had anticipated at least some of those changes and had counted on them to cause the Saudis to seek to restore their political-strategic connection with Egypt. However, not only did the Saudis fail to do so, but on the contrary they put continuing ostracism of Egypt and rejection of the Camp David accords at the basis of any maneuvers and responses they were compelled to make. The greater the pressure on their American security connection or the greater their need for it, the more they found it necessary to compensate by stressing their distance from the American-Egyptian relationship resting on Camp David. Sadat's angry but ultimately harmless reactions only played into their hands and confirmed them in their course.

In the summer of 1979 Sadat had helped defeat the Saudis' attempt to bypass the Camp David process by opening a way for an American-PLO dialogue. In the wake of that episode Sadat decided to bide his time and not press for progress on the autonomy talks until the Saudis were forced to rally to the Camp David process by the pressures that the Baghdad bloc was bound to exert on them on account of their American connection. Such pressures did develop at the November 1979 Tunis summit, but the Saudis managed to deflect them on that occasion by resorting to various devices, including confirmation of the ostracism of Egypt and subscription to sharp verbal attacks and threats directed at the United States.

The Soviet invasion of Afghanistan one month later appeared to Sadat as a likely occasion for the desired Saudi turnaround. The invasion came hard on the heels of the seizure of the Mecca mosque, which had rattled the Saudi establishment. It split the Baghdad bloc several ways and suggested a specific strategic role for the American-Egyptian connection. The United States sought Saudi cooperation in military arrangements to underpin the Carter Doctrine, and the Saudis responded that they favored a strong American military presence and military facilities elsewhere in the region, so long as the Kingdom was not openly associated with the endeavor. Both Sadat and the Americans understood this response to mean that the Kingdom desired American facilities in Egypt, among other places, and they viewed it as a first step toward a Saudi-Egyptian rapprochement. It soon transpired, however, that the Saudis wanted the benefits of American-Egyptian military cooperation without any reciprocal move on their part. Moreover, they continued to use the boycott of Egypt and denunciation of Camp David as a means to appease Syria and promote other aims, as they did in the Islamabad Islamic Conference, where they supported resolutions condemning Egypt and calling on the Muslim countries to penalize it because of its treaty with Israel. In disappointment, Sadat lashed out with redoubled fury against the Saudi royal family in a speech to his parliament on January 28, 1980. The Saudi media struck back, and the verbal hostilities reached a particularly intense level in February, when Egypt exchanged ambassadors with Israel.

In May 1980 Sadat thought he saw another sign of a possible Saudi change of heart. At that time the Egyptian-Israeli autonomy talks had ground to a halt, and President Carter was desperately trying to get them moving again or at least to create the impression that they were moving in order to help his election campaign. Also at that time, on May 25, Crown Prince Fahd told Catharine Graham in an interview with the *Washington Post* that Saudi Arabia would bring Arabs and Palestinians to the peace table if Israel promised to withdraw from Arab territory. Sadat saw in that statement a signal of Saudi willingness to break ranks with Syria and Iraq, if not actually to rally to the effort he was making with the American president to revive the peace talks, and he quickly praised it. Within three days, however, Fahd denied that Saudi Arabia was preparing its own peace initiative and reaffirmed his country's commitment to a "collective Arab position." Later it transpired that at about the same time the Saudis had approached the United States with a request for equipment to upgrade the capabilities of the F-15 aircraft they had acquired in 1978. Fahd's statement was meant to prepare the ground for favorable consideration of the request, and conformed to a pattern of Saudi behavior in similar circumstances.

The Gulf war and related events seemed to create almost ideal conditions for the Saudi turnaround long expected by Sadat. The Arab ranks were in total disarray, Saudi Arabia openly sought and received an American military presence, Syria signed a treaty with the Soviet Union, the Steadfastness Front boycotted the Amman summit, Syria and Jordan engaged in a military confrontation, and Iraq proved to be a security liability rather than an asset to Saudi Arabia and the Gulf emirates and was in no position to obstruct any move they might want to make. Egypt, especially with American cooperation, seemed to be the most obvious and logical strategic prop for Saudi Arabia in both the Gulf and the Arab arenas. However, the Saudis once more dashed Sadat's hopes. They preferred to deal with the situation through improvisations and piecemeal measures rather than in broad strategic terms: counting on the United States to secure oil transit routes for its own interest, calling for American military assistance when unavoidable, trying to isolate Syria and then quickly reverting to appeasing it, seeking to rally the Gulf emirates but without provoking either Iraq or Iran, pressing the exploration of possible Pakistani military support, and so on. Moreover, they once more used their continuing ostracism of Egypt to cloak their much greater dependence on the United States and to gain credence for their other policy moves. On January 14–30, 1981, they hosted a meeting of the Islamic Conference in Ta'if that espoused two sets of resolutions: one denouncing Camp David, asserting that Resolution 242 was not a suitable basis for peace, and calling for jihad against Israel; the other calling on Iraq and

Iran to cease fighting and accept mediation, and appointing a committee of Muslim leaders to promote that objective.

Strategic Consensus, U.S. Arms Deal, and Sequels

Although the Saudi-Syrian rift manifested at the Amman summit and in the Syrian military threat against Jordan was repaired on the surface, its underlying causes continued to operate. The Syrians continued to believe that the Saudis were determined to isolate them in order to be able to cooperate even more closely with the United States. They particularly retained their suspicion that the Saudis wanted to detach the PLO from them in order to be able to promote the kind of approaches to the United States they had attempted in the past, leaving Syria to face Israel alone.

The Saudis knew that the Syrians' suspicion was to a large degree valid, but they placed the blame for it on the Syrians themselves, whose extreme suspiciousness and obduracy had paralyzed all Arab peace initiatives. Similarly, in the Saudis' view, Syrian suspicions of their American connection had led Damascus to act in ways that tended to make its fears self-fulfilling. Syria's one-sided hostility to the United States and uncritical cooperation with the Soviet Union had tended to force the hand of other Arab parties and to promote polarization of the Arab world along East-West lines. In addition, the Saudis probably resented the lengths to which the Syrians were prepared to go in indulging their hostility toward Iraq, which was their ally in the Gulf, and were certainly shocked by the Syrians' willingness to resort to blunt military threats against Jordan, which was so close to them as to be their virtual proxy.

These contradictory perceptions and attitudes came into play in connection with a multitude of events that agitated the area over the next two years. But as far as Saudi policy is concerned they found their most relevant expression in connection with three episodes: the Saudi quest for American arms; the complex conflict in Lebanon, which culminated in war in June 1982; and the so-called Fahd Plan.

As mentioned earlier, in May–June 1980 the Saudis had approached the United States with a request for equipment to upgrade the capabilities of the F-15 combat aircraft they had previously acquired. President Carter, who was fighting an uphill election campaign and was engaged in efforts to revive the Egyptian-Israeli autonomy negotiations based on Camp David, had put off consideration of the Saudi request until after the elections. When these were over, the Saudis renewed their request and expanded it to include five AWACS aircraft as well as the F-15 enhancement equipment. The Reagan administration promptly agreed to the request: on March 6, 1981, it announced its agreement to sell the F-15 equipment, and on April 21 it announced its decision to sell the AWACS aircraft. However, the administration sought to relate its decisions to a broad Middle East policy, a key component of which was the concept of "strategic consensus," which was troublesome to the Saudis.

The concept was first unveiled by Secretary of State Alexander Haig in testimony before a Senate committee on March 19, 1981. Starting from an assumption of overriding concern among some key Middle Eastern countries about Soviet threats to the region, the promoters of the concept sought to use that concern as a lever to mobilize those countries into some kind of defense framework to counter the threats. Such an alignment, the advocates believed, should make it possible for countries of the area to transcend other disputes among themselves and thus facilitate their eventual resolution. The arms deal, though not explicitly linked to Saudi adherence to the strategic consensus, was supposed to provide an inducement to rally to it, and the Kingdom's agreement to do so was in turn supposed to make the Israelis less concerned about the deal itself. The secretary of state was scheduled to go to the Middle East in early April and visit Egypt, Israel, Jordan, and Saudi Arabia to explain and promote his policy.

The Saudis were pleased about the administration's positive responses to their arms request but not about the connection made between them and the concept of strategic consensus. They may have welcomed the new administration's determination to resist Soviet encroachments, but they definitely did not want to associate themselves openly with any doctrine that would polarize the Arab world into pro-American and pro-Soviet camps. They had barely managed to keep their critics at bay when they operated on the basis of the 1979 agreement to disagree with the United States on the Arab-Israeli conflict; they certainly did not want to take on the added dangers involved in agreeing to subsume the conflict to strategic cooperation with the United States, Israel, and Egypt. They were already regarded with suspicion by Syria and its allies because of their recently strengthened military connection with the United States, and they expected to have to do some explaining to rebut charges that the envisaged arms deal would make them even more dependent on America; they surely did not need the added burden of explaining away the explicit relationship that the administration established between the deal and the strategic consensus. Consequently, when Haig visited the Kingdom on April 7 and 8, 1981, they went out of their way to stress their dissociation from the concept. Privately, they conceded that they were seriously concerned about the Soviet threat but added that they were far more concerned about the problem of Israel. Publicly, they went to the extreme of asserting that the only threat to the area emanated from Israel.

Despite the vehemence of the Saudis' rejection of the notion of strategic consensus, the Syrians were not reassured and reacted, as they had at the time of the Amman summit, by mounting indirect pressure on the Saudis, this time in Lebanon. At the end of March and the beginning of April 1981, violence erupted between Muslims and Christians in Beirut, and Syrian forces tangled with Phalange militias around Zahle in the Bekaa Valley in the worst outburst of fighting since the 1975– 1976 civil war. The immediate causes of the eruption are obscure, but what is certain is that the Syrians kept it up by laying siege to Zahle and by seeking, to all appearances, to crush the Phalange forces. For the Saudis, this raised the specter of total Syrian hegemony over Lebanon, which would put Syria in position to install a radical regime and/or to achieve complete control over the PLO establishment in that country. Alternatively, the Syrians' action might provoke Israeli intervention, which would lead to a wider conflict and embroil the Saudis with the United States at a time when they badly needed the latter's cooperation. How to prevent these developments and advance the arms deal with the United States while dissociating themselves from the concept of strategic consensus was the problem the Saudis faced. The problem became tangled with developments involving Israel and the PLO, Iraq, and the United States as well as Syria.

In mid-April 1981 Israel escalated retaliatory action against PLO bombardment of its northern settlements by launching massive air attacks against PLO camps and installations and shelling PLO bases in southern Lebanon. The Israeli action was meant to pin down PLO forces to prevent them from joining the battle against the Phalanges and to warn Syria that Israel would not allow it to crush the Phalanges. The latter feature of Israel's action might have been helpful to the Saudis' aim to get Syria to desist but for the fact that the Phalange leader, Bechir Gemayel, chose that moment to reveal publicly his alliance with Israel. On April 16 he declared that his organization had been receiving military aid from Israel and that it would continue to do so until the Syrian forces left Lebanon. The Saudis could not ask the Syrians to cease their attacks on the Phalanges without demanding that the latter renounce their alliance with Israel. This the Phalanges found inexpedient to do while they were under attack.

A further complication developed when Israel and Syria became involved in direct confrontation. On April 25, 1981, Syria began a determined assault against Zahle in which it made use of its air force for the first time. Two days later, Israel's air force intervened and shot down two Syrian helicopters. The Syrians responded by deploying surface-to-air missiles in the Bekaa Valley for the first time since they had entered Lebanon. Israel viewed the missiles as endangering its control of Lebanon's airspace generally and its continuing campaign against the PLO in particular; consequently, on May 3 it threatened to attach and destroy the missiles if they were not removed by May 5. The danger of an Israeli-Syrian war was serious enough that on May 3 both the United States and the Soviet Union issued public calls to the parties to exercise restraint.[17] The next day President Reagan reiterated the appeal in a note to Israeli Prime Minister Begin, and on May 5 he announced that he was sending a special envoy, former Under Secretary of State Philip Habib, to the area to seek a peaceful settlement of the missile issue and a termination of the fighting. Begin agreed the same day to delay military action.

Before the missile complication, the Saudis had exerted themselves to persuade the Syrians to halt their campaign against the Phalanges on the grounds that to do so was essential to detach the latter from Israel. The Syrians had resisted, and the Saudis are said to have suspended their financial support for the Syrian forces in Lebanon.[18] The addition of the missile complication and the public call by the Soviet Union apparently made the Syrians more willing to deescalate the crisis. On May 14, for instance, Secretary Haig said that President Assad had agreed to discuss a pullout of Syrian troops from the peaks around Zahle.[19] However, the intrusion of the Israeli threats and the involvement of the United States led the Saudis to seek a collective Arab cover for their further exertions both in collaboration with Habib and independently. They arranged for a meeting of the Arab League foreign ministers in Tunis on May 26, which, after adopting a pro forma twelve-point resolution supporting Syria, appointed a follow-up committee composed of the Saudis, the Syrians, the Lebanese government, and Kuwait to promote a settlement of the ramified crisis. In addition, the Saudis got a June 1–5 meeting of the Islamic Conference in Baghdad to call for a cease-fire in Lebanon.

The first meeting of the follow-up committee, in Bait al-Din, Lebanon, on June 7 and 8, concentrated on ending the fighting between Syria and the Phalanges. Syria insisted on a Christian public disavowal of Israeli ties before desisting. While the committee was deliberating, Israeli aircraft launched a surprise attack on June 7 against Iraq's nuclear facilities near Baghdad and destroyed them. The Israeli action focused the attention of the world and the Arab countries on the American reaction and threatened both the possibility of Saudi-American cooperation and completion of the impending arms deal if that reaction appeared to be inadequate. As the United States verbally condemned the attack and decided to hold back delivery of four F-16 aircraft to Israel but resisted draft resolutions in the UN Security Council that would impose severe sanctions on Israel, the American reaction was definitely mild. However, Iraq itself came to the rescue when it agreed with the United States on a relatively moderate condemnatory resolution to which the latter could and did subscribe. The Saudis appreciated Iraq's care not to embarrass them, in diametrical contrast to the Syrians' behavior in Lebanon, and signified their gratitude by announcing on July 16 that they would pay the full cost of "repairing" the Iraqi reactor.

After the Israeli raid and its sequel, the Syrians showed greater responsiveness to the Saudi endeavors through the follow-up committee concerning their hostilities with the Phalanges. Under an accord arranged by the committee, they agreed on June 30 to end the siege of Zahle and to have Lebanese police replace the Phalange forces there. However, they remained adamant on the missile question, and the failure to resolve that issue, together with the continuing fighting between Israel and the PLO, kept the Lebanon crisis alive. The Saudis worked with Habib in trying to defuse both issues, but they were constrained by their vulnerability to charges of appeasing the United States and Israel or of failing to back Syria and the PLO against them. Then suddenly Israel took an action that precipitated change.

On July 17, 1981, the Israeli air force launched a massive attack on ostensible PLO targets in Beirut that was said at the time to have killed 300 people and to have injured 800, mostly innocent civilians. The United States promptly suspended indefinitely the delivery of ten more F-16s to Israel, joined the Security Council in unanimously condemning the attack and calling for a cease-fire, and directly pressed Israel to agree to a cessation of hostilities between it and the PLO. Confronted with this uproar, Israel was unable to resist, especially after Habib, working through the Saudis, secured the PLO's agreement to a cease-fire. On July 24 Israel agreed to end its raids, and in doing so gave effect to the first agreement ever achieved between it and the PLO, however tacit and indirect. Two days later the Arab League follow-up committee announced that Bechir Gemayel had agreed not to deal with Israel after Syria had agreed to reduce its presence in Lebanon. The missile issue remained unresolved, but with the end of fighting between Syria and the Phalanges and between Israel and the PLO, that problem could be temporarily ignored.

The Saudis regarded the management of the 1981 Lebanon episode and its attendant complications as a major diplomatic success for themselves. Unlike the case of the 1980 Syrian-Jordanian confrontation, for example, the Lebanon crisis was brought under control on terms that did not constitute flagrant appeasement of Syria. It was more a case of the Saudis' capitalizing on the consequences of Syria's rash actions to cause it to relent. Furthermore, in the course of working out a resolution of the crisis, the Saudis broke new diplomatic ground by collaborating with the United States in bringing about an unprecedented agreement between the PLO and Israel. Several times before, the Saudis had tried to advance diplomatic moves based on the idea of their "delivering" the PLO while the United States "delivered" Israel but had been frustrated by Syria; this time the idea seemed to work at last. Although the success was narrowly confined to a cease-fire agreement, it encouraged the Saudis to think that the approach might next be applied to wider issues. Finally, and most important from the Saudis' point of view, these successes were achieved without their exposing themselves to organized Arab opposition.

The Fahd Plan and Fiasco

Reinforced by their accomplishments in Lebanon, the Saudis next attempted a more ambitious move. On August 7, 1981, Crown Prince Fahd gave an important interview to the Saudi Press Agency in which he first dwelled on the Kingdom's role in bringing about a cease-fire in Lebanon and then expressed dissatisfaction with overall U.S. policy in the Middle East, especially regarding the Palestinian situation. He urged the United States to abandon the Camp David framework, end "unlimited" aid to Israel, promote Israeli withdrawal, recognize the PLO, and support the establishment of a Palestinian state. Then, in reply to an obviously rehearsed question as to whether he had a practical vision of an eventual settlement, Fahd said that, without entering into details just then, he had several principles in mind that had previously been espoused and reiterated many times by the United Nations, and proceeded to unfold an eight-point proposal.

The first six points called for Israeli withdrawal from all occupied territories, including Jerusalem; the dismantling of Israeli settlements built on Arab land after 1967; recognition of the right of the Palestinians to return home or to receive compensation; the creation of a Palestinian state with Jerusalem as its capital; and a transitional period of a few months under UN auspices. The seventh point asserted that *all states* in the region (implicitly including Israel) should be able to live in peace, and the final point called on the UN or member states of the UN to guarantee the execution of these principles.[20]

It is almost certain that when Fahd advanced his proposal his aim was to achieve some immediate tactical ends rather than to enunciate a major Saudi foreign policy program. One of those ends was to advance the prospects of the huge AWACS and F-15 equipment deal. After announcing its decision in favor of the deal in April, the Reagan administration had delayed submitting the statutory notification to Congress for fear that the deal would be turned down. The administration's apprehensions seemed to be confirmed when on June 24, 1981, a majority of the House passed a resolution opposing the sale, and fifty-six senators sent a letter to the president stating that in their view the sale was not in the interest of the United States. The president vowed to do his utmost to secure passage of the deal, and the Saudis thought that they could help the administration by putting forward, as they had on similar occasions in the past (for instance, in 1979 and 1977), ideas about a peaceful settlement. Although the Saudis probably realized that Fahd's proposals had little chance of being accepted in their entirety by the United States, let alone by Israel, they at least included two points that the administration could use in its endeavor on behalf of the deal: the implicit recognition of Israel's right to live in peace, and the absence of specific mention of the PLO.

Another tactical aim was related to the latest Egyptian initiative. Two days before the Fahd announcement, President Sadat had begun a formal visit to the United States during which he had sought to spur the Reagan administration to revive the Camp David peace process. Sadat had argued that the time was propitious for Washington to attempt to involve the Saudis and the Palestinians in the process. He had publicly praised the Saudis' role in achieving the cease-fire in Lebanon and the first agreement between Israel and the PLO, and had urged the United States to build upon that achievement by opening talks with the PLO. Fahd himself, as was evident from his own statement, was pleased with the Saudi accomplishment in Lebanon; but the last thing he wanted was for Sadat to use that development to promote the Camp David approach, and in the process implicate the Saudis by praising their role. By announcing his plan and explicitly calling on the United States to renounce the Camp David process, Fahd sought to undercut Sadat's endeavor and clearly dissociate Saudi Arabia from it.

Although initially Fahd's proposal was almost certainly limited in its aims, once it was announced it blended with other events and acquired a momentum of its own, and in the process gained substantial political-strategic significance. The day after Fahd made his statement, Khalil al-Wazir (Abu Jihad), a ranking colleague of Yasser Arafat, expressed approval in terms that accurately reflected one of Fahd's tactical purposes: Al-Wazir praised the statement because "it is very important to hear a high-ranking Arab voice saying no to the U.S. government and rejecting the U.S. course in the Middle East."[21] The next day, August 9, Sadat showed that he had been stung; he dismissed the plan as bringing nothing new and representing an "old stand which I do not approve and totally reject."[22] On August 10, however, Arafat told the Beirut daily *al-Nahar* that the "plan" was positive and added that a future Palestinian state could be federated with Jordan. On the seventeenth, Arafat reaffirmed to the *New York Times* his approval of Fahd's proposals as "a good beginning for a lasting peace in the Middle East." Sadat's rejection and Arafat's approval encouraged Morocco, Jordan, and the Gulf emirates to voice their support in the next few weeks, and all this prompted the Saudis to take their own proposals more seriously. On September 10 Fahd met with Secretary of State Haig in Málaga, Spain, discussed his plan, received reassurances that the administration expected to overcome congressional opposition to the AWACS deal, and accepted an invitation to visit Washington soon.

The Syrians had disliked Fahd's statement from the outset but had refrained from expressing any strong reaction to it because they initially viewed it as possibly having a limited tactical significance. However, as the proposal began to take on the character of a plan, with Arafat and other Arab parties expressing their support and with Fahd engaging in dealings about it with the United States, the Syrians began to worry. What concerned them most at this stage was not the substance of the plan, which was unexceptionable in principle, or its practical chances, which they deemed to be nil, but the old fear that the Saudis might use it to detach the PLO from them, isolate them in the Arab arena, and then proceed to work out a separate, perhaps different, Palestinian-Jordanian settlement with the United States that would exclude them. As soon as Fahd returned from Málaga, the Syrians sent Foreign Minister Khaddam to Riyadh to ascertain the Saudis' intentions and to remonstrate against their persisting with their initiative at this time.[23] Khaddam repeated the argument that it was necessary to restore the Arab strategic balance with Israel before talking about any kind of settlement and added that such restoration could be achieved only with Soviet arms. He asserted that the American-Saudi deal was unlikely to be approved, and that even if it were its usefulness would be limited because of America's commitment to Israel.

Shortly after Khaddam returned home, Israel's Prime Minister Begin concluded a visit to the United States during which the two countries concluded an agreement in principle on strategic cooperation. The Syrians viewed that development as a confirmation of their arguments, and their media reacted by indicating that if the agreement were realized Syria would conclude a strategic cooperation agreement of its own with the Soviet Union. Assad himself, in an implicit criticism of the Saudis, called upon the Arabs to seek Soviet, not American, arms.[24] The Saudis, too, denounced the Israeli-American agreement, but they also sent Prince Abdallah to Damascus on September 27, 1981, to try to pacify the Syrians. Abdallah tried in effect to work out a deal with Assad wherein the Kingdom would help Syria acquire arms from the Soviets by underwriting one-third of an envisaged $2 billion deal if Syria did not obstruct the Kingdom's quest for American arms.[25] Furthermore, in exchange for the Syrians' showing some understanding for the requirements of the Kingdom's dealings with America, which might call for statements such as Fahd's proposal, the Saudis would reciprocate by considering the establishment of diplomatic relations with the Soviet Union, thus bestowing legitimacy on Assad's close relationship with that country at a time when he was under attack on that score from his own Muslim fundamentalists.[26]

During the next month two developments gave the Fahd Plan further impetus. On October 6, 1981, President Sadat was assassinated by Muslim fanatics in the midst of a parade celebrating the anniversary of the 1973 war. The event put into question Egypt's policy course and future, and this uncertainty in turn brought to the surface the latent disagreements among Sadat's opponents and gave the Fahd Plan a new relevance. The Syrians, the Libyans, and the PLO, for instance, called upon Egypt to repudiate the Camp David accords and return to the Arab consensus, based, of course, on the common denominator defined by themselves. To the Saudis, however, such a reversion involved a serious danger of taking Egypt back to the Nasser era, destroying the Egyptian-American alliance, and undoing Faisal's great strategic achievement of weaning Egypt away from the Soviets.[27] To counter that danger they urged the Arab parties to refrain from pressing Sadat's successor, Husni Mubarak, to abrogate the peace treaty with Israel, and thus encouraged Mubarak to resist any temptation of doing so.[28]

The different reactions of the rejectionists and the Saudis underscored a related point that had been obscured by their common opposition to Sadat and his work. Whereas the Saudis had rejected the Camp David formula along with the others, they, unlike the Syrians, Libyans, and the PLO, had a vital interest in the underlying idea of an Arab-Israeli settlement worked out through American mediation and serving to consolidate American influence in the region. Consequently, when the Camp David formula appeared to to be shaken in the wake of Sadat's demise, the Saudis felt it all the more necessary to press the Fahd Plan as an alternative that would preserve the notion of an American-sponsored peace. This disposition was greatly strengthened by the success of President Reagan in overcoming Senate opposition and clearing the way for the AWACS and F-15 equipment deal on October 28, 1981. Apart from the intrinsic value of the deal to the Saudis, the administration's demonstration of its ability to take on and defeat Israel's supporters encouraged them to believe that Washington could do the same with the Fahd Plan if it decided to espouse it. And it so happened that immediately after passage of the deal, elements within the administration suddenly began to speak favorably of the plan, which had hitherto been almost entirely ignored.[29] The phenomenon was sufficiently important to prompt Begin to call upon the United States publicly to reject the plan as an "obstacle" to the Camp David process and to lead the Israeli ambassador to Washington to make a formal *démarche* to that effect with Secretary of State Haig.[30]

Prompted by the developments surrounding Sadat's death and the American arms deal, Crown Prince Fahd said that his eight-point plan was an alternative to the Camp David accords, which were at a "dead end," and that the establishment of a Palestinian state governed by the PLO was essential for the success of his program.[31] The day before, in an extensive interview on the Saudi radio, Fahd stated that Saudi Arabia considered his proposal to be an Arab plan derived from UN resolutions, that the United States had responded favorably to it, and that the Kingdom counted on further American support to make the plan a success.[32] At about the same time, Saudi Arabia formally proposed to put the plan on the agenda of the Arab summit due to meet in Fez on November 25, 1981, and began a campaign to rally support for it and to neutralize potential opposition.

The evolution of Fahd's statement from a tactical move to a serious peace plan confronted the Syrians with a severe dilemma. On the one hand, they did not want to risk a breach with the Saudis by opposing it, both because Abdallah had promised them benefits and because they were uncertain that they could effectively block it. On the other hand, they were barred from supporting it by their old apprehensions, which seemed to them to be confirmed by the passage of the American-Saudi arms deal and by the American noises in favor of the plan. In the ceaseless discussions they held with the Saudis, they reiterated their arguments about the inherent unreliability of America's support, the need to change the balance of power before engaging in any moves for settlement, and the importance of involving the Soviet Union; and in the end they urged the Saudis at least to put off summit discussion of their plan to allow for further study, the gathering of additional pertinent intelligence, and the formulation of possible adjustments. The Saudis responded with contradictory moves, reflecting their own dilemma and probably divided counsels. They tried simultaneously to accommodate the Syrians and to make their plan more appealing to the United States; to lure the Syrians into participation in the summit and at the same time to engineer their isolation there by detaching the PLO from them. Their endeavor ended in failure, the victim of its own complexity, last-moment desertion by the PLO, an untimely American move, and, ultimately, the Saudis' own loss of nerve.

Among the hectic activities in the weeks preceding the climax at Fez, the following landmarks shed some useful light on the mode of operation of the Saudis and relevant others.

1. On November 5, 1981, British Foreign Secretary Lord Carrington, who was visiting Riyadh, stated that Foreign Minister Saud al-Faisal had told him that Saudi Arabia was willing to recognize Israel if a settlement were reached on the basis of the Saudi plan.[33] At a press conference of his own, however, the Saudi foreign minister chose to dwell on other points, more to the liking of Syria. He stated that the Kingdom would seek UN support for the plan, and a subsequent international conference in which the Soviet Union would participate. The Palestinians would negotiate with Israel after the two recognized each other.[34]

2. On November 10 President Reagan renewed his praise of "aspects" of the Saudi peace plan. On the same day an aide to Egypt's President Mubarak did the same, while asserting that a positive view of the plan did not contradict the Camp David accords. On the twelfth the Saudis elicited from a Gulf Cooperation Council summit meeting a formal resolution supporting their plan. On November 14 the Saudi delegate to the UN, Ja'far Allaghany, stated that point 7 of the Fahd Plan clearly recognized Israel. On the sixteenth, however, the Saudi government declared that Allaghany was not authorized to interpret the Saudi plan. On the same day President Assad declared that Syria wanted peace based on justice in the Middle East, not on Israeli terms backed by the United States.[35]

3. On November 17 Saud al-Faisal met with Assad in Damascus. Assad reportedly suggested that, to avoid confrontation, the best course was to refer the plan to a committee, which would consider it at a later date along with other possible initiatives. The Saudis agreed to discuss other plans but refused postponement. They apparently misunderstood or misrepresented Assad's view as being not unfavorable to their plan, because on November 20 Syria's Foreign Minister Khaddam asserted vigorously that his country had never supported the plan and intended to oppose it at Fez.[36]

4. On November 22 the foreign ministers began their preparatory meetings for the summit due to open on the twenty-fifth. On the same day King Khaled and Crown Prince Fahd met with Arafat in their capital in a last-minute effort to ensure his support. Arafat flew on to Damascus for a meeting with Khaddam, while Assad's brother, the head of the regime's guard, shuttled in and out of Riyadh the same day. In the meantime, at Fez, Syria's Khaddam stated that his country would not accept any peace plan that implicitly recognized Israel, while Saud asserted that the Kingdom would not accept any compromise on its plan. At that time Saudi sources were expressing confidence that their plan would be adopted more or less intact by the summit.[37] On the same day Secretary of State Haig, concerned about the intrusion of previous American expressions of support for the plan on arrangements to secure the final stage of Israel's evacuation of Sinai, reasserted America's commitment to the Camp David process.[38]

5. On the day of the summit, November 25, the Syrian radio announced that Assad would not be attending and that Khaddam would head the Syrian delegation in his stead. The heads of state of the Steadfastness Front also boycotted the meeting, as did the Iraqi president, to the Saudis' surprise. But the decisive development was the PLO's last-moment decision to join opponents of the plan. After a stormy opening session marked by a shouting match between King Hassan and Khaddam, Crown Prince Fahd offered to withdraw his plan but was dissuaded from doing so by

Hassan, King Hussein, and the GCC bloc. Instead, after four hours of debate King Hassan simply adjourned the summit, ostensibly to allow for further study and preparation.

The defeat of the Fahd Plan had several important implications. In general, it reaffirmed the point, previously learned by Sadat but subsequently obscured by Saudi rhetoric, that to insist on Arab consensus before making any major diplomatic move was a sure prescription for Arab paralysis. The Saudis' futile attempt to secure such a consensus only revealed the fundamental limitation on their ability to play a leading role in Arab affairs, inasmuch as their one major peace initiative was frustrated by Syria and Iraq, which were beholden to them at that very moment for massive economic and political benefits, and ultimately by the extremists in the PLO, who vetoed the accommodating inclination of Yasser Arafat. Moreover, the Saudis showed no inclination after their frustrating experience to do what Sadat had done in similar circumstances and try to force the hand of the reticents by pressing ahead with their plan. Their immediate reaction was rather to try to divest themselves of it by proclaiming it to have been an Arab plan, and to revert to their basic approach of reacting defensively to events initiated by others rather than seeking to shape them themselves. And others kept their hands full in the next weeks and months.

The United States continued the effort begun on November 22 to repair the damage that its flirtation with the Fahd Plan might have done to its relations with Israel and to the prospects of completing the Israeli withdrawal from Sinai. Five days after the defeat of the plan it signed with Israel a specific memorandum of understanding on strategic cooperation, and three days later, on December 3, it issued with Israel a joint statement reaffirming the Camp David accords as "the only" basis for peace and for the Sinai Multilateral Force Organization.[39] On December 14, however, Begin's government rushed through the Knesset in a few hours a bill applying Israeli law to the Golan Heights, effectively annexing that territory. Among the motives that prompted Begin to act just then was, on the one hand, the desire to foreclose that issue after the Fahd Plan had stirred it with the point about return of all the territories;[40] and on the other hand, the endeavor to capitalize on the rift in the Arab ranks, particularly between Syria and Saudi Arabia, revealed by the fiasco at Fez.

The United States reacted by joining the UN Security Council in a resolution passed on December 15 that called the Golan move illegal and invalid and threatened sanctions if it were not rescinded. On the eighteenth it suspended the strategic pact signed at the end of the previous month, provoking a sharp verbal retort from Begin that expressed an unprecedented degree of strain in the relations between the two countries. The United States had probably reacted sharply partly in order to spare the Saudis any embarrassment in view of the impending visit of Crown Prince Fahd. If so, its concern proved to be irrelevant. On December 23, 1981, Fahd announced the indefinite postponement of the visit.

On the day Israel passed the Golan law, Syria stated that the move amounted to a "declaration of war,"[41] but was careful to refrain from taking any action that might provoke Israel at a time when its own forces were dispersed and when the regime was under intensified attacks by the Muslim Brethren. A week or so later, on December 22 and 23, Assad went to Riyadh to try to mend his relationship with the Saudis and to seek their help. The Saudis were prepared to suppress their resentment of Syria's key role in defeating their plan for the sake of securing its cooperation in dealing with the deteriorating situation on the Gulf front. In the interim since Fez, the Saudis had been made more acutely aware of the Iranian danger by the discovery of Iranian-fostered plots against their own regime and Bahrain's. On December 16 the two governments announced that fifty-two Bahraini and thirteen Saudi participants in the plot had been arrested.

In the Riyadh discussions the Saudis agreed to Assad's oft-repeated proposition that the Arabs had to change their basic strategic position before seeking any settlement. They accordingly agreed not to pursue the Fahd Plan any further on their own and to discuss it honestly with Syria when circumstances warranted its reconsideration. As an earnest of their sincerity they immediately announced the postponement *sine die* of Fahd's visit to the United States. The Saudis also confirmed their promise to support Syria's acquisition of new Soviet weapons and seriously to weigh again the establishment of diplomatic relations with the Soviet Union.[42] Finally, they promised to resume and intensify their mediation efforts in Lebanon in order to make possible an optimal deployment of Syria's forces against Israel. On the other hand, the Saudis used Assad's own basic proposition to press on him the view that righting the Arab strategic balance required the mobilization of all Arab forces and therefore a reconciliation among the Arab parties. For themselves, the Saudis said they were prepared to resume their broken relations with Libya, and they asked Assad to show the same spirit by conciliating Iraq and Jordan and thus helping to discourage Iranian adventurism to the extent that it fed on Arab disunity.[43] Assad agreed to do his part, starting with a promise to refrain from attacking those countries if they did likewise. Thus by the end of 1981 it appeared that the Syrian-Saudi strains that had escalated from the time of the Amman 1980 summit, through the Lebanon crisis of the first half of 1981, to the crisis in connection with the Fez summit, had finally been resolved in a comprehensive understanding at the highest level.

The understanding did not last long. The Saudis made no move toward the Soviet Union even though the United States, in an endeavor to secure the final Israeli withdrawal from Sinai, adopted in the next few months a straight pro-Israeli line. On January 20, 1982, for instance, it vetoed a Security Council resolution calling for sanctions against Israel for annexing the Golan Heights, even though it had voted with the other members on December 15 to threaten sanctions if Israel did not rescind its action. On April 2 it vetoed another resolution, demanding that Israel restore Arab authorities removed from office in three West Bank towns. On April 20 it vetoed a third resolution, condemning Israel for a shooting spree by an Israeli soldier in the Dome of the Rock that resulted in the death of two Arabs and the wounding of many. On the same day President Reagan sent Prime Minister Begin a letter promising help to maintain Israeli military superiority over the Arabs after its withdrawal from Sinai. Despite the embarrassment that these moves caused them, the Saudis felt that they could not afford to take any action which might seem hostile to the United States or which would stress closeness to Syria, because of other developments that were taking place simultaneously.

On January 30, 1982, the usually well-informed Kuwaiti press reported that earlier in the month Assad had crushed a serious military coup attempt against his regime.[44] On February 10 Syrian forces surrounded the town of Hama after Muslim Brethren rebels had seized it, and in the next eight days proceeded to level large sections of it with artillery and armor fire. The dead were subsequently estimated at about 10,000. The Saudis, embarrassed because of their past association with Assad, had a hard enough time keeping control over the media's reportings of the events, even without manifesting their new understanding with him. Assad did not make matters any easier when, in a nationwide address on March 7, he accused the United States of supporting the Muslim rebels in their effort to overthrow him.[45] Assad was, of course, using the alleged American complicity to "explain" to his people the plots and rebellions against his regime; but the accusation was also meant to implicate the Saudi friends of the United States and thus repay them for their reticence and "explain" their attitude, too.

Nor did the Syrians live up to their promise to refrain from attacking Iraq and Jordan. On the contrary, their troubles at home led them to redouble their assault on their opponents on the grounds that they had instigated or assisted the rebels, while Iraq and Jordan responded by denouncing the brutality of the Syrian regime toward its own people. The Syrians' vindictiveness reached a high point in April 1982. On March 22 the Iranians had launched a new counteroffensive that scored major successes in the Dezful area a week later, and went on to score a massive victory in Khuzistan. In the latter battle the Iranians recaptured Khorramshahr and allegedly took 30,000 Iraqi prisoners. In the midst of that campaign the Syrians deployed diversionary forces on their border with Iraq and then, on April 19, cut off the pipeline carrying Iraqi oil to the Mediterranean through Syrian territory and called upon the Iraqi people to overthrow Saddam Hussein.[46] The Saudis, already terrified at the prospect of a total Iranian victory, could not afford just then to retaliate against Syria's attacks on their Iraqi ally. However, events in Lebanon soon gave them the chance to get even.

Coping with the 1982 Lebanon War

Not long after the conclusion of the July 1981 cease-fire in Lebanon, Begin's government inaugurated a new policy in the West Bank aimed at the gradual, unilateral application of autonomy as it understood it. The policy called for mobilizing support for self-rule among the rural population through the organization of "village leagues," with a view to undermining and eventually destroying the dominant PLO influence in the towns. As the PLO countered with assassinations and acts of intimidation against the "collaborators," Israel's defense minister, Ariel Sharon, convinced his government that the success of its policy depended on dealing the main PLO forces and infrastructure in Lebanon a knockout blow. Sharon's work was made easier by the fact that Prime Minister Begin resented the widespread interpretations, critical or approving, that he had tacitly recognized the PLO by concluding a cease-fire agreement with it, by reports that the PLO had availed itself of the cease-fire to mass forces in southern Lebanon that held the settlements in northern Israel hostage to their artillery, and by the PLO's insistence that the cease-fire did not apply to other "battlefields," including the West Bank and Israeli targets in the world at large. At any rate, Israeli forces were already massed along the northern borders by early April 1982, and the Israeli government waited for the opportune moment to give the go-ahead order. That moment was adjudged to have arrived on June 3, when Israel's ambassador to London was shot and critically wounded by members of a dissident PLO grouping sponsored by Iraq.

On June 6, 1982, Israeli armor and infantry columns crossed the border into Lebanon, supported by large air strikes and sea landings. The declared aims of the action were to destroy PLO forces and to secure a buffer zone that would place Israel's northern settlements beyond the reach of long-range artillery. Subsequent information revealed that these were only the minimal objectives, in the unlikely case that the Syrian forces refrained from intervening, or in case of unforeseen military or diplomatic complications. If the Syrians intervened and circumstances were favorable, far wider objectives would be pursued: the Israeli forces, in cooperation with the Lebanese Phalange forces, would seek to destroy totally the PLO forces and political presence in Lebanon, to defeat the Syrian forces in the country or to render their position there untenable, and to place all of Lebanon under the control of a Phalange-dominated government formally or informally allied to Israel. But events did not conform to the neat anticipations of the planners. The expected brief, decisive campaign that was supposed to produce neat political results turned into one of the longest Arab-Israeli wars and produced a tangled political situation that had not been sorted out nearly a year later.

From the perspective of Saudi security and foreign policy, the developments related to the Lebanon war may be assessed in terms of two phases. Although King Khaled's death on June 13, 1982, marked the approximate end of the first phase, both phases will be considered here for the sake of continuity of analysis. Moreover, all the available evidence suggests that Khaled's death did not have an immediate effect on Saudi policy concerning the war, except perhaps to increase its relative passiveness.

The War of Movement: June 6–June 14

Militarily, the war unfolded initially in accordance with Israel's plans. The Israelis quickly overran the PLO positions in the entire southern sector and advanced northward along three axes. On the western axis, where they confronted the PLO, the Israeli columns moved rapidly toward Beirut, assisted by powerful air support and small amphibious operations. For three days the Syrian forces did not intervene, and the Israeli air force did not attack them, even as the Israeli armored columns advanced gingerly toward their main positions in the interior mountainous sectors. Then, on June 9, when the Israeli advances became threatening to their lines, the Syrians reacted, ignoring an assurance of innocent intent and an appeal to restrain their force made by Begin the previous day.[47] The principal battle focused on command of the air, and the Israelis won it totally. In two days their air force destroyed all the Syrian surface-to-air missiles and shot down eighty-three Syrian fighter aircraft without suffering a single loss. Without an air defense, the Syrian ground forces, which were simultaneously assaulted by Israeli armor, were henceforth exposed to utter annihilation. Consequently, on June 11 Syria agreed with Israel to a cease-fire independently of the PLO. The latter also accepted a cease-fire the next day but Israel found reasons to ignore it. On the fourteenth, Israeli forces linked up with the Phalange forces in east Beirut and thus surrounded and trapped the PLO, the Muslim militias allied with it, a Syrian formation in west Beirut, and an urban agglomeration of about one million people.

The Saudi rulers, like all other Arabs, were certainly outraged at this new episode of Israeli "aggression" and mass killing of fellow Arabs, notwithstanding the fact that Arab had been killing Arab in Lebanon for a long time. Beyond that, however, their specific concern about that war, as about others before it, centered on the fear of spontaneous or instigated pressure on them, from within and without, to take action deleterious to the vital interests of the Kingdom as they saw them[48] or to risk the consequences of external agitation combined with popular unrest at home. The danger in this instance was in some respects more serious, in others less than in the 1973 crisis. It was more serious because oil sanctions against the United States, for instance, were unlikely to be effective; the totally changed circumstances of the oil market had already caused a drastic, perhaps even painful, reduction in Saudi production. Even more important, the Saudi rulers, regardless of inclination, realized that the Kingdom could least afford to antagonize the United States just then, when the Iranians were in the midst of a successful offensive against Iraq, when American AWACS aircraft and support personnel were protecting the Kingdom's skies, and when the U.S. Navy was securing its transit routes.

On the other hand, the chances that the pressures on the Kingdom would become irresistible were considerably less in this than in previous wars because of the state of inter-Arab relations. Iraq's regime was fighting for its life and was in no position to pressure anyone, certainly not on account of the Syrians and their PLO satellite. The Syrians had alienated the majority of the Arab countries by supporting Iran against Iraq and had discredited themselves from the outset in the war by letting the PLO take a beating before intervening, and then leaving it to its fate and concluding a separate cease-fire after a brief and seemingly pathetic performance. The PLO itself, abandoned and fighting for its existence, was in no position to alienate its only remaining source of salvation with any threats or demands. PDRY was in one of its conciliatory phases (discussed in Chapter 15), and Algeria recognized that the Saudis were the only ones who could help because of their American connection. Only Qaddafi was intransigent, but by himself he could be ignored.

In the opening phase of the war the Saudi objectives were therefore twofold: to prevent the formation of pressures on themselves and to do what they could to bring the fighting to an end. They tried to achieve these aims by calling upon the Arabs to unite in the face of the Zionist aggression and at the same time making certain that no summit or other all-Arab emergency meeting took place by heeding, in the name of consensus, any party's objection to such a meeting. They did not even assemble the amenable GCC for fear that someone might force the hand of the others by proposing a drastic move or even a larger Arab meeting. At the same time they sent well-publicized messages of support to PLO Chairman Arafat on June 9,[49] and to Lebanon's President Sarkis on the eighth,[50] but with regard to Syria said only that Assad conferred with Fahd by phone on the eleventh.[51] Finally, on June 6 they announced that King Khaled had sent messages to President Reagan and other world leaders to intervene to halt the Israeli "massacre,"[52] and on the tenth Crown Prince Fahd promised to intervene with the United States.[53]

American policy regarding the war became gradually apparent in the first week. On June 6 the United States voted with all other members of the UN Security Council for the withdrawal of Israel's forces. On the seventh it sent special envoy Philip Habib back to the Middle East to begin discussions aimed at ending the hostilities. The next day it vetoed a resolution threatening Israel with sanctions for refusing to halt the invasion. On the tenth President Reagan met Saudi Foreign Minister Saud al-Faisal in Bonn, and on the same day an American announcement was made that President Reagan had sent a message to Prime Minister Begin calling for an end to the fighting. The enunciation of the effective American policy came finally on June 13, 1982. On that day Secretary of State Haig stated that the United States would seek the withdrawal of Israeli forces from Lebanon as part of a long-term solution in which all foreign troops would be pulled out of Lebanese territory.[54]

The Soviet Union kept a conspicuously low profile.[55] Apart from supporting the Security Council resolutions, the only significant independent public move it made was to issue a mild "warning" to Israel on June 14 — after the Syrian-Israeli cease-fire! — that military developments in Lebanon "cannot help affecting the interests of the USSR."[56] This surprisingly passive and mild reaction, particularly at a time when the Syrian forces were still exposed to destruction, was probably due to two factors: the Soviets' long-standing disapproval of the Syrian presence in Lebanon because it dispersed Syria's forces and entailed the danger of complications with the PLO and Israel; and their desire to avoid entanglement in the Levant war at a time when the Gulf war nearer home seemed to be moving to a climax that involved far greater potential opportunities and dangers to themselves.

As far as the Saudis were concerned, the American objective defined by Haig was highly desirable in principle but problematic in practice, since its pursuit entailed prolongation of the crisis. The Soviet position, however, was unambiguously welcome. It reduced the chances of superpower confrontation and the resultant complications; it weakened the Soviets' prestige in the area generally; it specifically undermined the Syrians' notion of strategic balance relying on the alleged unqualified commitment of the Soviet Union to the Arab side; and it was apt to make the Syrians less critical of the Kingdom's American connection, which now became critically relevant to their own fate. The Saudis knew the Syrian regime too well to hope for a repetition of the Egyptian scenario of the early 1970s, which had resulted in Sadat's leaving the Soviet and joining the American camp; but a rapprochement between Damascus and Washington mediated by themselves was not out of the question and could serve their interests no less.

The Siege of Beirut and the Fate of the PLO: June 15 – August 30

After the Israeli forces linked up with the Phalanges and surrounded west Beirut, the latter had second thoughts about fulfilling their part of the plan and storming the city. The Phalange leader, Bechir Gemayel, was surprised by the sudden emergence of the possibility of restoring the integrity and unity of Lebanon in the international forums and did not want to jeopardize it by engaging his troops in a bloody battle with the PLO and their allies in the thickly inhabited Muslim part of the city. Nor did the Israelis want to pay the toll of heavy casualties that would be involved in battling the enemy in a built-up area. Consequently they modified their objective and sought the disarming and removal of the PLO from the city rather than insisting on its destruction or surrender. To accomplish this they attempted a strategy of siege and attrition, leaving the option of storming the city as a last resort, after the enemy had been brought near the breaking point.

The Israelis applied that strategy over the next six weeks by means of constant harassment with artillery and air raids, punctuated by episodes of massive bombardment, shelling and bombing, and occasional ground assaults. One of the Israelis' secondary aims was to stir up the civilian population to demand the removal of the PLO and other armed militias; consequently, although they did not follow a systematic policy of indiscriminate attack, they did not particularly mind when civilian areas in which their military targets were ensconced were hit.

Diplomatically, the United States was the pacesetter during this phase. It sought to end the siege of Beirut by mediating through Philip Habib the removal of the PLO from the city, as part of the wider objective of seeking the withdrawal of all foreign forces from Lebanon. Its principal interlocutors were Israel on one side, and on the other a bewilderingly diffuse Arab side of which the Saudis were one of the most important components, albeit a remote one. The main asset of the United States in the pursuit of its objective was Israel's military pressure; its problem was that it could not control the amount that Israel's strong-headed government chose to apply, and this confronted it with a dilemma. If it condoned whatever violence Israel applied, it risked damage on the Arab/Saudi side;

and if it condemned it, it risked a confrontation with Israel with the consequence of either losing the chance to gain the acquiescence of the PLO and its allies to withdrawal, or of provoking an all-out Israeli assault on Beirut. The Reagan administration as a whole did not have that clear a conception of the problem and developed no deliberate policy to deal with it. Rather, it muddled through the situation amid division and crisis in its ranks.

The interplay of all these considerations produced three more or less distinct subphases. The first, lasting from the beginning of the siege until the resignation of Secretary of State Haig on June 25, was marked by the secretary's attempt to avail himself of Israel's military pressure to force the PLO's withdrawal in the face of attempts by other members of the administration to distance the United States from Israel for the sake of the Saudis. In the second, from June 27 through about the third week of July, the United States distanced itself decisively from the degree of violence used by Israel while continuing to seek the removal of the PLO. The strain between the United States and Israel relieved the pressure on the Saudis and made it easier for them to operate among key Arab parties in an attempt to secure agreement on a PLO withdrawal. However, the strain also encouraged reticence among the Arab parties and made agreement impossible. In the third subphase, from the last days of July through about mid-August, the realization by the relevant Arab parties that the United States remained wedded to its objective, coupled with the ruthless intensification of Israeli pressure in defiance of the United States, finally overcame all reticence and led to agreement on evacuation. The following paragraphs outline each subphase.

Once the Israelis surrounded Beirut on June 13, the Saudis' first concern was that the Israelis might storm the city. The Saudi rulers feared that the slaughter and destruction involved in such an assault would raise such a storm of outrage in the Arab world and at home that they would be compelled to take drastic action regardless of prospects and consequences, including sanctions against the United States, simply to appease the agitated public. The Israelis had assured Secretary Haig that they did not intend to storm the city, but wanted to keep the Arab side uninformed on this point as a means of exerting pressure to achieve removal of the PLO. On June 16, however, when Vice President Bush was told by Fahd and Saud during a Riyadh visit that American nonintervention would have a negative effect in one form or another on Saudi-American relations, he reassured them that the United States had secured Israel's word that it would not invade west Beirut and would see that it kept it. Reinforced by that assurance, the Saudis on June 19 "warned" Israel not to invade Beirut, saying that the Arabs "would defend their territories with all their means" and that "Saudi Arabia will be the first to answer the call of duty."[57]

On June 20 Prime Minister Begin met President Reagan in Washington and agreed with him on the Haig June 13 formula of withdrawal of all foreign troops from Lebanon. During the next two days, while Begin was still in Washington meeting with senior officials and members of Congress, Israeli artillery and aircraft pounded Syrian and PLO positions, including those located in the midst of refugee camps. On June 21 Fahd intimated at a meeting of his Council of Ministers that he was seeking the withdrawal of all forces under the formula of "restoring Lebanese territorial integrity,"[58] and the next day Saud met with the members of the PLO Central Committee to gauge their position. But the Israeli bombardments and bombings aroused in the Saudis the same kind of worries as the fear of an all-out Israeli assault on Beirut, and the American passiveness made their association with the United States and its goal embarrassing. Consequently, on June 25, after Israel mounted the biggest artillery barrage against the city so far, Fahd cabled Reagan to intervene, stressing that Israel's action would have "terrible consequences for the peace of the region."[59] As members of the White House staff rushed to reassure the Saudis, Secretary Haig protested that their interference sabotaged his policy and threatened to resign if they were not ordered to desist. To Haig's surprise the president did not yield, accepted his resignation, nominated George Shultz to succeed him, and asked him to serve during the transition period.

Two days after Haig's resignation the United States warned Israel against new attacks on Beirut, and for the next three weeks or so Israel confined itself to relatively small and infrequent harassments. The Israeli restraint was primarily due to the fact that on the same day, June 27, Begin announced a peace plan calling for the Lebanese army to enter west Beirut and promising safe passage to Palestinians who were willing to lay down their arms and leave the country. Nevertheless, the Saudis viewed the triple coincidence of Haig's resignation, the American warning, and Israel's relative restraint as a sign of change in American policy for which they took at least partial credit. On the strength of that credit, they assumed a more active role in Arab councils in trying to work out a solution based on the withdrawal of the PLO, with less fear of being branded as an accomplice of America and Israel. However, to the extent that other Arab parties believed in the efficacy of Saudi influence, their expectations about what was attainable were raised to levels that made success unlikely.

For instance, on June 27 the Arab League foreign ministers met in Tunis for the only all-Arab conference during the war. The PLO representative made the routine call for sanctions against the United States, and the conference failed to reach agreement on any joint reaction. The Saudis, however, managed to get the conferees to adopt their favorite device of appointing a small committee to follow developments and explore options. Its membership included representatives of the parties directly concerned — Lebanon, Syria, the PLO — plus Saudi Arabia, Kuwait, and Algeria. The committee met in Ta'if on June 30 and considered various aspects of the option of a PLO withdrawal, including scope, modalities, and places to which it might withdraw. It seems that at this stage the discussion centered on the first aspect and was based on a proposal by the PLO itself, involving the withdrawal of its fighters with their arms but the retention of the PLO economic and social infrastructure and a political presence in Lebanon. Although a representative of the Lebanese government was in attendance, the committee realized that his position on such a crucial matter was not of much value and decided to invite the leader of the Phalanges, Bechir Gemayel, to give his views. Gemayel came on July 1 and departed the next day after having pronounced the proposal totally unacceptable.[60] Although the committee was stymied in its first endeavor, the Saudis kept it alive in order to deflect calls for wider meetings and to provide a legitimizing cover for further discussion of withdrawal in the future.

In the meantime Habib was carrying on the negotiations at other levels. The PLO's agreement to pull out at least its fighters directed attention to the questions how and whither. On July 6 President Reagan indicated that the United States was willing "in principle" to contribute a small contingent of U.S. troops as part of a multinational force to facilitate the withdrawal process. Arafat immediately spurned "protection" by the United States but did not rule out a role for American troops in separating Israeli and Palestinian forces. The next day the Soviets, who had been quiet for some time, spoke through Brezhnev to caution Reagan against sending troops to Beirut. Two days later the Syrians weighed in with a complication of their own by indicating their rejection of any plans to transfer the PLO to their country. Ever since concluding a separate cease-fire four weeks before, the Syrians had been isolated and made to feel defensive by their fellow Arabs. Although they were represented in the Arab League ministerial committee and although Assad had met with Fahd on July 4, their views, particularly about the future of the PLO, which they had "deserted," were heavily discounted. By refusing to give haven to the PLO, they sought to force their way back into the center of things and compel all concerned to take their position into account, and at the same time to distance themselves from "defeatist" proposals.

The Syrians succeeded in their maneuver. Over the next few days the United States tried to persuade them to change their position, but the Syrians refused to view the question of a haven for the PLO in isolation. On July 14 Secretary of State designate Shultz made a statement in the course of his confirmation hearings about the centrality of the Palestinian problem and the necessity to satisfy their legitimate rights. The

Saudis viewed the statement as a direct result of their endeavors and as evidence that the United States was amenable to Arab concerns, and on that basis convinced the Syrians to send their foreign minister along with their own to Washington on July 20 for a comprehensive discussion of the Lebanon problem. The next day Saud and Khaddam jointly met the press, and Saud stated that the talks had been successful, that there was a serious desire to reach an early settlement of the Beirut problem, achieve an integration of Lebanese territory, and bring about the withdrawal of Israeli forces. Khaddam kept silent, presumably agreeing.

Apart from any substantive consideration, the Syrians probably had some tactical reasons for sending their foreign minister to Washington: they may have wanted to spur Moscow to be more forthcoming than it had been in its support by appearing to flirt with Washington; and by the same token they probably wanted to give the United States a reason to restrain Israel from attacking them at a time when their forces were highly exposed. If those were their aims, they failed to achieve them. On July 20, while Khaddam was in Washington, Brezhnev endorsed the sending of UN troops to Beirut "to end the impasse," and thus tacitly accepted the idea of the withdrawal of all foreign forces. And two days later the Israelis, frustrated by the endless and seemingly futile negotiations and concerned about an apparent American willingness to compromise, resumed their attacks on the Syrian positions as well as on Beirut, where the Israeli air force mounted a sustained weeklong bombing campaign on presumed PLO targets.

The Israeli attacks got the negotiations moving again. On July 28 the Arab League ministerial committee met in Saudi Arabia to form a common Arab negotiating stance, and the next day it endorsed a plan for complete PLO withdrawal once the PLO was guaranteed safe passage out of Beirut and the future security of Palestinians remaining in Lebanon was assured. On the thirtieth the PLO offered Habib a detailed plan for pulling out its 6,000 troops to Syria (if the latter agreed), Jordan, and Egypt over a one-month period. Israel saw in these proposals ample room for further procrastination and on the same day resumed its attacks by land, sea, and air. On August 1 its forces mounted the fiercest bombardment of Beirut since the beginning of hostilities, and on August 4 armored units under heavy air and artillery cover thrust into parts of the city.

On August 1 the Saudis had urged the United States to press Israel to stop the fighting and warned that relations between the two countries would "assume a negative trend" unless it did so.[61] On the fourth President Reagan appealed to Begin in a sternly worded statement to observe the truce. Begin replied that Israel would continue the siege as it saw fit regardless of international criticism; nevertheless, on the same day the

United States merely abstained in a Security Council vote that called for an immediate cease-fire and Israel's withdrawal to the August 1 positions, and censured Israel for failing to comply with earlier resolutions. On August 5 Fahd telephoned Reagan to ask him to prevent an all-out attack on Beirut, especially since a resolution of the problem was near. The president's answer is not known, but it was judged satisfactory by Fahd.[62]

On August 6 the PLO accepted all the main points of a withdrawal plan negotiated by Habib, and on the tenth the Syrians, after allowing time for the notion to sink in that they had not been a party to the American-mediated plan, agreed to provide a haven to the PLO. The day before, the United States had presented to Israel a plan for a multinational force to assist in the withdrawal of the PLO forces from Beirut. Israel accepted "in principle" but insisted on the departure of the PLO before the arrival of the peacekeeping troops, to avert the possibility that PLO forces would remain and shield themselves behind it. On August 12, while negotiations on this point and other loose ends were taking place, Israel launched an eleven-hour bombardment of west Beirut. Fahd called Reagan again, and Reagan called Begin to express his "outrage" and demand an end to the attacks. Begin called back and reported that an order for a complete cease-fire had been given.

During the next week arrangements were completed for the withdrawal of the Syrian forces, the PLO, and its allied militias, and on August 21 the first group of PLO fighters left for Cyprus as the first contingent of French troops, part of the multinational peacekeeping force, arrived. Other PLO groups went by land, sea, and air to Syria, Jordan, Iraq, Sudan, the Yemens, Tunisia, and Algeria. On August 30 Yasser Arafat departed for Greece with the last elements of the PLO. In the meantime, on August 23 the Lebanese parliament elected Bechir Gemayel president.

Throughout this last phase the United States cooperated with Israel in seeking the disarming and removal of the PLO from Beirut as part of its broader policy of seeking the withdrawal of all foreign forces. That point was made part of Philip Habib's mission. Washington also recognized, although it did not admit so publicly, that a certain amount of military pressure by Israel was necessary to achieve that aim. However, the United States thought that the pressure applied by Israel was sometimes excessive, and conveyed publicly the impression that it thought so more often, in an attempt to deflect criticism from itself and to assuage the anxieties of the Saudis and other friendly Arab parties.

The Saudis shared the end sought by the United States, although they were careful never to espouse it as their own. As the siege persisted they explored with other Arab parties the idea of a PLO withdrawal, but they presented that view as a necessity imposed by irresistible external forces, and put the stress on seeking ways to make that necessity more palatable. As to the means used by the Israelis or the extent of violence tolerated by the United States to bring about the PLO withdrawal, the Saudis only repudiated them, at all times, in all forums, without qualification. Moreover, whenever the level of violence reached a crescendo, they made it a point to appeal to the United States to curb Israel. In this way they sought to deflect any suspicion of their interest in the end result, to prevent the accumulation of pressure on themselves, and to demonstrate at one and the same time their distance from America and the usefulness of their connection with it.

14

The Gulf Arena, 1979–1982: Crosscurrents and Uncertainty

In the Gulf even more than in the Arab-Israeli arena, Saudi policy in the second stage of King Khaled's reign was buffeted by major events beyond the Saudis' control. However, in the Gulf the dangers confronting the Saudis were more immediate and clear and their reactions were therefore more consistent and coherent.

The collapse of the shah's regime confronted the Saudis with three problems. First, it replaced a rival but friendly government in Iran with an Islamic revolutionary regime that was potentially hostile and had a potential appeal to sectarian and fundamentalist elements of the population of the Kingdom and its small neighbors. Second, it replaced the convenient triangular power configuration which had come into being after 1975, and which the Saudis had effectively used to check and balance Iran and Iraq to their own advantage, with one that placed them in the middle of two antagonistic powers, exposing them to the hostility of one and diminishing their leverage with the other. It was a reversion to the pre-1975 situation with a major difference: instead of being aligned with the shah's Iran in the pro-American camp against an isolated Iraq aligned with the Soviets, the Saudis began to align themselves with an Iraq that had distanced itself from the Soviet Union but remained hostile to the United States, had managed to propel itself to the center of Arab affairs, and was driven by grandiose pan-Arab ambitions of its own. Finally, the change in the power configuration, coupled with Iran's potential hostility, presented a specific threat to the security of oil transit in the Gulf and through the Strait of Hormuz, vital for the Kingdom and its small neighbors. Although Iran's navy, like its armed forces generally, was then in disarray because of the revolution, it remained actually and potentially superior to Iraq's on account of its size and Iran's more advantageous geographic position.

Compounding these problems was the fact that just when the Saudis needed it most, their American security connection was heavily strained by the opposed positions taken by the two countries with respect to the Egyptian-Israeli peace treaty. Other complications stemmed from a certain loss of confidence among the smaller Gulf countries in the ability of the Saudi leadership to deal with the upheavals in the region (made worse by the troubles within the Saudi ruling establishment), and a consequent intensification of the divergent tendencies among those countries. Oman, for example, more than ever sought a closer American connection to replace its special relationship with the shah's Iran and went so far as to break ranks with the Baghdad consensus and refuse to ostracize Egypt on account of its peace with Israel. Kuwait, on the contrary, was anxious to find common grounds between the new regime in Iran and Iraq in order to be in a position to appease both. Bahrain was inclined to move closer to Saudi Arabia for security, while Qatar and the UAE were disposed to rely more heavily on Iraq.

To deal with all these problems the Saudis first tried to pursue a number of rather incompatible policy objectives simultaneously. They sought to appease Iran without antagonizing Iraq; to enlist American support for their Gulf security without incurring the hostility of the anti–Camp David Arab coalition, Iran, or Iraq; to rely on Iraq as a counterpoise to Iran without provoking the latter; and to rally the Gulf countries around themselves in competition with Iraq without arousing the latter's ire. The difficulties they encountered in pursuing these aims, coupled with the impact of major events on various elements of the configuration, compelled them to make choices they had sought to avoid and adjustments that entailed new problems as well as opportunities. That interplay between objectives and reality unfolded in four phases in the period from April 1979 until the time of King Khaled's death in June 1982. The following sections outline that evolution.

Initial Redefinition of Positions, April–November 1979

After the overthrow of the short-lived Bakhtiar government, Khaled and Abdallah, who conducted Saudi policy while Fahd sulked in Spain, took the first opportunity to try to appease Iran's revolutionary regime. On April 2, 1979, on the occasion of Khomeini's proclamation of the Islamic Republic of Iran, Khaled sent him a note of congratulations in which he stressed that Islamic solidarity could form the basis of close ties between the two countries. Later that month Abdallah elaborated on the potential for Saudi-Iranian cooperation in a long press interview (quoted in part at the end of Chapter 12), in which he indicated that Saudi Arabia actually preferred Iran's new regime to the shah's.

The formulation of the foreign policy of the new Iranian regime was at that time subject to a tug-of-war between the official government, headed by Mehdi Bazargan, and various coteries of revolutionary clerics and a few laymen clustered around Khomeini, the undisputed supreme leader. Bazargan defined Iran's role in the Gulf as one of promoting stability through cooperation with the countries bordering it, whereas some of the revolutionary leaders spoke of exporting the revolution and protecting the rights of the Shi'ites in neighboring countries. With regard to Saudi Arabia, however, the revolutionaries as well as the government were willing to test the Saudis' professed good intentions through their actions in the coming months. Even the militants, it seems, who betrayed no concern about driving some of the small Gulf countries into alignments with the larger ones, wanted to avoid driving Saudi Arabia into alignment with Iraq.

Another reason that probably contributed to the Iranians' willingness to adopt a wait-and-see attitude toward Saudi Arabia was the configuration of the two countries' relationship with the United States at that time. On the one hand, the Kingdom was clearly at odds with the United States over the Camp David accords and the Egyptian-Israeli peace; on the other hand, the United States was making a serious effort to get along with the new regime in Iran by cultivating Bazargan and his government.

That situation, however, was not to the liking of the Saudis and they were anxious to change it if they could. With regard to the Egyptian-Israeli peace issue, by May–June 1979 the Saudis managed to work out a formula for coming to terms with the United States based on an agreement to disagree (see Chapter 13); but the American effort to cooperate with Iran's new regime was beyond their power to change and was deeply disturbing to them. In their view it showed insufficient appreciation by Washington of the danger presented by Iran and of the need to take remedial action. It also provided clear confirmation of a point the Saudis already suspected: that in its dealings with the Gulf countries, Saudi Arabia included, the United States was prompted only by its interest in oil and would work with *any* regime that would serve that interest. America's refusal in September 1979 to provide asylum to the shah only underscored that point.

With regard to Iraq, Khaled and Abdallah, in opposition to Fahd, had deliberately counted on the Iraqi-Syrian entente and the projected union that emerged in connection with the Baghdad summit to provide protection against the consequences of the upheaval in Iran. As it turned out, however, the difference in Syria's and Iraq's attitudes toward the Iranian revolution — with the former fervently supporting it and the latter fearing it and seeking to exploit it — proved to be one of the reasons for the failure of the two countries to consummate their union in June 1979, and for their gradual reversion to mutual hostility.

When the break between the two countries occurred, the Saudis could still count on Iraq to counterbalance Iran. Militarily, such a calculation seemed plausible because Iraq's power still loomed much larger than Iran's, whose armed forces were thought to have been disrupted by the internal turmoil. However, there were two other difficulties with such an alliance. First, by June 1979 Iraqi-Iranian relations had deteriorated to outright hostility, including open attempts at mutual subversion and border skirmishing. On October 31, 1979, the Iraqi ambassador in Beirut voiced demands on Iran that included revision of the 1975 treaty, return of the three Gulf islands that the shah had seized in 1971, and self-rule for the minorities in Iran, notably for the Arabs of Khuzistan.[1] The Saudis, even while seeking Iraqi protection against Iranian mischiefmaking, had to be careful not to identify too closely with Iraq lest they encourage its belligerency and incur Iran's wrath. The other problem was that too obvious an alliance with Iraq would play into the latter's designs regarding the Gulf emirates, which clashed with the Saudis' own aspirations.

The crisis period preceding the downfall of the shah had accelerated the endeavors of various Gulf countries, including Saudi Arabia and Iraq, to promote various schemes for collective defense, but these activities had been interrupted by the final collapse of the Iranian monarchy. The next few months saw a great many nervous bilateral and multilateral consultations and unilateral defensive actions,[2] but no collective initiative developed because of the difficulty of excluding Iraq and the fear of provoking Iran by appearing to gang up against it. Finally, in June 1979 the Saudis devised a way to get around that problem. On June 27 they held military maneuvers at Khamis Mushayt, near the North Yemeni border, far from the Gulf, to which they invited leaders of the small Gulf countries and North Yemen, but not Iraq's and then used the occasion to hold an informal summit that considered common defense problems.

Reports of the meeting indicated that the participants agreed that the United States could be relied upon to look after its interests in matters relating to access to oil and resisting Soviet encroachments, but could not be expected to protect the established order or to keep a ruling house in power.[3] Against that background, the Saudis followed the display of their military power with a solemn promise that the Kingdom would use "all its human, material and military resources in support of any fraternal [Gulf] state facing a threat against its sovereignty and independence."[4]

After the meeting, Saudi officials asserted that the participants had agreed on a "unified strategy for confronting any danger or attack on any of their states";[5] however, judging by the one practical result that emerged from the meeting, it seemed that if there was a unified strategy, it was to bell the Iranian and Iraqi cats.

The conferees agreed that any attempt to cope with the external threats to the Gulf required the cooperation of both Iraq and Iran, and delegated the Kuwaiti deputy prime minister and foreign minister to present their views to Baghdad and Tehran and attempt to mediate an understanding between them. The Kuwaiti visited the two capitals in July 1979 and heard encouraging words from the government officials he met but accomplished little else. On the contrary, in the following months tension between Iran and the Gulf countries rose sharply as Shi'ite elements in the latter, stirred by the Islamic revolutionaries of Tehran, clashed with authorities. In August, for instance, elements of Bahrain's Shi'ite majority held demonstrations in response to Khomeini's appeal to mark "Jerusalem's day," and local Shi'ite clerics were arrested. Tehran demanded their immediate release, threatening that otherwise it might give open support to the Shi'ites against their tyrannical government. In September 1979 the Kuwaiti authorities arrested a nephew of Khomeini for making seditious speeches in mosques serving the country's 20 percent Shi'ite population. One of Iran's revolutionary clerics, Ayatollah Hussein Ali Montazeri, reacted by sending a note to the Kuwaiti ruler saying that leaders of neighboring Islamic countries should "learn a lesson" from events in Iran if they did not wish to "suffer the same fate that befell the Shah."[6] In Saudi Arabia itself, with its nearly 400,000 Shi'ites concentrated in the Eastern Province, mujtahids (Shi'ite religious scholars) of Qatif announced their intention to hold the 'Ashura ceremonies (commemorating the death of Imam Hussein) the coming November in defiance of a long-standing ban on such a demonstration, and thus prepared the way for major riots that broke out at the appointed time.

The strain between Iran and its smaller neighbors evoked parallel but competing responses from Iraq and Saudi Arabia. On September 22, 1979, Saddam Hussein sent his defense minister to Kuwait and Bahrain with a qualified Iraqi security guarantee. Hussein said later that the minister had reass·ured the Kuwaiti and Bahraini rulers that Iraq would not allow any "external" party "to harm Arab sovereignty, people or land" anywhere in the Gulf, and that they could call upon Iraqi help any time "to the degree they need it" and to the degree they allowed it.[7] The Saudis went Iraq one better: in the last week of September 1979 they sent two brigades to Bahrain at the latter's request, as the Iranian navy started a six-day exercise in the Gulf.[8] And on December 3 the Saudis announced plans to build a causeway to link the Kingdom and Bahrain.

In the meantime the sultan of Oman, as ever skeptical about purely

Arab Gulf defense projects (he did not participate in the June durbar organized by the Saudis), submitted a proposal in September for a collective organization to protect navigation and oil routes with Western participation. Iraq countered with a plan for a purely Arab collective security pact. The Saudis, already committed by their action to the defense of their neighbors and spurred by the rising tension, lost some of their inhibition about seeming to form a coalition against Iran and called for a conference at Ta'if for October 14–16 to discuss the Iraqi and Omani proposals. They remained sufficiently cautious to see to it that Iraq did not attend, on the grounds that its hostility to Iran had gone so far that its participation would be too provocative. At the conference itself the Saudis used those same grounds to table the Iraqi proposal but also invoked Iraq's opposition, sustained by Kuwait, to mete the same fate to the Omani proposal. Apart from thus neutralizing rival schemes, the Saudis were content at that point with the fact that the conference was held under their auspices and leadership, and hoped to build on that later. The future, however, held its own surprises.

Setbacks and Adjustments, November 1979–September 1980

In November and December 1979 three dramatic events set off a series of chain reactions that profoundly affected the Saudis' position and the prospects of the policies they had tried to promote in the previous seven or eight months. On November 4 Iranian militants, mostly students, angered by the arrival of the shah in the United States, stormed the American embassy in Tehran and held scores of its occupants hostage for the next 444 days. That action converted the American policy of striving to get along with Iran's new regime to one of open hostility and confrontation. Although the United States was constrained in what it could do itself by its predominant concern with the fate of the hostages, the change in its relationship with Iran had an important effect on Saudi Arabia's position, both directly and by way of its influence on Iraq's relations with Iran.

The second event occurred on November 20, 1979, when several hundred armed Muslim zealots[9] seized the Grand Mosque of Mecca, Islam's holiest shrine, barricaded themselves in the huge structure, proclaimed one of their own to be the leader of the Muslim nation, and broadcast over the mosque's public-address system attacks on the royal family, its alleged misdeeds, and the climate of moral collapse in the Kingdom. Only after two weeks of fighting and heavy casualties did the Saudi National Guard and army units subdue the rebels.[10] In the meantime, on November 28 the Shi'ites of Qatif attempted to celebrate the 'Ashura ceremonies in defiance of the provincial governor's ban. The National Guard's effort to stop them triggered large-scale riots that lasted for twenty-four hours and resulted in seventeen deaths. These two events exposed the vulnerability of the regime and shook its self-confidence. They also undermined the Kingdom's potential value as a strategic asset in the eyes of the United States just as it was giving up its previous illusions about Iran, and deepened the doubts of the small Gulf countries about the Kingdom's value as a security asset.

The third dramatic development was the Soviet invasion of Afghanistan on December 27, 1979. That event, coming in the wake of the turnabout in America's relations with Iran,[11] alarmed the United States and deepened its involvement in Gulf security. That involvement, in turn, coupled with the effects of the unrest in Saudi Arabia, intensified Iraq's bid for leadership in the Gulf, and all these events together added to the perplexities of the small Gulf countries and to the fragmentation of their tendencies. In another respect, however, the invasion gave the Saudis a chance to try to take the lead in organizing Muslim reaction against it and thus repair some of the damage to their image as a result of the Mecca incident. That effort, in turn, was of benefit to their position in the Arab arena.

Although the Saudis had been disillusioned with America's policy toward the shah and toward the revolutionaries who overthrew him, they welcomed its reversal of position on several counts. The seizure of the hostages caused the United States to despatch a carrier task force immediately to the vicinity of the Gulf. Although the purpose of the action was to deter the Iranians from harming the hostages, it also automatically deterred interference with the oil transit routes and other threats to oil facilities. Second, the confrontation absorbed the attention of the revolutionaries and led the United States to take other sanctions against Iran; and both developments seemed to the Saudis likely to weaken Iran's capacity for mischiefmaking. Third, the confrontation created a shared tactical interest between the United States and Iraq centered on their common hostility to Iran (Iraq duly condemned the seizure of the hostages as contrary to international law), which held the prospect of greater Iraqi tolerance of the Saudis' own security relationship with the United States. Welcome as these developments were, however, the Saudis felt no need to adopt a more positive attitude toward the United States in return, because the changes took place of their own accord. Indeed, the Saudis did just the opposite at the Tunis summit a short while later.

The opening of the Tunis summit on November 20, 1979, coincided with the seizure of the Grand Mosque. Although the Saudis tried to underplay the importance of the incident, their nervousness about it contributed to their agreement to a set of resolutions that strongly condemned the United States on account of Camp David and hinted at future sanctions against it (see Chapter 13). To be sure, the Saudis deflected, with

Iraqi help, more extreme proposals for using the oil weapon against the United States; but the fact that they went as far as they did underscored the complexity of their relationship with Washington and showed that a greater objective convergence of dispositions toward a particular issue, even one as important as Iran, did not necessarily translate into greater practical cooperation across the board.

The Soviet invasion of Afghanistan produced a further convergence of objective American and Saudi interests and also a certain convergence of practical policies, but once again, other factors inhibited any increase in cooperation and led the Saudis to look elsewhere for additional security support. At the diplomatic level, the Saudis welcomed the strong initial American reaction against the invasion and undertook a parallel initiative for their own reasons. The Mecca incident had severely undermined the Kingdom's standing in the Muslim world, which rested on the ostensible pursuit of Islamic values in the realm and its guardianship of Islam's holiest places. The invasion gave the Saudis a chance to recover some of their lost prestige by promoting a meeting of the Islamic Conference at Islamabad on January 26–29, 1980, at which they led the denunciation of the Soviet attack on a Muslim country and called for sanctions against Moscow and a boycott of the puppet Afghan regime. The condemnation of the Soviet Union also served the purposes of turning the tables on countries such as Syria and Libya, which cooperated with Moscow while chiding the Saudis for their association with the United States, and of widening the gap between Baghdad and Moscow through the former's association with the anti-Soviet initiatives.

At the strategic level the Saudis were more discreet in their first response to the American reaction to the invasion. They reacted with conspicuous silence to the proclamation of the Carter Doctrine on January 23, 1980, even though they obviously favored it. A few days later, on February 4–6, Crown Prince Fahd and Foreign Minister Saud received National Security Adviser Zbigniew Brzezinski on his way back from Pakistan, where he had sought to enlist support for Afghan resistance. Brzezinski wrote in his memoirs that both Saudi princes stressed their concern about the grave security situation that the region now faced and were "much more prepared than before to consider, *on a quiet basis,* enhanced American-Saudi cooperation." They stated their desire for closer military ties, asked for better intelligence about Soviet activity in the region, and expressed particular concern about "the growing Communist military presence in South Yemen."[12] Contemporary accounts mentioned that Fahd, specifically, indicated his support for a permanent U.S. force in the Gulf and for military facilities in the region, though not in the Kingdom, and for joint exercises and emergency use of Saudi bases.[13] However, as the United States proceeded with concrete efforts to project its power more effectively, it found that the Saudi cooperative disposition had cooled a great deal. American indiscretion, the disastrous failure of the hostage rescue attempt on April 24, 1980, and a tacit Saudi understanding with the South Yemeni regime (discussed in Chapter 15) had much to do with the change; but developments in the Gulf itself were also crucial.

The Saudis' discretion had been prompted in the first place by a desire to avoid provoking Iran and antagonizing Iraq, both of which had denounced the Carter Doctrine for different reasons. Iran saw the doctrine and the related intensification of America's quest for military facilities in the region as a direct threat to itself, while Iraq wanted to capitalize on the deepening sense of insecurity among the Gulf countries in the wake of the Soviet invasion in order to advance itself as protector of the region. On February 8, 1980, two weeks after Carter enunciated his doctrine, Saddam Hussein issued his Charter for Pan-Arab Action. The charter called for nonalignment and for inter-Arab solidarity to confront any aggression, and emphatically rejected any foreign military presence on Arab soil. It hinted at the possibility of a modus vivendi with Iran based on renunciation of the use of force, but implicitly threatened it by excepting cases in which the sovereignty, security, and basic interests of Arab countries were threatened.[14]

The charter intensified the hostility between Iran and Iraq and became a focus for their rival activity among the Gulf countries and elsewhere. The Iranian revolutionaries denounced the charter as a diabolical scheme intended to stem the Islamic tide in Arab countries,[15] and in the next months they responded with various confrontational actions against all the Gulf countries and Iraq. The Iranian government, for its part, viewed the Iraqi initiative as an attempt to rally the Arab countries into a hostile coalition and tried in April and May of 1980 to foil that design by conventional diplomatic action aimed at reassuring the smaller Gulf countries and enlisting the support of Arab opponents within Iraq. By that time, however, even the Iranian government appeared to have written off the Saudi regime as being irretrievably wedded to Iraq and the United States, particularly after the abortive American hostage rescue mission. Although the Saudi foreign ministry described the American operation as conflicting with "the norms of international law" and deplored the operation's "undesirable complications and harm to the region's stability and security,"[16] the fact that American aircraft used in the operation overflew Saudi territory implicated the Kingdom. The Saudis could do less than ever before to affect either Iran's hostility or Iraq's ambition, as the Mecca incident and the Shi'ite unrest undermined much of their credibility even with their weaker Gulf neighbors.

Thus, when the charter was first proclaimed, most of the smaller Gulf countries promptly expressed support for it; Kuwait did so on February 13, Qatar on the fifteenth, and Bahrain on the twentieth. Oman, on the other hand, went its own way as usual, ignored the charter, and contravened it by concluding an agreement with the United States on February 13 allowing it to use military facilities in its territory. The Iraqis claimed that the Saudis expressed their approval of the charter on February 13; but the Saudis themselves neither confirmed nor denied the allegation, in order to avoid offending Iraq, antagonizing Syria and Iran, or facilitating Iraq's endeavor to translate its verbal support from the Gulf countries into practical commitments to a defense scheme under its leadership. That passive position, coupled with Iranian diplomatic initiatives, helped cool the emirates' initial responsiveness to Iraq, but it did not avail the Saudis much with the government of Iran. On April 30 and May 1, 1980, Iranian Foreign Minister Ghotbzadeh toured Kuwait, Qatar, the UAE, and Bahrain in an attempt to reassure their rulers about his country's intentions and to undercut Iraq's endeavor to rally them, but made it a point to refrain from calling on Saudi Arabia. A week earlier Iran, which already enjoyed good relations with Syria and Libya, had established diplomatic relations with Marxist PDRY in an obvious diplomatic envelopment maneuver directed at Saudi Arabia and Iraq.

By May–June 1980 it was thus becoming increasingly apparent that the Saudis' policy of seeking simultaneously to appease Iran, align themselves with Iraq, strengthen their security bond with the United States, and maintain a predominant position with the Gulf emirates was breaking down under the weight of its inherent contradictions. The Saudis held a faint hope that the impending elections and political reorganization in Iran might still produce a coherent and reasonable leadership that would give one key part of that policy a new chance; Fahd expressed that hope when he stated on May 11, 1980: "We will just have to wait and see what will happen after the formation of the anticipated parliament."[17] However, even before that hope proved definitely to be illusory, the Saudis reluctantly accepted the Iraqi project for dealing with the Iranian problem by means of military action and began to prepare for its anticipated strategic consequences.

Just when the Saudis came around to supporting Iraq's war option is not known. This much, however, is clear: that Iraq's war project had ripened by May 18, 1980, when Jordan's King Hussein concluded a visit to Baghdad by aligning himself militarily with Iraq (see Chapter 13); that the Saudis probably endorsed that alliance; and that by August 1980 they had ceased to worry about provoking Iran, at least enough so as to make a number of moves that the latter was bound to view as confrontational. On August 5–6, 1980, for instance, they received Saddam Hussein at Ta'if for a major visit that was publicized as having achieved coordination of policies between the two countries on a whole range of issues.[18] On August 25 and 26 they countered Iran's move toward PDRY by receiving the YAR's President Saleh at Ta'if, mending their strained relations with him, and announcing agreement on all points at issue between the two countries.[19] On the next two days they hosted a conference of Arab interior ministers in which joint internal security measures were agreed upon.[20] On September 2, 1980, Iran accused Saudi Arabia and Iraq of conspiring to overproduce oil in order to enforce a lower price policy and threatened to boycott the forthcoming November OPEC meeting.

The Saudi preparations for the strategic consequences of the war centered on the implications of an Iraqi victory and disregarded problems that might arise from the hostilities themselves, since Iranian military power was expected to be swiftly neutralized by Iraqi action. The object of the preparations was twofold: to build up the Kingdom's own military capacity and a friendly capacity it could call upon to deal with the strategic configuration that would emerge in the wake of Iraq's victory; and to use the program for developing such a capacity as a means to prevent the smaller Gulf countries from slipping quickly into the Iraqi orbit. The instruments of that strategy were broached early in 1980, but the deterioration of Saudi-Iranian and Iraqi-Iranian relations accelerated the quest for them.

One of the instruments of the Saudi strategy was the major new arms deal with the United States involving the acquisition of F-15 enhancement equipment and AWACS aircraft. In February 1980 the Saudis had given Brzezinski a request for those arms,[21] and he had promised them a sympathetic response in return for their greater willingness to cooperate in certain security matters of common interest.[22] In April the Saudis renewed and expanded their request but received a somewhat evasive reply suggesting, among other things, a feasibility study for the AWACS. In June Defense Minister Sultan met Secretary of Defense Brown in Geneva and pressed hard for the deal but, with the American election season in full swing, received no firmer commitment than before.[23] The Saudis justified their request for the equipment on the grounds of the changed strategic situation; but their eagerness to gain immediate approval of their request was also due to their desire to impress the smaller Gulf countries in anticipation of the expected victory of Iraq in the forthcoming war against Iran.

Another instrument of the Saudi strategy was a defense connection with Pakistan. The idea of such a connection had first been broached by King Saud at the outset of his reign in the early 1950s, but was dropped when Pakistan joined the Baghdad Pact and SEATO. Since then, a considerable number of Pakistanis had served in the Saudi armed forces on an individual basis, particularly in technical positions. At the beginning of

February 1980, while Brzezinski was visiting Pakistan in connection with the Soviet invasion of Afghanistan, President Zia ul-Haq suggested to him that the United States use its good offices to increase Saudi-Pakistani military cooperation. Brzezinski raised the subject with Fahd and Saud during his visit to the Kingdom on February 4–6, and they agreed to facilitate Pakistani arms purchases in exchange for Pakistani "input to Saudi security."[24] Under the pressure of events in the following months, the Saudis' consideration of the Pakistani "input" led to a revival of the idea of a major Saudi-Pakistani strategic relationship, including the stationing of substantial Pakistani forces in the Kingdom to man its defenses.

In connection with the exploration of this option, Pakistan's Minister of Interior Mahmud Hassoon made a weeklong visit to the Kingdom starting May 3, 1980. President Zia himself came on July 9 and met with King Khaled, Fahd, and Abdallah, but not, significantly, with Defense Minister Sultan, who was unexplainably absent. Zia came back the next month as a pilgrim and held talks with Saudi leaders on August 8. On August 21, 1980, there were reports in the international press that the Saudi and Pakistani leaders were discussing the stationing of Pakistani forces in the Kingdom,[25] but on August 23 Saudi sources denied that such a deal had been concluded.[26] The absence of Sultan from the July discussions and the apparent sensitivity of the Saudi media on the issue reflected at least a partial perception by the Saudis that the option was inherently problematic.

On the face of it, the idea had some obvious major attractions. Pakistan had large and experienced ground, air, and naval forces but lacked the financial means to support and equip them adequately; Saudi Arabia had abundant financial means but lacked the manpower and level of technical development necessary to build substantial armed forces. An alliance between the two would be a logical symbiosis. Moreover, an alliance with Pakistan, a large Sunni Muslim, Third World, but non-Arab nation, would be free of both the taints that marred the Saudis' American connection and the dangers that attended any alliance with a large Arab power. Finally, Pakistan is located near enough to the Persian Gulf for strategic access, but not so near as to entertain the kind of ambitions upon it that Iran or Iraq did.

But the idea had also some major disadvantages. In the first place, Zia's government appeared to be highly unstable, having come to power through a military coup that overthrew a popular, duly elected government. That instability cast a shadow of uncertainty on any arrangement reached with him, and raised doubts about the future submission of any Pakistani forces in the Kingdom to the authority of the home government in case of conflict there. Second, a Saudi strategic alliance with Pakistan would gratuitously implicate the Kingdom in Pakistan's conflict with India and in the entire matrix within which that conflict was pursued, including the Soviet Union, China, and the United States. Third, the presence of large Pakistani forces in Saudi Arabia could be a source of great danger to the regime. Even if one were to rule out the possibility of their taking over power some day and establishing a kind of Mamluk state of their own, the Pakistani forces could well become the power behind the throne, making and unmaking rulers, as various mercenary forces had done through long periods of Islamic history. It is significant, and ominous, in that respect that the mere discussion of the issue stirred up a conflict between Abdallah and Sultan, the princes in charge of the National Guard and the regular forces respectively, over the desirability of bringing in such forces, the jurisdiction under which they would come, their putative size and deployment, and so on.

While the Saudis were struggling with measures to deal with the anticipated consequences of war, the Iraqis turned the war contingency into a reality. On September 9, 1980, their forces proceeded to "retrieve" the territories conceded to Iran in the 1975 agreement and claimed to have "liberated" them by September 12.[27] On September 17 Saddam Hussein, in a speech before the National Assembly, formally abrogated the 1975 agreement, asserted complete Iraqi sovereignty over Shatt-al-Arab, demanded the return of the Arab islands of Abu Musa and the Tunbs, and extended Iraq's support to Iran's minorities.[28] On the same day, Iraqi envoys visited all the countries of the Arabian Peninsula except PDRY to explain their government's plans and returned home claiming to have obtained the support of all the governments they visited. The Saudis, again, neither confirmed nor denied the claim. On September 22, 1980, the Iraqi air force launched a massive attack against ten Iranian airfields in an attempt to cripple the Iranian air force on the ground, and the next day Iraqi armored columns struck in the direction of Abadan and Khorramshahr, Ahwaz, and Dezful.

Gulf War Perils, Relief, Opportunities, September 1980 – June 1981

The Saudis' reluctant decision to support Iraq's war project discreetly was, typically, prompted by a desire to relieve short-term dangers even at the cost of intensifying long-term strategic threats. It counted on Iraq's defeating Iran quickly and thus removing the immediate problems presented by the latter, and put aside concern about the resulting Iraqi hegemony in the Gulf and Arab arenas. The actual course of the war, however, produced an opposite situation. On the one hand, Iraq's attempt to deal Iran a knockout blow failed, leaving the latter's air force and navy in a position to inflict immediate grievous damage on the oil facilities and shipping lanes of Iraq and its supporters, including Saudi Arabia. On the other hand, the stalemate that jelled in the battlefield after Iraq's failure relieved the Saudis of any major imminent strategic risks and gave them time and unexpected opportunities to strengthen themselves against likely eventualities.

The Saudi response to the immediate Iranian threat to their facilities and transit routes was to take the unprecedented step of openly calling for American military assistance. Once that threat was brought under control, the Saudis adjusted to the stalemate in the battlefield by restricting their commitment to Iraq so as not to provoke Iran, and by trying to play the role of indirect mediator between the belligerents through the Islamic Conference. They hoped to promote a settlement without victor or vanquished, which would have best served their long-term strategic interests; however, although that hope proved futile, their mediating endeavor served to advance several other objectives. It helped them maintain a safe semineutral position for a while. It helped them take advantage of the stalemate to advance their security connection with Pakistan. Most important from their point of view, it helped them capitalize on Iraq's and Iran's absorption in the war and on the fears of the Gulf countries to rally the latter to a disguised collective security organization under their aegis. Finally, it made their quest for more American arms less provocative to either of the belligerents than it might have been.

The Iraqi war plans envisaged a short, sharp campaign leading to the collapse of Iran's revolutionary regime or its acceptance of capitulatory terms. They called for an initial devastating blow against Iran's main airfields that would cripple them, destroy most of the air force on the ground and secure Iraqi control of the skies. Simultaneously, armored and mechanized formations were to advance rapidly to capture the eastern shore of Shatt-al-Arab with its ports and refineries, slice and seize Iran's oil-producing province of Khuzistan (called Arabistan by the Iraqis because of its majority of ethnic Arabs), defeat the main body of Iran's army, trigger secessions in the outlying provinces, and cause a breakdown of will at the center. The Iranian navy would have little opportunity to play an effective role before the whole campaign was over. In retrospect, Iraq's plans may appear to have been foolishly sanguine; but the consensus among analysts at the time was that revolutionary Iran was tottering and needed only a push to collapse. Iran's armed forces in particular, though large on paper, were supposedly in total disarray due to lack of coherent political leadership, decimation of the officer corps by executions and purges, mass desertions and demoralization among the ranks, deteriorated equipment through neglect, and a shortage of supplies and parts as a result of the American embargo. So confident were the Iraqis of their prognoses that they initially committed only three or four divisions of their thirteen divisions to the campaign.

Iraq's plans went wrong almost from the outset. In the air, the attempt to suppress Iran's air force in the first two days was a total failure. According to one American military analyst, "it did virtually no damage" and did not even significantly delay Iranian air force operations.[29] Indeed, on the second day of the war the Iranian air force struck back at Iraqi airfields so effectively as to compel the Iraqi high command to disperse its air force to bases in Jordan, Kuwait, Saudi Arabia, the UAE, Oman, and North Yemen.[30] Moreover, as Iraq's ground forces and artillery pounded Iran's oil outlets and commercial ports of Khorramshahr and Bandar Khomeini and its refinery at Abadan, the Iranian air force responded with effective attacks on Iraqi economic targets and oil facilities, civilian as well as military objectives in Baghdad, Mosul, Basra, Kirkuk, Khaniqin, and elsewhere. The Iraqi air force responded, of course, in kind, but it was clear a few days after the start of hostilities that the air war had got out of hand and that neither side's air defense was of much use in preventing indiscriminate ravages by the other.

On the ground, the Iraqi forces captured some border towns in the northern sector and probed toward Kermanshah, on the Baghdad-Tehran highway, for a few days before halting. In the central sector they attacked in two prongs: one toward Dezful, with its pumping station crucial to the pipelines from Iran's southern oil fields to Tehran, its air base, and its hydroelectric dam; and one toward Ahwaz, the provincial capital of Khuzistan. By the end of the first week both forces had reached the outskirts of their respective targets but were halted there by Iranian resistance. The heaviest battle took place in the Shatt-al-Arab sector, in the south. After ten days of fighting, Iraqi forces captured Khorramshahr's port area but were barred from entering the city itself. On the same day, October 2, 1980, the Iraqi high command announced that since its forces had "reached their basic objectives, their military activities will henceforth be limited to retaining the targets gained."[31] On October 11 the Iraqis bypassed Khorramshahr and tried to take Abadan after isolating it, but stubborn Iranian resistance forced them to content themselves with laying siege to the city. By that time the fighting had decidedly settled down to a war of attrition.

Even before the stalemate set in, Iraq's failure to neutralize Iran's air force raised some critical and urgent security problems for the Saudis. Much as they attempted to keep their support for Iraq discreet, Iran considered them to be Iraq's allies and might decide to turn against them any moment. Besides, when the Iraqi high command sought to disperse its air force after the successful attacks on its bases by the Iranian air force, the Saudis could not refuse to provide a haven for the Iraqi aircraft, and thus gave the Iranians specific reason to want to attack them. Were the Iranians to decide to do so, Saudi Arabia's oil facilities presented an easy and inviting target. Concentrated offshore and within forty miles of the coast, they could be struck with virtually no warning by aircraft approaching over Gulf waters. Selective attacks on them could either hurt Saudi Arabia badly and cripple its ability to help Iraq financially or, if that suited Iran's plans better, simply ignite an alarm signal that would internationalize the conflict.

Another critical problem confronting the Saudis had to do with oil transit in and through the Gulf. Iraq's war plans had ignored the far superior Iranian navy on the assumption that the war would be over before there was time for it to come into effective play. This assumption, in turn, had depended on the expectation that the Iranian air force would be promptly disposed of. The failure of those plans not only led to Iran's effective blockade of Iraq's ports at the head of the Gulf, but also left the Iranian navy in a position to interfere with the traffic of Iraq's allies, if and when that suited Iran's calculations. Again, the fact that Iraqi ships sought haven in Saudi and other Gulf ports provided an added provocation to the Iranian regime, which had in any case demonstrated an unpredictable pattern of behavior.

To meet those threats the Saudis felt compelled to seek American help. Urgent consultations between the two countries at the highest levels began shortly after the outbreak of hostilities and covered security issues as well as increased Saudi oil production to make up for some of the Iraqi and Iranian supplies disrupted by the war. The United States wanted its assistance to the Kingdom to be visible yet nonprovocative to the Iranians, lest they harm the American hostages. Washington therefore proposed to station four AWACS aircraft with several hundred support personnel on Saudi soil, to be backed up in case of need by American F-15 fighters, and to establish a joint American-Saudi naval task force to secure free navigation. At the same time it urged the Saudis not to permit Iraqi forces to launch any attacks from their own territory.[32] The Saudis were even more anxious to avoid provoking Iran and wanted the American help to be less visible. Consequently they rejected the idea of a joint naval task force, since they could count on the United States to secure the transit of oil on its own, for its own reasons. Regarding the deployment of American aircraft, however, their collaboration was inescapable, and they therefore yielded to American insistence that they announce that the deployment was made at their request. Accordingly, on September 30, 1980, the Saudi Press Agency reported that Saudi Arabia had requested and would receive AWACS aircraft "in order to consolidate the Kingdom's air defense capabilities."[33] The next day Washington made a similar announcement and also sent a note to Iran assuring it of its continued neutrality.[34]

Once the urgent and critical threats raised by the failure of Iraq's war plans were met, the ensuing stalemate was potentially much more advantageous to the Saudis than an Iraqi victory would have been. For one thing, the Saudis did not have to confront the serious strategic consequences of a triumphant Iraq, at least not for the time being; and time was a commodity the Saudis almost instinctively appreciated. For another thing, the longer the deadlock in the battlefield lasted, the greater the chances that the conflict would eventually be settled by negotiations and compromise, which would leave the belligerents in a state in which they checked and balanced each other indefinitely. (The idea that Iran might win the war was not even imagined at the time.) However, those potential advantages depended on some prior conditions, one of which was the Saudis' successful management of Iraqi demands for assistance, badly needed to sustain a prolonged war of attrition.

At the outset of the hostilities, when a quick Iraqi victory was taken for granted, Jordan and the YAR had immediately proclaimed their support for Iraq, whereas Iran's Arab friends, Syria, Libya, and the PLO, had called for an immediate cease-fire and mediation. The Saudis, although they had discreetly endorsed Iraq's war project, typically remained silent. The Iraqis had tried to force their hand by announcing over Baghdad Radio on September 25, 1980, that King Khaled had "affirmed Saudi Arabia's support for Iraq in its [Arab] national battle against the Persians";[35] however, the Saudis made it a point to correct that announcement the next day by stating through the Saudi Press Agency that King Khaled had expressed only "his interest and good fraternal feelings."[36] In a speech to the nation on September 28 Saddam Hussein had attacked proponents of "so-called mediation" but had expressed reluctant tolerance toward countries that adopted "stands of silence," understood to include Saudi Arabia and the smaller Gulf countries.[37] That tolerance probably reflected the Iraqi leader's recognition even then that he would need their practical support because of the situation that was developing in the battlefield.

The prospect of a prolonged war confronted Iraq with two crucial problems, both arising from Iran's blockade of Iraq's only ports: one had to do with military and civilian supplies, and the other with financing the war despite the disruption of oil exports. Even before the war, Jordan had agreed to put its only port, Aqaba, at Iraq's disposal; but Aqaba was already heavily taxed, and the goods and materiel arriving there had to be trucked a long distance to Iraq over a narrow and, for the most part, heavily used road. Traffic from Mediterranean ports was under the control of hostile Syria. The Iraqis therefore badly needed access to the ports of Saudi Arabia and the Gulf countries. Regarding exports, the only outlets for Iraqi oil apart from the blockaded port of Basra were two pipelines, one going through Syria, with a throughput capacity of 1.5

mbd, the other going through Turkey, with a throughput capacity of 700,000 barrels a day.[38] The first was clearly subject to Syria's mercy; the second could accommodate only a portion of Iraq's prewar export level of 3.5 mbd, and even it was not immune from disruption, for a section of it passed not far from the Syrian-Turkish border. If Iraq were to fight a long war, it needed massive financial assistance to compensate for the drastic cut in oil revenues, especially since its regime did not feel that the war was sufficiently popular and its own position sufficiently secure to permit it to suspend ongoing development projects, let alone impose drastic austerity measures.

The issues were brought to a head in the second and third weeks of October 1980. On October 9 the Iraqi oil minister visited Riyadh and met with all the top Saudi leaders — Khaled, Fahd, Abdallah, and Sultan — to discuss ways to help Iraq deal with the oil export problem, possibly including Saudi production on Iraq's account, to be repaid with future Iraqi production. On October 11 King Hussein of Jordan met the Saudi leaders in Riyadh, reportedly to discuss Jordanian-Saudi plans to help Iraq.[39] On October 20 it was the turn of the Iraqi defense minister to come to Riyadh and meet with the same team of Saudi chiefs. The specific results of these discussions are not known; however, subsequent events indicate that the Saudis endeavored to find ways to accommodate Iraq's needs without associating themselves so closely with that country as to provoke Iran.

On November 3, 1980, for instance, it was reported that the Saudis directed the firms in charge of marketing their oil to meet the needs of nations hurt by the war.[40] That meant primarily filling the gap left by Iraq under the production credit scheme, although in principle the directive was also applicable to customers of Iran, whose exports were affected much less than Iraq's. On the logistics question, it was reported on November 21 that the Saudis had made their Red Sea ports available for shipment of military equipment to Iraq.[41] Three weeks later, however, on December 13, Defense Minister Sultan denied specific reports that Yanbo was being used to supply Soviet arms to Iraq,[42] and about two months afterward Sultan again denied a report that Saudi Arabia was allowing a transshipment of Soviet tanks to Iraq.[43] It seems likely that at this stage the Saudis had worked out a division of labor between themselves and Jordan. While Jordan, as a declared ally of Iraq, made Aqaba available for the transshipment of weapons, the Saudis acted as a friendly neutral, allowing use of their Red Sea ports, but not their Gulf ports, for the transshipment of civilian supplies and perhaps of some nonlethal military equipment, but not of major combat weapons. As for the allegations and denials about the transshipment of tanks, the explanation may be that some ships put in both at Aqaba and at Saudi ports.

Whatever the actual arrangements made, it is clear that at this stage they were deemed acceptable by Iraq and tolerable by Iran. Iraq, for instance, cooperated fully with the Saudis on such issues as the convening of the eleventh Arab summit at Amman, which was boycotted by Syria and its Steadfastness Front allies, and supported the rump summit's resolutions calling for a peaceful settlement in the Gulf war and expressing only general support for Iraq's "legitimate rights" (see Chapter 13). Iran's attitude toward Saudi Arabia was reflected indirectly but clearly through the contrast of its behavior toward Kuwait, which cooperated more closely with Iraq for lack of choice.

On November 12, 1980, for instance, Iranian aircraft fired two missiles in the Abdali area in northern Kuwait, aimed at no specific target. The Kuwaiti media first reported that the missiles had been fired by "unidentified" aircraft, then that the Kuwaiti government had protested to Iran, and then that the attack had been inadvertent. On November 16, however, a larger attack was reported to have taken place in the same region. Kuwait protested again, and Saudi Arabia and the other Gulf countries expressed support. The Iranian government, however, denied the attacks and stressed its commitment to Kuwait's sovereignty.[44] The incident suggests clearly that at this stage the Iranian regime intended to signal the Kuwaitis that they were straining the limits of its tolerance in their support for Iraq, and sought to warn both them and their neighbors that it was capable of punishing them if they did not modify their behavior. At the same time, by denying responsibility for the attacks (which were to be repeated, targeted to hurt, and acknowledged at a later stage), Iran sought to avoid driving the Kuwaitis and the others, including the Saudis, irrevocably into Iraq's arms. Perhaps a related motive was the thought of sparing Iran's Arab allies—Syria, Libya, and the PLO—further embarrassment by openly attacking a country with which the latter were on friendly terms.

Iran's attitude toward Saudi Arabia at this stage was prompted by two additional motives. Until he was overthrown by the revolutionaries in June 1981, President Bani Sadr maintained secret contacts with the United States aimed at resolving the hostage problem and thus clearing the way for possible American supplies that would help Iran's war effort.[45] Avoiding a clash with the Saudis, if at all possible, was necessary for advancing that goal. Moreover, Bani Sadr hoped that by keeping relations with Saudi Arabia at a mutually tolerable level, he would preserve the possibility of direct or indirect Saudi mediation to end the conflict with Iraq, if and when the opportunity presented itself and Iran's internal politics permitted it.

The Saudis, for their part, had contemplated the possibility of attempting mediation through the Islamic Conference for some time but had looked for the appropriate moment to do so. At the outbreak of the war, foreign ministers of the member countries of the Islamic Conference who were in New York for the UN General Assembly meeting had consulted informally on the desirability of delegating Pakistan's President Zia ul-Haq and the secretary general of the organization, Habib Chatti, to act as mediators. The Saudis had favored a more formal meeting of conference foreign ministers to test the positions of the Iranian and Iraqi members first, since the situation on the battlefield was still fluid and both belligerents viewed mediation with apprehension; but the others had had their way and the Saudis had gone along. Zia and Chatti had gone to Tehran and Baghdad on September 29, 1980, and had quickly found that there was no basis for their effort. One month later, after the battlefront had become stabilized, Chatti met with Prince Abdallah in Riyadh on October 28 in an endeavor to reactivate the Islamic mediation effort on a more formal basis, but the Saudi leadership was in the midst of working out the delicate arrangements to assist Iraq and wanted to test them before undertaking a conference initiative. Moreover, Crown Prince Fahd and Interior Minister Nayef apparently wanted to undertake certain strategic initiatives with the smaller Gulf countries and with Pakistan before attempting to activate the Islamic Conference organization, and there was also the distraction caused by the Saudi split with Syria and its allies over the Amman summit and the Syrian-Jordanian military confrontation in late November and early December 1980 (see Chapter 13). By December the Saudis felt that the conditions were finally ripe for calling a formal conference, and arranged to have one scheduled to meet in Ta'if in January 1981.

The conference began with a preparatory meeting of foreign ministers on January 17–22, 1981, and was followed by a summit of organization members on January 24–30. The Iranians refused to attend either level because of the presence of Iraqi representatives, but they did not object to the conference and accepted its results, which included the formation of a mediation commission composed of the leaders of Bangladesh, Pakistan, Guinea, and the PLO. Although Saudi Arabia was not a member of the commission, it was the moving spirit behind the entire effort. Its representatives not only hosted the conference, chaired it, and steered it toward the resolutions it adopted, but they also presented to the commission specific ideas for approaching its task. The Iranian government acknowledged that role when it sent a delegation to Riyadh to discuss the mediation project with Fahd on February 16, before meeting with the formal commission. The latter did the same by meeting in Jidda on March 1 before setting off the same day for Tehran and Baghdad on its peace mission.

The commission presented the belligerents with a concrete two-part plan, one dealing with the principles for a settlement, the other containing specific proposals for a cease-fire, withdrawal, and negotiations. The Iranian government was reported to be receptive to the plan, but the Supreme Defense Council, dominated by the revolutionaries, rejected it on March 6 on the grounds that it did not provide for unconditional Iraqi withdrawal and investigation of Iraq's "aggression," and that it suggested that the Shatt-al-Arab issue was open to negotiation, when, in the Iranian view, the matter had been settled by the 1975 Algiers agreement. The commission went back to work and returned on March 31, 1981, with modified proposals to meet some of Iran's objections. This time Bani Sadr agreed, but by April 4 he was overruled by the Islamic hardliners, who insisted that Saddam Hussein must resign or be deposed as part of any settlement. The clash over the commission's proposals intensified the internecine political struggle in Iran during the next few months, which resulted in a total and final defeat of Bani Sadr. On June 11, 1981, he was dismissed by Khomeini from his post as commander-in-chief of the armed forces, and six days later he was impeached as president and went into hiding.

The downfall of Bani Sadr ended whatever hopes the Saudis had entertained of advancing, through the Islamic Conference mission, a settlement without victory or defeat for either side. However, the endeavor itself was quite rewarding in other respects. In the first place, it facilitated the Saudis' adjustment to the problem they confronted after the stalemate set in. The preliminary talks about an Islamic Conference meeting helped the Saudis justify their semineutral position toward the belligerents, and the Ta'if conference, which was accepted by Iran despite its refusal to attend, legitimized that position further. In that context, Saudi Arabia was able to extend financial assistance to Iraq, starting with a $4 billion loan in April 1981,[46] without provoking Iran, even though the latter reacted to a similar $2 billion loan from Kuwait at the same time by seizing a Kuwaiti ship.[47]

Second, the involvement of Pakistan as well as Saudi Arabia in the Islamic mediation endeavors, coupled with the underlying stalemate, facilitated the advancement of the strategic defense connection between those two countries by reducing or removing any implication that it was directed at either Iran or Iraq. The easing of that implication, together with an apparent resolution of the disagreement among the Saudi rulers on the issue, revived the Saudi-Pakistani talks interrupted the previous August and brought them to a successful conclusion. Thus, on December 2, 1980, Interior Minister Nayef visited Pakistan, reportedly to discuss a Saudi security plan. Crown Prince Fahd followed shortly thereafter with a longer visit, from December 6 to 8, at the conclusion of which it was reported that Pakistan would deploy one division in the Kingdom in exchange for $1 billion of Saudi aid annually.[48]

Third, and most important in the view of the Saudis, the Islamic mediation endeavor made it easier to take advantage of Iraq's and Iran's absorption in the conflict to advance the long-sought project of a collective Gulf security organization under their own aegis, excluding both belligerents. On November 26, 1980, for instance, at a time when the smaller Gulf countries were agitated about the Iranian attacks on Kuwait two weeks before, Interior Minister Nayef had declared that Saudi Arabia would complete a series of bilateral security agreements with all the Gulf states as a first step toward a unified Gulf security arrangement.[49] Both Iraq and Iran had promptly objected for different reasons. Iraq resented being left out, and its foreign minister declared on November 30 that the countries concerned did not need an Arab defense pact to protect the Gulf because they were already bound together by the all-Arab collective security pact.[50] Iran, seeing the envisaged pact as an effort to rally the Arab countries against itself, had threatened to "take all necessary steps" against any security pact. Kuwait, the target of the recent Iranian attacks, was duly intimidated and denied that any security pact was intended.[51] In the face of these reactions, the Saudis had shelved the idea as they had so many times on similar occasions in the past.

After the Islamic Conference at Ta'if was successfully concluded, however, and the Islamic peace commission was launched with the assent of both Iraq and Iran, the Saudis revived their project and moved swiftly toward its realization. On February 4, 1981, they assembled the foreign ministers of the Gulf countries at a conference in Riyadh, which endorsed a Saudi proposal for a Gulf Cooperation Council. Saudi officials insisted at that point that the GCC was not a military or political bloc.[52] Ten days later, formal documents were signed at Riyadh; less than a month later, on March 9, the foreign ministers met again in Muscat and approved the statutes of the council. Promptly thereafter "Saudi sources" were reported as saying that the GCC would soon begin negotiations to "pool" military resources.[53] On May 25–26 the Supreme Council of the GCC, comprising the heads of state of the member countries, held its first meeting in Abu Dhabi and formally launched the organization. The Saudis' success in rapidly establishing an organization that had eluded their efforts for several years required the exercise of indirect approach diplomacy and an unusual degree of transparent make-believe; but circumstances allowed them to get away with it.

Thus the communiqué issued at the end of the Abu Dhabi meeting stated that the participants recognized "the inevitability of economic integration among their countries and a social merger among their peoples." In view of this and "the current circumstances of their states and the similar issues and problems they face," they had decided to set up institutions "that will make this economic integration and social merger a living reality." Apart from those oblique allusions, the communiqué said nothing about defense and security cooperation, the *raison d'être* of the GCC, except to assert that it was the responsibility of the countries of the area, so as not to offend Iraq and Iran. However, since the GCC countries were linked by a network of bilateral security agreements, including agreements between Saudi Arabia and each of the others, the omission of specific reference to defense and security did not matter much once an integrative framework was established.

The communiqué also sought to allay apprehensions about a possible link between the GCC and the American-promoted Gulf security measures by affirming the GCC's "absolute rejection of foreign interference in the region from any source" and calling for keeping the region free of conflicts, "particularly the presence of military fleets and foreign bases" —this at a time when Oman had a facilities agreement with the United States, when American AWACS aircraft stationed on Saudi soil protected that country's oil facilities, and when American and Western fleets secured the vital oil routes of the GCC countries. Finally, to allay apprehensions stirred by the Reagan administration's notion of "strategic consensus," the communiqué asserted that Gulf stability was linked to achieving a "just solution" of the Palestine question; yet it went on to say that the Iran-Iraq war, which was obviously unrelated to the Palestine question, was "one of the problems that threaten the region's security" and stressed the need to redouble the efforts to settle it.[54]

Fourth, the stalemate and the indirect mediation endeavor gave the Saudis a chance to modify their posture of dependence on the United States as a result of their call for American military assistance. The deployment of American AWACS aircraft and personnel on Saudi soil in the critical first week of the war had occurred when the Saudis also had a request pending for a major American arms transaction and was followed on October 11 by an announcement that the United States was sending additional men and equipment to the region, including two KC-130 refueling planes and their personnel to Saudi Arabia and a missile cruiser to the Gulf.[55] Necessary as all these acts may have been, the Saudis felt uneasy about the reality and impression of increased dependence they conveyed, and about the effect of both on their own bargaining position with the United States and on the positions of Syria, Egypt, and the Gulf countries. The stalemate and the mediation endeavor gave the Saudis an opportunity to distance themselves from the United States and thus place themselves in a position to pursue additional American assistance without sacrificing room for maneuver.

At about the time the stalemate in the war had definitely set in and the Saudis had begun to work on the idea of an Islamic conference, President Carter had stated on October 23, 1980, that he had decided to reject the Saudi request for bomb racks for the F-15s.[56] The Saudis complained that

Carter had broken a pledge to defer the issue until after the election, and took advantage of the occasion to assert their independence by threatening to buy weapons elsewhere.[57] On December 10, 1980, President Brezhnev, addressing India's parliament, had proposed a series of principles to govern the superpowers' approach to the Persian Gulf, which would essentially neutralize the area.[58] The Saudis at first denounced the proposal by invoking the Soviet occupation of Afghanistan but then let out, on December 22, that they took a less critical view of it. They cited their support for the idea of keeping the Gulf out of international conflicts but also called on the USSR to demonstrate its good intentions by leaving Afghanistan.[59] At the Ta'if Islamic conference itself, Fahd included, in the opening speech he gave in the name of King Khaled, an appeal to the Muslim nations to resist military alliances with the superpowers, and sought to underscore the Kingdom's independent policy toward the United States and the Soviet Union by citing the occupation of Jerusalem and of Afghanistan as major challenges facing the Islamic world.[60]

Once they ostensibly corrected the impression of being a client of the United States, and once the Islamic mediation effort was launched, the Saudis pressed for a decision on their outstanding request for arms from the United States but were careful to avoid slipping back into a compromising position. Thus, when Secretary of State Haig tried, on his visit to the Kingdom on April 8, 1981, to elicit an endorsement of his "strategic consensus" concept in recognition of American past assistance and present willingness to meet their request, the Saudis resisted him strongly in private and even more strongly in public. When the Reagan administration on April 21 formally announced its decision to sell to Saudi Arabia the five AWACS aircraft and the F-15 equipment, Defense Minister Sultan welcomed the decision the next day and Interior Minister Nayef did the same four days later, but both were careful to couple their expressions of satisfaction with appeals to Iraq and Iran to end the conflict, and thus to underscore both the Kingdom's mediation role and its "innocent" motives in seeking the American arms.

New Perils and Anxious Temporizing,
June 1981–July 1982

The fall of Bani Sadr not only ended all hopes of a mediated settlement of the war but also decisively tilted the balance of power in Tehran in favor of the militant Islamic revolutionaries and began a period of unmitigated political confrontation between Iran and all its Arab Gulf neighbors. Initially the Saudis were not overly disturbed by the change. They took comfort in the fact that Iran remained paralyzed for a while by struggles among extremist factions, that the belligerents in the war continued to be locked in a stalemate, and that the American air and naval deployments protected their oil facilities and sea-lanes. The Saudis even tried to turn Iran's increased hostility toward the Arab Gulf countries and the first Iranian battlefield successes to advantage by seeking to develop the GCC into a more avowedly defense organization. This initial Saudi complacency was reinforced by the diplomatic success they were having at the same time in the Arab arena, which was reflected in their initiation and pursuit of the Fahd Plan (see Chapter 13).

In the last months of 1981, however, a series of new major threats developed that set the Saudis scurrying for means to meet them. At about the time that Syria defeated the Fahd Plan at the November 1981 Fez summit, Iran won a second major battle in two months, which portended a turn of the war tide in its favor. A few days later, the discovery of a major Iranian plot to destabilize Bahrain and Saudi Arabia brought to a climax a period of propaganda war and drove home to the Saudis the point that a victorious militant Iran would pursue its revolutionary goals in the Gulf by means of the dreaded combination of external pressure and internal subversion. The Saudis sought to meet that danger by trying to shore up Iraq and rally Syria to a united Arab front, or at least to neutralize its hostility to Iraq and its friends; but another major Iranian victory at the end of March 1982 foiled the Saudis' efforts, and yet another Iranian victory five weeks later made a final collapse of the Iraqi regime appear imminent.

The Saudis tried indirectly to enlist Egyptian military intervention to save Iraq and check Iran. When Egypt refused, the Saudis turned again to Syria, seeking its intercession with Iran, and looked to the United States for help but without giving any sign of seeking it. The United States responded with some indirect warnings to Iran, but these did not prevent the latter from launching an invasion of Iraq in July 1982 in an effort to deal its foe the coup de grâce. Washington next proposed joint military measures of a deterrent character, but these were particularly painful to the Saudis to contemplate because the United States appeared at the time to be implicated on Israel's side in the Lebanon war. Even as the Saudis struggled with the dilemma, fate came to their rescue, as it had on so many occasions before. On July 21, 1982, after a costly weeklong battle, the Iraqi forces, fighting on their own soil and enjoying the advantage of shortened lines of communication, were at last able to stop the Iranian offensive. King Khaled's successors thus got a reprieve, which they have enjoyed to the present.

On June 11, 1981, the day on which Khomeini dismissed Bani Sadr as commander-in-chief, Iranian aircraft attacked a Kuwaiti border post. The Kuwaitis were understandably agitated, but the Saudis took the matter in their stride after having registered the obligatory expression of support for their neighbor. Their lack of concern was partly due to the fact, itself rooted in the stalemate in the battlefield, that the Iranians did not admit to their action; this reticence suggested that they were continuing their policy of seeking to warn the Arab Gulf countries against excessive aid to Iraq but still wanted to avoid confrontation with them. But the Saudis' equanimity also stemmed from their belief that the raid at once served to justify their own resort to American AWACS assistance, their quest for American air defense equipment, and their endeavor to develop the GCC's military role. During the following weeks developments inside Iran reinforced, or at least did nothing to alter, the Saudis' relatively relaxed disposition. On June 29, 1981, the struggle among extremist factions reached a climax when an explosion shattered a meeting of the Islamic Republican party, killed and injured scores of leaders, and triggered a wave of assassinations, executions, and arrests that sucked the country into a whirlpool of terror and totally absorbed its attention.

In the summer of 1981 the Saudis still felt sufficiently confident about the situation in the Gulf to devote much of their attention and energy to the Arab arena, where they followed up their success in defusing the complex crisis in Lebanon with the atypically ambitious undertaking centered on the Fahd Plan (see Chapter 13). In late September and early October, however, developments nearer home gave them pause. On September 22 Iranian pilgrims clashed with Saudi police in the first of a series of incidents that spanned several weeks, during which the Saudis took sanctions against some Iranians for rowdy behavior and attempts to make political propaganda, while the Iranian authorities charged the Saudis with harassment and discrimination against Iranian pilgrims.[61] On September 29 Iranian forces launched their first major successful counterattack in the war, broke the siege of Abadan, and compelled the Iraqi forces to retreat in disorder. On October 1, 1981, Iranian aircraft attacked a Kuwaiti oil storage facility and the Iranian government for the first time acknowledged responsibility.

The Saudis promptly recognized Iran's switch to a confrontational approach but did not grasp for a while all the potential implications of its Abadan victory. They tended to view the latter more as a local success, which might soften Iraq's position and thus facilitate a settlement, than as a sign of a decisive turn in the tide of the war, which could have far-reaching strategic implications for themselves. Consequently, until further developments in the battlefield forced them to revise their view, their reaction concentrated on Iran's switch in style, and that reaction, typically, fluctuated.

The Saudi response to the first disturbance involving the Iranian pilgrims was prompt and firm. The agitators were forcibly restrained and expelled, and the minister of interior issued a stiff statement on September 26 that gave the lie to the Radio Tehran version of the incident and warned that anyone seeking to make propaganda or found carrying publications or photographs would be "returned to his point of origin."[62] As the incidents continued and the Iranian media sustained their attacks against the Saudis, King Khaled appealed directly to Khomeini on October 6, "reporting" to him the actions of the Iranian pilgrims and urging him to instruct their leaders to stop perpetrating acts that contravened the sanctity of the pilgrimage.[63] On October 19 Minister of Interior Nayef himself maintained the conciliatory tone while rebutting charges made by Radio Tehran on the demonstrations and clashes.[64] By early November, however, the Saudis gave up their attempts to appease Iran and switched to full-scale propaganda counterattack. On November 8, for instance, Radio Riyadh broadcast an unattributed commentary in which it denounced the Iranian rulers as "a disgrace to Islam," a rancorous group that "acts for the devil." They had set up gallows for children and daily ushered scores of men and women like herds toward the slaughterhouse. They had falsely charged that the AWACS planes had been flying over the holy mosques, when they had themselves been supplying themselves with arms from Israel, and so on. The diatribe concluded with a statement that the nooses of the gallows that the Iranian rulers had set up for others had begun to tighten around their own necks, and that they tried to escape by attacking others.[65] Attacks of this kind continued throughout the month.

The initial Saudi response to the October 1 attack on the Kuwaiti oil storage facilities was formulated when they were still trying to calm the pilgrims' dispute and was rather mild; the Saudi royal court merely issued a statement condemning the attack as "unjustified aggression."[66] As that dispute deteriorated, the Saudis availed themselves of the tension generated by it as well as by the Iranian attack on Kuwait in order to press the GCC to expand its aims explicitly to the military sphere, on the theory that there was nothing left to lose from such a development as far as Iran was concerned. Thus, on November 4 Defense Minister Sultan began discussing the need to form an "advanced defense group" to coordinate GCC military forces.[67] At the second meeting of the GCC summit, on November 9–11, the question of military cooperation was placed on the agenda for the first time, and a decision was taken to have the GCC defense ministers meet in Riyadh the following month to discuss plans to put the idea into effect.[68]

Before any such meeting took place, however, the Iranians launched another successful offensive, this time in the Bostan area of the central sector, starting on November 29, 1981. After a weeklong battle involving heavy losses on both sides, the Iranians reoccupied Bostan and seized control of its surroundings, thus cutting off communications and logistical links between the Iraqi forces at Dezful and Ahwaz and developing major threats to the two Iraqi bulges that were formed as a result. More-over, one week after the Iranian victory, on December 13, 1981, the Bahrain authorities announced that they had uncovered a major Iranian-instigated plot to overthrow the government and destabilize Saudi Arabia. The conspirators' plan was to use a "network of saboteurs" trained in Iran to set off explosions and assassinate officials in National Day dem-onstrations while Radio Tehran urged support for the disruptions. The authorities said that sixty people, including thirteen Saudis, had been arrested and that arms caches had been discovered. The leader of the conspiracy was said to be Hojjatolislam (a religious title below ayatollah) Hadi Modarresi, a Shi'ite cleric who had fled to Bahrain during the shah's rule.[69]

The Bahrain plot demonstrated to the Saudis the intent of Iran's ruling Islamic revolutionaries to go beyond the war of words and to export their revolution by instigating terrorism and subversion; the Bostan victory, following within two months that of Abadan, drove home to the Saudis the very real possibility that the Iranians might soon defeat Iraq alto-gether. The combination of those two developments was all the more frightening because it coincided closely with the blow inflicted on the Saudis by the Syrians and their allies on November 25, which led to the collapse of the Fahd Plan — a blow that was made all the more painful by Iraq's joining the plan's opponents (see Chapter 13). The Saudis' response to that conjuncture was rather surprising, reflecting perhaps the seesaw-ing of policy in moments of crisis that is inherent in collective leadership.

Immediately after the announcement of the discovery of the plot, Saudi Minister of Interior Nayef denounced Iran publicly, in contrast to the other small Gulf states, which expressed support for Bahrain but refrained from mentioning Iran's involvement.[70] On December 19 Nayef went to Bahrain to sign a bilateral security agreement with it and used the occasion to repeat the charge that the plot was engineered by the Iranian government, assert that the conspiracy was directed at Saudi Arabia, attribute to the Iranians the intent of exporting the revolution, and denounce them as "the Gulf's terrorists."[71] Surprisingly, however, the meeting of GCC defense ministers previously scheduled for December was not held; instead the GCC's secretary general announced on De-cember 21 that the council's *interior* ministers would meet in Riyadh on February 9 and 10 — seven weeks thence — to discuss internal security in light of the Bahrain plot.[72] In other words, just when the activation of the GCC as a defense and security body was most necessary, it was put off to a time when it might be less relevant. A similar pattern manifested itself on December 23, when, instead of activating the American security connection, the Saudis announced the cancellation of Crown Prince Fahd's previously scheduled visit to the United States.

Probably the Saudis postponed the GCC meeting because of their inability to rally some of the frightened members to what might look like a confrontational stance against Iran. That fear was sufficiently overcome in the next month to make possible a meeting of the GCC defense ministers on January 25, 1982, but not enough to permit the publication of any statement about the decisions reached. Most probably the decisions had something to do with the Kingdom's signing, in the last week of February, of separate bilateral security agreements with Qatar, the UAE, and Oman. Kuwait promised to follow suit but did not do so. Other decisions probably centered on ways to shore up Iraq's position without provoking Iran.

The immediate reason for the cancellation of Fahd's visit to the United States was his preoccupation with the ramifications of the Bahrain coup attempt, which a U.S. defense official later characterized as "a much closer thing than most people realize."[73] Basically, however, it stemmed from the decision of the Saudi rulers to pursue at that point an alternative response to the crisis they faced, which called for deemphasizing their American connection rather than stressing it. That alternative was to try to shore up their own and Iraq's positions through initiatives in the Arab arena and the Yemens, but particularly in their relations with Syria.

Syria's regime had recently been embarrassed by Israel's annexation of the Golan Heights on December 14, 1981, and faced mounting difficulties with the Muslim Brethren at home. The Saudis tried to take advantage of that situation to work out a deal with President Assad during a visit he made to Riyadh on December 22 and 23, 1981. They agreed to bury their grudge against Syria in connection with the Fahd Plan — indeed, to bury effectively the Fahd Plan itself — and to concede to various demands that they support Syria's arms acquisition efforts and change their attitude toward the Soviet Union. In exchange, Syria agreed to the need to close Arab ranks, and particularly to desist from any hostile acts toward Iraq and its Jordanian ally (see Chapter 13). In the wake of that understanding, Jordan's King Hussein felt sufficiently reassured about his Syrian flank to issue in January 1982 a call for volunteers to fight on Iraq's side, but not enough to send regular Jordanian forces, as the Saudis may have wished him to do.

The Saudi-Syrian understanding lasted long enough to affect the position the Saudis took in their discussions with U.S. Secretary of Defense Weinberger, who visited the Kingdom on February 5, 1982, as part of a tour that also included Oman and Jordan. The Saudis sought from Weinberger American assistance in establishing a Gulf arms industry, which would help them consolidate and develop the GCC, and urged him to supply Jordan with advanced weapons, which would strengthen its ability to withstand Syrian pressure and contribute to Gulf security. Weinberger expressed support for both requests and got the Saudis to agree, in return, to the creation of a joint Saudi-American defense planning committee. On February 8, however, immediately after Weinberger's visit, Saudi "officials and military officers" were cited as having expressed their concern to the secretary over "fundamental differences" between American and Saudi views on the Middle East.[74] On February 15, 1982, Saudi Information Minister Muhammad Yamani stated that the defense planning committee would be "confined to following up the Kingdom's purchases from abroad. Whatever else has been said has no foundation whatsoever."[75]

Not long thereafter, however, the Saudi-Syrian understanding unraveled completely, even as the war took yet another critical turn against Iraq. Around the time of Weinberger's visit, several Arab parties had accelerated efforts to bring Egypt back into the Arab fold despite its treaty with Israel, in order to secure its help in facing the Iranian danger. Iraq, which had presided over the March 1979 Baghdad conference that had decreed sanctions against Egypt, declared in the first week of February 1982 that it would welcome Egypt's return to the Arab fold, and specifically invited President Mubarak to attend the nonaligned summit scheduled to meet in Baghdad the following September.[76] Jordan's King Hussein enthusiastically chimed in with the Iraqi statement.[77] There were reports at the same time that several thousand Egyptians, including former army officers, had been recruited as volunteers to serve with Iraq's armed forces.[78] The Saudis followed a week later with a statement by the minister of information that the Kingdom was ready to welcome Egypt back into the Arab ranks.[79] These moves deeply troubled the Syrians, who saw them as an attempt, in the name of Arab detente, to isolate them and accept the Egyptian-Israeli treaty with all its strategic implications.

The efforts to reinstate Egypt reached a high point in March 1982, when a representative from Cairo attended the conference of the foreign ministers of nonaligned countries in Kuwait and there put forward a peace plan that was very close to the Fahd Plan and contained no reference to Camp David.[80] Syria's opposition to these efforts provoked the resentment of those who favored them. For instance, the well-informed London Arabic-language daily *al-Sharq al-Awsat* reported on March 18, 1982, that the GCC was considering cutting off all aid to Syria because of the latter's severe repression of the Muslim Brethren in Hama and its continuing hostility toward Jordan and Iraq. In the meanwhile, on March 22 the Iranians launched their third major offensive in the area of Dezful. Capitalizing on their previous victory at Bostan, they threw some 100,000 troops into a battle aimed at destroying the entire Iraqi central front, manned by some 70,000 troops. After a week of fighting the Iranians achieved their objective, captured 20,000 Iraqi prisoners, and placed themselves in a position either to advance into Iraq or to attack the remaining Iraqi forces in southern Khuzistan. Syria availed itself of the opportunity to help Iran's attempt to deal Iraq the final blow. It deployed diversionary forces on Iraq's borders, shipped arms to Iran, cut off the flow of Iraqi oil through the pipeline running across its territory, and called upon the Iraqi people to overthrow Saddam Hussein.[81]

These developments confronted the Saudi leaders with dilemmas that paralyzed their ability to make clear and sharp decisions. On the one hand, they were keenly aware of the danger of an Iraqi military collapse and were sensitive to the urgings of Iraq, Jordan, and their GCC partners as well as the United States to do everything possible to entice Egypt to come to the rescue. On the other hand, they were fearful of the consequences of breaking with Syria and giving further provocation to Iran precisely when the tide seemed to be going their way, and they were not even certain that Egypt would be willing and able to make enough of a contribution to alter the situation. They therefore decided to explore Egypt's intentions further and, in addition, to see if they could get Egypt to dilute its commitment to the autonomy part of the Camp David accords in order to weaken the cause for Syria's anticipated reaction.

Getting an open clarification of Egypt's position entailed some delay because of the nearness of the date for the completion of Israel's evacuation of Sinai. The statement of Egypt's representative at the Kuwait non-aligned conference had caused concern in Israel and the United States; as a result Egypt qualified its statement and was careful subsequently to avoid taking any public position that might endanger Israel's compliance. On April 25, 1982, Israel actually completed its pullout as scheduled, and the next day President Mubarak marked the occasion with a major speech before the National Assembly. Mubarak reaffirmed Egypt's commitment to the peace treaty with Israel but strongly qualified his country's position on the agreement regarding the Palestinian question. He criticized Israel's "colonization" plans for the West Bank and asserted that in seeking to resolve the Palestinian question Egypt must defer to the wishes of the Palestinian people. He then stressed the "historic links of destiny" between Egypt and the Gulf, stated that "we consider their security and stability an inseparable part of our strategic security," and concluded that "any threat to their safety will represent a dangerous situation which would be viewed by Egypt with profound concern."[82] Two days later, Egypt's Minister of State for Foreign Affairs Boutros Ghali made Mubarak's point somewhat stronger by stating that "Egypt is ready to defend any Arab state which is subjected to an invasion by a foreign country."[83]

While the Saudi leaders pondered the significance of Egypt's position for their own problem, the Iranians on April 30 launched their biggest offensive of the war in southern Khuzistan. In twenty-four days of fighting they drove the Iraqis into the port of Khorramshahr, surrounded them, and turned their attempt to escape into a total rout.[84] According to Iranian reports, 30,000 Iraqis were captured in a battle that essentially terminated the Iraqi invasion of Iran. The critical question was now whether Saddam Hussein would survive the defeat, and if he did, whether Iran would go after him by invading Iraq.

The Saudis, who had been conducting hectic consultations with Iraq, Pakistan, and their GCC partners, were spurred by the Iranian offensive to endorse a trip of Oman's Sultan Qabus to Egypt in the first week of May to find out if the Egyptians were specifically willing to intervene militarily on a large scale in the Gulf war and on what terms. After spending four days in Cairo, Qabus reported to a GCC meeting convened on May 15, 1982, that the Egyptians were studying the question and would respond soon, whereupon the GCC adjourned for two weeks to await Egypt's reply.

On May 17, 1982, the Egyptian defense minister, Field Marshal Abu Ghazala, announced his government's decision definitely not to send troops to Iraq.[85] As the situation in the battlefield deteriorated further, the Iraqis and others appealed to Egypt to reconsider, but on May 29 President Mubarak himself confirmed the decision.[86] Much as Egypt wished to return to the Arab fold and resume its position of leadership, the price asked for the privilege was more than it was willing or perhaps even able to pay.

With the failure of the Egyptian gambit, the Saudis were left with a few poor options or hopes. One was to turn to the Syrians again and, despite their unreliable recent behavior, urge them to intercede with their Iranian ally to refrain from invading Iraq, or at least to express their opposition to such action. The Syrians agreed, but not before exacting from the Saudis a public statement, made by Foreign Minister Saud al-Faisal, that Egypt could not return to the Arab ranks until the reasons for its isolation had disappeared.[87] Another option was to count on the United States, acting in its own interests, to restrain Iran without a specific Saudi request for aid or an open quid pro quo that would be compromising. A third was a hope that a combination of outside pressures on Iran, coupled with Iraqi amenability, would permit the ending of hostilities and open the way to mediation.

For a while it looked as though the Saudi hopes were going to be fulfilled. On May 21 Secretary of Defense Weinberger stated that an Iranian military victory over Iraq was not in America's interest;[88] on May 22 State Department officials were reported as saying that the United States was worried about the Iraqi setbacks and was quietly seeking help from Islamic nations such as Turkey, Malaysia, Pakistan, Indonesia, and

Algeria to put pressure on Khomeini to reach a settlement with Baghdad;[89] on May 26 Secretary of State Haig, in a major policy address in Chicago, stated that the United States would play "a more active role" in coming weeks in trying to end the war, and implicitly warned Iran that if it spread the conflict into neighboring nations, Washington would protect its "vital interests" in the Persian Gulf.[90] The American statements seemed to be having the desired effect on Tehran; two days after Haig's speech, the speaker of the Iranian parliament, Ali Akbar Rafsanjani, declared that Iran was not adventurous and would not seek to cut the flow of oil in the Gulf.[91] Finally, on May 29 Syria's President Assad asserted that he had had assurances from Iran that it would not invade Iraq.[92]

The Saudi hopes were further sustained when, on June 4, Iran made public its terms for ending the war. These were rather stiff and included a demand for $150 billion in reparations and a trial of Saddam Hussein; but the latter represented a "moderation" of Iran's previous insistence on the deposition of the Iraqi ruler, and the simultaneous acceptance of renewed Islamic mediation suggested that there might be room for further compromise on that question as well as on the amount of reparations. Moreover, on June 10, 1982, Saddam Hussein used the outbreak of the Lebanon war a few days earlier as an excuse to proclaim a unilateral cease-fire except if attacked; ten days later he sought to remove grounds for possible attack on his forces by declaring a unilateral withdrawal from all occupied Iranian territory.

All these hopes, however, came crashing down when Ayatollah Khomeini rejected on June 21, 1982, all the terms of settlement under discussion, and when Iranian forces began an invasion of Iraq on July 14, with a powerful thrust aimed at cutting off Basra and its vicinity. Syria, although it was itself caught in a losing war with Israel in Lebanon, expressed support for Iran.

In the midst of these developments King Khaled died on June 13, 1982. Although the succession itself proceeded smoothly, the issues of redistribution of power it opened up imposed an added measure of caution on the process of decision making, which was already half paralyzed by lack of agreement on specific reactions to the turn taken by the Gulf war, and strained by the demands made upon it by the Lebanon war. On July 16 the United States sought to give substance to its previous warnings to Iran by proposing to the Saudis joint military exercises of American, Saudi, and other GCC forces.[93] The Saudis, who had been playing a very delicate role in connection with the Lebanon war and were trying just then to serve as a bridge between Syria and the United States (see Chapter 13), did not want to jeopardize their effort by appearing to be more dependent than ever on the United States for their own security. At the same time, however, the failure of the "Arab strategy" and the reality of the Gulf situation pointed clearly to the need to activate the American last-resort option. Unable to resolve the dilemma, the Saudi rulers merely put off any decision and waited further upon events. These came to the rescue once more, in the shape of an unexpected failure of the Iranian offensive into Iraq and the onset of another long period of war of attrition.

15

The Yemens, 1979–1982: Living with the Problem

The March 1979 Kuwait pact terminating the war between the two Yemens confronted the Saudis with a new version of an old problem. Like the agreement that followed the 1972 war, the 1979 pact centered on an agreement between the two countries to merge. However, whereas the earlier union project had been actively supported mainly by Libya's Qaddafi under a loose Arab League sponsorship, the new agreement was the result of mediation by a strong Arab team representing countries of great strategic relevance to Saudi Arabia, such as Iraq, Syria, Algeria, Jordan, and Kuwait, and was embedded in the dynamics that produced the Baghdad core and anti–Camp David consensus.

The wide Arab support for the 1979 unity project compelled Saudi Arabia to endorse the idea formally, strengthened the hands of the two Yemens in pursuing it, and constrained the Saudis' ability to subvert it by manipulating North Yemen's political forces, as they had done with the 1972 project. But the Arab consensus against the American-promoted peace in which the 1979 agreement was embedded also introduced a new perspective into the behavior of PDRY, acting as a proxy for Soviet policy, which impelled it to seek to accommodate Saudi Arabia. Ironically, that perspective ultimately helped bail the Saudis out of the new version of their Yemen problem and by 1980 contributed to establishing a modus vivendi in southern Arabia that lasted beyond King Khaled's death. That modus vivendi, in turn, affected Saudi strategy in the Gulf and elsewhere.

The general pattern of development unfolded in two phases separated by a brief transitional period. The first phase, lasting from March 1979 until the end of the year, was characterized by mounting strain between Saudi Arabia and the YAR, and, paradoxically, an opposite tendency in Saudi-PDRY relations. At the turn of the year, the strain in Saudi-YAR relations reached the point of confrontation, even as the Soviet invasion of Afghanistan disrupted the incipient Saudi-PDRY detente. However, the very fears of intensified Soviet pressures in the region and of possible American-Saudi counterpressures against PDRY that had led to the disruption of the detente in Saudi-PDRY relations generated a renewed understanding that not only led to a resumption of the rapprochement but also helped repair the breach between Saudi Arabia and the YAR and usher in a modus vivendi phase among all three countries.

The strain between Saudi Arabia and the YAR was triggered by a familiar mechanism. Following the Kuwait agreement, President Saleh, confident in the support of radical Arab parties such as Iraq, Syria, and Algeria, sought to reinforce the central government and tried to reach an accommodation with the radical, pro-unity, anti-Saudi National Democratic Front opposition, with a view to advancing the unity project. The Saudis, resenting Saleh's attempt to conciliate their enemies so soon after they had helped him in the war against the NDF and PDRY, and fearing the assertion of central government control over the northern tribes, their ultimate source of leverage over Yemeni affairs, sought to constrain his power. They therefore restricted the supply of American arms to the YAR that they had acquired for it during the previous months of crisis and war and over which they had retained control. Saleh reacted by trying to deal directly with Washington in June 1979, and when that attempt failed, he turned to Moscow in July and August and concluded a major arms agreement with it. In the interim the Saudis had supported a revolt of their client tribes against Saleh, and when that attempt failed, they tried to bring his government to heel by cutting off all aid to it at the beginning of 1980.

The improvement in Saudi-PDRY relations was stimulated by the fact that President Abd al-Fattah Isma'il looked at the Kuwait agreement through the eyes of Moscow, and that Moscow, in turn, looked at it in a broad regional context that indicated a carefully conciliatory policy toward Saudi Arabia and the YAR. On the one hand, the Soviets were pleased by the emergence at Baghdad of an Arab consensus, to which PDRY was a party, against the American-promoted Camp David peace process. They wanted to keep the Yemeni unity project, about which they were rightly skeptical, from undermining the Saudis' adherence to that consensus and driving them back into close alignment with the United States. On the other hand, the Soviets also realized that the Baghdad consensus would also keep *them* out of the core area of the Middle East, especially if Iraq continued to play the leading role, and that the Yemeni situation offered them an opportunity to strengthen their positions at the periphery to compensate for their weakened position at the core. Consequently, the policy they pursued through PDRY was two-pronged: they took advantage of the constellation that produced and followed the Kuwait agreement in order to strengthen their position in PDRY and to develop a PDRY-YAR association with themselves; but they also used PDRY as a channel for a dialogue with the Saudis in which the two sides tried to explore possible areas of mutual understanding, and they backed up that endeavor by having PDRY refrain from pressing hard for realization of the unity agreement and demonstratively withhold support from the NDF, the Saudis' bête noire.

The Saudis' response to the Soviet-PDRY approach was initially receptive, especially after the failure of the tribal revolt against Saleh. In the fall of 1979 Saudi leaders were speaking of a Soviet role in the search for peace in the Middle East and even of the possibility of diplomatic relations between the two countries (see point 3 in the outline later in the chapter). By the turn of the year, however, that trend was disrupted. The Soviet invasion of Afghanistan, coming hard on the heels of the Mecca Grand Mosque takeover, prompted the Saudis to take the lead in assembling the Islamabad conference and promoting anti-Soviet resolutions. The invasion also seemed to have bestirred the United States to react against the Soviets' closing in on the Persian Gulf by proclaiming the Carter Doctrine, exploring measures for strengthening the defense of the Gulf, and organizing global sanctions against the Soviet Union. About that time, too, the Saudis had their showdown with Saleh by cutting off indispensable economic assistance to the YAR. For a moment, it looked as though the Saudis were ready to reverse their previous course and join the United States in an anti-Soviet campaign, including particularly an assault against the Soviet position in both PDRY and the YAR. But that moment soon passed.

Precisely because the Soviets feared that the Yemens were a convenient place for an American-led counterassault in response to their own action in Afghanistan, they made a special effort to dissuade the Saudis from joining such an undertaking, by a show of reasonableness on the part of PDRY as well as in their dialogue with the Saudis through Aden. The Soviets may have gone as far as to promise the Saudis to support a change of leadership in PDRY, replacing Isma'il with the more moderate Ali Nasser, in order to reassure them. At any rate, the Saudis developed their own reasons to respond favorably to the Soviet message. In the first place, they really had no stomach for taking on both the YAR and PDRY in any sustained confrontation. Moreover, although they were initially pleased when the United States appeared to have been finally aroused to the Soviet danger, they were disappointed with the concrete American response at the international level, and disturbed by the initiatives to which it led at the regional level. The American request for their assistance in obtaining bases and facilities in the area, coupled with talk about the development of a Rapid Deployment Force, raised for the Saudis immediate sharp problems that overshadowed the longer-term dangers that the American measures were supposed to address. Finally, the Saudis' Islamabad venture had already involved them in a clash with Syria on account of its relations with the Soviet Union, while the Carter Doctrine precipitated the opposition of Iraq on account of its own regional leadership ambitions (see Chapter 14). In these circumstances close, open association with the United States not only would have isolated the Saudis, but also would have caused them to incur the hostility of two antagonists they had hitherto played off against each other. Syria could then hurt them through support for PDRY and the NDF as well as in Jordan and Lebanon, while Iraq could hurt them through support for Saleh's regime, with which it had close relations.

Once they decided to pull back from open association with the United States against the Soviets and their clients, the Saudis availed themselves of the opening given them by the Soviets and PDRY to make a successful end run around the YAR. Saleh, faced with a Saudi-PDRY understanding and badly in need of Saudi financial assistance, was forced to come to terms in March 1980. In exchange for resumption of Saudi aid, Saleh agreed to restrict the Soviets' presence in the YAR and to renounce his plans to bring the NDF into the government. The agreement drove the NDF to revolt and led to a protracted armed clash between it and the forces of Saleh's government, in which the latter gradually reduced the NDF's power. That development further reassured the Saudis because the weakening of the NDF automatically strengthened the relative power of their client tribes and made them more willing to tolerate Saleh's continuing but slow quest for unity, especially since PDRY was maintaining a generally satisfactory cooperative disposition.

PDRY, even under Isma'il, refrained from objecting to Saleh's March 1980 reconciliation with the Saudis, despite its provision for restricting the Soviet presence in the YAR, for the sake of keeping Saudi Arabia from too close an association with the United States. The following month Ali Nasser overthrew Isma'il in a political coup d'état and, with the blessings of the Soviets, made great strides in the rapprochement with the Saudis and other Gulf countries. Ali Nasser not only refrained from supporting the NDF in its fight with Saleh but also helped legitimize the latter's position by agreeing to carry on the unity talks with him at a leisurely pace. With neither of the two Yemens disposed to precipitate matters, the Saudis learned to view the unity discussions as a useful instrument to help keep the peace between them and to facilitate their own relations with both.

Thus, by the latter half of 1980 the Saudis were essentially pursuing toward the Yemens the same basic policy they had attempted in 1976–1977, except that this time changed circumstances and a modification in the Saudis' attitude improved its chances of success. The modification was that whereas one of the aims of the Saudi 1976–1977 detente effort was to try to lure PDRY away from the Soviet Union and eventually transform its character, in 1979–1980 they for the first time accepted PDRY for what it was as well as its Soviet connection, and indeed tried to use that very connection to advance their policy. That change, in turn, had an important effect on PDRY's internal politics as they bore on the Saudis' policy. In 1976–1977 the Saudis had tried to work with Rubaya Ali, whose policy of rapprochement was suspect and who was strongly opposed, and eventually overthrown, by the more rigidly pro-Soviet Isma'il. In 1979–1980 Isma'il himself began the detente process at the instigation of the Soviets, who subsequently supported his displacement by Ali Nasser on the very grounds that the latter was better suited to continue the detente policy.

As for changes in the circumstances, in 1977 the war between Ethiopia and Somalia had forced Rubaya's hand and contributed to the alienation of the Saudis; whereas in 1980 the situation in the Horn of Africa was relatively quiescent, partly because the Soviets were pursuing there a policy similar to the one they were attempting toward the Yemens. Finally, in 1976–1977 the continuing Iranian military presence in Oman had kept up the tension between the latter and PDRY and thus undermined the PDRY-Saudi detente; by 1980 the Iranians had completely evacuated Oman. And although Oman's disposition to cooperate with the United States and its willingness to grant it facilities on its territory constituted a new source of tension between Oman and PDRY, the concern of the Soviets and PDRY not to drive Oman even further into alignment with the United States restrained their reaction against it. Moreover, the fact that the Saudis formally opposed Oman's policy and that other Gulf countries really did so acted as a check on Oman and helped prevent what strain did exist between it and PDRY from disrupting the general detente.

All this does not mean that the modus vivendi that took shape in 1980 was free of difficulties. PDRY, for instance, to the irritation of the Saudis, automatically sided with the Steadfastness Front led by Syria in virtually all matters. As part of that adherence, it formally supported Iran in its war with Iraq, while the YAR and Saudi Arabia actively supported Iraq. Saudi Arabia antagonized the YAR by not inviting it to join the GCC, and the YAR antagonized the Saudis by arresting one of their prominent supporters on charges of spying. PDRY suspected the Saudi-promoted GCC and, fearing that it might come to reflect Oman's pro-American views more than it might restrain them, reacted by forming a pro-Soviet alliance with Ethiopia and Libya, which was feared by the Saudis. Such difficulties and others, however, were tolerated by the parties involved for the sake of preserving the wider modus vivendi. Indeed, that aim came to constitute one of the main factors that determined the Saudis' crucial policy choices elsewhere. It contributed to their rejection of "strategic consensus," to the nonaligned orientation of the GCC charter, to the Saudis' attempt to follow an "Arab strategy" after the tide of the war turned against Iraq, and to their hesitation to call on American help after Syria torpedoed that strategy.

The remainder of this chapter highlights the main events and episodes documenting the preceding analytical overview.

1. On March 29, 1979, the Kuwait agreement on unity was announced. Saleh declared general amnesty for NDF members.

In April 1979 Saleh was reported to be seeking accommodation with the NDF. In that connection, he removed from cabinet posts two leaders hostile to the NDF, including Foreign Minister Abdallah al-Asnaj, but retained the latter as an adviser.

Saudi Arabia slowed down delivery of American arms.

Emir Abdallah declared in an interview on April 21, 1979, that Saudi Arabia "supports [unity] efforts without any reservations or conditions as long as they stem from our religion and traditions, because unity which does not stem from this is fabricated and dictated by foreign factors."[1] The declaration was clearly intended to express Saudi Arabia's compliance with the Kuwait agreement, while justifying its opposition to Saleh's overtures to the NDF.

A meeting scheduled for May 1979 between the presidents of the YAR and PDRY to advance unity did not take place. Opposition by Saudi client tribes was believed to be the cause.[2]

In June 1979 Saleh sent al-Asnaj to Washington to try to work out a direct arms agreement with the United States. The mission was a failure.[3]

In the same month Saleh initiated talks with NDF leaders aimed at forming a new government with NDF participation.[4]

On June 21 an attempted revolt by anti-NDF army elements said to be supported by the Saudis was put down and most of the leaders were executed. The attempt was followed by clashes between the army and northern tribal forces.[5]

On June 27 the YAR participated in the Khamis Mushayt durbar organized by Saudi Arabia despite the tension between the two countries. Presumably, the YAR's participation in an event involving military maneuvers near its borders could not be avoided.

2. In late July and early August 1979, a YAR delegation visited Moscow and concluded an arms deal on highly advantageous terms, including prompt delivery in the remainder of 1979 and early 1980. The deal report-

edly involved 500 T-55 tanks, 60 MIG-21 and SU-22 aircraft, 150 armored personnel carriers, and SAMs and antiaircraft guns.[6] Radio Moscow explained the deal in terms of Soviet friendship toward the people of North Yemen and interest in "the aspirations of the Yemeni people for unity."[7]

In September 1979 the USSR carried out a massive airlift exercise that was said to have demonstrated its capacity to airlift two fully equipped fighting divisions from Soviet and Bulgarian bases to PDRY and the Horn of Africa within thirty-six hours.[8]

In mid-September 1979 Soviet Premier Kosygin visited PDRY and Ethiopia. At the end of the month Abd al-Fattah Isma'il expressed PDRY's desire to establish "good and normal relations" with Saudi Arabia.[9]

3. In an interview with a Beirut weekly on October 11, 1979, Saudi Defense Minister Sultan said that diplomatic relations with the USSR would be possible if and when the Soviets realized that Saudi positions were based on Islamic principles.[10]

On October 25, during a visit to Moscow, PDRY's President Isma'il signed a treaty of friendship and cooperation with the Soviet Union. In the joint communiqué issued at the end of the visit, the Soviet side expressed "satisfaction with the development of peaceful relations between PDRY and the Yemen Arab Republic."[11] According to Kuwait's daily *al-Siyasah*, Isma'il undertook to deliver an oral message from the Soviet leadership to the Saudis regarding bilateral USSR-Saudi relations.[12]

4. In the meantime, on October 4, 1979, PDRY's Prime Minister Ali Nasser visited San'a and agreed with YAR President Saleh that the joint committees on unity "should be given sufficient time to complete the tasks entrusted to them."[13] The YAR's Constituent People's Assembly, including strong representation of pro-Saudi elements, approved the San'a statement but stressed that Yemeni unity must be based on "Islamic principles."[14]

On November 18–19 the YAR and PDRY signed an agreement on security cooperation and trade.[15]

5. From November 20 to December 5, 1979, there were the Mecca Grand Mosque episode and the Shi'ite riots, followed by the Soviet invasion of Afghanistan on December 27. The Saudis vehemently denounced the invasion, were the first to boycott the Moscow Olympics, and took the lead in assembling the emergency Islamic conference on January 26–29, 1980, which denounced the Soviet Union. The YAR was one of the few Arab countries to refrain from denouncing the Soviets. Three days before the conference, the United States proclaimed the Carter Doctrine (see Chapter 14).

At the end of December 1979 and the beginning of January 1980, Saleh resumed negotiations with the NDF aimed at forming a "national reconciliation" government including all groups and factions in the country to facilitate the advancement of unity.[16] The Saudis objected directly and through their client tribal leaders and suspended economic assistance.[17]

6. In an interview with *al-Hawadess* published on January 11, 1980, Crown Prince Fahd said that although Islam and communism were irreconcilable, Russia could not be ignored as a world power, and that it could play a constructive role in the search for peace in the Middle East. He expressed satisfaction with the progress of trade relations between the two countries and revealed that contacts had taken place through a third party (most probably PDRY).[18]

On January 12, 1980, the YAR's prime minister headed a delegation to Riyadh that unsuccessfully tried to persuade the Saudis to restore their financial aid. According to press reports, the Saudis demanded that the YAR break its military relations with the Soviet Union, ease out the Soviet experts, and denounce the Soviet invasion of Afghanistan.[19]

In an interview in *al-Watan al-'Arabi* of January 18, 1980, Crown Prince Fahd declared that cooperation between the YAR and the USSR had been blown out of all proportion, and asserted that Saudi Arabia and the YAR enjoyed "complete understanding on all matters of common interest."[20]

This statement was at variance with the fact of suspended aid to the YAR and with Saleh's subsequent action. Conceivably, Fahd's minimizing of the dispute with the YAR on account of its Soviet relations and his statement about the Soviet Union the previous week related to a debate within the Saudi ruling establishment.

On January 31, 1980, Saleh signed an agreement with NDF leader Sultan Ahmad Omar on the formation of a coalition government, the drawing up of a new, nonaligned constitution, the resumption of discussions on the unification of the armed forces of the YAR and PDRY, the release of all political prisoners, the ending of all forms of confrontation between the NDF and the regime, and the formation of a new committee to supervise general elections.[21]

On February 5, 1980, Secretary of State Vance declared before the Senate Foreign Relations Committee that Soviet influence in the YAR was "an important and troubling situation."[22] At the same time, Fahd and Saud expressed to Brzezinski, during his February 4–6 visit to Riyadh, their particular concern about the growing Communist military presence in South Yemen (see Chapter 14).[23] Yet on February 26, 1980, the Saudis disclosed that they had recently given permission to Soviet military planes to overfly their country on the way to PDRY.[24]

On March 3, 1980, *Newsweek* reported Crown Prince Fahd to have said that, contrary to his hopes, the United States seemed incapable of "taking urgent and bold action to stop the Communist thrust," and added that Saudi Arabia had never dreamed that "in the twentieth century this [the Soviet invasion] could take place with impunity."

7. On March 18 the Saudis reached an understanding with Saleh that

ended the confrontation with him and led to the resumption of Saudi financial assistance to the YAR. According to Saudi sources, the YAR agreed to remove the Soviet advisers, while Saudi Arabia agreed to provide substitute advisers and instructors to train the Yemeni army in the use of Soviet weapons, and to resume the supply of American weapons under Saudi auspices.[25] YAR sources claimed that the understanding involved only acceptance of the "principle" of phasing out Soviet advisers, and reassurances by the YAR that it was not drifting away from nonalignment toward a Soviet-oriented alliance with PDRY.[26]

In early April 1980, PDRY's foreign minister visited Jidda and returned with a Saudi invitation to Isma'il to visit Riyadh. Isma'il reportedly refused.[27]

On April 21 Ali Nasser overthrew and replaced Isma'il as president of PDRY and as secretary general of the Yemen Socialist party. The next day Brezhnev congratulated Nasser and invited him to come to Moscow the following month.[28] At the end of that visit the Soviet press reported "complete unanimity of views" between guest and hosts.[29]

8. On May 13, 1980, Saudi Defense Minister Sultan and Foreign Minister Saud visited San'a to follow up on the March understanding with Saleh.

In May and June a growing number of armed clashes were reported between YAR and NDF forces.[30] Presumably these were the result of the Saudi understanding with Saleh coupled with reduced PDRY support for the NDF. During the clashes Ali Nasser visited San'a on June 9–13 for talks with Saleh.

9. On June 28, 1980, Ali Nasser visited Riyadh for talks with the Saudi leaders that, according to the Kuwait News Agency, established "a new basis for relations based on equality, mutual respect and non-interference."[31]

On July 21 Foreign Minister Saud stated in an interview with a Beirut weekly that the end of the Soviet occupation of Afghanistan would remove "any inhibition" the Saudis might have about "evolving and developing good relations with the Soviet Union."[32]

10. On August 28, 1980, Saleh returned to San'a after a visit to Baghdad and Riyadh in connection with Iraq's impending invasion of Iran. Both Saleh and the Saudis claimed to have achieved "full understanding on all issues" (see Chapter 14).

11. In September 1980 Ali Nasser and Saleh met twice, on the first and the twenty-sixth. After the second meeting it was announced that a "draft plan for unity" had been formulated by the joint constitutional committee.[33]

Nine days later Ali Nasser declared in an interview that a gradual advance toward unity and careful work by the committees were the best guarantees for the success of the project.[34]

In mid-October there were changes in the governments of both PDRY and the YAR. The former reinforced Ali Nasser's position; the latter gave pro-Saudi elements greater weight.[35]

From mid-October 1980 to the end of the year, fighting intensified between YAR and NDF forces.

12. (In the meantime, on September 22, 1980, Iraq invaded Iran, and on September 30 Saudi Arabia announced its request for American-manned AWACS aircraft.)

On October 15, 1980, Saleh declared that any foreign military presence "undermine[d] the security, stability and peace of the area" and risked embroiling the Middle East in future global conflicts.[36] Saleh thus distanced himself from the Saudis' action for the sake of his relations with PDRY and the Soviets.

On November 29 the Saudi weekly *al-Majallah* stated, on the basis of a "top secret" report, that Moscow and Aden had concluded an agreement on military cooperation going far beyond their friendship and cooperation treaty. The agreement ostensibly allowed the Soviets to use PDRY facilities for their land, air, and naval forces in return for a Soviet pledge to protect the Aden regime.[37] The publication of the story reflected at once the Saudis' concern about Aden's action and their acknowledgment of the anxieties that prompted it.

In mid-December 1980 an NDF delegation visited Damascus for talks with Ba'th officials. The two sides announced "identical views" in condemning "Iraq's dirty war against Iran" and the Iraqi and Jordanian conspiracies against Syria. Syria also expressed "strong support" for "the struggle of the NDF in the YAR."[38] Syria, which in the same month had boycotted the Amman summit and massed troops against Jordan, thus showed its capacity to hurt Saudi interests in the Yemens, too.

13. (On February 14, 1981, the Riyadh conference of Gulf foreign ministers approved the Saudi proposal for a Gulf Cooperation Council. On March 9 the Muscat conference approved the statutes of the council.)

On March 3 Ali Nasser went on a visit to Moscow.

On March 16 Ali Nasser went to Ethiopia to coordinate policies, and the two sides reached agreement on an alliance "to safeguard their vital interests in the region."[39]

On March 25 Oman submitted to the Arab League a long list of complaints alleging PDRY "acts of aggression" during the previous months. Commentators believed Oman's complaints were exaggerated in order to influence the GCC to take a firmer pro-American, anti-Soviet stance. PDRY, in turn, charged Oman with provocations connected with the American involvement in Oman. The charges and countercharges led to abortive attempts at mediation by Kuwait and the UAE in May and September,[40] which did not prevent the Arab Monetary Fund from giving PDRY a $30 million loan in July.

Meanwhile, on March 25 President Saleh's pro-Saudi adviser, Abdallah al-Asnaj, was arrested on suspicion of having spied on Saleh in order to report to Saudi Arabia his attitude toward the USSR and PDRY.[41] The previous month the Egyptian press had reported that al-Asnaj and others had been implicated in a Saudi-supported coup attempt against Saleh.[42] The incident probably reflected the YAR's resentment over its exclusion from the GCC.[43] At any rate, neither this nor PDRY's alliance with Ethiopia was allowed to disrupt the rapprochement between the two countries and Saudi Arabia.

14. On April 11–14, 1981, the Saudi-YAR Coordination Council met in Jidda, with the participation of the Saudi defense minister and the YAR's foreign minister. The Saudis pledged SR 345 million (over $100 million) in budget support in addition to assistance for a multitude of projects.[44] The joint communiqué spoke of the determination of both sides to keep the peninsula removed from "international and ideological conflicts" and from "foreign influences — Eastern or Western" while stressing their "deep faith in Islam and Arabism."[45]

15. On August 19, 1981, PDRY, Ethiopia, and Libya concluded talks in Aden by signing a tripartite alliance. The YAR was presumably asked to join but refrained for the sake of its relations with Saudi Arabia.

On September 14, Saleh and Ali Nasser met at Tai'z to speed up unity talks. Fighting between YAR and NDF forces, which had been going on for some time, intensified in the following months.[46]

On October 26–28 Saleh visited Moscow. He apparently sought more arms, while the Soviets sought YAR support for their plan for the neutralization of the Persian Gulf–Red Sea–Indian Ocean area. The final communiqué suggested that both achieved their aims. It spoke of the desire of the two countries to continue "broadening and perfecting their advantageous cooperation" in the military field. Saleh expressed thanks to the USSR for its support for the YAR's "national independence and sovereignty," supported Moscow's call for an international conference on the Middle East and its peace plan for the Gulf and Indian Ocean, and condemned the establishment of foreign military bases in the Gulf.[47]

On November 8–9 Saleh visited Riyadh. (Presumably his quest for additional arms from Moscow was made easier to justify to the Saudis after the approval of their AWACS and other arms deal with the United States the previous month.) Saleh reportedly sought Saudi financial aid in fighting the NDF rebellion, which was raging through wide areas of the YAR.[48]

16. On November 13–15, 1981, Ali Nasser visited Bahrain and Qatar, with which PDRY did not yet have diplomatic relations.

On November 23 Ali Nasser and Saleh met in Kuwait, the seat of the 1979 unity agreement, to discuss further unity moves.

On November 26 the NDF claimed to have reached agreement with Saleh in Kuwait on a cease-fire, but San'a issued a denial.

On December 3 Ali Nasser and Saleh met in Aden and agreed to "wide ranging political and economic cooperation."[49] During the meeting, the YAR's military debt to the USSR was said to have been rescheduled.[50]

17. (On December 22–23, 1981, Syria's President Assad made his important visit to Riyadh following the strain over the Fahd Plan, the Israeli annexation of the Golan, the Iranian attempt to destabilize Bahrain, Fahd's cancellation of his trip to the United States, and the Iranian victories over Iraq. The visit resulted in a temporary Saudi-Syrian understanding and the Saudis' adoption of an "Arab strategy" to help Iraq and to deal with the intensified Iranian threat [see Chapter 14].)

On January 9, 1982, PDRY and Iraq restored diplomatic relations, broken since June 1979.

On the same day the secretary of PDRY's parliament announced that PDRY and the YAR had agreed on a draft constitution aimed at merger, which would be submitted to a referendum in each of the two states and then ratified.[51]

Hostilities between the YAR and the NDF were reported to have ceased some time before.

On March 3, 1982, the United States announced the easing of trade restrictions against Syria and PDRY. (This was probably a delayed response to a request by the Saudis in connection with their "Syrian-Arab strategy.")

18. On March 15, 1982, fighting resumed between YAR and NDF forces. NDF leader Sultan Ahmad Omar was reported to be in Beirut.[52]

(In the last week of March the Iranians launched another successful offensive, and the Syrian-Saudi understanding collapsed [see Chapter 14].)

On April 7 Defense Minister Sultan led a big Saudi delegation, comprising Foreign Minister Saud, Interior Minister Nayef, and four other cabinet ministers, to the Saudi-YAR Coordination Council. Saleh represented the YAR. The meeting led to a Saudi aid commitment of $206 million.[53]

On May 5 Saleh and Ali Nasser met in Ta'iz as fighting between YAR and NDF forces continued. The course of the fighting favored San'a, and diplomats reported that the purpose of the meeting was for Saleh to reassure Ali Nasser that YAR forces had no intention of carrying their offensive into PDRY territory.[54]

On the same day a GCC delegation visited Aden in an effort to renew mediation between the PDRY and Oman.[55]

On June 9 Saudi Interior Minister Nayef visited Aden and spoke of an imminent improvement in Saudi-PDRY relations.[56]

16

The American Connection, 1979–1982: Ambivalence, Improvisation, Drift

As in the first part of Khaled's reign, the Kingdom's relationship with America continued to unfold on two distinct levels. On the secondary or practical level, centering on trade, technical cooperation, and civilian and military contracts, the relationship prospered on the whole despite moments of tension in connection with massive oil price increases and major Saudi arms requests and acquisitions. Thus, Saudi trade with the United States grew from $10.2 billion in 1978 — the last full year of the first stage — to $22.8 billion in 1981 — the last full year of the second — averaging $19.1 billion annually in the second period. Much of the increase was due to the higher price of oil exports to the United States, which averaged $11.6 billion a year in 1979–1981, compared with less than $6 billion in 1978; but imports, too, increased to an average of $6.1 billion, compared with $4.3 billion in 1978.[1] Purchases of arms and military construction from the United States continued to average about $5 billion a year in the second stage. They amounted to $20.1 billion in 1979–1982, compared with $19.6 billion in 1975–1978.[2]

On the primary or high-policy level, Saudi Arabia's decision to go with the Baghdad powers in March 1979 produced the most intense strain in Saudi-American relations since the 1973 oil embargo. Like the earlier episode, the crisis of 1979 was formally repaired within a few months. As in 1974, the repairing of Saudi-American relations in 1979 at the diplomatic level did nothing to reverse the enormous damage to American, Western, and Third World interests in the form of a runaway increase in oil prices — some 250 percent in less than a year and a half — triggered by the Saudi decisions of January and April 1979. Yet, unlike the 1973–1974 reconciliation, the mending of Saudi-American relations in 1979 was not even very effective. The termination of the earlier crisis was based on a comprehensive agreement on broad strategic goals, which made possible a period of close cooperation on a new basis. The 1979 reconciliation, on the other hand, began with the flawed notion of agreeing to disagree on an issue of great importance to the two countries, and the uneven relations that ensued were made worse by developments in related features of Saudi policy at the same time. Underlying the difference between the two situations was the fact that in 1973–1974 the Kingdom's policy was ultimately decided by a single leader of unquestioned authority and ability, whereas in 1979 it was the product of the tugs and pulls, hesitations and compromises typical of a collective leadership.

The formula by which the 1979 crisis was ostensibly resolved was meant to prevent the disagreement between the Kingdom and the United States over the peace process from encroaching on other aspects of their relations. In fact, contending third-party pressures on the two sides — Egyptian, Israeli, and domestic in the case of the United States; the Steadfastness Front and Iraq in the case of Saudi Arabia — often defeated that purpose.

As far as Saudi Arabia was concerned, the formula was supposed to preserve the American strategic connection as an ultimate safeguard and otherwise allow it to pursue an "Arab strategy." In fact, the Arab strategy as initially conceived broke down under the weight of a combination of events and the ingrained Syrian-Iraqi hostility and was not replaced by a coherent alternative. Instead, residues of that strategy led the Saudis to make haphazard adaptations and improvisations in the various arenas, which undercut their ability to pursue a consistent policy toward the United States.

The reconciliation formula was also premised on the assumption that isolating the Arab-Israeli issue on which the Kingdom and the United States disagreed would facilitate cooperation between the two countries in other spheres, such as the Soviet threat, Gulf security, the Yemens, and military transactions, where their interests were thought to be compatible. In fact, partly because of the two reasons just cited but partly also because of differences in perspective and style, Saudi and American policies and actions in those other spheres diverged as often as they converged.

Finally, the formula itself was an outgrowth of a compromise agreement among senior members of the Saudi royal family that was supposed to give the Kingdom's policy a certain consistency of direction. In fact, the contending pressures, the breakdown of the Arab strategy, and the differences in American and Saudi perspectives stimulated the reassertion of those members' different inclinations, and in turn exacerbated the fluctuations and ambiguities in the Saudis' relations with America.

As a result of all this, Saudi "high policy" in the second stage of Khaled's reign was reduced to a set of disparate general objectives, unevenly shared by members of the ruling group and pursued through a mixture of ambiguous narrow policies and ad hoc responses to threats and opportunities. In that context, the American connection was only one important but constricted element. All the key leaders saw the United States' role as threefold: to protect certain Saudi interests as a by-product of protecting its own, as in resisting Soviet encroachments and safeguarding oil transit routes; to supply arms and military assistance; and to provide help in emergency situations — although this function was cast into grave doubt by America's failure to save the shah. To ensure fulfillment of that role, some leaders, particularly Abdallah and Khaled, thought that willingness to respond to American and Western oil needs was a sufficient compensation, whereas others, led by Fahd, felt it necessary to do more to secure the American connection.

For its part, the United States, whether under the Carter or the Reagan administration, failed to recognize that basic Saudi view of the relationship between the two countries, and consequently it sporadically but consistently attempted to press its own views upon the reluctant Saudis. Each time a situation arose that suggested that the Saudis needed or might need American help, Washington tried to use the occasion to move the Kingdom into an explicit or implicit comprehensive strategic association with it. The fact that some Saudi leaders sometimes listened sympathetically to these overtures tended to obscure the point that the different Saudi and American perspectives often pointed in opposite directions. Even when the two countries' views converged on some issue, as they did briefly in the case of the Soviet invasion of Afghanistan, the Saudis preferred to follow parallel rather than joint courses. In the case of arms deals, the Saudis tried to depict them as limited military transactions with no strategic implications. When the Saudis faced an inescapable necessity to call on direct American military assistance, as they did at the beginning of the Gulf war, they did their best to keep their association with the United States as discrete and limited as possible. Throughout the period they compensated for any manifestations of the American connection by reaffirming their dissociation from the United States' policy on the Arab-Israeli issue, either by criticizing it or by suggesting alternatives.

Because of the generally disconnected character of Saudi high policy in the latter stage of Khaled's reign, the limited role assigned to the American connection in that policy, the disparity in the Saudi and American perspectives, the divergent views among the Saudi leaders, and because of the impact on all this of major events, Saudi-American relations lacked the kind of continuity and coherence that were discernible in the first stage. Consequently, the following discussion focuses on a succession of more or less interrelated episodes rather than attempting a seamless analytical presentation.

Crisis and Turning Point, February–May 1979

Previous chapters (especially Chapter 12) have already discussed in various contexts the developments culminating in the crisis in the Saudis' relationship with the United States in the spring of 1979. However, the nature of that crisis deserves to be underscored because it marked a historic turning point in Saudi-American relations, and especially because, unlike the 1973–74 crisis, it was not perceived as such, especially on the American side, either at the time or later.

Although the 1979 crisis did not manifest itself in an open Saudi confrontation with the United States, as in the case of the 1973–74 embargo, its long-term impact on the relationship between the two countries was even more profound, for at least three reasons. First, although the 1979 crisis was brought to a head by the specific issue of the American-sponsored Egyptian-Israeli peace treaty, that issue became related, in the Saudi view, to America's place in the overall strategy of the Kingdom at a time when the entire Saudi strategic environment was being transformed by critical events such as the fall of the shah and the advent of an Islamic revolutionary regime in Iran, the eruption into war of the Yemeni problem, and diplomatic upheaval in the Arab arena in the shape of moves for Iraqi-Syrian union.

Second, because the problem between Saudi Arabia and the United States was thus ramified, it was less susceptible to accurate diagnosis and specific remedy than the dispute that had led to the 1973–74 crisis. Saudis and Americans were tempted to focus on their evident disagreement over the Egyptian-Israeli treaty issue, but that only served to obscure incompatibilities in the Saudi and American views on the other issues.

Third, in contrast to the situation in 1973–74, when Faisal was in firm control of policy, the issues in 1979 became entangled in the power and policy rivalries among the country's collegial leaders and caused a split in the royal family. This entanglement made the possibility of adjusting Saudi and American policies much more difficult, and tended sometimes to place the imperative of restoring and preserving family unity in competition with the imperative of pursuing a consistent, coherent policy.

Reflecting the nature of the crisis in the Saudi-American relationship was the Saudi decision in April 1979 to cut oil production by 1 mbd while

the international oil market was still in turmoil over the Iranian revolution. The effect was to send the spot market price soaring from $21.25 in
that month to $35.40 in June.[3] That decision was not particularly directed
at the United States with a view to achieving a specific policy aim regarding the Arab-Israeli issue, but was rather a consequence of the adoption of
the Khaled-Abdallah "Arab strategy" with its concomitant of appeasing
and balancing revolutionary Iran. The production decrease was primarily intended to avert criticism by Iran's revolutionary government by
acceding to its demand for room to increase its own production after the
big decline during the period of revolutionary turmoil (see Chapter 12).
The damage suffered by the United States (as well as Japan, Western
Europe, and the Third World) was simply a by-product of the Khaled-
Abdallah policy of shifting the emphasis of the Kingdom's quest for
security away from America toward regional actors.

American policymakers, however, remained riveted to the issue that
had brought the crisis in Saudi-American relations to a head and did not
recognize the structural change that had taken place in the relationship
between the two countries. When Secretary of State Vance told Congress
on May 8, 1979, that Saudi-American relations were at a low point, reflecting "clear and sharp" differences between the two countries,[4] he had in
mind the Egyptian-Israeli peace and the Saudi post – Baghdad II reaction
to it. National Security Adviser Zbigniew Brzezinski, even with the benefit of a few years' hindsight, referred in his memoirs to the 1979 problem
between the United States and Saudi Arabia exclusively in terms of the
Egyptian-Israeli peace. He incidentally also misread the facts when he
said that his "most important accomplishment" was to obtain a secret
Saudi pledge "that they would do nothing tangible to hurt Sadat," and
added that "in subsequent months they kept that promise."[5] The latter
statement was not accurate in any relevant sense. The Saudis may have
tried to restrict the sanctions against Egypt in the first two or three
months after Baghdad II, before turning to strict ostracism of Sadat until
the end of his life. However, the relative "moderation" of those early
months had no significant political relevance. President Carter, in his
memoirs, did not discuss the 1979 crisis but did refer to the Saudis'
position in connection with the November 1978 Baghdad conference. In
that context he said that he was "disturbed that the Saudis had not fulfilled their earlier commitment to me" to support the Camp David agreements and "to hold the Arab nations together in a positive attitude toward
us and Egypt" during the conference.[6]

The Saudis, for their part, had no reason to intimate to the United
States the extent of the change in their attitude toward it, and found it to
their advantage rather to keep the focus on the disagreement over the
peace treaty. They could thus gain credit with their fellow Arabs and help

deflect attention from the split among leading members of the royal family over the broader issues in which the issue of the treaty was embedded.

The CIA did gain some information about the dispute in the royal family that prompted Fahd's departure for Spain in March 1979, and a report about it was leaked to the press the next month.[7] However, the report indicated no clear connection between the quarrel and broad policy orientations beyond those possibly arising from the alleged weakening of the position of the "pro-American" crown prince. The exclusive emphasis on personality helped keep in obscurity the underlying conceptual political-strategic change that occurred and persisted even after Fahd and his fellow princes patched up their dispute.

The leaking of the CIA story was itself indicative of the strained state of Saudi-American relations at the time. There was no discernible reason for it other than the venting of anger at the Saudi position. William Quandt, Brzezinski's Middle East aide in the National Security Council, stated that around that time, President Carter, disappointed over the Saudi stance on the Camp David accords, also "ordered his ambassador [to Saudi Arabia] to speak bluntly and critically to the Saudis about the harm their position would have on bilateral U.S.-Saudi relations."[8] The Saudis, ever extremely sensitive about discussion of intrafamily quarrels, were incensed about the leak and served notice of their intent to declare the CIA station chief in Jidda, whom they identified as the source of the leaked story, persona non grata,[9] an act that would have worsened the already damaged relations between the two countries. In the following weeks they were persuaded to content themselves with a quiet withdrawal of the official as part of the reconciliation between the two governments.

Flawed Reconciliation, May–December 1979

The Saudi-American reconciliation around the middle of 1979 was a by-product of the personal and policy reconciliation within the royal family that led to Fahd's return home. The Khaled-Abdallah group had agreed to adjust its Arab-oriented strategy to satisfy Fahd's insistence on the need to preserve the American strategic connection, while Fahd, in the wake of Sadat's undifferentiated attacks on the the royal family, had agreed to an unequivocal break with Egypt that would facilitate pursuit of the Arab strategy. The break was made final on May 20, 1979, when Defense Minister Sultan repudiated his government's promise to finance Egypt's acquisition of fifty F-5 jet fighters from the United States (see Chapter 13).

Because the Saudi-American reconciliation ignored the broader Saudi policy orientation in which the issue of the Egyptian-Israeli peace was embedded, it proved to be problematic from the outset. The two countries, it turned out, did not necessarily see eye to eye on other issues, such as policy toward Iran. Moreover, the formula of agreeing to disagree on the peace question was itself flawed, since it was impossible in practice to isolate differences over so important an issue from other aspects of Saudi-American relations. The United States, for instance, repeatedly tried to induce the Saudis to adhere to its overall regional strategy, which was founded on the Egyptian-Israeli peace. Congress was particularly insistent in attempts to link arms sales requiring its approval to the Saudi position on peace. Key Arab countries, on the other hand, objected to the separation of issues for opposite reasons. They generally suspected any Saudi cooperation with the United States as implying or portending support for the treaty, and specifically pressed the Saudis to use their leverage with the United States to force it to change its policy on the Arab-Israeli question. Finally, although the reconciliation and policy compromise among the Saudi leaders held firm with regard to the ostracism of Sadat and Egypt, they did not hold so well when it came to other aspects of the formula or to issues related to it. The renewed tugs and pulls that ensued further complicated Saudi-American relations and added to their ambiguity. The consequences of all these problems manifested themselves throughout the remainder of Khaled's reign, but were expressed with particular intensity during the second half of 1979.

Perhaps the most conspicuous outcome of the Saudi-American reconciliation was the Saudi decision, announced in early July 1979, to increase oil production from 8.5 mbd to 9.5 mbd. This move helped ease for a while the speculative pressure and reduce slightly the spot market prices from the June 1979 high.[10] The U.S. government, for its part, announced on July 13, 1979, its approval of the sale of $1.2 billion of military equipment to the Saudi National Guard.[11] The previous month, the United States had complied with Saudi policy toward North Yemen, which at that point involved an attempt to curb President Saleh's endeavor to pursue an independent course, by refusing to establish a significant direct arms relationship with that country (see Chapter 15).

If the reconciliation formula worked with regard to Saudi oil production and American military supplies to the Kingdom and North Yemen, it did not work with regard to the all-important Gulf arena. Saudi policy in mid-1979, as expressed during the Khamis Mushayt durbar, sought to rally the small Gulf countries around the Kingdom on the basis of three propositions: mutual support for regime protection; Saudi power to balance Iran and Iraq for regional defense; and reliance on the United States, acting in its own interests, to assure the flow of oil and check the Soviets. That policy was beset from the start by doubts among some of the small

Gulf countries about the value of the Saudi defense umbrella, and these doubts increased in the next few months as tension between Iraq and Iran mounted, and as the Iranian revolutionaries spurned the appeasement efforts of Saudi Arabia and its neighbors and clashed with them over issues of Shi'ite rights and restrictions on pilgrims (discussed in Chapter 14).

The Saudis might have improved their credibility among the smaller Gulf countries and their deterrence vis-à-vis Iran if they could somehow have supplied proof that their strategic connection with America was working. Events at the time, however, tended to produce the opposite impression. Almost immediately after the final collapse of the shah's regime the United States began an effort to cultivate the Bazargan government, and it persisted in this endeavor after the Saudis' own appeasement efforts had failed, at least until the storming of the American embassy in Tehran in November 1979 (see Chapter 14). Thus, although the Saudis and the Americans had obvious shared interests in the Gulf, their specific policy courses diverged, despite the superficial initial similarity in their efforts to get along with the revolutionary Iranian regime.

All the Saudi leaders recognized the necessity of preserving the American strategic connection. Nine days after Fahd's June 21, 1979, statement affirming the formula for reconciliation with the United States (see Chapter 13), Abdallah issued a similiar statement of his own. In a June 30 interview with the Kuwait daily *al-Siyasah*, Abdallah declared that differences over the peace treaty would not affect "the continuity of friendship" with the United States, because Saudi-American relations "are based on mutual and common interests."[12] However, it seems that whereas Abdallah and his supporters were convinced of the adequacy of the formula to preserve that connection, Fahd continued to have doubts and therefore sought from the outset to find a way to resolve the Saudi-American differences on the peace process without accepting the Egyptian-Israeli peace treaty. In the same June 21 reconciliation statement, Fahd voiced a proposal to have the United States open a dialogue with the PLO on the basis of PLO acceptance of a modified version of UN Resolution 242, which, Fahd intimated, he had already secured. The Carter administration pursued that proposal, but by the end of August 1979 the entire endeavor had come to naught, and the attempt only cast a deeper shadow on Saudi-American relations. The United States had mismanaged the contacts with the PLO and yielded to Egyptian and Israeli opposition, while the Saudis had failed either to rally other key Arab parties to their endeavor or to deliver the PLO despite the others (see Chapter 13).

Fahd's doubts about the possibility of cooperating effectively with Washington while disagreeing with it over its peace policy were, paradoxically, shared by the Syrians. However, whereas Fahd feared that the disagreement might undermine the necessary cooperation with the United States, the Syrians feared that the Saudis' cooperation with the United States was apt to lead them to seek an accommodation with America's peace policy even if that accommodation ignored Syria's interests. Fahd's PLO initiative only confirmed them in their view. Consequently, the Syrians not only helped stir up trouble in Lebanon and put pressure on the PLO to reject that initiative, but also sought to cut the ground from under similar Saudi attempts in the future by trying to marshal pressures for collective Arab sanctions against the United States and harsher penalties against Egypt at the November 1979 Tunis summit. The Saudis foiled the Syrians' maneuver, but only at the cost of committing themselves to a collective Arab economic strategy and subscribing to a strong condemnation of the United States coupled with vague warnings (see Chapter 13).

The Saudis' endorsement of the Tunis summit conclusions may have been influenced by anxiety over the seizure of Mecca's Grand Mosque by Muslim fundamentalists the day the conference opened. In the subsequent weeks, as the fighting in the mosque continued and as clashes occurred between Shi'ites in the Eastern Province and the National Guard, the American media turned their attention on Saudi Arabia and, in the absence of reliable knowledge, engaged in widespread speculation about the country's conditions and the viability of its regime. To the Saudis, whose penchant for discretion borders on the fetishistic, such speculations appeared to be expressions of hostility; and although media throughout the world engaged in it, the indulgence of the American media was particularly rankling.

Faltering Strategic Cooperation, December 1979 – June 1980

The Soviet invasion of Afghanistan in late December 1979 provided a test of the reconciliation formula. Here was a threat to both American and Saudi interests that was seemingly unrelated to the Egyptian-Israeli peace issue and should therefore have provided a perfect occasion for strategic cooperation between the two countries. In fact both sides engaged in complementary or parallel initiatives for a while, but before long the Saudis detached themselves from the United States and reverted to their own course. One reason was that the ramifications of the position taken by the Saudis on the Egyptian-Israeli peace — what remained of the "Arab strategy" and the related Gulf policy — impinged on the Saudis' willingness or ability to translate their shared interest with the United States into a more substantial strategic cooperation, proving the difficulty of separating those issues.

Another reason was that the Saudis were tempted to use the *possibility* of greater strategic cooperation with the United States, raised by the pursuit of parallel initiatives, to reach an at least tacit understanding with the Soviets regarding the two Yemens, especially PDRY. The Saudis criticized Washington's inability to mount a forceful response to the Soviets' invasion in order to justify their going their own way, but they failed to see that their own reticence was crucial in making the American response as powerless as it seemed to be.[13] That failure, in turn, underscored the Saudis' detached attitude toward the United States and their disposition to seek whenever possible a "free ride" on its interests even when they shared in those interests.

Immediately after the invasion the Saudis, with Fahd in the lead, pressed for convening a meeting of the Islamic Conference at Islamabad in January 1980, which strongly condemned the Soviet Union and called for a boycott of the new puppet regime in Kabul. The Saudis had particular interests of their own attached to that move: they wanted to burnish their Islamic credentials after the Mecca mosque takeover and to reassure the smaller Gulf states that they were still able to conduct major foreign policy initiatives; and they also wanted to put the Syrians and other parties who cooperated with the Soviet Union despite its invasion of a Muslim country on the same footing as those who cooperated with the United States despite its support for Israel (see Chapter 13). Nevertheless, the United States viewed the Saudi initiative as a welcome indication of shared Saudi-American strategic interest and sought to build upon it. That was Brzezinski's purpose in visiting the Kingdom on February 4–6, 1980, on his way back from Pakistan, shortly after the proclamation of the Carter Doctrine on January 23.

Brzezinski's overall aim was to try to flesh out "a regional security arrangement with the Egyptians, the Saudis, the Pakistanis and the Turks."[14] On his visit to Saudi Arabia he was convinced that he had reached an understanding with Fahd, "the sensible and very pro-American head of government," and even with Prince Saud, "the articulate but somewhat more distant Foreign Minister," about greater American-Saudi military cooperation "on a quiet basis."[15] Actually, that understanding was wrapped with strong mental reservations on the Saudis' part and did not last long anyway. Just before Brzezinski's arrival, Fahd had publicly rejected a call by President Carter for a "Middle East security framework" and had repudiated any ideas for "pacts, defense belts, and areas of influence."[16] To the extent that Brzezinski had been briefed about Fahd's statement, he might have put it down as a smokescreen to conceal the kind of quiet understanding that he believed he had reached. In fact, however, the considerations underlying Fahd's public statement reflected real ambivalences among the Saudi rulers that soon nullified much of the privately achieved understanding.

Fahd's public statement was aimed, first of all, at appeasing the Syrians, who rightly suspected that the United States sought to use the Soviet invasion as a means to advance defense schemes including Egypt, which would nullify its ostracism and thus implicitly sanction its peace with Israel. Earlier the Syrians had vehemently opposed the Saudis' anti-Soviet Islamabad initiative, and Assad himself had gone to Riyadh on the eve of the conference to warn the Saudis against lending themselves to American attempts to divert Arab and Islamic peoples from their main object of liberating Palestine, polarize them, and drive a wedge between them and their Soviet friend (see Chapter 13). Fahd's statement was also meant to avoid antagonizing the Iraqis, who, although they denounced the Soviet invasion, sought to use the resentment and anxieties it aroused in order to advance their own schemes for collective defense and Gulf security. A few days after Brzezinski's visit, Saddam Hussein gave that aim a formal expression by issuing his Charter for Pan-Arab Action, which called for Arab nonalignment and for Arab solidarity as the means to oppose any aggression, and emphatically rejected any foreign military presence on Arab soil. The fact that the charter was quickly approved by most of the Gulf countries gave the Saudis the added motive of preventing Iraq from gaining an advantage over them in the competition for preeminence on the Arab side of the Gulf (see Chapter 14).

Yet another aim of Fahd's statement, which became apparent only in retrospect, was an attempt to reassure the Soviets about the Saudis' intentions, as part of an eventually successful effort to achieve an understanding with them concerning the Yemens. While the Saudis were pursuing the Islamabad initiative in January 1980, they had had a showdown with YAR President Saleh over his relations with the Soviet Union and the National Democratic Front (see Chapter 15). That initial Saudi militant stance led Moscow to make overtures to the Saudis, probably through PDRY, aimed at forestalling their cooperating with the United States to undermine the Soviet position in the Yemens in response to the invasion of Afghanistan. These overtures, it seems, led to an understanding that was manifested in the Saudis' allowing Soviet aircraft to overfly their territory on the way to PDRY, and in the Soviets' support for the replacement of the rigid and doctrinaire Abd al-Fattah Isma'il by the more moderate and accommodating Ali Nasser at PDRY's helm in March 1980. The understanding was also reflected in Saleh's conciliation of the Saudis in the same month, and in Ali Nasser's formal visit to Riyadh in June 1980 (see Chapter 15).

By that time, not only had the initial prospects of close American-Saudi strategic cooperation evaporated, but a whole array of incidents had marred the routine relations between the two countries. In late January 1980, for instance, before Brzezinski's departure for Pakistan and Saudi

Arabia, the CIA had completed a study on Saudi Arabia begun after the Mecca incident, in which it concluded that the Saudi regime might collapse within two years. The conclusion found its way into the March 3, 1980, edition of *Newsweek* and greatly angered the Saudis. The Saudi minister of industry and electricity, Dr. Ghazi al-Ghosaibi, still felt that anger when, in an address to the National Association of Arab Americans on May 3, he said that the fate of the Saudi regime depended on the feelings of the people toward it, and not on "the pronouncements of third-rate bureaucrats reading fourth-rate intelligence reports from fifth-rate spies."[17]

Coincidentally the same issue of *Newsweek* carried a statement by Crown Prince Fahd in which he expressed disbelief that such a thing as the Soviet invasion of Afghanistan could take place with impunity in the twentieth century, and voiced his disappointment that the United States seemed incapable of "taking urgent and bold action to stop the Communist thrust." Fahd showed no sign of awareness that Saudi Arabia's hesitation to cooperate with the United States had something to do with the latter's seeming incapability, nor did he seem to be bothered by the irony that at that very time Saudi Arabia was seeking an accommodation with the Soviets.

On a more concrete level, in February and March 1980 the Saudis rebuffed American requests to buy oil to fill the Strategic Petroleum Reserve, on the grounds that to do so would put further pressure on the already tight oil market.[18] In May and June 1980 it was Washington's turn to rebuff the Saudis by denying their request for prompt agreement to sell them F-15 enhancement equipment and AWACS aircraft, because of the imminent American election (see Chapter 13). While the Saudi request was pending, Fahd made yet another peace statement designed to appeal to the American public, when he told the *Washington Post* in an interview published on May 25, 1980, that Saudi Arabia would bring the Palestinians and other Arabs to the peace table if Israel agreed to withdraw from the occupied territories. Yet when Sadat, hoping or believing that the statement heralded a Saudi willingness to break ranks with Syria and Iraq, praised it, Fahd was quick to disabuse him and to reaffirm the Kingdom's commitment to the "collective Arab position," which left Egypt out in the cold (see Chapter 13).

One thing that the Saudis did do notwithstanding these fluctuations in their American connection was to maintain the high level of oil production they had begun the year before, even in the face of cutbacks by other OPEC members. In June 1980 they produced 9.8 mbd, the same amount as in July 1979, even as other producers were cutting down, so that the Saudi share of total OPEC output rose between those two dates from 31 to 36 percent.[19]

Open Strategic Cooperation in the Face of Danger, September – October 1980

The outbreak of the Iraq-Iran war and the initial course of the fighting made it imperative for the Saudis to activate openly the American strategic connection, and consequently provided a unique case study of the two parties' view of that connection. Whereas the United States viewed the particular measures of cooperation that were adopted as a turning point toward a stronger, open-ended strategic partnership, the Saudis viewed them as inevitable ad hoc measures and sought to restrict their implications to narrow confines and to escape them at the first opportunity.

By early August 1980 at the latest, the Saudis had come around to supporting Iraq's war design. Although they feared the long-term strategic consequences of an Iraqi victory, which they like everyone else took for granted, they comforted themselves with two thoughts: that the war would at least solve in a radical way the immediate problem of the threats emanating from revolutionary Iran, which had proved impervious to management by appeasement; and that the strengthening of the military capacity at their command, through additional American arms and the Pakistani option, would take care of the long-term problem (see Chapter 14). One consideration that did not occur to the Saudis was that the Iraqi war plans might go awry and expose their own vital oil facilities and the oil transit routes to danger, which is precisely what happened.

The Iraqis' initial failure to destroy the Iranian air force on the ground assured the prolongation of the conflict and created a grave double threat to the Saudis' vital interests. Their alignment with Iraq, made even more manifest by their allowing Iraqi aircraft to disperse in their own airfields to escape Iranian air force counterattacks, exposed them to Iranian reprisals against their vulnerable oil facilities. Moreover, the superior Iranian navy, which was to have been neutralized by a quick general Iranian collapse, was now in a position to interdict maritime traffic, including oil, in the narrow Gulf waters and through the Strait of Hormuz to and from Iraqi and allied ports. Faced with this grave, clear and present danger, the Saudis turned to the United States for help.

From the perspective of the Saudis, their appeal to the United States was no easy matter. It probably involved a loss of face for Abdallah and his allies, who had argued for a strategy based on minimal dependence on the American connection. It certainly meant a deviation from the policy that was being pursued, and created the risk of angering Syria and endangering the modus vivendi achieved with the two Yemens and the Soviets, not to speak of further antagonizing Iran and giving ammunition to its anti-Saudi propaganda. Yet, in the absence of any alternative, the Saudis took the step.

The United States, for its part, had always thought that it had a common vital interest with the Saudis in protecting the flow of oil and was therefore anxious to respond favorably to the Saudi appeal for help. However, because of the recent contretemps in the relations between the two countries, it sought to use the occasion to demonstrate their cooperation on vital security matters. Accordingly, the United States proposed to deploy a squadron of American-manned AWACS aircraft to Saudi bases to detect and track potentially hostile planes while they were still in international airspace, before they approached the Saudi oil facilities located near the coast. Ostensibly, Saudi fighters were to undertake the interception of enemy aircraft; but the potential enemy understood that its aircraft were likely also to be engaged by American personnel flying F-15 fighters previously acquired by the Saudis, backed up by carrier-based American aircraft. Washington also proposed to set up a joint Saudi-American naval task force to deter interference with the sea lanes and to defeat it should it occur. Although the Saudis could contribute little to such a force, their participation was meant to underscore the military cooperation between the two countries. For the same reason, the United States insisted that the Saudis announce that the envisaged deployment of the AWACS was being done at their request.

The Saudis welcomed the air defense proposal and agreed to having it announced that the AWACS deployment was made at their request, since the operation could not have been practically executed without their assent. Regarding the defense of the sea lanes, however, where their practical cooperation was not essential, they preferred to leave the matter entirely in the hands of the United States so as to minimize the extent to which they openly "compromised" themselves. The United States did not insist on Saudi participation, contenting itself with securing its own interests and with the quid pro quo that the Saudis offered for its timely assistance.

The Saudi quid pro quo took the form of increased oil production to counter the effect of the disruption of Iraqi and Iranian output by the war. In October 1980 the Kingdom raised its production from 9.7 mbd the previous month to 10.3 mbd — the highest level it could sustain — and kept it at or near that level for the following ten months. Physically, the Saudi increase of 0.5 mbd was hardly enough to make up for the shortfall caused by the war: Iraqi production dropped from 3 mbd to 0.15 mbd in October before inching back to 0.6 mbd in January 1981; Iranian production declined from 1.4 mbd to 0.6 mbd in October before moving up to 1.6 mbd in January 1981. Psychologically, however, the Saudi action was crucial in preventing the development of the kind of panic that had sent oil prices soaring after the fall of the shah and the Saudis' April 1979 decision to cut production by 1 mbd. Instead of a rush to stock up, dealers began to reduce the inventories they had overstocked during the previous year. Demand also decreased as a result of the previous massive price increases, while producers other than Saudi Arabia also increased their output. The result was that after the spot market price climbed from $32.92 in September to $41.25 in November 1980, it declined steadily to $32.00 in June 1981 — lower than the prewar level. The Saudis continued to maintain a high level of production a while longer and unwittingly contributed to the development of an oil glut.[20]

Reversion to Ambivalence as the Danger Subsides, November 1980 – November 1981

While the United States viewed the overt and concealed military coopera- tion with Saudi Arabia as marking the start of an upward trend in the continuing strategic relationship between the two countries, the Saudis viewed these developments with two minds — in more than one sense. On the one hand, the Saudi leaders — including Abdallah — felt fortu- nate to be able to call on the kind of help America provided at a critical moment for the Kingdom; on the other hand, they — including Fahd — were worried about the costs they might have thus incurred, and even more about the costs they might yet incur if they should sustain their association with the United States, either at the current level or at the higher level they knew the United States wanted.

The fortuitous turn in the Gulf war, with the conflict settling into a stalemate, largely resolved the Saudis' dilemma and restored them to a position in which they could control the extent of the American connec- tion with a view to their other concerns. They used that position to correct the tilt toward the United States, to repair the damage it might have caused, and to capitalize on unexpected opportunities that the new situation and related developments opened up. By March 1981, when the new American administration was proposing to use the Saudi connec- tion as a basis for a regional strategic alignment, dubbed "strategic con- census," the Saudis were totally unreceptive and had reverted almost entirely to their prewar reserved, instrumental, and essentially ambiva- lent attitude toward the United States. Although the American connection was preserved as a last resort, it was manipulated as a function of imme- diate fluctuations in the security situation and the related balance of influence and power among the Saudi leaders.

In the Gulf arena the stalemate was potentially more advantageous to Saudi security interests than an Iraqi victory. It relieved the Saudis' concern about the long-term strategic consequences of such a victory and created conditions favoring an eventual negotiated settlement that would balance the two Gulf powers against each other indefinitely. To capitalize on these potential advantages, the Saudis needed to distance themselves from Iraq enough to tempt Iranian interest, but not so much as to provoke Iraqi charges of betrayal and antagonistic reactions. The American military protection of Saudi Arabia, coupled with Washington's secret contacts with Iranian President Bani Sadr, helped make that feat possible. The Iranians found it preferable, on balance, to accept the Saudis' reduced association with Iraq than to confront them and their American protector, while Iraq was compelled to content itself with the assistance it could get from the Saudis and the emirates and looked to the former to help bail it out of the war. Thus, by December 1980 the Saudis had maneuvered themselves into a position in which they were able to play their favorite role of mediator through the Islamic Conference, which assembled at Ta'if in January 1981. Moreover, they had begun by then to take advantage of Iraq's and Iran's absorption in the conflict in order to promote, against objections from both and fears among some of the emirates, the first moves toward the eventual creation of the Gulf Cooperation Council (see Chapter 14).

In south Arabia, the deployment of the American AWACS, coupled with the two Yemens' alignment on opposite sides in the Gulf war and with their resentment and suspicion at being excluded from the Saudi-promoted Gulf pact, jeopardized the entire, painfully achieved, prewar modus vivendi. The stalemate, however, gave the Saudis the chance to sort out the situation and repair the damage. After using their financial and political leverage with the YAR, demonstrating their distance from the United States while making modest gestures toward the Soviet Union, and showing a tolerant understanding toward PDRY's reactive tightening of its Soviet connection and its relations with Ethiopia, they were able to restore the modus vivendi by April 1981 (see Chapter 15).

If the stalemate permitted the Saudis to reassert an independent policy in the Gulf, and if in the south it facilitated restoration of the modus vivendi that had been worked out independently of the United States, in the Arab arena it enabled the Saudis to revert to a fully ambivalent posture, reasserting their disagreement with Washington over the Arab-Israeli conflict while retaining or seeking its help in other matters. That process centered on a series of encounters with Syria, starting with the latter's hostile reaction to the deployment of the American AWACS.

Syria and Libya raised the strongest objections to the deployment, viewing it as a likely indication of American collusion in Iraq's war against Iran and of a Saudi inclination to join, or fall into, the overall American strategic design for the Middle East. Syria reacted by signing a Friendship and Cooperation Treaty with the Soviet Union on October 8, 1980, while Libya attacked the Saudis so sharply that they broke off diplomatic relations with it on October 28, 1980. Initially the Saudis tried to take advantage of the stalemate and of the fact that those two countries, along with PDRY, were the only ones in the Arab world that supported Iran against Iraq, in order to isolate them and, above all, to detach the PLO from Syria and thus undermine the latter's posture as guardian of the Palestinian cause. They pushed to convene the November 1980 summit in Amman and to place the Gulf war on its agenda despite Syrian objections and boycott threats. However, the Saudi maneuver backfired when Syria "persuaded" the PLO and even Lebanon to stay away from the summit and then went on to exert military pressure on Jordan, forcing the rump conference to adopt a mild position on the Gulf war and the Saudis to rush Emir Abdallah to Damascus in an endeavor to mollify it (see Chapter 13). In the meantime, the encounter prompted the Saudis to try to rebut Syrian charges by demonstrating their independence from the United States.

Thus, in the last week of October 1980, after President Carter announced his decision to reject the Saudi request for bomb racks for the F-15s, the Saudis threatened to buy their weapons elsewhere if the West refused to sell them.[21] The threat was particularly significant because it was made by the ostensibly pro-American Crown Prince Fahd a few weeks after Syria signed the friendship and cooperation treaty with the Soviet Union. In the last week of December 1980, the Saudis also made favorable comments about Brezhnev's proposal for the neutralization of the Persian Gulf after having previously denounced it. Finally, at the January 1981 meeting of the Islamic Conference at Ta'if, Fahd called on the Muslim nations to resist military alliances with the superpowers and supported a resolution rejecting Camp David and calling for jihad against Israel.[22]

The Saudis' demonstrations of their independence from the United States were, paradoxically, also designed to prepare the ground among the Arab constituency for renewing and pressing their request for American arms, including AWACS aircraft. They were meant to anticipate and counter charges that the envisaged arms deal was another indication of their being in thralldom to America. The newly installed Reagan administration, oblivious of these concerns and mindful only of the greater protective role played by the United States since the start of the Gulf war, indicated its willingness to accede to the Saudis' arms request but sought to link it tacitly to its attempt to organize an informal alignment based on "strategic consensus."

From the Saudis' point of view, that endeavor was ill conceived and could hardly have been worse timed. It was a transparent attempt to circumvent the Arab-Israeli conflict at a time when the Syrians were charging them with seeking to do just that and were following up on their accusation by making trouble in Lebanon and stirring up the radical NDF opposition in the YAR. The endeavor also came at a time when the Saudis were trying, on the one hand, to promote a mediated settlement of the Iran-Iraq war and, on the other hand, to put together the GCC in the face of objections from both Iran and Iraq, who were suspicious of an American link, and of apprehensions among some of the GCC members themselves. Finally, the American proposal was made while the Saudis were striving to restore the modus vivendi in the south, which was in danger of unraveling as a result of a chain reaction triggered by the earlier deployment of American AWACS. Little wonder that the Saudis promptly and categorically rejected the proposal publicly and made it a point to assert again and again that the main threat to the security of the region was Israel.

But the Saudis still needed the American arms for their long-term defense program and were concerned about the congressional opposition to the administration's willingness to sell them. Moreover, by the summer of 1981, as the Islamic mediation efforts failed, Bani Sadr was dismissed, and Iranian aircraft attacked Kuwait again, the Saudis were reminded of the importance of preserving the American security connection. Consequently, at least some Saudi leaders felt that a gesture was needed to offset the rebuff of the American "strategic consensus" initiative and the negative statements that preceded and followed it. The opportunity to do so came in the later months of the summer of 1981 and took the form of enunciating what came to be known as the Fahd Plan. By that time the modus vivendi in the south had been somehow restored, and in the north the Saudis had gained some credit with the Syrians by extricating them from a dangerous tangle in Lebanon when they mediated, with their approval, a comprehensive cease-fire in cooperation with the United States. The Fahd Plan appeared to be a particularly suitable instrument to accomplish the Saudi purpose without antagonizing the Syrians, because it also sought to undercut President Sadat's attempt, during his August 1981 visit to Washington, to revive the peace process on the basis of the Camp David formula (see Chapter 13).

Four points in the evolution of the Fahd Plan from a tactical move to a strategic initiative (see Chapter 13) were relevant to the Saudi-American connection. (1) The plan began to evolve after leaders of the PLO gave it their approval, and it acquired real momentum after the assassination of President Sadat on October 6, 1981, congressional approval of the AWACS deal later that month, and the Reagan administration's subsequent statements in favor of the plan. These developments encouraged Fahd to persevere, and particularly to seek to preserve the notion of an American-supported peace plan after the Camp David formula was shaken by Sadat's death. (2) That same process caused the Syrians to worry about losing their hold on the PLO and finding themselves either isolated or compelled to negotiate a settlement with Israel under American-Saudi aegis from a position of strategic weakness. This anxiety led them to move from a reserved position to one of opposition. (3) The Saudi efforts to overcome Syrian opposition involved several Saudi leaders and were not well coordinated, with the result that the Syrian and PLO positions were in doubt until the last moment and became known only at the opening of the November 1981 Fez summit called to consider the plan. (4) In the meantime Israel, which was preparing for the final evacuation of Sinai in April 1982, warned the United States that any deviation from Camp David could endanger the withdrawal. This threat led Secretary of State Haig to issue, three days before the opening of the Fez summit, a statement reasserting the American commitment to Camp David, which further undermined the Saudi endeavor. The net result was that President Assad refused to attend the conference, the PLO joined Syria in opposing the Fahd Plan, and the conference collapsed hours after it opened. Thus ended the most forward Saudi attempt in the second stage to find a common ground with the United States on the Arab-Israeli problem.

Opting for Syria and Relapsing into Improvisation, December 1981 – June 1982

Although the Syrians humiliated the Saudis by engineering the defeat of the Fahd Plan, the next major Saudi move was to try to conciliate rather than confront Syria and attempt to achieve a comprehensive strategic understanding with it. The reasons that prompted the Saudis to pursue that course included, on the one hand, their need for help in contending with a multifaceted crisis in the Gulf arena; and, on the other hand, their inability to turn to the United States for such help because of developments that compromised it in the Arab-Israeli arena. The politics of the royal family also probably played a role. Fahd having failed in the pursuit of the American-oriented plan that bore his name, Abdallah and others were more readily able to secure the agreement of the collective leadership to a broad entente with Syria aimed at reviving the "Arab strategy" in a revised version.

The gambit quickly proved to be a failure even as the Saudis faced a worsening strategic problem in the Gulf owing to the likelihood of an Iranian final victory. The Saudi leaders explored by proxy the possibility of bringing Egyptian military power to the rescue of Iraq; but after that attempt failed, they could not bring themselves to accept Washington's offer of greater, open military cooperation. They rather chose to content themselves with the existing discreet American help, to try again for an understanding with Syria despite its betrayal of the agreement concluded with it only months before, and to hope that events would turn their way. Not for the first time, events did so, at least for a while, as the Iranian offensive finally ground to a halt and as the Lebanon war diminished Syria's power, isolated it, and forced it to depend on the Kingdom's American connection as no previous event or Saudi initiative ever had. How the Saudis used or failed to use that opportunity goes beyond the reign of King Khaled, who died in the midst of these developments.

Even as the debate over the Fahd Plan was moving to its climax in November 1981, the stalemate in the Gulf war gave way to a very troublesome situation for the Saudis. In September and October 1981, clashes between Iranian pilgrims and the Saudi authorities and another Iranian air attack on Kuwait—this time on oil storage facilities—had led to a severe deterioration of Saudi-Iranian relations. The Saudis at first tried to put the tension in the region to advantage in order to develop their scheme for the GCC. Toward the end of November, however, even as the Fahd Plan went down to defeat, the Iranians' successful offensive in the Bostan area suddenly threatened the entire Iraqi front and made the likelihood of a total Iranian victory seem very real. The full implications of that prospect were frightening if somewhat obscure and complex, but one of them was made all too clear to the Saudis in the next two weeks. The discovery, announced on December 13, of an Iranian-supported plot to overthrow the regime of Bahrain and to destabilize their own raised the dreaded specter of a combination of external pressure and internal subversion to which the Saudis felt most vulnerable, and regarding which American help was of limited value. (For a full discussion of these developments, see Chapter 14.)

Seeking additional American aid in connection with that situation was in any case highly problematic if not impossible for the Saudis because of simultaneous developments in the Arab-Israeli arena. The United States, anxious to repair the damage that its flirtation with the Fahd Plan might have caused to the prospects of Israel's evacuation of Sinai, followed Haig's statement on the eve of the Fez summit with additional reassurances. On November 30, 1981, it signed with Israel a memorandum of understanding on strategic cooperation, and on December 3 it issued with Israel a joint statement reaffirming the Camp David accords as the only basis for peace and for the Multilateral Force Organization. Nevertheless, on December 14, Begin's government, partly in reaction to the earlier brouhaha about the Fahd Plan, rushed through the Knesset a bill annexing the Golan Heights. Although the United States joined other members of the UN Security Council the next day in voting for a resolution denouncing the Israeli move and threatening sanctions if it were not rescinded, and although it followed up by suspending the strategic cooperation agreement three days later, triggering a fierce verbal assault by

Begin, the Syrians believed that the annexation was a sequel to American-Israeli strategic cooperation, and in any case pronounced the act to be a virtual declaration of war (see Chapter 13).

Constrained in their ability, if not in their willingness, to turn to the United States, the Saudis swallowed their pride and turned to Syria for relief. Assad, faced with the American-Israeli challenge abroad and with mounting Muslim Brethren pressures and attacks at home, was disposed at that moment to make a deal anyway to retain Saudi support. The result was the comprehensive Saudi-Syrian understanding achieved during Assad's visit to Riyadh on December 22 and 23. The Saudis agreed to shelve indefinitely the Fahd Plan, to help Syria acquire additional Soviet arms as part of an effort to tilt the strategic balance vis-à-vis Israel to the Arab side, to cancel Fahd's planned trip to the United States, and to consider establishing diplomatic relations with the Soviet Union. In return Assad promised to refrain from criticizing Jordan and Iraq and to reach out to conciliate them as part of an effort to close Arab ranks and discourage Iranian adventurism (see Chapter 13). In the wake of the agreement, Jordan's King Hussein felt confident enough about his Syrian flank to call in January 1982 for volunteers to go fight on Iraq's side, but not enough to send regular Jordanian troops (see Chapter 14).

Neither side honored the understanding. The Saudis made no move toward the Soviet Union even though the United States vetoed anti-Israel resolutions in the Security Council in connection with the Golan and the West Bank and went on to reaffirm its determination to maintain Israel's military superiority after its envisaged withdrawal from Sinai. Moreover, the Saudis maintained a critical distance from Syria as its regime brutally suppressed the Muslim Brethren uprising in Hama while accusing the United States of supporting the rebels. The Syrians, reacting to condemnations of their repressive action, intensified their attacks on Jordan and Iraq. Worse still, as the Iranians launched yet another successful offensive in Khuzistan in March 1982, the Syrians deployed diversionary forces on Iraq's borders, cut off the flow of Iraqi oil through the pipeline running across their territory to the Mediterranean, and called upon the Iraqi people to overthrow Saddam Hussein (see Chapter 13).

Before the Syrian actions against Iraq in support of Iran's March offensive had totally defeated the purpose of the Saudis, the United States, in what had become a customary move, explored with the Saudis the possibility of greater military cooperation, in the expectation that the deteriorating situation in the Gulf would make them more receptive. Secretary of Defense Weinberger visited the Kingdom on February 5, 1982, to that end, in a tour that took him also to Oman and Jordan. The Saudis asked Weinberger for American help in establishing a Gulf arms industry, urged him to supply Jordan with advanced weapons, and agreed to his suggestion to set up a joint Saudi-American defense planning committee. Yet, because of the vestiges of their continuing concern with Syria, the Saudis went out of their way to indicate after Weinberger's departure that there were "fundamental differences" between the American and Saudi views of the Middle East, and to downplay the significance of the joint defense planning committee by stating that its only purpose was to follow up the Kingdom's arms purchases (see Chapter 14).

The rejection of the American offer of closer military cooperation was followed by the most successful Iranian offensive yet, which presaged the possibility of an Iranian invasion of Iraq and the latter's collapse. Dreading that prospect, Iraq and the Saudis' GCC partners sought to appeal to Egypt to intervene militarily to avert it. The Saudis, though fearful of Syrian and Iranian reactions, endorsed at least the exploration of that possibility by Sultan Qabus. When Egypt rejected the invitation,[23] the Saudis were left without any coherent policy to deal with the deteriorating situation. Perhaps they counted on the United States to do entirely on its own and for its own interest whatever could be done to stave off the dangers they faced. They may have been encouraged in such hopes by statements such as the one made by the American secretary of defense on May 21, 1982, that an Iranian victory over Iraq was not in the American interest, and another by the secretary of state on May 26 that warned Iran against spreading the conflict to neighboring nations and asserted that the United States would protect its "vital interests" in that area. Perhaps they hoped that the Iranians would be content with the ejection of the Iraqi invaders from their territory and be willing to negotiate a settlement. Noises to that effect did emanate from Iranian sources. Quite possibly, too, the tug-of-war among the Saudi leaders reached the point of paralysis in the last weeks of King Khaled's life and prevented agreement on any active course (see Chapter 14). At any rate it is clear that when King Khaled's reign ended, on June 13, 1982, the Saudis were sitting out the Gulf war crisis and hoping for the best, and that the eruption of a new war in Lebanon a week before could make matters either better or worse.

17

The Defense and Security Perspective, 1975–1982

Defense Allocations: Trends, Fluctuations, Significance

As in the reigns of Faisal and Saud, analysis of the budgetary allocations to defense and security under King Khaled confirms some of the main trends detected in the political-strategic analysis and sheds additional light on the Kingdom's defense and security concerns. However, partly because revenue was not a constraint throughout Khaled's reign, and partly because the Kingdom continued the pattern established by Faisal of planning for defense and security in terms of several years at a time, there are fewer revealing fluctuations in the data.

Table 13 provides the global data on defense and security allocations and its main components, both in absolute amounts in relation to total revenue, for all but the last year of Khaled's reign (the figures for which are not yet available).

1. Allocations to defense and security continued to increase by vast amounts. In the six years surveyed, they rose from about SR 36 billion to about SR 85 billion, a 133 percent increase. From fiscal 1973–74, the last year before the 1973 oil upheaval, to fiscal 1980–81, the allocations increased from SR 7.6 billion to SR 84.8 billion, an elevenfold increase in eight years.

In relation to revenue, defense and security allocations continued the pattern of Faisal's era. They fluctuated between 32 and 42 percent of revenue and averaged 36 percent a year, compared with 29 to 43 percent and an average of 37 percent under Faisal, excluding fiscal 1974–75, the first year after the upheaval. As in the Faisal era, a particularly large increase in revenue in a given year may cause the percentage allocated to

Table 13. Revenues and defense and security allocations, fiscal 1976–1982 (million SR and percent of revenue)

	1975–76	1976–77	1977–78	1978–79	1979–80	1980–81	1981–82
Revenues and allocations							
Total revenue	95847	110935	146493	130000	160000	261516	340000
Defense and security allocations[a]	35988	44735	47971	52516	66425	84822	
% of total revenue	(37.5)	(40.3)	(32.7)	(40.4)	(41.5)	(32.4)	
Specific defense and security allocations[b]							
1. Ministry of Defense	23725 (24.8)	31906 (28.8)	31601 (21.6)	35199 (27.1)	47060 (29.4)	59366 (22.7)	65084 (19.1)
2. National Guard	2613 (2.7)	4269 (3.8)	5603 (3.8)	5329 (4.1)	6217 (3.9)	7509 (2.9)	
3. Ministry of Interior	4880 (5.1)	5854 (5.3)	7986 (5.5)	9025 (6.9)	10247 (6.4)	12961 (5.0)	17280 (5.1)
4. Intelligence Bureau	221 (0.2)	206 (0.2)	281 (0.2)	400 (0.3)	398 (0.2)	486 (0.2)	
5. Emergency expenditures[c]	4500 (4.7)	2500 (2.3)	2500 (1.7)	2500 (1.9)	2500 (1.6)	4500 (1.7)	
6. Total 2–5	12263 (12.8)	12829 (11.6)	16370 (11.2)	17337 (13.3)	19364 (12.1)	25456 (9.7)	
Ratio of item 6 to item 1	.52	.40	.52	.49	.41	.43	

Source: Kingdom of Saudi Arabia, *Statistical Yearbooks,* 1976–1982.

a. Allocations for foreign aid are not included under defense and security expenditures because of the lack of a consistent series of data.

b. Items 1–5 are official Saudi budget categories.

c. Includes "contingency projects."

defense and security in that year to drop, but the percentage soon catches up with the increase. An interesting exception is fiscal 1978, discussed later.

During the same period, allocations to civilian welfare and development sectors also increased substantially in absolute amounts but on the whole maintained a constant, modest percentage of revenue. Allocations to the Ministry of Health, for instance, increased from SR 3.2 billion in fiscal 1975–76 to SR 5.7 billion in fiscal 1980–81, while as a percentage of revenue they fluctuated between 2.2 and 3.3 percent. Allocations to the Ministry of Agriculture and Water Resources increased from SR 1.3 billion in 1975–76 to SR 2.7 billion in 1979–80 before dropping to SR 1.6 billion in 1980–81, fluctuating between 1.6 and 2.7 percent of revenue.[1]

These contrasting patterns reveal a continuing high level of anxiety about defense and security among the Kingdom's rulers, and a continuing tendency to seek to allay that anxiety by devoting large financial resources to defense and security and then developing plans to spend those resources.

2. The bottom line of Table 13 also shows that the shift of emphasis from internal security instruments to the Ministry of Defense, initiated by Faisal in 1966–67, was maintained at roughly the same level under Khaled, reflecting a persistence of the intent to develop the regular armed forces despite any potential internal political risks.

As in the Faisal era, the notion that the National Guard was intended to balance the regular forces is not sustained by the data in items 1 and 2 of Table 13. On the other hand, the point previously made, that all the instruments of internal security were intended to balance the army, is sustained by the data for the Khaled period, as is shown in Table 14.

3. The proliferation of defense and security instruments noted in the reigns of Faisal and Saud finally stopped in Khaled's. Differentiation within existing instruments continued, albeit at a slower pace. The line allocations under the Ministry of Interior for "special security" and the National Security Council, begun at the end of Faisal's reign, continued and increased. Under the Ministry of Defense, a new line allocation was devoted to general staff, quaintly translated in the budgets as "staff officers presidency." The process of formal institutionalization and bureaucratization of the defense and security apparatuses seems thus to have been essentially completed.

Moving from the broad strategic level to the operational level, Table 15 shows the fluctuations in revenue and allocations to defense and security in terms of percentage of annual change. As for Faisal's reign, the composite category Ministry of Defense is broken into its components, and the survey of allocations to those components occasionally examines

Table 14. Comparative allocations to internal security and army, fiscal 1977–1982 (million SR and percent of revenue)

	1976–77	1977–78	1978–79	1979–80	1980–81	1981–82
Internal security	7714	10329	13870	14817	16862	20958
	(21.4)	(23.1)	(28.9)	(28.2)	(25.4)	(24.7)
Army	8888	15434	14822	17609	20143	23763
	(24.7)	(34.5)	(30.9)	(33.5)	(30.3)	(28.0)

Sources: Table 13 and Kingdom of Saudi Arabia, *Statistical Yearbooks,* 1977–1982.

Table 15. Annual revenues and allocations to defense and security instruments (million SR), with percent change from previous year, fiscal 1975–1982

	1974–75	1975–76	1976–77	1977–78	1978–79	1979–80	1980–81	1981–82
Total revenue	98247 (330.7)	95847 (−2.4)	110935 (15.7)	146493 (32.1)	130000 (−11.3)	160000 (23.1)	261516 (63.4)	340520[a] (30.2)
Total defense and security	14115 (85.3)	35988 (155.0)	44735 (24.3)	47971 (7.2)	52516 (9.5)	66425 (26.5)	84822 (27.7)	—
1. Ministry of Defense[b]	8814 (63.0)	23725 (169.2)	31906 (34.5)	31601 (−1.0)	35199 (11.4)	47060 (33.7)	59366 (26.1)	65084 (9.6)
a. Army	4122 (112.7)	8888 (115.3)	15434 (73.6)	14822 (−4.0)	17609 (18.8)	20143 (14.4)	23763 (18.0)	—
b. Air force	2363 (1.0)	5408 (128.9)	7024 (29.9)	7264 (3.4)	7581 (4.4)	11783 (55.4)	14177 (20.3)	—
c. Navy	240 (5.7)	2322 (867.5)	2564 (10.4)	2148 (−16.2)	3371 (56.9)	5166 (53.2)	5408 (4.9)	—
2. National Guard	1296 (99.7)	2613 (101.6)	4269 (63.4)	5603 (31.2)	5392 (−3.8)	6217 (15.3)	7509 (20.8)	—
3. Ministry of Interior	2307 (77.9)	4880 (111.5)	5854 (20.0)	7986 (36.4)	9025 (13.0)	10247 (13.5)	12961 (26.5)	17281 (33.3)
4. Intelligence	96 (50.0)	221 (130.2)	206 (−6.8)	281 (36.4)	400 (42.3)	398 (−0.5)	486 (22.1)	—
5. Emergency expenditures[c]	1600 (701.0)	4500 (180.9)	2500 (−44.4)	2500 (0.0)	2500 (0.0)	2500 (0.0)	4500 (80.0)	—

Source: Kingdom of Saudi Arabia, *Statistical Yearbooks,* 1975–1982.
a. Estimate by Kingdom of Saudi Arabia, Saudi Arabian Monetary Agency, *Annual Report, 1982* (Riyadh, 1982).
b. Items 1–5 are official Saudi budget categories.
c. Includes "emergency projects" and "contingent expenditures."

suballocations to salaries and projects. Figure 3 illustrates the relationship between percent annual changes in revenue and in defense and security.

4. Figure 3 and the data on defense and security in the table show comparatively low rates of increase in the allocations for defense and security in fiscal 1977–78 and 1978–79 (both beginning in June), which are not explainable by the changes in revenue in the two years taken together. This provides *prima facie* confirmation of the periodization adopted in the historical analysis, and is further sustained by a close comparison of the average allocations for those two years and those for the preceding year, presented in Table 16.

The data in Table 16 show that in fiscal 1977–78 and 1978–79 the average increases in defense and security allocations were exactly half

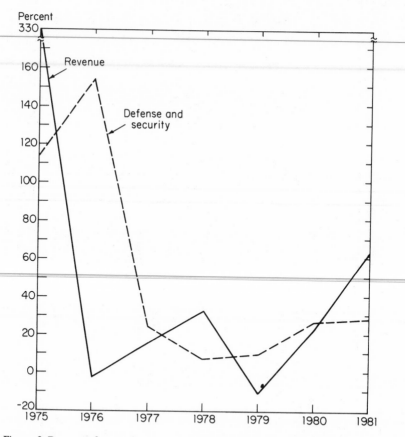

Figure 3. Percent change from previous year in revenues and defense and security allocations, fiscal 1975–1982 (Source: Table 15)

Table 16. Comparative allocations to defense and security instruments, fiscal 1977 and average fiscal 1978–1979 (million SR and percent change)

	1977	Average 1978–1979	Percent change
Total revenue	110935	138247	24.6
Total defense and security	44735	50244	12.3
Ministry of Defense	31906	33400	4.7
Army	15434	16216	0.5
Air force	7024	7423	0.6
Navy	2564	2760	0.8
National Guard	4269	5498	28.8
Ministry of Interior	5854	8506	45.3
Intelligence	206	341	65.5

Source: Table 15.

the average increases in revenue, indicating a comparatively relaxed attitude about security generally. The increases in allocations to the Ministry of Defense as a whole were a great deal lower, and those to the various branches of the armed forces remained virtually static. All of this confirms a major point made in the historical analysis, that 1977 and the first half of 1978 were the high water mark of the endeavor of Faisal's successors to pursue the coherent policy he had begun, before the onset of a second, troublesome stage.

5. It is noteworthy that, within the framework of relatively small average increases in allocations to overall defense and security in fiscal 1977–78 and 1978–79, there were very large increases in the allocations to instruments of internal security, in stark contrast to the virtually static allocations to the regular armed forces. This is probably yet another specific illustration of the relentless Saudi preoccupation with security. When the need or opportunity for greater effort in one direction is temporarily reduced, an outlet for such effort is sought in another direction.

6. By the time the budget for fiscal 1979–80 (May–May) was worked out, the "good" stage had come to an end with the multiple crises of the fall of the shah, the Egyptian-Israeli peace treaty, and the war between the Yemens. This is reflected in the substantial increase in the rate of allocations to defense and security generally in that year and the next (see Table 15, line 2). The increases would have been even more substantial if foreign subsidies were included as part of defense and security, which was not done because of the lack of a complete series of data. It is known, however, that allocations to "foreign aids" increased from SR 1 billion in

1978–79 to SR 7 billion in 1979–80 and SR 9 billion in 1980–81. Inclusion of these figures would raise the rate of increase in defense and security in 1979–80 over the previous year from 26.5 to 37 percent. For 1980–81 the percent increase over the previous year would remain basically unchanged, but the absolute amount would be SR 93.8 billion.

The *average* increases in allocations to the various instruments in the two years of the second stage for which there are complete data compared with the averages for the last two years of the first stage are summarized in Table 17.

7. The data show that despite enormous average increases in revenue during the second stage because of the surge in oil prices, allocations to defense and security generally increased by similar magnitudes. Allocations to the regular armed forces, represented by the Ministry of Defense, increased over that period by even higher averages. Allocations to the instruments of internal security remained at levels comparable to those of the previous stage, although in the previous stage they far exceeded the rate of increase in revenue whereas in the second stage they fell far short of it. The average rate of increase for intelligence dropped exceptionally sharply, reflecting the consequences of the dismissal of its chief, Kamal Adham, in the wake of the crisis in Egyptian-Saudi relations, which were under his personal ministration. As is shown in Table 15, in 1979–80 (May–May) the allocation to intelligence was reduced by 0.5 percent, from SR 400 million to SR 398 million, even as other security instruments were getting large increases.

Table 17. Comparative average percent change in allocations to defense and security instruments, fiscal 1978–1979 over fiscal 1977 and fiscal 1980–1981 over fiscal 1978–1979

	% change 1978–1979 over 1977	% change 1980–1981 over 1978–1979
Total revenue	24.6	52.5
Total defense and security	12.3	50.5
Ministry of Defense	4.7	59.3
Army	0.5	35.4
Air force	0.6	74.9
Navy	0.8	91.6
National Guard	28.8	24.8
Ministry of Interior	45.3	36.4
Intelligence	65.5	29.6

Source: Tables 15 and 16.

8. In terms of year-to-year fluctuations in particular items rather than the stage-to-stage, broad fluctuations previously discussed, the following points in Table 15 seem noteworthy.

8a. The huge across-the-board increases in allocations in 1975 – 76 (July – June). These, as was pointed out in the discussion of the Faisal era, reflect the "catching up" of defense and security allocations with the huge increase in revenue the previous year, following the decision to uphold the high oil prices.

However, the increases also reflect the anxiety of Faisal's successors at a moment of transition during which the regime was particularly vulnerable. This factor is specifically reflected in the exceptionally high increase in the allocation to "emergency expenditures" in 1975 – 76, which then drops and stays low in the "good" years and rises again sharply in 1980 – 81 (May – May), in the wake of the troubles of 1979.

The concern during the succession transition is also manifested in an increase of between 87 and 122 percent in the salaries titles for all the components and subcomponents of defense and security in that same year. Except for the case of the navy, this increase does not reflect an expansion of personnel, but an effort to maintain the goodwill of existing security personnel with salary raises. (See point 9, below.)

8b. Big year-to-year fluctuations in allocations to the Ministry of Defense and its principal components. These are due mainly to the flow of contracts for defense construction and equipment and the Saudi practice of allocating most of the amounts even for a multiyear contract in the year in which the contract is concluded. That practice is intended to protect defense and security programs against possible sharp drops in revenue and is thus part of the entire Saudi security complex.

8c. A drop in the allocation to the National Guard in 1978 – 79 (June – May). The point was made earlier that the budgets for that year and the year before reflected the relative relaxation of Saudi security anxieties; yet, although several components of defense and security received relatively small increases and "emergency expenditures" received no increase, the National Guard alone experienced a cut — the only one on record since 1962.

Was this an early reflection of the strain between Fahd and Abdallah that came to a head before the fiscal year was over, and did it contribute to the showdown? The answer must await further evidence.

8d. The Mecca mosque takeover and the Shi'ite disturbances of late 1979 are reflected in 1980 – 81 (May – May) in the very large, 80 percent, increase in the allocation to "emergency expenditures" — a good barometer of the Saudi sense of insecurity. Another reflection is in the allocation to the Ministry of Interior, which increases by the next highest percentage that year, 26.5 percent. Within the Ministry of Interior, "special security" receives an exceptional increase of 134 percent over the previous year, from SR 161 million to SR 377 million.

9. A systematic examination of the allocations to salaries for all the defense and security instruments after 1975–76 showed some puzzling fluctuations. In an attempt to decipher their significance, the percent annual changes in salaries were compared with the percent annual changes in total allocations to the defense and security components. Moreover, similar data for two civilian ministries were computed for control. The results are shown in Table 18.

Table 18 documents the nearly 100 percent increase in salary titles for all defense and security instruments in fiscal 1975–76 (July–June), which was explained before as being probably due to the anxiety of the succession period. A confirmation of that interpretation is the fact that salaries for the civilian ministries increase half as much or less, even though their total allocations — especially those for Health — increase by a very high percentage.

Table 18. Percent change from previous year in total and salary allocations to defense and security instruments and to Ministries of Agriculture and Health, fiscal 1976–1981

	1975–76	1976–77	1977–78	1978–79	1979–80	1980–81
Ministry of Defense	169.2	34.5	−1.0	11.4	33.7	26.1
	(90.1)	(−9.5)	(100.3)	(36.6)	(−1.2)	(33.2)
Army	115.3	73.6	−4.0	18.8	14.4	18.0
	(87.4)	(−9.5)	(94.8)	(17.8)	(−3.3)	(35.0)
Air force	128.9	29.9	3.4	4.4	55.4	20.3
	(96.4)	(−10.0)	(117.2)	(15.6)	(−3.4)	(24.2)
Navy	867.5	10.4	−16.2	56.9	53.2	4.9
	(121.7)	(−5.9)	(116.7)	(46.2)	(7.9)	(34.8)
National Guard	101.6	63.4	31.2	−3.8	15.3	20.8
	(100.0)	(−3.4)	(98.4)	(21.4)	(0.8)	(26.1)
Ministry of Interior	111.5	20.0	36.4	13.0	13.5	26.5
	(136.7)	(−0.8)	(105.3)	(64.7)	(0.2)	(30.1)
Intelligence	130.2	−6.8	36.4	42.3	−0.5	22.1
			(100.0)	(20.3)	(−1.8)	(33.1)
Ministry of Agriculture	67.2	7.3	−6.3	34.4	47.0	−3.7
			(53.5)	(13.8)	(9.5)	(32.5)
Ministry of Health	174.9	−7.0	13.5	19.8	19.5	17.2
	(52.2)	(6.6)	(56.2)	(37.6)	(15.1)	(50.7)

Sources: Table 15 and Kingdom of Saudi Arabia, *Statistical Yearbooks,* 1976–1981.

The most puzzling point in the table is the decrease in salary allocations to all defense and security instruments in the next year— 1976–77 (June–June)—followed by another increase of nearly 100 percent in 1977–78 (June–June). The decrease in 1976–77, though amounting to 10 percent or less, violates the pattern of mean increases of 20 percent or more. Furthermore, the cut in the salary title occurs when total allocations to the various defense and security instruments increase by very substantial percentages. It should be noted that here, too, the civilian ministries are not affected in the same way either in fiscal 1976–77 or in fiscal 1977–78, so the explanation must be specific to the defense and security instruments.

It is extremely unlikely that the decrease in the salary title in fiscal 1976–77 is due to an actual cut in personnel pay, wedged between two increases of about 100 percent each. It must indicate a reduction — and a rather substantial one — in the *number* of personnel. Because the reduction affects all the instruments, though in varying degrees, and occurs in the context of large increases in total allocations to those instruments, it is unlikely that the reduction in the number of personnel reflects a relaxation of security tension. The only remaining explanation is a purge affecting all the instruments of defense and security.

Such a hypothesis would also help explain the subsequent 100 percent increase in the salary title the following year. The increase could then be seen as an attempt to appease the security personnel after the shake-up of the purge. The only trouble with this hypothesis is that there is no satisfactory substantive confirmation of it from other sources. One informed observer, in a study published by the London International Institute for Strategic Studies (IISS), reported that in October and November 1977 seventeen officers and a large number of civilians were tried for plotting against the regime, including three air force officers who were tried in absentia after flying their planes to Iraq.[2] Even if those trials are assumed to reveal only the tip of the iceberg, there would still be a timing problem. Since the 1976–77 budget was finalized in May 1976 at the latest, the purges must have taken place earlier, which involves a gap of at least one and a half years between the purges and the trials. Not impossible, but not very satisfactory.

The table also shows slight decreases in the salary titles for army and air force and a negligible increase for the National Guard in 1979–80 (May–May). The hypothesis of a purge may be more plausible in that troublesome period, but again there is no corroborative evidence except for an unsatisfactory hint. The IISS annual *Military Balance* for 1979–80 reports global numbers for the Saudi army, air force, and National Guard that are 22 to 43 percent lower than those reported in the previous year but provides no explanation.

Strategic-Military Concepts and Programs:
Scope, Aims, Results

At the time of Faisal's death and Khaled's accession, Saudi Arabia was getting ready to launch its most ambitious defense program. For the first time, it had a comprehensive ten-year plan based on the 1974 U.S. Department of Defense (DoD) survey, including an overall strategic concept, an operational strategy, and specific force levels and armament programs for all the services. A separate seven-year plan was also worked out for the National Guard. Ample resources were available to finance the plans, and the domestic and international political climate highly favored close cooperation with the United States, which was indispensable for their realization.

However, typical of the circumstances under which the Kingdom has lived since the end of World War II, within four years of Khaled's accession and less than halfway through the ten-year plan, the strategic environment was abruptly transformed by major upheavals. The overthrow of the shah by Islamic revolutionaries turned Iran from a shield to Saudi Arabia and a pillar of Gulf security into a source of major threats to both. The United States, the ultimate security guarantor in the 1974 grand strategic concept, not only "failed," in the Saudis' view, to rescue the shah's regime but also placed itself in a position in which it could not restore a long-term strategic balance in the Gulf without immediately exposing the Kingdom to grave perils. The uproar caused among potentially dangerous Arab parties by the signing of the American-promoted Egyptian-Israeli peace not only prevented the Saudis from turning to the United States for greater strategic support but also compelled them, after bitter debate and a split among their leaders, to espouse an Arab-oriented strategy, which had the potential to damage permanently (insofar as anything can be permanent in that fluid region) the Kingdom's relationship with the United States.

Fear of the latter prospect, on the one hand, and the internal fragmentation of the Arab front that had formed as a result of the Egyptian-Israeli peace treaty, on the other hand, enabled the Saudis to shore up their American connection by "agreeing to disagree" on the peace issue. But their continuing fear of Syrian and other Arab reactions, together with their own accumulated doubts about the reliability of the United States, inhibited them from undertaking or depending on any explicit strategic association with Washington. So, rather than seeking to replace the tattered grand strategic conception of the 1974 plan with a neat, coherent alternative, the Saudis adopted piecemeal a set of disparate strategic goals and endeavored as best as they could to muddle their way through the resultant inconsistencies.

Chief among those goals was the attainment of a maximum independent self-defense capability to compensate for Iran's transformation from an asset to a liability, to contend with the possibility of Iraqi ascendency, and to avert the problems of close association with the United States. The problem here was twofold. First, to the extent that the Saudis were in fact capable of achieving that degree of independent capability in the long run, the endeavor to realize it involved greatly *increased* dependence on American arms and technical assistance in the intermediate run of ten years or so. Could such prolonged and increased dependence at the technical level be insulated and separated from the strategic level either in reality or in the perception of relevant others? Second, how were the Saudis to deal with threats likely to arise in the meantime without becoming visibly entangled with the United States at the strategic level?

The historical analysis has shown how the Saudis dealt with the second problem as it manifested itself in the Soviet invasion of Afghanistan, the Iran-Iraq war, and the Lebanon war. They essentially improvised and zigzagged, first tilting toward the United States then leaning toward neutralism; calling on American AWACS aircraft and personnel shortly after the outbreak of the Gulf war and then using the first opportunity to put some distance between themselves and the United States; making some attempts to isolate the Syrians and, at the first signs of failure, seeking to appease them again. Regarding the first problem, the Saudis tried as much as possible to downplay their technical connection with America and to obscure it by diversifying that kind of relationship to some extent to include other Western powers. However, because of the magnitude of the American role, these efforts had only limited success (even in the judgment of friends of the Saudis) and entailed additional problems.

A second major strategic goal adopted by the Saudis in the wake of the upheaval in the strategic configuration was to press for the creation of the GCC and then seek to turn it into an authentic regional security and defense organization. Such an organization was necessary for achieving coordination of antisubversion measures and providing for mutual regime support, and was indispensable for the development of an integrated regional air defense system, without which the Kingdom's own defense system would be vulnerable. The problem here, however, was that the Saudis met with resistance from some GCC members, especially Kuwait, because of the massive American technical involvement in the Kingdom's defense plans and programs, and they were unable to overcome that resistance by the end of Khaled's reign.

If the Saudis should eventually manage to overcome that opposition, their dependence on the United States would be increased and prolonged as new, integrated defense programs to include the GCC were adopted. If the Saudis should fail, they either would face a major gap in their own air defense scheme or would have to subscribe to a different or additional defense scheme acceptable to their GCC partners, involving powers other than the United States — say France and/or Britain. The latter alternative would not only involve heavy additional costs, which the Saudis might be less able to afford than previously, but it would also greatly complicate the already considerable problems of logistics, command, control, and coordination.

The same kind of inconsistency involved in the Saudi aim of achieving independent military capability with American help affected yet another Saudi strategic objective, relating to the security of oil transit. In 1977, before the upheavals in the regional strategic configuration, the Saudis had adopted a project to build a pipeline from the Ghawar oil fields, near the Gulf, across the Kingdom to the Red Sea port of Yanbo. The 750-mile, 48-inch pipeline, with a throughput capacity of 2.3 mbd, was meant to reduce the Kingdom's dependence on the Strait of Hormuz by providing an additional outlet. The oil loaded at Yanbo would be carried either through the Bab al-Mandeb choke point or through the Suez Canal and the SUMED pipeline, which runs from 'Ain al-Sukhna, on Egypt's Red Sea coast, to a point west of Alexandria and has a throughput capacity of more than 1.5 mbd. In 1978, when construction of the Saudi pipeline began, the latter route presented no problem. A year later, however, just when the Strait of Hormuz route began in fact to be endangered by the upheavals in the Gulf, the Saudis also severed relations with Egypt in the crisis over the peace with Israel. Nevertheless, the Saudis not only continued the project that depended on Egypt's goodwill, but also expanded it to include greater throughput capacity and vast, costly storage facilities near the western end of the pipeline to provide an economic-strategic petroleum reserve. So far both the Egyptians and the Saudis have conveniently ignored the inconsistency between the Saudis' greater dependence on Egypt and their actual clash with it; but the problem could become a source of trouble in the future.

A fourth strategic goal broached by the Saudis was that of a strategic connection with Pakistan. For a while such a connection, coupled with deployment of a substantial Pakistani force in the Kingdom, was considered as a possible centerpiece for a new coherent strategic concept. It would not only restore the balance in the Gulf, disrupted by the Iranian revolution, but would also provide an effective, tangible deterrent against a variety of threats and greatly increase the military options potentially available to the Saudis. That scheme, however, became entangled in jurisdictional-political disputes among members of the royal family, was opposed by the head of the regular armed forces as contrary to the principle of self-sufficiency and as demoralizing to the Saudi armed forces, and was ultimately reduced by compromise to a limited measure to ease the military manpower problem. The defense minister tabled his insistence on conscription, which was opposed by the chief of the National Guard, in exchange for bringing in some 5,000 to 10,000 Pakistani troops to serve under his jurisdiction.

In addition to pursuing these disparate major strategic goals, the Saudis adopted or improvised several more-limited strategic measures. The Iranian upheaval and the failure of the attempt to appease the Iranian revolutionaries revived the old Saudi dread, experienced in the heyday of Nasserism, of a combination of external military pressure and internal subversion. So, in 1980, following the Mecca mosque insurrection and the poor performance of the National Guard and the army in putting it down, they decided, among other things, to create yet another special internal security force, this one under the Ministry of Interior, to deal with similar contingencies. In addition, during a visit to the Kingdom at the beginning of 1982, the American secretary of defense proposed the creation of a small but powerful Jordanian rapid deployment force to help in certain contingencies, especially ones in which American intervention would be embarrassing or otherwise problematic. The Saudis secretly approved the project, although it is not known whether they also agreed to provide material support for it.

The changes in strategic goals in response to the transformation of the strategic configuration necessitated major revisions in the 1974 operational concepts. The principle of compensating for the Kingdom's dearth of manpower and vast distances with high technology remained central; but it was pushed to such lengths, in connection with the goal of maximum self-sufficiency, as to make it almost qualitatively different. The general operational strategy also continued to be centered on defending the central Dhahran-Riyadh-Jidda corridor; however, the prominence and nature of the threats from the direction of Iran led to an immensely increased emphasis on defense against air attacks, hostile naval action, and internal subversion. The revisions were reflected in the general pattern of arms acquisitions during Khaled's reign and in the specific defense programs adopted for the various forces of the Kingdom.

Table 19 presents the data on major arms acquisitions during Khaled's reign. The acquisitions of the National Guard are included with those of the army because the available sources do not permit complete separation. For instance, it is known that tanks are for the army and V-150 and AML-90 armored vehicles are for the National Guard; but TOW missiles and antiaircraft guns are used by both and no distinction is possible. The value of the equipment ordered and of related training and servicing programs is estimated at over $25 billion. In addition, contracts for about $17 billion worth of military construction were concluded with the U.S. government alone.[3]

Table 19. Major defense acquisition programs, 1975–1982[a]

Year[b]	Army[c]	Air force	Navy
1975	300 AMX-30 medium tanks (France) 250 AMX-10 armored personnel carriers (APCs) (France)	60 F-5E/B/F fighter/bombers 10 KC-130 Hercules transports 8 C-130 Hercules transports	4 MSC-322 coastal minesweepers 1 large missile patrol boat 14 patrol boats 100 Harpoon surface-to-surface missiles (SSMs)
1976	250 M-60 medium tanks 100 M-113 APCs 1650 TOW antitank guided weapons (ATGWs) 4000 Dragon antitank (AT) missiles 50–60 Vulcan antiaircraft (AA) guns 6 Hawk surface-to-air missiles (SAMs)	4 F-5F fighter/bombers 17 C-130 Hercules transports 11 BAC Strikemaster counterinsurgency/trainers 2000 Sidewinder air-to-air missiles (AAMs) 1650 Maverick air-to-surface missiles (ASMs) 200 Bell 209AHIS attack helicopters	6 large missile patrol boats 12 coastal patrol boats 8 patrol boats (France)
1977	? Redeye SAMs	10 miscellaneous helicopters (Italy, Japan)	4 Badr class corvettes 9 As-Sadiq class fast-attack craft
1978	250 AML wheeled armored reconnaissance vehicles (ARVs) (France) 94 V-150 wheeled ARVs/APCs with ATGWs 86 35 mm AA guns	60 F-15 Eagle fighters (various types)	9 Tacoma fast patrol boats
1979	118 M-60A1 tank chassis 200 AMX-10P tracked APCs (France) 26 M-113A1 tracked APCs 12 M-160A2 mortar carriers 1292 Dragon AT missiles	2 KC-130 Hercules transports 20–40 CASA Aviocar transports (Spain)	
1980	50 M-116A1 self-propelled howitzers 579 V-150 wheeled ARVs/APCs with ATGWs 86 SAMs	2 C-130 Hercules transports 2 F-15C Eagle fighters	4 ASW F-2000 class (2610 tons) frigates (France)[d] 2 Durance class (17800 tons) oilers (France)[d] 2 Atlantic II marine reconnaissance aircraft (France)[d] 24 Dauphin-2 helicopters (France)[d]

Table 19 (continued)

Year[b]	Army[c]	Air force	Navy
1980 (cont.)			200 AS-15TT ASMs (France)
			? Crotale SAMs (France)
			? Otomat SSMs (France)
1981	18 M-198 155 mm towed howitzers	5 E-3A Sentry AWACS aircraft[e]	
	72 FH-70 155 mm towed howitzers	18 ground radar installations[e]	
		6 KC-135 tanker aircraft[e]	
		101 "FAST" kits, conformal fuel tanks for F-15s[e]	
		1177 AIM-9L AAMs[e]	
1982	200 VCC-1 TOW armored fighting vehicles	10 RF-5E reconnaissance aircraft	
		5 F-5F training aircraft	

Sources: Stockholm International Peace Research Institute, *World Armaments and Disarmament: SIPRI Yearbook* (London and Philadelphia: Taylor and Francis, 1976–1978); International Institute for Strategic Studies, *The Military Balance, 1974–75* through *1982–83* (London, 1974–1982); U.S. Congress, House of Representatives, Committee on Appropriations, *Foreign Assistance and Related Agencies Appropriations for 1978*, 95th Cong., 1st sess., 1977; U.S. Congress, Senate, Committee on Foreign Relations, *U.S. Arms Sales Policy*, 94th Cong., 2d sess., 1976; U.S. Congress, House of Representatives, Committee on Foreign Affairs, *Proposed Arms Sales to Saudi Arabia*, 96th Cong., 1st sess., 1979; idem, *Proposed Arms Sales for Countries in the Middle East*, 96th Cong., 1st sess., 1979.

a. All acquisitions are from the United States unless otherwise indicated.
b. Years refer to initiation of orders or agreements.
c. Includes National Guard.
d. Parts of a $3.45 billion package deal.
e. Parts of an $8.5 billion package deal.

A comparison of the data in the table with the equipment prescribed by the 1974 DoD survey (see Chapter 7) shows that the great bulk of the equipment recommended for the three services was acquired or ordered by the end of 1976. The one major exception was the order for the F-15 Eagles, which was finalized only in 1978 because the United States delayed approval. The 1974 survey had indicated that the Saudis needed forty advanced interceptors to replace the aging Lightnings, and the Saudis had made it clear as early as March 1976 that they favored the F-15s. In October 1976 President Ford had agreed to the Saudi request, but the Carter administration had reopened the issue and then delayed the confirmation procedure until May 1978. In the meantime the Saudis had raised the number of aircraft requested from forty to sixty.[4]

The speed with which the Saudis ordered the equipment part of more comprehensive programs suggests a sense among Saudi leaders that security is enhanced by the mere accumulation of hardware. The fact that nearly all the transactions were completed by early 1978 also reflected the closeness of Saudi-American relations in those years and the no less important fact that Saudi relations with key Arab parties at the time were such that the Saudi rulers felt no inhibition in openly entertaining close relations with the United States.

The table shows that after the equipment recommended by the DoD survey had been acquired, there was a brief slowdown in the flow of acquisitions and then a second major spurt of agreements starting in 1980 and continuing into 1981 and 1982. This overall pattern confirms the one observed in the preceding analysis of allocations to defense and security and supports the periodization adopted in the historical analysis. The second spurt reflects the revisions wrought in the initial DoD operational concepts and related programs after the upheavals of 1979 and 1980.

The most significant and most ambitious of those programs involved the acquisition from the United States in 1981 of an air defense package worth $8.5 billion. The package included 5 E-3A Sentry AWACS aircraft, 18 related ground radar installations, 6 KC-707 tanker aircraft (with an option on two more), 101 conformal fuel tanks for the F-15 aircraft acquired in 1978, and 1,177 AIM-9L air-to-air missiles with an all-aspect guidance and control system. The package was intended to provide a much greater air defense capability than had been envisaged in the 1974 program, in order to meet the danger of air attacks on oil facilities and other high-value targets, such as those executed by Iran against Iraq, and generally to reinforce the overall deterrent and defensive capability of the Saudi armed forces.

American and Saudi defense planners justified the need for the AWACS by reference to geographic and topographical features affecting the defense of Saudi oil facilities. Those facilities are all located within forty miles of the coast — many are on the coast or at sea — in terrain that does not rise significantly above sea level. As a result, any ground-based radar can provide only about thirty to fifty miles of coverage against low-flying aircraft, or something like two to four minutes' warning. A fighter aircraft could not even theoretically scramble and arrive on the scene in response to such warning until the attacking aircraft had begun exiting after having struck its target.[5] The AWACS, it was argued, would extend the warning time to a minimum of seven minutes, which would allow the AWACS to vector in an F-15 fighter to make at least one pass on an attacker before it hit its target, vector the acquisition radars of the Saudi Hawk batteries and allow them to engage effectively, and allow some backup coordination of the Saudi F-5Es.[6]

The conformal fuel tanks, it was argued, would extend the radius of the F-15 by 65 to 93 percent, depending on the mode in which it was used. This would give Saudi Arabia's sixty-two such aircraft the endurance and range to maintain air combat patrol with a comparatively limited number of fighters, to mass in the Gulf area for short periods even if Saudi Arabia should lose the air base at Dhahran, and to do the same to reinforce other parts of the country as necessary. The KC-707 tankers would extend these capabilities by making it possible to refuel the AWACS, F-15, and F-5E aircraft, and would enable Saudi Arabia to accept reinforcements from U.S. carriers or air bases outside the Kingdom. The AIM-9L missiles, with their all-aspect capability, would give the F-15s, and the F-5Es when adapted to receive them, a weapon for use in near "head-on" intercepts against low-flying attackers without having to sacrifice the time and the probability of intercept in maneuvering into a long-stern or "dog fight" position — a valuable feature in view of the limited warning time the AWACS can provide.

Another revision in the 1974 plan involved the expansion and acceleration of the naval development program through an agreement with France worth $3.45 billion. The expanded program envisaged a fleet of thirty-four combat ships, including four French-built 2,000-ton frigates armed with Exocet surface-to-surface missiles and Crotale naval SAMs, plus twenty-four Dauphin-2 helicopters armed with AS-15TT missiles for deployment on the frigates. It also included OTO Melara-Matra Otomat coastal defense missile systems. The overall aim was to create two flotillas for coastal defense, one in the Gulf and one in the Red Sea, plus ocean surveillance capability. The Gulf flotilla was also meant specifically to guard against naval attack on the oil facilities and to provide an advance sea-based radar warning.

To protect the flanks of the eastern air defense line, the Saudis endeavored to persuade the smaller Gulf countries to extend the purview of the GCC from internal security and mutual regime protection and to adopt compatible air defense programs to be integrated with those of the Kingdom. The results of these endeavors were still uncertain at the end of Khaled's reign, partly because of disagreement over the role of the United States in the project.

Shortly before Khaled's death the Saudis were also considering bids for a C3I system for the air force that would be used to tie into a nationwide network of sensors with the land and naval forces. The estimated cost of the program was $3.8 billion. The system would utilize 17 GE FPS-117 Seek Igloo three-dimensional solid-state radars, which would be deployed around the periphery of the country, and would encompass a hardened underground command and control center at air headquarters in Riyadh and five hardened sector centers. Air surveillance, warning, and weapons control decisions would be from the sectors, and centralized command

and control would be from Riyadh.[7] Theoretically, according to a U.S. Air Force officer, the program would provide an area defense system incorporating all the land, air, and naval defense assets of the Kingdom in an overall battle management system, the like of which the United States itself has never been able to afford.[8] A decision on that program was reportedly delayed because of the softening of the world oil market.[9] This and the delay of some construction at Kharj air base were the only known major instances through 1982 showing the effect of the decline in oil revenues on major defense projects.

In contrast to the major air defense programs, the program for the army did not change much from the 1974 plan. Efforts were made to acquire the German Leopard II tank, but when Bonn proved reluctant to authorize the sale the Saudis temporized by acquiring 150 kits for converting the M-60A1 tanks in their possession to M-60A3 standard in addition to 100 M-60A3s on order. Combat mobility and antitank capability were further emphasized with substantial orders of French AMX-10P armored personnel carriers (APCs) and American VCC-1 TOW-armed armored fighting vehicles. Organic air defense was also promoted through orders for a derivative of the Crotale SAM (Shahine), mounted on an AMX-30 chassis.[10]

The programs for the National Guard continued to follow a rhythm of their own, related to royal family politics and the domestic security situation as much as to changes in the external strategic environment. At any rate, the guard felt no need to respond to the critical events of 1979 and 1980 in the environment and at home because it had adopted an expansion program before they occurred. Its relatively modest 1973 program, which had already been upgraded once in 1976 to provide for an elaborate base infrastructure (see Chapter 7), was upgraded again in 1978 to provide for the creation of eight, instead of four, mechanized infantry battalions with organic air defense and artillery support, plus one logistics battalion.[11] Procurement for the expanded program was delayed somewhat by the dispute with the United States over the Egyptian-Israeli peace treaty, but in July 1979, as soon as that quarrel was settled, the guard concluded an arms and training agreement with the United States worth $1.2 billion.[12]

The events of 1979 and 1980, especially the seizure of the Mecca mosque, affected the development of internal security instruments under the Ministry of Interior, which had hitherto followed their own plans. Toward the end of 1975, for instance, the General Intelligence Department had signed a contract with a computing subsidiary of British Petroleum known as Scientific Control Systems (Scicon) worth 24 million pounds sterling for the creation of a national network of computerized intelligence. The project called for twin computer centers in Riyadh and

Jidda to be connected over scrambled radio links to twenty-seven branch offices of the GID located at airports, frontier posts, industrial centers, and major towns. The branches would feed into the computer intelligence reports from a network of informants and agents, and obtain on request profile dossiers on any named individual. The system was designed to monitor foreign workers, foreign visitors, and above all the multitude of annual pilgrims to the holy cities and to check them against a surveillance list. The target date for completion of the project was 1981.[13]

The intelligence failures associated with the Mecca insurrection prompted acceleration of that project. More important, the dubious performance of the National Guard and the army in putting down the insurrection also led to a decision in 1980 to establish a new, 1,200-man special antiterrorist unit equipped with helicopters and APCs under the jurisdiction of the Ministry of Interior. French cooperation was sought and led to the creation of a Joint Security Commission and to the signing of an agreement in November 1980 whereby France would train and equip that force. In July 1981 plans were announced for the creation of an entire "security training city," following the pattern of the military cities of the regular armed forces and the National Guard.[14]

The revised and expanded defense programs, plausible or even impressive though they may appear on paper, proved to be highly problematic in practice. First of all, although the programs were devised with a view to the scarcity of Saudi manpower, which had frustrated several previous defense plans, the Saudis nevertheless ran into difficulty in meeting the minimal planned requirements. Military service was opened up to Hijazis and other elements that had formerly been partly excluded, thus expanding the military manpower pool, but the attraction of the opportunities offered by the booming civilian sector and an aversion to the discipline and regular work schedule of the military kept Saudi men away from the armed forces. Minister of Defense Sultan ibn Abd al-Aziz tried to overcome that problem by advocating conscription in March 1979, after the fall of the shah's regime,[15] and pressing for it again in 1980, after the Soviet invasion of Afghanistan. He was, however, successfully opposed by Abdallah ibn Abd al-Aziz, who sought to protect the tribal character of his National Guard and feared the infusion of discontented elements into the armed forces.

Sultan, on the other hand, opposed the alternative solution, proposed by some of his brothers, of enlisting the service of Pakistani forces in the context of a broad-based agreement on strategic cooperation with that neighboring Muslim country. He was concerned about suggestions that command of the proposed force should not reside exclusively in his ministry, and argued that the entire project was detrimental to the prestige of the Saudi government and the morale of the armed forces because it underscored their inability to look after the defense of the Kingdom independently. When the Gulf war further accentuated the Kingdom's defense problems, the Saudi leaders finally agreed on a compromise wherein the conscription plan was shelved but a relatively small Pakistani force, of one or two brigades according to various sources,[16] was brought into the country, placed under the control of the Ministry of Defense, and deployed in border areas, at Tabuk and Khamis Mushayt.[17] The compromise somewhat eased the manpower problem for the army but hardly resolved it for the armed forces generally, especially the air force.

In the case of the air force, the problem remained particularly acute because of the large numbers of technical personnel and skilled workers needed to operate, maintain, and support the equipment of that service, and because the Saudis piled up program upon program for that central component of their defense plan. In 1977, for instance, the comptroller general of the United States reported to Congress that the Peace Hawk program successfully provided the Saudi air force with F-5 aircraft and associated facilities, but that the maintenance and support parts of the program were encountering serious difficulties. The report observed that any future purchases of advanced aircraft would only add to the maintenance and support problems of the Saudi air force and recommended that, in reviewing any such future request, Congress should ask the secretary of defense to provide information on the Kingdom's progress in operating and maintaining its F-5 aircraft.[18]

The Department of Defense rejected as impractical the linkage that this report tried to establish, and a few months later the Saudis concluded the deal for the sixty F-15s. Those aircraft required not only additional skilled manpower; they needed twice as many skilled men per plane for operation, maintenance, and support as the F-5 — eighty instead of forty.[19] Moreover, the first F-15s had barely arrived in the Kingdom, in January 1981, when the Saudis were already pressing the United States to approve their request for the five AWACS aircraft, ground radars, tankers aircraft, and F-15 enhancement equipment, which was consummated later that year. Well before the first AWACS aircraft had been delivered, the Saudis were already calling for bids for the most advanced, integrated C3I system that money could buy. All this in addition to ongoing programs to absorb forty-three C-130 transport aircraft and scores of helicopters partly associated with plans for air mobility and heliborne troops for the army.

The Saudis made large-scale use of foreign technical personnel in an attempt to meet the problem. It has been estimated that in 1979 nearly 60,000 foreign advisers and technicians were engaged in defense work, equal to the total number of Saudi regular forces at the time.[20] These included Jordanians, Pakistanis, Egyptians, and others, hired directly or seconded by their governments, as well as Western technicians and advisers contracted for as part of the major arms transactions to provide training in operation, maintenance, and support and to undertake the latter two functions until Saudis could take over. In 1980 the number of American technicians involved in direct support of U.S. weapons systems was about 4,325, in addition to about 2,000 British and probably a larger number of French personnel involved in parallel programs.[21] In the air force alone, American direct support personnel before the 1981 AWACS deal exceeded 2,000 — one for every seven Saudis. The plans called for the number to peak at over 2,300 by 1985, after the AWACS aircraft had been delivered and other programs had been completed, and then to decline gradually to a plateau of about 1,500 until the mid-1990s.[22] This, of course, ran counter to the objective of Saudi self-sufficiency or put it off to the distant future. In the meantime the AWACS, the centerpiece of the air defense program, would not be able to operate for more than a few days without U.S. support.[23]

The shortage of qualified manpower, notwithstanding the importation of foreign personnel, and the persistence of political impediments and bureaucratic bungling caused the various programs to fall far short of their minimal targets. The 1974 plan, taking account of the manpower problem, had envisaged a modest quantitative expansion of the personnel of the armed forces over the next ten years. These were to increase from about 60,000 to about 98,000, while the National Guard's size was to remain stationary at 35,000. Seven or eight years later, the actual size of the armed forces had *decreased* from the 1974 level to about 52,000, and that of the National Guard to about 23,000.[24]

The air force in particular, which was supposed to increase its personnel from 14,000 in 1974 to 22,000 by 1984 even before the critical expansion of its role as a result of the changes in the strategic environment, was only 15,000 strong by the end of 1982. The navy, starting from a very small base of less than 1,000, did relatively better, reaching 2,200 by the end of 1982; but that was still far short of the 3,900 level envisaged in the 1974 plan before the post-1979 projects for further expansion of its mission. The army suffered a drastic reduction from 45,000 to 35,000 in the same period, falling more than 50 percent short of the 72,000 mark set for it in the 1974 plan. The National Guard also suffered a decline, from 35,000 in 1974 to 20,000 – 25,000 at the end of 1982.[25] Even as all these forces were suffering these manpower strains, the Saudis, typically, created yet another instrument, the special security force under the Ministry of Interior, to deal with internal security weaknesses revealed by the Mecca insurrection.

Within the limits of the sizes actually attained, the record of the Saudis' progress in realizing the programs in place during Khaled's reign is mixed. There is some evidence that, for the first time since the Saudis sought to develop regular armed forces, back in the early 1950s, some substantial formations with a presumed independent operational capability have been actually put into place. However, these achievements, realized at astronomical costs, were still considerably short of the designated targets. Moreover, the operational capability of these formations remains questionable in the absence of a real combat test, and in light of their performance in the few instances in which they were put to any kind of test.

According to the 1974 plan, for instance, the Saudis were to achieve full capability to operate, maintain, and support the 115 F-5s by 1979. By 1977, delivery of equipment and construction projects were on schedule, but training, maintenance, and support operations were encountering difficulties. Initially, civilian personnel of the Northrop Corporation taught the Saudis to fly the aircraft; but the instruction did not meet U.S. requirements or satisfy the commitments to the Saudis, so U.S. military pilots took over, and the training schedule was extended through 1981.[26]

In the spring of 1983 a survey team of the respected trade journal, *Aviation Week and Space Technology*, reported that three F-5 squadrons were actually deployed operationally at Dhahran, Khamis Mushayt, and Ta'if, with a fourth at Ta'if being used partly for training. The operation, maintenance, and support of the squadron at Khamis Mushayt were reported to be 100 percent Saudi, the others more or less nearly so. Overall, the journal reported, the Saudis had achieved approximately 80 percent capability to operate, maintain, and support the F-5s, which means that the realization of the original program, when completed, will have taken at least twice the length of time originally planned.[27]

The target date for completion of the 1974 naval program was 1981. But again, although acquisition and construction were on schedule in 1977, training was behind by 25 percent, and the original target date had to be extended to 1983.[28] Given that the overall manpower target for the navy was off by more than 40 percent in 1982, it is fair to suppose that the 1974 program will be further stretched, even without the added demands of the French package contracted for in 1980.

The 1974 program for the army, designed to enable it to maintain and operate two armored brigades, four mechanized brigades, plus an airborne brigade and three helicopter battalions (see Chapter 7), had no specified target date. Unlike the air force and navy programs, the army's was conceived so that Saudi training personnel, prepared by small American technical teams, should train the bulk of the Saudi personnel, and so that the entire program should progress at the Saudis' own speed. The U.S. mission chief feared at the time of the program's inception that the entire training program might fail without intensive American input (see Chapter 7). In fact, by the end of 1976 some selected equipment items had been identified, but other basic matters, such as an approved brigade table of organization and equipment configuration, a confirmed equipment delivery schedule, and a related training schedule, had not yet been defined.[29] By the end of 1982 the Saudi army had achieved less than half of the 1974 program, as may be seen from the order of battle in Table 20.

The 1973 National Guard modernization program aimed at converting four infantry battalions into mechanized battalions with their own artillery and antiaircraft support over a seven-year period. By August 1976, halfway through the plan period, only one battalion had completed training, and the selection of personnel for a second training battalion was in progress.[30] Nevertheless, two years later the program goal was expanded to eight mechanized battalions with all-arms capability. Typically, the equipment for the expanded program was promptly acquired but training lagged behind. By the end of 1982 only half of the eight battalions projected in 1978 were in place.

Table 20 compares the overall standing of the Saudi armed forces at the end of Khaled's reign and at the end of Faisal's. For weapons on order to supplement the inventory data in Table 20, see Table 19.

Although the Saudis clearly made modest progress in building up their armed forces in the period surveyed, the actual operational capability of these forces remained untested. Under Khaled, as under Faisal, the Saudis continued to be careful not to commit their forces to combat even when the situation and their interests called for doing so, for fear of the repercussions of a setback. The 1979 war between the Yemens best illustrates that point. The Saudis' interest in the conflict was vital beyond doubt. They were sufficiently concerned about the course of the hostilities to alert and deploy their armed forces, to call on American help for North Yemen, and even to harbor two American AWACS aircraft to exercise sky surveillance over the battlefield and to guide possible action by Saudi combat aircraft. Yet, although the fighting lasted for three weeks, the Saudis refrained from committing either their ground or their air forces to the battle. In another, less dramatic set of instances, the Saudis refrained from even voicing a threat when the Iranian air force attacked Kuwait on three occasions.

There were, however, several occasions when a limited test was imposed on the Saudi defense forces by others, and the results were not reassuring. The most important of these was the action of the National Guard and the army in putting down the Mecca insurgency. That action was admittedly rather unusual, in that it required combat in a built-up area and the sanctity of the mosque imposed limitations on the kind of weapons and tactics that could be used. Nevertheless, a careful sifting of the mass of reports on the event points to excessive confusion at the

Table 20. Order of battle and inventory of weapons, 1975 and 1982 (brackets show JCSS data when these differ substantially from IISS data)

	1975	1982	
Personnel			
Army	40,000	35,000	
Navy	1,500	2,200	
Air force	5,500	15,000	
National Guard	28,000	25,000	[20,000]
Coast Guard and Frontier Guard	6,500	6,500	
Organization			
Army			
Infantry brigades	4	2	[4]
Armored brigades	1	2	[1]
Mechanized brigades	—	2	[1]
Royal Guard battalions	1	1	
Parachute battalions	1	2 + 1 Company	
Artillery battalions	3	4	
SAM batteries	10	18	
National Guard			
Infantry battalions	20	16 regular	
		4 all-arms plus irregulars	
Air force			
Fighter/bomber squadrons	2 (F-5E)	3 (F-5E)	
Counterinsurgency (COIN)/ training squadrons	2 (BAC-167)		
Interceptor squadrons	2 (Lightnings)	1 (Lightning)	
		1 (F-15, forming)	
Transport squadrons	2 (C-130)	3 (C-130)	
Helicopter squadrons	2 (AB-206, AB-205)	2 (AB-206, AB-205, AB-212)	
Operational conversion units		2 (with 40 F-5F/B; 6 F-15C/D)	

highest command levels, lack of coordination between National Guard and army formations, bad tactical decisions, inept execution, and low morale and poor discipline among the troops, especially in the National Guard, where commanders from modernized formations were reportedly disobeyed by still "unreformed" troops. All this was reflected in the fact that the operation lasted for two weeks and that the Saudi security forces suffered 578 casualties, including 127 killed, out of an engaged force of about 3,000. The Saudi losses were thus more than twice those of the rebels, who according to official Saudi sources lost 272 men, captured or killed.[31]

The Saudis themselves implicitly acknowledged the bad overall performance of the army and National Guard when they subsequently decided to establish yet another special security force under the Ministry of

Table 20 (continued)

1975	1982
Inventory of weapons	
Army 150 AMX-30 main battle tanks 85 M-47 medium and M-41 light tanks	300 AMX-30 main battle tanks [400]
200 AML-60/90 armored cars (plus some Staghounds, Greyhounds, and Ferret Scouts) 150 mm guns; 75 mm recoilless rifles (RCLs); SS-11 Harpoon antitank guided weapons, (ATGWs); antiaircraft (AA) guns Hawk surface-to-air missiles (SAMs)	200 AML-60/90 armored cars 100 Fox/Ferret armored cars [200] 105 mm and 155 mm howitzers; 75 mm, 90 mm, 106 mm RCLs; TOW, Dragon, HOT ATGWs; AA guns Redeye, Shahine, improved Hawk SAMs 150 M-60A1 tank chassis 250 AMX-10P tracked armored personnel carriers (APCs) [200] 600 M-113 Panhard APCs [1000]
Navy 1 patrol boat 3 fast patrol boats (Jaguar class) 50 small patrol boats 8 SRN-6 hovercraft (under Coast Guard)	1 patrol boat 3 Jaguar fast-attack craft 53 coastal patrol boats [38] 8 SRN-6 hovercraft [Coast Guard, 10] 6 landing craft [12] 4 PLG-1 corvettes 5 PGG-1 fast-attack craft missiles [7] 4 MSC-322 minesweepers
Air force 35 F-5Es 20 F-5Bs	65 F-5Es } [80] 24 F-5Fs } 16 F-5Bs
30 BAC-167 COIN/trainers 3 Lightning T-55 trainers	46 BAC-167 COIN/trainers 2 Lightning T-55 trainers 4 F-15C trainers 2 TF-15D trainers
35 Lightning F-52/F-53s	32 Lightning F-52/F-53s 14 F-15s
21 C-130 transports 4 KC-130 transports	63 C-130 transports [50] 6 KC-130 transports 2 C-140 Jet Star transports 12 Cessna 172 light transports
45 AB-206 and AB-205 helicopters 6 Alouette III helicopters	25 AB-206 and AB-205 helicopters 10 AB-22 helicopters 2 Alouette III helicopters [6 KV-107/IIA-17]

Sources: International Institute for Strategic Studies (IISS), *The Military Balance, 1975 – 76* and *1982 – 83* (London, 1975 and 1982); The Jaffee Center for Strategic Studies (JCSS), *The Military Balance in the Middle East, 1983* (Tel Aviv: Tel Aviv University, 1983).

Interior and replaced the army chief of staff, the commander of the land forces, the commander of the air force, the director of military operations, the chief of the Frontier Guard, and the director of public security at the Ministry of Interior. The governor of Mecca, Emir Fawwaz ibn Abd al-Aziz, also resigned, citing "health reasons."[32]

Two other revealing incidents are known to have occurred. The Saudi air force based at Dhahran uses what is known locally as the "Fahd Line," after Director of Operations Colonel Fahd ibn Abdallah al-Saud, in its contingency plans. The line runs from Abadan, at the north end of the Gulf, along the middle of the waterway to the Strait of Hormuz, at the south end. Unidentified aircraft crossing that line are considered hostile and are supposed to be intercepted by Saudi fighters prepared for a combat engagement.[33] The American-manned AWACS aircraft and ground-based gap-filler radar would ostensibly ensure detection and activate the Saudi-manned interceptors, with which they are tied by voice communication. Yet in 1982 a defecting Iranian F-4 Phantom crew flew across the Gulf and took their aircraft — capable of carrying 9.75 tons of bombs — directly over the vital oil terminal at Ras Tannura. The Saudi F-5s were scrambled only at the last minute and were vectored at a spurious radar track. The Iranian F-4 entered the landing pattern just as the F-5s were taking off.

The explanation given for that failure was that the AWACS on patrol was at the far end of its orbit and that commercial aircraft were operating in the area at the same time. Yet in the same year another defecting Iranian air crew, flying a Boeing 707 cargo aircraft with a capacity of 43 tons or 180 passengers, crossed the Gulf and the entire width of Saudi Arabia and landed in Cairo without being detected by the orbiting AWACS or the ground-based radar. The first anyone knew about the flight was when the aircraft landed.[34] No explanation was given this time.

Clearly the Saudis are not to be blamed entirely for those failures. Perhaps the American personnel operating the AWACS bear the brunt of the responsibility. Nevertheless, the two events point out the vulnerability of the entire sophisticated air defense program centered on the AWACS, radars, and C3 systems that the Saudis eagerly bought, and altogether underscore the folly of analysts and defense planners who expect high-technology systems to operate in real situations in accordance with their paper capabilities.

Although the Saudis refrained from deliberately using their available forces in combat, they continued to use them in noncombat deterrent or policy-support roles. The most notable example was the large-scale deployment of land and air forces in connection with the 1979 Yemen war, already mentioned. That action was probably relevant in deterring South Yemen from pressing its advantage in the war and agreeing to a political "settlement." Although the settlement was not to the liking of the Saudis (see Chapters 11 and 15), it was still far better than a decisive South Yemeni military victory.

Later in 1979 the Saudis displayed some of their armed forces in maneuvers attended by leaders of the smaller Gulf countries and North Yemen, during the Khamis Mushayt durbar, in an endeavor to raise morale in the face of the Iranian revolution and to promote regional defense cooperation. Although the endeavor produced no tangible results at that time (see Chapter 14), the display of the Saudi forces, together with some more specific armed demonstrations before and afterward, may have contributed to persuading those who witnessed it to join the GCC eventually.

One of those more specific demonstrations consisted of joint military maneuvers involving Saudi paratroopers and Bahraini armed forces in June 1979. In October 1979 there were reports following a meeting between Crown Prince Fahd and Bahrain's chief, Khalifa ibn Salman, that a Saudi force would be stationed in the island emirate. The Saudi defense minister denied the reports but affirmed that "Saudi strength is strength for Bahrain."[35]

As in the Faisal era, the Saudis continued to deploy elements of their armed forces in a noncombat role in the Arab arena, except that under Khaled they did so less often and on a more limited scale. Indeed, in 1977 they deployed a force of only some 700–1,200 in Lebanon as part of the predominantly Syrian Arab Deterrent Force,[36] and they recalled even that limited contingent in connection with the mobilization and deployments relating to the 1979 war between the Yemens.

Yet another use of the Saudi military establishment should perhaps be mentioned in this connection. The Saudis have built military facilities and ordered or acquired military equipment with an eye not only to their use by their own, actual or planned, armed forces, but also with a view to their possible use by friendly forces in case of need. Military bases were built that could accommodate existing Pakistani troops and the potential Jordanian rapid deployment force. Airfields were constructed with redundant runways and other facilities to accommodate possible American air force units, and aircraft, radar, and communication equipment were acquired with an eye to their compatibility with possible American intervention forces. The use of these capabilities for deterrent purposes has been somewhat constrained by the Saudis' contradictory need to conceal or downplay their dependence on others; but it may be assumed that the potential enemy must know about them and take them into account.

Conclusions:
Retrospect and Prospect

Khaled's Reign and the Quest for Security

Khaled's reign epitomized Saudi Arabia's position after the 1973–74 watershed. It was the first reign to unfold entirely in the post-1973 era of superabundant wealth. Indeed, in the relatively brief span between 1975 and 1982, the Kingdom received $435 billion in oil revenues, more than ten times the $41.7 billion it had received in the entire period since 1938, when oil was discovered. In the course of acquiring that revenue and spending most of it on the second five-year plan and half of the third, the physical and social profile of the Kingdom was transformed, and the country was thrust into the center of regional politics and international trade, finance, and influence.

But Khaled's brief reign also demonstrated the fundamental limitations of the Kingdom's strategic position. In the first place, it underscored the extent to which the Kingdom was a prisoner of its own wealth. Egypt, for instance, could choose to go its own way in pursuing peace, ally itself with America, and sit out the Gulf war and the Lebanon war. Little Jordan could decide to refrain from taking sides in the quarrels between Syria and Egypt, avoid involvement in the Lebanon civil war, and watch the 1982 Lebanon war from the sidelines. Saudi Arabia, in contrast, could not avoid being drawn into all these and other issues regardless of its rulers' wishes, and had to bear the consequences of whatever stances it adopted. It was simply too rich and ostensibly influential to be ignored by others, and too weak and cautious to be able to ignore them.

As the Saudi leadership grappled with the issues thrust upon it, the

Kingdom's security position, which had been on the ascent since 1973, peaked sometime in 1978 and then took a dive in 1979 from which the country never fully recovered. Moreover, such were the reasons for that decline that a reversal of the trend in the foreseeable future is highly unlikely. The Kingdom's moment as a secure, major regional and world actor lasted only five years, although that fact remained unrecognized for some time longer.

Three interrelated fundamental reasons underlay that reversal. The first had to do with the inherent extreme fluidity of the Kingdom's external strategic environment. In the brief eight-year period of Khaled's reign, critical developments all around the Kingdom repeatedly altered the strategic configuration and posed new problems that sapped its position: Egypt and Syria turned from wartime allies to peacetime antagonists and caught the Kingdom in the middle; Iran turned from a shield for the Kingdom to a dagger pointed at its heart after the fall of the shah; Egypt's peace treaty with Israel polarized the Arab world and forced the Saudis to choose between alternative highly costly courses; the Yemens turned from would-be partners in unity to active belligerents and again to unity partners as a result of chaotic processes that defied Saudi control; the Soviets used their own armed forces for territorial expansion in Afghanistan for the first time since the end of World War II, threatening to bring their forces there closer to those of their proxies in PDRY and the Horn of Africa and to catch the Arabian Peninsula and the Gulf in a huge pincer; the Gulf war caught the Saudis and their small neighbors between Iraq and Iran and exposed their vital oil facilities and oil transit to grave danger; finally, each of these developments, in turn, caught the Saudis between their own interest in the American strategic connection and the hostility of others to that connection.

Important as the factor of instability of the external environment is, however, it does not in itself suffice to explain the decline in the Kingdom's position during Khaled's reign. Faisal, after all, confronted in a comparable period a no less drastic series of upheavals around the entire perimeter of the Kingdom, yet he managed to maneuver the Kingdom through them all to the high point of wealth, influence, and security it attained in 1974 and 1975. Between early 1967 and the time of his death in early 1975, there occurred the ongoing proxy war with Egypt in Yemen; the British withdrawal from Aden and the emergence of PDRY; the war of attrition; the emergence of radical regimes in the Sudan, Libya, and Iraq; the civil war in Jordan; the withdrawal of the British from the Gulf; the Dhofar rebellion; the 1972 war between the Yemens; and the October 1973 war. That comparison suggests that, in addition to the instability of the environment, the change in the quality of leadership after 1975 also had much to do with the decline in the Kingdom's position.

The change in the quality of leadership was not merely a matter of personality. Although Faisal was beyond doubt a leader of exceptional ability, the crucial element in his handling of the kaleidoscopic changes in the external environment was the fact that he was the uncontested effective leader and thus was able to pursue a coherent policy, keep his objectives and priorities steadily in view even while making necessary tactical detours, and act decisively when the moment was ripe. That capability was lost, probably irretrievably, when he was succeeded by a de facto collective leadership, which was structurally incapable of acting in the same way.

Ironically, the foundations of a collective leadership were laid by Faisal himself, as part of his endeavor to create and sustain a coalition that would support his sole leadership without threatening it. Whether or not he had any alternative is a moot question; the fact is that by the time of his death the members of that coalition had become entrenched in their positions, and that fact made it almost impossible for another single leader to assert himself without plunging the dynasty into a potentially disastrous internecine struggle. The persistence of that condition throughout Khaled's reign has only reinforced it and made its modification in the future highly unlikely.

The effects of an unstable strategic environment and of an indecisive, slow, ambiguous collective leadership were, in turn, particularly telling because of the Kingdom's limited endowment in power and the resources of power. The Kingdom's principal resources were oil and oil wealth, and on the whole it made effective use of them; but oil and "riyal diplomacy" by themselves could go only so far toward addressing the kind of contingencies that the Saudis faced. It is significant in this respect that, although oil revenue increased nearly threefold in the second half of Khaled's reign over the first half, $306 billion in 1979–1982 compared with $126 billion in 1975–1978, the Kingdom fared far less well in the second period than in the first. Throughout Khaled's reign, the Kingdom invested huge sums in an effort to build a military capability to buttress its security and backstop its diplomacy, but its attempt to convert wealth into military power was limited by the paucity of the population and the vastness of the territory. The resort to foreign labor on a massive scale helped somewhat, although it created new security burdens; but the hiring of foreign personnel for direct defense functions in the numbers needed to make a difference was constrained by the danger of complications worse than the problem in need of remedy.

In addition to those structural geographic and demographic constraints, political apprehensions among its leaders prevented the Kingdom from making optimal use of the potential military resources that were at its disposal. For instance, under the pressure of the needs created by the unfavorable changes in the strategic environment, Defense Minister Sultan and his professional staff sought periodically to rationalize the use of the Kingdom's resources by enforcing conscription or unifying all its armed forces. However, the ingrained fear of potential military coups if the checks and balances were eliminated, the constant, at least latent, concern about determination of the succession if the armed forces were unified and under single control, and fear of upsetting the current balance of influence among members of the royal family always led other princes to combine to defeat those projects. The opposition may well have been justified, but the result was nonetheless to perpetuate multiple defense and security apparatuses under independent leaderships, which competed for the scarce manpower resources, pursued disparate strategies, restricted optimal deployment and potential use of forces, and thus ultimately limited the Kingdom's diplomatic leverage.

The general effect of the combination of these three factors — frequent major changes in the strategic environment, divided or indecisive collective leadership, and inadequate military power — was to erode the coherence and purposiveness that Faisal had imparted to the Kingdom's political strategy since 1973 and to set it adrift from 1979 on. By the end of Khaled's reign and the beginning of Fahd's, that strategy had been reduced to a set of improvised, often inconsistent, short-term policies designed to cope with troublesome situations in the various arenas.

The most crucial change centered on the relationship with the United States. A critical reason for the Kingdom's success in the period 1973–1978 had been its ability to maintain good relations with Washington as well as with the parties to several regional axes: Cairo and Damascus, Tehran and Baghdad, San'a and Aden. That ability had rested on the fact that at least one party to each of the regional axes shared the Kingdom's strategic relationship with America and supported it. This configuration changed drastically in 1979, when Egypt was drummed out of the Arab fold by parties hostile to the United States, and when the revolution in Iran replaced the pro-American regime with one that was implacably hostile to the United States and weary of the Saudi connection with it. The Saudis did not dare cast their lot entirely with the United States in defiance of all the parties that opposed it, nor could they afford to rely exclusively on regional alliances and renounce the American connection altogether in view of the role it might play in various contingencies. Now and then, factions of the leadership tried to resolve the dilemma by pulling the Kingdom's policy in one direction or the other; but on the whole the leadership as a collectivity endeavored to muddle its way through it on a case-by-case basis. The net result was that the American connection ceased to be the hub of the Kingdom's strategy and instead became merely one of several problematic relationships requiring constant careful management.[1]

By the end of Khaled's reign two mutually contradictory tendencies were discernible in the Saudis' relationship with the United States. One was an increasing dependence at the practical level, expressed in the discreet American role in ensuring navigation and assisting in the Kingdom's air defense in the context of the seemingly endless Gulf war, and even more in the explicit long-term American contracts to equip and develop its armed forces. The other tendency was for greater separation from the United States at the policy level, which found expression in the understanding the Saudis reached with the Soviets regarding the Yemens, the Saudis' willingness to underwrite Syria's closer military connection with the Soviet Union, and their receptivity to Syrian arguments urging the establishment of formal diplomatic relations with that superpower. That tendency was also expressed in the conscious Saudi efforts to avoid identification with various American initiatives, such as "strategic consensus" and the Reagan peace plan, and to shun offers of American help at difficult moments in the Gulf war, preferring instead to try their own uncertain remedies. Both tendencies are expected to continue in contention, until there is a radical change in the domestic and strategic configuration underlying them.

In the Arab-Israeli arena, Saudi policy at the end of Khaled's reign and the beginning of Fahd's was almost completely enthralled to Syria's basic policy. Assad relentlessly played on the Kingdom's vulnerability and on the sympathy he enjoyed among some Saudi leaders, headed by Abdallah, to prevent it from falling in with American strategic designs for the Arab-Israeli area and the region as a whole, and to extract from it support for his own conception of the necessity to build up Syria's power with Soviet help as a strategic counterbalance to Israel's. Syria's defeat in the 1982 Lebanon war, its desertion of the PLO, and its nearly total isolation in the Arab world had created a unique opportunity for the Saudi leadership as a whole to break free from Syria and to promote, in cooperation with the United States, a more favorable political-strategic configuration in the area. However, excessive caution, intensified by a desire to avoid straining relations within the leadership during the delicate post-succession period, and the accumulated doubt about America's reliability, caused them to forgo the opportunity. Syria's subsequent recovery and the patent failure of America's own efforts to advance a new order indicate that the Kingdom's enthrallment to Syria is likely to continue, at least as long as Assad or his basic policy endures.

In the Gulf arena, at the time of Khaled's death and Fahd's accession the Kingdom was mesmerized by the perils presented by the continuation of the Gulf war. One danger it feared was a renewal of attempts to subvert it and its smaller neighbors. Another was the possibility of successful attacks on its oil facilities despite the air defense screen centered on the American-manned AWACS. The worst peril was that of an Iranian final victory over Iraq, which might immediately loose an Islamic revolutionary tidal wave that would either sweep the whole region or establish a stifling Iranian hegemony in the Gulf.

In the face of all these real dangers, the Kingdom occupied itself with prodding its even more terrified GCC partners into closer defense cooperation, which at best was relevant only to checking subversion. Regarding the other perils, the Kingdom's policy seemed to be to lie low and hope that exhaustion of the belligerents would finally produce a definitive stalemate. This, despite the probability that such a stalemate would entail the full restoration of Iraqi and Iranian oil exports, worsen the glut in the oil market, and create serious problems for OPEC. The Saudis dared not contemplate any precautionary or deterrent measures in cooperation with the United States beyond the ones already in place, and only timidly explored by proxy the possibility of bringing Egypt's strategic weight into play, for fear of further provoking Iran, angering Syria, or displeasing the Soviet Union. Against the possibility that the worst should come to pass, the Saudis seemed resigned to relying on America to come to the rescue of its own accord, in pursuit of its own interests.

This approach worked for the Saudis in the past and may work again in the future. On the other hand, the United States may well be unable to help effectively in some future contingencies any more than it was able to do when the shah's regime faced its fatal crisis, notwithstanding President Reagan's brave declaration of October 1981 that the United States would not allow that kind of thing to happen. Moreover, even if the United States had the material capability to act in a given contingency, its ability to do so may be politically constrained, especially if the crisis should occur while there is still a glut in the oil market and while there is a comfortable strategic petroleum reserve. Thus, the fear-induced failure to anticipate plausible future dangers with timely strategic provisions may well, next time, have tragic consequences for the Kingdom.

Beyond specific policies, the analysis of the Khaled era suggests the following observations about the Saudis' mode of operation in the sphere of defense and foreign policy.

1. Saudi policy even in the best of circumstances is essentially defensive, stemming from a recognition of the Kingdom's limitations. The Saudi quest for Arab "consensus" and unity since 1973 has often been interpreted in terms of an attempt to exert leadership; in fact it flows from the realization that they cannot remain aloof, and that divisions are likely to catch them in a cross fire between the contending parties. This syndrome has been illustrated in the episodes of rift between Cairo and Damascus, and in some similar episodes between Damascus and Baghdad.

When division better serves their interests, the Saudis are not averse to stimulating it, as they did in the various attempts, however halfhearted, to isolate Syria and the Steadfastness Front. When division fragments the Arabs' ranks so much that the danger of being caught in the middle is minimal, as at the time of the 1982 Lebanon war, the Saudis have used the slogan of consensus to prevent the crystallization of a consensus that might lead to pressure on them to take undesired action.

2. The defensive disposition, the inability to stay aloof, and the desire to avoid getting caught in the middle strongly motivate the Saudis to seek to play the role of mediator. But the same factors equally strongly disqualify them from playing the role of policy initiator or leader, especially when opposition is anticipated. Exceptions such as the Fahd Plan and the creation of the GCC only prove the rule. The former was withdrawn when it encountered strong opposition; the latter project was discussed inconclusively for a long time, and was finally brought to a head only when Iraqi and Iranian opposition to it became neutralized.

3. In situations involving a choice between incurring short-term danger to advance long-term interests or seeking to avoid the former at a risk to the latter, the Saudis invariably opt for the second course. This was illustrated in their early 1979 decision, against their own established judgment about the best long-term oil policy, to cut oil production in order to avoid Iran's wrath. It was also illustrated by their decision, at about the same time, to break with Egypt, disrupting the strategic alliance that Faisal had painstakingly cultivated with it and putting the American connection at risk, in order to avert the immediate anger of Iraq, Syria, and the PLO. In a somewhat different context, in October 1980 they risked the policy they had been evolving in the Arab arena, the Gulf, and the Yemens by calling on American military assistance to meet the immediate danger presented by the Iraq-Iran war.

In situations involving a choice between equally risky short-term or long-term courses, the Saudis either *deliberately* refrain from decision and play for time (more true of the Faisal than of the Khaled era) or are virtually paralyzed (true of the Khaled era). This tendency was illustrated by the Saudis' almost passive reaction to several of the successful Iranian counteroffensives in the Gulf war, when all the effective theoretically available options seemed to be risky.

4. The Saudis' defensive disposition manifests itself often in the extreme form of seeking to appease a powerful opponent regardless of basic ideological or strategic incompatibilities in order to avoid short-term confrontation and in the hope that the dangerous configuration might change with time. As practiced by Faisal toward Nasser's Egypt, appeasement was coupled with active efforts to bring about the desired change. As practiced by Faisal's successors toward Khomeini's Iran, or toward Syria for that matter, appeasement was merely coupled with the hope that time by itself might alter the problematic situation.

5. While practicing appeasement toward a powerful opponent, the

Saudis also tend to "take liberties" with parties whose strategic interests are locked with theirs. In some cases, that tendency merely takes the form of trying to get a "free ride" on the other party's endeavor to protect its interests, or of paying for the other party's contribution to the shared interest with noncontroversial coin. In other cases, however, the Saudis may even twit the other party for the sake of tactical advantages in their relations with third parties, even while benefiting from the second party's contribution to the shared interests.

The first form of that tendency was illustrated in the Saudis' relying on the United States to check Soviet threats and to secure navigation in the Gulf while refusing to contribute anything themselves. The second form was illustrated by the Saudis' cutting of oil production in January and March 1979 even while counting on the United States to continue to fulfill those same strategic functions. In a similar vein, the Saudis condemned and penalized Egypt after March 1979, even while they enjoyed the strategic benefits afforded by the Egyptian-Israeli peace and the Egyptian-American informal alliance.

6. As a corollary of the general defensive disposition and of the tendencies just described, the Saudis pursue a diplomatic style that is characterized by a preference for caution over maximization of potential gains; a passion for discretion and a low profile; attempts to follow several contradictory courses simultaneously; willingness to make sharp tactical reversals; and limited concern with the principle of consistency, either in reality or in appearance. Illustrations of this style pervade the historical analysis in the preceding chapters.

Prospects for the 1980s

Given the frequency and scope of past changes in the Kingdom's security position, any attempt to make precise forecasts about it for the distant or even near future would be foolhardy. Nevertheless, from a review of the major variables identified in this study from the vantage point of the end of Khaled's reign and the first years of Fahd's, it is possible to discern certain general trends that may be of use to scholars, governments, and business people who have dealings with the Kingdom. These trends add up to a picture of dangerous *immobilisme* at home and virtual paralysis abroad that does not bode well for the Kingdom's long-term prospects.

Nearly three years after Fahd's accession to the throne, it was apparent that the structural change, from single to collective leadership, that had taken place at the center of power during the Khaled era had become irreversible. Fahd's succession and the designation of Abdallah as crown prince and deputy prime minister and of Sultan as second deputy prime minister took place promptly and smoothly; but the hopes or fears entertained by many that Fahd would assert himself as a leader more in the Faisal than in the Khaled mold have proved to be misplaced. Collective leadership seems to have become so entrenched that Fahd did not even bother to make any major reshuffle of his government upon acceding to the throne and the prime ministership, as his predecessors were wont to do. Now and then he voiced some bold ideas, such as a proposal to assemble a conference of learned men from throughout the Islamic world to consider issues pertinent to Islam and modern life, including the question of the position and role of women; but his failure to follow up on them, indeed the very fact that he put such ideas in the form of a public appeal, indicated the extent to which he felt hemmed in by his more conservative fellow leaders.

The rigidity at the center of power owing to divided collective leadership is particularly ominous because it reinforces a syndrome that is pregnant with the most dangerous consequences for the Kingdom's future. That syndrome consists of a combination of a political system that is locked in immobility at a time when the social and economic systems are experiencing far-reaching changes at a dizzying pace. The failure of the political system to make even minimal adaptations to the economic and social changes was illustrated by the continuing inability of the collective leadership to enact a basic law more than twenty years after many of its members recognized the need for one that would carefully open up the system to participation by newly emerged classes. After his accession to the throne, Fahd repeated the promise several times, and on at least two occasions even indicated that the law would be promulgated "within two months," but more than two years into his reign the promise remained unfulfilled. It is conceivable that such a law will be finally put into place before long, but the strength of the resistance that has prevented its enactment for all these years does not bode well for the experiment in political participation if it should take place.

Another cause for concern for the future is the sudden, sharp deterioration of the Kingdom's principal asset. In the first half of 1981, Saudi Arabia was exporting oil at the rate of 10.2 mbd, near its maximum productive capacity. As a result of the glut in the world market, it cut its exports to an average of 6.5 mbd in 1982, 5 mbd in 1983, and 4–4.5 mbd in the first quarter of 1984.[2] Concomitantly, Saudi revenues from oil, which came to $101.2 billion in 1981, representing a fifty-three-fold increase during the previous decade, dropped to $76 billion in 1982 and $37.1 billion in 1983.[3] No one really knows how long these trends are likely to continue or how far an eventual reversal, if it should occur, is likely to go. The variables involved are so numerous and uncertain that a vast number of radically different but equally plausible scenarios can be imagined. From the perspective of the Kingdom's defense and security posture, however, the persistence of these trends for only a few years can cause grave damage.

The glut in the oil market has already substantially reduced the Kingdom's diplomatic influence. For instance, although the question whether Secretary of State Haig gave Israel the "green light" to invade Lebanon in 1982 is highly debated, there is little disagreement that he did not do all he could to prevent Israel from going to war or to bring the fighting promptly to a halt. He may have had good reasons for doing what he did, but it is hard to imagine any secretary of state pursuing such a line if the oil market were tight, when the mere outbreak of war could have set off talk of oil sanctions and sent oil prices soaring. Haig's successors in managing the crisis evinced greater concern for the Kingdom's sensitivities as they understood them; but it is hard to imagine them simultaneously adopting some of the same objectives as Israel's and showing the degree of patience they did toward actions that outraged them as well as Arab and world opinion, but for easy world oil conditions. In a different context, it is hard to imagine that a serious American presidential contender would make an unequivocal commitment to oppose the use of American troops to secure access to Gulf oil under any circumstances, as Senator Gary Hart did, without the background of a couple of years of an oil buyers' market.

The purely financial side of the decline in revenue has presented no serious problem so far. The Saudis have simply reduced expenditures to some extent by stretching out some of the development programs and have dipped into their very substantial reserves — estimated at over $100 billion in 1981 — to bridge the remaining revenue gap. Thus the budget for fiscal 1983–84, passed in April 1983, envisaged revenues of $63.9 billion and expenditures of $73.2 billion, allowing for a deficit of nearly $10 billion to be financed from the general reserves. Actual revenues amounted to only $53.2 billion and actual expenditures were cut to $63.1 billion, leaving about the same amount of deficit. The budget for fiscal 1984–85, approved in April 1984, estimated revenues at $60.9 billion and expenditures at $73.8 billion, leaving a deficit of $13 billion to be financed from the general reserves.[4]

The real question, however, is how long the regime can dip into the reserves and how much it can cut into expenditures without causing policy dissensions within the leadership, stirring up disputes among the myriad princes, interest groups, and government departments over the relative burden of "sacrifices," and provoking the new middle class generally and elements of the defense and security establishment in particular. Certainly the circumstances of the 1980s are different from those of the 1950s; but the fact that the dispute over King Saud's management of the Kingdom's finances blended with rivalries within the royal family and the turmoil of the times to expose the Kingdom to enormous dangers is suggestive of what may happen if the process continues for several more years. One possible straw in the wind in this respect was the resignation in 1983 of the veteran technocrat who headed the Saudi Arabian Monetary Agency, apparently in protest against dipping into the reserves. Also of possible significance is the fact that the budget for 1983–84 cut the allocations to instruments of defense and security collectively by 18.5 percent from those of the previous year, despite previous assurances by Fahd that these would not be affected by budgetary retrenchment.[5]

The armed forces will probably continue to make modest progress in the 1980s under the tutelage of foreign instructors. However, because of the ingrained geographic, personnel, and political limitations they are unlikely to develop in that period to a level where they can constitute a significant deterrent against major potential enemies, or provide greater leverage to Saudi diplomacy. The Kingdom may command enough power, in theoretical calculations, to outweigh an adversary such as PDRY; but even in that case the regime's very low tolerance for defeat will constrict the practical usefulness of that advantage. Against the variety of threats emanating from powers such as Iran, Iraq, Israel, or even a Jordan turned hostile, the Saudi armed forces will be able to play only such marginal roles as raising the threshold of determination the enemy must muster before contemplating attack, and imposing delay and caution on his operations in order to permit possible outside intervention or negotiations.

In the sphere of security-relevant foreign policy, the persistence of an unstable environment, collective leadership, and limited military capability, coupled with a decline in the importance of the oil resource, are likely to turn the strategic indecisiveness that characterized the latter part of the Khaled era into a virtual strategic paralysis. The Kingdom will confront dangers by appealing to the United States for help only at the last moment, only when they could not possibly be evaded or avoided, and only if the United States would not act on its own. This disposition will be particularly relevant to the Gulf situation and the dangers inherent in the continuation of the Iran-Iraq war. Potential opponents such as Syria will be appeased rather than confronted, and probably fewer attempts will be made to capitalize on fleeting opportunities, such as Fahd tried with the plan that bore his name, or with the various diplomatic raids that aimed at detaching the PLO from Syria's control. Troublesome demands by friendly powers such as Iraq and Jordan will probably go unheeded, and existing obligations to them may be whittled down. Efforts will be made to preserve the current modus vivendi regarding the Yemens, and probably to extend the underlying understanding with the Soviets to other spheres at the cost of further distancing the Kingdom from the United

States. Use of "mercenary" forces, such as Pakistani troops, may be increased piecemeal, without the adoption of any new strategic decision. Greater reliance may be placed on covert intelligence operations, as in the pre-1973 era of limited options.

In view of these anticipated trends and of the entire record of Saudi-American relations since 1979, strong voices will probably be raised in the United States to deal with the Kingdom by issuing it ultimatums and by confronting it with either/or strategic choices. These will probably be countered by louder reiterations of the conventional argument that the Kingdom's natural place is on America's side if only Washington would free itself from the influence of the Jewish lobby and do what is just and right about the Palestinian question. It is obvious from this study that the first approach would seriously risk losing the Kingdom or precipitating its demise by demanding from it what it simply cannot do; and that the second is based on simplistic assertions about the American political process and on assumptions about the Kingdom's problems that are unrelated to its actual history. If a sound alternative approach is to be suggested in one sentence or two, it would call on the United States to deal deliberately with the Kingdom in the way the Kingdom has almost unwittingly come to deal with it. America's long-term aim should be to disengage its vital interests from the policy and fate of the Kingdom. Its short-term policy should be designed with an eye to achieving that goal while cooperating with the Kingdom in dealing with problems on a case-by-case basis and advancing shared interests on the basis of reciprocity.

Appendix. Sample of a Summary of a Saudi Budget

ميزانية الدولة ــ الاعتمادات حسب الفصول والفروع والأبواب ١٤٠١/١٤٠٠ هـ

(بملايين الريالات)

Government Budget: Appropriations by Chapters, Items and Sections, 1400/1401 A.H.

Table 10-4   (Million S.R.)

Chapter	Item	Chapter & Item	Total	Section 4 Projects	Section 3 Other Expenditures	Section 2 General Expenditures	Section 1 Salaries	الفصول والفروع	فرع	فصل
1		**Royal Cabinets:**						الدواوين :		١
	1	Royal Cabinet	23,4	—	—	2,6	20,8	الديوان الملكى	١	
	2	Special office (His Majesty the King)	32,0	7,6	—	3,0	21,4	المكتب الخاص لجلالة الملك	٢	
	3	Crown Prince Office	78,0	—	—	66,4	11,6	ديوان سمو ولى العهد	٣	
	4	Protocol	213,1	195,2	—	2,3	15,6	ادارة المراسم الملكية	٤	
	5	Bedouins Affairs Office	3,6	—	—	0,7	2,9	مكتب شئون البادية	٥	
	6	Private Affairs Office	151,5	—	—	104,2	47,3	مكتب الشئون الخاصة	٦	
	7	Crown Prince Office Affairs	45,4	6,0	—	20,3	19,1	الشئون الخاصة بديوان سمو ولى العهد	٧	
2		**Council of Ministers:**						رئاسة مجلس الوزراء :		٢
	1	Council of Ministers. Presidency	62,7	—	—	21,5	41,2	ديوان رئاسة مجلس الوزراء	١	
	2	General Secretariat	48,9	25,0	—	3,5	20,4	الامانة العامة لمجلس الوزراء	٢	
	3	Experts' Branch	9,2	—	—	1,8	7,4	شعبة الخبراء	٣	
	4	Technical Assistance Agency	19,5	—	—	16,3	3,2	ادارة التعاون الفنى	٤	
	5	Military Branch	—	—	—	—	—	الشعبة العسكرية	٥	
3		**National Guards**	7,509,0	4,496,4	—	658,0	2,354,6	الحرس الوطنى		٣
4		**Intelligence Bureau**	486,0	197,1	—	71,8	217,1	الاستخبارات العامة		٤
5		**Consultative Council**	3,2	—	—	0,1	3,1	مجلس الشورى		٥
6		**Civil Service Bureau**	132,5	35,0	—	38,5	59,0	ديوان الخدمة المدنية		٦
7		**Ministry of Planning**	86,0	3,7	—	59,9	22,4	وزارة التخطيط		٧
8		**State Audit Department**	100,0	18,5	—	18,2	63,3	ديوان المراقبة العامة		٨
9		**Grievance Court**	17,0	00,8	—	2,5	13,7	ديوان المظالم		٩
10		**Investigation & Disc. Dept:**						هيئة التحقيق والتأديب:		١٠
	1	Investigation Department	64,4	22,0	—	5,4	37,0	هيئة التحقيق	١	
	2	Discipline Department	9,7	—	—	2,2	7,5	هيئة التأديب	٢	
11		**Ministry of Municipal & Rural Affairs**	19745,1	16597,3	26,7	1,417,7	1,703,4	وزارة الشئون البلدية والقروية		١١
12		**Ministry of P.W. & H.**						وزارة الاشغال العامة والاسكان		١٢
	1	Public Works	151,2	61,4	—	14,4	75,4	الاشغال العامة	١	
	2	Housing	5607,7	5512,4	—	76,0	19,3	الاسكان	٢	
13		**Ministry of Information**	1,442,6	878,1	—	294,5	270,0	وزارة الاعلام		١٣
14		**Ministry of Foreign Affairs**	736,2	287,9	10,0	231,2	207,1	وزارة الخارجية		١٤
15		**Ministry of Defence and Aviation:**						وزارة الدفاع والطيران :		١٥
	1	General Bureau	84,0	—	—	44,2	39,8	الديوان العام	١	
	2	Army	23678,9	19,202,4	—	898,9	3,577,6	القوات البرية	٢	
	3	Royal Air Force	14177,2	12,883,3	—	261,0	1,032,9	القوات الجوية	٣	
	4	Royal Navy	5,407,8	5,024,1	—	162,4	221,3	القوات البحرية	٤	
	5	Military Factory	576,5	412,2	—	20,5	143,8	المصانع الحربية	٥	
	6	Civil Aviation	10993,4	10,644,6	—	194,4	154,4	مصلحة الطيران المدنى	٦	
	7	Meteorological Department	386,1	278,3	—	65,2	42,6	مصلحة الارصاد الجوية	٧	
	8	King Abdul Aziz Military Academy	74,9	10,2	—	23,8	40,9	كلية الملك عبدالعزيز الحربية	٨	
	9	King Faisal Air Academy	137,7	36,2	—	26,7	74,8	كلية الملك فيصل الجوية	٩	
	10	Medical Services	3528,9	3189,4	—	111,3	228,2	الخدمات الطبية	١٠	
	11	Staff Officers Presidency	320,1	—	—	165,4	154,7	رئاسة الاركان العامة	١١	

ميزانية الدولة ــ الاعتمادات حسب الفصـــول والفـــروع والأبـــواب ١٤٠٠/١٤٠١ هـ

(بملايين الريالات)

Government Budget: Appropriations by Chapters, Items and Sections, 1400/1401 A.H.

(Million S.R.)

Table 10-4 (Cont'd)   جدول ١٠ ــ ٤ (تابع)

Chapter	Item	Chapter & Item	Total المجموع	Section 4 Projects الباب الرابع المشاريع	Section 3 Other Expenditures الباب الثالث المصروفات الأخرى	Section 2 General Expenditures الباب الثاني المصروفات العامة	Section 1 Salaries الباب الأول الرواتب	الفصول والفروع	رقم
								وزارة الداخلية :	١٦
16		Ministry of the Interior:							
	1	General Bureau	2095,5	1580,1	—	349,8	165,6	الديوان العام	١
	2	Public Security	4994,9	1568,0	—	750,8	2676,1	الأمن العام	٢
	3	Civil Defence	696,0	215,0	—	45,2	435.8	الدفاع المدني	٣
	4	Investigation Department	993,6	265,1	—	85,8	642,7	المباحث العامة	٤
	5	Frontiers & Coast Guards	1497,6	765,0	—	103,6	629,0	سلاح الحدود وخفر السواحل	٥
	6	Public Security College	154,9	79,0	—	34,7	41,2	كلية قوى الأمن الداخلي	٦
	7	Special Security Department	376,5	247,0	—	16,9	112,6	قوة الأمن الخاصة	٧
	8	National Security Council	15,4	—	—	2,7	12,7	مجلس الأمن الوطني	٨
								الجوازات والأحوال المدنية	١٠
	10	Passport and Civil Status	363,6	82,0	—	33,1	248,5	ادارة المجاهدين	١١
	11	White Army	248,5	4,3	—	13,2	231,0	امارة الرياض	١٢
	12	Emirate of Riyadh	199,0	68,6	—	38,8	91,6	امارة مكة المكرمة	١٣
	13	Emirate of Makkah	186,6	79,3	—	32,7	74,6	امارة المنطقة الشرقية	١٤
	14	Emirate of Eastern province	162,5	95,3	—	18,4	48,8	امارة المدينة المنورة	١٥
	15	Emirate of Medina	116,9	62,5	—	12,7	41,7	امارة حائل	١٦
	16	Emirate of Hail	119,3	72,9	—	12,9	33,5	امارة الحدود الشمالية	١٧
	17	Emirate of North Frontiers	59,9	37,0	—	6,6	16,3	امارة القصيم	١٨
	18	Emirate of Quaseem	95,0	32,7	—	17,8	44,5	امارة عسير	١٩
	19	Emirate of Aseer	140,5	63,9	—	20,5	56,1	امارة تبوك	٢٠
	20	Emirate of Tabouk	84,0	42,2	—	10,5	31,3	امارة الجوف	٢١
	21	Emirate of Al-Jouf	66,9	31,8	—	9,9	25,2	امارة الباحة	٢٢
	22	Emirate of Al-Baha	76,5	38,1	—	11,2	27,2	امارة القريات	٢٣
	23	Emirate of Al-Qurayyat	58,6	17,4	—	13,2	28,0	امارة جيزان	٢٤
	24	Emirate of Jizan	66,7	17,4	—	12,9	36,4	امارة نجران	٢٥
	25	Emirate of Najran	91,7	42,0	—	16,5	33,2	وزارة العمل :	١٧
17		Ministry of Labour:						الديوان العام	١
	1	General Bureau	4,9	—	—	0,6	4,3	شئون العمل	٢
	2	Labour Affairs	1118,8	826,6	15,0	97,3	179,9	الشئون الاجتماعية	٣
	3	Social Affairs Department	179,5	75,0	20,0	38,5	46,0	الضمان الاجتماعي	٤
	4	Social Security Department	1189,6	26,0	1100,0	11,0	52,6	الرعاية الاجتماعية	٥
	5	Social Welfare	342,5	186,8	50,0	41,5	64,2	وزارة الصحة :	١٨
18		Ministry of Health	5656,4	2420,0	—	1021,4	2215,0	وزارة المعارف :	١٩
19		Ministry of Education:						الديوان العام	١
	1	General Bureau	9568,2	2591,7	79,0	2214,5	4683,0	مدارس الثغر بجدة	٢
	2	Thaghr Model School. Jeddah	81,1	1,4	—	8,0	11,7	معهد العاصمة النموذجي	٣
	3	Al-Asma Model Institute	46,9	34,0	—	5,1	7,8	الرئاسة العامة لتعليم البنات	٢٠
20	1	Presidency of Girls School	3871,4	1131,7	11,3	524,8	2203,6	كلية التربية للبنات	١
	2	Teacher Training College for Girls	258,1	88,2	—	69,4	100,5	وزارة التعليم العالي : ديوان الوزارة	٢٢
22	1	Ministry of Higher Education	608,3	18,4	26,7	340,0	223,2	دارة الملك عبدالعزيز	٢
	2	Darat Al-Malik Abdul Aziz	9,6	—	—	4,0	5,6	وزارة المواصلات	٢٣
23		Ministry of Communications	7594,6	7365,0	19,0	27,9	182,7	وزارة البرق والبريد والهاتف	٢٤
24		Ministry of P.T.T.						البرق والهاتف	١
	1	T.T	7695,5	7120,2	—	216,3	359,0	البريد	٢
	2	Post	798,1	350,3	—	127,9	319,9	وزارة المالية والاقتصاد الوطني	٢٥
25		Ministry of Finance & N.E.						الديوان العام	١
	1	General Bureau	2879,6	2649,0	—	59,8	170,8	مصلحة الجمارك	٢
	2	Customs Department	442,3	158,0	—	39,2	245,1	مصلحة الزكاة والدخل	٣
	3	Income Tax Department	41,2	10,0	—	3,9	27,3	ادارة قصور الضيافة الحكومية	٤
	4	Department of Guest Palace	180,3	—	—	121,6	58,7	مصلحة الاحصاءات العامة	٥
	5	Central Department of Statistics	71,8	16,6	—	31,6	23,6	مباني ومرافق حكومية عامة	٦
	6	Gov. Public Utility	7805,0	7805,0	—	—	—		

ميزانية الدولة ــ الاعتمادات حسب الفصول والفروع والأبواب ١٤٠١/١٤٠٠ هـ
(بملايين الريالات)

Government Budget: Appropriations by Chapters, Items and Sections, 1400/1401 A.H.

Table 10-4 (Cont'd)   (Million S.R.)   جدول ١٠ ــ ٤ (تابع)

Chapter	Item	Chapter & Item	Total	Section 4 Projects	Section 3 Other Expenditures	Section 2 General Expenditures	Section 1 Salaries	الفصول والفروع		
26		Ministry of Petroleum and Minerals Resources:						وزارة البترول والثروة المعدنية :		٢٦
	1	Petroleum	393,4	334,4	—	11,6	47,4	البترول	١	
	2	Mineral Resources	831,1	763,9	—	36,3	30,9	الثروة المعدنية	٢	
27		Ministry of Commerce	120,2	42,2	2,0	17,8	58,2	وزارة التجارة		٢٧
28		Ministry of Industry & Electricity	1827,7	275,0	1500,0	9,3	43,4	وزارة الصناعة والكهرباء		٢٨
29		Ministry of Agriculture and Water	4160,5	3470,3	140,0	228,2	322,0	وزارة الزراعة والمياه		٢٩
30		Ministry of Pilgrims and Endowments:						وزارة الحج والأوقاف :		٣٠
	1	Endowments Affairs	1220,5	750,3	4,1	103,8	362,3	شئون الأوقاف	١	
	2	Pilgrim Affairs	86,9	36,3		12,0	38,6	شئون الحج	٢	
31		Ministry of Justice	556,0	177,2	—	63,8	315,0	وزارة العدل		٣١
32		Presidency of Religious Juristic, Preaching and Guidance Affairs	183,5	40,0		67,2	76,3	رئاسة ادارات شئون البحوث العلمية والافتاء والدعوة والارشاد		٣٢
33		Presidency of Religious Guidance Groups	140,0	1,0		30,3	108,7	الرئاسة العامة لهيئات الأمر بالمعروف		٣٣
35		Presidency of Religious Supervision in the holy Mosques	209,6	40,0	—	119,8	49,8	الرئاسة العامة لشئون ادارة الحرمين الشريفين		٣٥
36		Presidency of Youth Welfare	2679,8	2377,5	120,0	105,5	76,8	الرئاسة العامة لرعاية الشباب		٣٦
39	1	Islamic Affairs	150,0	—	150,0	—	—	الشئون الاسلامية	١	٣٩
	2	Islamic World Bond	67,1	—	—	46,5	20,6	رابطة العالم الاسلامي	٢	
40		Civil Employees Salaries and General Rools	350,0	—	350,0	—	—	الرواتب الذاتية والقواعد العامة		٤٠
41		Governments' Share in the Retirement Pension Fund & Social Insurance	950,0	—	950,0	—	—	حصة الحكومة فى معاشات التقاعد والتامينات الاجتماعية		٤١
42		Contingent Expenditures	2500,0	—	2500,0	—	—	مصروفات الطوارىء		٤٢
43		General Budget Reserve	4101,0	—	4101,0	—	—	احتياطى عام الميزانية		٤٣
44		Emergency Project	2000,0	2000,0	—	—	—	المشاريع الطارئة		٤٤
45		Foreign Aids	9000,0	—	9000,0	—	—	الاعانات الخارجية		٤٥
46		Foodstuffs Subsidies	1500,0	—	1500,0	—	—	اعانة المواد الغذائية		٤٦
47		Gas Collection programme	2710,0	2710,0	—	—	—	برنامج تجميع الغاز		٤٧
		Public Establishments Subsidies	49768,5	43312,4	542,7	3189,2	2724,0	اعانة المؤسسات العامة		
		Total Budget	244993,5	174736,1	22,217,5	15822,8	32,216,9	اجمالى الميزانية		

Source: Budget Volumes.   المصدر : مجلدات الميزانية

Notes

Abbreviations

FBIS   Foreign Broadcast Information Service, *Daily Report*
GAO   U.S. General Accounting Office
IISS   International Institute for Strategic Studies
MECS   Colin Legum et al., *Middle East Contemporary Survey,*
        1976–77 through *1980–81* (New York: Holmes and Meier,
        1978–1982)
MEED   *Middle East Economic Digest*
MEES   *Middle East Economic Survey*
MEJ   *Middle East Journal*
OPEC   Organization of Petroleum Exporting Countries
SAMA   Saudi Arabian Monetary Agency
SIPRI   Stockholm International Peace Research Institute

Introduction

1. Exxon Corporation, *Middle East Oil*, 2d ed. (n.p., September 1980), 13.

2. For the statistical data, see Table 13 and IISS, *The Military Balance, 1981–82* (London, 1981).

Introduction to Part One

1. The official name of the state in foreign languages is the Kingdom of Saudi Arabia, specifying the *territory* of Arabia and the dynastic qualifier; but the Arabic name, *al-mamlaka al-'arabiyya al-Su'udiyya*, the Saudi Arab Kingdom, stresses the ethnic Arab character in addition to the dynastic qualifier. In the

Arabic language media, the country is commonly referred to simply as *al-Su'udiyya* — Saudia — with exclusive reference to the dynastic component.

2. The lowercase *al* is the Arabic definite article. With a capital *A*, it means "of the family or house of."

1. The Rise and Fall of the First Two Realms

1. Literally, *shaikh* means "elder." In addition to this sense, however, it is used to designate a tribal leader, as in the present context, and a religious leader, as in its application to Muhammad ibn Abd al-Wahhab. In the latter case the term is often used with the definite article *al* to signify the shaikh par excellence. In this book *Shaikh* designates Muhammad ibn Abd al-Wahhab, and references to the Shaikh family are to his descendants.

2. H. St. John Philby, *Saudi Arabia* (London: Benn, 1955), 39–40.

3. Sir John Bagot Glubb, *War in the Desert* (New York: Norton, 1961), 44.

4. Ibid.

5. Beginning with the compact between Muhammad ibn Saud and the Shaikh, the Saudi rulers assumed the title *imam*, which means "the leader in prayers," and, by extension, the leader of the Muslim community. In addition, the leaders assumed the title *emir*, which stresses military leadership.

6. Hafiz Wahba, *Arabian Days* (London: Arthur Barker, 1964), 106.

7. Glubb, *War in the Desert*, 48–50.

8. Ibid., 51–52; R. Bayly Winder, *Saudi Arabia in the Nineteenth Century* (New York: St. Martin's Press, 1965), 16.

9. Understood in those days in a much narrower and looser sense than subsequently. The title was typical of Ottoman vagueness and of their standard policy of playing off the tribes against one another to minimize their danger.

10. Colonel Lewis Pelly, who visited Faisal in 1865, estimated that the ruler's revenue amounted to 2,826,000 Maria Theresa thalers — 2 million of which were derived from pilgrim fees, 806,000 from taxes, and 20,000 from tribute. He estimated the total settled population at 115,000, yielding 7,900 fighting men, and the total bedouin population at 20,300. See his *Report on a Journey to the Wahabee Capital of Riyadh in Central Arabia, 1865* (1866; reprint ed., Cambridge: Oleander/Falcon, 1978); cited in Winder, *Saudi Arabia*, 212–213.

11. Winder, *Saudi Arabia*, 264–265.

12. Ibid., 270–271.

13. Ibid., 277.

14. Ibid., 22–23.

2. The Third Realm

1. H. St. John Philby, *Arabia* (New York: Scribner's, 1930; reprint ed., Beirut, 1968), xi.

2. *Parliamentary Debates*, 4th ser., vol. 121 (1903), 1438; quoted in Gary Troeller, *The Birth of Saudi Arabia* (London: Frank Cass, 1976), 11.

3. Troeller, *Birth of Saudi Arabia*, 21–22.

4. This is how John Bagot Glubb viewed it in *War in the Desert*, 56, where he

explained it in terms of Ibn Saud's loss of nerve in the face of his own heavy losses and Turkey's superior potential power.

5. Philby, *Saudi Arabia*, 255–259.

6. Troeller, *Birth of Saudi Arabia*, 38–39.

7. Ibid., 22–24.

8. Ibid., 39–42.

9. Philby, *Saudi Arabia*, 267–269.

10. Troeller, *Birth of Saudi Arabia*, 44.

11. Ibid., 86–89; Philby, *Saudi Arabia*, 271–272.

12. Amin al-Mumayiz, *al-Mamlaka al-'Arabiyya al-Sa'udiyya kama 'Ariftuha: Mudhakarat Diblumasiyya* [Saudi Arabia as I have known it: Diplomatic memoirs] (Beirut, 1963), 228.

13. This number is given by Amin Rihani, *Ibn Sa'oud of Arabia: His Land and People* (London: Constable, 1928), 198–99. Rihani was a Christian Arab who visited Abd al-Aziz's domain in the 1920s. H. St. John Philby, *Arabian Jubilee* (London, 1954), 23, gives a much more conservative estimate of 25,000, and never more than 5,000 on any particular mission. Philby paints a glowing picture of the Ikhwan as noble warriors of the faith; Rihani presents a more balanced account. For a distinctly negative description of the Ikhwan as ignorant, intolerant, and uncultured, see Wahba, *Arabian Days*. Wahba, an Egyptian, served as an adviser to Abd al-Aziz.

14. Troeller, *Birth of Saudi Arabia*, 142.

15. Minute by Curzon, October 6, 1920, no. 9/E 12 144, FO 371/5064; quoted in ibid., 152.

16. One British official who was opposed to his government's design went to the length of alerting Ibn Saud to it and urging him to take action to defeat it. Philby reports in *Arabian Jubilee* that in the summer of 1920, while participating in a conference between Sir Percy Cox and Ibn Saud at 'Uqair, he held "a number of private meetings with Ibn Saud and his principal officials" in which "I warned them of the situation likely to arise in the immediate future, unless immediate steps were taken to eliminate Ibn Rashid as a political factor in Arabia. Within twelve months the Ibn Rashid dynasty had ceased to exist . . . " (p. 66).

17. High Commissioner Baghdad to Secretary of State for Colonies, September 15, 1922, (T) no. 3860; L/P and S/10,7251/1920 Pt. 1; cited by Troeller, *Birth of Saudi Arabia*, 178.

18. Troeller, *Birth of Saudi Arabia*, 219.

19. Wahba, *Arabian Days*, 131.

20. Ibid., 151.

21. See Arnold Toynbee, *Survey of International Affairs*, vol. 1, *1925* (London: Royal Institute for International Affairs, 1927), 300.

22. An Islamic conference was eventually held during the first pilgrimage after the occupation of Jidda. The delegates wrangled, were critical of most of what had been done so far, and dispersed without achieving any concrete results. Gerald De Gaury, *Faisal: King of Saudi Arabia* (New York: Praeger, 1967), 44–45.

23. Wahba, *Arabian Days*, 133.

24. Ibid., 136.

25. Ibid.; emphasis added.

26. This pure "power lust" interpretation is advanced by Glubb in *War in the Desert* and is supported by the subsequent events culminating in the rebel leaders' seeking asylum in Iraq, the country over which the Ikhwan clashed with Ibn Saud.

27. Ibid., 245.

28. Wahba, *Arabian Days*, 138.

29. Ibrahim Abd al-Rahman Al Khamis provides an interesting eyewitness description of the plots to trap Ibn Saud and of the battle of Sibla in *Usud Al Sa'ud* [The lions of the House of Saud] (Beirut: Dar al-Najah, 1972), 169–187.

30. Philby, *Saudi Arabia*, 311–312; Glubb, *War in the Desert*, 343–344.

31. Philby, *Saudi Arabia*, 322–324.

32. A similar situation began to develop in the 1950s and 1960s when King Saud sought to use Arab nationalism against the Iraqis and when he alternately supported "conservative" and "modernizing" forces in his struggle against his brother Faisal. The pattern could easily recur in the future and get out of hand.

33. Philby says about Ibn Saud and the Ikhwan: "The Frankenstein of his own creation would surely have destroyed him, if he had not taken the initiative of destroying it himself"; *Saudi Arabia*, 313. This statement expresses metaphorically the point about the Ikhwan's danger but does not make sufficient allowance for the help they provided through their excesses. Glubb, *War in the Desert*, 282, 293–294, rightly emphasizes the latter point. Wahba, *Arabian Days*, 134–142, supports Glubb's point indirectly with an extensive narrative of Ibn Saud's futile efforts to rally decisive support against the Ikhwan before the latter committed their excesses against "unbelievers."

34. Philby surely goes too far when he implies in a fuzzy conclusion that thereafter Wahhabism somehow became no different from Islam in more "modernized" Muslim countries. He writes: "Slowly at first, but with ever developing momentum, it [the Ikhwan movement] sank into oblivion: as the processes of assimilation kneaded the heterogeneous elements of the Sa'udi realm into a secular community, based as a matter of course on the faith and culture of Islam, but less conscious than before of the Almighty's constant interest in the daily activities of His creatures"; *Saudi Arabia*, 313.

3. Preserving the Empire, 1932–1953

1. Walmsley, Jr., to Secretary of State, no. 91 in Ibrahim al-Rashid, ed., *Documents on the History of Saudi Arabia*, vol. 3 (Salisbury, N.C.: Documentary Publications, 1976), 130.

2. Ibid., 131.

3. Ibid., Document no. 162, 169.

4. Ibid., 168.

5. Philby, *Arabian Jubilee*, 238–239.

6. Hafiz Wahba, *Khamsun 'Am fi al-Mamlaka al-Sa'udiyya* [Fifty years in the Saudi kingdom] (Cairo: Mustafa al-Babi, 1960), 105.

7. Philby, *Saudi Arabia*, 333.

8. Reproduced in Kingdom of Saudi Arabia, Ministry of Finance and

National Economy, Central Department of Statistics, *Statistical Yearbook, 1965* (Jidda, 1965; all *Statistical Yearbooks* cited hereafter by year only).

9. al-Mumayiz, *al-Mamlaka*, 229.

10. Cited in Harvey O'Connor, *World Crisis in Oil* (New York: New York Monthly Review Press, 1962), 327; Malcom Peck, "Saudi Arabia in United States Foreign Policy to 1958: A Study in the Sources and Determinants of American Policy (Ph.D. diss., Harvard University, 1970), 85.

11. OPEC, *Annual Report, 1978* (Vienna, 1978), 162. Figures rounded to the nearest million.

12. Dean Acheson, Memorandum to the President, February 18, 1947, in al-Rashid, *Documents*, 3: 73.

13. Childs to Secretary of State, December 4, 1947, no. 539 in ibid., 114–117.

14. Childs to Secretary of State, December 15 and 16, 1947, nos. 563 and 569 in ibid.

15. Childs to Secretary of State, April 19, 1948, no. 210 in ibid., 175.

16. Loy W. Henderson to Mr. Lovett, May 18, 1948, in ibid., 184.

17. Ibid.

18. Meloy to Secretary of State, May 10, 1949, no. 159 in ibid., 196–198.

19. Ibid.

20. David Holden and Richard Johns, *The House of Saud* (New York: Holt, Rinehart and Winston, 1981), 146–147.

21. "Memorandum for the President," May 9, 1950, in Declassified Documents Reference Service, *1979 Collection* (Washington, D.C.: Carrollton Press, 1979), 317 C.

22. Childs to Secretary of State, May 1950, Confidential File, Harry S. Truman Library, Independence, Mo.

23. al-Mumayiz, *al-Mamlaka*, 280.

24. Philby, *Saudi Arabia*, 353; Edgar O'Ballance, "Saudi Arabia," *Army Quarterly and Defense Journal*, 77 (January 1959), 178.

25. O'Ballance, "Saudi Arabia," 178.

26. Ibid., 186–187.

27. *New York Times*, December 30, 1953.

28. Ibid.

29. Ibid.

30. "Arabian Fledgling: The Royal Saudi Air Force," *Air Enthusiast*, no. 2 (June 1972), 301–302; an authoritative article based on firsthand knowledge.

31. SIPRI, *Arms Trade Register* (Cambridge, Mass.; MIT Press, 1975), 61.

4. Tribulations under the First Successor

1. Department of State, Division of Research for Near East, South Asia and Africa, "Saudi Arabia: A Disruptive Force in Western-Arab Relations," Intelligence Report 7144, January 18, 1956, p. 10 (hereafter cited as Intelligence Report 7144). From Declassified Documents Reference Service, *1979 Collection*, 318 A.

2. A detailed account of this episode can be found in Holden and Johns, *The House of Saud*, 180–182.

3. al-Mumayiz, *al-Mamlaka*, 422.

4. Ibid., 363–364. This report is confirmed by O'Ballance, "Saudi Arabia," 190.

5. Intelligence Report 7144.

6. George Lenczowski, *The Middle East in World Affairs*, 3d ed. (Ithaca, N.Y.: Cornell University Press, 1962), 561.

7. José Arnold, *Golden Swords and Pots and Pans* (London: Gollancz, 1962), 134.

8. Saudi revenue from oil was $341 million in 1955, 44 percent higher than the previous year. It dropped to $290 million in 1956 and did not regain the absolute level of 1955 until 1961, when it reached $378 million. OPEC, *Annual Statistical Review, 1978*, table III, p. 162.

9. Sherman Adams, *Firsthand Report* (New York: Popular Library, 1961), 278.

10. Joint Chiefs of Staff, "Memorandum for Admiral Radford," August 14, 1957, in Declassified Documents Reference Service, *1979 Collection*, 380 C. See also Department of State, "Draft Statement Resulting from Discussions between King Saud and President Eisenhower," February 7, 1957, in Declassified Documents Reference Service *1982 Collection* (Woodbridge, Conn.: Research Publications, 1982), no. 000329.

11. Lenczowski, *Middle East in World Affairs*, 296.

12. al-Mumayiz, *al-Mamlaka*.

13. *New York Times*, January 20, 1957.

14. John Bagot Glubb, *Soldier with the Arabs* (London: Hodder and Stoughton, 1957), 434.

15. Chronology, *MEJ*, Summer 1957; Amin Sa'id, *Tarikh al-Dawla al-Sa'udiyya* [History of the Saudi state], vol. 3, *'Ahd Sa'ud ibn Abd al-Aziz* (The reign of Saud ibn Abd al-Aziz] (Beirut: Dar al-Kitab al-'Arabi, 1964), 203–206.

16. Chronology, *MEJ*, Autumn 1957.

17. Adams, *Firsthand Report*, 290.

18. Department of State, Office of Intelligence, Research, and Analysis, Division of Research and Analysis for Near East, South Asia and Africa, "Background and Implications of the Conflict within the Royal Family," Intelligence Report 7692, April 1, 1958 (cited hereafter as Intelligence Report 7692). From OSS/State Department Intelligence and Research Reports Series, vol. 12, *The Middle East 1950–61*, Supplement (Frederick, Md.: University Publications of America, 1979), Reel III.

19. Yaacov Caroz, *The Arab Secret Services* (London: Corgi Books, 1978), 243–252, provides details on the episode. Some of those are evidently the results of poetic license; but the essential points are quite plausible and are borne out by the logic of known events.

20. OPEC, *Annual Report, 1978*, 162.

21. Arnold, *Golden Swords*, 130, describes the September 1957 unity talks among Nasser, Saud, and Kuwatly in Riyadh. Ahmad Shuqairy, an adviser to Saud who went on to become the first chairman of the PLO, refers to Saud and Faisal's making use of Arab parties in their power struggle. Shuqairy, *'Ala Tariq al-Hazima* [On the road to defeat] (Beirut: Dar al-'Awda, 1972), 112 ff. See also the description later in this chapter of the August 1958 meeting between Faisal and Nasser.

22. King Hussein related in his memoirs, *Uneasy Lies the Head* (New York: Random House, 1962), 202, that the Saudis were so fearful that Faisal turned down his desperate pleas to allow American transport planes to carry some badly needed oil to Amman to fuel its power generators.

23. Chronology, *MEJ*, Autumn 1958.

24. Ibid.

25. On August 22, 1958, a few days after Faisal's visit, Radio Mecca reported that a "responsible source denied reports from Cairo that President Nasser had told Prince Faisal that no country would join the UAR while it had foreign bases on its soil." The broadcast went on to say that Saudi Arabia was not bound by any agreement with a foreign country that made it subservient, and that there was no secret agreement with the United States. Ibid.

26. FBIS, October 24, 1958.

27. A U.S. National Security Council policy directive to all departments and agencies dated November 4, 1958, clearly hints at Saud's approaches. It says among other things: "Recognizing the position of reduced influence of King Saud, continue friendly contacts with him and consider direct requests from him to the extent that such requests do not seriously prejudice U.S. relations with the Saudi Arabian Government. Recognize that King Saud continues to have important support from elements in Nejd." The same directive incidentally called for cultivating groups from which "elements of leadership may emerge, particularly in the armed forces and the middle level . . . officials." National Security Council, "U.S. Policy toward the Near East," NSC 5820/1, November 4, 1958. From Declassified Documents Reference Service *1980 Collection* (Washington, D.C.: Carrollton Press, 1980), 386 B.

28. See Shuqairy, *'Ala Tariq al-Hazima*, opposite pp. 112 and 135.

29. Details in *Middle East Record, 1960* (London: Weidenfeld and Nicolson for the Israel Oriental Society), 375–376.

30. For the content of the speech see Sa'id, *Tarikh al-Dawla*, 3: 247–248.

31. Ibid.

32. Dana Adams Schmidt, *Yemen: The Unknown War* (New York: Holt, Rinehart and Winston, 1968), 51.

33. Central Intelligence Agency, "The President's Intelligence Checklist," October 15, 1962, in Declassified Documents Reference Service, *1978 Collection* (Washington, D.C.: Carrollton Press, 1978), 143 A.

34. Central Intelligence Agency, "The President's Intelligence Checklist," October 18, 1958, in ibid., 143 C.

35. Reproduced in Mohammad H. Heikal, *Ya Sahib al-Jalalah* [Your Majesty] (Cairo: al-Dar al-Qawmiyya lil-Tiba'a wal-Nashr, 1963 [?]), 80–82.

36. "Arabian Fledgling," 302–306.

37. Reported in Sa'id, *Tarikh al-Dawla*, 3: 288–291.

38. *New York Times*, January 24, 1964.

39. *New York Times*, March 29, 1964.

40. Interview with *London Observer*, reported in Chronology, *MEJ*, Spring 1964.

41. *Mideast Mirror*, April 4, 1964, pp. 2–3, citing "reliable Beirut sources."

42. *New York Times*, March 29, 1964.

43. De Gaury, *Faisal,* 101.

44. Text in *MEJ,* Summer 1964.

45. Edgar O'Ballance, *The War in Yemen* (Hamden, Conn.: Archon Books, 1971), 130.

46. Sa'id, *Tarikh al-Dawla,* 3: 392.

47. Amin Sa'id, *Faisal al-'Azim* [Faisal the Great] (Beirut: Dar al-Kutub al-'Arabiyya, 1965), 86–88.

48. Sources for all the preceding: SIPRI, *Arms Trade Register;* "Arabian Fledgling," 302–303.

49. Richard Nyrop et al., *Area Handbook for Saudi Arabia,* 3d ed. (Washington, D.C.: Government Printing Office, 1977), 334.

50. SIPRI, *Arms Trade Register,* 62.

51. Intelligence Report 7144, p. 6.

52. Intelligence Report 7692.

53. Ibid. The report noted as early as April 1958 that "most of the 40-odd officers in the air force are secret sympathizers with Nasser," as were some of the officers of the regular army.

54. Joint Chiefs of Staff, "A Report by the Joint Committee on Programs for Military Assistance and Military Aid for the Middle East," JCS 1887/340, February 1, 1957 (hereafter cited as JCS 1887/340); in Declassified Documents Reference Service, *1980 Collection,* 153 B.

55. See note 53 above.

56. The higher estimate is in Intelligence Report 7692, p. 7; the lower is in JCS 1887/340.

57. Again, the high and low estimates were given by Intelligence Report 7692 and JCS 1887/340, respectively.

58. Intelligence Report 7692, pp. 7–8.

59. "Arabian Fledgling," 303.

60. Intelligence Report 7692, p. 8.

Introduction to Part Three

1. The figures are based on revenue estimates of the Saudi budgets in *Statistical Yearbook,* relevant years.

5. Strivings and Probings, 1964–1973

1. For a discussion of this episode see Gary Samore, "Royal Family Politics in Saudi Arabia (1953–1982)" (Ph.D. diss., Harvard University, 1983), 241–244.

2. Badr was appointed deputy commander of the National Guard; Fawwaz, deputy governor of Mecca; Nawwaf, royal adviser; Abd al-Muhsin had earlier been appointed governor of Madina, a senior-sounding but traditionally not very desirable position.

3. See Chapter 4.

4. Schmidt, *Yemen,* 281–282; Chronology, *MEJ,* Spring 1967.

5. Chronology, *MEJ,* Summer 1967.

6. J. B. Kelly, *Arabia, the Gulf, and the West* (New York: Basic Books, 1980), 132.

7. Some of those arrested had connections with Egyptian intelligence; at least that is what Faisal told Nasser on December 18–19, 1969. Abd al-Majid Farid, *Abd al-Nasir's Secret Papers,* Joint Publications Research Service, no. 72223 (Washington, D.C., 1978), 126. Most reports (such as the *New York Times,* September 9, 1969) put the number of those arrested at between 200 and 300, but some (including *Facts on File, 1969*) gave a figure as high as 2,000.

8. *New York Times,* September 9, 1969; U.S. Congress, House of Representatives, Committee on International Relations, *U.S. Arms Sales to the Persian Gulf,* 94th Cong., 1st sess., 1975, 19. According to Nyrop et al., *Area Handbook for Saudi Arabia,* 339, the National Guard put down a rebellion by air force officers.

9. Holden and Johns, *The House of Saud,* 281.

10. Robert Stookey, *Yemen: The Politics of the Yemen Arab Republic* (Boulder, Colo.: Westview Press, 1978), 253.

11. *Arab World Weekly,* July 21, 1973.

12. *New York Times,* December 23 and 24, 1969.

13. Resolution 242 in its preamble referred to the "inadmissibility of the acquisition of territory by war and the need to work for a just and lasting peace in which every state in the area can live in security." It called for the withdrawal of Israeli forces "from territories occupied in the recent conflict," for termination of "all claims or states of belligerency," and for the "acknowledgment of the sovereignty and political independence of each state in the region within secure and recognized boundaries." The resolution also called for guarantees of free navigation through international waterways, for achieving "a just settlement of the refugee problem," and for guarantees of security and territorial inviolability.

14. William Quandt, *Decade of Decisions* (Berkeley: University of California Press, 1977), 87–88.

15. Henry Kissinger, *White House Years* (Boston: Little, Brown, 1979), chap. 15.

16. Ibid.; Nadav Safran, *Israel: The Embattled Ally* (Cambridge, Mass.: Harvard University Press, 1978), 451–455; Yitzhak Rabin, *The Rabin Memoirs* (Boston: Little, Brown, 1979), chap. 9.

17. Edgar O'Ballance, *Arab Guerrilla Power* (Hamden, Conn.: Archon Books, 1973), 207, 281.

18. Mohammad H. Heikal, *The Road to Ramadan* (London: Collins, 1975), 119–120.

19. *Arab World Weekly,* July 3, 1971.

20. Heikal, *The Road to Ramadan,* 159. Saad El Shazly, the Egyptian army's chief of staff from 1971 to 1973, says that the offer of two squadrons was made in November 1971; *The Crossing of the Suez* (San Francisco: American Mideast Research, 1980), 148. Perhaps the Saudis renewed the offer immediately before Sadat's departure.

21. Heikal, *The Road to Ramadan,* 159.

22. Ibid., 178.

23. Anwar Sadat, *In Search of Identity* (New York: Harper and Row, 1978), 238.

24. Adeed Dawisha, *Saudi Arabia's Search for Security*, Adelphi Papers, no. 158 (London: IISS, 1979), 5.

25. According to Heikal, *The Road to Ramadan*, 200, Qaddafi contributed $1 billion to Egypt's preparation for the Yom Kippur War, presumably between July 1972 and August 1973.

26. See Chapter 5.

27. See Chapter 5.

6. Upheaval and Its Aftermath, 1973–1975

1. See the relevant chapters in Henry Kissinger's *White House Years* and *Years of Upheaval* (Boston: Little, Brown, 1982).

2. U.S. Congress, Senate, Committee on Foreign Relations, Subcommittee on Multinational Corporations, *U.S. Oil Companies and the Arab Oil Embargo: The International Allocation of Constricted Supplies*, Report prepared by the Federal Energy Administration, Office of International Energy Affairs, January 27, 1975, 13.

3. Chronology, *MEJ*, Summer 1973.

4. U.S. Congress, Senate, Committee on Foreign Relations, Subcommittee on Multinational Corporations, *Multinational Petroleum Companies*, 93d Cong., 2d sess., 1974; cited in Robert Stobaugh and Daniel Yergin, *Energy Future* (New York: Random House, 1979), 27.

5. *New York Times*, April 15, 1973.

6. Chronology, *MEJ*, Autumn 1973.

7. *New York Times*, May 26, 1973.

8. Chronology, *MEJ*, Autumn 1973.

9. Heikal, *The Road to Ramadan*, 181; El Shazly, *The Crossing of the Suez*, 31–32, 172–181.

10. Heikal, *The Road to Ramadan*, 275.

11. Quandt, *Decade of Decisions*, 188.

12. Heikal, *The Road to Ramadan*, 270–273.

13. Ibid., 232.

14. The summary of the proceedings is based on ibid., 232–234, and on Quandt, *Decade of Decisions*, 189–190. The two accounts agree on the essentials but differ in tone and detail, reflecting the different recorded perceptions of the American and Arab participants. Interestingly, the impression of a pleading attitude on the part of the Arabs emerges more from Heikal's account than from Quandt's.

15. Mohammad H. Heikal, *The Sphinx and the Commissar* (New York: Harper and Row, 1978), 259. Heikal maintains that misuse of this line by one panicked Saudi officer to say that the Russians were about to descend en masse on the Middle East probably contributed to the U.S. alert on October 25.

16. Heikal, *The Road to Ramadan*, 198.

17. Heikal reports that at least 270 Israeli tanks or armored vehicles could be identified in the pictures produced by Kosygin; ibid., 231–232, 246.

18. Ibid., 235.

19. Ibid., 238–239.

20. George Lenczowski, *Middle East Oil in a Revolutionary Age* (Washington, D.C.: American Enterprise Institute, 1976), 14; quoted from a Saudi government document.

21. On October 19 Abu Dhabi and Libya had jumped the gun by announcing total stoppage of exports to the United States; *New York Times*, October 19, 1973.

22. Senate Subcommittee on Multinational Corporations, *U.S. Oil Companies and the Arab Oil Embargo*, 7.

23. Ibid., 8.

24. *Platt's Oil Price Handbook* and the *Petroleum Intelligence Weekly* during that period.

25. *Petroleum Intelligence Weekly*, September 24, 1973.

26. Based on OPEC, *Annual Report, 1977* (Vienna, 1977).

27. *New York Times*, October 26, 1973.

28. *New York Times*, December 15, 1973.

29. *New York Times*, December 16, 1973.

30. *New York Times*, October 20, 1973.

31. Marvin Kalb and Bernard Kalb, *Kissinger* (New York: Dell, 1974), 582–583.

32. *New York Times*, November 22, 1973.

33. *New York Times*, November 29, 1973.

34. *New York Times*, December 10, 1973.

35. Kalb and Kalb, *Kissinger*, 589.

36. *New York Times*, December 24 and 26, 1973.

37. *New York Times*, January 4, 1974.

38. *New York Times*, January 23, 1974.

39. *New York Times*, January 31, 1974.

40. *New York Times*, January 28, 1974.

41. OPEC, *Annual Report, 1977*, 162.

42. Stobaugh and Yergin, *Energy Future*, 28.

43. *New York Times*, September 10, 1974.

44. *New York Times*, June 9, 1974.

45. *New York Times*, September 10, 1974.

46. *New York Times*, September 24, 1974.

47. *New York Times*, November 3, 1974.

48. *New York Times*, January 10, 1975.

49. *New York Times*, February 10, 1975.

50. Holden and Johns, *The House of Saud*, 359.

51. *New York Times*, February 16, 1981.

52. Kelly, *Arabia, the Gulf, and the West*, 210.

7. The Defense and Security Perspective, 1963–1975

1. See "Arabian Fledgling."

2. Anthony Cordesman, "Defense Planning in Saudi Arabia," in *Defense Planning in Less-Industrialized States*, ed. Stephanie Neuman (Lexington, Mass.: Lexington Books, 1984), 75.

3. Chronology, *MEJ*, Spring 1965.

4. Anthony Cordesman, "Saudi Arabia, AWACS, and America's Search for Strategic Stability in the Near East," Wilson Center International Security Studies Program, Working Paper 26A, September 1981, 46. See also his "Defense Planning in Saudi Arabia," 75–76.

5. Shazly, *The Crossing of the Suez*, 148.

6. GAO, *Perspectives on Military Sales to Saudi Arabia*, Report to Congress, October 2, 1977, 8–9.

7. *Washington Post*, October 19, 1974.

8. U.S. Congress, House of Representatives, Committee on International Relations, *The Persian Gulf, 1975: The Continuing Debate on Arms Sales*, 94th Cong., 1st sess., 1975, 221; and GAO, *Military Sales to Saudi Arabia*, 17.

9. Based on a garbled report in the *Washington Post*, November 7, 1974.

10. House Committee on International Relations, *The Persian Gulf, 1975*, 240; GAO, *Military Sales to Saudi Arabia*, 19.

11. GAO, *Military Sales to Saudi Arabia*, 23.

12. Ibid.

13. Ibid., 17; House Committee on International Relations, *The Persian Gulf, 1975*, 240; Cordesman, "Defense Planning in Saudi Arabia," 76.

14. GAO, *Military Sales to Saudi Arabia*, 28.

8. A Time of Change

1. For a comprehensive description and analysis of Saudi royal family politics see Samore, "Royal Family Politics."

2. Ibid., 230–235.

3. Max Weber, *The Theory of Social and Economic Organizations* (New York: Oxford University Press, 1947), 402.

4. For an elaboration of the preceding points, see Mark Heller and Nadav Safran, *The New Middle Class and Regime Stability in Saudi Arabia*, Harvard Middle East Papers Series, forthcoming.

5. See United States–Saudi Arabian Joint Commission on Economic Cooperation, *Summary of Saudi Arabian Five-Year Development Plan, 1980–1985* (n.p., 1975), 15; J. A. Shaw and D. E. Long, *Saudi Arabian Modernization*, Washington Papers 89 (New York: Praeger, 1982), 28.

6. U.S.-Saudi Joint Commission, *Summary of Five-Year Development Plan*, 9–10.

7. The data are derived from Kingdom of Saudi Arabia, Ministry of Planning, "Financial Summary," *Second Development Plan, 1975–1980* (Springfield, Va.: U.S. Department of Commerce, Bureau of International Commerce, 1975); U.S.-Saudi Joint Commission, *Summary of Five-Year Development Plan*, 88; SAMA, *Annual Report, 1979*, 160, and *1980*, 173.

8. Interview with *Iqraa* magazine, February 10, 1983, cited in FBIS, February 14, 1983.

9. SAMA, *Annual Report, 1979*, 150–151, and *1981*, 154–155.

10. "Pipelines versus Tankers," *Petroleum Economist*, February 1978.

11. "Saudi Arabia: Economic Report," *Christian Science Monitor,* March 30, 1983; SAMA, *Annual Report, 1981,* 167.

12. *Statistical Yearbook, 1981,* 313.

13. "A Survey of Saudi Arabia," *Financial Times,* April 26, 1982.

14. *al-Siyasah,* cited in FBIS, March 23, 1983.

15. U.S. Department of Commerce, Bureau of the Census, *Statistical Abstract of the United States,* (Washington, D.C., 1979), 643.

16. Israel had 8,000 miles of paved roads in 1978. Central Bureau of Statistics, *Statistical Abstract of Israel, 1981* (Tel Aviv, 1982), 509.

17. Kingdom of Saudi Arabia, *Second Development Plan, 1975–1980,* 63.

18. Based on *New York Times,* March 7, 1980 and March 23, 1981; *Wall Street Journal,* June 4, 1981; and indirect private communication by Saudi Minister of Planning Hisham Nazer.

19. Based on a combination of sources, including J. S. Birks and C. A. Sinclair, *Arab Manpower* (New York: St. Martin's Press, 1980), 115; Ghassane Salameh, *al-Siyassa al-Kharijiyya al-Sa'udiyya mundhu 'Am 1945* [Saudi foreign policy since 1945] (Beirut: Ma'had al-'Inma al-'Arabi, 1980), 134; *Financial Times,* March 21, 1981; *Times,* May 22, 1980; Joseph Kraft, "Letter from Saudi Arabia," *New Yorker,* July 4, 1983, 42; Shaw and Long, *Saudi Arabian Modernization,* 47. Shaw and Long's list somehow omits the Britons.

20. The lack of a more definite figure in a country that is now in its third five-year plan serves as one interesting commentary on the Kingdom. The Saudi authorities have been highly sensitive on that issue and have tried to hold back or alter the information they had on the subject, with the result that figures cited by various commentators have ranged from 3.3 to 9 million, and even 15 million. Every serious author who has addressed the question has had to open an extensive investigation and conclude it by giving his or her own estimate. See, for instance, Birks and Sinclair, *Arab Manpower,* 92ff.; Nyrop et al., *Area Handbook for Saudi Arabia,* 62ff.; Shaw and Long, *Saudi Arabian Modernization,* 46; Salameh, *al-Siyassa al-Kharijiyya,* 122ff. In 1962–63 a census taken in connection with Faisal's ten-point reform program showed a population of 3.3 million; but the government rejected the finding as "unacceptably" low, even while independent investigators—such as Birks and Sinclair, *Arab Manpower,* 94—thought it to be too high. Another census was taken in 1974–75, when the second plan was being prepared. The results were kept secret, held under armed guard for three years before being published, and then amended. Kingdom of Saudi Arabia, Ministry of Finance and National Economy, Central Department of Statistics, *Population Census, 1974,* 14 vols. (Dammam, 1977), showed a national population of 5.9 million, which also appeared to analysts such as Birks and Sinclair to be too high; corrections based on internal evidence from the census data led the latter to revise the official figure downward to 4.59 million; *Arab Manpower,* 96–97. I take the lower figure for the population in 1977 as a basis for my estimate for 1980. It should be added that the Saudi authorities sought to "get away" with the higher estimates for the national population for planning purposes by understating the actual number of foreign workers taken into account—in other words, by counting foreign workers as natives for planning purposes.

21. *Christian Science Monitor,* July 17, 1981.
22. *Statistical Yearbook, 1978,* 36, and *1980,* 42.
23. *Statistical Yearbook, 1978,* 87, and *1980,* 97.
24. See Heller and Safran, *The New Middle Class,* 4–9.
25. Ibid., 12–13.
26. Ibid., table IV, p. 16.
27. Ibid., 16–27.

9. The Arab-Israeli Arena, 1975–1979

1. Holden and Johns, *The House of Saud,* 422.
2. Chronology, *MEJ,* Autumn 1975.
3. Adeed Dawisha, *Syria and the Lebanese Crisis* (New York: St. Martin's Press, 1980), 118.
4. The expression "red line" had more than a territorial connotation, as Rabin indicated in response to inquiries. It presumably referred also to action to crush the rightist-Christian forces, although Rabin refused to clarify this point. It is noteworthy that the expression was used in a similar sense by President Assad in a telephone conversation with President Franjieh on January 19, 1976, in reference to the Palestinians. In explaining why he had sent in the PLA the previous day, Assad reportedly said that, with respect to the Palestinians, Syria maintained that "there is a red line beyond which we will not permit anybody to go at all"; ibid. Had the Israelis intercepted the phone conversation between the two presidents? Did Rabin intend, in using the same expression, to impress Assad with that fact as well as to convey to him a message Rabin knew he would perfectly understand?
5. Ibid., 113.
6. *al-Thawra* (Baghdad), June 2, 1976; quoted in ibid., 136.
7. *al-Thawra* (Baghdad), June 9, 1976; quoted in ibid.
8. Brezhnev's note cited in ibid., 137.
9. *New York Times,* October 3, 1976.
10. *MEES,* May 30, 1977.
11. See Chronology, *MEJ,* Autumn 1977.
12. Moshe Dayan, *Breakthrough: A Personal Account of the Egypt-Israel Peace Negotiations* (New York: Knopf, 1981), chap. 4.
13. Saudi News Agency, November 18, 1977; Holden and Johns, *The House of Saud,* 481.
14. *New York Times,* June 22, 1979.
15. *al-Hawadess* (Beirut), December 9, 1977; cited in *MECS,* 2 (1977–78), 165.
16. Saudi News Agency, December 15, 1977; cited in ibid., 166.
17. Radio Riyadh; cited in ibid., 686.
18. Interview with *al-Siyasah* (Kuwait), August 23, 1978; cited in ibid., 166.
19. Saudi News Agency, September 19, 1978; cited in ibid., 167; emphases added.
20. Saudi News Agency, September 25, 1978; cited in ibid.
21. FBIS, October 24 and 25, 1978; *Washington Post,* October 29, 1978.

10. The Gulf Arena, 1975–1979

1. Chronology, *MEJ*, Autumn 1975.
2. Holden and Johns, *The House of Saud*, 425.
3. Ibid., 426.
4. *MECS*, 1 (1976–77), 343–344.
5. Ibid., 345.
6. See ibid., 332, for characterization of the atmosphere by the Omani minister of state for foreign affairs.
7. For the Saudi explanations of their position see Holden and Johns, *The House of Saud*, 450–453.
8. Ibid., 451–452.
9. *MECS*, 1 (1976–77), 394.
10. FBIS, July 5, 1977.
11. See Chapter 11.
12. *MECS*, 2 (1977–78), 238.
13. *Newsweek*, July 17, 1978; cited in ibid., 527.
14. *MECS*, 3 (1978–79), 538, 579.
15. For a summary of the Iraqi call and a description of the proceedings of the first Baghdad summit see ibid., 214–217.
16. Ibid.
17. Holden and Johns, *The House of Saud*, 501; see also *MECS*, 3 (1978–79), 249.
18. *Washington Post*, May 5, 1979; cited in *MECS*, 3 (1978–79), 752.
19. *Arab Report and Record*, March 28, 1979; cited in Holden and Johns, *The House of Saud*, 504.
20. *MECS*, 3 (1978–79), 220–221.
21. *Fiches du monde arabe*, quoted in Holden and Johns, *The House of Saud*, 505.
22. *al-Kifah al-'Arabi*, May 7, 1979; cited in *MECS*, 3 (1978–79), 739. See also Chapter 12.

11. The Yemens, Oman, and the Horn of Africa, 1975–1979

1. *MEED*, February 7, 1975.
2. *MEED*, March 28 and April 25, 1975.
3. *MEED*, March 21, 1975.
4. *MEED*, May 23, 1975.
5. *MECS*, 1 (1976–77), 652.
6. *MEED*, August 22, 1975.
7. *MEED*, June 20, 1975.
8. *Washington Post*, August 3, 1975.
9. *Middle East*, September 1977.
10. *MEED*, November 21, 1975.
11. *MEED*, December 19, 1975.
12. *MEED*, April 30, 1976.

13. U.S. Congress, House of Representatives, Committee on Foreign Affairs, *Proposed Arms Transfers to the Yemen Arab Republic,* 96th Cong., 1st sess., 1979, especially p. 30. Also cited in Chronology, *MEJ,* Autumn 1976.

14. *MEED,* April 2, 1976.

15. *MEED,* May 7, 1976.

16. *MECS,* 1 (1976–77), 45.

17. *Middle East,* July 1977.

18. *al-Siyasah,* April 16, 1977.

19. *MEED,* May 13, 1977.

20. *MEED,* June 17, 1977.

21. *MEED,* July 1, 1977.

22. *MEED,* July 15, 1977.

23. *MEED,* July 1, 1977.

24. Fred Halliday, "Yemen's Unfinished Revolution: Socialism in the South," *MERIP Reports,* no. 81 (October 1979), 17.

25. *MECS,* 1 (1976–77), 655.

26. For details of the last months of Hamdi's rule and his death, see ibid., 653–659.

27. See William Quandt, *Saudi Arabia in the 1980s* (Washington, D.C.: Brookings Institution, 1981), 27.

28. *MECS,* 1 (1976–77), 660.

29. From the Arabic press, cited in *MECS,* 2 (1977–78), 799.

30. Halliday, "Yemen's Unfinished Revolution," 17.

31. *MECS,* 2 (1977–78), 241.

32. See ibid.

33. House Committee on Foreign Affairs, *Proposed Arms Transfers to the Yemen Arab Republic,* 8.

34. *MECS,* 3 (1978–79), 248, 721.

35. Ibid., 247–250.

12. The American Connection, 1975–1979

1. International Monetary Fund (IMF), *Direction of Trade Yearbook* (Washington, D.C., 1982).

2. U.S. Congress, House of Representatives, Committee on International Relations, *U.S. Arms Policies in the Persian Gulf and Red Sea Areas: Past, Present, and Future,* Staff Report, 95th Cong., 1st sess., 1977, 28.

3. U.S. Department of Defense, Security Assistance Agency, *Foreign Military Sales, Foreign Military Construction Sales, and Military Assistance Facts,* (Washington, D.C.: Government Printing Office, 1982).

4. Cited in Barry Rubin, *Paved with Good Intentions: The American Experience and Iran* (New York: Oxford University Press, 1980), 230.

5. FBIS, December 8, 1978; *International Herald Tribune,* April 23, 1979.

6. *MECS,* 3 (1978–79), 785; William Quandt, *Saudi Arabia's Oil Policy* (Washington, D.C.: Brookings Institution, 1982), 14.

7. Quandt, *Saudi Arabia's Oil Policy,* 14.

8. *Arab News,* January 29, 1979.

9. FBIS, February 26, 1979; cited in *MECS*, 3 (1978–79), 752.

10. U.S. Congress, Senate, Committee on Foreign Relations, *Arms Sales Package to Saudi Arabia—Part 2*, 97th Cong., 1st sess., 1981, 113. Until that information became available it was assumed that the United States, not the Saudis, had requested the AWACS deployment.

11. *Washington Post*, March 19, 1979.

12. Brzezinski was reported in the *New York Times*, March 20, 1979, as saying that his mission had assured him that Saudi Arabia and Jordan would cooperate with U.S. diplomacy in the area. In his memoirs, Brzezinski said that during his mission he obtained "a secret Saudi pledge not to adopt any damaging sanctions against Egypt. The Saudis would confine themselves to a formally negative reaction"; *Power and Principle* (New York: Farrar, Straus and Giroux, 1983), 286. It is interesting that Brzezinski noted on the same page of his memoirs that "in subsequent months the Saudis kept that promise." In fact they did not—unless one takes "subsequent months" to mean two, in which case his remark would be true but pointless.

13. In a generally well-informed article, Tawfiq Mishlawi identifies additional members of the Khaled-Abdallah "faction" at the time as including Foreign Minister Saud al-Faisal, National Security Council head Mut'ib ibn Abd al-Aziz, and Riyadh's governor, Salman ibn Abd al-Aziz. Fahd's supporters included Interior Minister Nayef and Defense Minister Sultan. See "Saudis Tip the Balance," *Middle East*, May 1979, p. 25. Other reports agree with this list except with regard to Sultan, who is reported to have sided with Khaled and Abdallah on that occasion.

14. In *al-Jazirah*, January 6, 1979, Fahd asserted his support for the shah as the legitimate ruler of Iran. The comment about the Communists appeared in *Newsweek*, January 22, 1979.

15. *MEES*, April 2, 1979.

16. Shaul Bakhash, *The Politics of Oil and Revolution in Iran* (Washington, D.C.: Brookings Institution, 1982), 10.

17. *MEES*, April 2, 1979.

18. FBIS, April 25, 1979.

13. The Arab-Israeli Arena, 1979–1982

1. FBIS, April 24, 1979; cited in *MECS*, 3 (1978–79), 748.

2. *New York Times*, May 2, 1979.

3. See, for instance, *al-Jazirah*, May 2, 1979; *al-Riyadh*, May 3, 1979. Cited in *MECS*, 3 (1978–79), 748.

4. See, for instance, *New York Times*, April 30, 1979; Gulf News Agency, April 21, 1979, cited in *MECS*, 3 (1978–79), 740.

5. *New York Times*, June 22, 1979.

6. Ibid.

7. *New York Times*, August 13, 1979.

8. See *New York Times*, August 23, 1979.

9. For information about the conference see *MECS*, 4 (1979–80), 170–175.

10. Text of the communiqué in ibid., 216–218.

11. Details in ibid., 180. Text of statement of Damascus meeting in app. III, 220–221.

12. Text in ibid., 224–225.

13. Text in ibid., 222–224.

14. Details of the conference in ibid., 175–177. Statement in app. II, 218–220.

15. Saudi Minister of Interior Nayef ibn Abd al-Aziz declared to Kuwait's *al-Ra'y al-Amm* on November 26, 1980, just after the conference, that the absence of the PLO was "an unpleasant and unexpected surprise"; FBIS, November 28, 1980.

16. *MECS*, 4 (1979–80), 198.

17. Chronology, *Foreign Affairs*, 60, no. 3 (1981).

18. Quandt, *Saudi Arabia in the 1980s*, 9.

19. Chronology, *Foreign Affairs*, 60, no. 3 (1981).

20. Saudi Press Agency, interview read on Radio Riyadh, August 7, 1981.

21. FBIS, citing Radio Monte Carlo, August 8, 1981.

22. "Meet the Press," NBC-TV, August 9, 1981.

23. Chronology, *MEJ*, Winter 1982.

24. *London Sunday Telegraph*, October 25, 1981.

25. Ibid.

26. Kuwaiti News Agency, January 25, 1982.

27. The extent to which the Saudis viewed Egypt as a strategic asset despite their bitter quarrel with Sadat is shown in certain developments on a very practical level. In an effort to avoid exclusive dependence on the Strait of Hormuz for the transit of their oil, the Saudis launched, in the very midst of their dispute with Sadat, the construction of a pipeline across Arabia designed to carry 1.85 mbd from the eastern coast to Yanbo on the Red Sea; for further transit to Europe the oil would have to go through either the Suez Canal or the Sumed (Suez-Mediterranean) pipeline, both controlled by Egypt. Sumed itself had been built with the help of Saudi financing, and its capacity was brought up to its peak of 1.7 mbd in October 1979. Pipeline data in *Petroleum Economist*, August 1982, 314.

28. *New York Times*, October 29, 1981.

29. See *New York Times*, October 31, 1981.

30. *New York Times*, November 1, 1981; Chronology, *Foreign Affairs*, 60, no. 3 (1981).

31. *New York Times*, November 3, 1981.

32. Interview with the Saudi Press Agency, Saudi Radio, FBIS, November 2, 1981.

33. ABC News, November 6, 1981.

34. *Washington Post*, November 6, 1981.

35. *New York Times*, November 11, 13, 15, and 17, 1981.

36. *al-Mustaqbal* (Paris), November 21, 1981.

37. UPI, November 23, 1981.

38. "This Week," ABC News, November 22, 1981.

39. Chronology, *Foreign Affairs*, 60, no. 3 (1981).

40. On December 25, 1981, Defense Minister Ariel Sharon declared that the annexation was prompted by a U.S. plan to return all the occupied land; ibid.

41. Ibid.

42. Assad interview on Damascus TV, December 23, 1981; Kuwaiti News Agency, January 26, 1982.

43. Saudi Press Agency, December 31, 1981; *New York Times*, January 2, 1982.

44. Chronology, *Foreign Affairs*, 60, no. 3 (1981).

45. Ibid.

46. *New York Times*, April 14 and 19, 1982.

47. After the war, some evidence came to light showing that Defense Minister Ariel Sharon actually forced the Syrians' hand, contrary to the Israeli cabinet's inclination; Zeev Schiff, *Israel's War in Lebanon* (New York: Simon and Schuster, 1984).

48. That the Saudis' fear was not unfounded is shown by the fact that, as early as June 8, Arabic-language broadcasts on the Soviet radio, Peace and Progress, called upon the Arab states to help the Palestinians by using the oil weapon; Galia Golan, *The Soviet Union and the Israeli War in Lebanon*, Research Paper 46 (Jerusalem: Soviet and East European Research Center, 1982), 13.

49. Saudi Press Agency in FBIS, June 10, 1982.

50. Saudi Press Agency in FBIS, June 9, 1982.

51. Riyadh Domestic Service in FBIS, June 11, 1982.

52. Radio Riyadh in FBIS, June 7, 1982.

53. Saudi Press Agency in FBIS, June 11, 1982.

54. Chronology, *Foreign Affairs*, 61, no. 3 (1982).

55. On the Soviet attitude in the war, see Golan, *Soviet Union and Israeli War;* and Ammnon Sella, *The Soviet Attitude towards the War in Lebanon*, Research Paper 47 (Jerusalem: Soviet and East European Research Center, 1982).

56. Chronology, *Foreign Affairs*, 61, no. 3 (1982).

57. *New York Times*, June 19, 1982.

58. Saudi Press Agency in FBIS, June 22, 1982.

59. FBIS, June 28, 1982.

60. Chronology, *Journal of Palestinian Studies*, Summer/Fall 1982, 157–158.

61. Radio Monte Carlo in FBIS, August 2, 1982.

62. *New York Times*, August 6, 1982.

14. The Gulf Arena, 1979–1982

1. *al-Nahar*, October 31, 1979; cited in *MECS*, 4 (1979–80), 516.

2. The Kuwaiti rulers, for example, set in motion a process aimed at renewing parliament, suspended since 1976 under Saudi pressure; introduced military conscription; and exerted themselves to mediate disputes among their small neighbors. Some leaders of the UAE tried to reinforce the power of the federal government and precipitated instead a crisis that threatened the continued existence of the union.

3. *Financial Times*, July 19, 1979; *Newsweek*, July 25, 1979. Cited in *MECS*, 3 (1978–79), 751.

4. Qatar News Agency, June 30, 1979; cited in ibid., 437.

5. *al-Fajr* (Abu Dhabi), June 30, 1979; cited in ibid., 751.

6. Associated Press, September 11, 1979; cited in ibid., 451.

7. Interview with *al-Mustaqbal* (Paris), October 13, 1979; cited in *MECS*, 4 (1979–80), 200–201.

8. Reuters, September 27, 1979; cited in *MECS*, 3 (1978–79), 441.

9. The number of insurgents reported by different sources varied from the official figure of "about 210," cited in the *New York Times* on February 25, 1980, to 700, cited in *Der Spiegel* as reported in *Haaretz* on December 5, 1979. What is definitely known is that at the end of the fighting 175 rebels were seized, and somewhat less definitely that an additional 75 were killed in the fighting. Sixty Saudi troops and 25 bystanders were also reported killed.

10. The French magazine *Le Point* reported on January 27, 1980, that five Frenchmen from an elite antiterrorist unit took command of the foundering Saudi effort on November 23. The French government issued a lukewarm denial. *International Herald Tribune*, January 29, 1980; cited in *MECS*, 4 (1979–80), 686–687.

11. Was the Soviet invasion causally related to the crisis in American-Iranian relations? Did the Soviets invade because they felt certain that American-Iranian joint efforts to counter them in Afghanistan had become highly unlikely? No evidence is yet available to answer that question either way.

12. Brzezinski, *Power and Principle*, 450; emphasis added.

13. *New York Times*, February 5, 1980.

14. Text of charter in *MECS*, 4 (1979–80), 224–225.

15. Radio Tehran in Arabic, February 22, 1980; BBC, February 25, 1980. Cited in ibid., 486.

16. Saudi News Agency, April 27, 1980; cited in ibid., 705.

17. FBIS, May 12, 1980.

18. FBIS, August 7, 1980.

19. FBIS, August 27, 1980. See Chapter 15.

20. FBIS, August 29, 1980.

21. Senate Committee on Foreign Relations, *Arms Sales Package to Saudi Arabia*, 114.

22. Brzezinski, *Power and Principle*, 450.

23. Senate Committee on Foreign Relations, *Arms Sales Package to Saudi Arabia*, 114.

24. Brzezinski, *Power and Principle*, 449–450.

25. For example, *New York Times*, August 21, 1980.

26. FBIS, August 25, 1980.

27. FBIS, September 10, 1980; *New York Times*, September 16, 1980.

28. Text in FBIS, September 18, 1980.

29. Anthony Cordesman, "Lessons of the Iran-Iraq War: Part Two," *Armed Forces Journal International*, June 1982, p. 83.

30. William O. Standenmaier, "Military Policy and Strategy in the Gulf War," *Parameters: The Journal of the Army War College*, 12 (June 1982).

31. Radio Baghdad, October 2, 1980. cited in *MECS*, 4 (1979–80), 19.

32. See Jimmy Carter, *Keeping Faith* (New York: Bantam, 1982), 559, for points about AWACS, F-15s, and restraining Iraqis. On AWACS and the joint naval task force, see *Washington Post*, September 28, 1980; *New York Times*, September 30, October 1 and 2, 1980.

33. FBIS, October 1, 1980.

34. *New York Times*, October 1 and 2, 1980.

35. Baghdad Domestic Service, September 25, 1980; cited in FBIS, September 30, 1980.

36. FBIS, September 26, 1980.

37. Text in FBIS, September 29, 1980.

38. *Petroleum Economist*, August 1982, p. 314.

39. *Washington Post*, October 13, 1980.

40. *Washington Post*, November 3, 1980.

41. *New York Times*, November 21, 1980.

42. *al-Jazirah*, cited in FBIS, December 15, 1980.

43. *New York Times*, February 4, 1981; FBIS, February 5, 1981.

44. See FBIS, November 13, 17, 24, 1981.

45. See Carter, *Keeping Faith*, 485ff.

46. *al-Watan*, cited in FBIS, April 15, 1981.

47. Kuwait News Agency, cited in *MECS*, 5 (1980 – 81), 480.

48. *New York Times*, December 9, 1980.

49. *al-Bayan*, November 26, 1980; cited in FBIS, December 5, 1980.

50. FBIS, December 1, 1980; quoted in Stephen R. Grummon, *The Iran-Iraq War*, Washington Papers 92 (New York: Praeger, 1982), 55.

51. FBIS, December 2, 1980.

52. FBIS, February 6, 1981.

53. *al-Ra'y al-Amm*, cited in FBIS, March 15, 1981.

54. Text in FBIS, May 27, 1981.

55. *New York Times*, October 6 and 12, 1980.

56. *New York Times*, October 24, 1980.

57. *New York Times*, October 31, 1980.

58. *New York Times*, December 11, 1980.

59. FBIS, December 23, 1980.

60. FBIS, January 26, 1981.

61. *Washington Post*, September 23, 1981; *New York Times*, September 25, 1981.

62. FBIS, September 30, 1981.

63. FBIS, October 8, 1981.

64. FBIS, October 20, 1981.

65. FBIS, November 9, 1981.

66. FBIS, October 3, 1981.

67. *al-Siyasah*, November 4, 1981.

68. *Washington Post*, November 12, 1981.

69. *New York Times*, December 17, 18, 19, 1981.

70. FBIS, December 15, 1981.

71. FBIS, December 20 and 22, 1981.

72. FBIS, December 22, 1981.

73. *Washington Post*, February 15, 1982.

74. *New York Times*, February 8 and 19, 1982.

75. FBIS, February 17, 1982.

76. *MEES*, February 8, 1982.

77. See ibid., where King Hussein is reported to have declared that Jordan would welcome Mubarak's participation in the Fez II summit.

78. Ibid.

79. *Middle East Monitor,* February 15, 1982.

80. Ibid.

81. *New York Times,* April 14, 19, 25, 1982.

82. *MEES,* May 3, 1982.

83. Ibid.

84. *New York Times,* May 9 and 25, 1982.

85. *MEES,* May 24, 1982.

86. *New York Times,* May 30, 1982.

87. *MEES,* June 7, 1982.

88. *New York Times,* May 22, 1982.

89. *New York Times,* May 23, 1982.

90. *New York Times,* May 27, 1982.

91. *New York Times,* May 29, 1982.

92. *New York Times,* May 30, 1982.

93. *New York Times,* July 17, 1982.

15. The Yemens, 1979–1982

1. Interview with Gulf News Agency, in FBIS, April 23, 1979.

2. *MECS,* 4 (1979–80), 210.

3. See ibid., 832–833, for al-Asnaj's retrospective description of the failure.

4. Ibid., 895.

5. Ibid., 895–896.

6. IISS, *The Military Balance, 1980–81* (London, 1980), 105.

7. Cited in *MECS,* 3 (1978–79), 66.

8. See ibid., 65.

9. Radio Aden, September 30, 1979; cited in ibid., 723.

10. *al-Jumhur,* October 11, 1979; cited in *MECS,* 4 (1979–80), 706.

11. *Pravda,* October 27, 1979; cited in *MECS,* 3 (1978–79), 65.

12. *al-Siyasah,* October 29, 1979; cited in ibid.

13. Radio San'a, October 3 and 4, 1979; cited in *MECS,* 4 (1979–80), 211.

14. Radio San'a, October 8, 1979; cited in ibid.

15. Ibid.

16. *MECS,* 4 (1979–80), 828; *Washington Post,* February 20, 1980.

17. *New York Times,* March 19, 1980.

18. Cited in *MECS,* 4 (1979–80), 706.

19. Ibid., 699.

20. Cited in ibid.

21. Ibid., 828.

22. *New York Times,* February 6, 1980.

23. Brzezinski, *Power and Principle,* 450.

24. *New York Times,* February 27, 1980.

25. *New York Times,* March 19, 1980.

26. *Washington Post,* June 5, 1980.

27. *Financial Times,* April 22, 1980; cited in *MECS,* 4 (1979–80), 665.

28. *Pravda,* April 23, 1980; cited in ibid., 66.

29. *Pravda,* May 29, 1980; cited in ibid.

30. *MECS,* 4 (1979–80), 829.

31. Kuwait News Agency, June 30, 1980; cited in ibid., 666.

32. *Monday Morning,* July 21–27, 1980; cited in ibid., 707.

33. *MECS,* 5 (1980–81), 722.

34. *al-Fajr al-Jadid,* October 5, 1980; cited in ibid., 720.

35. *MECS,* 4 (1979–80), 663–664; Chronology, *MEJ,* Winter 1981.

36. *al-Sharq al-Awsat,* October 15, 1980; cited in *MECS,* 5 (1980–81), 874.

37. *al-Majallah,* November 29, 1980; cited in ibid., 724.

38. *MECS,* 5 (1980–81), 874.

39. Ibid., 873.

40. Ibid., 720–721.

41. *MEED,* March 27, 1981. Also, *Daily Telegraph,* April 16, 1981; cited in *MECS,* 5 (1980–81), 270.

42. *MECS,* 4 (1979–80), 831.

43. Saleh lamented in an interview with *al-Hawadess,* April 3, 1981, that he did not understand why the GCC had refused to admit the YAR despite its strategic importance. The YAR media condemned Saudi Arabia more sharply. See *MECS,* 5 (1980–81), 873.

44. *MECS,* 5 (1980–81), 270.

45. Radio Riyadh, April 14, 1981; cited in ibid.

46. *Middle East International,* no. 164.

47. *Pravda,* October 29, 1981; cited in *MECS,* 5 (1980–81), 71.

48. *Christian Science Monitor,* November 20, 1981.

49. *New York Times,* December 4, 1981.

50. *MEED,* December 11, 1981.

51. Chronology, *MEJ,* Spring 1982.

52. *MEED,* March 19, 1982.

53. *MEED,* April 9, 1982.

54. *MEED,* May 7, 1982.

54. Ibid.

56. *New York Times,* June 10, 1982.

16. The American Connection, 1979–1982

1. IMF, *Direction of Trade Yearbook.*

2. U.S. Department of Defense, Security Assistance Agency, *Foreign Military Sales, Foreign Military Construction Sales, and Military Assistance Facts.* Washington, D.C.: Government Printing Office, 1982.

3. Quandt, *Saudi Arabia's Oil Policy,* table 1, p. 14.

4. *New York Times,* May 8, 1979.

5. See Brzezinski, *Power and Principle,* 286. On the Saudis' action against Egypt, see above, Chapter 13.

6. Carter, *Keeping Faith,* 408, 410.

7. See story by Jim Hoagland in *Washington Post,* April 15, 1979.

8. Quandt, *Saudi Arabia's Oil Policy,* 17–18.

9. *Washington Star,* May 5, 1979; cited in *MECS,* 3 (1978–79), 753.

10. The spot market price came down from $35.40 in June to $33.13 in July, $33.80 in August, $35.00 in September, before climbing to $38.00 in October and $41.00 in November. See Quandt, *Saudi Arabia's Oil Policy,* table 1, p. 14.

11. *New York Times,* July 14, 1979.

12. Cited in *MECS,* 3 (1978–79), 253.

13. Actually, the Soviet invasion had far-reaching long-term effects on American policy. It precipitated, among other things, Washington's "tilt" toward China and contributed to killing the Salt II agreement. See Brzezinski, *Power and Principle,* 423–424; 431ff. But the Saudis looked at the situation only in immediate, local terms, and the United States did not instruct them about its global response, probably because that response developed in a pragmatic fashion and in connection with many other factors.

14. Brzezinski, *Power and Principle,* 444.

15. Ibid., 449–450; see also above, Chapter 14.

16. FBIS, February 6, 1980, cited in *MECS,* 4 (1979–80), 704.

17. *Washington Post,* July 22, 1980.

18. *New York Times,* February 21, 1980; FBIS, March 5, 1980.

19. Quandt, *Saudi Arabia's Oil Policy,* table 1, p. 14.

20. Data on production and prices from Quandt, *Saudi Arabia's Oil Policy,* table 1, p. 14 and passim; also, Department of Energy, *Monthly Energy Review,* May 1981.

21. *New York Times,* October 31, 1980. Also, *MECS,* 5 (1980–81), 749.

22. FBIS, January 26, 1981; see also Chapter 13.

23. *New York Times,* May 30, 1982.

17. The Defense and Security Perspective, 1975–1982

1. See *Statistical Yearbook,* relevant years.

2. Dawisha, *Saudi Arabia's Search for Security,* 7.

3. Department of Defense, *Foreign Military Sales.* The figures for U.S. military sales for fiscal 1975 through fiscal 1982 add up to $21.9 billion, to which was added $3.5 billion for a naval development package deal with France. The figure for military construction does not include foreign or non-U.S. government agencies.

4. Details in U.S. Congress, Senate, Committee on Foreign Relations, *Middle East Arms Sales Proposals,* 95th Cong., 2d sess., 1978, 238ff.

5. See Cordesman, "Saudi Arabia, AWACS, and America's Search," ix.

6. Ibid., xi.

7. "Special Report, Middle East Aerospace: Saudi Arabia," *Aviation Week and Space Technology,* May 23, 1983, pp. 48, 52.

8. Ibid., 53.

9. Ibid.

10. *International Defense Review,* 16 (1983), 1408–1409.

11. *Defense Monitor,* 9 (1981), 6.

12. See Chapter 13 and ibid., 7.

13. For a detailed story of the project, see *New Statesman,* March 23, 1979, pp. 384ff.

14. Additional details and sources in Samore, "Royal Family Politics," 457–458.

15. FBIS, March 6, 1979.

16. The Jaffee Center for Strategic Studies (JCSS), *The Middle East Military Balance, 1983* (Tel Aviv: Tel Aviv University, 1983), 205, says that 10,000 Pakistani troops were stationed in Saudi Arabia. Samore, "Royal Family Politics," 459, cites several newspapers and periodicals that spoke of two brigades.

17. See Samore, "Royal Family Politics," 433, 457–460.

18. GAO, *Military Sales to Saudi Arabia,* 2–3.

19. The estimate of forty men per plane for the F-5 is given in SIPRI, *World Armaments and Disarmament: SIPRI Yearbook, 1978* (London and Philadelphia: Taylor and Francis, 1978). The estimate for the F-15 is given in U.S. Air Force, HQ Tactical Air Command, "Manning Document for the F-15" (Langley Air Force Base, n.d.). According to that document, a wing of F-15s, about equal to the number of aircraft ordered by the Saudis, needs 4,760 personnel, nearly half of them characterized as "essential forces" — crews, maintenance, and operations staff — and the other half as "base support forces."

20. *New York Times,* March 26, 1979.

21. Cordesman, "Saudi Arabia, AWACS, and America's Search," 16.

22. See figure in ibid., 18.

23. Ibid., 26A, p. xii.

24. IISS, *The Military Balance, 1982–83* (London, 1983); JCSS, *Middle East Military Balance, 1983,* 199, gives similar figures: 55,000 for the armed forces, 20,000 for the National Guard.

25. IISS, *The Military Balance, 1982–83;* JCSS, *Middle East Military Balance, 1983,* gives comparable figures.

26. GAO, *Military Sales to Saudi Arabia,* 23, 25, 32.

27. "Special Report, Middle East Aerospace," 54, 83.

28. GAO, *Military Sales to Saudi Arabia,* 18.

29. Ibid., 20.

30. Ibid., 30.

31. Saudi News Agency, January 9, 1980; cited in FBIS, January 10, 1980.

32. Good summaries of reports on the Mecca incident, including the military operations, are found in *MECS,* 4 (1979–80), 682–688, 694–697; and Samore, "Royal Family Politics," 439–442. On pp. 442–459 Samore discusses the internal political repercussions of the incident.

33. "Special Report, Middle East Aerospace," 81.

34. Both incidents reported in ibid., 82.

35. *MECS,* 4 (1979–80), 701.

36. *MECS,* 1 (1976–77), 571.

Conclusions

1. It is often argued that the deterioration of the Saudi-American relationship is entirely due to America's policy toward Israel and the Arab-Israeli con-

flict. This summary shows that although the Israel problem was certainly an important factor in the equation, it was far from being the only one. Israel surely had nothing to do with the fall of the shah and little to do with the orientation of the regime that succeeded him. Moreover, Iraq under Saddam Hussein opposed the United States because it had its own pan-Arab designs, which precluded any significant American position in either the Gulf or the Arab-Israeli arena. That ambition was also a crucial motive for Iraq's invasion of Iran, which confronted the Kingdom with mortal dangers having nothing to do with the Israeli question.

2. Arthur N. Young, *Saudi Arabia: The Making of a Financial Giant* (New York: New York University Press, 1983), 125. See also Saudi Press Agency, "Major News Events," April 30, 1984, p. 2.

3. Saudi Press Agency, "Major News Events," April 30, 1984, p. 2.

4. Ibid., April 9, 1984, p. 1.

5. *MEES*, April 18, 1983, p. B2.

Bibliography

Official Documents and Source Material

Conant, Melvin A., and Fern Racine Gold. *Access to Oil: The U.S. Relationship with Saudi Arabia and Iran.* Washington, D.C.: Government Printing Office, 1977.

Declassified Documents Reference Service. *Retrospective Collection.* Washington, D.C.: Carrollton Press, 1977.

——— *1978 Collection.* Washington, D.C.: Carrollton Press, 1978.

——— *1979 Collection.* Washington, D.C.: Carrollton Press, 1979.

——— *1980 Collection.* Washington, D.C.: Carrollton Press, 1980.

——— *1981 Collection.* Washington, D.C.: Carrollton Press, 1981.

——— *1982 Collection.* Woodbridge, Conn.: Research Publications, 1982.

——— *1983 Collection.* Woodbridge, Conn.: Research Publications, 1983.

——— *1984 Collection.* Woodbridge, Conn.: Research Publications, 1984.

International Institute for Strategic Studies. *The Military Balance.* London, various years.

International Monetary Fund. *Direction of Trade Yearbook.* Washington, D.C., 1982.

Kingdom of Saudi Arabia. Ministry of Finance and National Economy. Central Department of Statistics. *Population Census.* 14 vols. Dammam, 1977.

——— *Statistical Yearbook, 1964* through *1981* (annual). Jidda, 1964–1981.

Kingdom of Saudi Arabia. Ministry of Planning. *Second Development Plan, 1975– 1980.* Springfield, Va.: U.S. Department of Commerce, Bureau of International Commerce, 1975.

——— *Third Development Plan, 1980–85.* Riyadh: Ministry of Planning Press, 1980.

Kingdom of Saudi Arabia. Saudi Arabian Monetary Agency. Research and Statistics Department. *Statistical Summary, 1980* through *1984* (annual). Riyadh, 1980–1984.

Organization of Petroleum Exporting Countries. *Annual Report.* Vienna, various years.

al-Rashid, Ibrahim, ed. *Documents on the History of Saudi Arabia.* 3 vols. Salisbury, N.C.: Documentary Publications, 1976.

―――― *Saudi Arabia Enters the Modern World: Secret U.S. Documents on the Emergence of the Kingdom of Saudi Arabia as a World Power: 1936–49.* 2 vols. Salisbury, N.C.: Documentary Publications, 1980.

Stockholm International Peace Research Institute. *Arms Trade Register.* Cambridge, Mass.: MIT Press, 1975.

―――― *World Armaments and Disarmament: SIPRI Yearbook, 1975* through *1981.* London and Philadelphia: Taylor and Francis, 1976–1982.

U.S. Congress. House of Representatives. Committee on Appropriations. *Foreign Assistance and Related Agencies Appropriations for 1978.* 95th Cong., 1st sess., 1977.

U.S. Congress. House of Representatives. Committee on Foreign Affairs. *Activities of the U.S. Corps of Engineers in Saudi Arabia.* 96th Cong., 1st sess., 1979.

―――― *Proposed Arms Sales for Countries in the Middle East.* 96th Cong., 1st sess., 1979.

―――― *Proposed Arms Transfers to the Yemen Arab Republic.* 96th Cong., 1st sess., 1979.

―――― *Proposed U.S. Arms Sales to Saudi Arabia.* 96th Cong., 1st sess., 1979.

―――― *U.S. Interests in, and Policies toward, the Persian Gulf, 1980.* 96th Cong., 2d sess., 1980.

―――― *Saudi Arabia and the United States.* Congressional Research Service Report. 97th Cong., 1st sess., 1981.

U.S. Congress. House of Representatives. Committee on Foreign Affairs and Joint Economic Committee. *U.S. Policy toward the Persian Gulf.* 97th Cong., 2d sess., 1983.

U.S. Congress. House of Representatives. Committee on International Relations. *The Persian Gulf, 1975: The Continuing Debate on Arms Sales.* 94th Cong., 1st sess., 1975.

―――― *U.S. Arms Sales to the Persian Gulf.* 94th Cong., 1st sess., 1975.

―――― *U.S. Arms Policies in the Persian Gulf and Red Sea Areas: Past, Present, and Future.* Staff report. 95th Cong., 1st sess., 1977.

U.S. Congress. Senate. Committee on Energy and Natural Resources. *The Geopolitics of Oil.* Staff report. 96th Cong., 2d sess., 1980.

U.S. Congress. Senate. Committee on Foreign Relations. *U.S. Arms Sales Policy.* 94th Cong., 2d sess., 1976.

―――― *Middle East Strategic Problems.* 95th Cong., 1st sess., 1977.

―――― *Middle East Arms Sales Proposals.* 95th Cong., 2d sess., 1978.

―――― *Fiscal Year 1980 International Security Assistance Authorization: State Department Briefing on the Situation in Yemen.* 96th Cong., 1st sess., 1979.

―――― *The Future of Saudi Arabian Oil Production.* Staff report. 96th Cong., 1st sess., 1979.

————— U.S. *Foreign Policy Objectives and Overseas Military Installations*. 96th Cong., 1st sess., 1979.

————— U.S. *Security Interests and Policies in Southwest Asia*. 96th Cong., 2d sess., 1980.

————— *Arms Sales Package to Saudi Arabia — Part 2*. 97th Cong., 1st sess., 1981.

————— *Persian Gulf Situation*. 97th Cong., 1st sess., 1981.

————— Subcommittee on Multinational Corporations. *Multinational Petroleum Companies*. 93d Cong., 2d sess., 1974.

————— U.S. *Oil Companies and the Arab Oil Embargo: The International Allocation of Constricted Supplies*. Report prepared by the Federal Energy Administration, Office of International Energy Affairs, January 27, 1975.

U.S. Department of Defense. Security Assistance Agency. *Foreign Military Sales, Foreign Military Construction Sales, and Military Assistance Facts*. Washington, D.C.: Government Printing Office, 1982.

U.S. Department of Energy. *Monthly Energy Review*. Washington, D.C.: U.S. Department of Energy, Energy Information Administration, various issues.

U.S. General Accounting Office. *Perspectives on Military Sales to Saudi Arabia*. Report to Congress, October 2, 1977.

U.S. Joint Publications Research Service. "History and Current Status of Royal Saudi Air Force." JPRS 56531, no. 794. July 18, 1972.

————— "Political Opposition within Nation Is Described at Length." JPRS 60197, no. 1039. October 3, 1973.

————— "Inauguration of National Guard Training Center." JPRS 65287, no. 1383. July 22, 1975.

U.S. OSS/State Department Intelligence and Research Reports Series. Vol. 12, *The Middle East, 1950–61*, Supplement. Frederick, Md.: University Publications of America, 1979.

United States–Saudi Arabian Joint Commission on Economic Cooperation. *Summary of Saudi Arabian Five-Year Development Plan, 1980–1985*. N.p., 1975.

Books

Abir, Mordechai. *Oil, Power, and Politics: Conflict in Arabia, the Red Sea, and the Gulf*. London: Frank Cass, 1974.

Adams, Sherman. *Firsthand Report*. New York: Popular Library, 1961.

Ajami, Fouad. *The Arab Predicament*. New York: Cambridge University Press, 1981.

Ali Sheikh Rustum. *Saudi Arabia and Oil Diplomacy*. New York: Praeger, 1976.

Alireza, Marianne. *At the Drop of a Veil*. Boston: Houghton Mifflin, 1971.

Almana, Mohammad. *Arabia Unified: A Portrait of Ibn Saud*. London: Hutchinson Benham, 1980.

Amirie, A., ed. *The Persian Gulf and Indian Ocean in International Politics*. Tehran: Institute for Political and Economic Studies, 1976.

Amirsadeghi, Hossein, ed. *The Security of the Persian Gulf*. New York: St. Martin's Press, 1981.

Anderson, Irvine. *Aramco, the United States, and Saudi Arabia: A Study of the Dynamics of Foreign Oil Policy, 1933–1950.* Princeton: Princeton University Press, 1981.

Anderson, Norman. *The Kingdom of Saudi Arabia.* London: Stacey International, 1978.

Anthony, John Duke. *The States of the Arabian Peninsula and Gulf Littoral: A Select and Annotated Bibliography.* Washington, D.C.: Middle East Institute, 1973.

——— *Arab States of the Lower Gulf: People, Politics, and Petroleum.* Washington, D.C.: Middle East Institute, 1975.

——— *The Middle East: Oil, Politics, and Development.* Washington, D.C.: American Enterprise Institute, 1975.

Arabian-American Oil Company. *Directory of the Royal Family, Officials of the Government, Diplomats, and Other Prominent Persons.* Dhahran, Saudi Arabia: Aramco, Local Government Relations Department, 1964.

——— *Handbook of Oil and the Middle East.* Dhahran, Saudi Arabia, 1968.

Arnold, José. *Golden Swords and Pots and Pans.* London: Gollancz, 1962.

Assad, Mohammed Moshen Ali. "Saudi Arabia's National Security: A Perspective Derived from Political, Economic, and Defense Policies." Ph.D. diss., University of Michigan, 1981.

Bakhash, Shaul. *The Politics of Oil and Revolution in Iran.* Washington, D.C.: Brookings Institution, 1982.

Barker, Paul. *Saudi Arabia: The Development Dilemma.* Special Report 116. London: Economist Intelligence Unit, 1982.

Beling, Willard, ed. *King Faisal and the Modernization of Saudi Arabia.* Boulder, Colo.: Westview, 1980.

Benoist-Mechin, Jacques. *Arabian Destiny.* London: Elek Books, 1957.

——— *Le Roi Saud.* Paris: Michel, 1960.

——— *Faysal: Roi d'Arabie.* Paris: Michel, 1975.

Bill, James, and Carl Leiden. *The Middle East: Politics and Power.* Boston: Allyn and Bacon, 1974.

Blandford, Linda. *Oil Sheikhs.* London: Weidenfeld and Nicolson, 1976.

Bradley, C. Paul. *Recent United States Policy in the Persian Gulf.* Hamden, Conn.: Shoe String Press, 1982.

Brossard, E. B. *Petroleum, Politics, and Power.* Tulsa, Okla.: Pennwell Books, 1983.

Brown, William. *Can OPEC Survive the Glut?* Croton-on-Hudson, N.Y.: Hudson Institute, 1981.

Brzezinski, Zbigniew. *Power and Principle.* New York: Farrar, Straus and Giroux, 1983.

Burke's Royal Families of the World. Vol. 2, *The Middle East and Africa.* London: Burke's Peerage, 1980.

Burrell, R. M. *The Persian Gulf.* Beverly Hills, Calif.: Sage for the Georgetown University Center for Strategic and International Studies, 1972.

Buschow, Rosemarie. *The Prince and I.* London: Futura, 1979.

Caroz, Yaacov. *The Arab Secret Services.* London: Corgi, 1978.

Carter, Jimmy. *Keeping Faith.* New York: Bantam, 1982.

Carter, J. R. L. *Leading Merchant Families of Saudi Arabia*. London: Scorpion, 1977.

Centers of Influence in Saudi Arabia. Princeton: East-West Group, 1978.

Chamieh, Jebran, ed. *Saudi Arabia Yearbook*. Beirut: Research and Publishing House, 1981.

Childs, J. Rives. *Foreign Service Farewell: My Years in the Near East*. Charlottesville: University Press of Virginia, 1969.

Chubin, Shahram. *Soviet Policy towards Iran and the Gulf*. Adelphi Papers, no. 157. London: International Institute for Strategic Studies, 1980.

—— *Security in the Persian Gulf*. Vol. 1, *Domestic Political Factors*. Montclair, N.J.: Allanheld for the International Institute for Strategic Studies, 1981.

—— *Security in the Persian Gulf*. Vol. 4, *The Role of Outside Powers*. London: International Institute for Strategic Studies, 1982.

Clayton, Sir Gilbert. *An Arabian Diary*. Berkeley: University of California Press, 1969.

Clements, F. A. *Saudi Arabia*. World Biographical Series. Oxford: Clio, 1979.

—— *Oman: The Reborn Land*. New York: Longman, 1980.

Cleron, Jean-Paul. *Saudi Arabia 2000: A Strategy for Growth*. London: Croom Helm, 1978.

Clifford, Mary. *Land and People of the Arabian Peninsula*. New York: Harper and Row, 1977.

Cole, Donald. *Nomads of the Nomads: The Al Murrah Bedouin of the Empty Quarter*. Chicago: Aldine, 1975.

Conant, Melvin A. *The Oil Factor in U.S. Foreign Policy, 1980–1990*. Lexington, Mass.: Lexington Books, 1982.

Copeland, Miles. *The Game of Nations*. London: Weidenfeld and Nicolson, 1969.

Cordesman, Anthony. *Jordanian Arms and the Middle East Balance*. Washington, D.C.: Middle East Institute, 1983.

Cottrell, Alvin, ed. *The Persian Gulf: A General Survey*. Baltimore: Johns Hopkins University Press, 1980.

Crane, Robert. *Planning the Future of Saudi Arabia: A Model for Achieving National Priorities*. New York: Praeger, 1978.

Dawisha, Adeed. *Saudi Arabia's Search for Security*. Adelphi Papers, no. 158. London: International Institute for Strategic Studies, 1979.

—— *Syria and the Lebanese Crisis*. New York: St. Martin's Press, 1980.

Dayan, Moshe. *Breakthrough: A Personal Account of the Egypt-Israel Peace Negotiation*. New York: Knopf, 1981.

Deese, David A., and Joseph Nye, eds. *Energy and Security*. Cambridge, Mass.: Ballinger, 1981.

De Gaury, Gerald. *Arabia Phoenix*. London: Harrap, 1946.

—— *Rulers of Mecca*. London: Harrap, 1951.

—— *Faisal: King of Saudi Arabia*. New York: Praeger, 1967.

De Planhol, Xavier. *Les Fondements géographiques de l'histoire de l'Islam*. Paris: Flammarion, 1968.

Dequin, H. F. E. *The Challenge of Saudi Arabia*. Hamburg: D. R. Gotze, 1976.

Doughty, Charles. *Travels in Arabia Deserta*. 2 vols. London: Jonathan Cape, 1964.

Dycus, Billy L., and Joseph Fiorillo. "An Investigation of the Scope, Purpose, and Effects of United States Foreign Military Sales to Saudi Arabia." Master's thesis, Air Force Institute of Technology, 1977.

Eisenhower, Dwight D. *The White House Years, Part I: Waging Peace*. Garden City, N.Y.: Doubleday, 1965.

Eveland, Wilbur Crane. *Ropes of Sand: America's Failure in the Middle East*. New York: Norton, 1980.

Fahmy, Ismail. *Negotiating for Peace in the Middle East*. Baltimore: Johns Hopkins University Press, 1983.

Farid, Abd al-Majid. *'Abd al-Nasir's Secret Papers*. Joint Publications Research Service, no. 72223. Washington, D.C., 1978.

——, ed. *Oil and Security in the Arabian Gulf*. London: Croom Helm, 1981.

al-Farsy, Fouad. *Saudi Arabia: A Case Study in Development*. London: Stacey International, 1980.

Fesharaki, Feridun, and David T. Isaak. *OPEC, the Gulf, and the World Petroleum Market*. Boulder, Colo.: Westview, 1983.

Ford Foundation. *A Time to Choose: America's Energy Future*. Cambridge, Mass.: Ballinger, 1974.

Freeman-Grenville, G. S. P., ed. *Memoirs of an Arabian Princess*. London: Salem House, 1982.

Ghaith, Abdelhakim. *The Marching Caravan: The Story of Modern Saudi Arabia*. Jidda, Saudi Arabia: Almedina Almonawarra, 1967.

Glubb, Sir John Bagot. *Soldier with the Arabs*. London: Hodder and Stoughton, 1957.

—— *War in the Desert*. New York: Norton, 1961.

Golan, Galia. *The Soviet Union and the Israeli War in Lebanon*. Research Paper 46. Jerusalem: Soviet and East European Research Center, 1982.

Grayson, Benson Lee. *Saudi-American Relations*. Washington, D.C.: University Press of America, 1982.

Grummon, Stephen. *The Iran-Iraq War*. Washington Papers 92. New York: Praeger, 1982.

Habib, John. *Ibn Saud's Warriors of Islam: The Ikhwan of Nejd and Their Role in the Creation of the Saudi Kingdom, 1910–1930*. Leiden: Brill, 1978.

Haig, Alexander. *Caveat*. New York: Macmillan, 1984.

Halliday, Fred. *Arabia without Sultans: A Survey of Political Instability in the Arab World*. New York: Vintage, 1974.

Hanks, Robert. *The U.S. Military Presence in the Middle East: Problems and Prospects*. Cambridge, Mass.: Institute for Foreign Policy Analysis, 1982.

Heikal, Mohammad Hassanein. *Ya Sahib al-Jalalah* [Your Majesty]. Cairo: al-Dar al-Qawmiyya lil-Tiba'a wal-Nashr, 1963[?].

—— *The Road to Ramadan*. London: Collins, 1975.

—— *The Sphinx and the Commissar*. New York: Harper and Row, 1978.

Heller, Mark, and Nadav Safran. *The New Middle Class and Regime Stability in Saudi Arabia*. Harvard Middle East Papers. Cambridge, Mass.: Harvard University Center for Middle Eastern Studies, forthcoming.

Helms, Christine Moss. *The Cohesion of Saudi Arabia*. Baltimore: Johns Hopkins University Press, 1981.

Hirst, David, and Irene Beeson. *Sadat*. London: Faber and Faber, 1981.

Hobday, Peter. *Saudi Arabia Today*. London: Macmillan, 1978.

Holden, David, and Richard Johns. *The House of Saud*. New York: Holt, Rinehart and Winston, 1981.

Hopwood, Derek, ed. *The Arabian Peninsula: Society and Politics*. Totowa, N.J.: Rowman and Littlefield, 1972.

Howarth, David. *The Desert King: Ibn Saud and His Arabia*. New York: McGraw-Hill, 1964.

Hussein ibn Talal, King of Jordan. *Uneasy Lies the Head*. New York: Random House, 1962.

Ibrahim, Saad Eddin. *The New Arab Social Order: A Study of the Social Impact of Oil Wealth*. Boulder, Colo.: Westview, 1982.

Iqbal, Sheikh Muhammad. *Emergence of Saudi Arabia: A Political Study of King Abd al-Aziz ibn Saud, 1901–1953*. Kashmir: Saudiyah Publications, 1977.

Ismael, Tareq. *Iraq and Iran: Roots of Conflict*. Syracuse, N.Y.: Syracuse University Press, 1982.

The Jaffee Center for Strategic Studies. *The Middle East Military Balance, 1983*. Tel Aviv: Tel Aviv University, 1983.

Johany, Ali. *The Myth of the OPEC Cartel: The Role of Saudi Arabia*. New York: Wiley, 1980.

Johnson, Lyndon B. *The Vantage Point*. New York: Holt, Rinehart and Winston, 1969.

Kalb, Marvin, and Bernard Kalb. *Kissinger*. New York: Dell, 1974.

Katakura, Motoko. *Bedouin Village: A Study of Saudi Arabian People in Transition*. Tokyo: University of Tokyo Press, 1975.

Kedourie, Elie. *Arabic Political Memoirs and Other Studies*. London: Frank Cass, 1974.

Keegan, John, ed. *World Armies*. New York: Facts on File, 1979.

Kelly, J. B. *Eastern Arabian Frontiers*. New York: Praeger, 1964.

————— *Arabia, the Gulf, and the West*. New York: Basic Books, 1980.

Kerr, Malcolm. *The Arab Cold War*. 3d ed. New York: Oxford University Press, 1971.

Kerr, Malcolm, and El Sayed Yassin, eds. *Rich and Poor States in the Middle East*. Boulder, Colo.: Westview, 1982.

Khalib, Abdul Hamid. *The Harbinger of Justice: Biography of His Majesty King Abdul Aziz*. Karachi: al-Arab Press, 1951.

Khalidi, Walid. *Conflict and Violence in Lebanon*. Cambridge, Mass.: Harvard University Center for International Affairs, 1979.

Al Khamis, Ibrahim Abd al-Rahman. *Usud Al Sa'ud* [The lions of the House of Saud]. Beirut: Dar al-Najah, 1972.

Kissinger, Henry A. *White House Years*. Boston: Little, Brown, 1979.

————— *Years of Upheaval*. Boston: Little, Brown, 1982.

Knauerhase, Ramon. *The Saudi Arabian Economy*. New York: Praeger, 1975.

Koury, Enver. *The Saudi Decision-Making Body: The House of Saud*. Washington, D.C.: Institute of Middle Eastern and North African Affairs, 1978.

Lacey, Robert. *The Kingdom: Arabia and the House of Saud*. New York: Harcourt Brace Jovanovich, 1981.

Lackner, Helen. *A House Built on Sand: The Political Economy of Saudi Arabia*. London: Ithaca, 1979.

Lees, Brian. *A Handbook of the Al Sa'ud Ruling Family of Saudi Arabia*. London: Royal Genealogies, 1980.

Legum, Colin, et al., eds. *Middle East Contemporary Survey*. Vols. 1–5, *1976–77* through *1980–81*. New York: Holmes and Meier, 1978–1982.

Lenczowski, George. *The Middle East in World Affairs*. 3d ed. Ithaca, N.Y.: Cornell University Press, 1962.

—— *Middle East Oil in a Revolutionary Age*. Washington, D.C.: American Enterprise Institute, 1976.

Lipsky, George. *Saudi Arabia: Its People, Its Society, Its Culture*. New Haven: Hraf Press, 1959.

Litwak, Robert. *Security in the Persian Gulf*. Vol. 2, *Sources of Inter-State Conflict*. Montclair, N.J.: Allanheld for the International Institute for Strategic Studies, 1981.

Long, David. *Saudi Arabia*. Washington Papers 39. Beverly Hills, Calif.: Sage for the Georgetown University Center for Strategic and International Studies, 1976.

—— *The Hajj Today: A Survey of the Contemporary Makkah Pilgrimage*. Washington, D.C.: State University of New York Press, 1979.

Looney, Robert. *Saudi Arabia's Development Potential*. Lexington, Mass.: Lexington Books, 1982.

Macro, Eric. *Bibliography of the Arabian Peninsula*. Coral Gables, Fla.: University of Miami Press, 1958.

McDonald, John, and Clyde Burleson. *Flight from Dhahran*. Englewood Cliffs, N.J.: Prentice-Hall, 1981.

El Mallakh, Ragaei. *Saudi Arabia: Rush to Development*. Baltimore: Johns Hopkins University Press, 1982.

——, et al. *Saudi Arabia: Energy, Development Planning, and Industrialization*. Lexington, Mass.: Lexington Books, 1982.

Maull, Hans. *Oil and Influence: The Oil Weapon Examined*. Adelphi Papers, no. 117. London: International Institute for Strategic Studies, 1975.

Miller, Aaron. *Search for Security: Saudi Arabian Oil and American Foreign Policy, 1939–49*. Chapel Hill: University of North Carolina Press, 1980.

Moliver, Donald, and Paul Abbondante. *The Saudi Arabian Economy*. New York: Praeger, 1980.

Monroe, Elizabeth. *Philby of Arabia*. London: Farber and Farber, 1973.

Montagne, R. *La Civilization du desert*. Paris: Hachette, 1947.

al-Mumayiz, Amin. *al-Mamlaka al-'Arabiyya al-Sa'udiyya kama 'Ariftuha: Muzakkirat Diblumasiyya* [Saudi Arabia as I have known it: Diplomatic memoirs]. Beirut, 1963.

Nakhleh, Emile. *The United States and Saudi Arabia: A Policy Analysis*. Washington, D.C.: American Enterprise Institute, 1975.

—— *The Persian Gulf and American Policy*. New York: American Enterprise Institute, 1982.

Niblock, Tim, ed. *Social and Economic Development in the Arab Gulf*. New York: St. Martin's Press, 1980.

———— *State, Society, and Economy in Saudi Arabia.* New York: St. Martin's Press, 1982.

Nixon, Richard M. *RN: The Memoirs of Richard Nixon.* New York: Grosset and Dunlap, 1978.

Noyes, James. *The Clouded Lens: Persian Gulf Security and U.S. Policy.* Stanford: Stanford University Hoover Institution, 1979.

Nutting, Anthony. *Nasser.* London: Constable, 1972.

Nyrop, Richard, et al. *Area Handbook for the Persian Gulf.* 3d ed. Washington, D.C.: Government Printing Office, 1977.

———— *Area Handbook for Saudi Arabia.* 3d ed. Washington, D.C.: Government Printing Office, 1977.

O'Ballance, Edgar. *The War in Yemen.* Hamden, Conn.: Archon Books, 1971.

———— *Arab Guerrilla Power.* Hamden, Conn.: Archon Books, 1973.

O'Connor, Harvey. *World Crisis in Oil.* New York: New York Monthly Review Press, 1962.

Peck, Malcolm. "Saudi Arabia in United States Foreign Policy to 1958: A Study in the Sources and Determinants of American Policy." Ph.D. diss., Harvard University, 1970.

Pelly, Lewis, *Report on a Journey to the Wahabee Capital of Riyadh in Central Arabia, 1865.* 1866. Reprint. Cambridge: Oleander/Falcon, 1978.

Peterson, J. E. *Yemen: The Search for a Modern State.* Baltimore: Johns Hopkins University Press, 1982.

Philby, H. St. John. *Arabia of the Wahhabis.* London: Constable, 1928.

———— *Arabian Jubilee.* London, 1954.

———— *Saudi Arabia.* London: Benn, 1955.

———— *Arabia.* New York: Scribner's, 1930. Reprint. Beirut, 1968.

Plascov, Avi. *Security in the Persian Gulf.* Vol. 3, *Modernization, Development, and Stability.* London: International Institute for Strategic Studies, 1982.

Quandt, William. *Decade of Decisions.* Berkeley: University of California Press, 1977.

———— *Saudi Arabia in the 1980s.* Washington, D.C.: Brookings Institution, 1981.

———— *Saudi Arabia's Oil Policy.* Washington, D.C.: Brookings Institution, 1982.

Rabin, Yitzhak. *The Rabin Memoirs.* Boston: Little, Brown, 1979.

Record, Jeffrey. *The Rapid Deployment Force and U.S. Military Intervention in the Persian Gulf.* Cambridge, Mass.: Institute for Foreign Policy Analysis, 1980.

Riad, Mahmoud. *The Struggle for Peace in the Middle East.* New York: Quartet Books, 1981.

Rihani, Amin. *Ibn Sa'oud of Arabia: His Land and People.* London: Constable, 1928.

Rubin, Barry. *Paved with Good Intentions: The American Experience and Iran.* New York: Oxford University Press, 1980.

———— *The Arab States and the Palestinian Conflict.* Syracuse, N.Y.: Syracuse University Press, 1981.

Rustow, Dankwart. *Oil and Turmoil: America Faces OPEC and the Middle East.* New York: Norton, 1982.

Sadat, Anwar. *In Search of Identity.* New York: Harper and Row, 1978.

Safran, Nadav. *From War to War.* Indianapolis: Bobbs-Merrill, 1969.

———— *Israel: The Embattled Ally.* Cambridge, Mass.: Harvard University Press, 1978.

Sa'id, Amin. *Tarikh al-Dawla al-Sa'udiyya* [History of the Saudi state]. Vol. 3, 'Ahd Sa'ud ibn Abd al-Aziz [The reign of Saud ibn Abd al-Aziz]. Beirut: Dar al-Kutub al-'Arabiyya, 1964.

———— *Faisal al-'Azim* [Faisal the Great]. Beirut: Dar al-Kutub al-'Arabiyya, 1965.

Salameh, Ghassane. *al-Siyassa al-Kharijiyya al-Sa'udiyya mundhu 'Am 1945* [Saudi foreign policy since 1945]. Beirut: Ma'had al-'Inma al-'Arabi, 1980.

Samore, Gary. "Royal Family Politics in Saudi Arabia (1953–1982)." Ph.D. diss., Harvard University, 1983.

Sanger, Richard. *The Arabian Peninsula.* Ithaca, N.Y.: Cornell University Press, 1954.

Sarhan, Samir, ed. *Who's Who in Saudi Arabia.* London: Europa Publications, 1977.

Schiff, Zeev. *Israel's War in Lebanon.* New York: Simon and Schuster, 1984.

Schmidt, Dana Adams. *Yemen: The Unknown War.* New York: Holt, Rinehart and Winston, 1968.

Scoville, Sheila, ed. *Gazetteer of Arabia: A Geographical and Tribal History of the Arabian Peninsula.* 3 vols. Graz: Akademische Druck, 1979.

Sella, Ammnon. *The Soviet Attitude towards the War in Lebanon.* Research Paper 47. Jerusalem: Soviet and East European Research Center, 1982.

Shabon, Anwar N. *The Political, Economic, and Labor Climate in the Countries of the Arabian Peninsula.* Philadelphia: Wharton School, Industrial Research Unit, 1981.

Shaw, John A., and David E. Long. *Saudi Arabian Modernization.* Washington Papers 89. New York: Praeger, 1982.

El Shazly, Saad. *The Crossing of the Suez.* San Francisco: American Mideast Research, 1980.

Sheean, Vincent. *Faisal: The King and His Kingdom.* Tavistock, England: University Press of Arabia, 1975.

Shuqairy, Ahmad. *Min al-Qimmah* [From the summit]. Beirut: Dar al-'Awda, 1971.

———— *'Ala Tariq al-Hazima* [On the road to defeat]. Beirut: Dar al-'Awda, 1972.

Stephens, Robert. *Nasser: A Political Biography.* London: Penguin, 1971.

Stevens, J. H., and R. King. *A Bibliography of Saudi Arabia.* Durham, England: Centre for Middle East and Islamic Studies, 1973.

Stobaugh, Robert, and Daniel Yergin. *Energy Future.* New York: Random House, 1979.

Stookey, Robert. *Yemen: The Politics of the Yemen Arab Republic.* Boulder, Colo.: Westview Press, 1978.

Tahtinen, Dale. *National Security Challenges to Saudi Arabia.* Washington, D.C.: American Enterprise Institute, 1978.

Talal ibn Abd al-Aziz. *Risalah ila Muwatin* [Letter to a fellow citizen]. Beirut, 1962.

Taylor, Alan. *The Arab Balance of Power.* Syracuse, N.Y.: Syracuse University Press, 1982.

Thesiger, Alfred. *Arabian Sands.* New York: Dutton, 1959.

Tillman, Seth. *The United States in the Middle East.* Bloomington: Indiana University Press, 1982.

Toynbee, Arnold. *Survey of International Affairs*. Vol. 1, *1925*. London: Royal Institute for International Affairs, 1927.

Troeller, Gary. *The Birth of Saudi Arabia*. London: Frank Cass, 1976.

Twitchell, K. S. *Saudi Arabia, with an Account of the Development of Its Natural Resources*. Princeton: Princeton University Press, 1953.

Vance, Cyrus. *Hard Choices*. New York: Simon and Schuster, 1983.

Van Dam, Nikilaos. *The Struggle for Power in Syria*. New York: St. Martin's Press, 1979.

Van der Meulen, D. *The Wells of Ibn Saud*. New York: Praeger, 1957.

Wahba, Hafiz. *Khamsun 'Am fi al-Mamlaka al-Sa'udiyya* [Fifty years in the Saudi kingdom]. Cairo: Mustafa al-Babi, 1960.

——— *Arabian Days*. London: Arthur Barker, 1964.

Weizman, Ezer. *The Battle for Peace*. New York: Bantam, 1981.

Wells, Donald. *Saudi Arabian Development Strategy*. Washington, D.C.: American Enterprise Institute, 1976.

Williams, Kenneth. *Ibn Saud: The Puritan King of Saudi Arabia*. London: Jonathan Cape, 1933.

Winder, R. Bayly. *Saudi Arabia in the Nineteenth Century*. New York: St. Martin's Press, 1965.

Yergin, Daniel, and Martin Hillenbrand, eds. *Global Insecurity*. Boston: Houghton Mifflin, 1982.

York, Valerie. *The Gulf in the 1980s*. London: Royal Institute for International Affairs, 1981.

Young, Arthur N. *Saudi Arabia: The Making of a Financial Giant*. New York: New York University Press, 1983.

Articles

Ajami, Fouad. "Between Cairo and Damascus." *Foreign Affairs*, 54 (April 1976).

——— "Stress in the Arab Triangle." *Foreign Policy*, no. 29 (Winter 1977–78).

——— "The End of Pan-Arabism." *Foreign Affairs*, 57 (Winter 1978/79).

Alyami, Ali Hassan. "The Coming Instability in Saudi Arabia." *New Outlook*, 20 (September 1977).

Amuzegar, Jahangir. "Oil Wealth: A Very Mixed Blessing." *Foreign Affairs*, 60 (Spring 1982).

Anthony, John Duke. "Foreign Policy: The View from Riyadh." *Wilson Quarterly*, 3 (Winter 1979).

——— "The Gulf Cooperation Council." *Journal of South Asian and Middle Eastern Studies*, 5 (Summer 1982).

"Arabian Fledgling: The Royal Saudi Air Force." *Air Enthusiast*, no. 2 (June 1972).

Bligh, A., and S. Plant. "Saudi Moderation in Oil and Foreign Policies in the post-AWACS Sale Period." *Middle East Review*, 14 (Spring–Summer 1982).

Bloomfield, Lincoln. "Saudi Arabia Faces the 1980s: Saudi Security Problems and American Interests." *Fletcher Forum*, 5, no. 2 (1981).

Bouteiller, Georges. "L'Arabie Saoudite: Aujourd'hui et demain." *Défense internationale*, November 1978.

Braibanti, Ralph, and Fouad Abdul Salem. "Saudi Arabia: A Development Perspective." *Journal of South Asian and Middle Eastern Studies*, 1, no. 1 (Fall 1977).

Carus, W. Seth. "Defense Planning in Iraq." In *Defense Planning in Less-Industrialized States*, edited by Stephanie Neuman. Lexington, Mass.: Lexington Books, 1984.

Chubin, Shahram. "Gains for Soviet Policy in the Middle East." *International Security*, 6 (Spring 1982).

Churba, Joseph. "The Eroding Security Balance in the Middle East." *Orbis*, 24 (Summer 1980).

Collins, Michael. "Riyadh: The Saud Balance." *Washington Quarterly*, Winter 1981.

Cooley, John. "Iran, the Palestinians, and the Gulf." *Foreign Affairs*, 57 (Summer 1979).

Cordesman, Anthony. "The Changing Military Balance in the Gulf and Middle East." *Armed Forces Journal International*, September 1981.

———— "Saudi Arabia, AWACs, and America's Search for Strategic Stability in the Near East." Wilson Center International Security Studies Program, Working Paper 26A. Washington, D.C., September 1981.

———— "The U.S. Search for Strategic Stability in the Persian Gulf." *Armed Forces Journal International*, September 1981.

———— "After AWACs: Establishing Western Security throughout Southwest Asia." *Armed Forces Journal International*, December 1981.

———— "Lessons of the Iran-Iraq War: Part One." *Armed Forces Journal International*, April 1982.

———— "Lessons of the Iran-Iraq War: Part Two." *Armed Forces Journal International*, June 1982.

———— "Oman: The Guardian of the Eastern Gulf." *Armed Forces Journal International*, June 1983.

———— "The 'Oil Glut' and the Strategic Importance of the Gulf States." *Armed Forces Journal International*, October 1983.

———— "Defense Planning in Saudi Arabia." In *Defense Planning in Less-Industrialized States*, edited by Stephanie Neuman. Lexington, Mass.: Lexington Books, 1984.

Crecilius, D. "Saudi Arabian–Egyptian Relations." *International Studies*, 14 (1975).

Dawisha, Adeed. "Internal Values and External Threats: The Making of Saudi Foreign Policy." *Orbis*, 23 (Summer 1979).

———— "Iraq and the Arab World: The Gulf War and After." *The World Today*, March 1981.

Dawisha, Karen. "Moscow's Moves in the Direction of the Gulf—So Near and Yet So Far." *Journal of International Studies*, Fall/Winter 1980/81.

———— "The USSR and Middle East Crises: 1973 and 1980." *International Affairs* (London), Winter 1980/81.

De Marino, Donald. "Royal Factionalism and Saudi Foreign Policy." Letter to the editor. *Foreign Affairs*, 58 (Fall 1979).

Dunn, Keith. "Constraints on the USSR in Southwest Asia: A Military Analysis." *Orbis*, 25 (Fall 1981).

Edens, David. "The Anatomy of the Saudi Revolution." *International Journal of Middle East Studies*, 5 (January 1974).

Eilts, Hermann. "Social Revolution in Saudi Arabia, Part I." *Parameters: The Journal of the Army War College*, 1 (Spring 1971).

———— "Social Revolution in Saudi Arabia, Part II." *Parameters: The Journal of the Army War College*, 1 (Fall 1971).

———— "Security Considerations in the Persian Gulf." *International Security*, 5 (Fall 1980).

Epstein, Joshua. "Soviet Vulnerabilities in Iran and the RDF Deterrent." *International Security*, 6 (Fall 1981).

Erb, Richard D. "The Gulf Oil Producers: Overview and Policy Implications." *AEI Foreign Policy and Defense Review*, 2, nos. 3–4 (1980).

Feith, Douglas. "The Oil Weapon De-Mystified." *Policy Review*, Winter 1981.

Fukuyama, Francis. "Nuclear Shadowboxing: Soviet Intervention in the Middle East." *Orbis*, 25 (Fall 1981).

Goldberg, Jacob. "How Stable Is Saudi Arabia?" *Washington Quarterly*, Spring 1982.

Halliday, Fred. "Yemen's Unfinished Revolution: Socialism in the South." *MERIP Reports*, no. 81 (October 1979).

Harrington, Charles. "The Saudi Arabian Council of Ministers." *Middle East Journal*, 12 (Winter 1958).

Hayan ibn Bayan [pseud]. "Poor Little Rich Nation: Open Letter to Saudi Arabia." *The Nation*, April 4, 1981.

Hogarth, D. G. "Wahhabism and British Interests." *Journal of the British Institute of International Affairs*, 4 (1925).

Hottinger, Arnold. "Does Saudi Arabia Face Revolution?" *New York Review of Books*, June 28, 1979.

———— "Behind the Grand Mosque Incident." *Swiss Review of International Affairs*, 39 (January 1980).

Howarth, H. M. F. "The Impact of the Iran-Iraq War on Military Requirements in the Gulf States." *International Defense Review*, 16, no. 10 (1983).

Humphreys, Stephen. "Islam and Political Values in Saudi Arabia, Egypt, and Syria." *Middle East Journal*, 33 (Winter 1979).

Ignotus, Miles [pseud]. "Seizing Arab Oil." *Harper's*, March 1975.

Iseman, Peter. "The Arabian Ethos." *Harper's*, February 1978.

Jordan, Amos. "Saudi Arabia: The Next Iran." *Parameters: The Journal of the Army War College*, 9 (March 1979).

Karawan, Ibrahim. "Egypt's Defense Policy." In *Defense Planning in Less-Industrialized Countries*, edited by Stephanie Neuman. Lexington, Mass.: Lexington Books, 1984.

Kashkett, Steven. "Iraq and the Pursuit of Nonalignment." *Orbis*, 26 (Summer 1982).

Kelidar, Abbas. "The Problem of Succession in Saudi Arabia." *Asian Affairs*, 65 (February 1978).

Kerr, Malcolm. "Rich and Poor in the New Arab Order." *Journal of Arab Affairs*, 1 (October 1981).

Knapp, Wilfrid. "Stabilité et instabilité dans le golfe arabo-persique." *Maghreb-Machrek*, no. 77 (July–September 1977).

Knauerhase, Ramon. "Saudi Arabia's Economy at the Beginning of the 1970s." *Middle East Journal*, 28 (Spring 1974).

Kraft, Joseph. "Letter from Saudi Arabia." *New Yorker*, October 20, 1975.

—— "Letter from Saudi Arabia." *New Yorker*, June 1, 1978.

—— "Letter from Saudi Arabia." *New Yorker*, July 4, 1983.

Kuniholm, Bruce. "What the Saudis Really Want: A Primer for the Reagan Administration." *Orbis*, 25 (Spring 1981).

Lenczowski, George. "The Soviet Union and the Persian Gulf: An Encircling Strategy." *International Journal*, 37, no. 2 (1982).

Levy, Walter. "The Years That the Locust Hath Eaten: Oil Policy and OPEC Development Prospects." *Foreign Affairs*, 57 (Winter 1978/79).

Long, David. "Kingdom of Saudi Arabia." In *The Middle East: Its Governments and Politics*, edited by Abid al-Marayati. Belmont, Calif.: Duxbury Press, 1972.

Maddy-Weitzman, Bruce. "The Fragmentation of Arab Politics: Inter-Arab Affairs since the Afghanistan Invasion." *Orbis*, 25 (Summer 1981).

—— "Islam and Arabism: The Iraq-Iran War." *Washington Quarterly*, Autumn 1982.

Malone, Joseph. "America and the Arabian Peninsula: The First Two Hundred Years." *Middle East Journal*, 30 (Summer 1976).

Mansur, Abdul Karim [pseud.]. "The American Threat to Saudi Arabia." *Armed Forces Journal International*, September 1980.

—— "The Military Balance in the Persian Gulf: Who Will Guard the Gulf States from Their Guardians?" *Armed Forces Journal International*, November 1980.

McHale, T. R. "A Prospect of Saudi Arabia." *International Affairs* (London), 56 (Autumn 1980).

Melikian, Levon, and Juhaina Al-Easa. "Oil and Social Change in the Gulf." *Journal of Arab Affairs*, 1 (October 1981).

Moran, Ted. "Modeling OPEC Behavior: Economic and Political Alternatives." *International Organization*, 2 (Spring 1981).

Nevo, Joseph. "The Saudi Royal Family: The Third Generation." *Jerusalem Quarterly*, no. 31 (Spring 1984).

Newsom, David. "America EnGulfed." *Foreign Policy*, no. 43 (Summer 1981).

Nimir, S. A., and M. Palmer. "Bureaucracy and Development in Saudi Arabia: A Behavioral Analysis." *Public Administration and Development*, April–June 1982.

Nollet, Richard. "Regard sur le clan des Al Saud." *L'Afrique et l'Arabie moderne*, no. 118 (Trimestre 1978).

Nolte, R. H. "A Tale of Three Cities: Dhahran, Riyadh, and Jeddah." *American University Fieldstaff Reports*, Southwest Asia Series, 6, no. 4 (1957) and 7, no. 2 (1958).

O'Ballance, Edgar. "Saudi Arabia." *Army Quarterly and Defense Journal*, 77 (January 1959).

—— "The Iraqi-Iranian War: The First Round." *Parameters: The Journal of the Army War College*, 11 (March 1981).

Paul, Jim. "Insurrection at Mecca." *MERIP Reports*, no. 86 (October 1980).

Peck, Malcolm. "Saudi Arabian Wealth: A Two-Edged Sword." *New Middle East*, January 1972.

Peterson, J. E. "Tribes and Politics in Eastern Arabia." *Middle East Journal*, 31 (Summer 1977).

———— "The Yemen Arab Republic and the Politics of Balance." *Asian Affairs*, 12 (October 1981).

Philby, H. St. John. "A Survey of Wahhabi Arabia, 1929." *Journal of the Royal Central Asian Society*, 16, no. 4 (1929).

———— "The New Reign in Saudi Arabia." *Foreign Affairs*, 32 (April 1954).

———— "Saudi Arabia: The New Statute of the Council of Ministers." *Middle East Journal*, 12 (Summer 1958).

———— "Riyadh: Ancient and Modern." *Middle East Journal*, 13 (Spring 1959).

Pipes, Daniel. "Increasing Security in the Persian Gulf." *Orbis*, 26 (Spring 1982).

Quandt, William. "Riyadh between the Superpowers." *Foreign Policy*, no. 44 (Fall 1981).

Ramazani, Rouhollah K. "Iran's Search for Regional Cooperation." *Middle East Journal*, 30 (Spring 1976).

———— "Security in the Persian Gulf." *Foreign Affairs*, 57 (Spring 1979).

Rentz, George. "Literature on the Kingdom of Saudi Arabia."·*Middle East Journal*, 4 (Spring 1950).

———— "Saudi Arabia: The Islamic Island." *Journal of International Affairs*, 19, no. 1 (1965).

Rondot, Philippe. "Les Hommes au pouvoir en Arabie Saoudite." *Magreb*, no. 89 (juillet–septembre 1980).

Rosenfeld, Henry. "The Social Composition of the Military in the Process of State Formation in the Arabian Desert." *Journal of the Royal Anthropological Institute*, 95, no. 1 (1965).

———— "The Military Forces Used to Achieve and Maintain Power and the Meaning of Its Social Composition: Slaves, Mercenaries, and Townsmen." *Journal of the Royal Anthropological Institute*, 95, no. 2 (1965).

Ross, Dennis. "Considering Soviet Threats to the Persian Gulf." *International Security*, 6 (Fall 1981).

Rubinstein, Alvin. "The Soviet Union and the Arabian Peninsula." *The World Today*, November 1979.

———— "The Evolution of Soviet Strategy in the Middle East." *Orbis*, 24 (Summer 1980).

———— "Afghanistan: Embraced by the Bear." *Orbis*, 26 (Spring 1982).

Rugh, William. "The Emergence of a New Middle Class in Saudi Arabia." *Middle East Journal*, 27 (Winter 1973).

———— "A Tale of Two Houses." *Wilson Quarterly*, 3 (Winter 1979).

Rustow, Dankwart. "U.S.-Saudi Relations and the Oil Crisis of the 1980s." *Foreign Affairs*, 53 (April 1977).

Safran, Nadav. "Arab Politics, Peace and War." *Orbis*, 18 (Summer 1974).

Salameh, Ghassane. "Political Power and the Saudi State." *MERIP Reports*, no. 91 (October 1980).

———— "Monarchical Institutions in the Face of Modernization." *Politica internazionale*, 2 (Spring 1981).

———— "Saudi Arabia: Development and Dependence." *Jerusalem Quarterly*, no. 20 (Summer 1981).

al-Salem, Faisal. "The United States and the Gulf: What Do the Arabs Want?" *Journal of South Asian and Middle Eastern Studies*, 6 (Fall 1982).

Sayigh, Yusif. "Problems and Prospects of Development in the Arabian Peninsula." *International Journal of Middle East Studies*, 2 (January 1971).

Schechterman, Bernard. "Political Instability in Saudi Arabia and Its Implications." *Middle East Review*, 14 (Fall–Winter 1981–82).

Shaw, John. "Saudi Arabia Comes of Age." *Washington Quarterly*, Spring 1982.

Singer, Fred. "Limits to Arab Oil Power." *Foreign Policy*, no. 30 (Spring 1978).

Smart, Ian. "Oil, the Superpowers, and the Middle East." *International Affairs*, 53 (January 1977).

Solaim, Soliman. "Legal Review: Saudi Arabia's Judicial System." *Middle East Journal*, 25 (Summer 1971).

"Special Report, Middle East Aerospace: Saudi Arabia." *Aviation Week and Space Technology*, May 23, 1983.

Standenmaier, William O. "Military Policy and Strategy in the Gulf War." *Parameters: The Journal of the Army War College*, 12 (June 1982).

Stork, Joe. "Saudi Oil and the U.S.: Special Relationship under Stress." *MERIP Reports*, no. 91 (October 1980).

"A Survey of Saudi Arabia." *Economist*, February 13, 1982.

Tahir-Kheli, Shirin, and William Standenmaier. "The Saudi-Pakistani Military Relationship: Implications for U.S. Policy." *Orbis*, 26 (Spring 1982).

Thompson, Scott. "The Persian Gulf and the Correlation of Forces." *International Security*, 7 (Summer 1982).

Tinnin, David. "Saudis Awaken to Their Vulnerability." *Fortune*, 101 (March 1980).

Tucker, Robert. "The Persian Gulf and American Power." *Commentary*, November 1980.

Turner, Louis, and James Bedore. "Saudi Arabia: The Power of the Purse Strings." *International Affairs*, 54 (July 1978).

van Creveld, Martin. "The Making of Israel's Security." In *Defense Planning in Less-Industrialized Countries*, edited by Stephanie Neuman. Lexington, Mass.: Lexington Books, 1984.

Van Hollen, Christopher. "Don't Engulf the Gulf." *Foreign Affairs*, 59 (Summer 1981).

———— "North Yemen: A Dangerous Pentagonal Game." *Washington Quarterly*, Summer 1982.

Wahba, Hafiz. "Wahhabism in Arabia, Past and Present." *Journal of the Royal Central Asian Society*, 16, no. 4 (1929).

Wenner, Manfred. "Saudi Arabia: Survival of Traditional Elites." In *Political Elites and Political Development in The Middle East*, edited by Frank Tachau. New York: Schenkman, 1975.

Wissa-Wassef, C. "L'Arabie Seoudite et le conflit israelo-arabe." *Politique étrangère*, 39, no. 2 (1974).

Wright, Claudia. "Iraq: New Power in the Middle East." *Foreign Affairs*, 58 (Winter 1979/80).

Yegnes, Tamar. "Saudi Arabia and the Peace Process." *Jerusalem Quarterly*, no. 18 (Winter 1981).

Selected Newspapers and Periodicals

American-Arab Affairs (Washington, D.C.)
Arab News (Riyadh, Saudi Arabia)
Arab Report and Record (London)
Arab World Weekly (Beirut)
Christian Science Monitor (Boston)
Defense Monitor (Washington, D.C.)
Financial Times (London)
Foreign Affairs (New York) — especially chronology section
Foreign Broadcast Information Service Daily Report (Washington, D.C.)
International Defense Review (Geneva)
International Journal of Middle East Studies (New York)
Journal of Palestinian Studies (Beirut and Kuwait)
London Sunday Telegraph
Mideast Mirror (Beirut)
Middle East (London)
Middle East Economic Digest (London)
Middle East Economic Survey (Cyprus)
Middle East International (London)
Middle East Journal (Washington, D.C.) — especially chronology section
Middle East Monitor
Middle East Record (London)
Middle East Review (New York)
New Statesman (London)
New York Times
Petroleum Economist (London)
Petroleum Intelligence Weekly (New York)
Platt's Oil Price Handbook (New York)
Strategic Survey (London)
Washington Post
Washington Star

Index